G 60° H 30° J 0° K 30° L 60° M
Lincoln Sea
Ellesmere Island
Etah
GREENLAND
(Den.)
Thule
BAFFIN BAY
Baffin Island
Foxe Basin
Arctic Circle
Str. of Denmark
Julianehaab
C. Farewell
FRANZ JOSEF LAND
(U.S.S.R.)
SVALBARD
(Nor.)
GREENLAND SEA
BARENTS SEA
NOVAYA ZEMLYA
KARA SEA
North Cape
Jan Mayen
(Nor.)
NORWEGIAN SEA
ICELAND
Reykjavík
Faeroerne
(Den.)
Murmansk
Archangel
Dudinka
Yenisei
Salekhard
Ob
NORWAY
SWEDEN
FINLAND
Helsinki
Leningrad
Oslo
Stockholm
Baltic Sea
North Sea
GREAT BRITAIN
Glasgow
IRELAND
London
DEN.
Berlin
NE.
GER.
BEL.
POL.
Warsaw
Moscow
Volga
UNION OF SOVIET SOCIALIST REPUBLICS
EUROPE
ASIA
Sverdlovsk
Omsk
Novosibirsk
Kharkov
Stalingrad
Paris
FRANCE
SW.
AU.
HUN.
CZ.
RUM.
YUGO.
ITALY
BUL.
Black Sea
Caspian
Aral Sea
Baku
Tashkent
Tihwa
SINKIANG
TIBET
PORTUGAL
Madrid
Rome
Lisbon
SPAIN
GR.
Istanbul
TURKEY
Athens
Mediterranean Sea
Beirut
SYRIA
Damascus
Baghdad
Tehran
IRAQ
IRAN
AFGH.
Kabul
PAK.
ISR.
Jerusalem
Persian G.
Karachi
New Delhi
INDIA
Calcutta
Bombay
B. of Bengal
GOA
(Port.)
Madras
CEYLON
Rabat
Casablanca
MOROCCO
Algiers
TUNISIA
Alexandria
Tripoli
LIBYA
Cairo
EGYPT
Nile
Canary Is.
(Sp.)
SP. W. AFRICA
ALGERIA
(Fr.)
SAHARA
SAUDI ARABIA
Mecca
Red Sea
OMAN
ADEN
(Br.)
G. of Aden
ARABIAN SEA
FR. W. AFRICA
AFRICA
SUDAN
Dakar
NIGERIA
(Br.)
GHANA
Lagos
FR. EQUAT. AFRICA
Addis Ababa
ETHIOPIA
SOM'LD.
Mogadiscio
SIERRA LEONE
(Br.)
LIBERIA
Equator
UGANDA
KENYA
Nairobi
BELG. CONGO
Brazzaville
Leopoldville
TANGANYIKA
Dar es Salaam
Seychelles
(Br.)
Luanda
ANGOLA
(Port.)
MOZAMBIQUE (Port.)
FED. OF RH. & NY.
Mozambique Chan.
MADAGASCAR
(Fr.)
Mauritius (Br.)
Réunion
(Fr.)
S.W. AFRICA
Windhoek
BECH.
Johannesburg
U. OF SO. AFR.
Lourenço Marques
Capetown
C. of Good Hope
Ascension
(Br.)
St. Helena (Br.)
Cape Verde Is.
(Port.)
Azores
(Port.)
Newfoundland
St. John's
C. Race
Montreal
Halifax
Boston
New York
Philadelphia
NORTH ATLANTIC OCEAN
Tropic of Cancer
WEST INDIES
Hispaniola
PUERTO RICO
(U.S.)
Caribbean Sea
Caracas
VEN.
BR. G.
SUR.
FR. G.
COL.
Manaus
Belém
Amazon
SOUTH AMERICA
BRAZIL
PERU
Natal
Salvador
BOLIVIA
La Paz
Brasília
PAR.
Asunción
Rio de Janeiro
São Paulo
Tropic of Capricorn
Córdoba
URU.
Montevideo
Buenos Aires
Santiago
CHILE
ARGENTINA
SOUTH ATLANTIC OCEAN
INDIAN OCEAN
Tristan da Cunha
(Br.)
Gough I.
(Br.)
FALKLAND IS.
(Br.)
S. Georgia
(Br.)
Cape Horn
SCOTIA SEA
SOUTH SANDWICH IS.
(Br.)
SOUTH ORKNEY IS. (Br.)
Bouvet I.
(Nor.)
Pr. Edward Is.
(U. of S. Afr.)
Crozet Is.
(Fr.)
Amsterdam I.
(Fr.)
St. Paul I.
(Fr.)
Kerguelen
(Fr.)
McDonald I.
(Australia)
Heard I.
(Australia)
1 2 3 4 5 6 7 8
80° 60° 40° 20° 0° 20° 40° 60°
Longitude East of Greenwich

Great CITIES of the WORLD

Great CITIES of the WORLD

C. S. HAMMOND and COMPANY
MAPLEWOOD, NEW JERSEY
NEW YORK CHICAGO LOS ANGELES

TABLE OF CONTENTS

THE key references of United States and Canadian cities refer to the map of the UNITED STATES AND SOUTHERN CANADA on the **back** lining sheet of book. Key references of other cities refer to the WORLD MAP on the **front** lining sheet. However, the key reference for Edmonton, Canada refers to the WORLD MAP on the **front** lining sheet.

PRINCIPAL CITIES OF THE UNITED STATES

PRINCIPAL CITIES OF THE UNITED STATES (Cont.)

OTHER CITIES OF THE AMERICAS

CITIES OF EUROPE

CITIES OF EUROPE (Cont.)

CITIES OF AFRICA

CITIES OF ASIA AND OCEANIA

FOREWORD

Cities began when men left their caves and began to live with others in cooperative groups rather than wandering alone in search of creature comforts. Through the centuries man has been absorbed with building and rebuilding as villages grew into towns and eventually expanded to city proportions. Cities reflect the spirit and history of the people who built them and these builders expressed the feeling of their times through the media of stone, steel, brick, marble and glass. In street names, monuments, public buildings, parks, in quiet side streets and broad, splendid avenues it is possible to piece together a great deal of the fascinating story behind the development of not only a city, but a whole nation.

But more than just history is evidenced in a city. It is the culmination of all that is good and, according to some, that is bad in any culture, attracting from the surrounding area those who aspire to success in their chosen field. Each city is a world itself, a planet within a planet, and, though many similarities occur, each is unique. Some cities, such as London, Paris or New York, become the epitome of a national way of life, showing a cross section of how the people live, work and play. Their vitality is such that they affect trends the world over. Other smaller cities, such as Luxembourg, are unique because of their charm or historic importance.

Only a comparatively few people are ever able to realize the dream of seeing these cities at first hand and it is for that reason the maps and pictures are here collected to help picture the world today as glimpsed through the streets of each nation's cities.

CITIES
of the
UNITED STATES

ALL-AMERICAN SOAP BOX DERBY draws huge crowds to famed "Derby Downs," a course especially constructed for this annual event

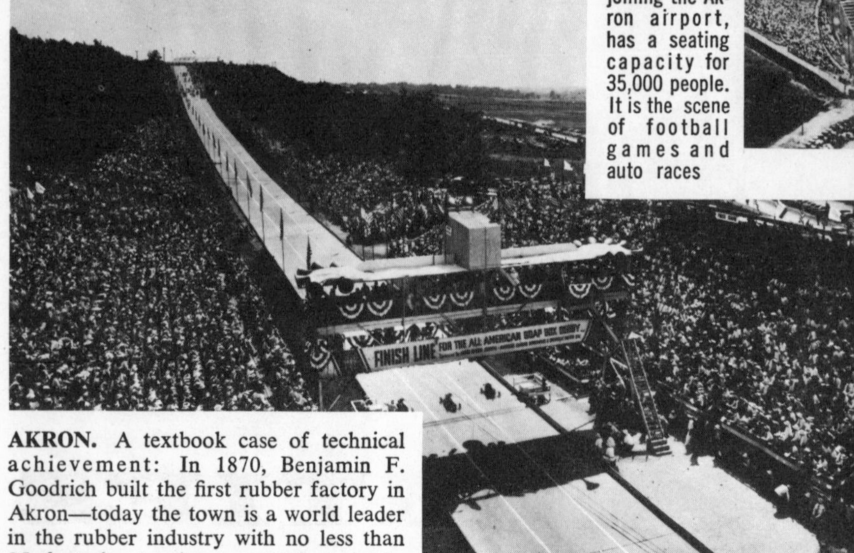

THE RUBBER BOWL located near the edge of town, adjoining the Akron airport, has a seating capacity for 35,000 people. It is the scene of football games and auto races

AKRON. A textbook case of technical achievement: In 1870, Benjamin F. Goodrich built the first rubber factory in Akron—today the town is a world leader in the rubber industry with no less than 25 factories turning out rubber goods, especially auto tires. A large number of other industries, notably plastics and cereals, contribute to the town's industrial importance. Akron attracted many workmen from other parts of the country, especially the South, as well as from abroad. With their varying backgrounds, ways of life and often typical accents of speech, they brought variety and colorful detail to the growing town. A green forest belt sparkling with lakes surrounds the city, whose recreational facilities are exceptional. There are 3,612 acres included in the metropolitan park area, and the Portage Lakes offer 75 miles of shore front. Three rivers run through the city and carry in their names—Cuyahoga, Little Cuyahoga and the Tuscarawas—the memory of the Indians whose portage path passed through this country. In its own name, Akron, (which like the Greek word, *akropolis,* means "high place,") the city indicates its elevation, one of the highest in the State of Ohio, (874 ft.). As a truly modern industrial town, with its laboratories and its university, Akron makes valuable contributions to science and research, especially in the field of rubber, plastics and lighter-than-air aviation, the latter in continuation of the pioneer work done here where America's two largest dirigibles were constructed.

THE GOODYEAR AIRDOCK, largest building in the world without interior supports, was built for the construction and housing of giant airships

Photos: Akron C. of C., Firestone News Service.

THE WORLD'S RUBBER CAPITAL is also the birthplace of the trucking industry, home of the world's biggest fishing tackle factory and one of the nation's largest cereal mills

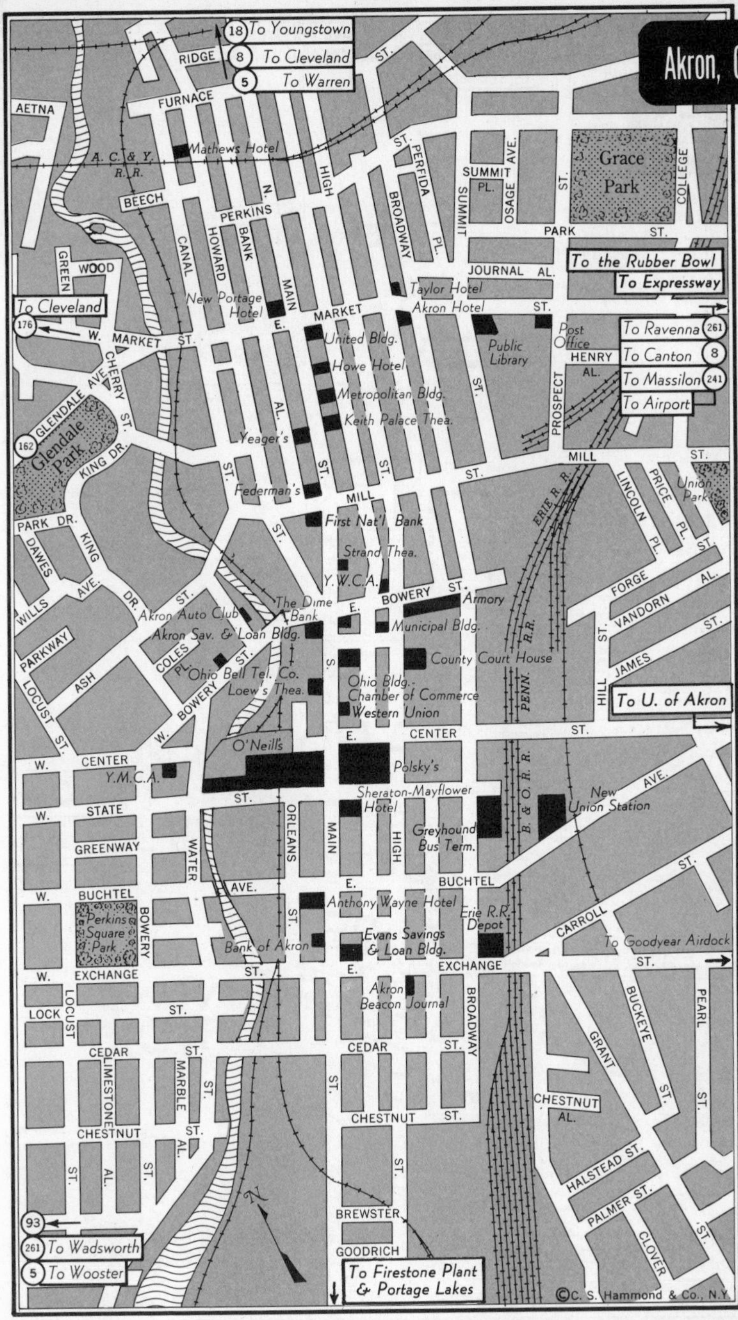

Akron, Ohio

18 To Youngstown
8 To Cleveland
5 To Warren
RIDGE
ST.
FURNACE
AETNA
A. C. & Y. R. R.
Mathews Hotel
N.
HIGH
ST.
PERFIDA
SUMMIT PL.
SUMMIT
OSAGE AVE.
Grace Park
ST.
COLLEGE
BEECH
PERKINS
BANK
HOWARD
CANAL
BROADWAY
PL.
PARK ST.
To the Rubber Bowl
To Expressway
GREEN
WOOD
JOURNAL AL.
New Portage Hotel
MAIN
Taylor Hotel
Akron Hotel
ST.
To Cleveland
176
W. MARKET ST.
E. MARKET
United Bldg.
Howe Hotel
Metropolitan Bldg.
Keith Palace Thea.
Public Library
Post Office
ST.
To Ravenna 261
HENRY AL.
To Canton 8
To Massilon 241
To Airport
PROSPECT
CHERRY ST.
GLENDALE AVE.
162
Glendale Park
KING DR.
AL.
Yeager's
ST.
ST.
ST.
Federman's
MILL ST.
MILL
ST.
LINCOLN PL.
PRICE PL.
Union Park
ERIE R. R.
PARK DR.
DAWES
KING DR.
First Nat'l Bank
Strand Thea.
Y.W.C.A.
ST.
WILLS AVE.
Akron Auto Club
The Dime Bank
E. BOWERY ST.
Armory
FORGE
AL.
VANDORN
ST.
PARKWAY
Akron Sav. & Loan Bldg.
Municipal Bldg.
COLES PL.
ST.
County Court House
S.
JAMES
Ohio Bell Tel. Co.
Loew's Thea.
PENN. R.R.
HILL ST.
LOCUST ST.
ASH
BOWERY
Ohio Bldg.-Chamber of Commerce
Western Union
To U. of Akron
W.
E. CENTER ST.
O'Neill's
W. CENTER
Y.M.C.A.
Polsky's
B. & O. R. R.
ST.
Sheraton-Mayflower Hotel
New Union Station
AVE.
W. STATE
ORLEANS
MAIN
HIGH
Greyhound Bus Term.
GREENWAY
WATER
W. BUCHTEL AVE.
E. BUCHTEL
ST.
Perkins Square Park
BOWERY
Anthony Wayne Hotel
Erie R.R. Depot
CARROLL
ST.
Bank of Akron
Evans Savings & Loan Bldg.
To Goodyear Airdock
W. EXCHANGE ST.
E. EXCHANGE ST.
Akron Beacon Journal
LOCK
LOCUST
ST.
BROADWAY
GRANT
BUCKEYE
PEARL
CEDAR ST.
CEDAR ST.
LIMESTONE
MARBLE
ST.
ST.
CHESTNUT AL.
ST.
ST.
CHESTNUT ST.
CHESTNUT
AL.
ST.
ST.
AL.
ST.
ST.
HALSTEAD ST.
PALMER ST.
CLOVER
ST.
N
BREWSTER
GOODRICH
93
261 To Wadsworth
5 To Wooster
To Firestone Plant & Portage Lakes
©C. S. Hammond & Co., N.Y.

RESEARCH BUILDING of the Firestone Tire and Rubber Company is one of the world's largest and most complete laboratories devoted to rubber and plastic research.

Albany, N. Y.

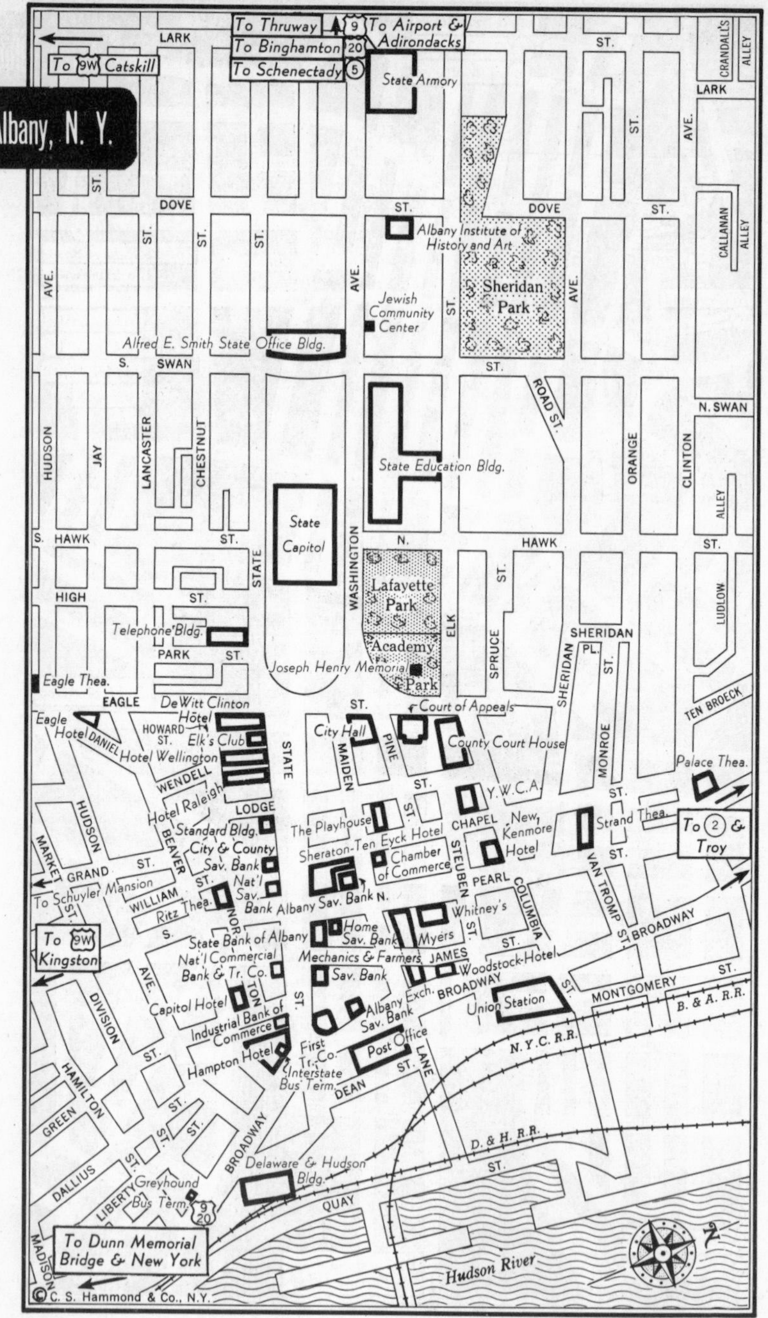

Photos: New York State Dept. of Commerce.

NEW YORK STATE'S CAPITOL which was built over a period of thirty years represents an expenditure of more than 25 million dollars. The great Western Staircase is noted for its architectural beauty.

ALBANY'S SKYLINE as it appears from Rensselaer, an industrial suburb, on the opposite bank of the Hudson River. The Dunn Memorial Bridge connects the two cities

ALBANY. The visitor to Albany, the capital of New York State, can read on a plaque in the center of town that here was the beginning of a famous Indian trail to the Middle West. The location where Albany was to rise was thus remarkable even before the settlers came. And it is its location which, today, gives this town its commercial importance. The waterways from the Atlantic Ocean to the Great Lakes and from the Hudson to the St. Lawrence River, both pass through Albany (or nearby Troy). The Port of Albany, one of America's inland seaports farthest removed from the coast, with its many docks and warehouses lining both banks of the river, possesses nearly every facility of a seaport, including the world's largest single-unit grain elevator. The city is one of the oldest to operate under its original charter and also one of the first to be settled in this country. In 1609, Henry Hudson, in search of a western passage to China, sailed his little ship "Half Moon" up the river to this point, where the Dutch later established a fur trading post. The first permanent settlement was made in 1624 by a group of eighteeen families, mostly Walloons, sent over by the Dutch East India Company. The city recalls its Dutch past in many street names and memorial statues. With its imposing government buildings and attractive residential sections, surrounded by fertile, undulating hills, it is a dignified and beautiful center of the government of the Empire State.

SCHUYLER MANSION, built in 1762, was the scene of many noted events. Here General Burgoyne was a prisoner guest following the battle of Saratoga. Here also, Alexander Hamilton married Schuyler's daughter in 1780.

IN ACADEMY PARK stands the Joseph Henry Memorial Building where Joseph Henry conducted the first practical experiments in electromagnetism. Herman Melville, author of "Moby Dick," attended school here.

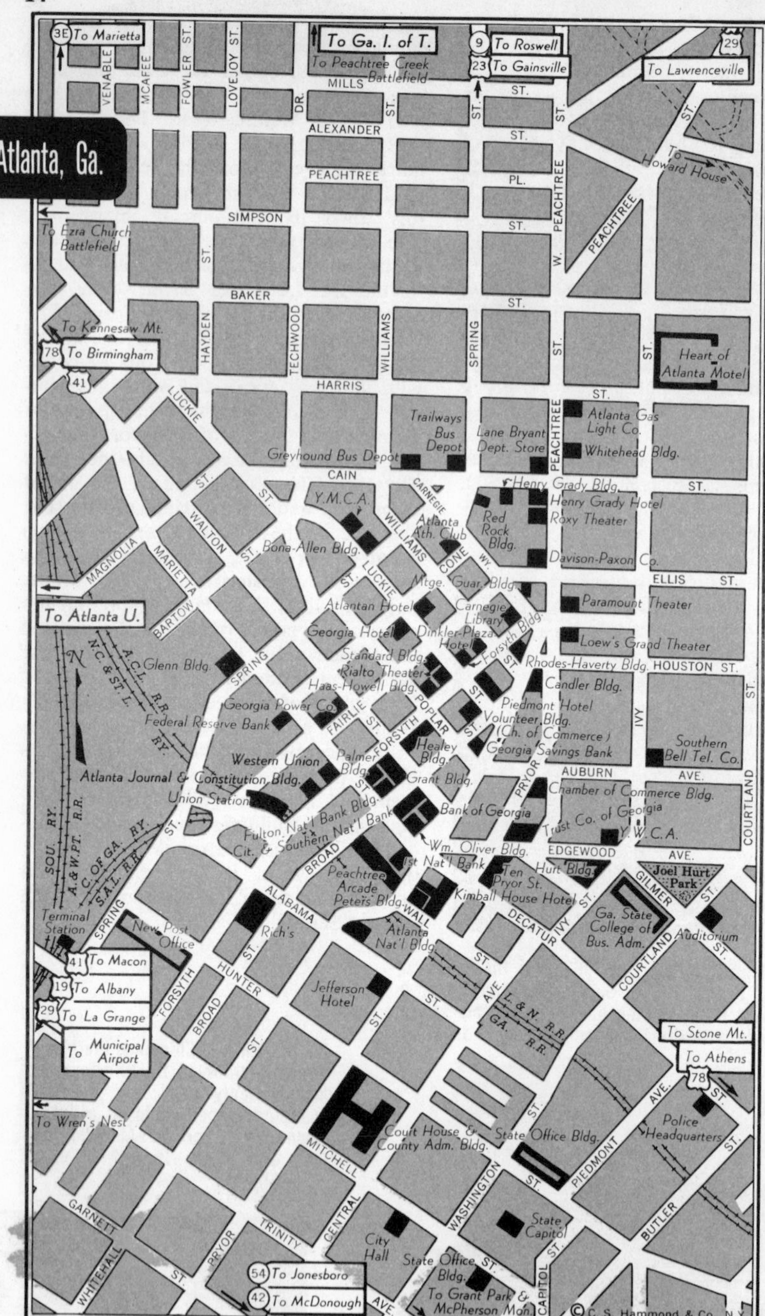

Photos: Atlanta Chamber of Commerce

ON CELEBRATED PEACHTREE STREET, looking north through Five Points, where a railroad surveyor named Stephen Harriman Long drove a surveyor's stake into the ground in 1837 and Atlanta was born

ATLANTA. Atlanta's brief history is drama-packed. By the time of the Civil War, she had become an important Southern center for communications and supplies. In the spring of 1864, Grant sent General William Sherman to cut off the western area from Lee and isolate the Confederate granary of Georgia. In Sherman's view, Atlanta was the key to the entire campaign and her "capture would be the death-knell of the Confederacy." During the summer he conducted his careful maneuver, fighting four tough contests — the Battles of Kennesaw Mountain, Peachtree Creek, Atlanta and Ezra Church — and finally captured her on September first. These hotly contested battlegrounds may be visited today, along with the monument erected upon the spot where General James B. McPherson, commanding the Army of the Tennessee, was killed on July 22nd; Howard House, Sherman's headquarters during the same battle; Fort Walker, a Confederate defense battery; General Joseph E. Johnston's headquarters at Marietta; National Cemetery at Marietta and Oakland Cemetery, final resting places for thousands of soldiers killed during the sieges. Reconstructed Atlanta now has regained her position as chief rail center of the South. In addition, her twenty-three inviting courses have made her a noted year-round golf resort.

ODD-LOOKING STONE MOUNTAIN, a favorite tourist sight on the outskirts of Atlanta, is said to be the largest exposed body of solid granite in the world

WREN'S NEST, home of Joel Chandler Harris, creator of the "Uncle Remus" and "Br'er Rabbit" stories for children, when he worked on the staff of the Atlanta Constitution

CITY HALL was built on the site of Sherman's headquarters during the Federal occupancy of the city in 1864, before he destroyed it by fire

GEORGIA STATE CAPITOL, on the site of the camping ground of the Union Army during the Battle of Atlanta, contains the State Museum of natural sciences. Statue is of John Brown Gordon, a Confederate general and governor of Georgia

ATLANTIC CITY. Atlantic City has been described as an "Amusement Factory," and in truth the City's major industry is the entertainment of visitors, who each year flock by the millions to its beaches and boardwalk. Located on Absecon Island, it is separated from the New Jersey mainland by broad expanses of salt marsh. The city began its growth as a year-round resort with the building of the Atlantic and Camden Railroad early in the 1850's. Atlantic City's sheltered location and its mild climate, tempered by the Gulf Stream, contribute to its popularity in winter as well as in summer. Today the city presents a glittering front along more than five miles of boardwalk lined by an extravagance of hotels, restaurants, hot dog stands, souvenir shops, shooting galleries, auction houses and side shows. The original idea for a boardwalk was conceived in 1870 by a hotel man and a railroad conductor; it was at first only 8 feet wide and laid directly upon the sand. The present structure is 60 feet wide and built of steel and concrete, covered by pine planking. Unique features of Atlantic City are its several amusement piers. Widely spaced by stretches of beach, these piers, set atop pilings, reach from the shore like long steel arms. Among Atlantic City's many crowd-drawing attractions is the annual Miss America Beauty Contest.

Photos: Atlantic City Press Bureau

PONY RIDES on the beach provide a thrill for youngsters from October through May. A year-round resort, Atlantic City has many pleasant diversions to offer the visitor during the winter months

ABSECON LIGHTHOUSE at Rhode Island and Pacific Avenues has been an Atlantic City landmark since 1854. Inactivated in 1933, the 167-foot beacon has recently been restored

THE BEACH AT ATLANTIC CITY with its sparkling white sands, gay umbrellas and rows of cabanas attracts throngs of bathers and sunworshippers

Atlantic City, N. J.

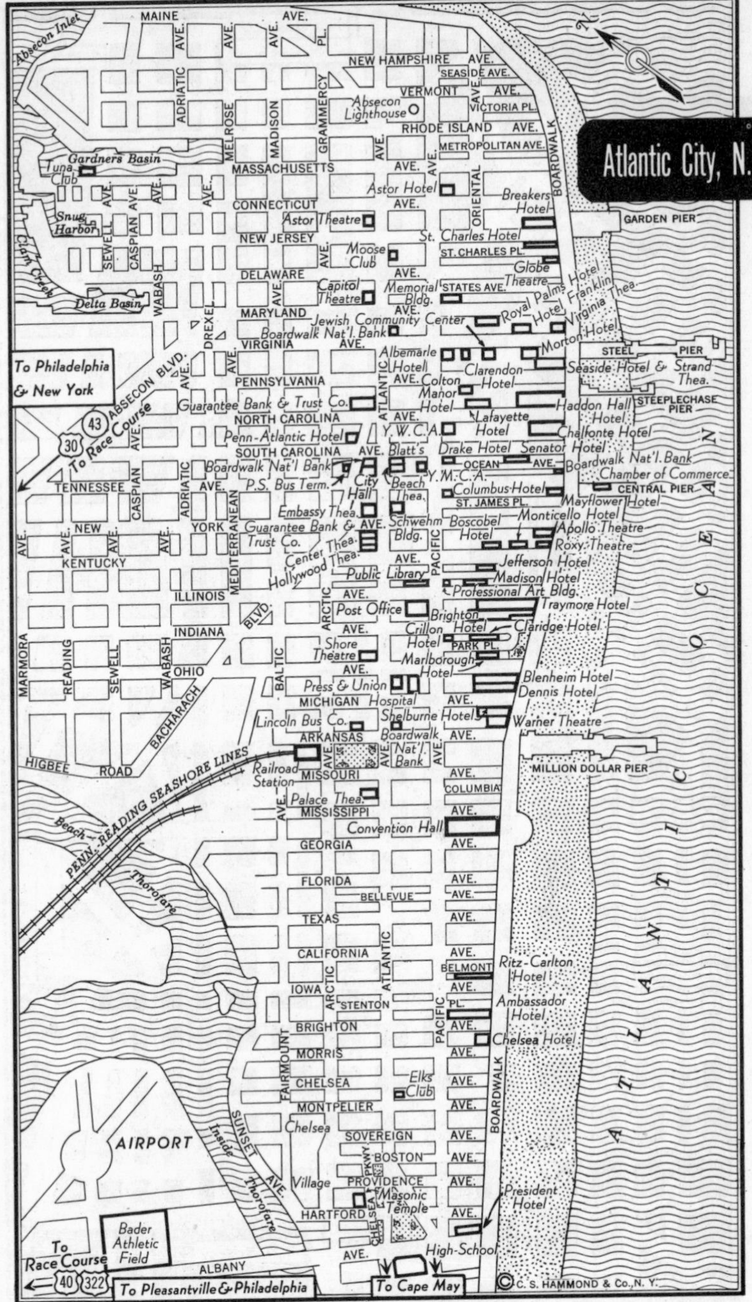

THE BOARDWALK is the axis around which the activities of Atlantic City revolve. This unique thoroughfare with its planks laid in a striking herring-bone pattern is lined with a dazzling array of hotels, shops and amusement palaces

Baltimore, Md.

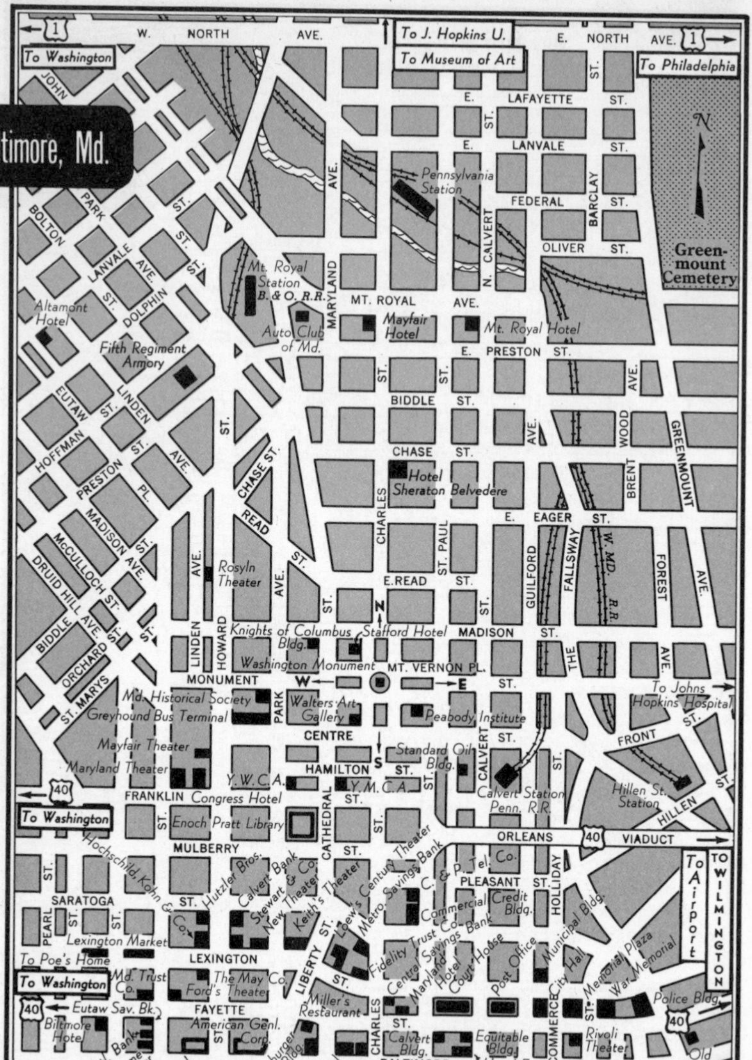

W. NORTH AVE.
To Washington
To J. Hopkins U.
To Museum of Art
E. NORTH AVE.
To Philadelphia
JOHN
E. LAFAYETTE ST.
E. LANVALE ST.
Pennsylvania Station
FEDERAL ST.
BARCLAY ST.
OLIVER ST.
Green-mount Cemetery
BOLTON
PARK
LANVALE
AVE.
DOLPHIN
Mt. Royal Station B. & O. R.R.
MARYLAND AVE.
N. CALVERT ST.
Altamont Hotel
Fifth Regiment Armory
Auto Club of Md.
MT. ROYAL AVE.
Mayfair Hotel
Mt. Royal Hotel
E. PRESTON ST.
EUTAW ST.
LINDEN
HOFFMAN
PRESTON
PL.
BIDDLE ST.
CHASE ST.
Hotel Sheraton Belvedere
BRENT
WOOD AVE.
GREENMOUNT
MADISON
McCULLOCH ST.
DRUID HILL AVE.
READ ST.
CHARLES ST.
ST. PAUL ST.
E. EAGER ST.
GUILFORD
FALLSWAY
W. MD. R.R.
FOREST AVE.
Rosyln Theater
E. READ ST.
BIDDLE AVE.
ORCHARD ST.
LINDEN AVE.
HOWARD
Knights of Columbus Bldg.
Stafford Hotel
MADISON ST.
THE AVE.
ST. MARYS
MONUMENT
Washington Monument
MT. VERNON PL.
Md. Historical Society
Greyhound Bus Terminal
PARK
Walters Art Gallery
Peabody Institute
To Johns Hopkins Hospital
CENTRE ST.
Mayfair Theater
Maryland Theater
Standard Oil Bldg.
FRONT ST.
HAMILTON ST.
Y.W.C.A.
Y.M.C.A.
Calvert Station Penn. R.R.
Hillen St. Station
HILLEN ST.
FRANKLIN
Congress Hotel
To Washington
Enoch Pratt Library
CATHEDRAL ST.
ORLEANS 40 VIADUCT
MULBERRY ST.
Hochschild, Kohn & Co.
Hutzler Bros.
Calvert Bank
Stewart & Co.
New Theater
Keith's Theater
Loew's Century Theater
Metro. Savings Bank
C. & P. Tel. Co.
PLEASANT ST.
HOLLIDAY
To Airport
TO WILMINGTON
SARATOGA ST.
PEARL
Lexington Market
Commercial Credit Bldg.
Fidelity Trust Co.
Central Savings Bank
Maryland Hotel
Court House
Post Office
Municipal Bldg.
City Hall
Memorial Plaza
War Memorial
To Poe's Home
LEXINGTON
LIBERTY ST.
To Washington
Md. Trust Co.
The May Co.
Ford's Theater
Miller's Restaurant
Police Bldg.
Eutaw Sav. Bk.
FAYETTE ST.
American Genl. Corp.
COMMERCE ST.
Biltmore Hotel
Western Natl. Bank
Hippodrome Theater
Hamburger Bldg.
Calvert Bldg.
Equitable Bldg.
Rivoli Theater
Old Shot Tower
BALTIMORE ST.
Hotel Emerson
New Howard Hotel
Trailways Bus Term.
REDWOOD
Lord Baltimore Hotel
B. & O. R.R.
Md. Life Ins. Co.
Safe Deposit & Trust Co.
PACA
Hopkins Pl. Sav. Bank
Sun Newspaper
Savings Bank of Balt.
Balt. Realty Tr. Co.
First Natl. Bank
Southern Hotel
Md. Trust Co.
Mercantile Trust Co.
Keyser Bldg.
Garrett Bldg.
GAY
MARKET
Univ. of Maryland
LOMBARD
HOPKINS PL.
LIGHT
Fidelity & Guar. Fire Corp.
GREENE
SOUTH ST.
Baltimore News Post & American
PRATT ST.
Pratt Street Wharves
SHARP ST.
To Annapolis
To Ft. McHenry
CAMDEN ST.
Camden Station
B. & O. R.R.
Light Street Wharves
© C. S. Hammond & Co., N.Y.

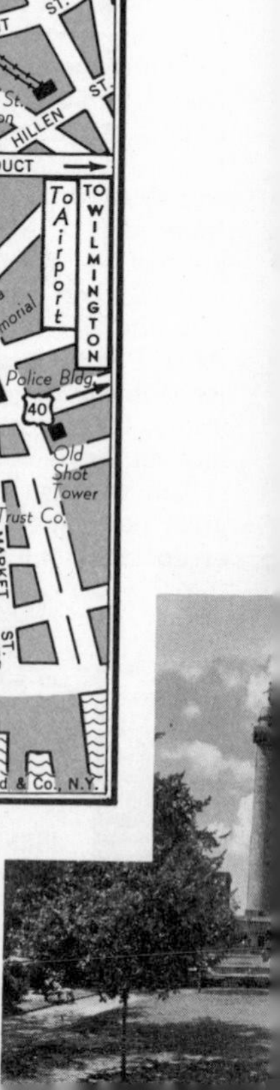

MT. VERNON PLACE, gracious hub of a favored residential district, radiates from the towering Washington Monument, the first large formal statue to the first President. In the foreground is the statue of Severn Teackle Wallis, lawyer, poet and wit

ORE PIER of the Baltimore and Ohio Railroad is one of the fastest unloading piers on the Eastern seaboard in a seaport whose import business ranks second only to New York's

BALTIMORE MUSEUM OF ART houses valuable collections of old furniture, miniatures, silver, cut glass, old laces, bronzes, the Antioch mosaics, over 40,000 prints and paintings, including some by Raphael, Rubens, Rembrandt and Millet

BALTIMORE. A city proud of her historic past, this "Monumental City" is crammed with mementos and memorials of her storied record. A picturesque city, the old sections are patterned with block after block of identical, narrow, red-brick houses with spotlessly scrubbed, white-marble steps. An old city which sprouted from a tiny colony, her hilly, clamorous, twisting, bursting downtown streets are a modern motorist's frustrating anathema. An unusual city where medical men are counted among the elite and the influential, her amazing Johns Hopkins University has earned an astonishing preeminence in the scientific field. A city of cherished social traditions, her strictly ruled society is dominated by long-standing institutions like the exclusive Bachelors' Cotillon, founded in 1796. A city of wealth—and poverty — she abounds with splendid mansions of many architectural styles. The city of H. L. Mencken and Edgar Allen Poe, her advanced artistic achievements have been primarily in the field of music, for her notable Peabody Institute has an enviable reputation as an excellent conservatory. This is Maryland's great port on the Chesapeake — proud, aristocratic, but rowdy, Baltimore.

STAR-SHAPED FORT MC HENRY, overlooking the Patapsco River, where the British attack on September 13, 1814, inspired the lawyer, Francis Scott Key to write the "Star-Spangled Banner," also confined over 6,000 prisoners during the Civil War

Photos: Maryland Department of Information, M. E. Warren

JOHNS HOPKINS HOSPITAL, an ugly red-brick building trimmed with sandstone, shares its world-famous reputation with the Medical School, first in the country to have a curriculum comparable to the finest in Europe

Birmingham, Ala.

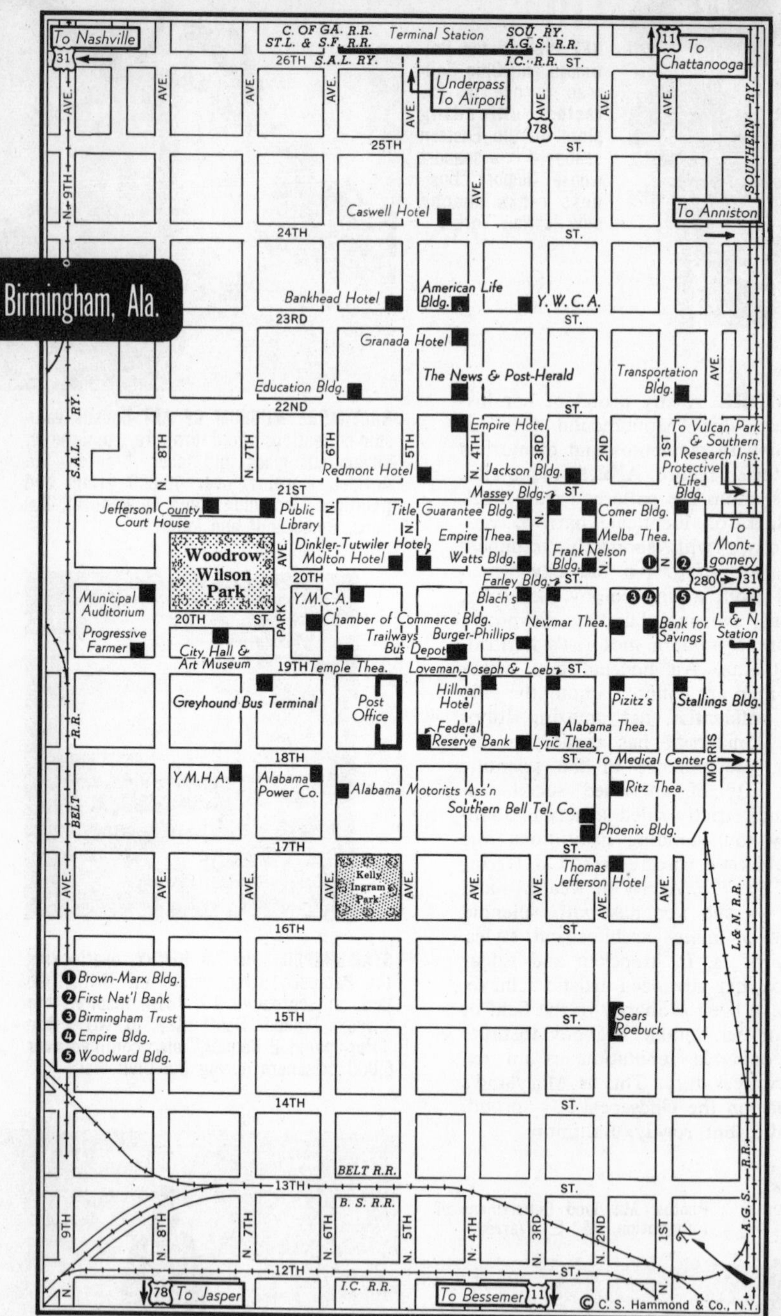

Photos: Black Star

NINETEENTH STREET, the main street of Birmingham, is a part of the city's highly important business section

THE HANDSOME CITY HALL rises above Woodrow Wilson Park in downtown Birmingham

THE VULCAN STATUE, on Red Mountain, looks down on Birmingham. Second in size only to the Statue of Liberty in New York Harbor, the iron Vulcan, an emblem of the city's industrial importance, is 40 feet high and stands atop a 120-foot tower

A REPLICA OF THE STATUE OF LIBERTY, presented to Birmingham by the Boy Scouts, stands in Woodrow Wilson Park. Behind the statue is the Jefferson County Court House

BIRMINGHAM (Ala.) Birmingham, the youthful, brisk-paced "Pittsburgh of the South," emerged from the Alabama wilderness within the memory of living man. It was incorporated in 1871 and named for the industrial city of Birmingham, England. The city's rapid growth has come about through the wealth of its mountains red with iron ore, black with coal and its valley white with limestone—the one place in the world where the three essential ingredients for making steel are found in such generous quantities. Diversified industrial center of the Southeast, Birmingham produces large portions of America's steel, pig iron and related products. Culturally and spiritually, Birmingham proudly proclaims a newly gained national fame for her fine Symphony Orchestra, Art Museum, Music Series, civic ballet and theater groups. She has long cherished wide prominence in the architecture and landscaping of her numerous churches and beautiful homes. Mountainous terrain, tall pine trees and green lawns characterize the city's famed residential areas to the east and south. Birmingham substantially contributes to modern world medical and industrial research through the South's fastest growing Medical Center and through Southern Research Institute widely known for its cancer and industrial experimentation.

BOSTON. Boston stands out among the cities of America because of her place in history and the extraordinary men whose lives have so enriched her exalted halls. Along her narrow, winding streets are the mellowed landmarks of high adventure. Here history comes to life amid cherished memories of early Puritan fathers, of troops mustering for the French and Indian Wars, of freedom-loving colonists rallying at fiery meetings, of a tradition echoing with glowing names like Revere, Adams, Emerson, Longfellow, Alcott, Thoreau and Holmes. As you walk through the ancient, cobblestoned streets, lined with quaint antique shops and musty bookstalls, or along elm-shaded walks of Boston Common, you cannot help but feel the presence of those patriots and scholars of another day, whose deeds still live to praise them. At one corner of the Common, which was set aside in 1634 for a "trayning field" and "feeding of cattell," is Granary Burying Ground, where lie John Hancock, Sam Adams and Robert Treat Paine, all signers of the Declaration of Independence, Paul Revere and the victims of the Boston Massacre. Boston has

BUNKER HILL MONUMENT on Breed's Hill, Charlestown, commemorates the heroic stand of raw American militia against the cream of British troops. A statue of Col. William Prescott stands at the base

FANEUIL HALL, epitomizing all the drama and struggle of America's earliest days, was given its popular name of the "Cradle of Liberty" by James Otis because of the many important protest meetings held here. It is the headquarters of the Ancient and Honorable Artillery Company, oldest military organization in the U. S.

Photos: Massachusetts Department of Commerce.

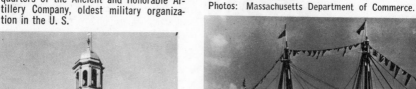

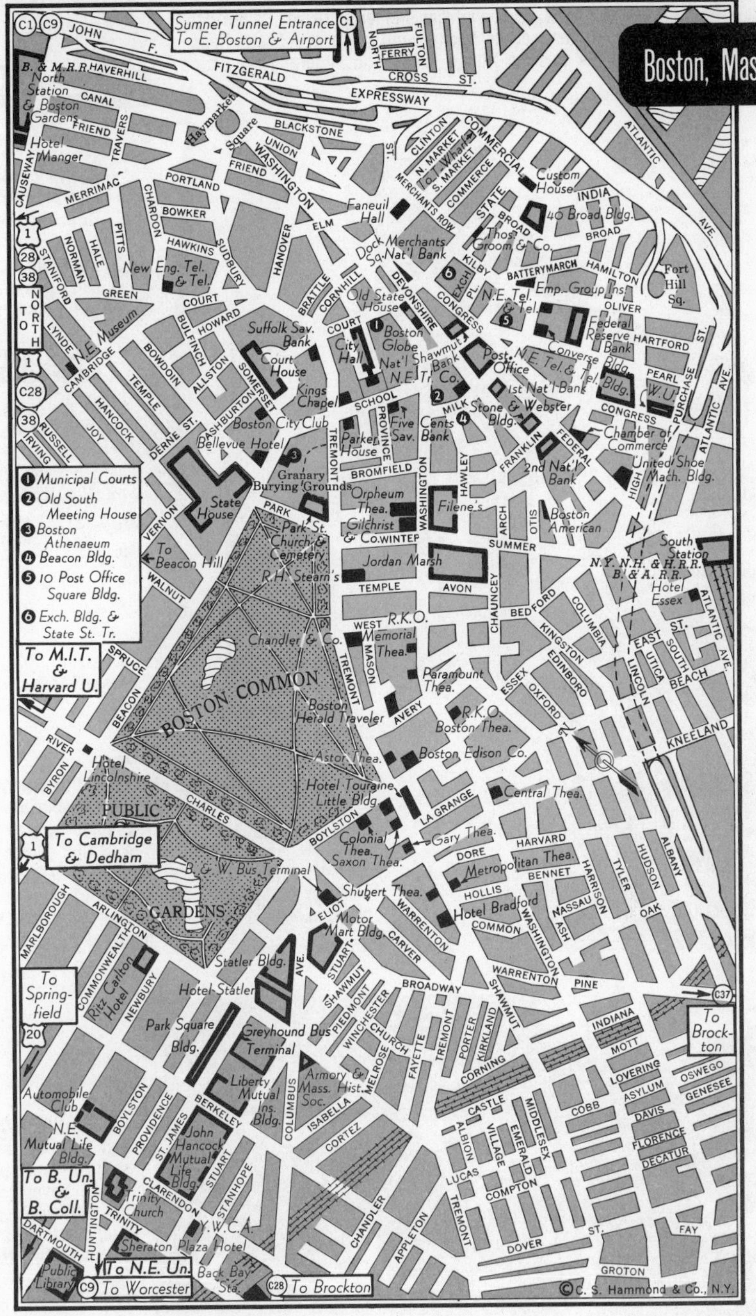

"OLD IRONSIDES," the U. S. Frigate "Constitution" rides today in the Boston Navy Yard just as she did in 1797 when chasing pirates and in her historic battles of the War of 1812

CHARLES RIVER BASIN as seen from Memorial Drive, Cambridge. Beacon Hill is in the center background, with the State House dome between the Custom House Tower and Federal Post Office

Photos: Massachusetts Department of Commerce

WELL-KNOWN EQUESTRIAN STATUE on Paul Revere Mall is dominated by the slender spire of Christ Church, or "Old North Church," where the signal lanterns, warning of the march of British troops to Lexington and Concord, were hung on the night of 18 April, 1775

LARS ANDERSON ESTATE has an outstanding museum of antique automobiles. Several times during the year, owners of such autos gather here to show off their paces

BOSTON Continued

in truth been termed the hotbed of the Revolution. Led by the Committee of Correspondence and Samuel Adams, it was the revolutionary protests of these solid Bostonians which inflamed the other colonies into sympathetic response and ultimately into open rebellion. A favorite meeting place of these fervid citizens was Old South Meeting House, within whose plain brick walls James Otis delivered his ringing oration against the Writs of Assistance and the Boston Tea Party was organized. On the unique paving of State Street, beneath the windows and stepped gables of the influential Old State House, fell the five victims of the explosive Boston Massacre. A center of American Puritanism, with notable ministers and statesmen, Boston — whose ships and fisheries early made her the colonies' commercial leader — soon provided for her intellectual life. The city's nickname, "Hub of the Universe," is derived from her nineteenth-century position of intellectual, political and commercial leadership. This was the literary center of the United States and

FAIRBANKS HOUSE in suburban Dedham, built in 1636, is the oldest frame dwelling in America. Shaded by giant elms, the long, low, weatherbrown house is furnished with family heirlooms

KING'S CHAPEL, whose restful interior is perhaps the finest colonial church interior in existence, has a unique background. It was the first Episcopal Church in America and later, the country's first Unitarian Church. The adjacent burial ground, first in Boston, contains the grave of John Winthrop, first governor of Massachusetts

ON COPLEY SQUARE, the massive Romanesque architecture of Trinity Church, the masterpiece of Henry Hobson Richardson, contrasts sharply with the starkly simple, yet graceful modern lines of the city's largest office building, home of John Hancock Mutual Life Insurance Company

PICTURESQUE T-WHARF, somnolent in the early afternoon sun, where colorful fishing boats bob lazily to every ripple from passing harbor craft. Along the wharf are small restaurants specializing in New England fish dinners, and in the apartments above, quaint artists' studios

LOUISBURG SQUARE on Beacon Hill is one of the oldest and best-known residential areas. Its cobblestone roadway, well-kept old homes, some with the priceless original lavender windowpanes, and its quaint private park, with the wrought-iron fence, form a pleasant link with the past

Photos: Massachusetts Department of Commerce

AN EXCURSION BOAT on the Charles River passes Dunster Hall on the beautiful campus of Harvard University in Cambridge, the oldest in America, founded in 1636

BOSTON Continued

America's chief essayists, historians, poets, philosophers and novelists lived in and around the city. Boston Public Library is one of the world's most famous, for not only does it possess a significant assortment of Americana and notable mural paintings, but architecturally it was the epochal achievement of the century. Besides many other high-ranking collections, the Museum of Fine Arts is unsurpassed for the quality, comprehensiveness and continuity of its Asiatic art. As a creative musical center, Boston is today in many respects unrivaled. The venerable Boston Symphony Orchestra, with a string section reputed to be the finest in the world, performs in Symphony Hall, and its offspring, the famous Boston Pops Concerts and the more-recently established Esplanade Summer Concerts, rank with the finest musical presentations. This, then, is Boston, storied city whose name will be eternally preserved in the language of the country — from Boston baked beans and Boston cream pie to Boston terriers. Hub of New England commerce, hallowed shrine of American liberty, seat of education and culture, city of battlegrounds and monuments immortalized by the gallant deeds of men whose names are etched forever in the pages of history — this is legendary, dignified, traditional, uncompromising Boston, and paradoxically, still the famous city of imagination, impassioned vitality and unquenchable liberalism.

TRADITIONAL "MUST" for Boston visitors is a quiet ride in one of the famous swan boats on the lagoon in the Public Gardens, next to the Common

BUFFALO. On October 26, 1825, a fleet of canal boats led by the *Seneca Chief* left Buffalo on an historic trip to New York City, via Albany, on the newly completed Erie Canal. Booming cannon and cheering crowds welcomed the fleet at every stop. The canal's opening made Buffalo an inland "seaport" and paved the way to its present eminence as second largest city in New York State. Although unhappily associated with the assassination of President McKinley in 1901, Buffalo has with good reason attained the reputation as the "City of Good Neighbors." It was an important station on the Underground Railroad; the building which served as temporary shelter for many of these Negro slaves making their dash to Canada for freedom is now the Michigan Avenue Baptist Church. The Charity Organization Society, now the Family Service Society, founded here in 1877, was the first of its kind in the country. And the Peace Bridge over the Niagara River at Buffalo, one of the busiest points of entry between the United States and Canada, commemorates the long friendship between these two great countries.

ALBRIGHT ART GALLERY in beautiful Delaware Park features a distinguished collection of paintings and sculpture, including Wilhelm Lehmbruck's famed "Kneeling Woman" and the mysterious "Roman Poet"

MASSIVE CITY HALL faces McKinley Circle. Two statues flanking the building honor Millard Fillmore and Grover Cleveland, both citizens of Buffalo who rose to the Presidency of the U. S.

Photos: New York State Department of Commerce

KLEINHANS MUSIC HALL, home of the Buffalo Philharmonic Orchestra, is one of the finest concert halls in the world. Functional in both interior and exterior design, the acoustical and lighting research which preceded its design make it ideal for musician and actor

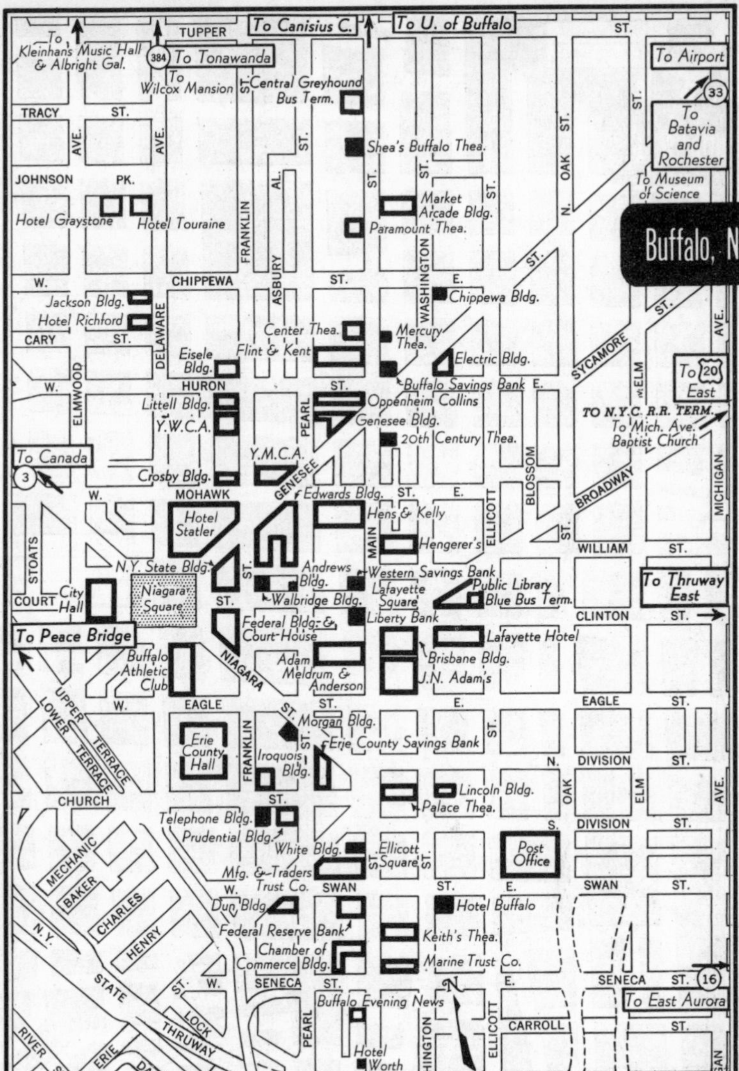

Buffalo, N. Y.

To Kleinhans Music Hall & Albright Gal.
TUPPER ST.
To Canisius C.
To U. of Buffalo
384 To Tonawanda
To Wilcox Mansion
Central Greyhound Bus Term.
To Airport
33
To Batavia and Rochester
To Museum of Science
TRACY ST.
JOHNSON PK.
Shea's Buffalo Thea.
Hotel Graystone
Hotel Touraine
Market Arcade Bldg.
Paramount Thea.
W. CHIPPEWA ST.
E. Chippewa Bldg.
Jackson Bldg.
Hotel Richford
CARY ST.
Center Thea.
Mercury Thea.
Flint & Kent
Eisele Bldg.
Electric Bldg.
Buffalo Savings Bank
W. HURON ST.
E. HURON ST.
Oppenheim Collins
Genesee Bldg.
Littell Bldg.
Y.W.C.A.
20th Century Thea.
To 20 East
TO N.Y.C. R.R. TERM.
To Mich. Ave. Baptist Church
To Canada
3
Y.M.C.A.
Crosby Bldg.
GENESEE
SYCAMORE ST.
BROADWAY
W. MOHAWK
Edwards Bldg.
E. MOHAWK ST.
Hotel Statler
Hens & Kelly
Hengerer's
WILLIAM ST.
N.Y. State Bldg.
Andrews Bldg.
Western Savings Bank
Public Library
To Thruway East
COURT ST.
City Hall
Niagara Square
Walbridge Bldg.
Lafayette Square
Blue Bus Term.
CLINTON ST.
Liberty Bank
Federal Bldg. & Court House
To Peace Bridge
Lafayette Hotel
Buffalo Athletic Club
Adam Meldrum & Anderson
Brisbane Bldg.
J.N. Adam's
NIAGARA
W. EAGLE ST.
E. EAGLE ST.
Morgan Bldg.
Erie County Savings Bank
Erie County Hall
Iroquois Bldg.
N. DIVISION ST.
Lincoln Bldg.
Palace Thea.
UPPER TERRACE
LOWER TERRACE
CHURCH ST.
Telephone Bldg.
Prudential Bldg.
S. DIVISION ST.
White Bldg.
Ellicott Square
Post Office
Mfg. & Traders Trust Co.
W. SWAN ST.
E. SWAN ST.
Dun Bldg.
Hotel Buffalo
Federal Reserve Bank
Keith's Thea.
Chamber of Commerce Bldg.
Marine Trust Co.
MECHANIC
BAKER
CHARLES
HENRY
N.Y. STATE ST.
W. SENECA ST.
E. SENECA ST.
16
Buffalo Evening News
To East Aurora
LOCK
THRUWAY
CARROLL ST.
RIVER ST.
ERIE
DANTE PL.
Hotel Worth
EXCHANGE ST.
Dante Housing Development
Buffalo Memorial Auditorium
QUAY ST.
SKYWAY
WATER ST.
D.L. & W. R.R.
HANOVER
SCOTT ST.
5
To Dunkirk
BUFFALO RIVER
TO D.L. & W. R.R. B. & O. R.R. & N.Y.C. & ST.L. R.R. STA.
DELAWARE AVE.
ELMWOOD AVE.
STOATS
FRANKLIN ST.
ASBURY AL.
PEARL ST.
MAIN ST.
WASHINGTON ST.
ELLICOTT ST.
BLOSSOM ST.
OAK ST.
ELM ST.
MICHIGAN AVE.

BUFFALO MUSEUM OF SCIENCE arranges its main exhibits to tell the story of science in natural sequence. The "Glass Man," showing the working of the human body, is one of its most popular attractions

Charlotte, N. C.

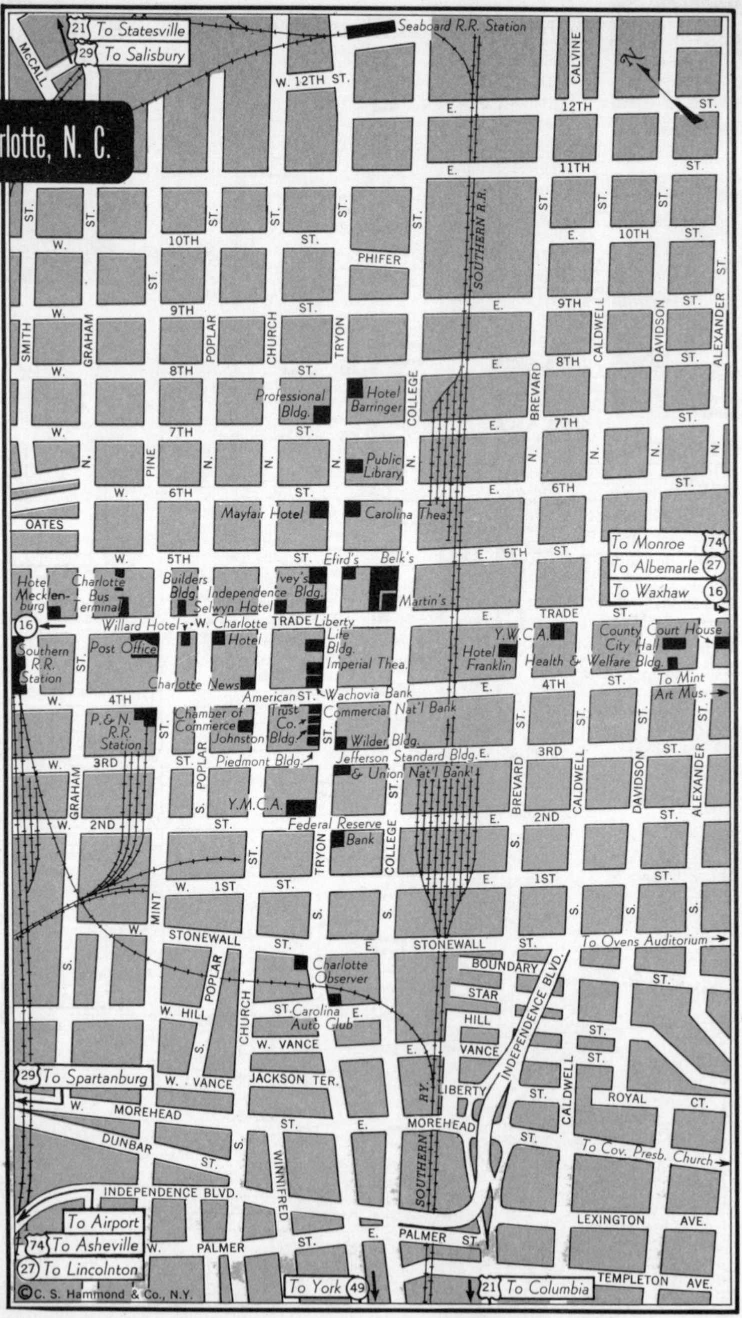

MINT MUSEUM OF ART was once a branch of the United States Mint which operated here from 1837 to 1861. After the Civil War it was used as an Assay Office until 1913. Completely restored from its original materials, it is now used as a museum

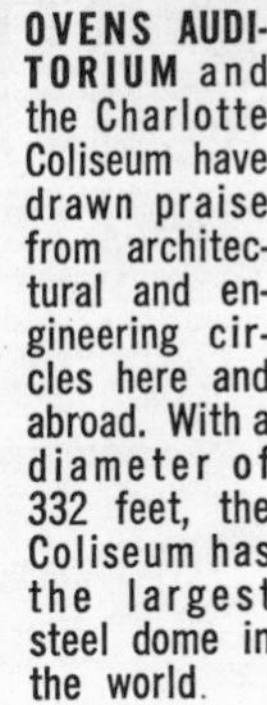

OVENS AUDITORIUM and the Charlotte Coliseum have drawn praise from architectural and engineering circles here and abroad. With a diameter of 332 feet, the Coliseum has the largest steel dome in the world.

CHARLOTTE. Charlotte, the largest city of the Carolinas, lies in the fertile hills of the central North Carolina Piedmont. The "Queen City" is named for Charlotte of Mecklenburg-Schwerin, wife of George II of England. Here in 1775, irate colonists, dissatisfied with British rule, wrote America's first declaration of independence. May 19th, the anniversary of the signing of the Mecklenburg Declaration, is to this day celebrated as a state holiday. When British forces under Cornwallis occupied the area, his Lordship referred to Charlotte as a "damned hornet's nest" because his troops were continually harassed by local patriots. The city's seal proudly immortalizes the "hornet's nest" epithet. Until gold was discovered in California, Charlotte, with over 100 gold mines in the vicinity, was the center of America's principal gold-producing area; also the scene of this country's first gold rush. Although the city's location is many miles from the sea, it served as a Confederate Navy Yard during the War Between the States. In the early 1900's, cotton gins, cotton mills and hosiery factories sprang up around the margins of the city. With the Catawba River supplying abundant hydro-electric power for its more than forty large textile mills, Charlotte has become one of America's leading textile centers.

DOUGLAS MUNICIPAL AIRPORT houses the facilities for five airlines in this modern, one and a half million dollar terminal.

JAMES JACK MONUMENT was erected in memory of Captain Jack, the "Paul Revere of the South," who rode on horseback to Philadelphia to carry the Mecklenburg Declaration to the Continentall Congress

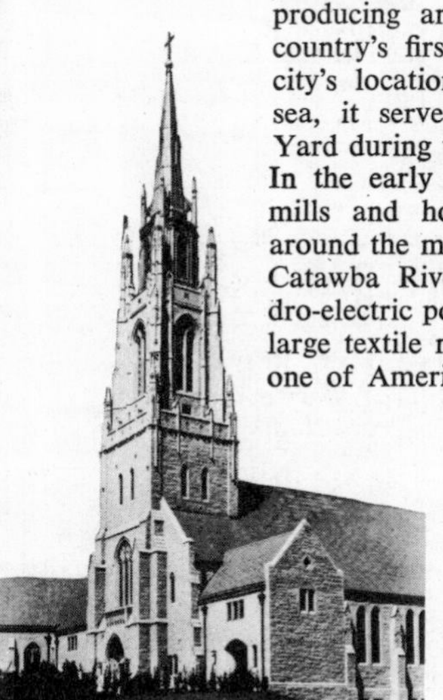

COVENANT PRESBYTERIAN CHURCH is one of the many that have caused Charlotte to become known as a city of churches. Its uncontested claim is that it has more churches per capita than any other city in the world with the exception of Edinburgh, Scotland

Photos: Charlotte Chamber of Commerce

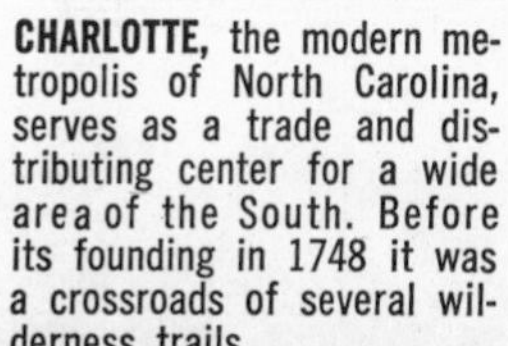

CHARLOTTE, the modern metropolis of North Carolina, serves as a trade and distributing center for a wide area of the South. Before its founding in 1748 it was a crossroads of several wilderness trails

Chicago, Ill.

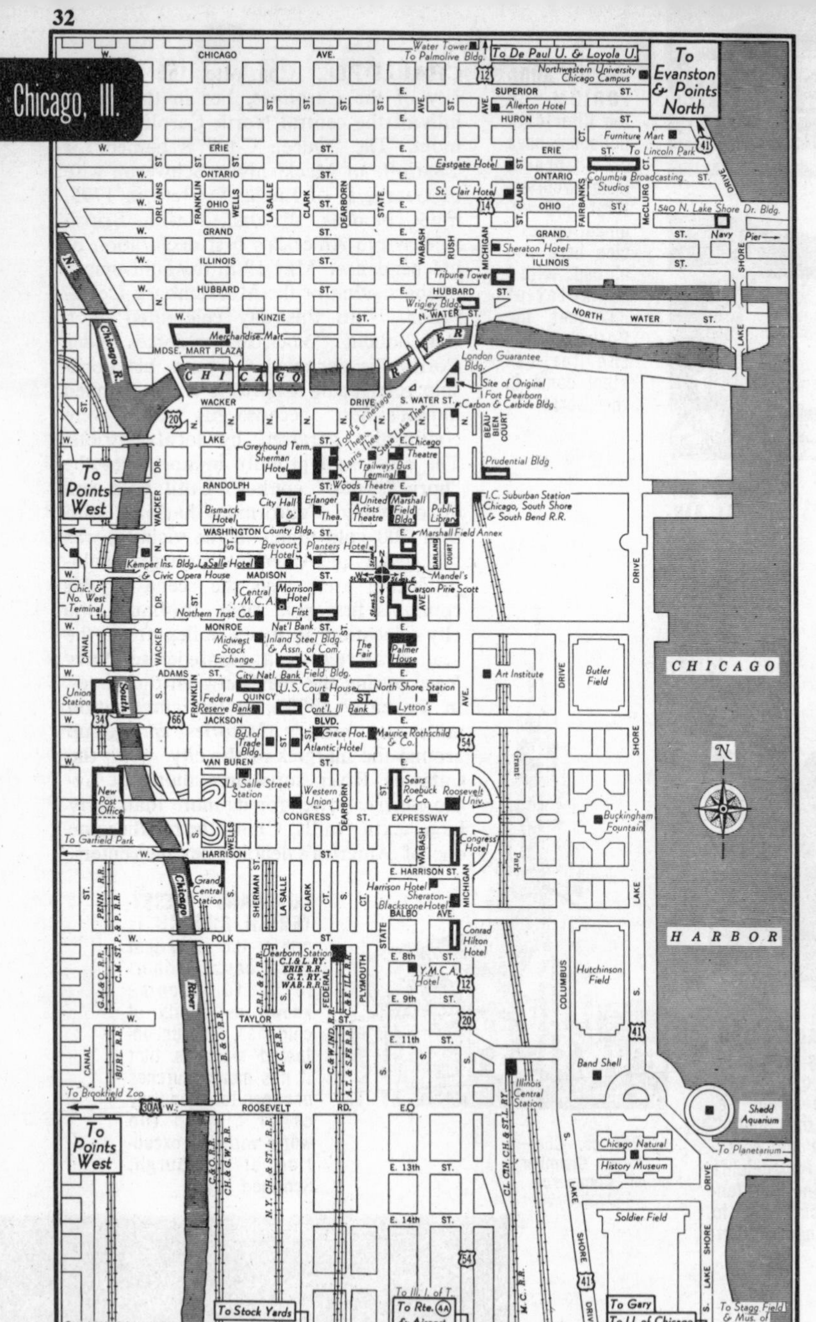

Photos: Chicago Park District

GRANT PARK which serves as Chicago's handsome front yard is backed by the familiar profile of the city's skyline. A newcomer to Chicago's great cluster of skyscrapers is the 41-story Prudential Building

CLARENCE BUCKINGHAM FOUNTAIN suggests something out of Wonderland. By day, lacy jets of water spurt heavenward and fall in spray-bordered torrents over the lips of 3 circular basins. At night the display is a miracle of changing color and light

CHICAGO. Chartered in 1833, Chicago is relatively young as cities go, yet its growth has been phenomenal. In keeping with its motto—"I Will"—Chicago has risen from a remote frontier outpost to become the nation's second largest city with a population of over 3½ million people. The great fire of 1871, which completely wiped out the business district, scarcely interrupted the city's progress. The tremendous task of rebuilding—in steel and stone instead of wood—started immediately, and by 1877 recovery was complete, with the Old Water Tower and the legend of Mrs. O'Leary's cow kicking over a lantern about the only remnants of the older city redeemed from the ashes. Standing at the nation's transportation crossroads, Chicago has become the business capital of mid-America—the most productive, the best balanced region on earth in terms of industry, commerce and agriculture. In the words of the poet Carl Sandburg, Chicago is:

> "Hog Butcher for the World,
> Tool Maker, Stacker of Wheat,
> Player with Railroads and the
> Nation's Freight Handler."

More people or more tons of freight can be transported to the rest of the nation from Chicago in less time, at less cost and with fewer transfers than from any other major city. Today, its 22-mile lake front is lined by great masses of towering buildings in a striking setting of handsome parks, broad boulevards, white sand beaches and the sparkling waters of Lake Michigan. The stretch north of the Chicago river is particularly impressive

CHICAGO Continued

with its apartment houses, big hotels and such landmarks as the Tribune Tower, the Wrigley Building and the Palmolive Building. Here is found the Furniture Mart with its office and display facilities for the nation's leading home furnishers; the Merchandise Mart, the second largest office building in the world; the nationally famous Marshall Field's department store with its spectacular dome composed of millions of pieces of Tiffany glass, and the Chicago Campus of Northwestern University with its schools of law, medicine and dentistry. At the northern end of Lake Shore Drive is Lincoln Park — 25 acres of which house the Lincoln Park Zoo of TV fame with its extensive collection of birds, mammals and reptiles representing almost every part of the earth. The zoo's many attractions draw an average annual attendance of more than four million men, women and children. The center of Chicago's downtown section is an area, seven blocks long by five blocks wide, known as the Loop—the heart of the city—where elevated railway lines actually loop around the financial and commercial buildings. South of the Loop, the Chicago Board of Trade rises 44 stories and is topped by a massive statue of the goddess Ceres—an appropriate symbol, since the building contains the world's largest grain exchange. Here one may witness the various types of grain being bought and sold by means of rapid and—to the layman—often mysterious signals. East of the Loop, stretching along Chicago's filled-in shoreline, is Grant Park with its formal gardens and the Chicago Institute of Art. Works of Goya and El Greco are among the masterpieces in the Institution's collection of paintings. The Chicago Institute is also

SYMPHONY CONCERTS under the stars are presented four times a week during July and August at the Band Shell in Grant Park. Programs feature the Grant Park Symphony Orchestra as well as nationally famous soloists and noted conductors

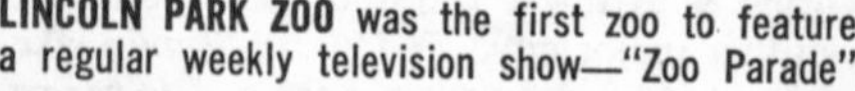
LINCOLN PARK ZOO was the first zoo to feature a regular weekly television show—"Zoo Parade"

SOLDIER FIELD, located in Burnham Park, has long been recognized as one of the greatest sports stadiums of all times. The entire structure is designed to harmonize with other classic buildings in Chicago's lake front development plan

Photos: Chicago Park District

Photos: Chicago Park District

CHICAGO NATURAL HISTORY MUSEUM, where the story of the earth and mankind is pictured from the beginning to the present, ranks among the world's finest museums. Distinguished among the exhibits is Malvina Hoffman's series of life-size bronzes depicting the "Races of Mankind"

ADLER PLANETARIUM is in reality an Astronomical Museum of which the planetarium instrument is the principal exhibit. The museum contains one of the finest collections of antique astronomical and mathematical instruments in the world

MUSEUM OF SCIENCE AND INDUSTRY has many exhibits showing the application of science to a wide variety of American industries. Among the museum's popular attractions is a full-sized working model of a coal mine

CHICAGO Continued

a leading art school of the Middle West. For scientific museums, Chicago offers The Chicago Museum of Natural History, the Shedd Aquarium and the Adler Planetarium — each outstanding in its field and all located on the south side of Grant Park. Further south, Michigan Avenue leads to the University of Chicago with its handsome Gothic buildings and its 100-acre campus. The University's Stagg Athletic Field is an atomic age landmark. Here beneath one of its stands the first controlled nuclear chain reaction was demonstrated. To the south and southwest are two widely scattered points of special interest—the Union Stockyards, center of the world's livestock marketing and meat packing industries, and the Brookfield Zoo with its fine natural-habitat exhibits of animals. The city's amazing development could not have been accomplished without great citizens as well as great circumstances. Chicago has always been fortunate in the industry and dynamic vitality of its people. To them and to their leaders—the business giants of the past and the capable leaders of the present—the city owes a large measure of credit for its remarkable record over the years.

SHOW HOUSE at the Garfield Park Conservatory is so called because it always features fine displays of flowers and foliage plants. Among the five major shows held annually is the autumn Chrysanthemum Show, a gorgeous display of bloom which includes many of the Conservatory's own hybrids

SKYLINE OF CINCINNATI as it appears from across the Ohio River in northern Kentucky. Cincinnati, the second largest city in Ohio, was originally called Losantiville.

CINCINNATI. Cincinnati, Ohio's second largest city, owes much of its importance as a commercial and industrial center to its favorable location on the banks of the Ohio River, midway between Pittsburgh and Cairo. Long before the coming of the white man, this site had been a favorite river-crossing for the Indians. Cincinnati, starting the 19th century as a tiny backwoods settlement, grew rapidly in size and by the time 1860 rolled around, ranked as the country's sixth largest city. In charm, gaiety and culture it was the talk of the nation and the world. A large part of its population were German and Irish immigrants, and to Cincinnati they brought a devotion to the arts, a willingness to be gracefully tolerant and a progressive spirit that made the city grow and prosper at an unbelievable rate. That progressive spirit is, even today, one of its most distinctive qualities. Spreading along the river's edge are its factory and business districts dominated by the 48-story Carew Tower and the massive Union Terminal Building whose utilitarian beauty is admired by visitors from all parts of the world. Behind the business district, the hills rise in a series of terraces, a setting for Cincinnati's handsome residential area. One of the nation's most beautiful inland cities, Cincinnati is particularly proud of its many parks.

Photos: Cincinnati Chamber of Commerce.

TYLER DAVIDSON FOUNTAIN, executed in ornamental bronze, rises in tiers to a height of 43 feet and is topped by a figure depicting the "Genius of Water." Other groups of figures symbolize man's need and uses of water

TAFT MUSEUM, an excellent example of Federal architecture, has been called the "most pleasing sight in Cincinnati." Its collection of fine art includes paintings by such masters as Rembrandt, Turner, Goya and Gainsborough.

EDEN PARK with its miniature lake, rolling lawns and steep hills, is the site of the Cincinnati Art Museum, the Art Academy and the Eden Park Conservatory

Cincinnati, Ohio

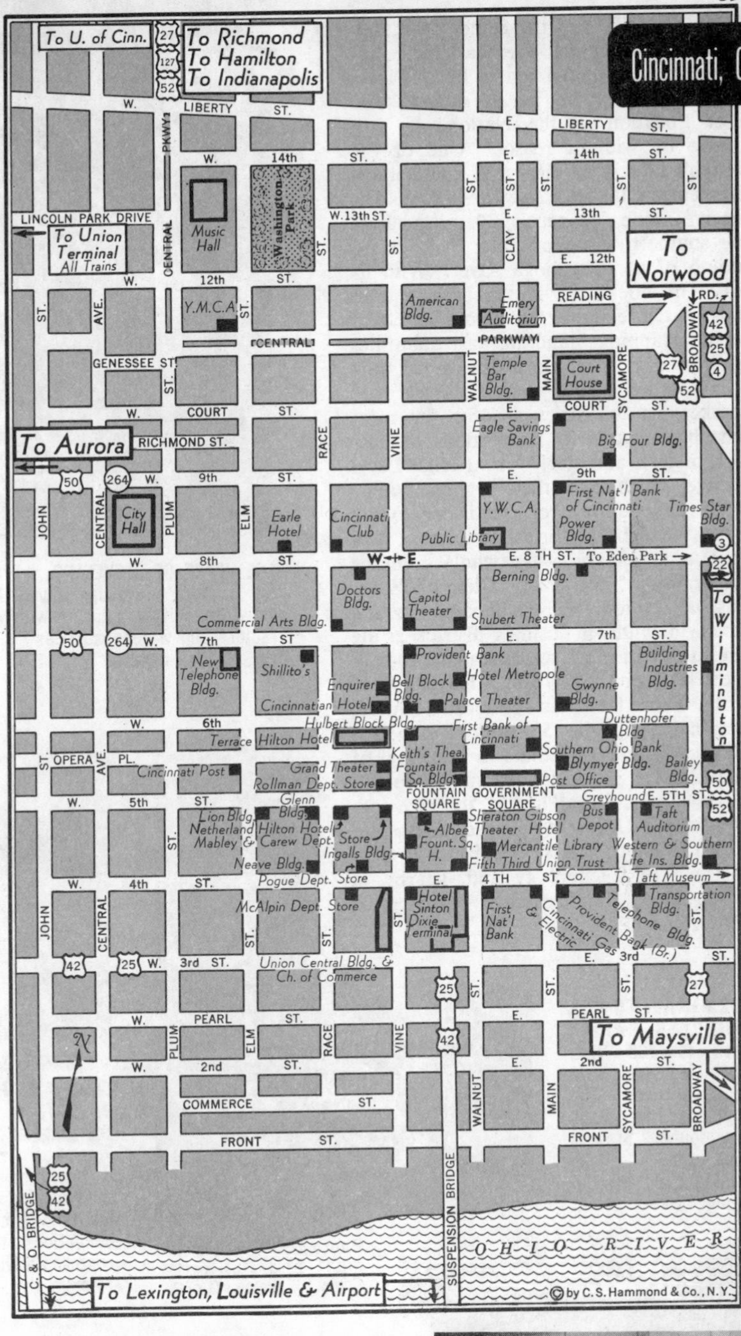

THOR JOHNSON conducts the world-renowned Cincinnati Symphony Orchestra. Founded in 1895, the orchestra gives concerts on Fridays and Saturdays from October through April at the Cincinnati Music Hall.

CLEVELAND. As the center of a 500-mile radius in which over half the population of the United States lives, Cleveland did not come by its slogan "The Best Location in the Nation" by just rhyme or without reason. One of the nation's largest business and manufacturing centers, the city stretches out its extensive scene for nearly 30 miles along the southern shore of Lake Erie, at the mouth of the Cuyahoga River. With its miles of docks, its natural river-mouth harbor, Cleveland is a key port for Great Lakes' shipping, handling vast quantities of iron ore, coal, grain and other bulk commodities. The world's largest ore market, its industries are for the most part based upon its tremendous production of iron and steel. From High Level Bridge, which spans the Cuyahoga Valley 96 feet above the river, one is confronted by a scene of factories, foundries, steel mills and refineries—the whole immense panorama of the Flats, Cleveland's industrial section. Public Square, the hub of the downtown business district, is the site of the original settlement—a 10-acre plot laid out by Moses Cleaveland in 1796. From this centrally located square, dominated by the 52-story Terminal Tower Building, radiate a number of Cleveland's most important thoroughfares. The cultural life of the city centers about University Circle where are found Western Reserve University, Case Institute of Technology and, nearby in Wade Park, the Cleveland Museum of Fine Art.

THE HEART OF CLEVELAND, the valley of the winding Cuyahoga River, has provided the city's industry with excellent factory and warehouse sites

TERMINAL TOWER BUILDING, which rises to 708 feet, dominates the entire Terminal Group. The sightseeing boat (foreground) makes trips along the lake front and up the Cuyahoga River.

CLEVELAND MUSEUM OF ART, overlooking the lagoon of the Fine Arts Garden, is a beautiful building of gleaming Georgia marble. It contains collections that are representative of art through the ages.

Photos: Ohio Development and Publicity Comm., Cleveland C. of C.

SEVERANCE HALL is the home of the nationally famous Cleveland Symphony Orchestra. Besides its regular winter concerts, the orchestra gives a series of informal "pop concerts" during the summer season.

Cleveland, Ohio

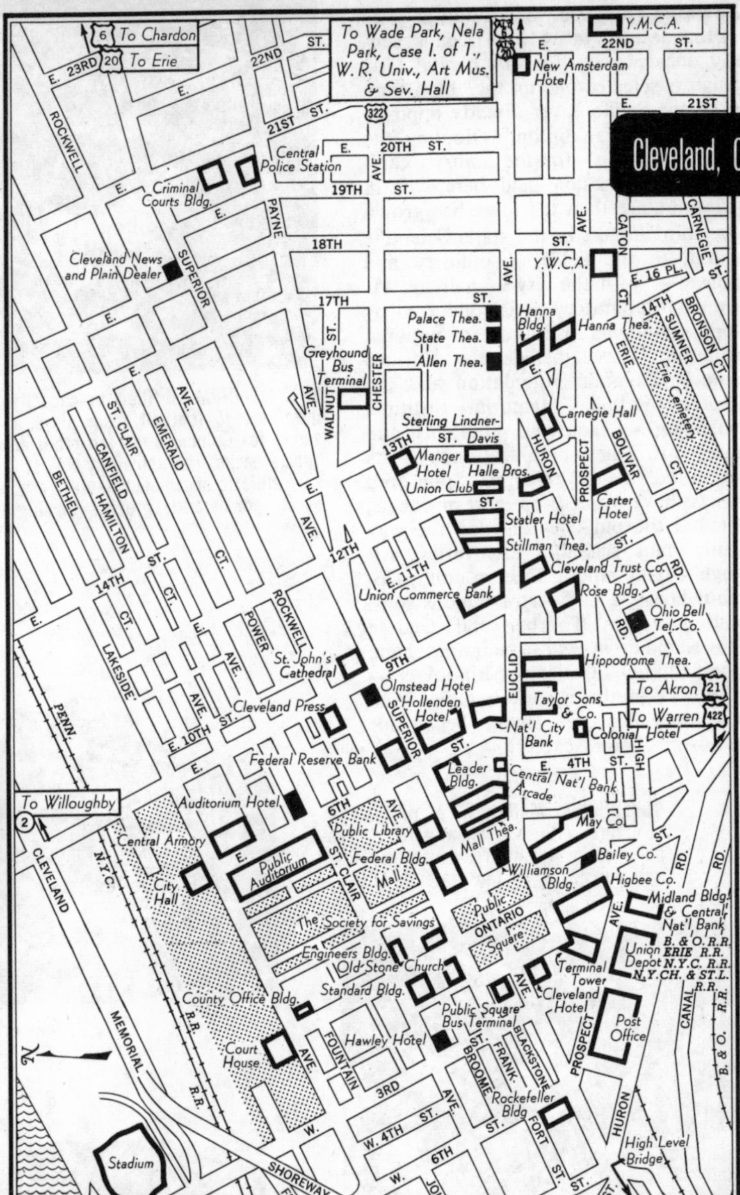

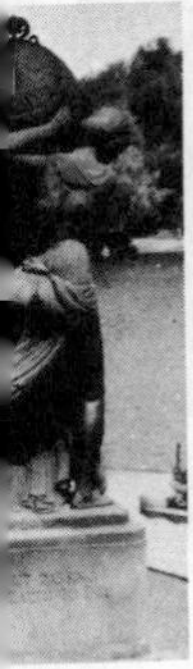

To Chardon 6
To Erie 20
To Wade Park, Nela Park, Case I. of T., W. R. Univ., Art Mus. & Sev. Hall
Y.M.C.A.
New Amsterdam Hotel
Central Police Station
Criminal Courts Bldg.
Cleveland News and Plain Dealer
Y.W.C.A.
Palace Thea.
State Thea.
Allen Thea.
Hanna Bldg.
Hanna Thea.
Greyhound Bus Terminal
Erie Cemetery
Carnegie Hall
Sterling Lindner-Davis
Manger Hotel
Halle Bros.
Union Club
Carter Hotel
Statler Hotel
Stillman Thea.
Cleveland Trust Co.
Union Commerce Bank
Rose Bldg.
Ohio Bell Tel. Co.
Hippodrome Thea.
St. John's Cathedral
Olmstead Hotel
Hollenden Hotel
Cleveland Press
Taylor Sons & Co.
To Akron 21
To Warren 422
Nat'l City Bank
Colonial Hotel
Federal Reserve Bank
Leader Bldg.
Central Nat'l Bank
Arcade
To Willoughby 2
Auditorium Hotel
Public Library
May Co.
Central Armory
Public Auditorium
Federal Bldg.
Mall
Mall Thea.
Bailey Co.
City Hall
Williamson Bldg.
Higbee Co.
Public Square
The Society for Savings
Midland Bldg. & Central Nat'l Bank
B. & O. R.R.
ERIE R.R.
N.Y.C. R.R.
N.Y.CH. & ST.L. R.R.
Union Depot
Engineers Bldg.
Old Stone Church
Terminal Tower
Standard Bldg.
Cleveland Hotel
County Office Bldg.
Public Square Bus Terminal
Post Office
Court House
Hawley Hotel
Rockefeller Bldg.
High Level Bridge
Stadium
LAKE ERIE
Donald Gray Gardens
To Medina 3
To Lorain 6
To Elyria 20
To Airport 42
To Lorain 2

NELA PARK, lighting headquarters of the General Electric Co. in Cleveland, has been responsible for the development of many new types of electric lamps and the "Science of Seeing." It is a beautiful example of the campus-type laboratory.

COLUMBUS. When the youthful state of Ohio decided in 1812 to seek a centrally located site for its capital, the legislators selected one on the "high bank east of the Scioto River directly opposite the town of Franklinton," adopting the name "Columbus" for the embryo capital. The first session held here was in 1816 and since then the town has grown to be third largest in the state. Scientific research in the fields of industry and business — with the city as a living experimental laboratory — is conducted by several Columbus institutions of national reputation. These include the Edward Orton Jr. Ceramic Foundation and the non-profit Battelle Memorial Institute, specializing in industrial problems and leading all other organizations of its kind in volume of research. Sponsored projects have turned up new products, improved the old ones and led the way to important scientific discoveries. Although a baby among Eastern cities, Columbus boasts a number of famous sons, including James Thurber and George Bellows, many of whose paintings hang in the Columbus Gallery of Fine Arts — and it was in the notorious Ohio State Penitentiary that O. Henry began his noteworthy literary career.

OHIO STADIUM is filled to capacity when the Buckeye football team plays a home game, for Columbusites are rabid armchair quarterbacks. The university's most impressive athletic accomplishments are achieved by its consistently great swimming teams

GOVERNOR'S MANSION, a thirty-room structure with a sunken garden, was built as a private residence in 1904 and purchased by the state in 1919

LOOKING WEST toward the Scioto River, there are the State Capitol, considered one of the purest examples of Doric architecture in the U. S., with its annex; the Departments of State Building, at the river's edge, and the LeVeque-Lincoln Tower

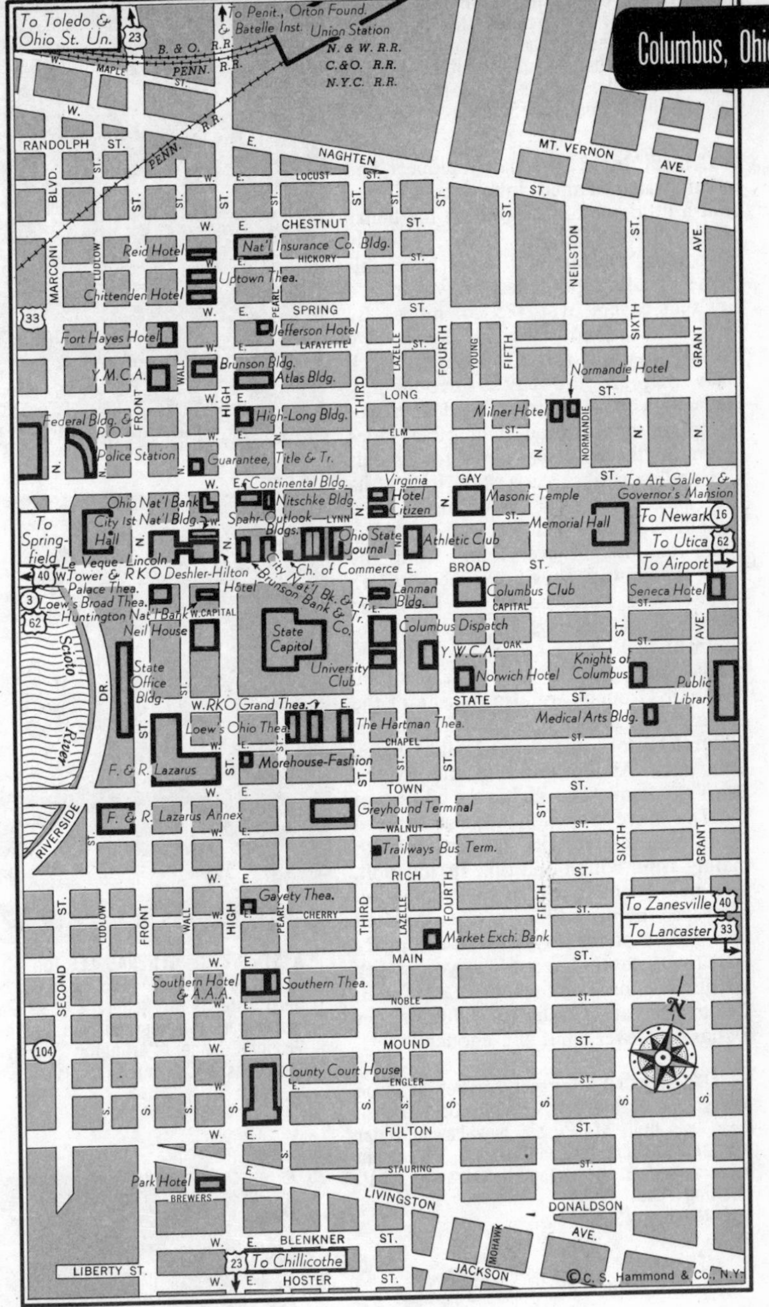

SPANKING NEW Medical Health Center on the campus of Ohio State University is one of the foremost in the field of medicine. At the university, 7th largest in the country, many departments conduct research in different fields

Photos: Columbus Chamber of Commerce

ENTRANCE TO THE TEXAS STATE FAIR leads to 195 acres of fair grounds—the home of the world's largest annual exhibition. In addition to many permanent exhibit buildings, the Fair's facilities include a year-round midway and the Cotton Bowl Stadium

DALLAS. In 1814, a hardy pioneer and Indian trader named John Neely Bryan built a little one-room cabin on the banks of the Trinity River. Today, scarcely more than one hundred years later, this former trading post has grown into a city that covers over 185 sq. miles. By leaps and bounds, the buildings have soared skyward above the rich black lands that are the city's surroundings. Dallas is a modern streamlined metropolis; more sophisticated than other cities of the Southwest, it is known for its culture and urbanity. As a style leader, its luxurious stores rival New York's most fashionable and expensive shops. Dallas offers the visitor everything from the latest Broadway shows to the nation's largest state fair. Begun in 1886, the State Fair of Texas is an annual attraction which draws a crowd of 2,500,000 people during its two-week exposition. The Fair Grounds are also the site of the Dallas Art Museum, the Museum of Natural History, the Texas Hall of State, Fair Park Auditorium and the Cotton Bowl Stadium. "Big D," as the citizens of Dallas have affectionately nicknamed their city, derives its colossal wealth mainly from cotton and oil. Its location, with nearly one-fourth of the population of Texas living within a one hundred mile radius of the city, has also contributed to its development. The young city admits one problem; as the late G. B. Dealey so aptly put it, "Nothing in Dallas was ever built big enough!"

A STATUE OF GENERAL LEE, on his favorite mount, "Traveler," accompanied by an orderly, stands in Robert E. Lee Park. Also in the park is a reproduction of the General's Virginia home, "Arlington," which serves Dallas as a Community House

BRYAN'S LOG CABIN, a reconstruction of which now stands on the Dallas County Court House lawn, was built of 12-inch, hand-hewed cedar logs and was about 16 feet square. The Cabin once served as a combination trading post, dwelling, post office and temporary court house

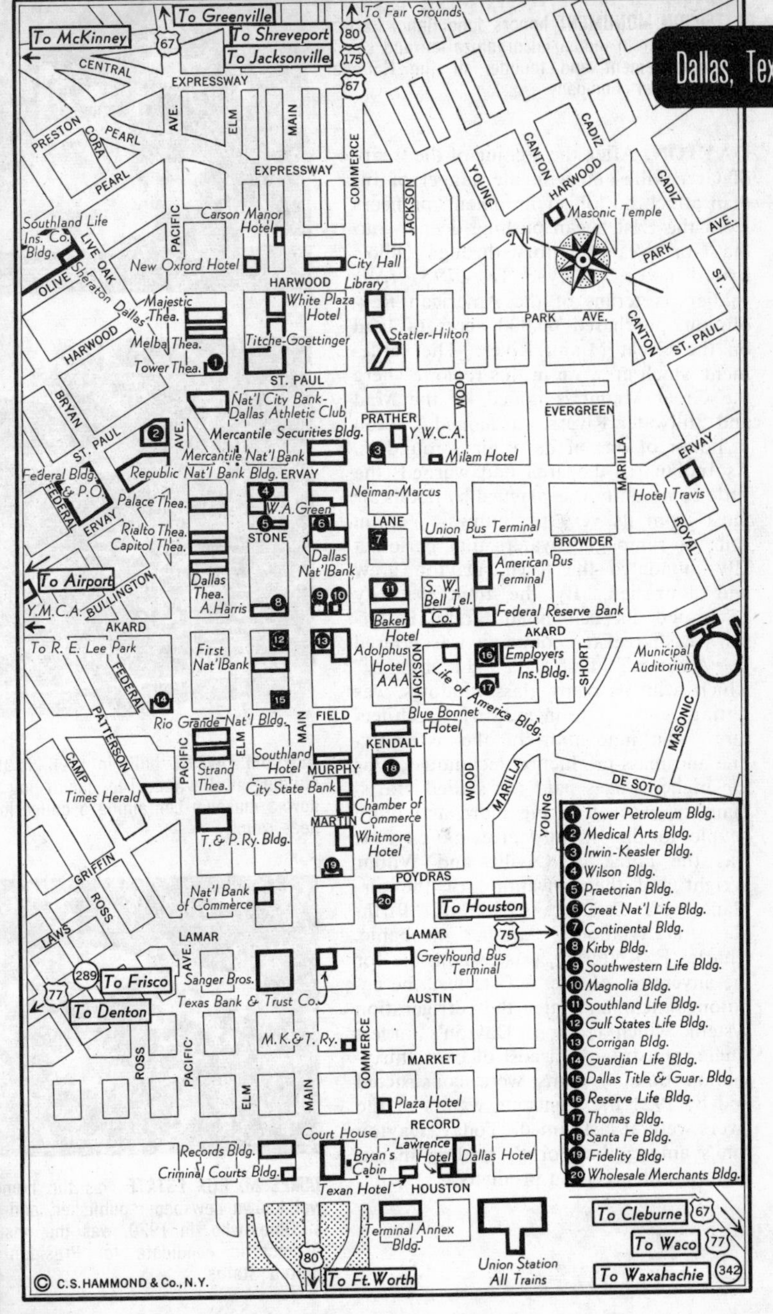

A STREAMLINED CITY, Dallas is more compact than the other large cities of Texas. Instead of sprawling outward, this city has thrust its tall buildings, story upon story, into the air. Growing by leaps and bounds, Dallas is now one of the largest inland cities in America

Photos: Dallas Chamber of Commerce, Texas Highway Dept

PATTERSON MONUMENT honors John Henry Patterson, a pioneer in industrial organization and scientific management and founder of the National Cash Register Company

DAYTON. After the signing of the treaty of Greenville and with the danger of Indian attack no longer imminent, pioneers from the East began pushing deeper into the Northwest Territory through Ohio's broad river valleys. In 1795, four soldiers, veterans of the American Revolution, purchased 60,000 acres of land on the Great Miami River. The settlement which grew up in this region, where the Great Miami is joined by the Mad and Stillwater Rivers, was named Dayton in honor of one of its original founders. As Indians in the area had warned, the little community was plagued by floods almost from its very beginnings. Yet, in spite of rampaging waters that periodically inundated the town, Dayton grew and flourished. By the time the city celebrated its centennial, John Patterson's cash register company was housed in America's first "daylight factory" which, with its many glass windows, was setting a new style in industrial architecture. The innovation of the assembly-line and mass-production techniques, plus the higher wages paid for skilled craftsmanship, was attracting more and more people to this rapidly growing city. It was the home of Orville and Wilbur Wright and their invention of the airplane gave Dayton its title of "Birthplace of Aviation." Another mechanic, Charles F. Kettering, was responsible for the invention of the self-starter, the ignition system and later the refrigeration system, which today is Dayton's largest single industry. At a cost of over thirty-million dollars, dams were constructed and by 1921 the menacing waters of the rivers were at last tamed. Today, Dayton ranks among the world's leading manufacturers of precision products.

NEWCOM TAVERN, built in 1796, is the oldest building in Dayton. The quaint log house is now a museum containing a collection of pioneer relics

JAMES M. COX ESTATE was the home of the well-known newspaper publisher, and Governor of Ohio, who, in 1920, was the unsuccessful Democratic candidate for President of the United States

WRIGHT BROTHERS MEMORIAL was erected in memory of Orville and Wilbur Wright. After the brothers made their historic flight at Kitty Hawk on December 17th, 1903, they returned to Dayton and set up a research airplane plant

Dayton, Ohio

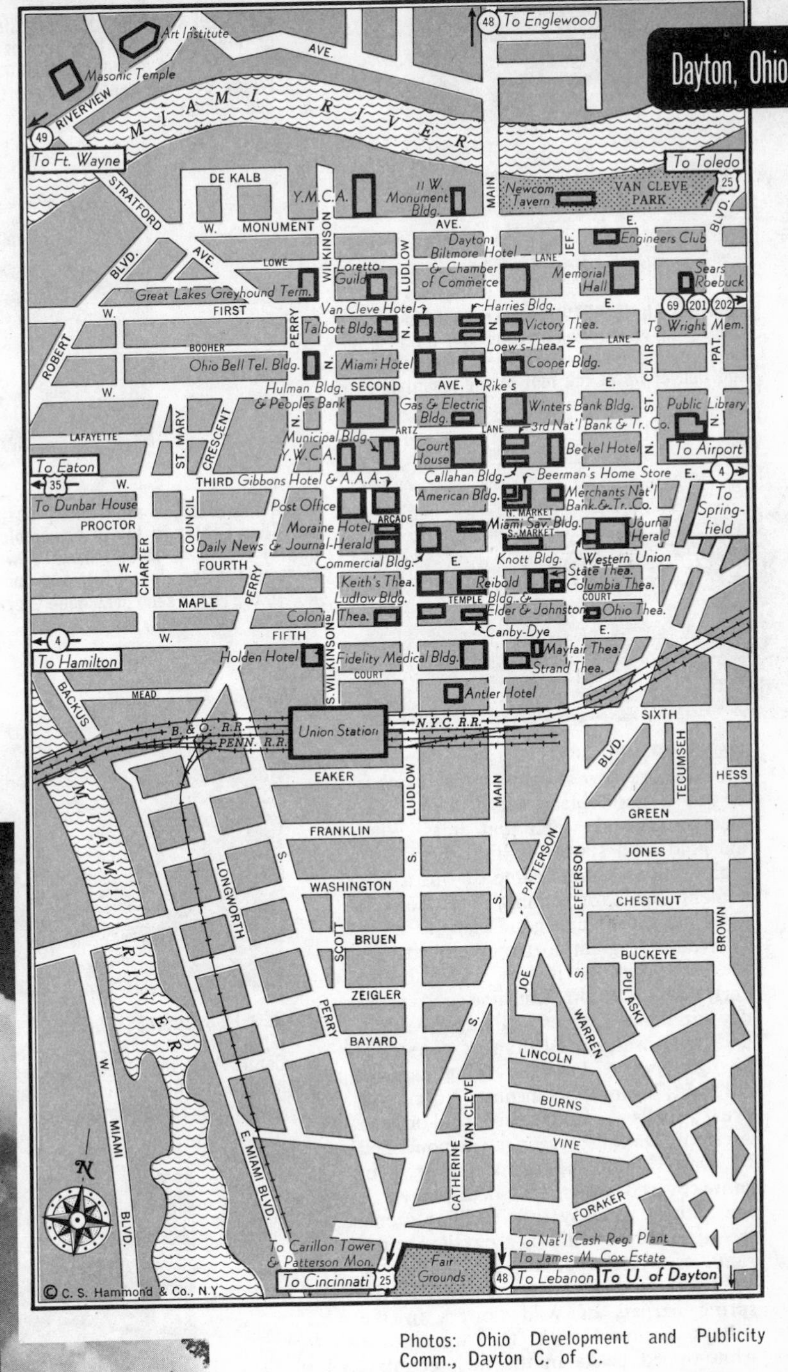

Photos: Ohio Development and Publicity Comm., Dayton C. of C.

CARILLON TOWER, in which hangs the 32-bell Deeds Carillon given to the city of Dayton by Mrs. E. A. Deeds, is one of the best examples of tower architecture in the country

BUFFALO BILL'S GRAVE atop Lookout Mountain is on ground selected by him for his final resting place. The cities of Golden and Denver lie at the foot of the mountain

AMPHITHEATER in the magnificent Park of the Red Rocks has perfect acoustics. The Denver Symphony Orchestra presents Friday evening concerts here during July and August

FROM THE STEPS of the Capitol, looking across the Civic Center to the incomparable Rockies, one of America's most famous views. On the west side is the classic City and County Building. To the left is seen the unique Greek Theater

DENVER. In 1857 a trapper built a cabin where two streams come together. It was a good place for a home, with plenty of wood, water and grass. When the gold rush started to the Pike's Peak region, more settlers came. It was a convenient base for mining operations, a good place to live, a good place to trade. Denver is a great metropolitan city for the same reasons it was settled in the early days. Bright sunshine and clear, dry air make Denver's climate healthful and invigorating. Pleasant seasonal changes occur, but one thing remains constant: Colorado sunshine. No cloudy, dreary spells — no excessive cold or heat. A city of fabulously green lawns, nourished by water from the giant backdrop of snow-covered peaks, mile-high Denver is the natural gateway to a thrilling scenic treasury. Winter unfolds a dazzling panorama of white splendor, enticing to the sight-seer, irresistible to the skier. In the spring carpets of wild flowers in the valleys contrast with the wonder of white-tipped peaks in the high country. Brilliant blue skies frame the lush green beauty of summer. And fall ushers in a spectacular fairyland of color, as entire mountainsides turn to shimmering gold.

DENVER'S BUSINESS DISTRICT includes the city's two new skyscrapers, the Mile High Center and the Denver Club, at left and center. The historic towering landmark, the Daniel and Fisher Tower, is at upper right

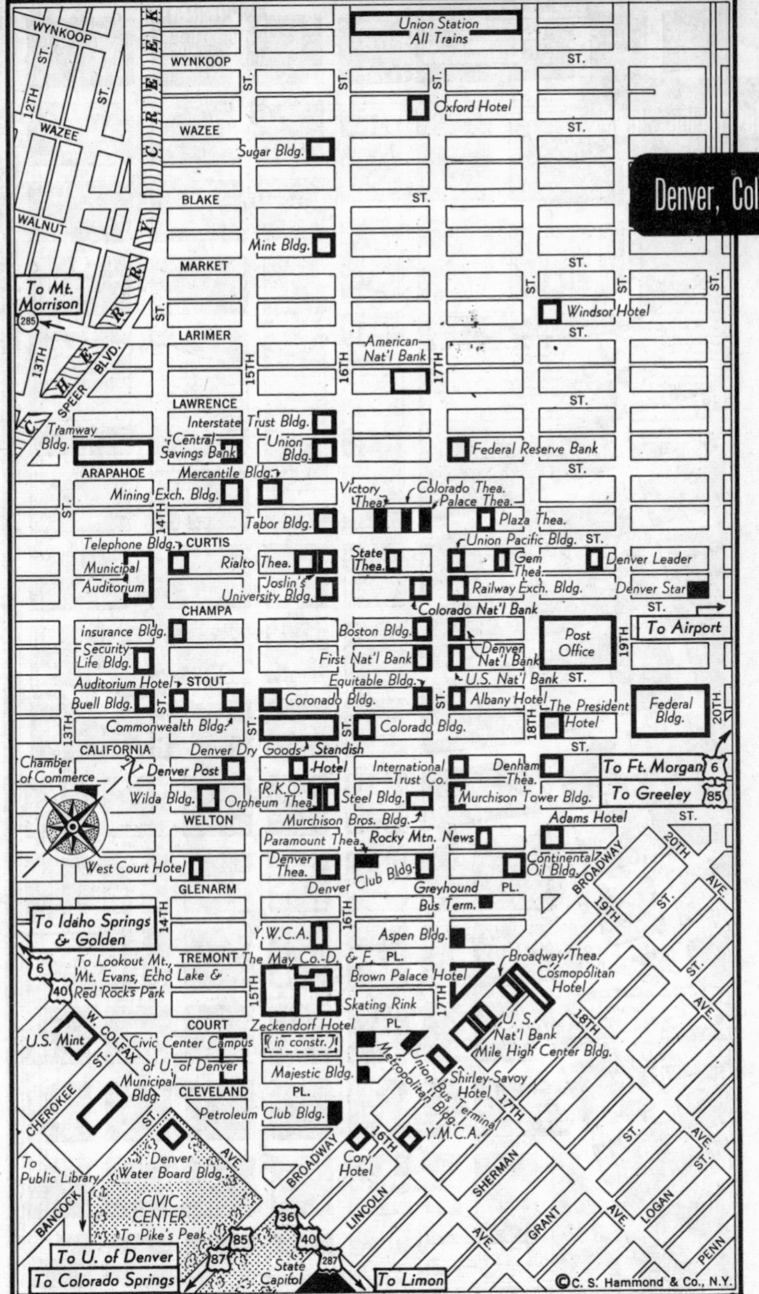

ECHO LAKE, in Denver Mountain Parks System, is greatly beloved by trout fishermen. The highest automobile mountain road in the world winds to the top of Mt. Evans at an elevation of 14,260 feet, past Echo and Summit Lakes

Photos: Denver Convention & Visitors Bureau

Des Moines, Iowa

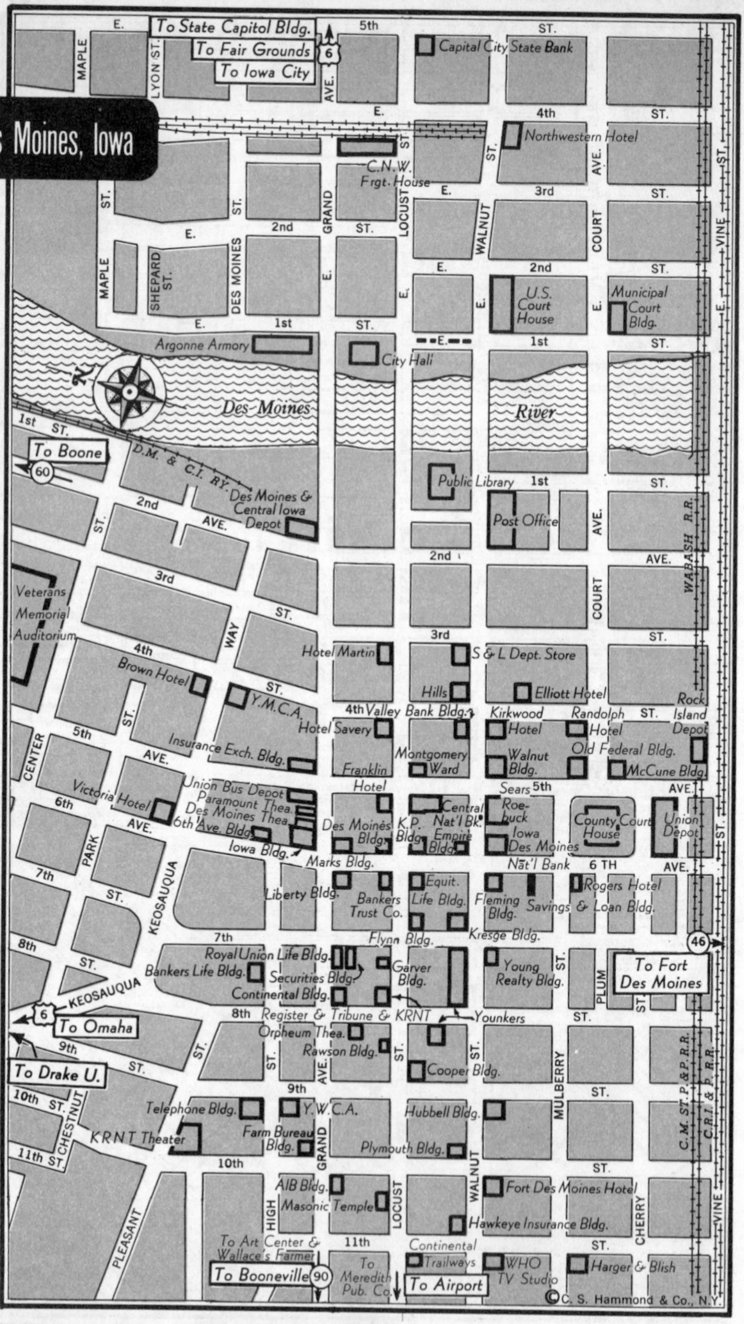

To State Capitol Bldg.
To Fair Grounds
To Iowa City
To Boone
To Omaha
To Drake U.
To Fort Des Moines
To Booneville
To Airport
To Art Center & Wallace's Farmer
To Meredith Pub. Co.

Capital City State Bank
Northwestern Hotel
C.N.W. Frgt. House
U.S. Court House
Municipal Court Bldg.
Argonne Armory
City Hall
Des Moines River
D.M. & C.I. RY.
Des Moines & Central Iowa Depot
Public Library
Post Office
Veterans Memorial Auditorium
Hotel Martin
S & L Dept. Store
Hills
Elliott Hotel
Brown Hotel
Y.M.C.A.
Valley Bank Bldg.
Kirkwood Hotel
Randolph Hotel
Rock Island Depot
Hotel Savery
Insurance Exch. Bldg.
Montgomery Ward
Franklin Hotel
Walnut Bldg.
Old Federal Bldg.
McCune Bldg.
Victoria Hotel
Union Bus Depot
Paramount Thea.
Des Moines Thea.
6th Ave. Bldg.
Iowa Bldg.
Des Moines Bldg.
K.P. Bldg.
Central Nat'l Bk.
Empire Bldg.
Sears Roebuck
Iowa Des Moines Nat'l Bank
County Court House
Union Depot
Marks Bldg.
Liberty Bldg.
Bankers Trust Co.
Equit. Life Bldg.
Fleming Bldg.
Savings & Loan Bldg.
Rogers Hotel
Flynn Bldg.
Kresge Bldg.
Royal Union Life Bldg.
Bankers Life Bldg.
Securities Bldg.
Garver Bldg.
Young Realty Bldg.
Continental Bldg.
Register & Tribune & KRNT
Younkers
Orpheum Thea.
Rawson Bldg.
Cooper Bldg.
Telephone Bldg.
Y.W.C.A.
Hubbell Bldg.
Farm Bureau Bldg.
KRNT Theater
Plymouth Bldg.
AIB Bldg.
Masonic Temple
Fort Des Moines Hotel
Hawkeye Insurance Bldg.
Continental Trailways
WHO TV Studio
Harger & Blish
Wabash R.R.
C.M. St. P. & P. R.R.
C.R.I. & P. R.R.

©C. S. Hammond & Co., N.Y.

DES MOINES ART CENTER, located in Greenwood park, houses many fine paintings and also provides the best of facilities for those interested in becoming artists.

IOWA STATE CAPITOL stands on a hill in the eastern part of the city, surrounded by a large park. The magnificent old building contains many beautiful and valuable paintings as well as an outstanding collection of war flags

NEW TERMINAL BUILDING at the Des Moines Municipal Airport is one of the finest in the United States. The city has become an important air center, being one of the main stops on a transcontinental air mail route

Photos: Greater Des Moines Chamber of Commerce

IOWA STATE FAIR GROUNDS are the home of one of the world's largest agricultural expositions, held annually during the last week in August. The fair grounds are located at the eastern end of Grand Avenue

DES MOINES. Des Moines, capital of Iowa and the "Farm Capital of America," is centrally located within the state at the heart of what is probably the nation's richest agricultural region. A marketing and manufacturing center, its varied industries include meat packing, flour milling and the production of farm implements and equipment. More than fifty insurance companies are located in Des Moines, giving the city the title of "Hartford of the West." Des Moines is also the home of a number of large printing and publishing companies which specialize in the publication of farm journals and periodicals including the famous "Wallace's Farmer." The Iowa State Fair held here is one of the world's premier agricultural expositions. Farmers from Iowa and neighboring states bring in their prize horses, prima donna steers and giant hogs, also their grains, fruits and over-size vegetables; the womenfolk compete for honors in baked goods, jams, preserves and various types of needlework. The huge midway of rides and thrills adds a carnival atmosphere to the proceedings. Drake University, one of the city's several institutions of higher learning, holds the Drake Relays, a national track event. One of Des Moines' most outstanding cultural institutions is the Des Moines Public Forum. Dealing with current problems, it was originally carried out as an experiment in adult education. The Forum has been so successful that it has set a pattern for similar projects in other cities.

BANKERS LIFE COMPANY is one of the many large insurance companies which have their home offices at Des Moines. Hundreds of thousands of people throughout the country carry policies in these companies.

To U. of Detroit
To Cranbrook, Zoo & Inst. of Arts
To Wayne U.
To Pontiac
To Lansing & Ann Arbor
To Dearborn
TO M.C.R.R. DEPOT
To Toledo
To Mt. Clemens & Airport
To Belle Isle

① David Stott Bldg.
② Lafayette Bldg.
③ Majestic Bldg.
④ Shubert Lafayette Thea.
⑤ City Hall
⑥ Bk. of the Com'nwealth
⑦ Penobscot Bldg.

ELIOT
PETERBORO
Imperial Hotel
ERSKINE
WATSON
CHARLOTTE
Ft. Wayne Hotel
EDMUND
TEMPLE
ALFRED
LEDYARD
SPROAT
Park Ave. Hotel
ADELAIDE
SIBLEY
HENRY
WINDER
DUFFIELD
VERNOR HWAY.
CHERRY
COLUMBIA
PLUM
ELIZABETH
Detroit Edison Bldg.
BEECH
JONES
Detroit Leland Hotel
BAGLEY
STATE
Detroit Times
PORTER
Mich. Bell Tel. Bldg.
MICHIGAN
ABBOTT
HOWARD
Detroit News
Ft. Shelby Hotel
Union Depot
C. & O.
WABASH, PENN.
R.R.
JOHN C. LODGE EXPRESSWAY
FOURTH
THIRD
SECOND
FIRST
CASS
PARK
WOODWARD AVE.
JOHN R.
BRUSH
BEAUBIEN
ST. ANTOINE
GRAND RIVER
MONTCALM
Rex Hotel
Fairbairn Hotel
Y.W.C.A.
Y.M.C.A.
Fox Bldg.
Wolverine Hotel
Mutual Bldg.
Kales Bldg.
Park Ave. Bldg.
Briggs Hotel
Tuller Hotel
Auto. Club of Mich.
United Artists Bldg.
Michigan Bldg.
Mich. Consol. Gas Co.
Greyhound Bus Term.
Statler Hotel
David Whitney Bldg.
David Broderick Tower
ADAMS
WITHERELL
Fred M. Butzel Mem. Bldg.
MADISON
CROSS
BEACON
Detroit Athletic Club
Broadway Capital Theater
Madison-Lenox Hotel
Metropolitan Bldg.
CLIFFORD
WASHINGTON BLVD.
PARK PL.
Book Tower Bldg.
Manuf. Nat'l Bank
GRAND RIVER
BROADWAY
GRATIOT AVE.
College of Medicine
MULLETT
Police Hdqs.
CLINTON
Wash. Blvd. Bldg.
Sheraton-Cadillac Hotel
Board of Commerce
Recreation Bldg.
Detroit Free Press
American Legion
Detroit Bank
J.L. Hudson Co.
Public Library
LIBRARY
FARMER
Crowley-Milner
MACOMB
Municipal Courts Bldg.
MONROE
Ernst Kern Co.
Family Theater
Cadillac Tower
LAFAYETTE
GRISWOLD
Detroit Water Board Bldg.
BATES
CADILLAC SQ.
Barlum Hotel
FORT
Post Office
Detroit Trust Co. Bldg.
Lawyers Title Ins. Bldg.
SHELBY
Manuf. Nat'l Bank
Nat'l Bank of Detroit
County Bldg.
CONGRESS
Ford Bldg.
BLVD.
Buhl Bldg.
Union Guardian Bldg.
Greyhound Term. (Site)
WAYNE
LARNED
Federal Bldg. (Site)
City-County Bldg.
Exhibition Hall (Site)
EXPRESSWAY
JEFFERSON
RANDOLPH
CIVIC CENTER
Pool (Site)
Mariners Church
Veterans Memorial
Convention Hall
WOODBRIDGE
Canada Tunnel
FRANKLIN
Henry & Edsel Ford Auditorium
ATWATER
Grand Trunk Western Depot
DETROIT RIVER
Detroit Windsor Tunnel
R.R.T. Ferry
N

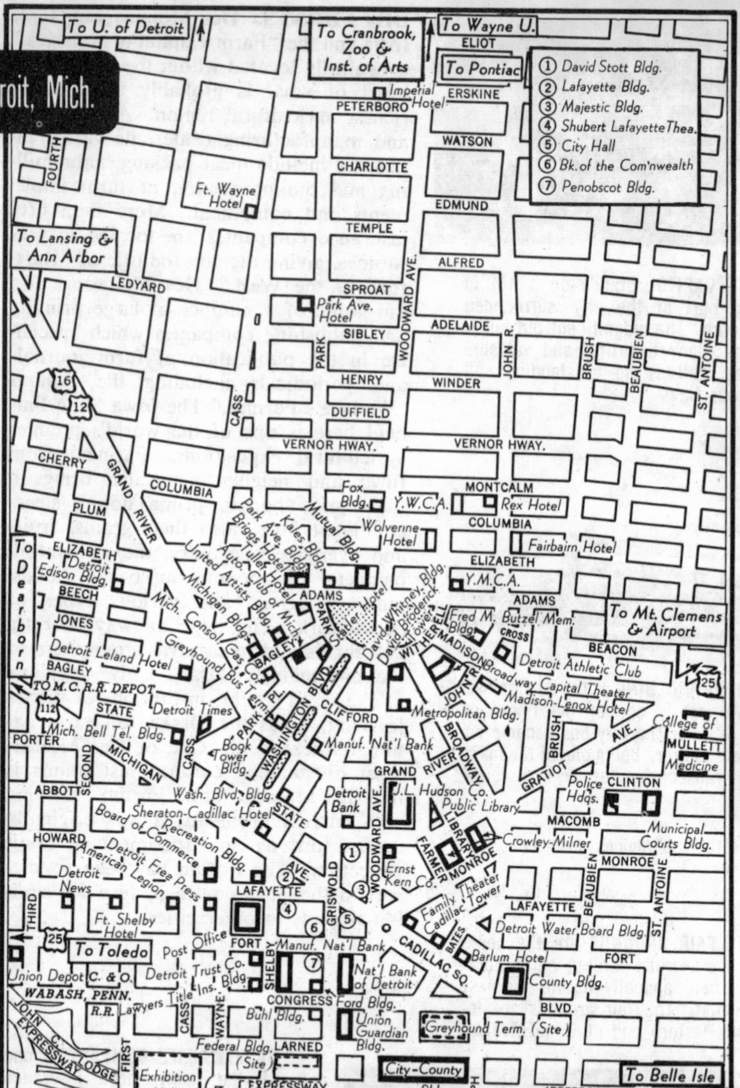

DETROIT'S DOWNTOWN SKYLINE as it is seen from Windsor, Canada shows, at the right, two of the newly completed buildings in the city's emerging Civic Center—the City County Building and the Henry and Edsel Ford Memorial Auditorium

NBROOK, just north of Detroit, is a world fa-
s combination of beautifully landscaped park
outstanding museums, schools and church.
ured is the peristyle breezeway linking the
ary of the Cranbrook Academy with the Cran-
ok Museum of Art

E PLANT of the
Motor Company
e world's great-
ndustrial concen-
on. Here are
d 1,200 acres of
ories, foundries,
l mills, paper
, glass plant,
er plants, coke
s, ship docks and
te railroad lines

CITY-COUNTY BUILDING is one of America's outstanding approaches to the housing of local government functions. The 20-story towering white marble slab is one of the impressive units of Detroit's Civic Center which is taking shape along the river front

DETROIT. Detroit is known throughout the world as the producer of the chrome-plated symbol of modern civilzation, the automobile. Settled by the French in 1701, it is one of the oldest cities west of the original thirteen colonies. Facing Canada across the Detroit River, the world's busiest marine highway, Detroit's situation has been advantageous to its development as one of the great industrial cities of the nation. The vast wealth amassed from its automotive industry has played an important role in supporting many social, educational and cultural institutions. The Henry Ford Museum and Greenfield Village at Dearborn, a part of the Detroit industrial area, are among the numerous attractions of the "Motor Capital." Divided into three sections, the Ford Museum contains a gallery of Fine Arts, a Street of Early American Shops and the Mechanical Arts Hall devoted to displays of antique and modern automobiles, historic airplanes, steam engines, old carriages, bicycles and the like. In the calm, peaceful atmosphere of Greenfield Village the pages of early American history unfold. Here an old windmill, a blacksmith shop, replicas of the homes of Stephen Foster, Noah Webster and William McGuffy are reminders of the days when life was a lot simpler. Also of interest is the Detroit Institute of Arts where art forms, old and new, ancient and modern, meet. Located on Woodward Avenue and Ten Mile Road is the Detroit Zoological Park, one of the most attractive animal displays in the country. A smaller zoo and an aquarium are found near the center of beautiful Belle Isle Park, situated on an island in the Detroit River.

LANDMARKS OF AMERICAN HISTORY are collected at Detroit's Greenfield Village. Founded by Henry Ford, it is now the world's greatest collection of Americana. Pictured is part of the collection of over 165 early automobiles in the Henry Ford Museum

Photos: Detroit Convention and Tourist Bureau

Fort Worth, Tex.

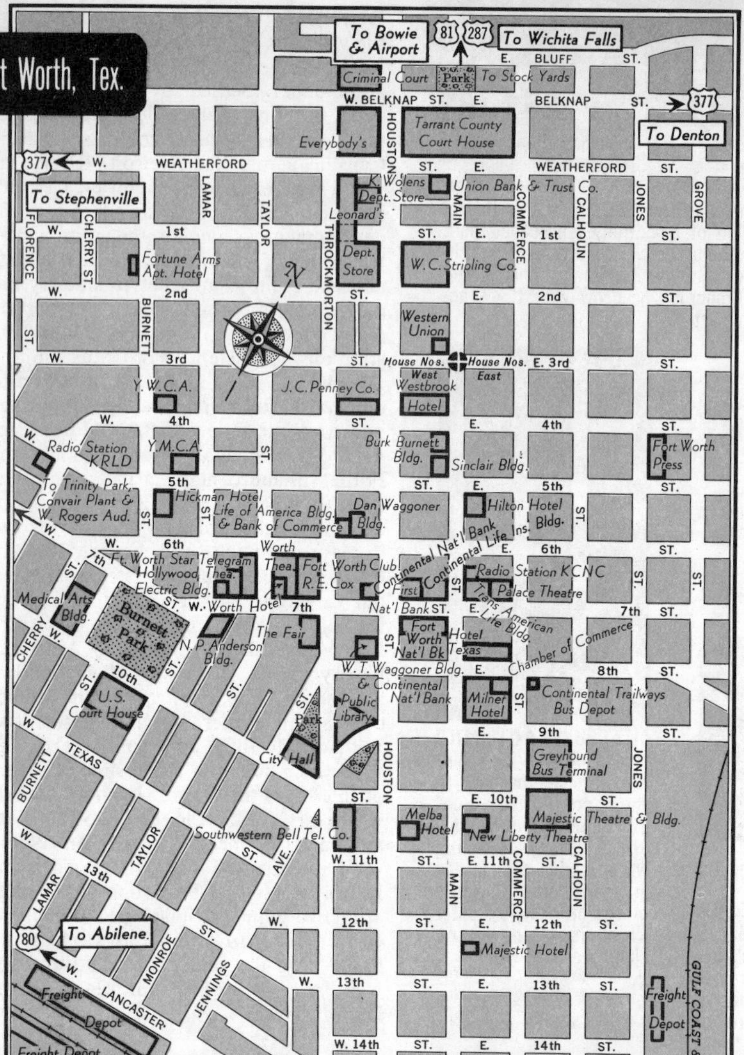

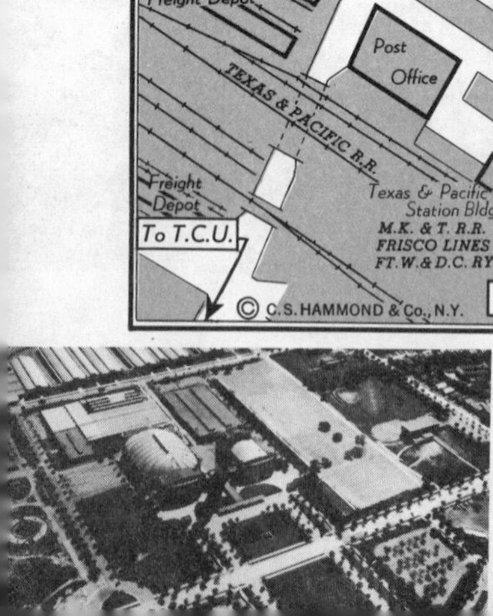

To Bowie & Airport
81
287
To Wichita Falls
E. BLUFF ST.
Criminal Court
Park
To Stock Yards
W. BELKNAP ST.
E. BELKNAP ST.
377
To Denton
Everybody's
Tarrant County Court House
377
W. WEATHERFORD ST.
E. WEATHERFORD ST.
To Stephenville
K. Wolens Dept. Store
Union Bank & Trust Co.
Leonard's Dept. Store
W. 1st ST.
E. 1st ST.
Fortune Arms Apt. Hotel
W. C. Stripling Co.
W. 2nd ST.
E. 2nd ST.
Western Union
W. 3rd ST.
House Nos. West
House Nos. East
E. 3rd ST.
Y.W.C.A.
J.C. Penney Co.
Westbrook Hotel
W. 4th ST.
E. 4th ST.
Radio Station KRLD
Y.M.C.A.
Burk Burnett Bldg.
Sinclair Bldg.
Fort Worth Press
W. 5th ST.
E. 5th ST.
To Trinity Park, Convair Plant & W. Rogers Aud.
Hickman Hotel
Life of America Bldg. & Bank of Commerce
Dan Waggoner Bldg.
Hilton Hotel Bldg.
Continental Nat'l Bank
Continental Life Ins. Bldg.
W. 6th ST.
E. 6th ST.
W. 7th ST.
E. 7th ST.
Ft. Worth Star Telegram
Hollywood Thea.
Electric Bldg.
Worth Thea.
Fort Worth Club
R. E. Cox
First Nat'l Bank
Radio Station KCNC
Palace Theatre
Trans American Life Bldg.
Medical Arts Bldg.
Burnett Park
Worth Hotel
The Fair
Fort Worth Nat'l Bk
Hotel Texas
Chamber of Commerce
N. P. Anderson Bldg.
W. T. Waggoner Bldg. & Continental Nat'l Bank
E. 8th ST.
10th ST.
U.S. Court House
Public Library
Park
Milner Hotel
Continental Trailways Bus Depot
E. 9th ST.
City Hall
Greyhound Bus Terminal
E. 10th ST.
Melba Hotel
Majestic Theatre & Bldg.
New Liberty Theatre
Southwestern Bell Tel. Co.
W. 11th ST.
E. 11th ST.
W. 12th ST.
E. 12th ST.
Majestic Hotel
13th ST.
W. 13th ST.
E. 13th ST.
To Abilene
80
W. LANCASTER
Freight Depot
Freight Depot
W. 14th ST.
E. 14th ST.
Freight Depot
Post Office
Santa Fe R.R. Station
SOU. PAC. R.R.
C.R.I. & P. RY.
FRISCO LINES
W. 15th ST.
TEXAS & PACIFIC R.R.
GULF COAST & SANTA FE R.R.
E. 16th ST.
Freight Depot
Texas & Pacific R.R. Station Bldg.
M.K. & T. R.R.
FRISCO LINES
FT.W. & D.C. RY.
E. 17th ST.
E. LANCASTER ST.
To T.C.U.
To Corsicana
81
287
To Waco
80
To Dallas
FLORENCE ST.
CHERRY ST.
LAMAR
BURNETT
TAYLOR
THROCKMORTON
HOUSTON
MAIN
COMMERCE
CALHOUN
JONES
GROVE
TEXAS
MONROE
JENNINGS
AVE.
CHERRY

FEW CITIES possess a civic center as spacious and functional as the Will Rogers Auditorium, Coliseum and Exhibit Halls

Photos: Fort Worth Chamber of Commerce

STOCKYARDS, packing plants and allied industries make Fort Worth the largest livestock marketing and processing center south of Kansas City

FORT WORTH. When Major Ripley Arnold and his Second Dragoons established Camp Worth on the banks of the Trinity River in 1849, the country to the west was inhabited only by a few settlers, warlike Comanches, and buffalo. Later the name of the post was changed to Fort Worth and a small trading settlement grew up around it. Citizens with a real pioneering spirit followed, and when the army post was abandoned in 1853, these first Fort Worthians stayed on. The old cavalry stables became Fort Worth's first hotel and stores, and homes were soon built up around it. An important station on cattle trails leading to railheads in Kansas, Fort Worth had grown from a village to a town's estate when the Texas and Pacific Railroad reached here in 1876. Indeed, it was already experiencing the initial growing pains that someday would make it a great city. The cattle industry gave Fort Worth its packing houses and its first real boom, while oil also played an important role in the city's economy. However, it was the manufacture of aircraft that accelerated Fort Worth's growth more than any other factor. Today this big, bustling, industrial city still manages to maintain the informal flavor of a cattle town, yet its cultural and recreational facilities have matched its tremendous industrial development. Fort Worth is proud of its frontier heritage of strength, courage and friendliness, equalled by few communities.

CONVAIR—FORT WORTH AIRCRAFT PLANT is the home of big bombers. Fort Worth is the second largest producer of aircraft in the United States.

THE MAGNIFICENT BOTANIC GARDEN adjoining Trinity Park is a library of living plants only 2 miles from the heart of the Fort Worth business-district

IN STEEL AND CONCRETE, new buildings are rushed to completion in hustling, bustling Fort Worth, one of America's fastest growing cities

GRAND RAPIDS. Although a large manufacturing center, Grand Rapids is located in the heart of the great recreational area of southwestern Michigan. This district in the valley of the Grand River — in Indian lore called *Wash-te-nong Sebe,* "the river that takes you to far places" — offers fishing, boating and outdoor life in abundance. In the spring and summer there is fishing for pike, pickerel, bass and smaller panfish in the lakes and brooks and brown trout are found in the streams. In the fall, hunters have good pheasant, duck and small-game shooting, in addition to some deer hunting. Picnicking is a special favorite of all Grand Rapids' dwellers, particularly in one of the fifty-three municipal parks encircling the business area. In this country, the name Grand Rapids is synonymous with the making of furniture. Starting as a lumber-milling town, it made a natural evolution into a furniture-manufacturing city. Her numerous factories, whose doors are open to touring visitors, still lead the United States field in furniture design; the Ryerson Public Library has a unique, comprehensive collection on such design and manufacture and two art schools specialize in furniture designing.

MODERN CIVIC AUDITORIUM, most important public building, serves as the entertainment and education center of this convention city

FURNITURE MUSEUM, only one of its kind, displays the evolution of American household furniture from the earliest colonial times to the present, including outstanding pieces by Grand Rapids' craftsmen

JOHN BALL PARK, with its acres of forested hills, is a wonderful place to spend a leisurely afternoon. The extensive park system is so well planned that no home is farther than a fifteen-minute walk from one of these playgrounds

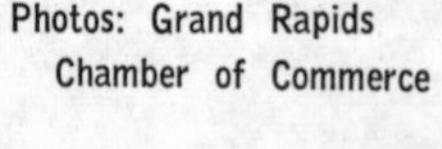

Photos: Grand Rapids Chamber of Commerce

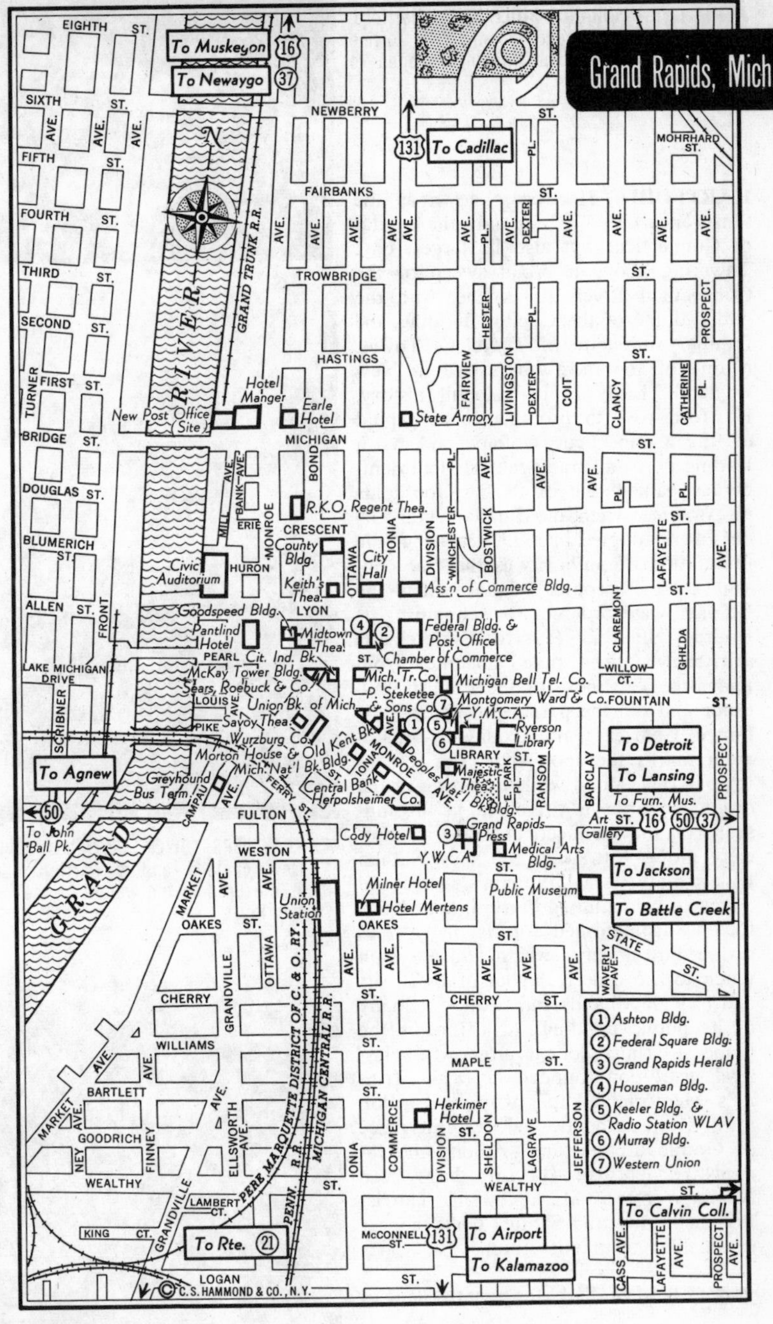

CALVIN COLLEGE was founded as a seminary of the Christian Reformed Church, a living memorial to the many Dutch immigrants who settled here

AETNA LIFE INSURANCE BUILDING, at Hartford, is the world's largest Colonial-style office building. The handsome building is open to visitors

HARTFORD. Hartford, known as the "Insurance City," is not only the capital of Connecticut but also its largest city. Towering above a broad sweep of the Connecticut River, its skyline, with the gilded dome of the Capitol Building, the familiar silhouette of Traveler's Tower, is one of the most impressive in New England. Early in its colorful history, Hartford rose to prominence as capital of the Connecticut Colony and as a leading port and trade center. Here democracy gained one of its first footholds in America when the Fundamental Orders were adopted in 1639, declaring "the foundation of authority is the free consent of the people." Later when the Colony was ordered to relinquish its liberal charter, Hartford's citizens spirited away the disputed document from under the very nose of the English governor and hid the parchment in the now famed Charter Oak. Today, a monument marks the spot where the spreading oak once stood while a portion of the original charter is preserved in the museum of the Connecticut Historical Society along with such relics as Nathan Hale's diary, Israel Putnam's sword and a bicycle belonging to Mark Twain. Hartford is distinguished for its many trees and beautiful parks which add a sylvan touch to the orderly layout of its streets and provide a handsome setting for many of its public buildings. Hartford is the home of Trinity College, a renowned classical institution founded in 1823. Trinity's Memorial Chapel with its carillon tower is an authentic and exquisite piece of Gothic architecture. Among the famous residents of Hartford have been Noah Webster, Mark Twain, Harriet Beecher Stowe and Samuel Colt, pioneer in small-arms manufacture.

Photos: Hartford Park Department, Hartford Chamber of Commerce

TRAVELERS TOWER, the tallest building in New England and a Hartford landmark, is mirrored in the waters of the Connecticut River

ELIZABETH PARK is famous for its many beautiful roses and the Rose Festival held here each June. The park contains over 500 varieties of roses

Hartford, Conn.

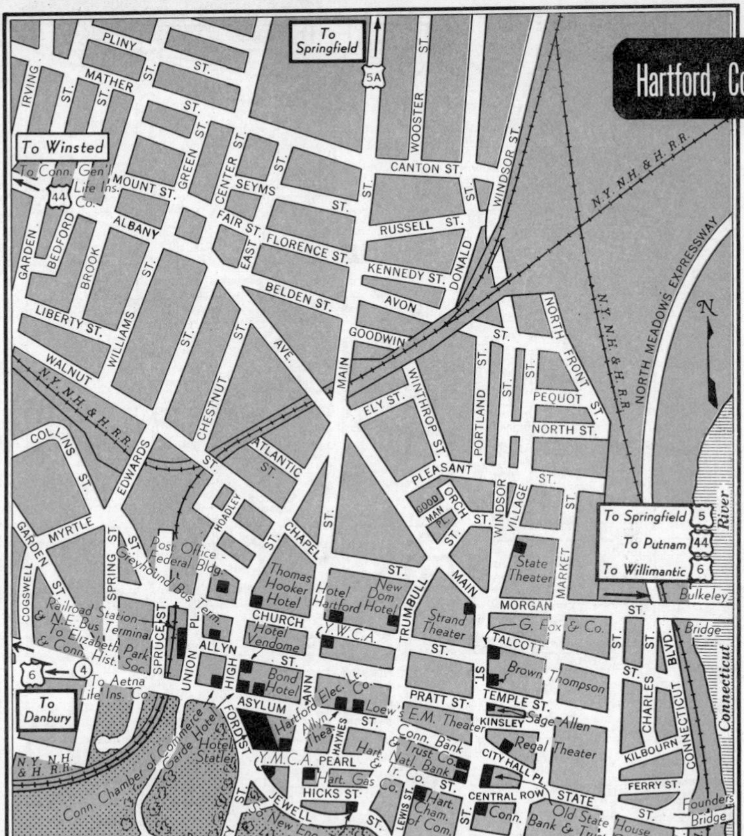

THE NEW HOME OFFICE of the Connecticut General Life Insurance Company is now nearing completion in suburban Hartford

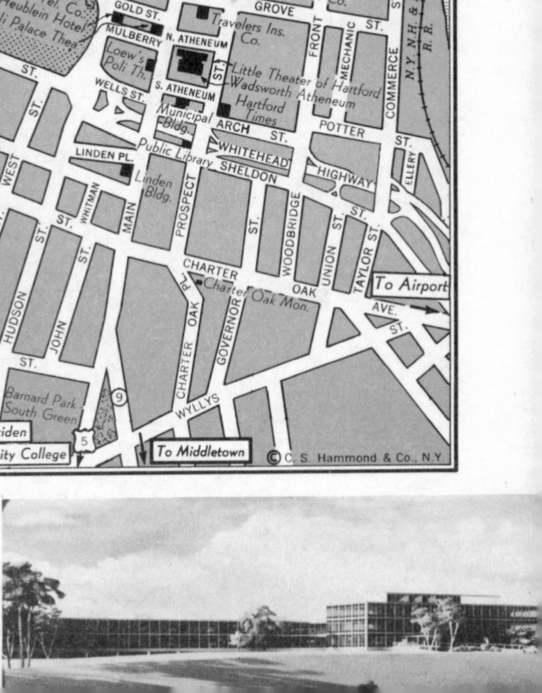

Houston, Tex.

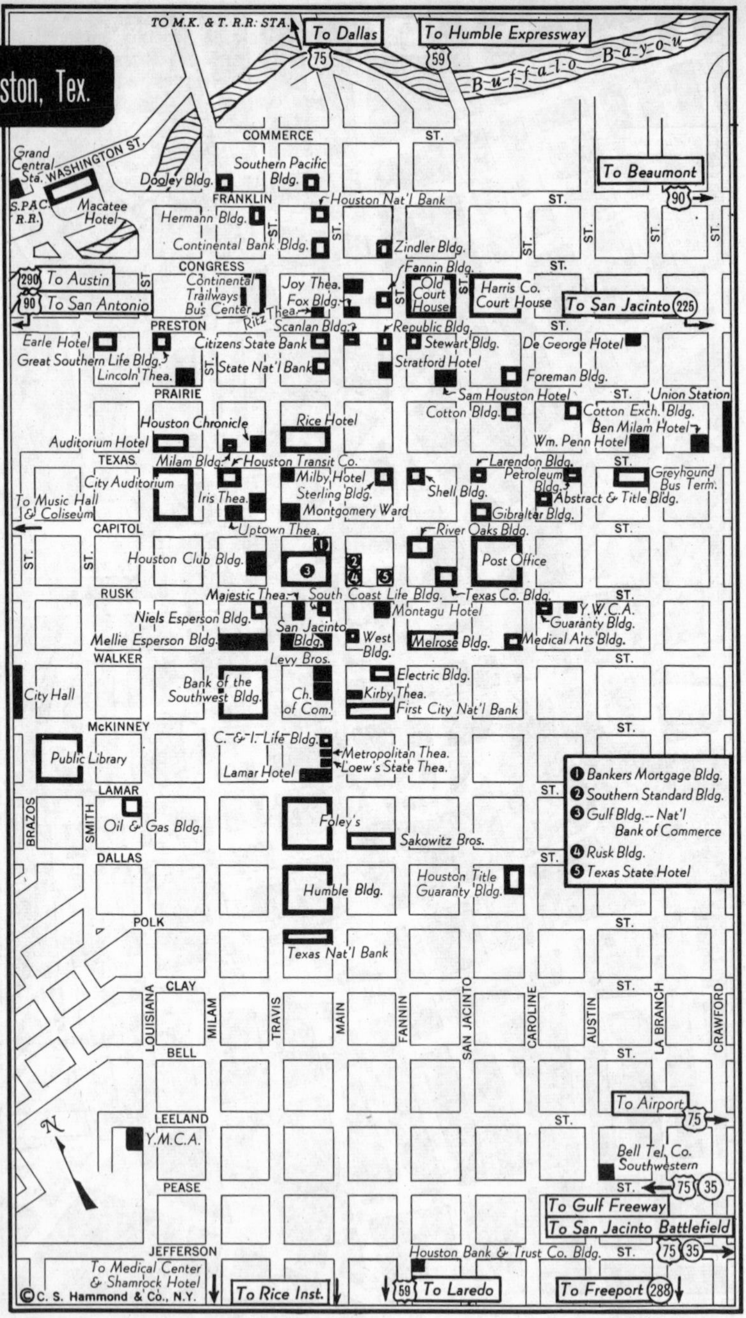

TO M.K. & T. R.R. STA.

To Dallas 75

To Humble Expressway 59

Buffalo Bayou

COMMERCE ST.

To Beaumont 90

Grand Central Sta.

WASHINGTON ST.

S.PAC. R.R.

Macatee Hotel

Dooley Bldg.

Southern Pacific Bldg.

FRANKLIN ST.

Houston Nat'l Bank

Hermann Bldg.

Continental Bank Bldg.

Zindler Bldg.

CONGRESS ST.

Fannin Bldg.

290 To Austin

90 To San Antonio

Continental Trailways Bus Center

Joy Thea.

Fox Bldg.

Ritz Thea.

Old Court House

Harris Co. Court House

To San Jacinto 225

PRESTON ST.

Scanlan Bldg.

Republic Bldg.

Earle Hotel

Citizens State Bank

Stewart Bldg.

De George Hotel

Great Southern Life Bldg.

Lincoln Thea.

State Nat'l Bank

Stratford Hotel

Foreman Bldg.

PRAIRIE ST.

Sam Houston Hotel

Union Station

Cotton Bldg.

Cotton Exch. Bldg.

Houston Chronicle

Rice Hotel

Ben Milam Hotel

Auditorium Hotel

Wm. Penn Hotel

TEXAS ST.

Milam Bldg.

Houston Transit Co.

Larendon Bldg.

City Auditorium

Milby Hotel

Petroleum Bldg.

Greyhound Bus Term.

To Music Hall & Coliseum

Iris Thea.

Sterling Bldg.

Shell Bldg.

Abstract & Title Bldg.

Montgomery Ward

Gibraltar Bldg.

Uptown Thea.

CAPITOL ST.

River Oaks Bldg.

Houston Club Bldg.

Post Office

RUSK ST.

Majestic Thea.

South Coast Life Bldg.

Texas Co. Bldg.

Niels Esperson Bldg.

Montagu Hotel

Y.W.C.A.

Guaranty Bldg.

San Jacinto Bldg.

Mellie Esperson Bldg.

West Bldg.

Melrose Bldg.

Medical Arts Bldg.

Levy Bros.

WALKER ST.

Electric Bldg.

City Hall

Bank of the Southwest Bldg.

Ch. of Com.

Kirby Thea.

First City Nat'l Bank

McKINNEY ST.

C. & I. Life Bldg.

Metropolitan Thea.

Public Library

Loew's State Thea.

Lamar Hotel

LAMAR ST.

❶ Bankers Mortgage Bldg.
❷ Southern Standard Bldg.
❸ Gulf Bldg.-- Nat'l Bank of Commerce
❹ Rusk Bldg.
❺ Texas State Hotel

Oil & Gas Bldg.

Foley's

Sakowitz Bros.

DALLAS ST.

Houston Title Guaranty Bldg.

Humble Bldg.

POLK ST.

Texas Nat'l Bank

CLAY ST.

BRAZOS, SMITH, LOUISIANA, MILAM, TRAVIS, MAIN, FANNIN, SAN JACINTO, CAROLINE, AUSTIN, LA BRANCH, CRAWFORD

BELL ST.

To Airport 75

LEELAND ST.

Y.M.C.A.

N

Bell Tel. Co. Southwestern

PEASE ST. 75 35

To Gulf Freeway

To San Jacinto Battlefield

JEFFERSON ST. 75 35

Houston Bank & Trust Co. Bldg.

To Medical Center & Shamrock Hotel

To Rice Inst.

59 To Laredo

To Freeport 288

SAM HOUSTON COLISEUM, with 51,000 feet of exhibit space, and the adjoining Music Hall are among the excellent facilities which have made Houston one of the leading convention cities of the South

U.S.S. TEXAS is now permanently anchored at San Jacinto State Park as a Texas shrine. The gallant old battleship was saved from being scrapped after valiant service in both World Wars

HOUSTON. Houston, "Giant of the Golden Bend," is an adolescent among American cities. Though founded in 1836, Houston's greatest period of development has been within the last ten years. Construction—commercial, industrial and residential—is seemingly completed overnight. Visitors don't have to be told of the city's amazing growth—on every hand they can see the visible signs of it for themselves. Dynamic Houston is literally booming with new skyscrapers, lavish stores, apartment buildings and such flamboyant establishments as the Shamrock Hotel. Adjoining Hermann Park is the 100-million-dollar Texas Medical Center, one of the world's greatest concentrations of medical facilities for research, teaching and treatment. The city's giant petrochemical industry, which has mushroomed into being since World War II, presents a spectacular sight with its maze of vari-colored pipes and gleaming spherical-shaped tanks. The Port of Houston, linked with the Gulf by the 50-mile length of the Houston Ship Channel, ranks tonnagewise as our country's second largest port. Houston serves as gateway to an area which extends from Canada to Mexico and from the Mississippi to the Rockies. Located along the channel, about 18 miles southeast of the city, is the San Jacinto Battleground. Here a stately monument, topped by a lone star, commemorates the victory which won for Texas its independence from Mexico on April 21st, 1836.

Photos: Houston C. of C., Texas Highway Dept.

HOUSTON EXPRESSWAY is one of the modern urban expressways built by the Texas Highway Department to transport heavy traffic into and away from large cities

TURNING BASIN of the Houston Ship Channel provides facilities for ships from all nations. Houston is an inland port, protected against the dangers of wind and sea yet connected with the world's shipping lanes by a 50 mile channel

A TYPICAL OIL FIELD SCENE showing Humble production operations near Houston. Pictured are pumping wells, a tall separator, where gas is taken from oil, and storage tanks with walkways

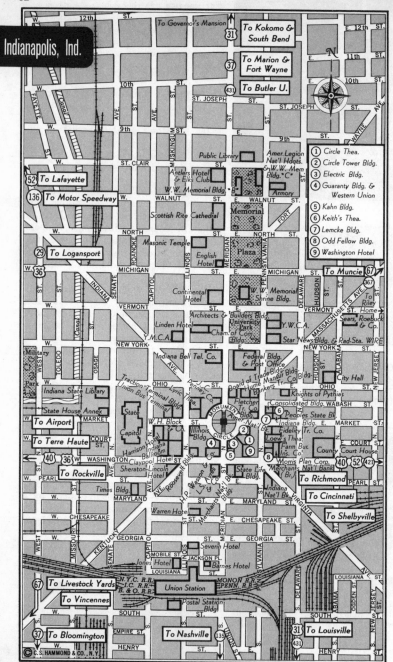

Indianapolis, Ind.

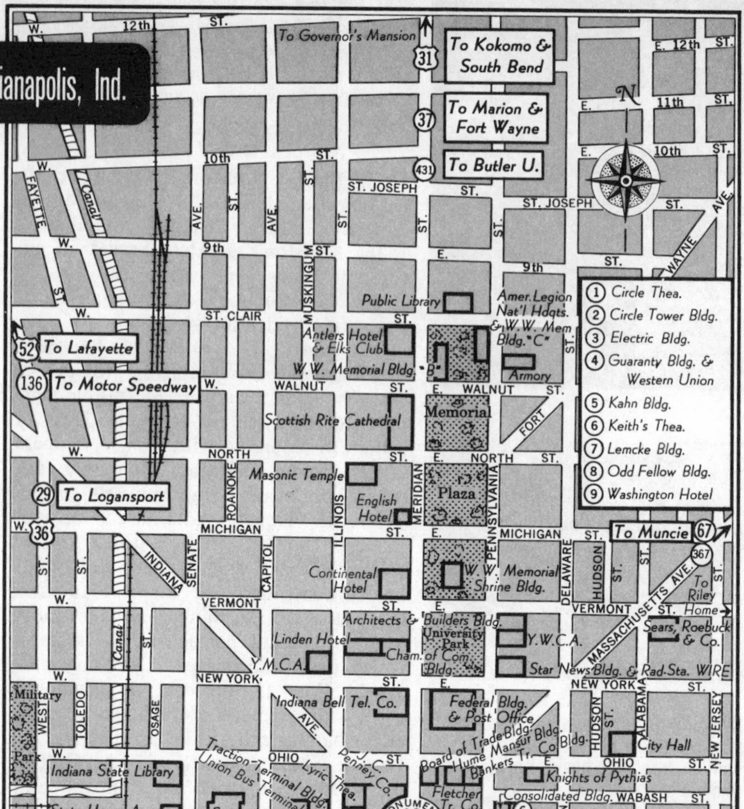

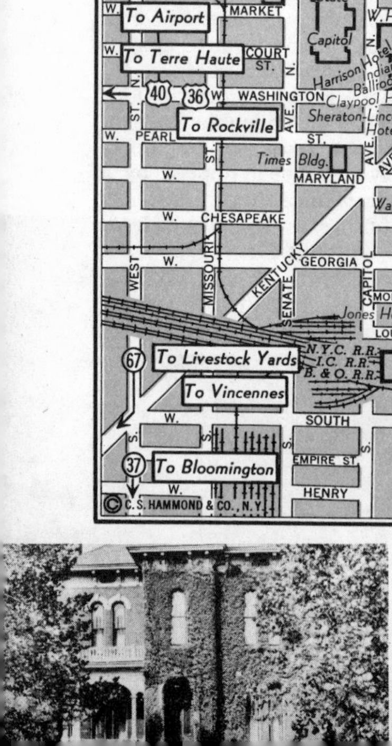

To Governor's Mansion
To Kokomo & South Bend
To Marion & Fort Wayne
To Butler U.
To Lafayette
To Motor Speedway
To Logansport
To Muncie
To Riley Home
To Airport
To Terre Haute
To Rockville
To Richmond
To Cincinnati
To Shelbyville
To Livestock Yards
To Vincennes
To Bloomington
To Nashville
To Louisville

Public Library
Amer. Legion Nat'l Hdqts. & W.W. Mem Bldg. "C"
Antlers Hotel & Elks Club
W.W. Memorial Bldg. "B"
Armory
Scottish Rite Cathedral
Memorial
Masonic Temple
English Hotel
Plaza
Continental Hotel
W.W. Memorial Shrine Bldg.
Architects & Builders Bldg.
University Park
Linden Hotel
Cham. of Com. Bldg.
Y.W.C.A.
Y.M.C.A.
Star News Bldg. & Rad. Sta. WIRE
Sears, Roebuck & Co.
Military Park
Indiana Bell Tel. Co.
Federal Bldg. & Post Office
City Hall
Indiana State Library
State House Annex
Traction Terminal Bldg.
Union Bus Terminal
Lyric Thea.
J. C. Penney Co.
Board of Trade Bldg.
Hume Mansur Bldg.
Bankers Tr. Co. Bldg.
Knights of Pythias
Consolidated Bldg.
Fletcher Tr. Co. Bldg.
Monument Circle
Amer. Nat'l Bk.
Peoples State Bk.
Indiana Bldg.
Fidelity Tr. Co.
Loew's Thea.
Farm Bur. Ins. Co.
County Court House
State Capitol
W. H. Block & Co.
Illinois Bldg.
Harrison Hotel
Indiana Ballroom
Claypool Hotel
Sheraton-Lincoln Hotel
Roosevelt Bldg.
H. P. Wasson & Co.
L. S. Ayres & Co.
Merchants Nat'l Bk. Bldg.
State Life Bldg.
Morris Plan Corp.
Merchants Nat'l Bank (Br.)
Indiana Nat'l Bk.
Times Bldg.
Warren Hotel
Severin Hotel
Jones Hotel
Barnes Hotel
Union Station
N.Y.C. R.R.
I.C. R.R.
B. & O. R.R.
Monon R.R.
Penn. R.R.
Postal Station Bldg.

1. Circle Thea.
2. Circle Tower Bldg.
3. Electric Bldg.
4. Guaranty Bldg. & Western Union
5. Kahn Bldg.
6. Keith's Thea.
7. Lemcke Bldg.
8. Odd Fellow Bldg.
9. Washington Hotel

Photos: Black Star

THE HOME OF JAMES WHITCOMB RILEY, the "Hoosier Poet," is one of the famous landmarks of Indianapolis. The house is preserved as it was during the poet's life-time

THE HOOSIER CAPITOL at Indianapolis, is built of rock from Indiana's own limestone hills. Begun in 1878, it enjoys the distinction of having cost less than the sum appropriated for it

INDIANAPOLIS. Indianapolis owes much of its stately beauty and spaciousness to the fact that it is a "made-to-order" city. In 1820, wishing to locate the capital as close to the geographic center of the state as possible, the Indiana State Legislature selected its site on the West Branch of the White River. Patterned after the national capital the city's streets were laid out around a circular plaza in a conventional grid, cut diagonally by four broad avenues. Rising above the central circle where the governor's mansion formerly stood, is the Indiana State Soldiers' and Sailors' Monument—a 284-foot shaft, topped by a bronze statue of Liberty. Indianapolis's central location has been a prime factor in its commercial development. An important rail center, it is served by 16 lines of 6 railroads. Its major industries include meat-packing, milling and the processing of food. Indianapolis is internationally known for the Memorial Day racing classic—the 500-mile race at the Indianapolis Motor Speedway. This grueling race around a 2.5-mile course not only provides the thrill of ultra-high speed but also acts as a proving ground for the latest in automotive developments; innovations such as balloon tires, rear-vision mirrors and four-wheel brakes were introduced here.

THE SCOTTISH RITE CATHEDRAL is a magnificent building ornamented with emblematic designs in cut stone. Its tower houses a carillon of 63 "singing bells"

THE GOVERNOR'S MANSION is a handsome home in an attractive setting of tree-shaded lawns and beautiful gardens

Jacksonville, Fla.

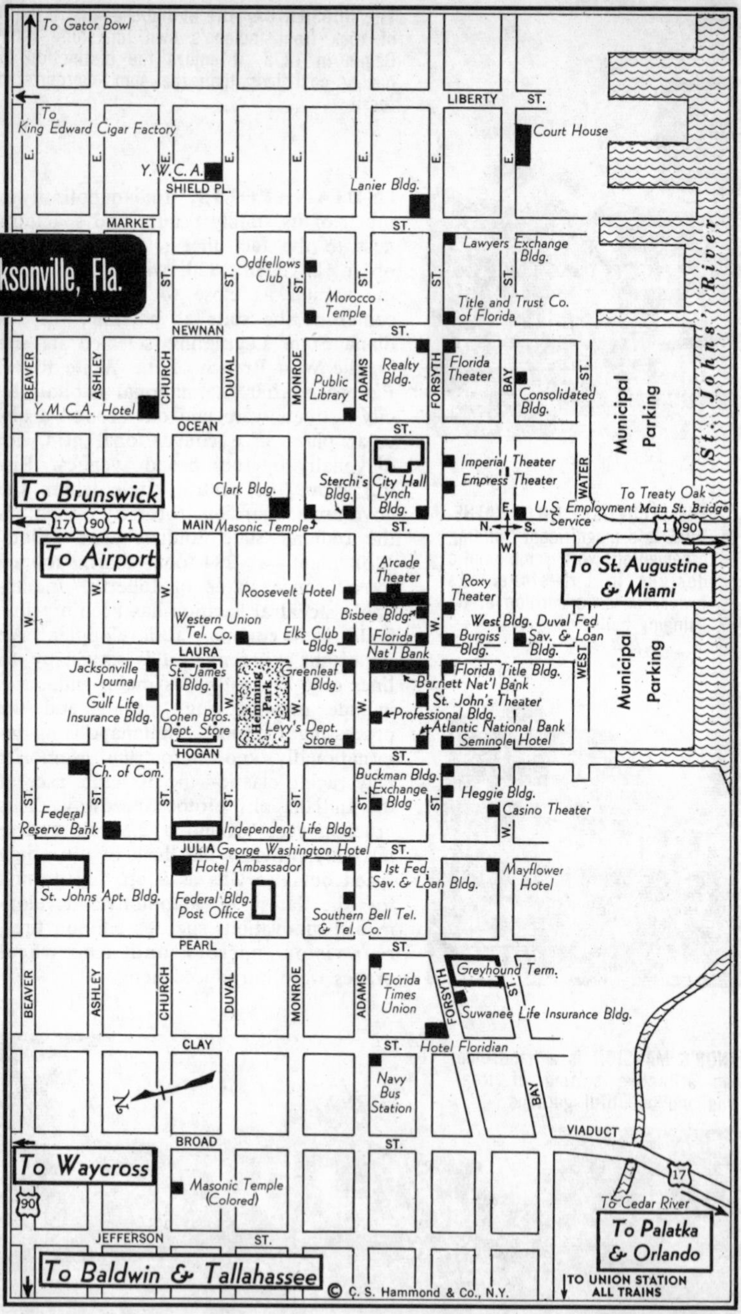

To Gator Bowl
To King Edward Cigar Factory
LIBERTY ST.
Court House
Y. W. C. A.
SHIELD PL.
Lanier Bldg.
MARKET ST.
Lawyers Exchange Bldg.
Oddfellows Club
Morocco Temple
Title and Trust Co. of Florida
NEWNAN ST.
BEAVER
ASHLEY
CHURCH
DUVAL
MONROE
ADAMS
FORSYTH
BAY
Public Library
Realty Bldg.
Florida Theater
Consolidated Bldg.
Y.M.C.A. Hotel
OCEAN ST.
WATER ST.
Municipal Parking
St. Johns River
Imperial Theater
Empress Theater
To Brunswick
17 90 1
Clark Bldg.
Sterchi's Bldg.
City Hall
Lynch Bldg.
U.S. Employment Service
To Treaty Oak
Main St. Bridge
MAIN ST.
Masonic Temple
N. S. E. W.
To Airport
To St. Augustine & Miami
Arcade Theater
Roxy Theater
Roosevelt Hotel
Bisbee Bldg.
Western Union Tel. Co.
Elks Club Bldg.
Florida Nat'l Bank
West Bldg.
Burgiss Bldg.
Duval Fed Sav. & Loan Bldg.
WEST ST.
LAURA
Jacksonville Journal
St. James Bldg.
Hemming Park
Greenleaf Bldg.
Florida Title Bldg.
Barnett Nat'l Bank
St. John's Theater
Gulf Life Insurance Bldg.
Cohen Bros. Dept. Store
Levy's Dept. Store
Professional Bldg.
Atlantic National Bank
Seminole Hotel
HOGAN ST.
Ch. of Com.
Buckman Bldg.
Exchange Bldg.
Heggie Bldg.
Casino Theater
Federal Reserve Bank
Independent Life Bldg.
JULIA ST.
George Washington Hotel
Hotel Ambassador
1st Fed. Sav. & Loan Bldg.
Mayflower Hotel
St. Johns Apt. Bldg.
Federal Bldg. Post Office
Southern Bell Tel. & Tel. Co.
PEARL ST.
Greyhound Term.
Florida Times Union
Suwanee Life Insurance Bldg.
CLAY ST.
Hotel Floridian
Navy Bus Station
BAY
VIADUCT
BROAD ST.
To Waycross
90
Masonic Temple (Colored)
17
To Cedar River
To Palatka & Orlando
JEFFERSON ST.
To Baldwin & Tallahassee
TO UNION STATION ALL TRAINS

BOATING ON THE CEDAR RIVER near Jacksonville is a favorite pastime of outdoor lovers. The rivers and nearby lakes are famous for black bass fishing

THE TREATY OAK—tradition has it that under this 800-year old tree Florida Indians held their powwows. Today, its spreading branches could shade at least 4,000 people

JACKSONVILLE (Fla.). The great metropolitan seaport of Jacksonville has long held the reputation for making friends out of strangers. The normal hospitality of the Deep South, the cosmopolitan character of its industry and culture, its vast store of entertainment and the natural friendliness of its people, add up to a warm welcome sensed by even the most casual visitor. Jacksonville is an "outdoor-weather town." There is just enough difference between June and January to define the seasons. Summers are cooled by ocean breezes and winter frost is pushed back by the warm waters of the St. John's River which rises 200 miles to the south. In the vicinity of "Florida's Gateway City" are numerous historic spots where quite literally the inspiring pages of American history were first written in the blood of Spanish Conquistadors, French Huguenots, English adventurers and pirates of the Spanish Main. St. Augustine and many of the name-places were old when the timbers of the Mayflower still bore leaves. Outdoor sports, theaters, parks, playgrounds and gardens gay with exotic bloom are also among the many attractions of Jacksonville. Of the city's many industries one of the most fascinating is the King Edward cigar plant, the world's largest cigar factory. Tours through the plant are conducted daily.

HARD-PACKED SANDS stretch for some 30 miles outside Jacksonville. Here visitors enjoy driving on the beach and the pleasure of swimming in fine surf

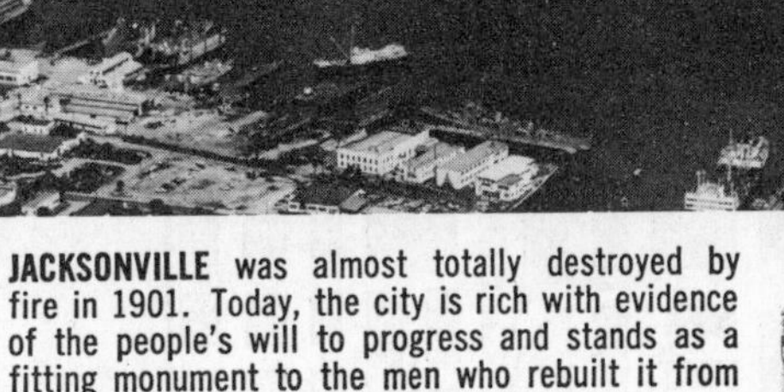

JACKSONVILLE was almost totally destroyed by fire in 1901. Today, the city is rich with evidence of the people's will to progress and stands as a fitting monument to the men who rebuilt it from the ashes

Photos: Crisp and Harrison agency

GATOR BOWL is the scene of the annual New Year's Day football classic. The stadium is a perfect setting for sports and thrilling outdoor events which include rodeos and professional ice shows

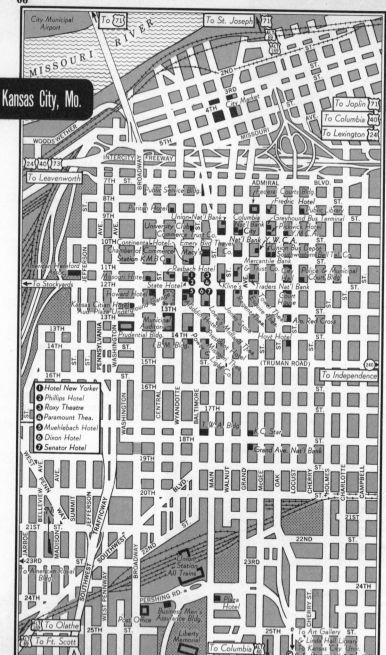

Kansas City, Mo.

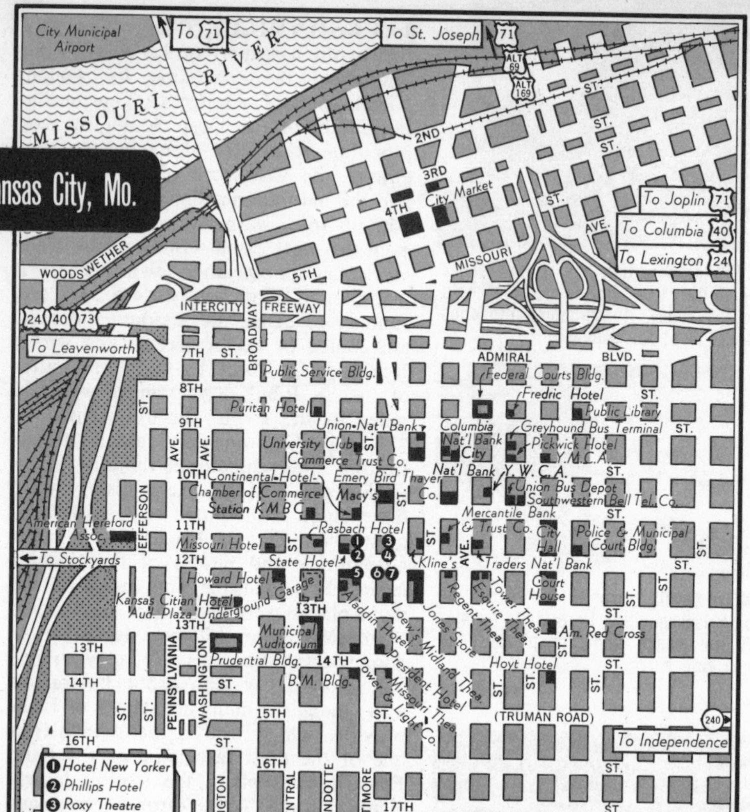

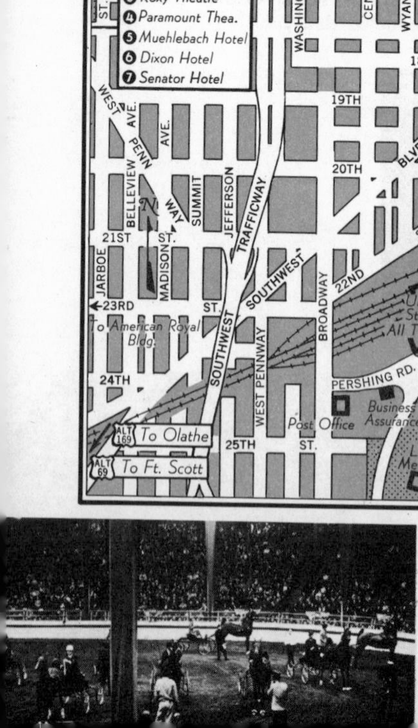

THE HORSE SHOW, one of the main attractions at the American Royal, always draws a large crowd. Here the finest saddle and harness classes of American horses appear before the critical eyes of equine lovers

FAMOUS STOCKYARDS at Kansas City are known the world over—being the nation's largest stocker and feeder market. They extend into Kansas City, Kansas, which lies across the river

KANSAS CITY (Mo.). There is a thrill in entering a city across a huge bridge over a wide river, and this thrill is enhanced when you approach Kansas City across the Missouri, for you face west and you seem to sense the wide-open spaces, deserts and mountain ranges, and the Pacific beyond. In the heart of the modern traveler is thus repeated what the pioneers and settlers felt whose wagon trains journeyed west along the Sante Fe and Oregon trails and who came here to cross the Missouri. Known as Westport Landing, the town there at the big bend of the Missouri was boisterous, whiskey-drinking and gun-toting, as befitted its role as caterer to wagon trains and gateway to the West. When, in 1844, a flood destroyed nearby Independence, Kansas City added the trade on the river to its business activities. And when the railroads came, it was quick to assure its importance as a crossroads in this new era—it built, in 1865, the first railroad bridge across the Missouri. Today, with its twin-city, Kansas City, Kansas, it is America's second largest cattle market and its primary market for winter wheat. Culture and gracious living have followed in the wake of commercial expansion, and little is left of the old wild spirit. But in spite of fine streets, modern stores and beautiful residential sections, the lure of pioneer days still is felt, to the south down the river, and to the west toward the setting sun.

BEAUTIFUL COLUMNS in the main foyer of the Nelson Gallery of Art frame a knight in armor. The halls of this famed museum contain over 10,000 works of art

Photo: Massie-Missouri Resources Division, American Hereford Assoc.

HEADQUARTERS for the American Hereford Association is an ultra-modern building, inside and out. The bull atop the 90-foot pylon is made of 1,000 lbs. of plastic and 4,500 lbs. of steel. It is lighted from the inside at night

LIBERTY MEMORIAL is dedicated to those who died in World War I. Visitors who ride to the top of the 217-foot shaft receive a rewarding view of the city

LINDA HALL LIBRARY of Science and Technology is a portent of the city's bid for greatness. Founded in 1946, it already has more than 175,000 scientific volumes

LITTLE ROCK. Little Rock, capital of Arkansas, has the distinction of owning three capitol buildings. The Territorial Capitol, now restored, was constructed of hand-hewn logs and cypress sidings; the reconstruction project includes several frontier homes complete with gardens and furnishings of the period. The Old State House, considered to be one of the best examples of classic architecture in the United States, dates from the ante-bellum era; today, this beautiful building serves as a war memorial. The present Capitol, built of gleaming white Arkansas marble, is noted for its photo-mural rotunda and exhibitions of minerals and historical relics. Back in Little Rock's frontier-trading-post days, when most of its citizens toted six-shooters, the town could also boast a law which read, "No shooting in the streets on Sundays." At one time, shooting matches were a favorite form of entertainment in Little Rock; in this manner, the townspeople celebrated a visit to their community by the famed American frontiersman, Davy Crockett. The distinguished Colonel who was passing through town on his way to fight for Texas liberty, was aptly described in a Little Rock newspaper as a "raal critter." A hero of more recent times, General Douglas MacArthur, commander of Allied forces in the Far East, was born in Little Rock.

Photos: Little Rock Chamber of Commerce

LITTLE ROCK is a growing medical center. Pictured is the new University of Arkansas Medical Center, housing schools of medicine, pharmacy and nursing

TERRITORIAL CAPITOL, built in 1820, served as the Capitol of Arkansas Territory before Arkansas was admitted to the Federal Union

OLD STATE HOUSE is considered a classic among buildings constructed in the anti-bellum period. It was used as Arkansas' Capitol during and after the Civil War

THE PRESENT STATE CAPITOL is patterned after the nation's Capitol in Washington, D.C. In the background are several of the buildings housing various state offices

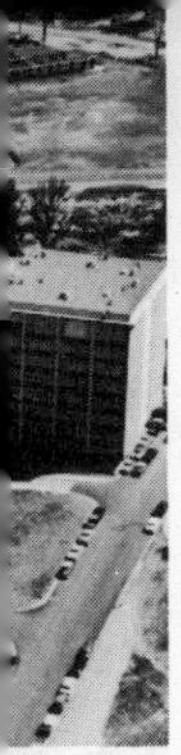

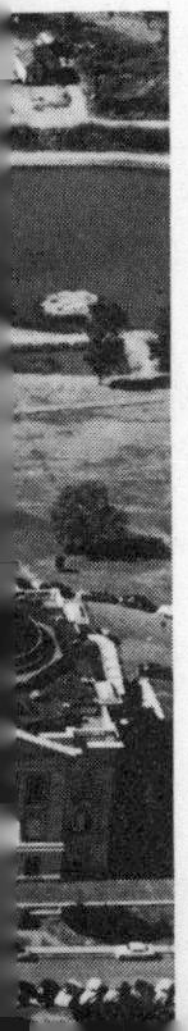

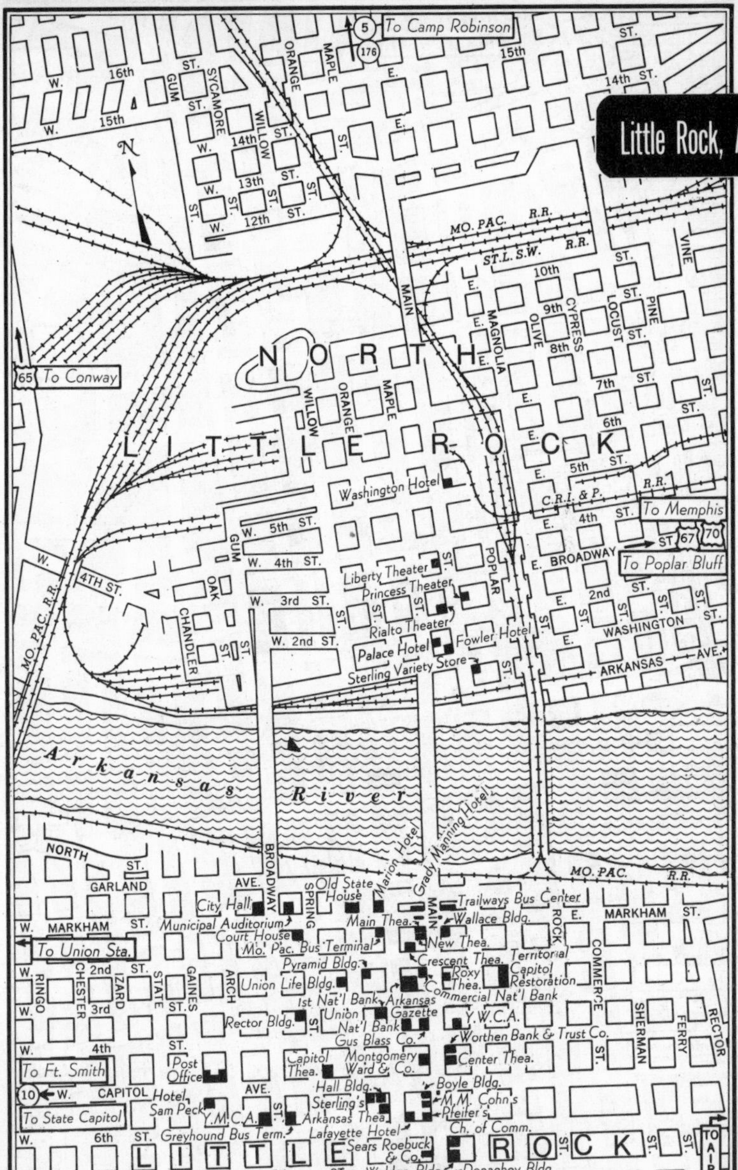

Little Rock, Ark.

To Camp Robinson
To Conway
NORTH LITTLE ROCK
Washington Hotel
Liberty Theater
Princess Theater
Rialto Theater
Palace Hotel
Fowler Hotel
Sterling Variety Store
To Memphis
To Poplar Bluff
MO. PAC. R.R.
ST.L. S.W. R.R.
C.R.I. & P. R.R.
Arkansas River
Marion Hotel
Grady Manning Hotel
Old State House
City Hall
Municipal Auditorium
Court House
Mo. Pac. Bus Terminal
Trailways Bus Center
Wallace Bldg.
Main Thea.
New Thea.
Pyramid Bldg.
Crescent Thea.
Territorial Capitol Restoration
Roxy Thea.
Union Life Bldg.
Commercial Nat'l Bank
1st Nat'l Bank
Arkansas Gazette
Union Nat'l Bank
Rector Bldg.
Y.W.C.A.
Gus Blass Co.
Worthen Bank & Trust Co.
Post Office
Capitol Thea.
Montgomery Ward & Co.
Center Thea.
Hall Bldg.
Boyle Bldg.
Sterling's
M.M. Cohn's
Hotel Sam Peck
Y.M.C.A.
Arkansas Thea.
Pfeifer's
Lafayette Hotel
Ch. of Comm.
Greyhound Bus Term.
Sears Roebuck & Co.
LITTLE ROCK
Waldon Bldg.
Donaghey Bldg.
Albert Pike Hotel
Public Library
Southwestern Bell Tel. Co.
Masonic Temple
Gem Theater
Fine Arts Museum
MacArthur Birthplace
To Union Sta.
To Ft. Smith
To State Capitol
To Univ. Medical Center
To Livestock Show Grounds
To Benton
To Sheridan
To Pine Bluff
To Hot Springs
TO AIRPORT

T. H. BARTON COLISEUM, located at the Livestock Show Grounds, is a 9,000 seat air-conditioned auditorium which is used for conventions, sporting events and livestock shows

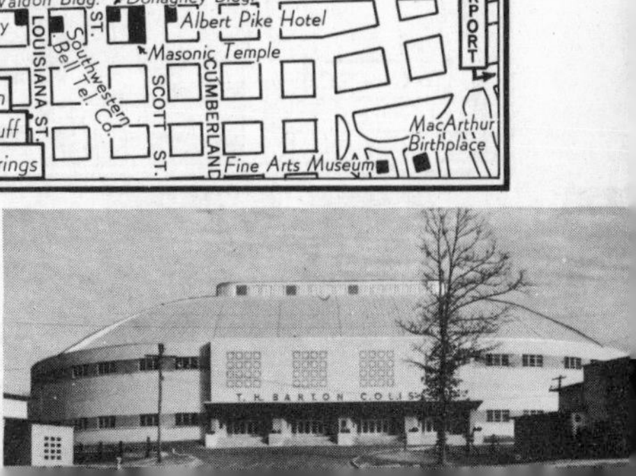

Los Angeles, Cal.

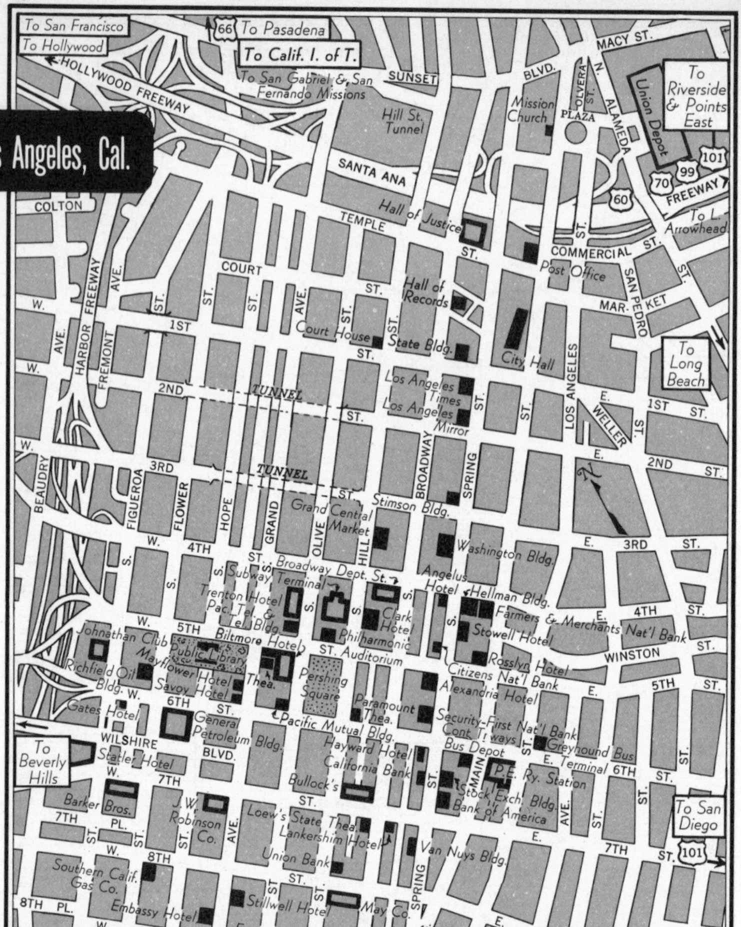

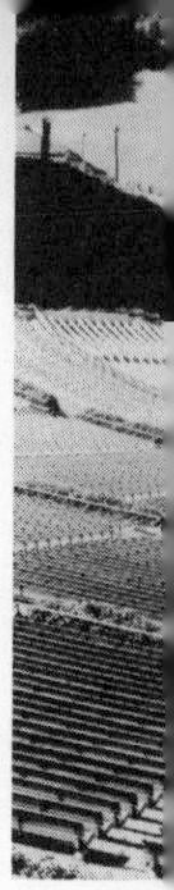

MISSION SAN FERNANDO REY DE ESPANA, located just south of San Fernando, is among California's treasured relics of Spanish occupation. Dating from the year 1797, the quaint adobe building is now completely restored. A statue of its founder Junipero Serra, stands in the lovely mission garden

HOLLYWOOD BOWL, a natural amphitheater set in the barren hillside above Hollywood, is the scene of the impressive Easter sunrise services. Symphony concerts are presented here during the summer months

LOS ANGELES. Los Angeles, popularly known as "L.A.," is the nation's third largest city. Situated on the southern California coast, it possesses a metropolitan area so vast it encompasses almost seventy outlying cities and nearly three times that many smaller towns and villages. Altogether Los Angeles spreads out over an area of 452 square miles. A decentralized metropolis, one community seemingly melting into another, it was once described by a humorist as "19 suburbs in search of a city." This great sprawling mass is tied neatly together into one great urban package by an amazing network of roads and superhighways. Los Angeles began its history as a sleepy little pueblo founded in 1781 by Felipe de Neve, the Spanish governor of California. The total population of El Pueblo de Nuestra Senora la Reina de Los Angeles de Porciuncula, as Los Angeles was then known, consisted of eleven Indian and Mexican families. Until 1881 its growth was unspectacular; then, with the coming of the railroads and the land-booms that followed, Los Angeles rapidly expanded its perimeter, swallowing up neighboring towns at a phenomenal rate. The growing of citrus fruit, the discovery of oil, the making of motion pictures and the manufacture of aircraft, all contributed to its spectacular development. An exceptionally fine climate and the grandeur of its setting, with the San Gabriel Mountains on one hand and the blue waters of the Pacific on the other, make Los Angeles a popular spot with tourists.

SOUTHERN CALIFORNIA'S ROCKY COAST is broken at intervals by little sandy coves and exquisite palm-dotted beaches. Pictured is one of the many fine beaches which lie within a short distance of the heart of Los Angeles

Photos: Los Angeles County Chamber of Commerce

HOLLYWOOD FREEWAY is a part of a complicated network of roads, expressways and super-highways that bind many small surrounding towns and villages into the huge urban mass that is Greater Los Angeles

LOS ANGELES Continued

In downtown Los Angeles, the new Civic Center with the gleaming white tower of City Hall is one of the city's most impressive groups of buildings. Nearby, Pershing Square serves as the nearest thing to a general business center. The Plaza, the original heart of the city, and the Old Mission Church, its most historic building, are preserved as relics of early pueblo days. Olvera Street, too, recalls the past. Crowded with little shops, gay with colored lanterns and Latin music, the narrow street, closed to all but pedestrian traffic, is a replica of a Mexican street of a century ago. Avila Adobe on Olvera Street is Los Angeles' oldest building, dating back to 1818. Wilshire Boulevard runs westward for some 17 miles, passing Hancock Park, where the famous La Brea Tar Pits have yielded the remains of prehistoric monsters trapped millions of years ago in the oozing asphalt pools. The boulevard leads on through Beverly Hills, home of many notable screen stars, to Santa Monica, where it ends at the Pacific Ocean. Hollywood, the city's most famous district, lies northwest of the downtown area. The large motion picture studios are located here as well as the western headquarters of most of the major radio and television networks. The main streets of the glittering film capital are Sunset Boulevard and Hollywood Boulevard, while the busy intersection of Hollywood and Vine serves as its main center. The Hollywood area is probably Los Angeles' biggest tourist attraction. Just north of Hollywood proper lies Griffith Park, which includes within its 4,253 acres an observatory, a planetarium and a zoo.

THE COUNTRY'S LARGEST PRODUCER OF AIRCRAFT, the Los Angeles area is also a major hub of air transportation. Six large airlines provide the city with both domestic and foreign service. Pictured is the busy Los Angeles International Airport

DISNEYLAND is one of the newest and most popular attractions of the Los Angeles area. Opened in 1955, this children's "wonderland come to life" is visited by thousands from all over the country annually

UNION STATION is a handsome structure of California mission style architecture, notable for its charming landscaped innercourt. Four large railroads link Los Angeles with cities on the East coast

SKIING AT LAKE ARROWHEAD is one of the many pleasant and varied diversions offered in the Los Angeles area. Lake Arrowhead, a resort in the mountains above San Bernardino, is noted for its excellent fishing and facilities for winter sports

MISSION SAN GABRIEL ARCANGEL, founded in 1771, is an outstanding example of mission architecture. San Gabriel is one of a chain of 21 missions that stretched from San Diego to Sonoma and played so important a role in early California history

CITY HALL, located just south of the Plaza, is the tallest building in southern California. The 452-foot-high tower offers an unsurpassed view of the city and its surroundings. City Hall is one of the buildings that comprise the new Los Angeles Civic Center

Louisville, Ky.

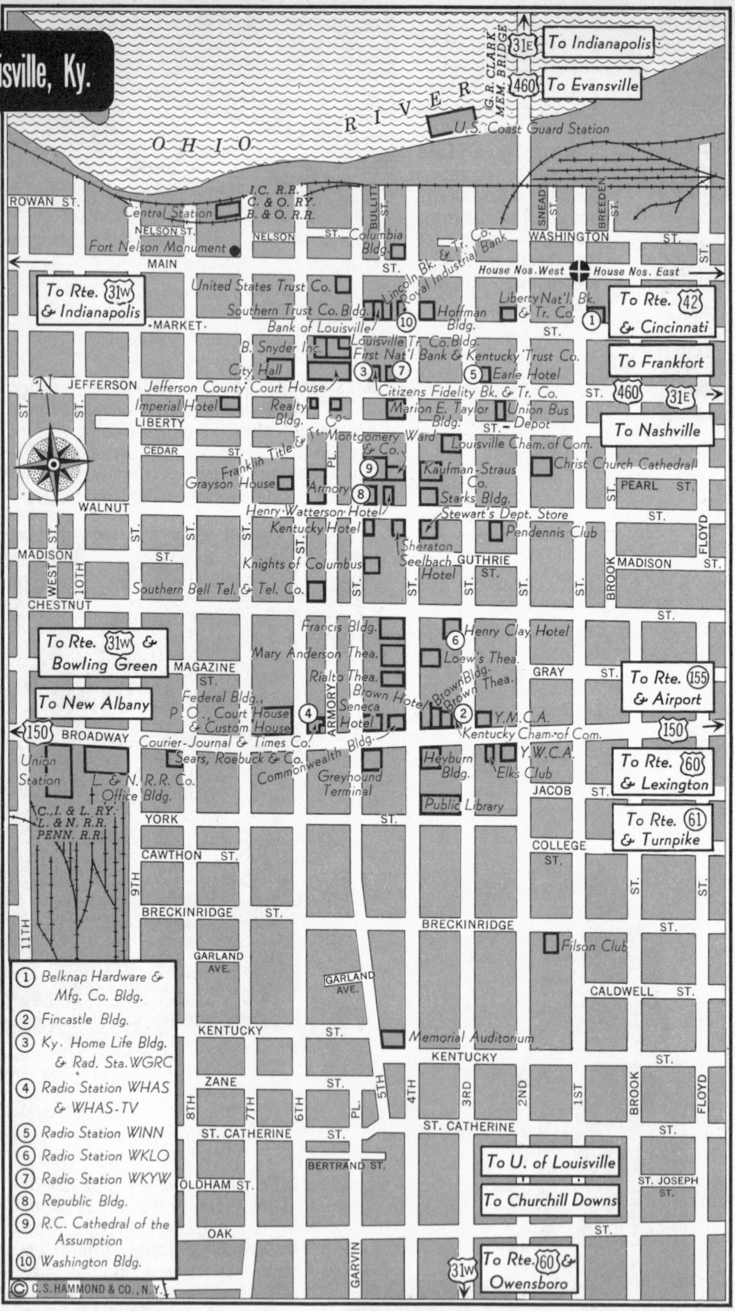

OHIO RIVER
G.R. CLARK MEM. BRIDGE
31E To Indianapolis
460 To Evansville
U.S. Coast Guard Station
I.C. R.R.
C. & O. RY.
B. & O. R.R.
Central Station
ROWAN ST.
NELSON ST.
NELSON ST.
Fort Nelson Monument
MAIN ST.
BULLITT ST.
Columbia Bldg.
WASHINGTON ST.
SNEAD ST.
BREEDEN ST.
House Nos. West
House Nos. East
To Rte. 31W & Indianapolis
United States Trust Co.
Southern Trust Co. Bldg.
Lincoln Bk. & Tr. Co.
Royal Industrial Bank
Hoffman Bldg.
Liberty Nat'l. Bk. & Tr. Co.
To Rte. 42 & Cincinnati
MARKET ST.
Bank of Louisville
B. Snyder Inc.
Louisville Tr. Co. Bldg.
First Nat'l Bank & Kentucky Trust Co.
To Frankfort
City Hall
Earle Hotel
JEFFERSON ST.
Jefferson County Court House
Citizens Fidelity Bk. & Tr. Co.
460 31E
Imperial Hotel
Realty Bldg.
Marion E. Taylor Bldg.
Union Bus Depot
To Nashville
LIBERTY ST.
Franklin Title & Tr. Co.
Montgomery Ward & Co.
Louisville Cham. of Com.
CEDAR ST.
Kaufman-Straus Co.
Christ Church Cathedral
Grayson House
Armory
PEARL ST.
Starks Bldg.
WALNUT ST.
Henry Watterson Hotel
Stewart's Dept. Store
Kentucky Hotel
Pendennis Club
Sheraton Seelbach Hotel
MADISON ST.
GUTHRIE ST.
Knights of Columbus
MADISON ST.
WEST ST.
10TH ST.
Southern Bell Tel. & Tel. Co.
CHESTNUT ST.
Francis Bldg.
Henry Clay Hotel
To Rte. 31W & Bowling Green
Mary Anderson Thea.
Loew's Thea.
MAGAZINE ST.
Rialto Thea.
Brown Bldg.
Brown Thea.
GRAY ST.
To Rte. 155 & Airport
To New Albany
Federal Bldg., P.O., Court House & Custom House
ARMORY PL.
Seneca Hotel
Brown Hotel
Y.M.C.A.
150 BROADWAY
Courier-Journal & Times Co.
Commonwealth Bldg.
Kentucky Cham. of Com.
150
Union Station
Sears, Roebuck & Co.
Heyburn Bldg.
Y.W.C.A.
Elks Club
To Rte. 60 & Lexington
L. & N. R.R. Co. Office Bldg.
Greyhound Terminal
JACOB ST.
Public Library
C., I. & L. RY.
L. & N. R.R.
PENN. R.R.
YORK ST.
To Rte. 61 & Turnpike
COLLEGE ST.
CAWTHON ST.
9TH ST.
BRECKINRIDGE ST.
BRECKINRIDGE ST.
11TH ST.
Filson Club
GARLAND AVE.
GARLAND AVE.
CALDWELL ST.
KENTUCKY ST.
Memorial Auditorium
KENTUCKY ST.
ZANE ST.
8TH 7TH 6TH PL. 5TH 4TH 3RD 2ND 1ST BROOK FLOYD
ST. CATHERINE ST.
ST. CATHERINE
BERTRAND ST.
To U. of Louisville
To Churchill Downs
ST. JOSEPH ST.
OLDHAM ST.
OAK ST.
GARVIN
31W To Rte. 60 & Owensboro

1. Belknap Hardware & Mfg. Co. Bldg.
2. Fincastle Bldg.
3. Ky. Home Life Bldg. & Rad. Sta. WGRC
4. Radio Station WHAS & WHAS-TV
5. Radio Station WINN
6. Radio Station WKLO
7. Radio Station WKYW
8. Republic Bldg.
9. R.C. Cathedral of the Assumption
10. Washington Bldg.

HARBOR, one of the finest along the entire river, played a vital part in the city's location and its subsequent growth, as well as in the development of the surrounding countryside

Photos: Kentucky Division of Publicity

LOUISVILLE. Situated on a broad bend of the Ohio, just below the river falls, Louisville was founded on trade and has never lost sight of this cold economic fact. Beneath a fine veneer of magnolias, plantation culture and drowsy Southern charm, it is a shrewd, hard-headed, business-conscious city in which the legendary frock-coated Louisvillian with goatee and string tie exists primarily on the labels of whiskey bottles. Louisville is proud to be the home of Hillerich and Bradsby, world's largest manufacturers of baseball bats; proud of its eight distilleries which turn out the amber Bourbon, leached through willow charcoal in the true native tradition. The city is well aware of the tremendous annual tonnage handled by its river canal and of the smog which issues from the stacks of rubber plants on its western boundaries. Even Louisville's more cultural activities manage to be self-supporting. These include a fine public library and the Louisville Philharmonic Orchestra. Equally important as a big-business enterprise is the Derby. Besides being the greatest of American turf classics, the Derby is a combination fiesta and civic mardi gras with floats, parades and thousands of racing fans pouring into the city from all over the nation.

COURIER-JOURNAL AND TIMES BUILDING houses the staff and plant of one of the South's most influential newspapers, whose journalistic achievements have won a number of Pulitzer prizes

WIDE OHIO RIVER, along whose banks the city lies, supports on her languid surface many kinds of shipping, from attractive excursion cruisers and passenger steamers to chugging tugs and loaded flatboats

CHURCHILL DOWNS, scene of the historic "run for the roses," the Kentucky Derby, Louisville's renowned institution, is not far from the resplendent farms of the Bluegrass country, where turf greats are raised and trained

SPEED MEMORIAL MUSEUM, on the campus of the University of Louisville, contains collections of pottery, porcelain, miniatures, portraits and other paintings

Memphis, Tenn.

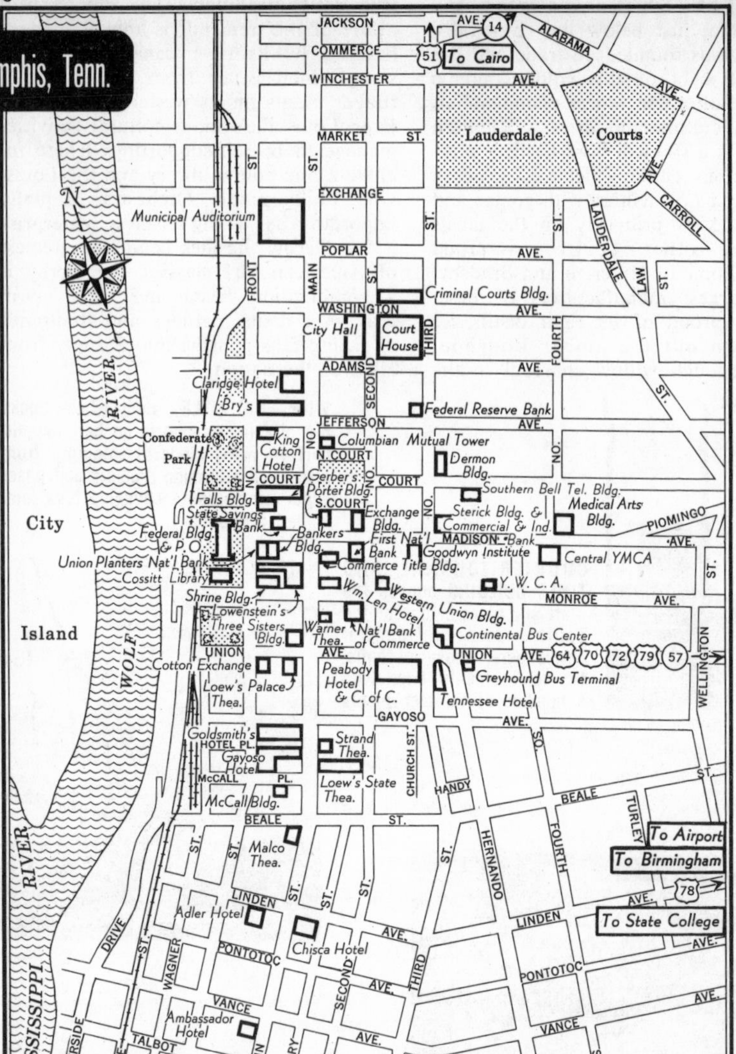

JACKSON AVE. 14
51 To Cairo
COMMERCE
WINCHESTER AVE.
ALABAMA AVE.
MARKET ST.
Lauderdale Courts
EXCHANGE
CARROLL AVE.
Municipal Auditorium
POPLAR AVE.
LAUDERDALE ST.
LAW ST.
FRONT ST.
MAIN ST.
SECOND ST.
THIRD ST.
FOURTH ST.
N
Criminal Courts Bldg.
WASHINGTON AVE.
City Hall
Court House
ADAMS AVE.
Claridge Hotel
Bry's
Federal Reserve Bank
JEFFERSON AVE.
Confederate Park
King Cotton Hotel
Columbian Mutual Tower
N. COURT
Dermon Bldg.
COURT
Gerber's
Porter Bldg.
Southern Bell Tel. Bldg.
Falls Bldg.
S. COURT
Medical Arts Bldg.
State Savings Bank
Exchange Bldg.
Sterick Bldg. & Commercial & Ind. Bank
City
Federal Bldg. & P.O.
Bankers Bldg.
First Nat'l Bank
MADISON
PIOMINGO AVE.
Union Planters Nat'l Bank
Goodwyn Institute
Central YMCA
Cossitt Library
Commerce Title Bldg.
Shrine Bldg.
Wm. Len Hotel
Y. W. C. A.
Lowenstein's
Western Union Bldg.
MONROE AVE.
Three Sisters Bldg.
Warner Thea.
Nat'l Bank of Commerce
Continental Bus Center
Island
WOLF RIVER
UNION AVE. 64 70 72 79 57
WELLINGTON ST.
Cotton Exchange
Peabody Hotel & C. of C.
Greyhound Bus Terminal
Loew's Palace Thea.
Tennessee Hotel
GAYOSO AVE.
Goldsmith's
HOTEL PL.
Strand Thea.
Gayoso Hotel
CHURCH ST.
SO.
McCALL PL.
Loew's State Thea.
HANDY
McCall Bldg.
BEALE ST.
TURLEY
HERNANDO ST.
FOURTH
To Airport
To Birmingham
Malco Thea.
78
LINDEN AVE.
Adler Hotel
To State College
Chisca Hotel
PONTOTOC AVE.
DRIVE
WAGNER
VANCE AVE.
Ambassador Hotel
RIVERSIDE
TALBOT
MULBERRY
AVERY
To Memphis Museum
MISSISSIPPI RIVER
TENNESSEE ST.
HULING AVE.
61 64 70 79
NETTLETON AVE.
BUTLER AVE.
HADDEN ST.
I.C. R.R.
Union Station
ST.L. S.W. RY.
MO. PAC. R.R.
CALHOUN
ST. PAUL
To Memphis-Arkansas Bridge
Grand Central Station
ST.L.& S.F. RY.
C.R.I.& P. RY.
P.O. Sub Station
L. & N. RY.
SOU. RY.
N.C. & ST. L. RY.
61 To Jackson
©C.S. HAMMOND & Co., N.Y.

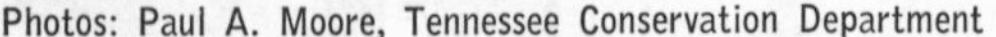

Photos: Paul A. Moore, Tennessee Conservation Department

BRIDGE over the Mississippi connects the city on the Fourth Chickasaw Bluff, traditionally the site where Hernando de Soto first saw the mighty river, to the Arkansas shore

"PINK PALACE" Museum of Natural History and Industrial Arts includes many interesting exhibitions, rare specimens and extensive rose gardens and houses the accomplished Memphis Little Theater

MEMPHIS. Memphis, the largest city of Tennessee, stands on the Fourth or Lower Chickasaw Bluff overlooking the waters of the Mississippi. Its site has long been important, not only from a stand point of river trade, but in our nation's history as well. From the bluff rising 40 feet above the high-water mark, the explorer De Soto looked down on the mighty river below—the first white man to view the "Father of Waters." Later, the British, French and Spanish each sought control of the strategic bluff. During the Civil War, Memphis, which was by then a booming river town, again became the scene of a bitter struggle, this time between the fleets of the Union and the Confederacy. Incorporated in 1826, the city, from its very beginning, has flourished. One of the greatest inland ports in North America, Memphis is also the world's largest cotton and hardwood lumber market. Its excellent transportation facilities make it the metropolis of the mid-South serving the rich garden and cotton regions of western Tennessee, eastern Arkansas and northern Mississippi. Memphis is also the famed home of the "blues." Here W. C. Handy composed the first blues basing it on the melancholy folk songs of the Southern Negro.

COURT SQUARE, one of the original four squares laid out in 1819 for public use, is a favorite resting place for shoppers and office workers. The fountain is a copy of Antonio Canova's celebrated statue, **Hebe Pouring Nectar**

"COTTON ROW," the section of Front Street running south from the Cotton Exchange Building, economic heart of the city, is filled with offices of cotton agents and brokers

Miami, Fla.

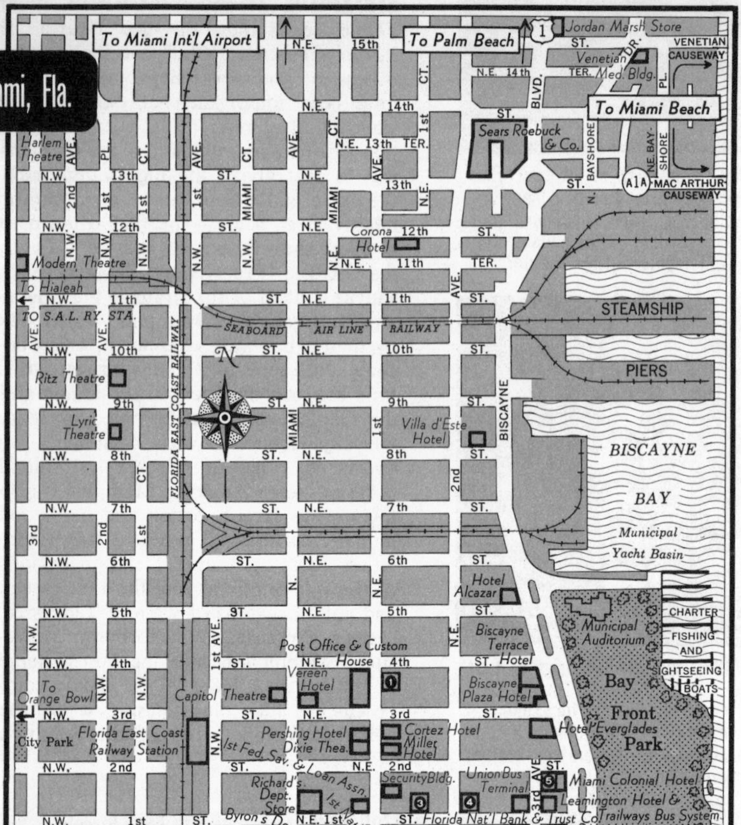

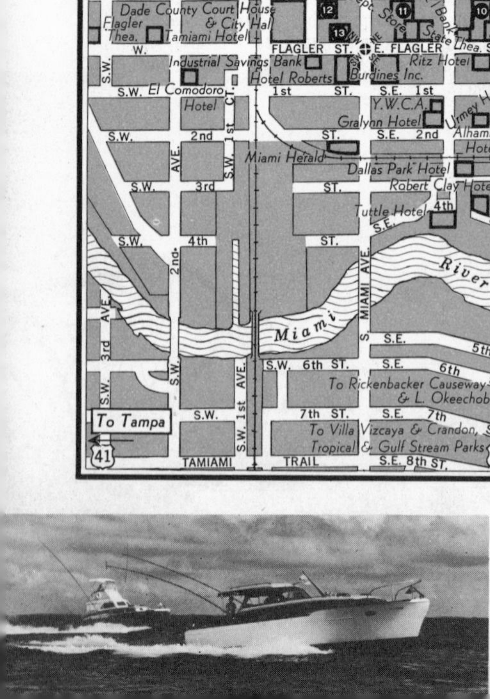

To Miami Int'l Airport · To Palm Beach · To Miami Beach · To Hialeah · To S.A.L. RY. STA. · To Orange Bowl · To Tampa · To Key West · To Rickenbacker Causeway & L. Okeechobee · To Villa Vizcaya & Crandon, Tropical & Gulf Stream Parks

1. Pacific Bldg.
2. Pan American Bank Bldg.
3. Dade Commonwealth Bldg.
4. Congress Bldg.
5. Chamber of Commerce Bldg.
6. Calumet Bldg.
7. Ingraham Bldg.
8. Huntington Bldg.
9. Du Pont Bldg.-Sta. WQAM
10. Shoreland Bldg.
11. Seybold Bldg.
12. Civic Bldg.
13. Biscayne Bldg.

SPORT FISHING BOATS head for the nearby Gulf Stream and some of the world's finest fishing. Sailfish, marlin, dolphin, kingfish, wahoo, bonito, albacore — you never know what may rise and strike your lure as you ride the waves

DOWNTOWN MIAMI with its many fine buildings towers above the shimmering waters of Biscayne Bay. The city serves as hub for all of fabulous southeastern Florida

IT'S "VACATION" EVERY DAY in Miami, with sunwashed beaches and miles of tempting blue-green water just around the corner

Photos: Florida State News Bureau, City of Miami News Bureau

MIAMI. Miami, Florida's largest city, lavishly spreads its vast panorama along the palm-fringed shores of Biscayne Bay where less than a century ago a trading post was all that stood amid a tropic wilderness. In 1896, H. M. Flagler, an enterprising railroad builder, extended his East Coast Railway to the southeastern tip of the Florida peninsula. Flagler at the same time built a hotel next to the old Indian storehouse and, seemingly overnight, Miami sprang from a lonely mangrove swamp to top rank among the nation's leading resort cities. Today, hundreds of hotels—luxurious establishments, each with its own beach, pool, cabanas and sundeck—crowd along the water's edge, while in the heart of the city, lofty buildings thrust their shafts of steel and concrete skyward. Among the many reasons for Miami's tremendous growth, its increasing popularity as a year-round playground, are the gentle trade winds which give the city a winter-warm, summer-cool climate duplicated in only five other small regions of the world. Besides its affable climate, the Miami area possesses a sub-tropical beauty not found elsewhere in the continental United States. Miami's "big city" facilities, entertainment and services

DADE COUNTY COURTHOUSE, a famous Miami landmark, was completed in 1927. The building, 27 stories high, is one of the tallest in the downtown business area

BAND CONCERTS held twice weekly are among the free entertainments presented at the Municipal Bandshell in downtown Miami's Bayfront Park

VILLA VIZCAYA, the $50,000,000 estate of the late James Deering, harvester magnate, is now the Dade County Museum. The mansion is replete with ancient and medieval works of art and furnishings

MIAMI Continued

make it the center for all of Florida's fabulous Gold Coast region. The Tamiami Trail leads across the sawgrass wilderness of the Everglades, connecting Miami with Tampa and the Gulf, while the unique Florida Freeway angles seaward, linking the city with Key West. The Bahamas are a scant half hour away by air; Cuba about an hour; other Caribbean, Central and South American countries only a few minutes or hours. Sightseeing boats, berthed at the City Yacht Basin in Bayfront Park, take visitors through Biscayne Bay, up canals and rivers, past palatial estates on man-made islands, Indian villages and tropical jungles. Some are equipped with glass bottoms so tropical fish and marine gardens may be inspected. The waters around Miami abound with more than 600 varieties of fresh and salt water fish providing incomparable fishing dividends for the sportsman. Crandon Park, the largest offshore park on the eastern seaboard, is reached via the Rickenbacker Causeway, which takes the motorist right out into Biscayne Bay. Here are coconut palms and miles of golden sand beaches. Crandon Park also contains a zoo of growing importance and complete facilities for picnicking as well as a yacht harbor. Spectator sports of all types, including horse racing at Tropical Park, Gulfstream Park and Hialeah, are among the numerous diversions offered. Notable among Miami's sporting events is the annual Orange Bowl football classic, with its dazzling pre-game and half-time spectacles, held on New Year's Day.

WORKERS HARVEST BEANS on one of the huge farms of the Redlands District, a few miles southeast of Miami. Here intensive winter farming is carried on and hundreds of acres of beans, tomatoes, as well as citrus, avocado and papaya groves may be seen under cultivation

TWELVE CHAMPIONSHIP COURSES as well as several driving ranges, putting ranges and miniature courses provide year-round golfing facilities. Included in the major golf tournaments is the $12,500 Miami Open, held each December

SIGHTSEEING AND SPORTS FISHING BOATS await the pleasure of the visitor at Miami's Municipal Docks on the edge of Bayfront Park

Photos: City of Miami News Bureau

MANY OF MIAMI'S LAVISH HOTELS face Biscayne Boulevard and 43 acre Bayfront Park

FLORIDA BEAUTY QUEEN, 1968 model, holds a string of Florida large-mouth beauties. The fresh waters around Miami abound with game fish, and within two hours drive of the city lies one of the world's greatest large-mouth black bass lakes — Lake Okeechobee

SAILBOAT RACES are held almost every weekend throughout the year on Biscayne Bay. The bay's 370 square miles of sheltered waters make Miami the four-seasons center of the nation for sailing and motor boating

FOUR HUGE STEAM TURBINES built by Allis-Chalmers, one of Milwaukee's famed industrial organizations, make the Wisconsin Electric Power Company's Oak Creek plant the largest in Wisconsin

Photos: Allis-Chalmers, Milwaukee Association of Commerce

MILWAUKEE. Milwaukee is a metropolis of character and stability. It is also a city of many moods and interests. Situated on the western shore of Lake Michigan at the confluence of three rivers—the Milwaukee, the Menominee and the Kinnickinnic, the city has managed to preserve its richest heritage—natural beauty. With its many parks, the tree-shaded velvet of its lawns and the handsome drives that sweep along the curve of its lake front, the whole aspect of Milwaukee is seemingly more suburban than metropolitan. Its excellent harbor protected by breakwaters, makes the city a leading lake port. Milwaukee's manufactured goods have carried its name throughout the world; its steam shovels helped to dig the Panama Canal; its turbines turn the flow of Niagara Falls into electric power. German immigrants who began arriving here in 1836, brought with them their homeland's skill of brewing fine beer. This industry, more than any other, has made Milwaukee famous. Today, the city boasts four of this country's largest breweries. Milwaukee's record in health, in accident and fire prevention is unique. As for crime, a congressional committee report reads: "Milwaukee is often cited as a city free of crime or where a criminal is speedily detected, arrested, promptly tried and sent on his way to serve his time. No other city has such a record."

WISCONSIN AVENUE, often referred to as Milwaukee's "magnificent mile," is a fast-moving downtown thoroughfare, uncluttered by streetcar tracks or trolley wires. The Court of Honor in the foreground is a lasting memorial to the veterans of all wars in which Milwaukee's citizens have been engaged

THE MILWAUKEE CLIPPER, which carries automobiles as well as business and vacation travelers, glides gracefully through the entrance of Milwaukee Harbor upon completion of a fast trip across Lake Michigan from Muskegon, Michigan

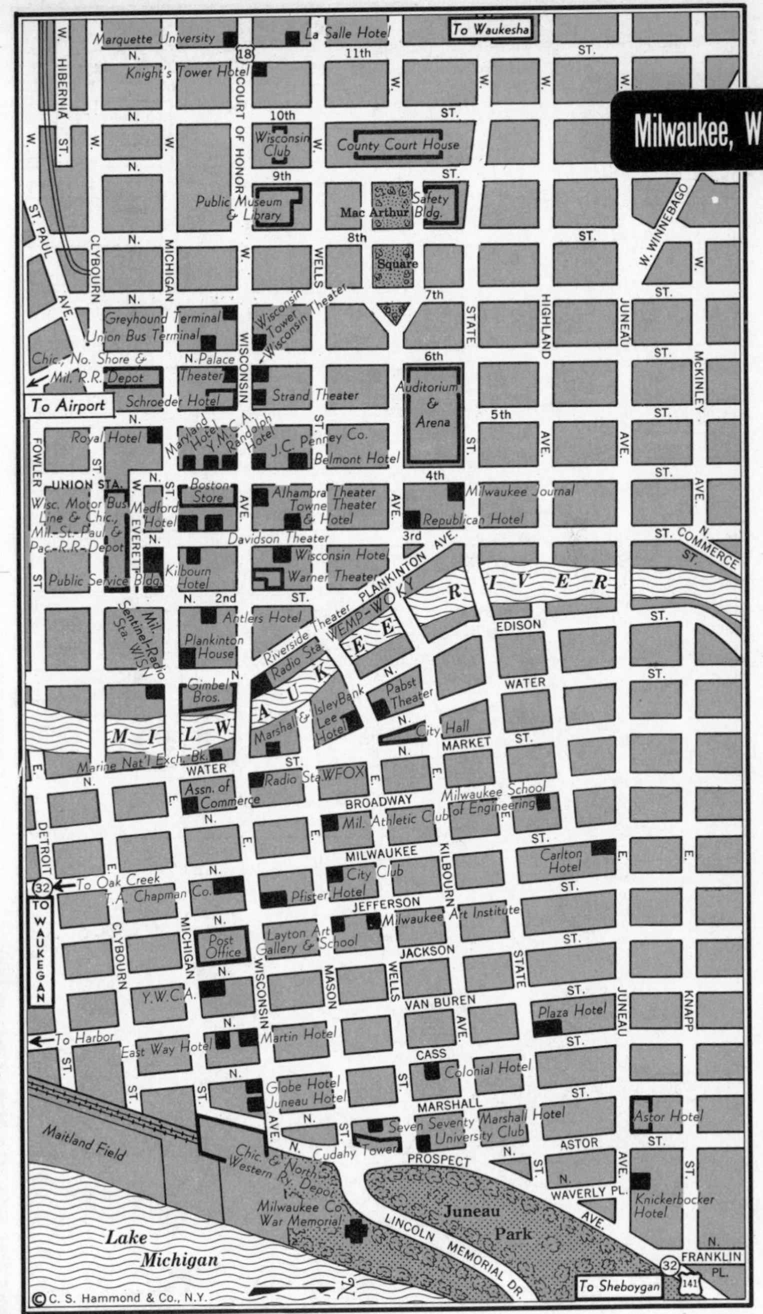

THE CITY HALL, built in 1896, is Milwaukee's tallest building. A sign which proclaims a personalized greeting to all visitors seems to reflect the "Old World" hospitality for which Milwaukee is famous

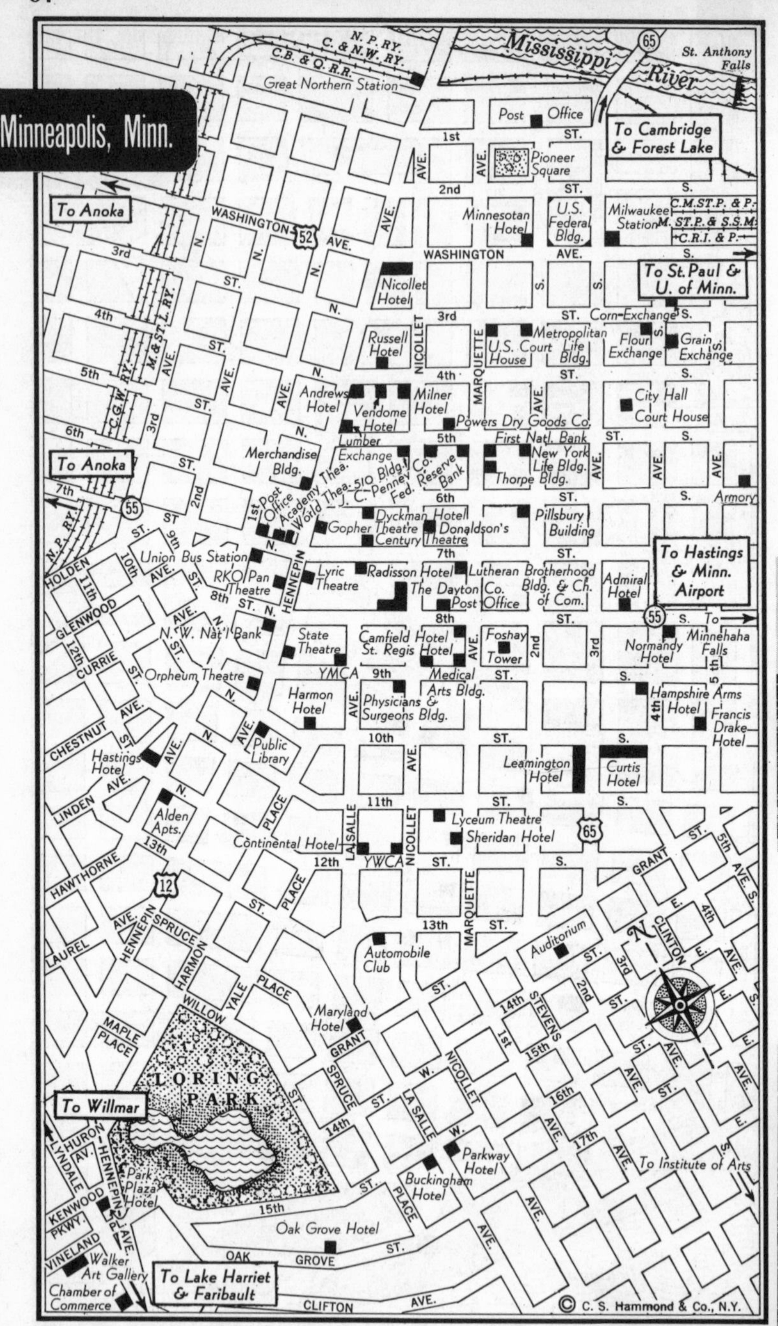

Minneapolis, Minn.
Mississippi River
St. Anthony Falls
N. P. RY.
C. & N. W. RY.
C.B. & Q. R.R.
Great Northern Station
Post Office
Pioneer Square
To Cambridge & Forest Lake
To Anoka
Minnesotan Hotel
U.S. Federal Bldg.
Milwaukee Station
C.M.ST.P. & P.
M. ST.P. & S.S.M.
C.R.I. & P.
To St. Paul & U. of Minn.
Nicollet Hotel
Corn Exchange
Russell Hotel
U.S. Court House
Metropolitan Life Bldg.
Flour Exchange
Grain Exchange
Andrews Hotel
Vendome Hotel
Milner Hotel
City Hall
Court House
Powers Dry Goods Co.
First Natl. Bank
Lumber Exchange
Merchandise Bldg.
New York Life Bldg.
Thorpe Bldg.
Academy Thea.
World Thea.
510 Bldg.
J. C. Penney Co.
Fed. Reserve Bank
Post Office
Armory
Dyckman Hotel
Gopher Theatre
Donaldson's
Century Theatre
Pillsbury Building
Union Bus Station
To Hastings & Minn. Airport
RKO Pan Theatre
Lyric Theatre
Radisson Hotel
Lutheran Brotherhood Bldg. & Ch. of Com.
Admiral Hotel
The Dayton Co.
Post Office
N. W. Nat'l Bank
State Theatre
Camfield Hotel
St. Regis Hotel
Foshay Tower
Normandy Hotel
To Minnehaha Falls
Orpheum Theatre
YMCA
Medical Arts Bldg.
Harmon Hotel
Physicians & Surgeons Bldg.
Hampshire Arms Hotel
Francis Drake Hotel
Public Library
Hastings Hotel
Leamington Hotel
Curtis Hotel
Alden Apts.
Lyceum Theatre
Sheridan Hotel
Continental Hotel
YWCA
Auditorium
Automobile Club
Maryland Hotel
LORING PARK
To Willmar
Parkway Hotel
Buckingham Hotel
To Institute of Arts
Park Plaza Hotel
Oak Grove Hotel
Walker Art Gallery
Chamber of Commerce
To Lake Harriet & Faribault
WASHINGTON AVE.
HENNEPIN
NICOLLET
MARQUETTE
LASALLE
HOLDEN
GLENWOOD
CURRIE
CHESTNUT
LINDEN
HAWTHORNE
LAUREL
SPRUCE
HARMON
WILLOW
YALE
MAPLE PLACE
GRANT
CLINTON
STEVENS
HURON
LYNDALE
KENWOOD PKWY.
VINELAND
OAK GROVE ST.
CLIFTON AVE.
© C. S. Hammond & Co., N.Y.

HUGE FLOUR MILLS are located in the Milling District which lines both banks of the Mississippi River in the vicinity of historic St. Anthony Falls.

MINNEHAHA FALLS which are immortalized in Longfellow's poem, the "Song of Hiawatha," are located in lovely Minnehaha Park. Also in the park is the Stevens House, the first frame dwelling in the city.

MINNEAPOLIS. Minneapolis, the largest city in Minnesota, takes its name from "minne," an Indian word meaning water, and "polis," the Greek word for city. In truth, Minneapolis is a "water-city," for not only does it lie at the head of navigation on the Mississippi River, but within its limits are found some twenty-two lakes. Water power furnished by the Falls of Saint Anthony in the Mississippi supplies electricity for its many mills and factories and has been responsible for much of the city's industrial development. Cascading from a height of 53 feet, Minnehaha (Laughing Waters) Falls, immortalized in Longfellows Hiawatha, are among its many scenic attractions. The city's cultural facilities are extensive: The Walker Art Galleries, the Minneapolis Institute of Art and the University of Minnesota Art Gallery offer well-balanced exhibits of both traditional and modern painting, while the Minneapolis Symphony Orchestra, one of the nation's better-known musical organizations, presents its concerts at the Northrup Auditorium. In July, the famous Aquatennial takes over the city with colorful parades, water shows and a Mardi Gras atmosphere. Besides its cultural, recreational and industrial advantages, Minneapolis has many beautiful homes and charming residential areas. "Grand Rounds," linking lakes, parks and river bridges, encircle the city with 61 miles of scenic boulevards.

THE SKYLINE of Minneapolis as seen from Loring Lake, another of the charming lakes within the Minneapolis Park System.

Photos: Minneapolis Chamber of Commerce.

BEAUTIFUL LAKE HARRIET, one of Minneapolis' 22 lakes and lakelets where residents and visitors alike may enjoy such sports as sailboating, fishing, bathing, canoeing, skating and iceboating.

NASHVILLE. On Christmas Day in 1779, James Robertson established a settlement on the west bank of the Cumberland River destined to become Nashville, the capital of Tennessee. Fort Nashborough, authentic replica of the pioneer stockade, cabins and blockhouses, stands on the original site. Surrounding modern Nashville are wide stretches of fertile farm lands and blue-ribbon stock farms of the blue-grass section and the wooded slopes of the gently rolling foothill country of the Middle Tennessee Basin. So momentous was this area's contributions to horse-breeding through the years of the great Southern plantations that the state's name came to be associated with a breed of saddle horse developed exclusively in America. One of the gaits of the Tennessee walking horse is the running walk, in which all four feet strike the ground separately, while the horse nods its head in time with the hoof beats. Since this gait is very easy on the rider, the Tennessee walking horse is known as the smoothest gaited saddle animal. Because of her many buildings of classic design, her interest in the arts and in education, Nashville is known as the Athens of the South. The spacious, Greek-Doric War Memorial Building and noted Fisk University greatly promote this distinction.

CAPITOL HILL and Memorial Square, at its foot, from the air shows the beautiful State Capitol, following the lines of a Greek Ionic temple; the tomb of James K. Polk, the 11th President of the U.S.; the odd-shaped State Office Building and other state monuments

PARTHENON in Centennial Park contains the Cowan Collection of American painters. To the right is the John W. Thomas Memorial

THE HERMITAGE, an impressive mansion of colonial architecture in a setting of sylvan loveliness remindful of days gone by, was the home of Andrew Jackson, 7th President of the U.S. Its stately halls and chambers are furnished throughout with the articles used by the general and his family

Nashville, Tenn.

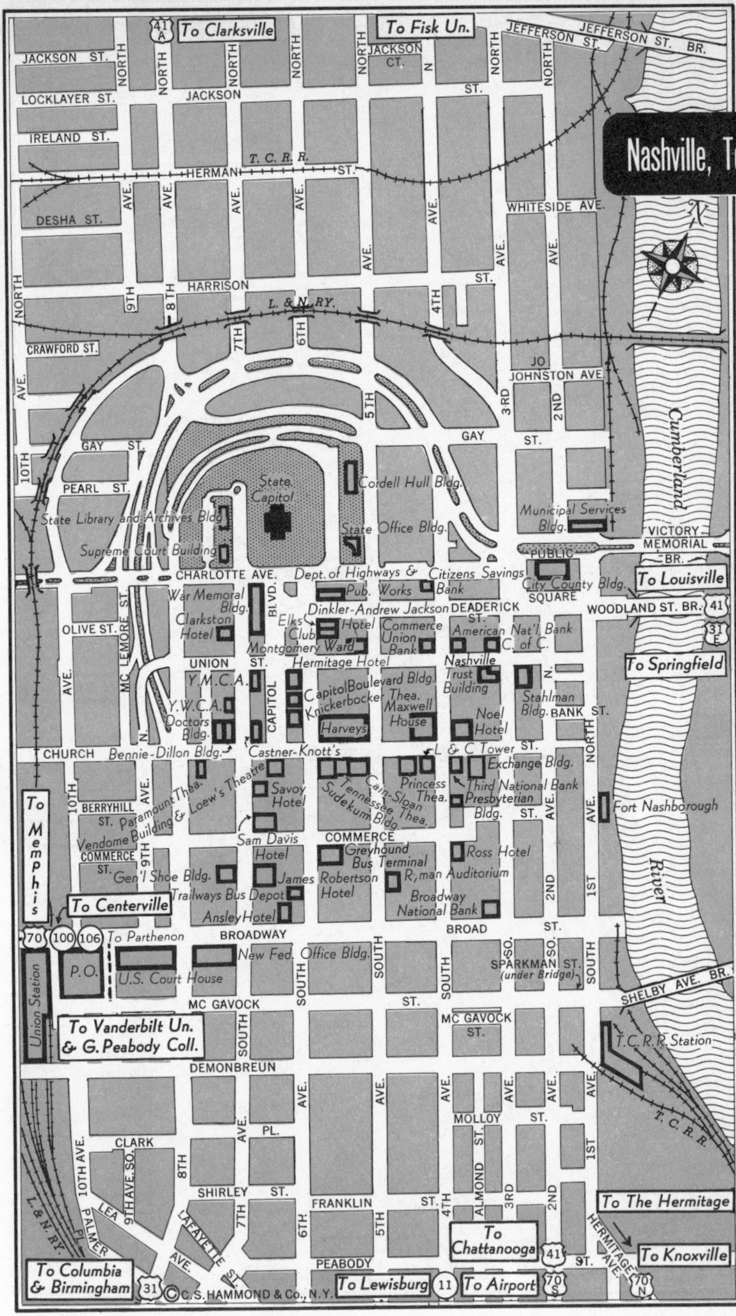

TOWER of Kirkland Hall at Vanderbilt University casts a protective shadow over the many buildings on the sprawling campus of one of the nation's best known universities

Photos: Paul A. Moore, Tennessee Conservation Department, Nashville Chamber of Commerce

Newark, N. J.

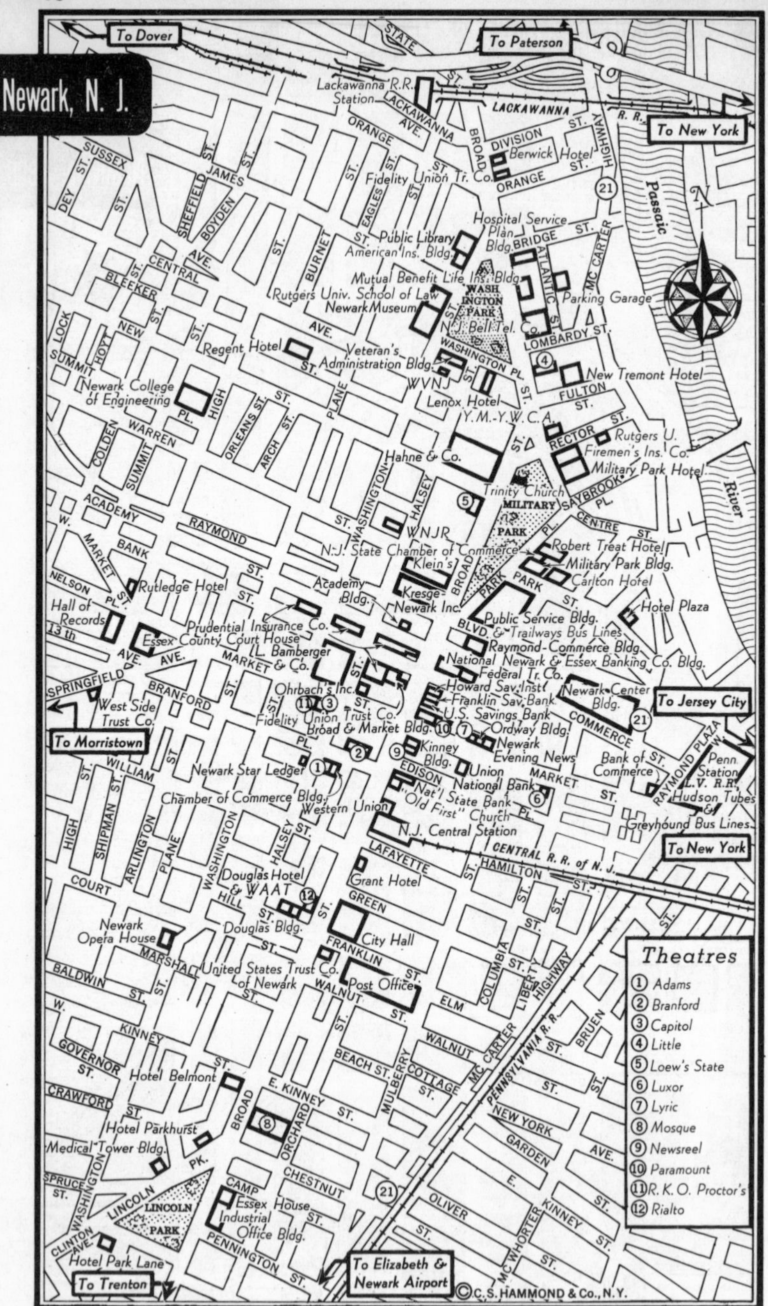

Photos: Newark Museum, Lockwood, Kessler and Bartlett, Inc., Philip Gendreau

NEWARK, the hub of northern New Jersey, spreads its extensive panorama of industry and commerce along the banks of the Passaic River

BORGLUM'S STATUE OF LINCOLN ranks among Newark's finest works of art. Many consider it second only to Daniel Chester French's statue of the great emancipator in the Lincoln Memorial in Washington, D.C.

THE NEWARK MUSEUM since its founding in 1909 by John Cotton Dana, has been a dynamic force in the cultural life of the community

TRINITY EPISCOPAL CHURCH, founded in 1733, is among the oldest churches in Newark. The present structure which stands in Military Park at Broad and Rector Streets, dates from 1809 when the church was rebuilt following a fire.

NEWARK. Newark, New Jersey's great sprawling industrial metropolis, ranks among the nation's leading cities not only because of its large population, but because of the volume and diversity of its manufactured goods and its importance as a rail and transportation terminus. From its beginning as a small seaport town only eight miles from Manhattan, Newark has grown up almost in the shadows of its famous skyscrapers, absorbing an overflow of its inhabitants and industries and in the process pushing its own boundaries, its suburbs, westward in an ever-widening semi-circle. Many immigrants from nearby Ellis Island have settled in Newark, bringing their skills to its industries and adding a cosmopolitan flavor to the original Anglo-Saxon community. Today, Newark is a modern metropolis with a growing skyline of tall buildings. Most of the reminders of its colonial past have been gradually overcome, crowded out by the present. Such landmarks as Trinity Episcopal Cathedral and "Old First"—the original church of the town's Puritan founders, stand bravely among Newark's newer structures, gazing serenely out across the seething maelstrom of traffic that is Broad Street. Gutzon Borglum's seated, bronze statue of Lincoln also surveys a scene of surging vehicles from the plaza in front of the Essex County Court House. Perhaps the city's most famed institution is its museum, a classic limestone structure which houses collections of painting, sculpture and natural history subjects. The museum is widely known for its children's workshop programs. Recently a fine planetarium has been added to its attractions. The city is the home of several noted educational institutions including the Newark colleges of Rutgers University and Newark College of Engineering.

NEW BEDFORD. Incorporated in 1847, New Bedford is one of New England's oldest and most famous cities. As long ago as the 19th century, it was known as the largest whaling port in the world. Later Yankee craftsmanship made it a great cotton textile center and the home of many diversified industries. The discovery of petroleum marked the passing of the whaling era, yet many reminders of those romantic days are still found in and around the city. The Whaling Museum of the Old Darmouth Historical Society intimately records the birth, life and death of this great industry. Here also are replicas of the old shops that carried on trade in the city during the whaling era, magnificent collections of ship models and the Navigation Book of the Bounty brought to New Bedford from Pitcairn by a sea captain. In Public Library plaza on Pleasant Street stands the famous Whaleman's statue, designed by Bela Pratt and inscribed with New Bedford's old slogan "A Dead Whale or a Stove Boat." On Johnny Cake Hill, the Mariner's Home is a typical mansion of the whaling period, while next door at Seamen's Bethel, made famous by Herman Melville in his "Moby Dick," one may see the unique Cenotaphs to the Sea Dead. Point Drive offers beautiful views of Buzzard's Bay and the ever-active, always fascinating harbor, home port of one of the great North Atlantic fishing fleets.

NEW BEDFORD is one of New England's oldest and most famous cities. It also serves as the gateway to Cape Cod and is the big-city shopping center for the entire area including the Islands of Martha's Vineyard, Nantucket and the Elizabeth Islands

NEARLY EVERY RESORT REQUIREMENT is to be found in New Bedford. Besides a comfortable and modern hotel the city has four golf courses, three bathing beaches, two yacht harbors, fresh and salt water fishing, riding and hunting. Many quaint and lovely scenes in and around the city make it an artist's paradise

BEAUTIFUL LAKES which provide New Bedford with its excellent drinking water are located twelve miles north of the city. The landscaped grounds rival many parks and are notable for a magnificent clipped white pine hedge, one of the few in existence

Photos: McGee's Photo Supply

New Bedford, Mass.

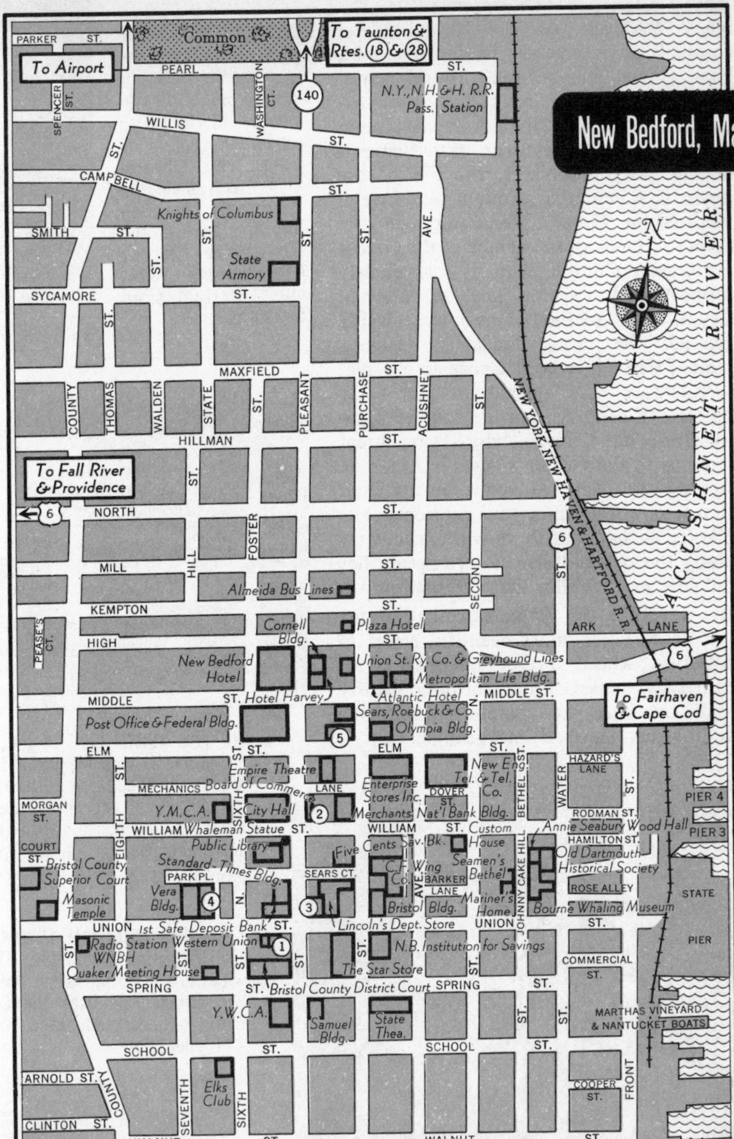

1. Bookstore Bldg.
2. John Duff Bldg.
3. Masonic Bldg.
4. New Bedford Thea.
5. Olympia Thea.

© C. S. HAMMOND & CO., N.Y.

A PROMINENT PORT of southern New England, New Bedford is also the home port of a great fishing fleet. Its bustling wharves, Coast Guard cutters, lighthouse tenders, cargo and naval vessels add much interest for the visitor

NEW HAVEN. An old New England colonial town steeped in historic lore, New Haven has been a cultural center since her founding in 1638 and still exudes an air of quiet dignity and profound scholarship. Characteristic of settlements of the early colonizers, the life of the town has centered around her lovely, picturesque Green. Remaining on the common land, in the center of the Green, are Center Church, with its marvelously proportioned interior and its unusual Crypt, a part of the colony's first burying ground; the more delicately designed United Church, whose Georgian-colonial architecture was typical of the early nineteenth century, and the somber Trinity Episcopal Church, which gave great impetus to the Gothic revival in America. Adding to New Haven's beauty and charm are the numerous ancient elms planted throughout the town, particularly along the original streets, prompting her old title as the "Elm City." Most impressive is Hillhouse Avenue, called in the last century the most beautiful street in America, whose former splendor is recalled by majestic elms forming a lofty arch overhead and imposing manors adding distinguished background.

CHARMING LIBRARIANS COURT of the monumental Sterling Memorial Library, whose interior is a model of good planning. This library, along with Memorial Quadrangle, the Gallery of Fine Arts and the notable Peabody Museum, are Yale's most distinguished treasures

ON THE NORTH SIDE of the Green are, to the left, Ives Memorial Library, designed in the early 20th-century, neoclassic style, and the austere, marble County Courthouse, with some Yale buildings beyond

SOARING WREXHAM TOWER is a part of Memorial Quadrangle. Third oldest and one of the greatest American universities, Yale uses the Oxford-Cambridge undergraduate college system of education

New Haven, Conn.

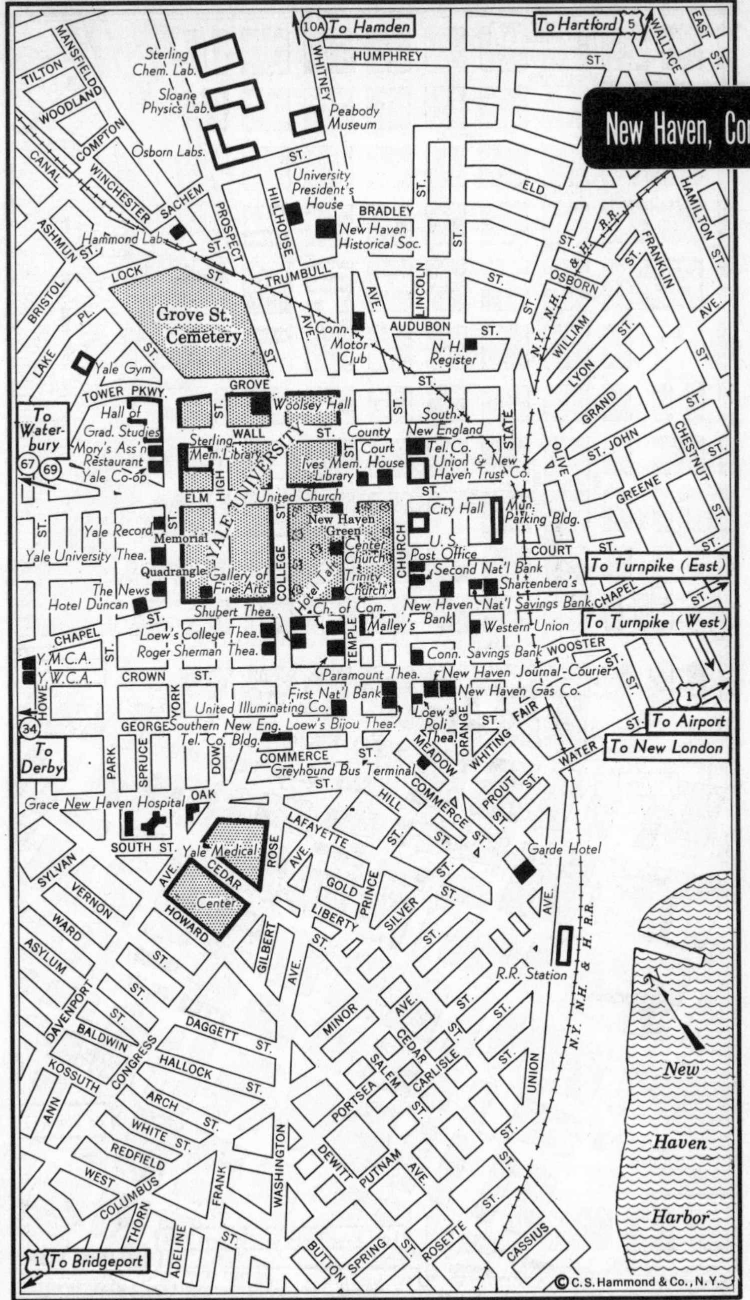

Photos: New Haven Chamber of Commerce

STREET SCENE in downtown New Haven illustrates how this old Pilgrim colony has grown into a large industrial city

New Orleans, La.

Photos: Bureau of New Orleans News, Port of New Orleans

A QUIET PATIO reflects the early influence of Spain on the city's architecture. Almost every home in the original section of New Orleans has its own charming patio garden

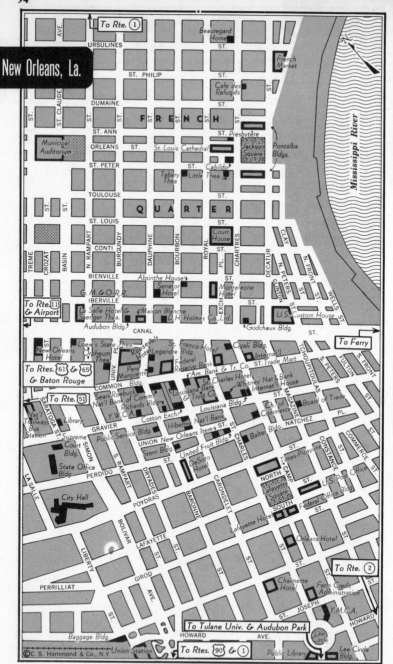

IRON LACEWORK is a notable characteristic of most of the balconies in the old section of New Orleans. While some of the ironwork was forged in the city, most of it was imported from Spain

SACKS OF COFFEE are unloaded from a ship anchored in the Port of New Orleans. Besides handling over 23% of the nation's coffee imports, large quantities of sugar, bananas, bauxite and molasses enter the country through this busy port

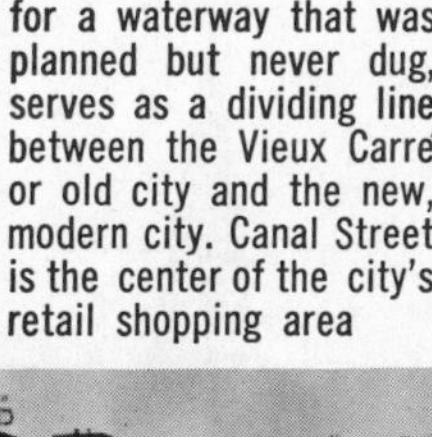

CANAL STREET, named for a waterway that was planned but never dug, serves as a dividing line between the Vieux Carré or old city and the new, modern city. Canal Street is the center of the city's retail shopping area

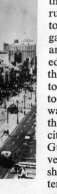

NEW ORLEANS. Having flourished in the past under both French and Spanish rule, New Orleans with its colorful history, its saga of pirates and gentlemen-gamblers, its legends of duels at dawn and black magic at midnight, is undoubtedly one of the most romantic cities in the United States. Serving as a gateway to the Mississippi Valley and with access to almost 15,000 miles of navigable waterways, New Orleans is also one of the nation's leading ports. Though the city lies 110 miles upstream from the Gulf, it is easily reached by large ocean vessels. Spreading along a wide crescent-shaped bend of the Mississippi River, its terrain is flat, unbroken by even the smallest of hills and scarcely more than a foot above the level of the sea. Thick mounds of earth hold back the waters of the Mississippi and ships anchored along the levees, high above the surrounding streets, present a strange picture. New Orleans is a city of contrasts where, on one hand, modern skyscrapers rise above their foundations of piles driven deep into the Mississippi muck, and on the other hand are found the delicate iron lace, the stuccoed walls, the balcony-hung streets of the Vieux Carré. Canal Street, one of the widest business streets in the nation, sharply divides the old from the new. The heart of the French Quarter or Vieux Carré is Jack-

MADRI GRAS PARADE, flamboyant with color and sound, winds its way through the streets of New Orleans where thousands jam the line of march for a glimpse of America's most extravagant festival

ANDREW JACKSON, hero of the Battle of New Orleans, is honored by this statue in Jackson Square. Incised on the base of the monument are Jackson's ringing words, "The Union Must and Shall Be Preserved"

Photos: Bureau of New Orleans News, State of Louisiana, Dept. of Commerce and Industry

MOSS-DRAPED LIVE OAKS cast their shadows across the lawns of Audubon Park. This park includes a portion of the old De Boré plantation where sugar was first granulated. It also includes the only hill in New Orleans and a man-made one at that

A SIDEWALK CAFÉ is a familiar sight in the Vieux Carré. Besides these little establishments which serve the famed black Louisiana coffee, the city is a gourmet's paradise of fine restaurants specializing in Creole cookery

THE PRESBYTERE, with its twin the Cabildo, flanks St. Louis Cathedral, and serves as the Louisiana State Museum. Built about 1813, it was originally called the Casa Curial. Its architecture combines both the French and Spanish influences

NEW ORLEANS Continued

son Square, formerly the Place d'Armes, where the flag of the United States was raised for the first time over the Louisiana Territory. The formal ceremonies surrounding the Louisiana Purchase took place nearby, in a room of the cabildo—an ancient Spanish government building which today serves as a museum. Flanking Jackson Square are the two beautiful, block-long Pontalba buildings. Excellent examples of Creole architecture, these were the first American apartment houses. Also on Jackson Square is St. Louis Cathedral. Originally a Spanish provincial church, the brick and stucco Cathedral built in 1794 is now somewhat altered from the original design by the many changes made over the years. The Old Absinthe House on Bourbon Street is famous as the one-time haunt of the pirates Pierre and Jean Lafitte. The U.S. Customs House at Decatur and Canal Streets is interesting for its Egyptian architecture. This old building once served as a Confederate prison. The French Market, which covers six city blocks, is a traditional New Orleans haunt for early risers and late merrymakers desiring "coffee and doughnuts." The New Orleans Mardi Gras is probably the city's greatest tourist attraction. This prelenten bacchanal begins early in January with masked-balls and other festivities. As the season progresses, the carnival spirit grows in intensity to break forth in a full week of unrestrained revelry. The merrymaking is climaxed on Shrove Tuesday when King Comus—the Lord of Misrule—reigns over the city.

ST. LOUIS CATHEDRAL, built in 1794 with funds supplied by a wealthy Spanish nobleman, continues to be one of the most famous religious structures in America

NEW YORK. New York is the world's largest city and its financial and entertainment capital. It is also the richest and perhaps the greatest of the world's great cities. If any one city could be said to be the embodiment of the "American Dream," it is most certainly this tremendous, shining metropolis. By comparison with such places as Rome, Paris or London, New York is still a young city; here you will find no crumbling ruins, no monuments of an ancient civilization, no patina of age to gild the flaws or hide the blemishes behind an aura of antiquity. Scarcely 350 years have passed since Peter Minuit, in one of history's most fabulous real estate transactions, purchased Manhattan from the Indians for sixty guilders (about $24) worth of trade goods. New York, the modern city, did not come into being until 1898 when five separate boroughs were consolidated into one government. The smallest borough is Richmond, which occupies Staten Island down the harbor in New York Bay. Best known is Manhattan, also an island. New York in fact is a city of islands, for the only part of the city located on the mainland is the Bronx, a residential area. Two other residential and industrial boroughs are Brooklyn and Queens on Long Island. Today, New York points with pride to the multiplicity of its accomplishments to its staggering vital statistics; to an eminence in world affairs all out of proportion to its size. Now with the headquarters of the United Nations located here, New York has the added distinction of being the world's political capital. New York is a

STATUE OF LIBERTY, proudly holding aloft the torch of freedom, rises 305 feet above the New York harbor. This 225-ton statue was a gift from the French people to the United States in 1884

Photos: New York Coliseum, New York Visitors and Convention Bureau

NEW YORK COLISEUM and Office Tower at Columbus Circle is a striking example of conservative modern architecture. This $35,000,000 building is devoted to the staging of expositions, trade shows, sales fairs and product displays

BROOKLYN BRIDGE, built by John Roebling, made engineering history when it was opened in 1883. It is still the 9th longest suspension bridge in the world and a famous New York landmark

New York, N. Y.

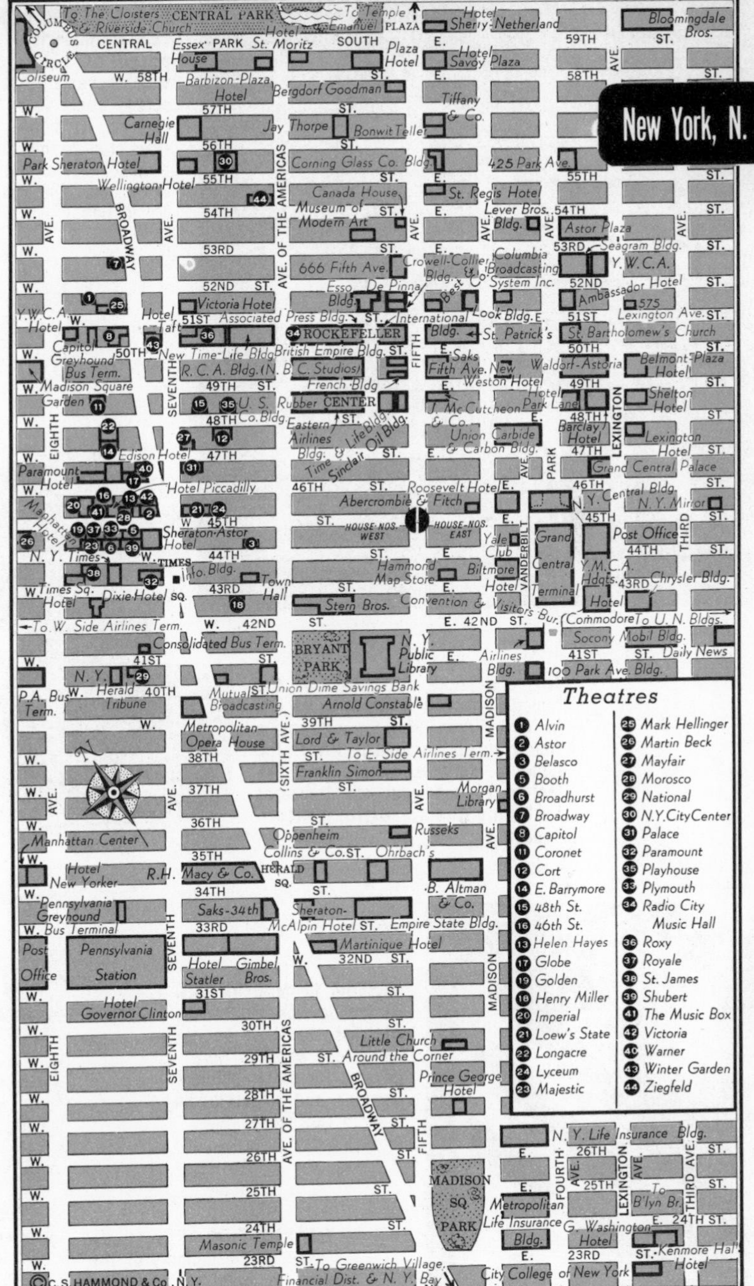
To The Cloisters & Riverside Church
CENTRAL PARK
To Temple Emanuel
COLUMBUS CIRCLE
CENTRAL PARK SOUTH
Coliseum
Essex House
Hotel St. Moritz
Plaza Hotel
PLAZA
Hotel Sherry-Netherland
Hotel Savoy Plaza
Bloomingdale Bros.
Barbizon-Plaza Hotel
Bergdorf Goodman
Tiffany & Co.
Carnegie Hall
Jay Thorpe
Bonwit Teller
Park Sheraton Hotel
Corning Glass Co. Bldg.
425 Park Ave.
Wellington Hotel
Canada House
St. Regis Hotel
Museum of Modern Art
Lever Bros. Bldg.
Astor Plaza
Seagram Bldg.
666 Fifth Ave.
Crowell-Collier Bldg.
Columbia Broadcasting System Inc.
Y.W.C.A.
Best & Co.
Esso Bldg.
De Pinna
Ambassador Hotel
575 Lexington Ave.
Victoria Hotel
Y.W.C.A. Hotel
Hotel Taft
Associated Press Bldg.
International Bldg.
Look Bldg.
St. Patrick's
St. Bartholomew's Church
Capitol
ROCKEFELLER
New Time-Life Bldg.
British Empire Bldg.
Saks Fifth Ave.
New Weston Hotel
Waldorf-Astoria
Belmont-Plaza Hotel
Greyhound Bus Term.
R. C. A. Bldg. (N. B. C. Studios)
French Bldg.
Hotel Park Lane
Shelton Hotel
Madison Square Garden
U. S. Rubber Co. Bldg.
CENTER
J. McCutcheon & Co.
Barclay Hotel
Eastern Airlines Bldg.
Time & Life Bldg.
Sinclair Oil Bldg.
Union Carbide & Carbon Bldg.
Lexington Hotel
Edison Hotel
Grand Central Palace
Paramount Hotel
Roosevelt Hotel
Hotel Piccadilly
Abercrombie & Fitch
N. Y. Central Bldg.
N. Y. Mirror
Manhattan Hotel
HOUSE NOS. WEST
HOUSE NOS. EAST
Sheraton-Astor Hotel
Yale Club
Grand Central Terminal
Post Office
N. Y. Times
TIMES SQ.
Info. Bldg.
Hammond Map Store
Biltmore Hotel
Y.M.C.A. Hdqts.
Chrysler Bldg.
Times Sq. Hotel
Dixie Hotel
Town Hall
Stern Bros.
Convention & Visitors Bur.
Hotel Commodore
To U. N. Bldgs.
To W. Side Airlines Term.
Consolidated Bus Term.
BRYANT PARK
N. Y. Public Library
Airlines Bldg.
Socony Mobil Bldg.
Daily News
100 Park Ave. Bldg.
N. Y. Herald Tribune
P.A. Bus Term.
Mutual Broadcasting
Union Dime Savings Bank
Arnold Constable
Metropolitan Opera House
Lord & Taylor
To E. Side Airlines Term.
Franklin Simon
Morgan Library
Oppenheim Collins & Co.
Russeks
Ohrbach's
Manhattan Center
Hotel New Yorker
R.H. Macy & Co.
HERALD SQ.
B. Altman & Co.
Pennsylvania Greyhound Bus Terminal
Saks-34th
Sheraton-McAlpin Hotel
Empire State Bldg.
Post Office
Pennsylvania Station
Martinique Hotel
Hotel Statler
Gimbel Bros.
Hotel Governor Clinton
Little Church Around the Corner
Prince George Hotel
N. Y. Life Insurance Bldg.
MADISON SQ. PARK
Metropolitan Life Insurance Bldg.
To B'lyn Br.
G. Washington Hotel
Kenmore Hall Hotel
Masonic Temple
To Greenwich Village, Financial Dist. & N. Y. Bay
City College of New York
©C.S. HAMMOND & Co., N.Y.
Theatres
1 Alvin
2 Astor
3 Belasco
5 Booth
6 Broadhurst
7 Broadway
8 Capitol
11 Coronet
12 Cort
14 E. Barrymore
15 48th St.
16 46th St.
13 Helen Hayes
17 Globe
19 Golden
18 Henry Miller
20 Imperial
21 Loew's State
22 Longacre
24 Lyceum
23 Majestic
25 Mark Hellinger
26 Martin Beck
27 Mayfair
28 Morosco
29 National
30 N.Y. City Center
31 Palace
32 Paramount
35 Playhouse
33 Plymouth
34 Radio City Music Hall
36 Roxy
37 Royale
38 St. James
39 Shubert
41 The Music Box
42 Victoria
40 Warner
43 Winter Garden
44 Ziegfeld

ROCKEFELLER CENTER, a "city-within-a-city," is composed of 15 skyscrapers which cover an area of 12½ acres from 48th to 52nd Streets. It houses the offices of more than 900 firms, a major radio and TV network and the Radio City Music Hall

THE CLOISTERS, a branch of the famed Metropolitan Museum of Art, in Fort Tryon Park, commands a fine view of the Hudson River. The building contains a renowned collection of medieval art treasures including the beautiful Unicorn Tapestries

MUSEUM OF MODERN ART— its façade stands out in bold contrast to the buildings alongside of it. Here is housed, for better public enjoyment and understanding, "Art in Our Time"

WASHINGTON ARCH, dedicated to the memory of the first president of the United States, was built in 1895. To the west is Greenwich Village, while a half-block north is MacDougal Alley, a private thoroughfare lighted by the city's only remaining gas street lamps

RIVERSIDE CHURCH resembles the 13th-century cathedral of Chartres, France. Its many stained glass windows are among the finest in the city and the 72-bell carillon, the largest in the world, is housed at the top of the 22 story tower. It is an interdenominational church

NEW YORK Continued

complex metropolis, one of many moods and aspects; a city of unusual contrasts where New Yorkers often take for granted things at which visitors marvel—the skyscrapers, subways, art galleries, theaters, museums, nightclubs. Manhattan Island, the vital, pulsing heart of the metropolis, is little more than twelve miles in length and only about two and one-half miles across at the widest point. With no chance of expanding its boundaries outward, the city of necessity built upwards, thrusting into the sky the most incredible pile of steel, glass and masonry to be found anywhere in the world. New York has also burrowed beneath its asphalt and concrete surface, honeycombing the solid rock of Manhattan Island with a maze of tunnels, tubes, wires, pipes, conduits, cables, sewers and gas mains. Across the mighty rivers that sweep around the island, the city has flung the silver spans of bridges linking it with Long Island and the mainland of New Jersey and the Bronx. This largest seaport of the nation has 755 miles of waterfront, fringed by the slender steel fingers of many docks and piers. New York's spacious harbor is a scene of restless activity where a never-ending procession of the world's merchant shipping passes in review. The settlement of Man-

Photos: New York Visitors and Convention Bureau, N. Y. State Dept. of Commerce

AN HEROIC STATUE OF WASHINGTON, on the steps of the Sub-Treasury Building, seems to watch the pulse of the nation's economic life —The New York Stock Exchange

A NIGHT WATCHMAN'S EYE VIEW of the New York metropolitan area from the top of the Empire State Building is a galaxy of jeweled lights. Observation terraces on the building's 86th and 102nd floors attract a million and a half visitors each year

Photos:
New York Visitors and Convention Bureau, N. Y. State Department of Commerce

"HISTORY IN THE MAKING." The glass, steel and marble United Nations Building, containing the offices of the Secretariat, towers above the East River. Other structures of the group include a Council and Committee Meeting Hall and the domed General Assembly Building

SKYSCRAPER APARTMENT HOUSES tower above the country scene that is Central Park. Busy New Yorkers find pleasant moments of relaxation in this 840-

TEMPLE EMANUEL is the largest synagogue built in modern times. It was completed in 1929 and has a seating capacity of 2,350. Its exterior is a modern version of Early Romanesque architecture as it was used in Syria and the Near East

GRAND CENTRAL—rays of sunlight penetrate the vast interior of the main waiting room of the world-famous railroad terminal where hundreds of trains arrive and depart daily for places as far away as St. Louis and Chicago

acre park containing gardens, lakes, sculpture, playgrounds, bridle paths and a charming zoo. Band concerts are featured on the tree-enclosed Mall

NEW YORK Continued

hattan was begun at the southern tip of the island. Spreading northward from the Battery, at first the city grew without any particular intention as to the location and proportion of its streets. The site of the original Dutch settlement is now overgrown with the towers of the financial section. Here the streets are narrow, often crooked and the sunlight scarcely filters into the sepulchral gloom of their concrete canyons. Historic landmarks such as Trinity Church stand courageously in the shadows of 20th-century skyscrapers. After 1811, when a formal plan for the city was devised, Manhattan laid out its streets and avenues to conform to a conventional grid pattern, most of them being designated by number rather than by name. Mid-Manhattan contains the city's major shopping section where the fabulous emporiums of fashion crowd sophisticated 5th Avenue. Here also is the breathtaking spectacle of the Times Square theater district which sets the blackness of night ablaze with a million lights. The uptown area is given over to apartment dwellings, museums, the famed halls of learning and, in the midst, Central Park is set like a cool green emerald. Besides more than 8,000,000 permanent inhabitants, New York has a large transient population. At rush hours at least one and a half million commuters from outside the city and from three neighboring states pour out of its ferry, bus, rail and subway stations as ants from an anthill. New York is so large and varied in its character that it appeals to all kinds of people; its thousands of unique attractions draw more than 13,000,000 visitors here each year. Yet New York, as with any other great city, requires more than a brief acquaintanceship to be fully appreciated and perhaps a lifetime to be understood.

HAMPTON ROADS exports more coal than any other port in the world. Seen here are the Norfolk and Western coal piers at Lamberts Point on Hampton Roads

THE U.S.S. NORFOLK, named after Virginia's largest city, is just one of many hundreds of capital ships assigned to the Hampton Roads Area. The Norfolk Naval Base is the largest of its kind in the world

NORFOLK. Norfolk, with Hampton, Portsmouth and Newport News, possesses the world's greatest natural harbor —Hampton Roads, a channel through which the James, Nansemond and Elizabeth Rivers flow into Chesapeake Bay. Here are to be seen the restless comings and goings of ships of almost every description: tankers, trawlers, ferries, barges, tugs, naval vessels, pleasure craft, fishing boats and an occasional passenger liner. America's foreign commerce was born in the James River and cradled in its infancy at Norfolk. With the building of railroads, Norfolk's importance increased as the products of Virginia's farms, forests and mines passed through the city, bound for foreign and domestic markets. Commerce too, has played a major role in the growth of Norfolk's varied industry, boosting the city to a place among the leading manufacturing centers of the South. Commanding a strategic position on the American coast, Norfolk and her twin-city Portsmouth, have been prominent in the defenses of this country since Colonial times and are the site of enormous shipyards, naval installations and naval training stations. Because of its many recreational assets and with many fine, white sand beaches close at hand, Norfolk is the unofficial capital of one of the most historic resort areas in this country.

OLD ST. PAUL'S CHURCH, built in 1739, is the only building in Norfolk which survived the fire of 1776. Imbedded in its wall is a cannon ball fired from a British man-of-war

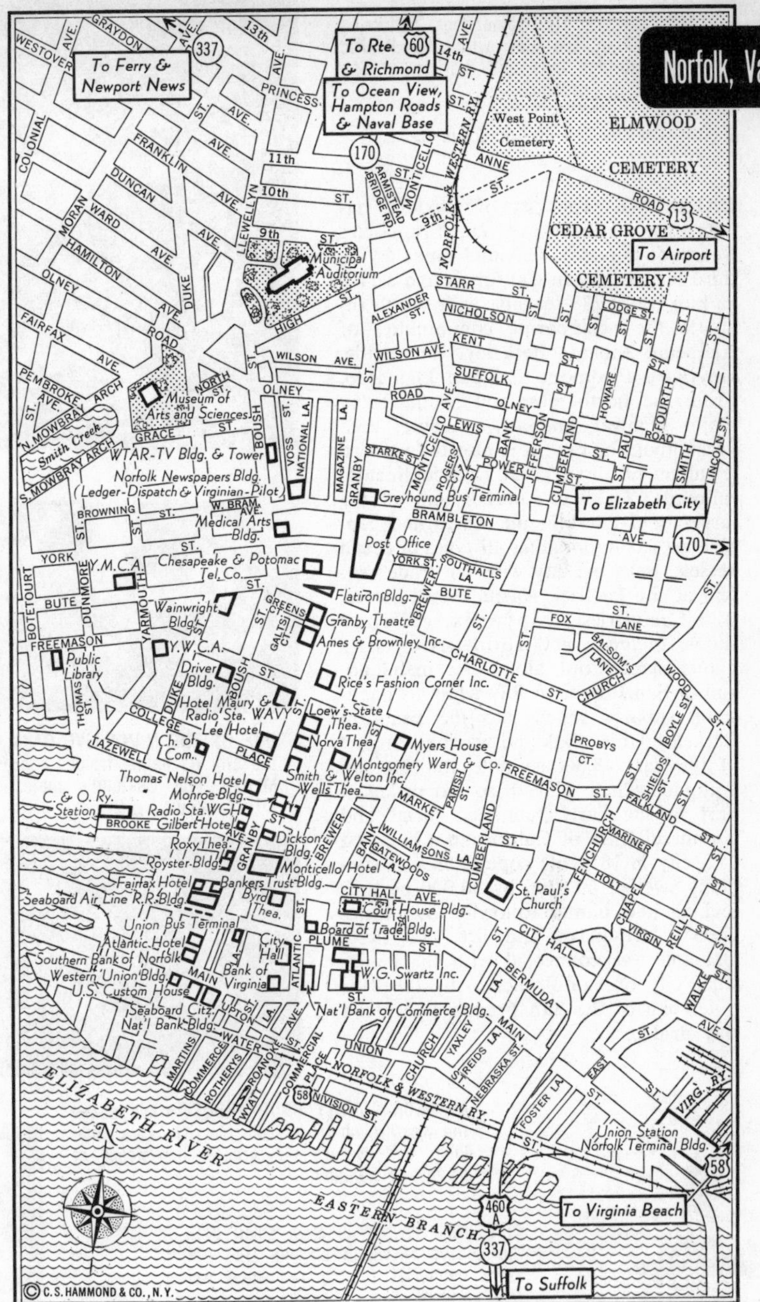

SACLANT, headquarters Supreme Allied Command, Altantic, is the only oceanic command in the western hemisphere. Seen here is SACLANT'S famous ring of NATO flags

Photos: Norfolk Chamber of Commerce

OAKLAND spreads its tremendous panorama along San Francisco Bay with the Pacific Ocean, the Golden Gate and the city of San Francisco in the distance.

Photos: Oakland Chamber of Commerce.

OAKLAND. The city of Oakland has outgrown its role as "San Francisco's Bedroom." Today, Oakland ranks as the third largest city in California and serves as hub for a 733-sq.-mile area which includes the neighboring communities of Alameda, Albany, Berkeley, Emeryville, Hayward, Piedmont and San Leonardo. From the north, east and south, many major highway and airway routes converge upon the city; it is also the western terminus of three great transcontinental railroads. Oakland's harbor, one of the largest and finest in the world and capable of accommodating all types of ocean vessels, links the city with the trade centers of the Pacific. An industrial center, its oil refineries, shipyards, railroad shops, factories and food-processing plants spread out along the mainland-rim of San Francisco Bay while its handsome suburbs reach into the beautiful Berkeley Hills. Oakland was once a part of the vast 48,000-sq.-mile Rancho San Antonio which played so important a part in the early religious, social and commercial life of California. Chartered as a city in 1854, its population was suddenly swelled in 1906 by 50,000 persons seeking new homes following San Francisco's earthquake and fire. In 1936, Oakland was connected with the peninsular city of San Francisco by the 8¼-mile span of the San Francisco-Oakland Bay Bridge.

ONE OF THE MANY LIVE OAKS which give the city its name, frames a scene of Lake Merritt and Oakland's majestic Scottish Rite Temple.

ALAMEDA COUNTY COURT HOUSE rises above the western shore of Lake Merritt. This mile-long, salt water lake graces the heart of downtown Oakland.

CITY HALL towers above a small park in the center of which an oak tree stands as a memorial to the renowned writer, Jack London.

FAIRYLAND, a land of fantasy, where everything is scaled to child's size, is located in the heart of Oakland. Fairyland is a community project developed by the Park Department.

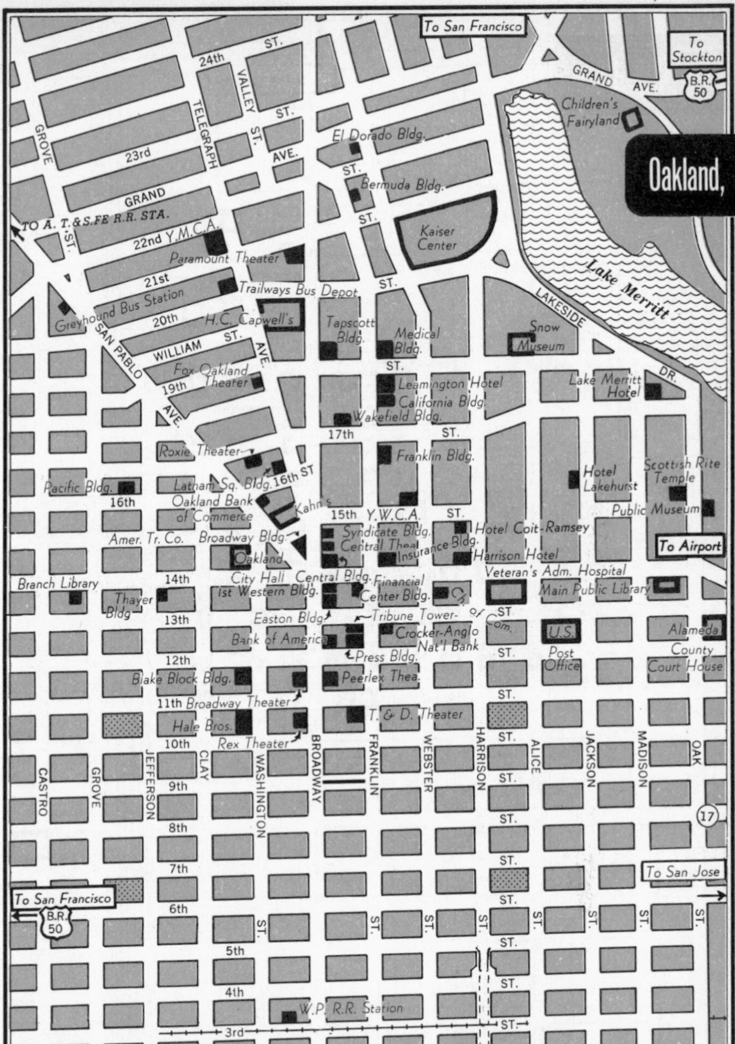

Oakland, Cal.

To San Francisco
To Stockton
B.R. 50
GRAND AVE.
Children's Fairyland
Lake Merritt
LAKESIDE DR.
24th ST.
VALLEY ST.
TELEGRAPH
GROVE
23rd
AVE.
El Dorado Bldg.
Bermuda Bldg.
Kaiser Center
GRAND
TO A. T. & S.FE R.R. STA.
22nd Y.M.C.A.
Paramount Theater
21st
Trailways Bus Depot
Greyhound Bus Station
20th
H.C. Capwell's
Tapscott Bldg.
Medical Bldg.
Snow Museum
SAN PABLO AVE.
WILLIAM ST.
Fox Oakland Theater
19th
Leamington Hotel
California Bldg.
Lake Merritt Hotel
Wakefield Bldg.
17th ST.
Roxie Theater
Franklin Bldg.
Hotel Lakehurst
Scottish Rite Temple
Pacific Bldg.
Latham Sq. Bldg.
16th ST
Oakland Bank of Commerce
Kahn's
Public Museum
15th Y.W.C.A. ST.
Amer. Tr. Co.
Broadway Bldg.
Syndicate Bldg.
Central Theal.
Insurance Bldg.
Hotel Coit-Ramsey
Harrison Hotel
To Airport
Oakland City Hall
Central Bldg.
Veteran's Adm. Hospital
Branch Library
14th
Thayer Bldg
1st Western Bldg.
Financial Center Bldg.
Ch. of Com.
Main Public Library
13th
Easton Bldg.
Tribune Tower
Bank of America
Crocker-Anglo Nat'l Bank
U.S. Post Office
Alameda County Court House
12th
Press Bldg.
Blake Block Bldg.
Peerless Thea.
11th Broadway Theater
Hale Bros.
T. & D. Theater
10th
Rex Theater
CASTRO
GROVE
JEFFERSON
CLAY
WASHINGTON
BROADWAY
FRANKLIN
WEBSTER
HARRISON
ALICE
JACKSON
MADISON
OAK
9th
8th
17
7th
To San Jose
To San Francisco
B.R. 50
6th
5th
4th
W.P. R.R. Station
3rd
2nd
S.P. R.R. Station
S.P. R.R.
1st
JACK LONDON WATER ST.
SQUARE
N
Inner Harbor
Tunnel To Alameda
©C. S. Hammond & Co., N.Y.

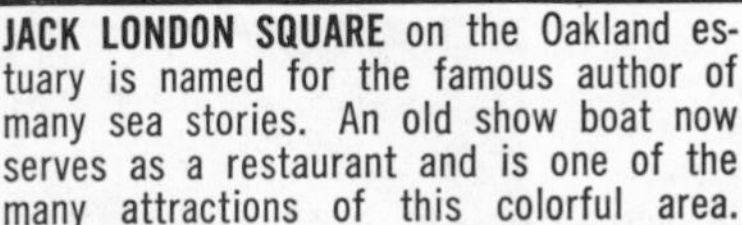
JACK LONDON SQUARE on the Oakland estuary is named for the famous author of many sea stories. An old show boat now serves as a restaurant and is one of the many attractions of this colorful area.

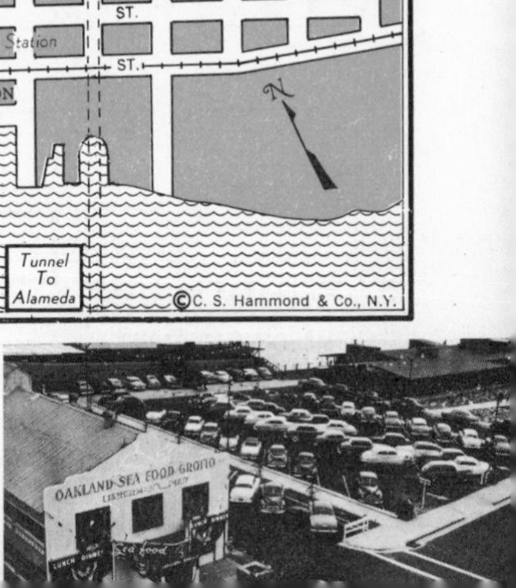

Oklahoma City, Okla.

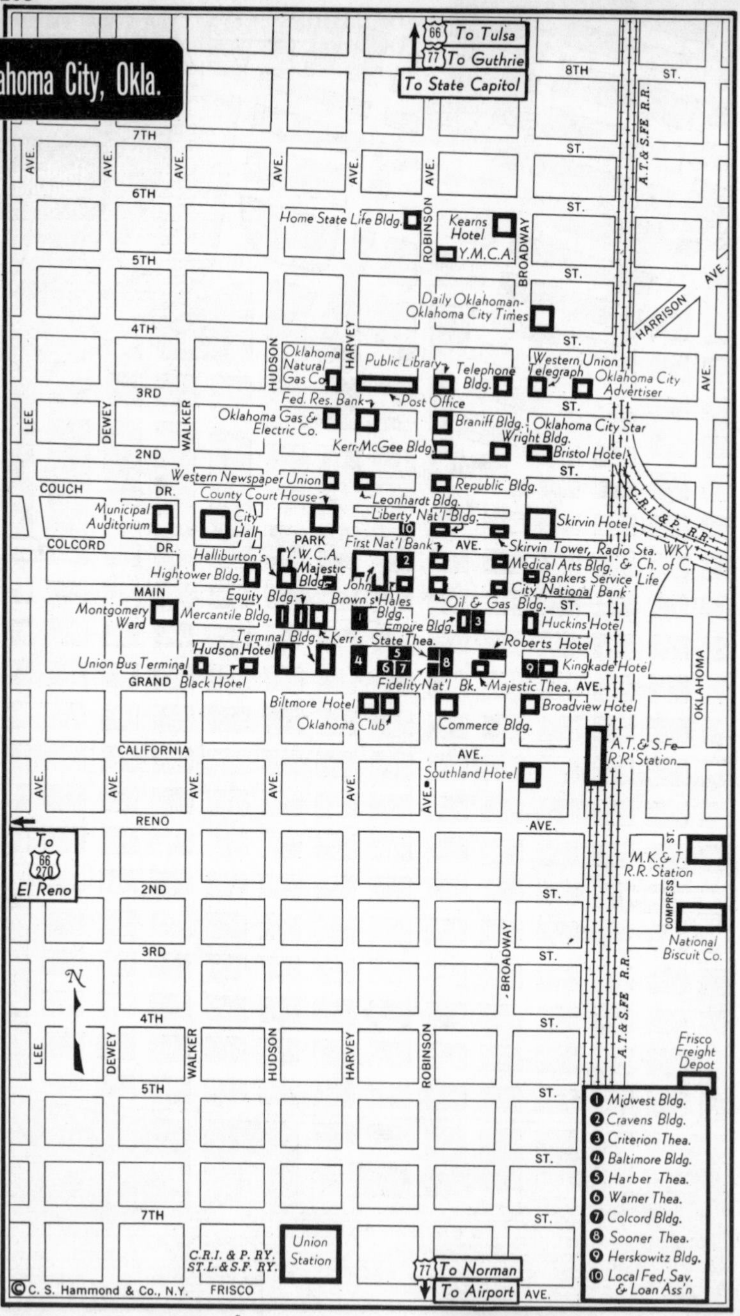

To Tulsa
To Guthrie
To State Capitol
To El Reno
To Norman
To Airport

1. Midwest Bldg.
2. Cravens Bldg.
3. Criterion Thea.
4. Baltimore Bldg.
5. Harber Thea.
6. Warner Thea.
7. Colcord Bldg.
8. Sooner Thea.
9. Herskowitz Bldg.
10. Local Fed. Sav. & Loan Ass'n

OKLAHOMA CITY LIBRARIES' new main library at Northwest 3rd and Robinson streets is one of the most modern in the nation. Its three branches include an Historical Library which is an unusually complete collection of source material on early Indian and white settlers

THE BEAUTIFUL MUNICIPAL BUILDING is one of four buildings that make up the handsome four-square-block Civic Center area of downtown Oklahoma City. This area was once a railroad switch yard

OKLAHOMA CITY. The beginnings of Oklahoma City are unique in American history. Between noon and sundown on April 22, 1889, a city of 10,000 persons sprang into being along the banks of the Canadian River where that morning stood only a Santa Fe station and three rude frame buildings. By train, by wagon, on foot and on horseback, people came to stake out claims, when the broad, central section of what is now Oklahoma was thrown open to settlement. In less than 70 years, Oklahoma City has grown from a city of tents to one of towers. A major factor in the city's spectacular development, was the discovery, in 1928, that its buildings literally stood atop one of the world's richest oil fields. Oil rigs erected to tap the riches of this deposit have appeared on the lawns of private homes as well as on the grounds of the State Capitol Building. Despite its oil wells and its many industries, Oklahoma City is noted for its sparkling cleanliness. No pall of smoke hangs over the city, no soot or grime discolors its fine buildings. Here natural gas and crude oil—both smokeless—are used exclusively for fuel. In 1955, in competition with 400 cities of the West, Oklahoma City was chosen as the permanent site for the National Cowboy Hall of Fame. One of its residents invented parking meters and Oklahoma City was the first town in the world to install them along its streets.

OKLAHOMA CITY has grown from teepees to towers in less than 70 years. Its central location, importance as a political center, the discovery of oil and development of manufacturing, wholesaling and retailing have all contributed to its position of leadership

Photos: Oklahoma City Chamber of Commerce

OKLAHOMA'S CAPITOL has two particularly interesting distinctions: it is the only capital in the nation that has no dome and it is the only one in the world with producing oil wells under it

OMAHA. In the heart of a rich and resourceful region — the breadbasket of America — is Omaha, Nebraska, virtually the geographical center of the United States. In effect, her fame and fortune stem from this auspicious location at the nation's crossroads. It was the Mormons who first contributed to this distinction, when they camped here during the winter of 1846-47 on their heroic trek to Utah. The famed bronze statue, *Winter Quarters,* in Omaha's Mormon Cemetery, commemorates the six hundred pioneers who died here. In the 'forties this Mormon or California Trail became a principal route for westward migration. Today the city is the world's largest cattle market and one of the nation's leading grain markets. Here, too, at Offutt Air Force Base is the headquarters of the Strategic Air Command, nerve center of our global bombing operations. Unique among civic organizations is the Knights of Ak-Sar-Ben (Nebraska spelled backwards), an association devoted to agricultural and educational activities, recognized as one of the greatest factors in the area's growth. Each fall Ak-Sar-Ben coliseum is the scene of the world's largest 4-H Baby Beef Show and the World Championship Rodeo.

UNION STOCKYARDS comprise more than 100 acres of buildings and paved pens and alleys. In the center of the yards is the Livestock Exchange Building, where hundreds of marketing transactions are conducted daily, while on the periphery are many leading packing plants

ADMINISTRATION BUILDING of Creighton University, a coeducational Jesuit institution founded in 1878 and excelling in the teaching of medicine and law

NEW MUNICIPAL AUDITORIUM provides the latest in convention and entertainment accommodations. Its four principle facilities handle any sports or entertainment event

ENTRANCE PYLON to internationally famed Boys Town, a community for homeless and underprivileged boys. Since its founding in 1917 by the late Father Edward J. Flanagan, more than 7,000 boys from every state have called Boys Town their home

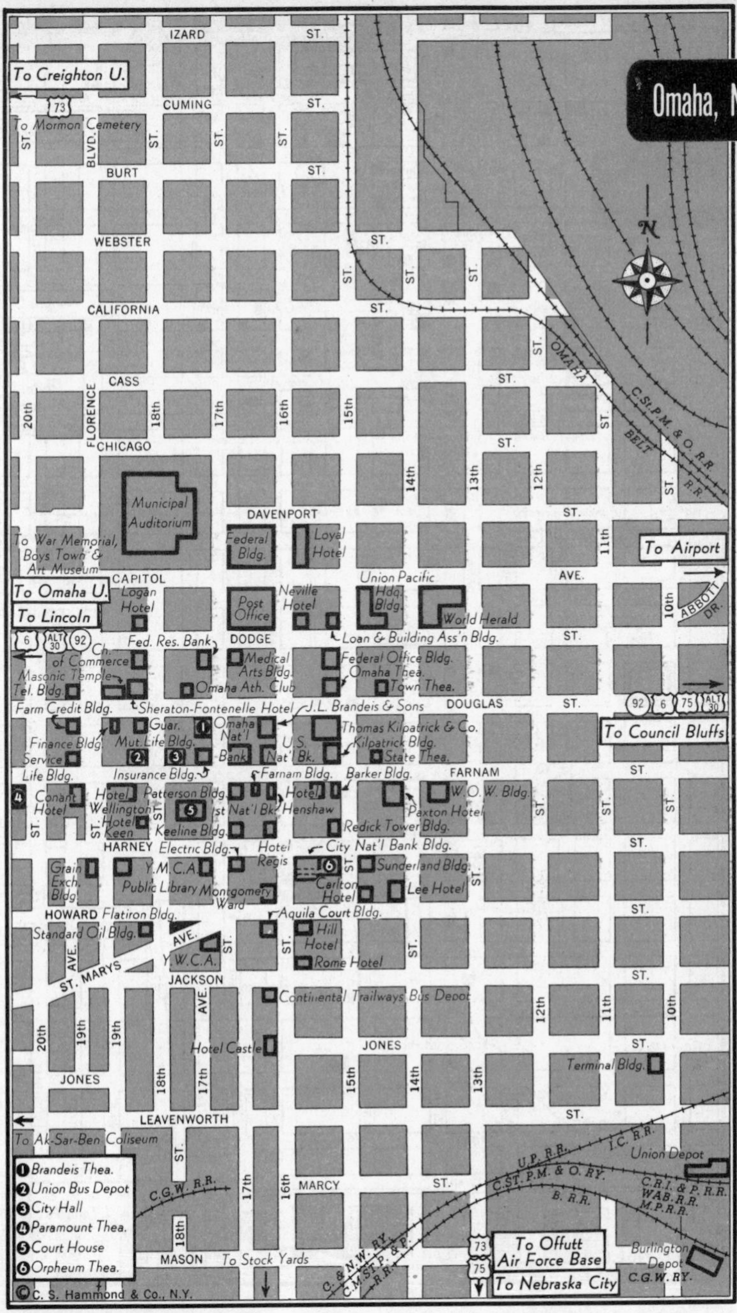

Omaha, Neb.

To Creighton U.
To Mormon Cemetery
To War Memorial, Boys Town & Art Museum
To Omaha U.
To Lincoln
To Airport
To Council Bluffs
To Ak-Sar-Ben Coliseum
To Stock Yards
To Offutt Air Force Base
To Nebraska City

IZARD ST.
CUMING ST.
BURT ST.
WEBSTER ST.
CALIFORNIA ST.
CASS ST.
CHICAGO ST.
DAVENPORT ST.
CAPITOL AVE.
DODGE ST.
DOUGLAS ST.
FARNAM ST.
HARNEY ST.
HOWARD ST.
JACKSON ST.
JONES ST.
LEAVENWORTH ST.
MARCY ST.
MASON ST.
ST. MARYS AVE.
ABBOTT DR.
20th ST.
FLORENCE BLVD.
19th ST.
18th ST.
17th ST.
16th ST.
15th ST.
14th ST.
13th ST.
12th ST.
11th ST.
10th ST.

Municipal Auditorium
Federal Bldg.
Loyal Hotel
Logan Hotel
Post Office
Neville Hotel
Union Pacific Hdq. Bldg.
World Herald
Loan & Building Ass'n Bldg.
Fed. Res. Bank
Ch. of Commerce
Masonic Temple
Tel. Bldg.
Medical Arts Bldg.
Omaha Ath. Club
Federal Office Bldg.
Omaha Thea.
Town Thea.
Farm Credit Bldg.
Sheraton-Fontenelle Hotel
J.L. Brandeis & Sons
Thomas Kilpatrick & Co.
Kilpatrick Bldg.
State Thea.
Finance Bldg.
Guar. Mut. Life Bldg.
Omaha Nat'l Bank
U.S. Nat'l Bk.
Service Life Bldg.
Insurance Bldg.
Farnam Bldg.
Barker Bldg.
W.O.W. Bldg.
Conant Hotel
Hotel Wellington
Hotel Keen
Patterson Bldg.
1st Nat'l Bk.
Keeline Bldg.
Hotel Henshaw
Paxton Hotel
Redick Tower Bldg.
Electric Bldg.
Hotel Regis
City Nat'l Bank Bldg.
Sunderland Bldg.
Grain Exch. Bldg.
Y.M.C.A.
Public Library
Montgomery Ward
Carlton Hotel
Lee Hotel
Flatiron Bldg.
Standard Oil Bldg.
Aquila Court Bldg.
Hill Hotel
Rome Hotel
Y.W.C.A.
Continental Trailways Bus Depot
Hotel Castle
Terminal Bldg.
Union Depot
Burlington Depot

OMAHA BELT R.R.
C.St.P.M. & O. R.R.
U.P. R.R.
I.C. R.R.
C.ST.P.M. & O. RY.
B. R.R.
C.R.I. & P. R.R.
WAB. R.R.
M.P. R.R.
C.G.W. RY.
C.G.W. R.R.
C. & N.W. RY.
C.M.ST.P. & P. R.R.

1 Brandeis Thea.
2 Union Bus Depot
3 City Hall
4 Paramount Thea.
5 Court House
6 Orpheum Thea.

JOSLYN MEMORIAL ART MUSEUM, a rose-marble design of extreme simplicity, is one of the finest art galleries in the Mid-West and provides a concert hall for the Omaha Symphony Orchestra

Photos: Walter S. Craig, Omaha Chamber of Commerce

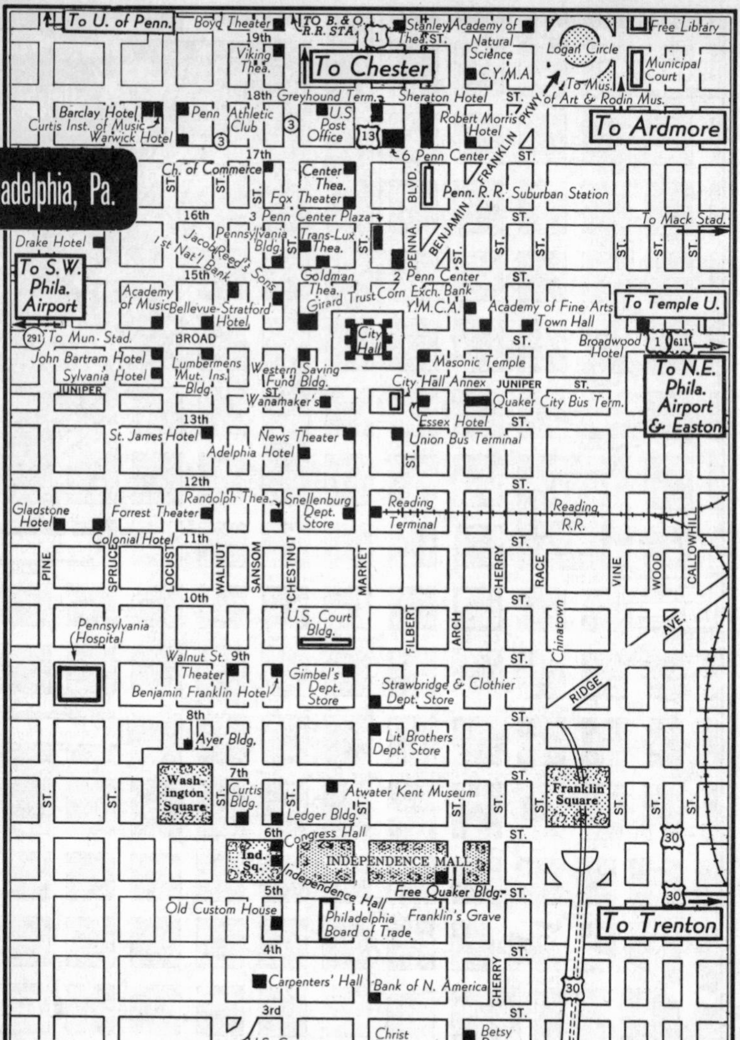

Philadelphia, Pa.

To U. of Penn.
Boyd Theater
TO B. & O. R.R. STA.
1
Stanley Thea.
ST.
Academy of Natural Science
Logan Circle
Free Library
19th
Viking Thea.
To Chester
C.Y.M.A.
Municipal Court
18th
Greyhound Term.
Sheraton Hotel
ST.
To Mus. of Art & Rodin Mus.
Barclay Hotel
Curtis Inst. of Music
Warwick Hotel
Penn Athletic Club
3
U.S. Post Office
13
Robert Morris Hotel
FRANKLIN PKWY
To Ardmore
17th
6 Penn Center
ST.
Ch. of Commerce
Center Thea.
Fox Theater
BLVD.
Penn. R.R. Suburban Station
16th
3 Penn Center Plaza
ST.
To Mack Stad.
Drake Hotel
Jacob Reed's Sons
1st Nat'l Bank
Pennsylvania Bldg.
Trans-Lux Thea.
PENNA.
BENJAMIN
To S.W. Phila. Airport
15th
Goldman Thea.
2 Penn Center
ST.
Academy of Music
Bellevue-Stratford Hotel
Girard Trust
Corn Exch. Bank
Y.M.C.A.
Academy of Fine Arts
Town Hall
To Temple U.
291
To Mun. Stad.
BROAD
City Hall
ST.
Broadwood Hotel
1
611
John Bartram Hotel
Sylvania Hotel
Lumbermens Mut. Ins. Bldg.
Western Saving Fund Bldg.
Masonic Temple
To N.E. Phila. Airport & Easton
JUNIPER
ST.
Wanamaker's
City Hall Annex
JUNIPER
ST.
Quaker City Bus Term.
13th
St. James Hotel
News Theater
Essex Hotel
ST.
Union Bus Terminal
Adelphia Hotel
12th
ST.
Gladstone Hotel
Forrest Theater
Randolph Thea.
Snellenburg Dept. Store
Reading Terminal
Reading R.R.
Colonial Hotel
11th
ST.
PINE
SPRUCE
LOCUST
WALNUT
SANSOM
CHESTNUT
MARKET
CHERRY
RACE
VINE
WOOD
CALLOWHILL
10th
ST.
Pennsylvania Hospital
U.S. Court Bldg.
FILBERT
ARCH
Chinatown
AVE.
Walnut St. Theater
9th
Benjamin Franklin Hotel
Gimbel's Dept. Store
Strawbridge & Clothier Dept. Store
ST.
RIDGE
8th
Ayer Bldg.
Lit Brothers Dept. Store
ST.
Washington Square
7th
Curtis Bldg.
Atwater Kent Museum
Ledger Bldg.
Franklin Square
6th
Congress Hall
ST.
30
Ind. Sq.
INDEPENDENCE MALL
Independence Hall
5th
Free Quaker Bldg.
ST.
30
Old Custom House
Philadelphia Board of Trade
Franklin's Grave
To Trenton
4th
ST.
Carpenters' Hall
Bank of N. America
CHERRY
30
3rd
ST.
Head House
U.S. Customs
Christ Church
Betsy Ross House
2nd
ST.
PINE
SPRUCE
DOCK
WALNUT
CHESTNUT
MARKET
ARCH
ELFRETH'S ALLEY
RACE
VINE
WOOD
CALLOWHILL
FRONT
ST.
To Old Swede's Church
DELAWARE
AVE.
Penn. R.R.
Benj. Franklin Bridge
To Camden & N.J. Turnpike
PENN.-READ. S. LINES
N

Delaware River

INDEPENDENCE HALL, America's birthplace, contains the Liberty Bell, the ink stand used in signing the Declaration of Independence and displays of other historic memorabilia

Photos: Philadelphia Convention and visitors Bureau

PHILADELPHIA. Birthplace of the nation, Philadelphia is an industrial giant that William Penn, its founder, would never recognize as the "greene countrie towne" he laid out in 1682. Named by Penn for an ancient Biblical town in Asia Minor, *Philadelphia* in Greek means "City of Brotherly Love." This city, which today covers almost 130 square miles, ranks as the third largest in the United States, yet its original area of two square miles was once considered ample space for its growth and expansion. Situated on the Delaware at its junction with the Schuylkill, Philadelphia's extensive frontage on the two rivers has been an important factor in its development as a leading world port while its large piers and excellent rail connections facilitate the rapid and efficient handling of marine cargos. Philadelphia's importance in finance and insurance was early established. The Bank of North America, the first bank chartered by Congress, began business here in 1782 and still exists under a

PHILADELPHIA MUSEUM OF ART, contains one of the largest and finest collections of art in the United States. Rugs, textiles, ceramics, glass, jewelry and illuminated books are also on display

RODIN MUSEUM contains 245 casts of the French sculptor, Auguste Rodin. The building is a replica of the Rodin Museum at Meudon, France

CONGRESS HALL was used by the National Congress during the period Philadelphia served as seat of the Federal Government. Here George Washington was inaugurated for his second term as President

PHILADELPHIA Continued

slightly altered name. The Curtis Publishing Company is one of the largest publishers in the magazine field. Within the bustling modern city, with its tall buildings, hotels and fine stores, are many reminders of the old Philadelphia of Penn and Franklin—the quaint little alleys paved with cobblestones, the neat Colonial dwellings and such landmarks as Independence Hall, familiar to every American, where a new nation was cradled in its infancy. Besides the numerous historical associations, Philadelphia has been renowned since prerevolutionary times for its cultural achievements and its educational facilities in the arts and sciences. The University, which began as a humble experiment in education, has long been outstanding in many fields of academic achievement and boasts one of the finest archaeological collections in existence. Other notable Philadelphia institutions include Temple University, Drexel Institute, the Philadelphia Museum School of Art, the Pennsylvania Academy of Fine Arts and the Curtis Institute of Music. Philadelphia has never lacked for amusements. The Academy of Music is a leading opera house and the city is the birthplace of the world-famed Philadelphia Symphony Orchestra. Always an important town for sporting events, it offers such true national classics as the annual Army-Navy football game at Franklin Field Stadium and Connie Mack Stadium is the home of two major league baseball teams. Although its site, in 1682, was mostly open field and forest, Philadelphia is one of the few cities whose founders had enough foresight to include a system of parks in its original plan. Today, Fairmount Park is considered to be the largest natural park within a city's limits.

ELFRETH'S ALLEY runs from Front to 2nd Street. This tiny street, one of the nation's oldest, has a quaint Colonial flavor and houses that date from 1690

BENJAMIN FRANKLIN PARKWAY runs from Fairmount Park to Broad Street, joining Philadelphia's largest park area with the heart of the city. City Hall Tower topped by a statue of Willian Penn can be seen in the background

OLD CUSTOM HOUSE, erected between 1819 and 1824, was designed by Latrobe and executed by William Strickland, one of our first great architects. A free-copy of the Parthenon, it is one of the finest examples of Greek architecture in the country

PHILADELPHIA'S FIRST SETTLERS worshipped at the Old Swedes' Church, built in 1700. The Mummers Parade on New Year's Day is one of the last surviving folk customs of these early dwellers in the Delaware Valley

UNIVERSITY OF PENNSYLVANIA, founded by Benjamin Franklin, occupies a 123-acre campus in West Philadelphia. Its Schools of Law and Medicine were the first in the United States

Photos: Philadelphia Convention and visitors Bureau

BETSY ROSS HOUSE stands at 239 Arch Street. Here the skilled needle of Mrs. Elizabeth Ross made our first American flag. Relics on display, depict the life and times of the famous seamstress

CARPENTERS' HALL was built by the Carpenters' Company of Philadelphia, one of America's oldest trade guilds. Here the sessions of the first Continental Congress were held in 1774

PHOENIX. Phoenix, the capital of Arizona, is appropriately named, for, like the legendary phoenix bird of Egypt, it rose from the ashes of an ancient city. Situated in the great saucer-shaped Salt River Valley, popularly known as the "Valley of the Sun," the city is the center of a year-round vacation area which attracts an estimated 1,000,000 visitors throughout each year. Phoenix also serves as the center of a fabulously rich, irrigated farm empire of 435,000 acres which yields citrus fruits, dates, olives, flax, cotton and a variety of truck crops. Each year the Valley is becoming recognized more and more as the source of fine breeding cattle, including the hump-backed Brahman. According to the United States Weather Bureau's 55-year record, Phoenix can boast the driest, clearest, sunniest climate in America. A typical winter day is refreshingly dry, gloriously sunny and shirt-sleeve warm. The city gives an overall impression of cosmopolitan shops, delightfully smart eating places and lovely homes bordering palm-lined streets. Within a short distance lie such marvelous attractions as huge, colorful Indian reservations and the Superstition Mountains, site of the legendary $20,000,000 Lost Dutchman gold mine. Each Sunday during the winter season the Dons, an organization of Phoenix businessmen keenly interested in Southwestern history and culture, lead motorcades to Arizona sites rich in tradition and lore.

ROOSEVELT DAM, east of Phoenix on the scenic Apache Trail, was the first of the great reclamation dams to be constructed in the Salt River Valley. Water stored by the dams has turned the once arid desert into a rich garden area

PICNIC RAMADAS or shelters are among the facilities offered the visitor to South Mountain Park, a 15,000-acre tract which includes Hieroglyphic Canyon. The strange symbols and inscriptions carved in the canyon's walls have never been deciphered

Photos: Phoenix Chamber of Commerce

ST. FRANCIS CHURCH, built along colonial Spanish lines, is located in beautifully landscaped grounds which also serve as the site of Brophy Prep School. Phoenix is noted for its wide variety of church architecture ranging from traditional to ultra-modern

PUEBLO GRANDE RUIN is one of the interesting and unusual remains of the Hohokam Indian civilization. The partly excavated mound is nearly 300 feet long and 150 feet high and unique for the large amount of stone in the crumbling walls. The museum (foreground) displays ancient Indian relics

A THRIVING DESERT METROPOLIS and capital of Arizona, Phoenix boasts a wide variety of industries and agriculture as well as many famed vacation resorts

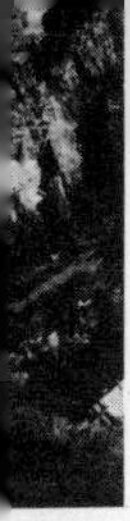

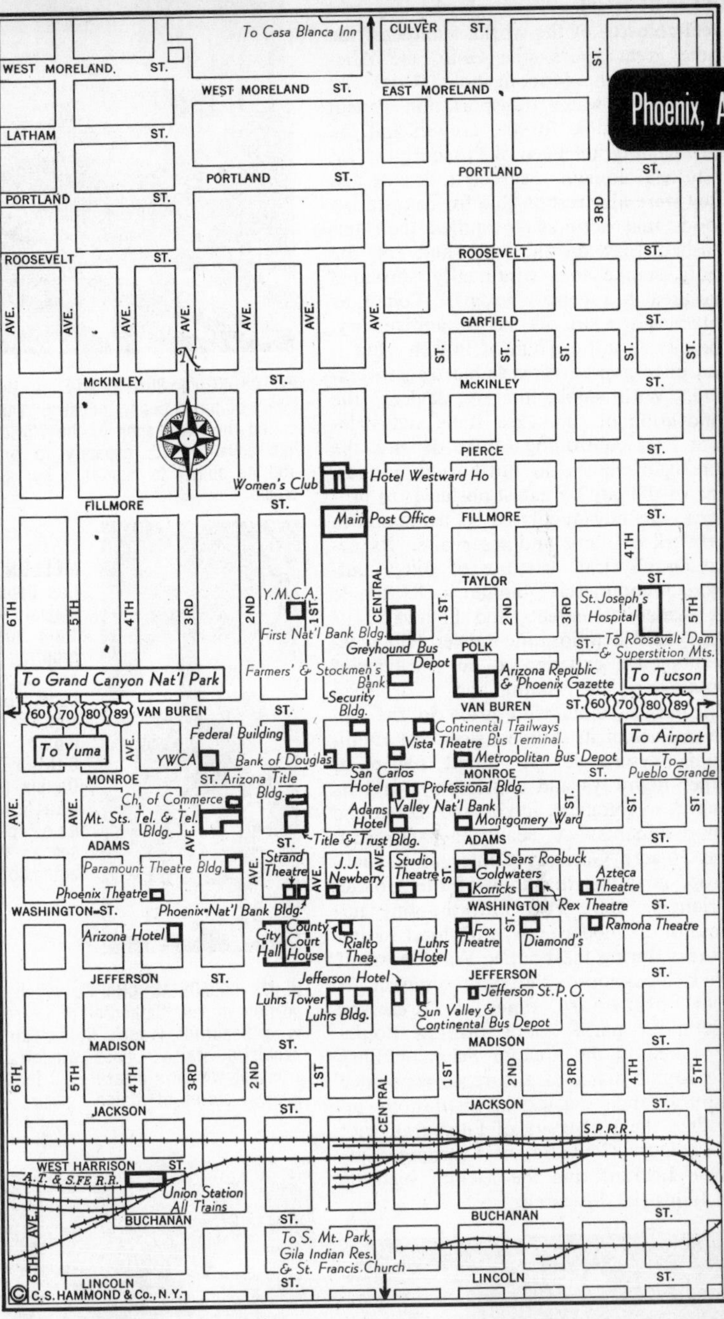

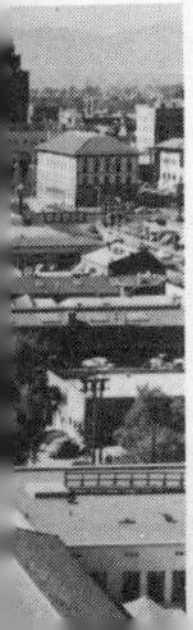

To Casa Blanca Inn
CULVER ST.
WEST MORELAND ST.
EAST MORELAND
LATHAM ST.
PORTLAND ST.
ROOSEVELT ST.
GARFIELD ST.
McKINLEY ST.
PIERCE ST.
Women's Club
Hotel Westward Ho
FILLMORE ST.
Main Post Office
TAYLOR ST.
Y.M.C.A.
First Nat'l Bank Bldg.
St. Joseph's Hospital
Greyhound Bus Depot
POLK ST.
To Roosevelt Dam & Superstition Mts.
To Grand Canyon Nat'l Park
Farmers' & Stockmen's Bank
Arizona Republic & Phoenix Gazette
To Tucson
Security Bldg.
VAN BUREN ST.
60 70 80 89
To Yuma
Federal Building
Continental Trailways Bus Terminal
Vista Theatre
To Airport
YWCA
Bank of Douglas
Metropolitan Bus Depot
To Pueblo Grande
MONROE ST.
Arizona Title Bldg.
San Carlos Hotel
Professional Bldg.
Ch. of Commerce
Mt. Sts. Tel. & Tel. Bldg.
Adams Hotel
Valley Nat'l Bank
Montgomery Ward
ADAMS ST.
Title & Trust Bldg.
Paramount Theatre Bldg.
Strand Theatre
J.J. Newberry
Studio Theatre
Sears Roebuck
Goldwaters
Korricks
Azteca Theatre
Phoenix Theatre
WASHINGTON ST.
Phoenix Nat'l Bank Bldg.
Rex Theatre
Ramona Theatre
Arizona Hotel
City Hall
County Court House
Rialto Thea.
Luhrs Hotel
Fox Theatre
Diamond's
JEFFERSON ST.
Jefferson Hotel
Luhrs Tower
Luhrs Bldg.
Jefferson St. P.O.
Sun Valley & Continental Bus Depot
MADISON ST.
6TH 5TH 4TH 3RD 2ND 1ST AVE.
CENTRAL AVE.
1ST 2ND 3RD 4TH 5TH ST.
JACKSON ST.
S.P.R.R.
WEST HARRISON ST.
A.T. & S.FE R.R.
Union Station All Trains
BUCHANAN ST.
To S. Mt. Park, Gila Indian Res. & St. Francis Church
LINCOLN ST.

CASA BLANCA INN, with its gleaming white Moorish tower rising out of the desert, is one of many fine resorts in the region of Phoenix. Beautifully landscaped, it has its own landing strip, swimming pool, stable, tennis courts, putting green and other recreational facilities

PITTSBURGH. Pittsburgh, the iron and steel colossus of the world, stands astride three great rivers—the Ohio, the Allegheny and the Monongahela. Coal and this mighty water transportation system were responsible for the growth and the far-reaching influence of Pittsburgh's vast industrial domain. Scarcely a decade ago they were also responsible for devastating floods that periodically spilled their unleashed fury on the city, and for the sooty smoke that continually shrouded the area in a dense black pall. Today, as Pittsburgh nears its 200th anniversary, the city is still a Titan of industry but it has undergone a remarkable transformation. With smoke-filtering devices, the innovation of smokeless fuels and stringent laws controlling smoke density, the sun again shines on Pittsburgh. Floods, one of the city's greatest obstacles to progress, are now regulated by a mammoth network of dams and reservoirs. Its decaying physical structure of dingy outmoded commercial buildings, its tangle of inadequate streets and highways, its seedy and deteriorating Lower Hill tenements have experienced an extravagant renaissance. A shining and refurbished Pittsburgh points with pride to the tall clean lines of its stainless steel and aluminum skyscrapers, its broad sweep of super highways and expressways and its many sociological, civic and economic improvements. A beautiful park, with the 36-acre Gateway Center as a backdrop, now fills the apex of the Golden Triangle. Here Fort Pitt, the tiny nucleus of the modern city, withstood Indian attacks during the Pontiac War. A small brick blockhouse, the only remnant of prerevolutionary times, is preserved within the park. Along Bigelow Boulevard and in the area of Schenley Park are found many of the city's renowned cultural and educational institutions including the University of Pittsburgh with its 42-story Cathedral of Learning, Carnegie Institute and the Mellon Institute of Industrial Research.

PITTSBURGH'S SOUTH SIDE is the throbbing heart of basic heavy industry. The city, often called the "Workshop of the World," zealously has advanced its capacity to produce steel and its ability to market it by rail, river and truck

MELLON SQUARE has brought the majestic beauty of trees and shrubs, erupting fountains and cascades accented by colored lights into the heart of the Golden Triangle. On six levels beneath the park are parking spaces for 1,000 automobiles

HEINZ MEMORIAL CHAPEL which occupies a portion of the Cathedral of Learning campus is a beautiful French Gothic structure with exquisite stained glass windows. The four transept windows measure 70 feet the worlds' longest series of stained glass

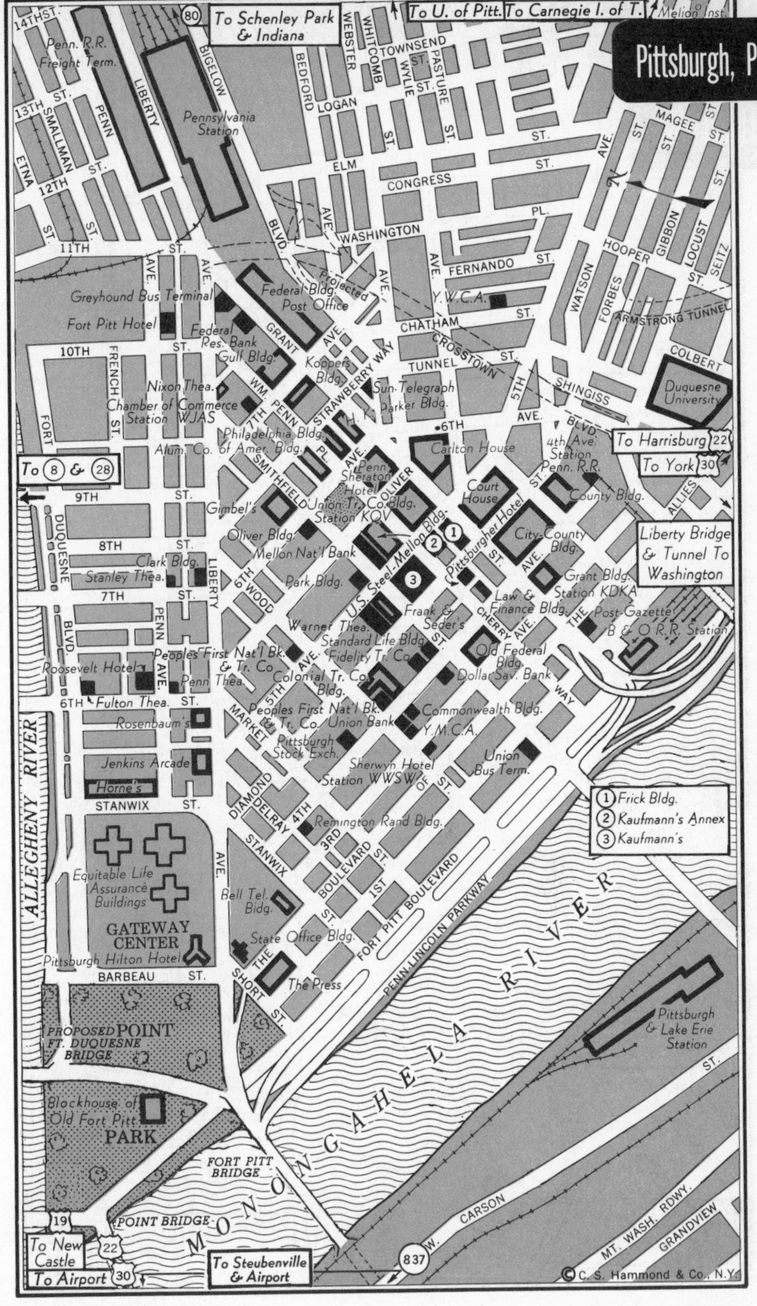

THE GOLDEN TRIANGLE, where the Allegheny and the Monongahela Rivers meet to form the Ohio, is the center of the city's handsome business district. Recently it has undergone a complete face-lifting

Portland, Me.

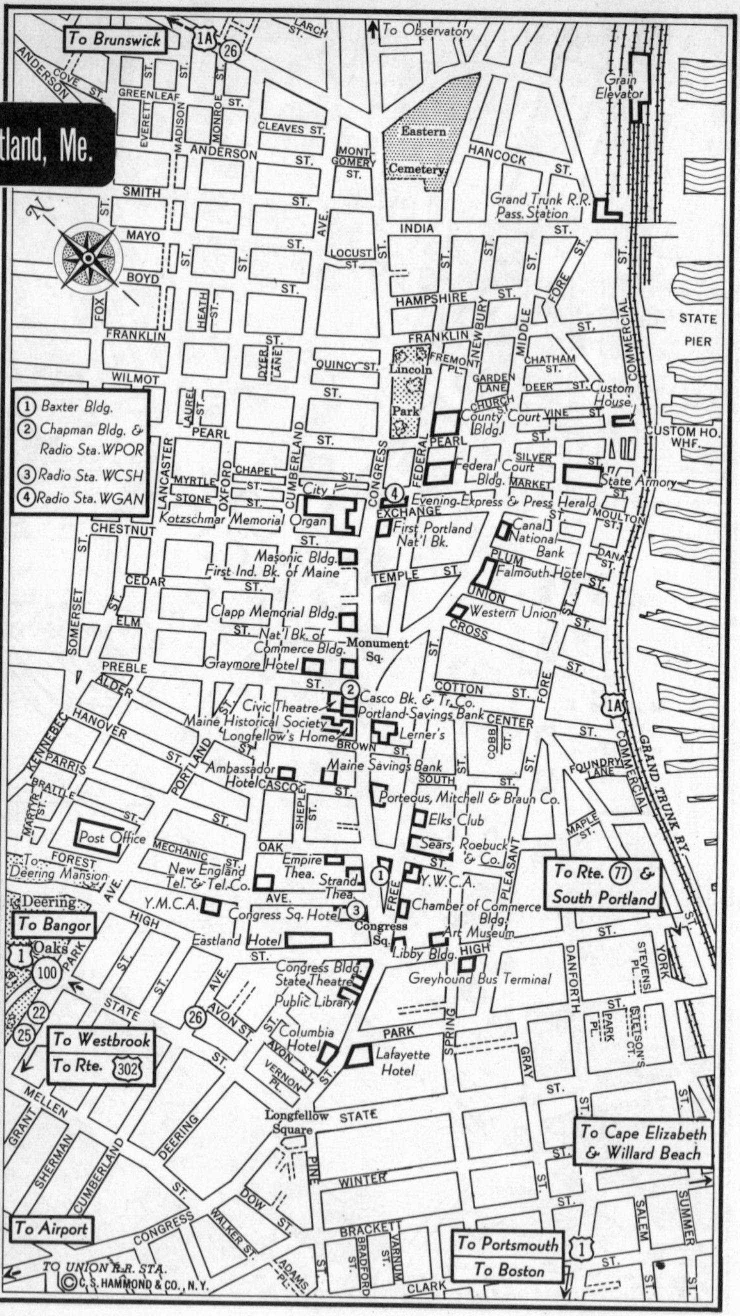

1. Baxter Bldg.
2. Chapman Bldg. & Radio Sta. WPOR
3. Radio Sta. WCSH
4. Radio Sta. WGAN

PORTLAND AIRPORT, municipally owned, is a modern airstrip serviced by Northeast Airlines. From here, Boston is but 40 minutes away by air and New York 80 minutes

PORTLAND HEAD LIGHT at Cape Elizabeth is one of the most familiar and most photographed lighthouses in the United States. This historic beacon was desgined by George Washington who also appointed its first keeper in 1791

PORTLAND. Portland, the largest city in Northern New England, occupies a narrow peninsula at the head of Casco Bay. This island-filled arm of the sea which curves inland from the rugged Maine coast provides Portland with the fine, sheltered harbor which has won it recognition since early Colonial days as one of our great Atlantic shipping ports. Noted for the scenic beauty of its location and the warm "down east" hospitality of its people, the city and its surroundings attract many vacationists during the summer season. Portland is a city of dignified public buildings and simple but charming homes, mostly built in the architectural styles of the 18th and early 19th century. Probably the most historic of these is a three-storied brick dwelling where the poet Henry Wadsworth Longfellow spent his childhood, boyhood and early manhood. Hallowed by its associations, the Wadsworth-Longfellow house contains a wealth of furnishings, records and personal possessions of the large and famous family. Also of interest is the Deering Mansion, the fine old Colonial home of one of Portland's oldest families, for which the town of Deering, later a part of Portland, was named. Portland Observatory, a relic of clipper ship days and originally used to signal their approach, offers a panoramic view of the Portland area. Sightseeing boats, sailing daily from Custom House Wharf, make delightful, scenic cruises around Casco Bay and through the Calendar Islands, so named because they total 365, "one for each day of the year."

AT MONUMENT SQUARE in the heart of Portland's business district, the traffic swirls around the site of old City Hall where today stands the impressive Soldiers and Sailors Monument, the work of sculptor Franklin Simmons

Photos: State of Maine Publicity Bureau

WILLARD BEACH, in the Portland area, is but one of the many sandy stretches of shoreline which offer the lure of tangy, salt water bathing

PORTLAND. The deep, cool green of Oregon's forests add distinction to the fresh-water port of Portland, the very capital of the lumber industry, for in the surrounding territory grows a fourth of the nation's saw timber. A huge new exhibit of the forest-products industry, the "Gallery of Trees," is housed in the famous old Forestry Building, the world's largest log cabin, with a hall supported by a colonnade of massive, fifty-four-feet-high, perfect fir logs. Like few other industrial cities, however, Portland is notable as a wonderful setting for enjoyable, peaceful living. A kind climate allows the cultivation of a variety of flowers and shrubs equalled in but few places in the world. Most small homes, as well as mansions, have inviting yards set off by luxuriant growth, and the delightful parks range from natural forests to garden show places of unparalleled beauty. Roses grow everywhere and rhododendrons, azaleas and other blooms provide a riot of glowing color. Rising to heights commanding magnificent views of the Cascade Range and the valleys, surrounded by deep evergreen stands, rich lands and great rivers, it is no wonder this spectacular, rambling city is the nerve center of the vast Columbia domain.

BRILLIANT, COMPLETELY FLORAL FLOATS make the Grand Floral Parade the climax of Portland's annual Rose Festival in June, one of the most colorful celebrations in the nation

INTERNATIONAL ROSE TEST GARDENS cover a large acreage in a perfect setting in the city's Washington Park, which also features a rose theater. The world-famous gardens are at their peak of bloom in June

MEDICAL CENTER, crowning the heights of Marquam Hill in Sam Jackson Park, includes the University of Oregon Medical School, Doernbecher Memorial Hospital for Crippled Children, Multnomah County Hospital and the Veterans Hospital

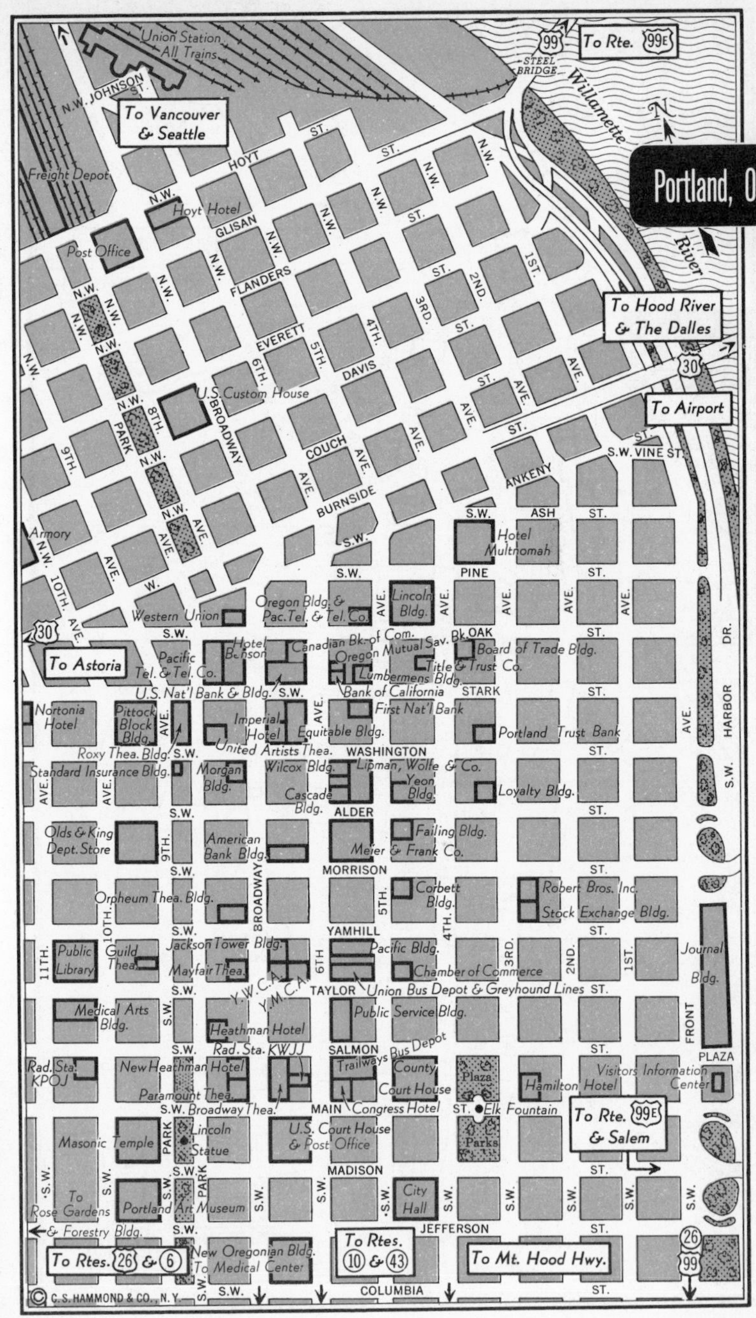

MAJESTIC, snow-powdered summit of Mount Hood stands silent, faithful guard over the precious "City of Roses" at its foot, the leading wheat- and lumber-shipping port on the Pacific coast

Photos: Chamber of Commerce, Oregon State Highway Comm.

Providence, R. I.

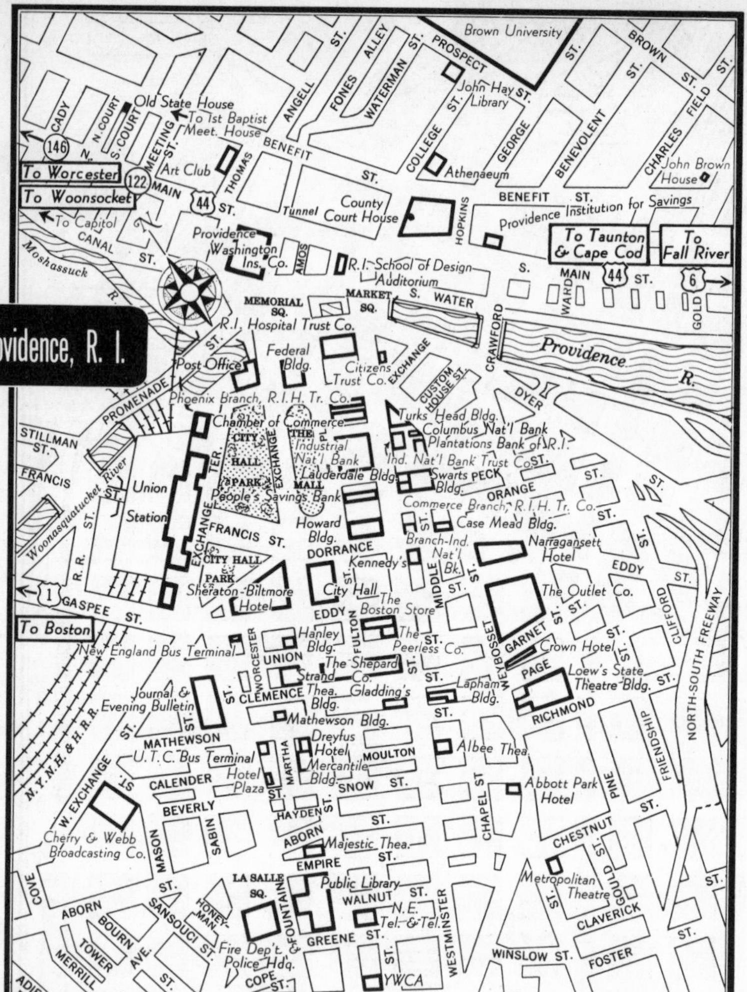

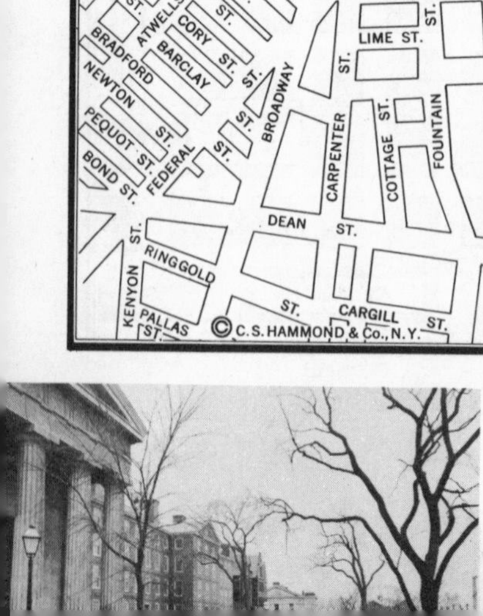

BROWN UNIVERSITY, chartered in 1764, is the seventh oldest of American colleges. Once its historic buildings stood in the midst of extensive pasture lands and cows grazed on the campus

RHODE ISLAND STATE CAPITOL, considered one of the most beautiful capitols in this country, possesses the world's second largest marble dome

PROVIDENCE COUNTY COURT HOUSE, dedicated in 1933, is a modern adaption of Early Republican architecture designed to harmonize with Providence traditions

PROVIDENCE. Banished from the Massachusetts Bay Colony because of religious and civil beliefs and the resulting conflict with the colony's Puritan leaders, Roger Williams founded Providence, naming the city in gratitude "for God's merciful providence unto me in my distress." In names such as Hope, Faith, Peace, Friendship and Benevolent, many of Providence's older streets reflect the piety of the town's early inhabitants while other streets such as Pound, Dollar and Shilling mirror their shrewd sense of business. Rhode Island's capital grew up at the confluence of the Woonasquatucket and Moshassuck Rivers at the head of Narragansett Bay. Originally a farming community, Providence soon turned to commerce and by the 18th century its harbor was described as being a "Forest of Masts." Shipping enterprises, including the triangular trade in slaves, rum and molasses, brought wealth to local merchants. Gradually in turn commerce gave way to industry and the wealth gained by trade was invested in the city's growing industries. Today, Providence, the second largest city in New England, has long been a leader in the manufacture of woolen textiles, knitted cotton goods, silverware and recently has become the world's leading center for the manufacture of jewelry.

FIRST BAPTIST MEETING HOUSE, is a memorable feature of Old Providence and the mother church of the denomination on this continent. Funds donated by John D. Rockefeller Jr. assure structural integrity of the church built in 1775

Reno, Nevada

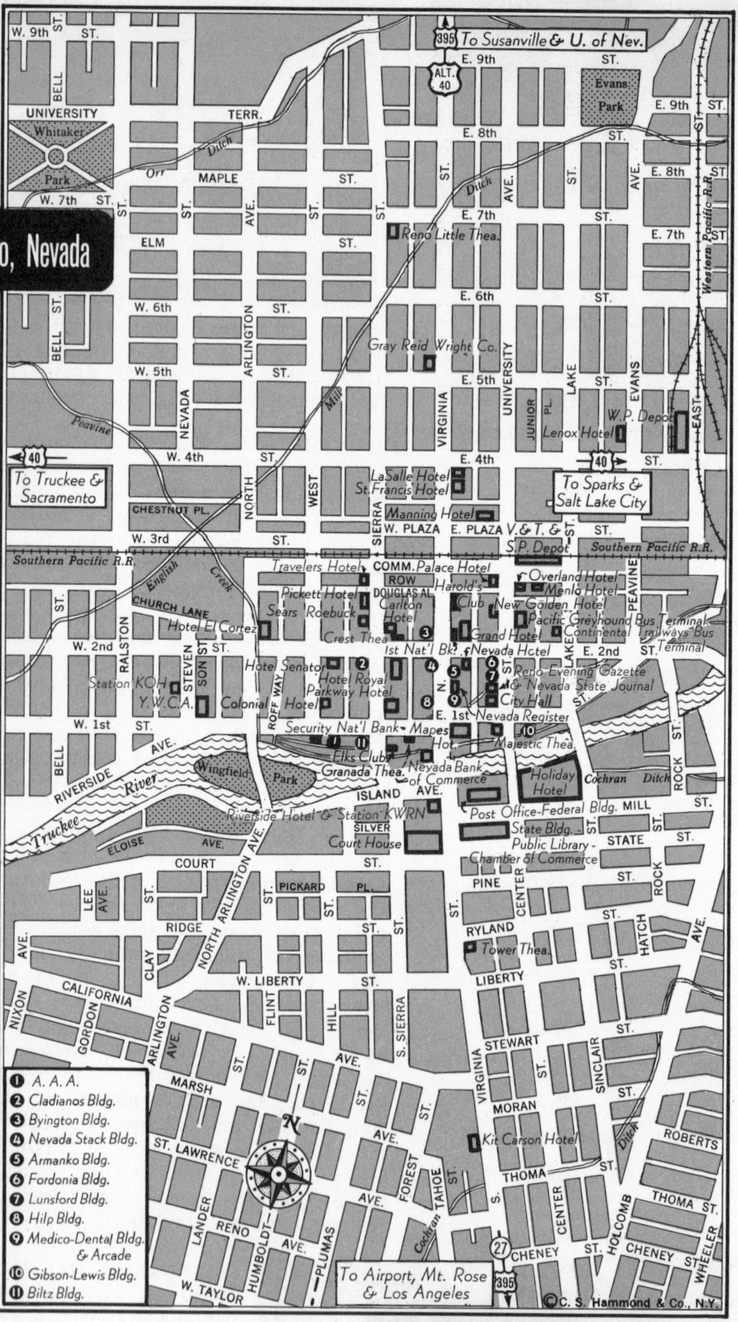

To Susanville & U. of Nev.

To Truckee & Sacramento

To Sparks & Salt Lake City

To Airport, Mt. Rose & Los Angeles

1. A. A. A.
2. Cladianos Bldg.
3. Byington Bldg.
4. Nevada Stack Bldg.
5. Armanko Bldg.
6. Fordonia Bldg.
7. Lunsford Bldg.
8. Hilp Bldg.
9. Medico-Dental Bldg. & Arcade
10. Gibson-Lewis Bldg.
11. Biltz Bldg.

THE TRUCKEE RIVER winds its way quietly through the very heart of Reno, Nevada's largest and most important business center

MOUNT ROSE lies only 17 miles southwest of Reno and is reached by the excellent Mount Rose Highway. Here the tourist can get an unexcelled view of mountains, forests, lakes, deserts and canyons from its 10,800-foot summit

RENO. Reno, the financial center and a vacation playground for the State of Nevada, regards itself as "the Biggest Little City in the World." Though small in regard to population, even counting those temporary residents who for six short weeks call Reno home while awaiting divorce decrees, it does have a certain big-city atmosphere, particularly in the gaudy, brightly-lighted district bordering Virginia and Center Streets where, within a few acres, are crammed most of the city's gambling houses. Here such establishments as the widely advertised Harold's Club, which boasts a bar encrusted with 2,000 silver dollars, invite the visitor to chance a dollar or stake a bankroll at a wide variety of card and dice games, not to mention the proverbial "one-armed bandit"—the slot machine. Reno was founded in 1868 during the building of the Central Pacific Railroad and named by railway officials for the Civil War hero, General Jesse Reno. A neat and pleasant town, encircled by mountains, it lies at an elevation of almost a mile. The city is noted for its fine residential sections, excellent schools, many churches and the lovely parks bordering the Truckee River. The University of Nevada with its world-famous Mackay School of Mines occupies a 60-acre campus on the northern heights overlooking the city. Ideally situated near the eastern slopes of the snow-capped Sierra Nevada, Reno is increasing in popularity as a winter-sports center.

ALL OUT FOR RENO! Southern Pacific's eastbound San Francisco Overland pulls to a stop at the beckoning entrance to "The Biggest Little City in the World"

Photos: Southern Pacific R. R.

FUN TOWN with liberal laws allowing the diversions of an "open town," Reno's sky is brightened at night by the neon lights of its many gambling casinos

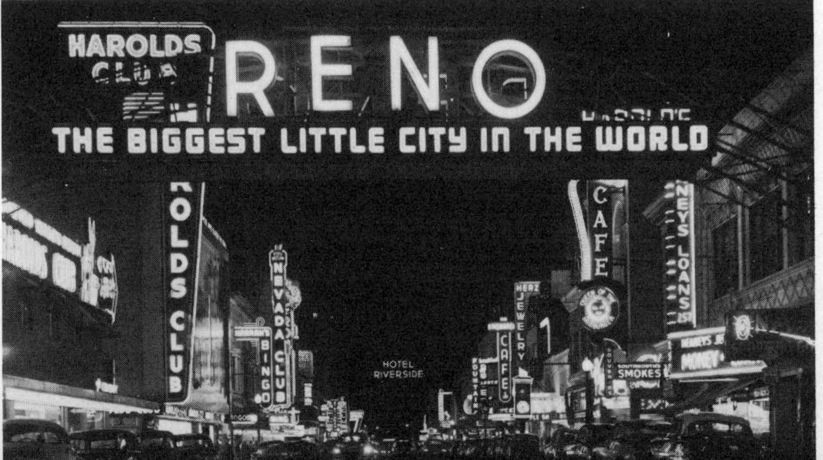

Richmond, Va.

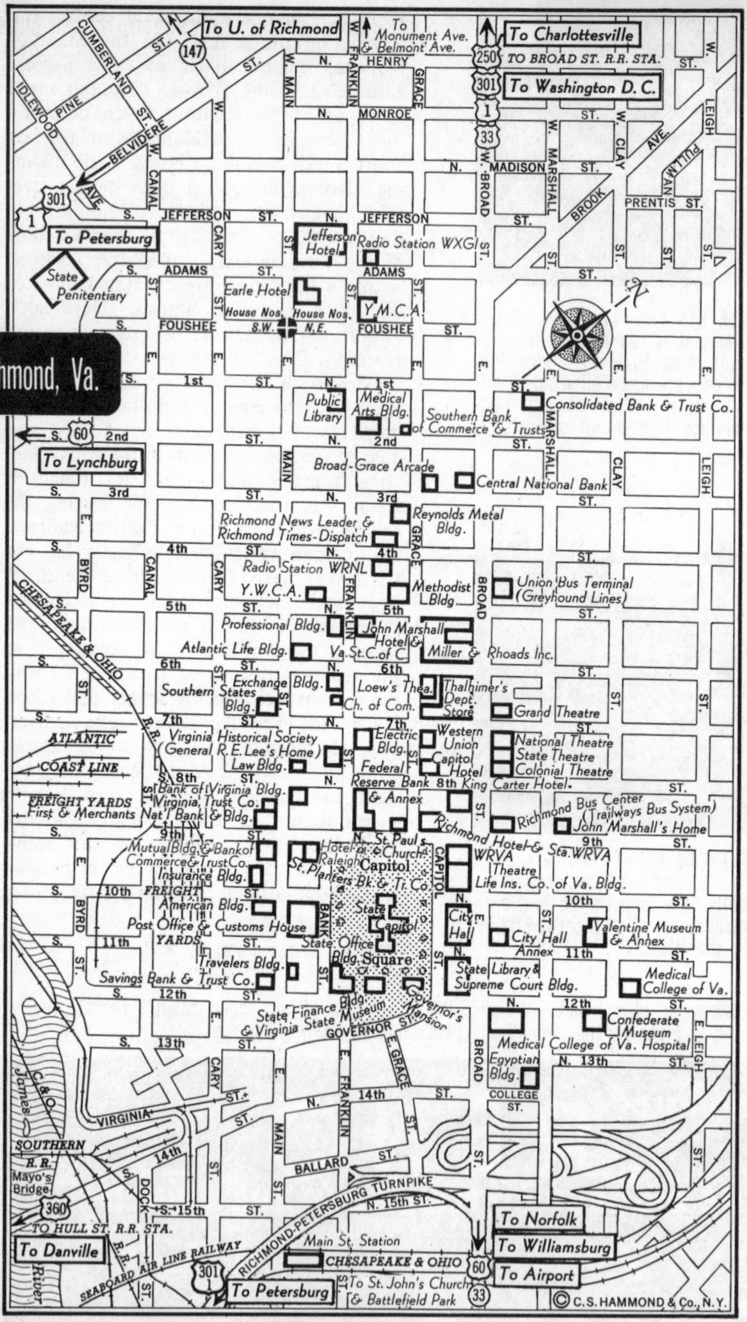

To U. of Richmond
To Monument Ave. & Belmont Ave.
To Charlottesville
TO BROAD ST. R.R. STA.
To Washington D.C.
To Petersburg
State Penitentiary
To Lynchburg
Jefferson Hotel
Radio Station WXGI
Earle Hotel
House Nos. S.W.
House Nos. N.E.
Y.M.C.A.
Consolidated Bank & Trust Co.
Public Library
Medical Arts Bldg.
Southern Bank of Commerce & Trusts
Broad-Grace Arcade
Central National Bank
Reynolds Metal Bldg.
Richmond News Leader & Richmond Times-Dispatch
Radio Station WRNL
Y.W.C.A.
Methodist Bldg.
Union Bus Terminal (Greyhound Lines)
Professional Bldg.
John Marshall Hotel
Atlantic Life Bldg.
Va. St. C. of C.
Miller & Rhoads Inc.
CHESAPEAKE & OHIO
Exchange Bldg.
Southern States Bldg.
Loew's Thea.
Ch. of Com.
Thalhimer's Dept. Store
Grand Theatre
ATLANTIC COAST LINE FREIGHT YARDS
Virginia Historical Society (General R.E. Lee's Home)
Law Bldg.
Electric Bldg.
Western Union
Capitol Hotel
National Theatre
State Theatre
Colonial Theatre
Federal Reserve Bank & Annex
King Carter Hotel
Bank of Virginia Bldg.
Virginia Trust Co.
First & Merchants Nat'l Bank & Bldg.
Richmond Bus Center (Trailways Bus System)
John Marshall's Home
Richmond Hotel & Sta. WRVA
Mutual Bldg. & Bank of Commerce & Trust Co.
Hotel Raleigh
St. Paul's Church
Capitol
WRVA Theatre
Insurance Bldg.
St. Planters Bk. & Tr. Co.
Life Ins. Co. of Va. Bldg.
FREIGHT YARDS
American Bldg.
Post Office & Customs House
State Capitol
City Hall
City Hall Annex
Valentine Museum & Annex
State Office Bldg.
Square
Travelers Bldg.
Savings Bank & Trust Co.
State Library & Supreme Court Bldg.
Medical College of Va.
State Finance Bldg.
& Virginia State Museum
Governor's Mansion
Confederate Museum
Medical College of Va. Hospital
Egyptian Bldg.
GOVERNOR ST.
COLLEGE ST.
VIRGINIA
C. & O.
James River
SOUTHERN R.R.
Mayo's Bridge
TO HULL ST. R.R. STA.
To Danville
SEABOARD AIR LINE RAILWAY
RICHMOND-PETERSBURG TURNPIKE
BALLARD
Main St. Station
CHESAPEAKE & OHIO
To Petersburg
To St. John's Church & Battlefield Park
To Norfolk
To Williamsburg
To Airport
© C.S. HAMMOND & Co., N.Y.

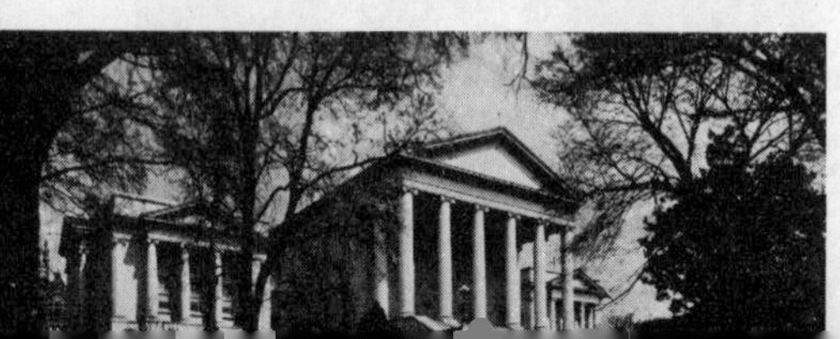

DESIGNED BY THOMAS JEFFERSON, the central building of Virginia's capitol is a modified replica of the Maison Carrée, a Roman Temple at Nîmes, France.

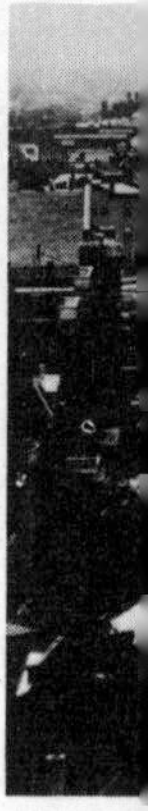

THE ONLY LIFE-SIZE STATUE of George Washington stands beneath the dome of the Capitol's rotunda. This priceless sculpture in marble is by the French artist Houdon.

ST. JOHN'S EPISCOPAL CHURCH is the oldest church in Richmond. Here in 1775, in a speech before the Virginia Convention, Patrick Henry uttered those immortal words, "Give me liberty or give me death"

MONUMENT AVENUE, a beautiful residential thoroughfare in the West End section of Richmond, is lined with monuments to numerous leaders of the Confederacy.

Photos: Richmond Chamber of Commerce

"PATHFINDER OF THE SEAS," Matthew Fontaine Maury, lived for a time in Richmond. The statue of the great oceanographer, seated beneath a bronze globe, stands at Belmont Avenue

RICHMOND. Richmond, the capital of Virginia, stands at the fall line of the James River, 90 miles from the sea. The center of the most historic section of Virginia, Richmond is filled with world-famous shrines; its streets in the older section are virtually lined with buildings which are monuments to the city's illustrious role in the molding of a nation. Here are the halls where once walked such men as George Washington, Thomas Jefferson, Patrick Henry and John Marshall. Vital in the War Between the States, Richmond served as the capital of the Confederacy from 1861 to 1865 and was the prime objective of the Union attack. The former Confederate White House, residence of Jefferson Davis, is now Richmond's Confederate Museum and contains many historical relics of the South's great heroes. The State Capitol, where Robert E. Lee accepted command of the Virginia forces, housed the Confederate House of Representatives. Earlier in 1807, Aaron Burr was tried here before Chief Justice Marshall, on charges of treason. The Richmond Battlefield, six miles east of the city, embraces the fields of the Seven Days Campaign and other battles of the war. Today, the city has retained its quiet charm of yesteryear and tangible evidences of the glorious past while becoming one of the principal industrial cities of the nation.

Rochester, N. Y.

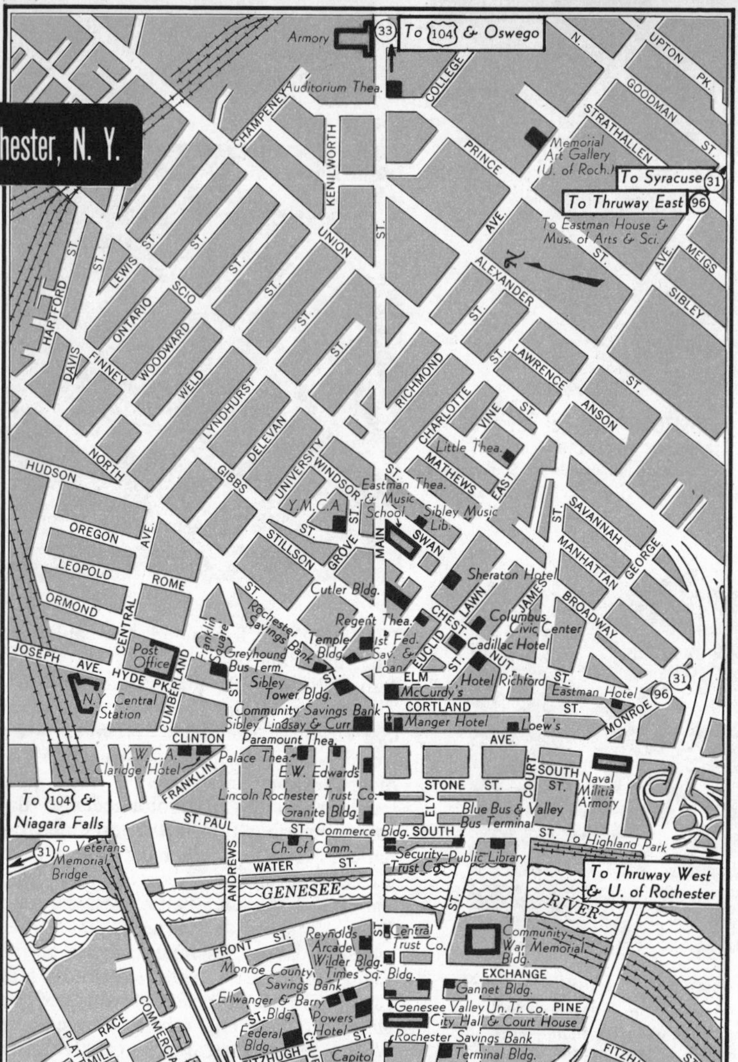

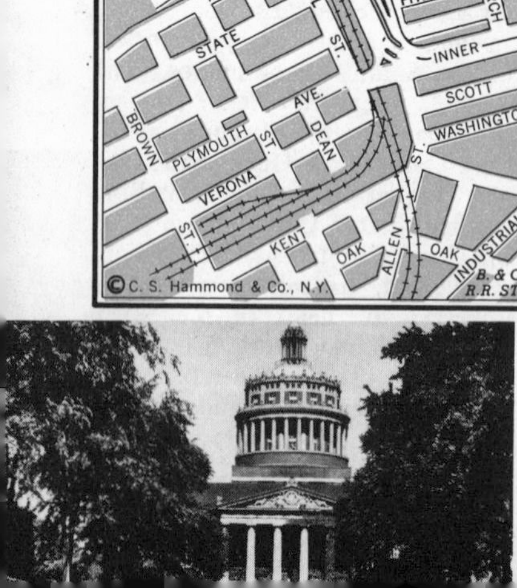

UNIVERSITY OF ROCHESTER is among the most heavily endowed colleges of America. It includes not only a College of Arts and Sciences but also a School of Medicine and Dentistry and the renowned Eastman School of Music. Pictured is the University's Library on the River Campus

GENESEE RIVER bisects the heart of Rochester and plunges in a shower of foaming white water over three immense falls. In pioneer times this water power led to the founding of the town where wheat from the rich farms of the valley was ground into flour

ROCHESTER. Through the heart of Rochester flows the Genesee River, dropping 261 feet in three cataracts to meet Lake Ontario. To the south, the river's wide banks are arched by trees and form the green margins of some of the city's lovely parks. Farther north, the river's banks are bordered by the dull-red brick walls of industrial plants whose specialized products have made Rochester's name famous throughout the country. Here are the world's largest film and camera plants; here are leading manufacturers of optical goods, dental equipment, thermometers, check-writers and glass-lined steel containers. Once the Genesee River provided power for mills that gave Rochester the name "Flour City." Later, when the flour-milling industry moved westward and was succeeded in importance by the nursery business, Rochester still retained the title of "Flower City" with only a slight change in the former spelling. Highland Park, part of which was given to the city by Ellwanger and Barry, early Rochester nurserymen, displays over 400 varieties of lilacs during the annual Lilac Festival in May. The park also contains some 370 varieties of evergreens. With the establishment of the Eastman School of Music, Rochester acquired renown as a center of music and culture. The Sibley Musical Library, opened in 1938, is devoted exclusively to music.

ROCHESTER, the third largest city in New York State, is an important industrial center. Pictured is one of the city's big petroleum processing plants

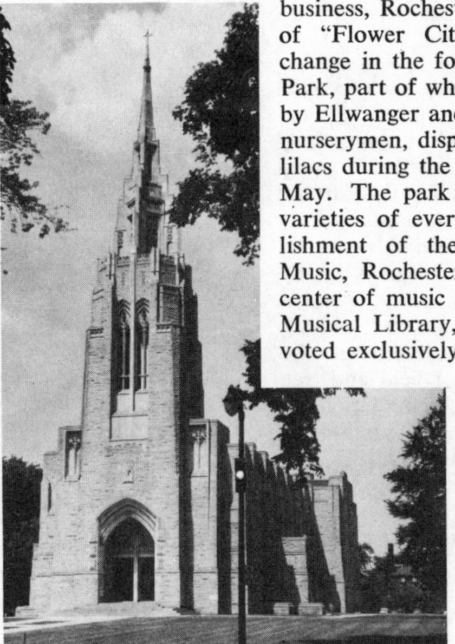

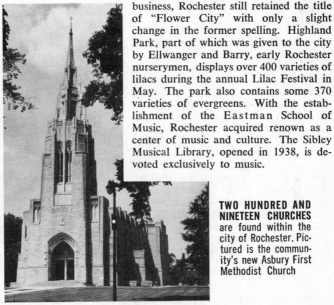

TWO HUNDRED AND NINETEEN CHURCHES are found within the city of Rochester. Pictured is the community's new Asbury First Methodist Church

Photos: N.Y. State Dept. of Commerce, Div. Public Information, City of Rochester

GEORGE EASTMAN HOUSE, a world famous photographic museum, is devoted to the history of photography and offers excellent displays and demonstrations of photographic equipment and processes

CALIFORNIA STATE CAPITOL BUILDING is thought by many to be America's outstanding state structure. At night, the brilliantly lighted dome may be seen for miles and has become a beautiful "trademark" for Sacramento

STATE GOVERNMENT BUILDING is one of several large state office buildings located around the Capitol of California. "Bring me men to match my mountains," is the inscription inscribed across its facade

SACRAMENTO. Sacramento stands amid a lush setting of orchards, vineyards and fruitful fields whose immensely fertile soil makes this northern sweep of the Great Central Valley California's richest agricultural region. Protected on the east by the snow-covered peaks of the Sierra Nevada and on the west by the Coastal Ranges, the valley is noted for its mild equable climate and its long growing season where throughout the year there is harvesting of field and tree crops. A center for the shipping of fresh fruits and vegetables, Sacramento is also the home of tremendous canning and food processing industries. Here, at the junction of the American and Sacramento Rivers, Captain John Sutter established his fort on a land grant from the Mexican government. Famed for its prosperity, its warm hospitality, Sutter's Fort was the largest trading post in California when in 1848, John Marshall found gold in the millrace of Sutter's sawmill. News of the discovery brought thousands of gold-seekers pouring into the once peaceful valley. In 1854, Sacramento, a raw little mining town which had mushroomed upon Sutter's claim, became the capital of California. Today Sacramento cherishes its many mementos of the past including a restoration of Sutter's Fort and the Pony Express Museum where are preserved relics of the days when the town served as western terminus for this pioneer mail route.

SUTTER'S FORT, founded more than a century ago, stands in a park in the heart of Sacramento. Built of adobe bricks, the fort is now a museum of historic relics

Photos: Sacramento Chamber of Commerce

SHOPPING CENTERS in the outlying districts of Sacramento blend into the familiar suburban living. Pictured is one of the popular rustic-style centers which contains 75 shops of all types

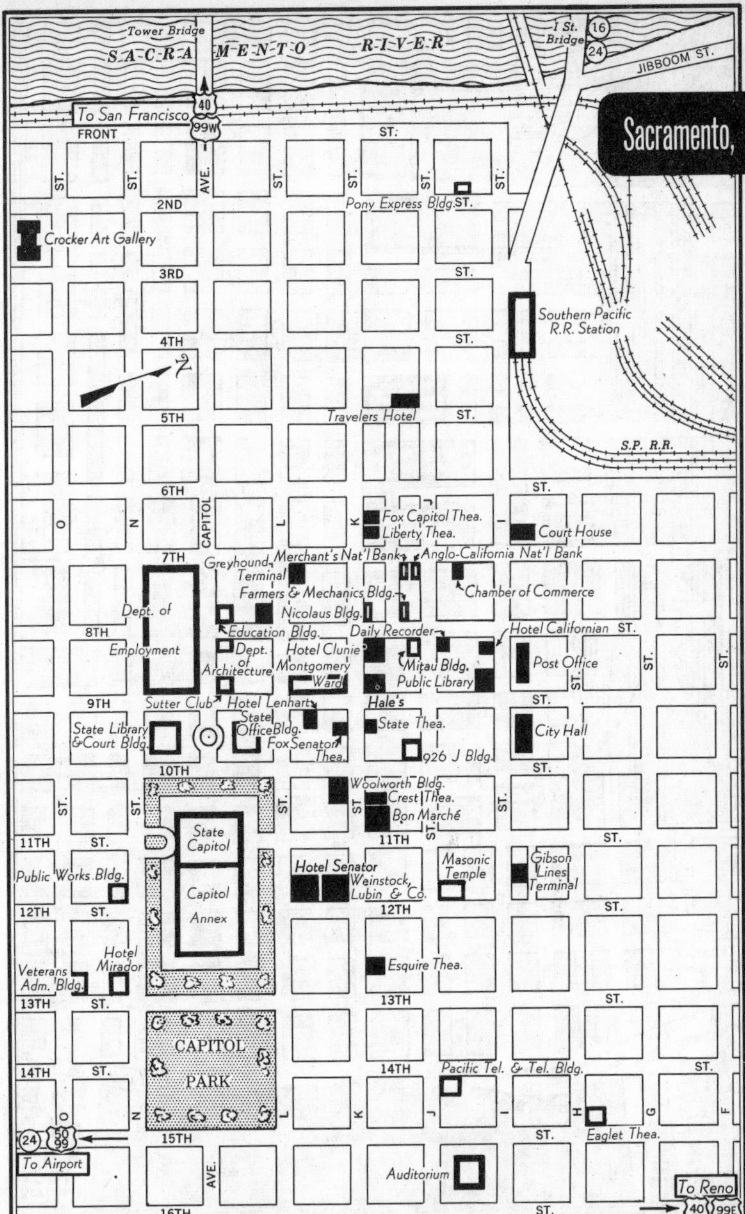

Sacramento, Cal.

Tower Bridge
SACRAMENTO RIVER
I St. Bridge
16
24
JIBBOOM ST.
To San Francisco
40
99W
FRONT ST.
2ND ST.
Pony Express Bldg.
Crocker Art Gallery
3RD ST.
Southern Pacific R.R. Station
4TH ST.
5TH ST.
Travelers Hotel
S.P. R.R.
6TH ST.
O ST.
N ST.
CAPITOL AVE.
L ST.
K ST.
J ST.
I ST.
H ST.
G ST.
F ST.
Fox Capitol Thea.
Liberty Thea.
Court House
7TH ST.
Greyhound Terminal
Merchant's Nat'l Bank
Anglo-California Nat'l Bank
Farmers & Mechanics Bldg.
Chamber of Commerce
Dept. of Employment
Nicolaus Bldg.
Education Bldg.
Daily Recorder
Hotel Californian
8TH ST.
Dept. of Architecture
Hotel Clunie
Montgomery Ward
Mitau Bldg.
Public Library
Post Office
9TH ST.
Sutter Club
Hotel Lenhart
Hale's
State Library & Court Bldg.
State Office Bldg.
Fox Senator Thea.
State Thea.
926 J Bldg.
City Hall
10TH ST.
Woolworth Bldg.
Crest Thea.
Bon Marché
State Capitol
Capitol Annex
11TH ST.
Public Works Bldg.
Hotel Senator
Weinstock, Lubin & Co.
Masonic Temple
Gibson Lines Terminal
12TH ST.
Hotel Mirador
Veterans Adm. Bldg.
Esquire Thea.
13TH ST.
CAPITOL PARK
14TH ST.
Pacific Tel. & Tel. Bldg.
Eaglet Thea.
15TH ST.
24
50
99
To Airport
Auditorium
16TH ST.
To Reno
40
99E
To Marysville
Y.W.C.A.
17TH ST.
50
16
To Sutter's Fort
TO W. PAC. R.R. STA.

90% OF THE RICE produced in California is processed near Sacramento. This huge rice plant is located along the Sacramento River. Bulk rice is shipped by barge to San Francisco where it is loaded into the hulls of Asia-bound ships

St. Louis, Mo.

To Jefferson 40 City
To St. Charles and Airport
To Forest Park
To St.L. U. & Wash. U.
Union Station • All Trains
Aloe Plaza
Claridge Hotel
20th
19th
18th ST.
17th
16th
15th
14th ST.
13th
12th ST.
11th ST.
10th
9th
8th
7th ST.
6th
4th ST.
2nd
1st
ST.
DELMAR
Post Office
OLIVE
ST. CHARLES
WASHINGTON
LUCAS
BLVD.
POPLAR
SPRUCE
BELMONT
CLARK
MARKET
CHESTNUT
PINE
LOCUST
Y.M.C.A.
Campbell House
Warwick Hotel
Y.W.C.A.
Municipal Auditorium
Municipal Courts
Soldiers Memorial
Public Library
Lucas Garden
Christ Church Cathedral
Police Hdqs.
Area Support Center
City Hall
Missouri Pacific Bldg.
Shell Bldg.
Sheraton-Jefferson Hotel
TO ALTON
30
66
67
TO SPRINGFIELD
Union Electric Co.
Federal Bldg.
Civil Courts Bldg.
St. Louis Post Dispatch & Radio Sta. KSD
Illinois Terminal R.R.
WALNUT
Bell Tel. Bldg.
Laclede Gas Lt. Co.
S. G. Adams
Scruggs-Vandervoort-Barney
AVE.
Western Union
Frisco Bldg.
Bd. of Educ. Bldg.
Bank of St. Louis
Orpheum Theater
Lennox Hotel
Paul Brown Bldg.
Arcade Bldg.
Customs House
Statler Hotel
Mayfair Hotel
Security Natl. Bank
Mark Twain Hotel
Mutual Bk. & Tr. Co.
Mercantile Trust Co.
Loew's Theater
To Anheuser-Busch Brewery
Ambassador Theater
CERRE ST.
Famous Barr & Ry. Exch. Bldg.
Stix, Baer & Fuller
Boyd's
York Hotel
First Natl. Bank
Mercantile Library
Union Market & Bus Depot
Federal Land Bank
Ch. of Com. Bldg.
BROADWAY
Commerce Bldg. & Ch. of Com.
Boatmen's Bank Bldg.
To Poplar Bluff
VALENTINE
Old Court House
Veterans Adm. Bldg.
Federal Reserve Bank
Missouri Athletic Club
Merchants La Clede Bldg.
Skinner Kennedy
VINE
ELM
Pierce Bldg.
JEFFERSON
CEDAR ST.
MEMORIAL HIGHWAY
MARK TWAIN EXPRESSWAY
Old Cathedral
PLUM
Jefferson National Expansion Memorial
Automobile Parking
EADS BRIDGE (TOLL)
40
50
Old Rock House
Streckfus Lines Dock - Excursion Boats
Mississippi River
To East St. Louis

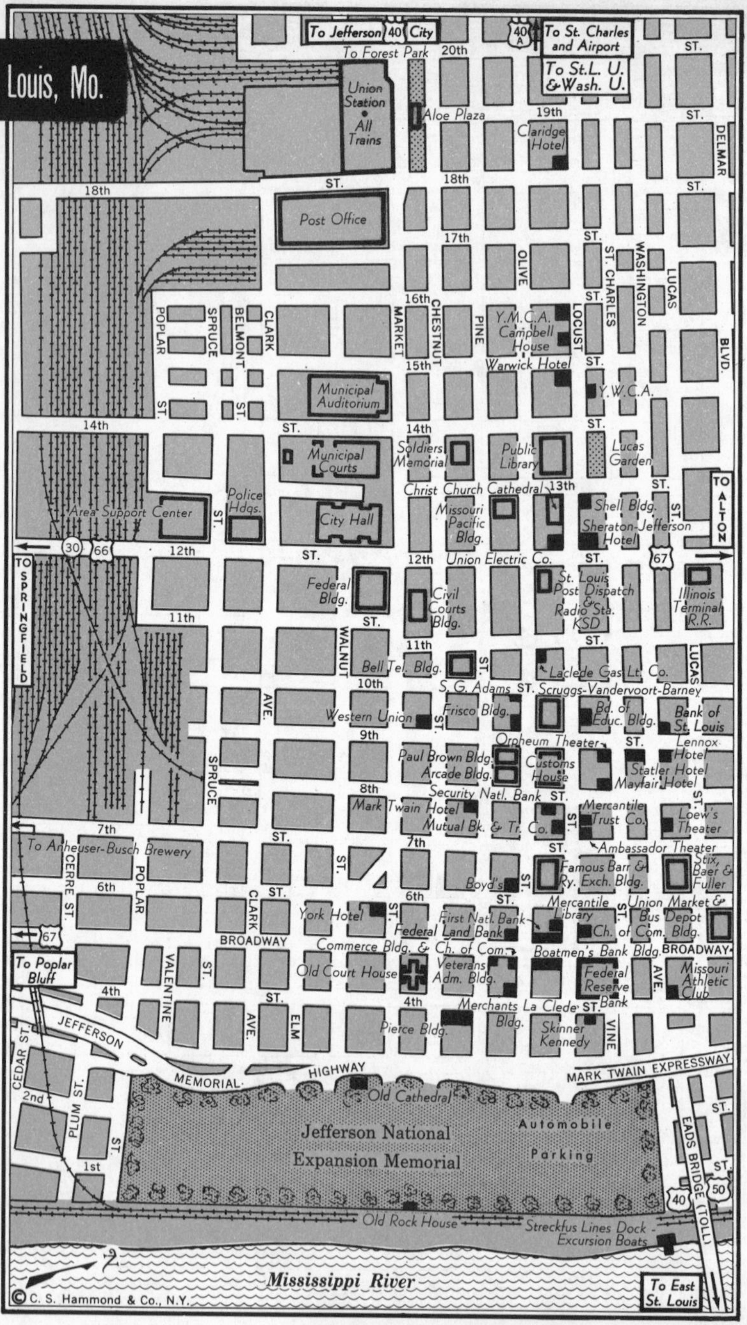

TRAINED ELEPHANTS put on regular shows at the famed Forest Park Zoological Gardens. Besides elephants, the zoo has an extensive collection of birds and other animals

JEWEL BOX in Forest Park faces a series of lily pools. This $60,000 conservatory with its seasonal display of flowers and plants has been called a "cathedral of waterfalls and flowers"

CARL MILLES FOUNTAIN GROUP in Aloe Plaza has 14 bronze figures symbolizing the meeting of the Mississippi and Missouri. In the background is the 230-foot tower of Union Station

ST. LOUIS. There is a pleasant lilt to the name of "St. Louis, Missouri," and in it a town of a romantic and memorable past asserts itself. Founded by a New Orleans merchant, Pierre Laclède, and named after Saint Louis, holy crusader-king of France, St. Louis soon left its modest beginnings behind and became the queen of the river, holding jealously on to its role as the ruler of traffic up and down the broad Mississippi. When the Lewis and Clark expedition, which set out from here, opened a route to the Pacific, St. Louis became gateway of migration. While encouraging settlements all around it, the town opposed the construction of railroad bridges across the Mississippi (losing the case in a suit regarding the Rock Island Bridge, in which the attorney for the railroad was Abraham Lincoln). But bridges were built, the railroad took over, and the traffic on the river lost some of its importance. This development, instead of lessening the city's energies, gave them a broader field. Today, St. Louis is a leading industrial metropolis and a center of a liberal, cosmopolitan culture. There is art in St. Louis, the opera has an excellent standing, and the zoological garden deserves notice. In honoring Thomas Jefferson in a new development on the site of the original settlement, the city not only honors the man who concluded the Louisiana Purchase (the actual transfer of the northern portion of the Purchase took place in St. Louis in 1804) and the organizer of the Lewis and Clark expedition, but his democratic spirit as well.

Photos: Anheuser-Busch, Massie-Missouri Resources Division

LUCAS GARDEN is a green oasis sunk amid interesting downtown structures. At extreme right is Central Public Library next to it is Christ Church Cathedral

BREW HOUSE of the Anheuser-Busch Brewery has been a well-known St. Louis landmark for many years. It is headquarters for the country's largest beer producer. Free tours are conducted through the brewery daily

ST. PAUL. Twin city to Minneapolis, St. Paul, capital of Minnesota, is actually the older of the two. Like most Western cities, the first tiny settlement grew up in the early nineteenth century around a trading post, but despite this and her later fame as the trading nucleus of the Northwest, she is a conservative city, mellow and dignified like the older Eastern cities rather than those of the younger West. Even her physical aspect is a reminder of this traditionalism, for her hilly terrain has created narrow, concentrated streets instead of broad boulevards. In one respect, though, she has abandoned her decorous mien: Since the time when the first family built their home here along the Mississippi, St. Paul has been a pioneer in modern education and culture. Symbol of this leadership is the lofty City Hall and Ramsey County Courthouse and its dramatic, three-story Memorial Hall, with its light-marble floor, blue-marble (almost black) walls and gold mirror ceiling. At one end of the striking concourse stands a majestic tribute to the Indian, the famous forty-four-foot-high, white, solid-onyx statue called the "Indian God of Peace," considered Carl Milles' most successful expression in stone.

STATE CAPITOL, a marble-domed renaissance design by Cass Gilbert, a St. Paul native son, achieves a harmony of detail rarely found in public buildings. Within are notable murals by Edward Simmons

SIBLEY HOUSE in suburban Mendota was built of native stone in 1835 as the home of the state's first governor, General Henry Sibley. This was the first stone house in Minnesota

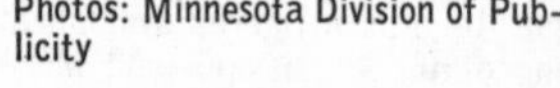

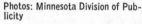

Photos: Minnesota Division of Publicity

SKYLINE VIEW shows how the city's buildings cluster together, clinging tenaciously to her hills, as the closely knit community clings to its cherished traditions. St. Paul has always made much of her attractive shoreline

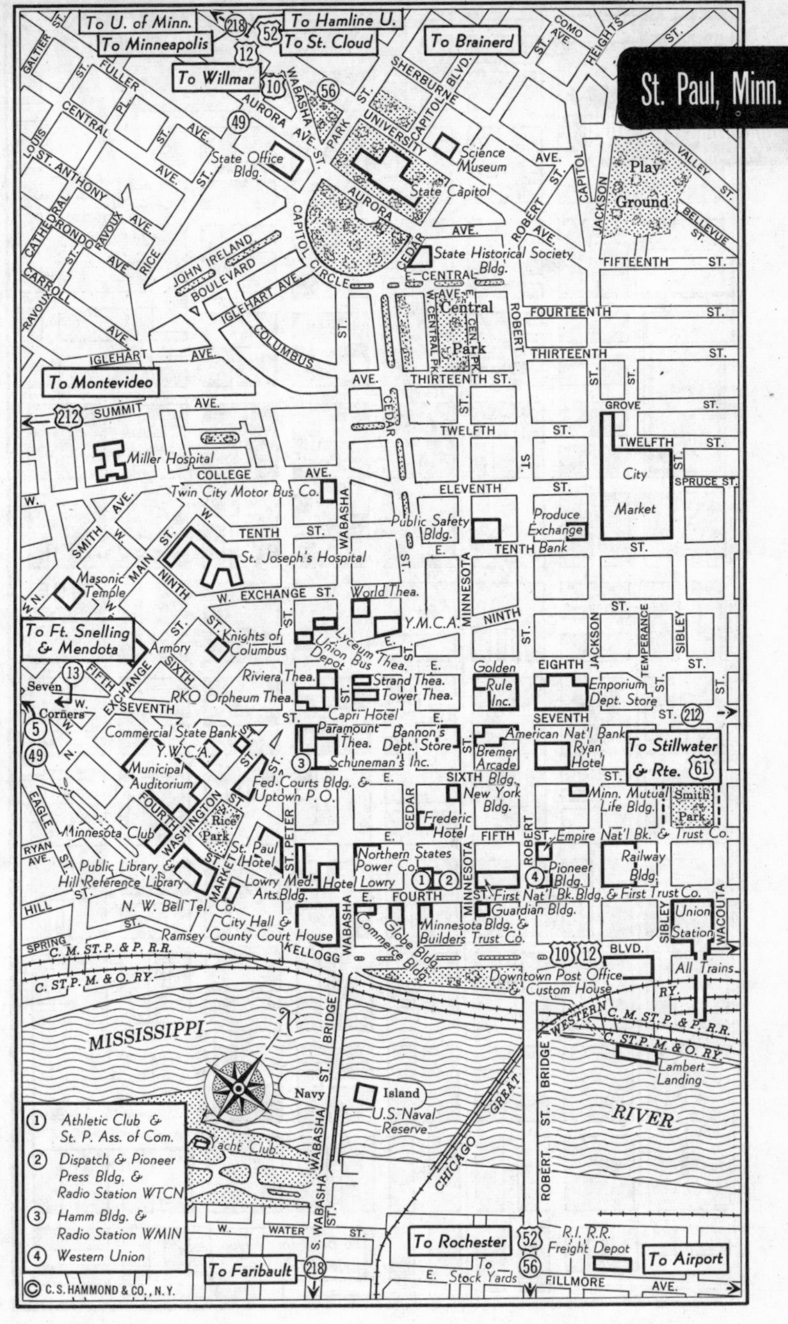

SOUTH ST. PAUL STOCKYARDS is the second largest livestock center in the United States. Tours through individual plants may be arranged

Salt Lake City, Utah

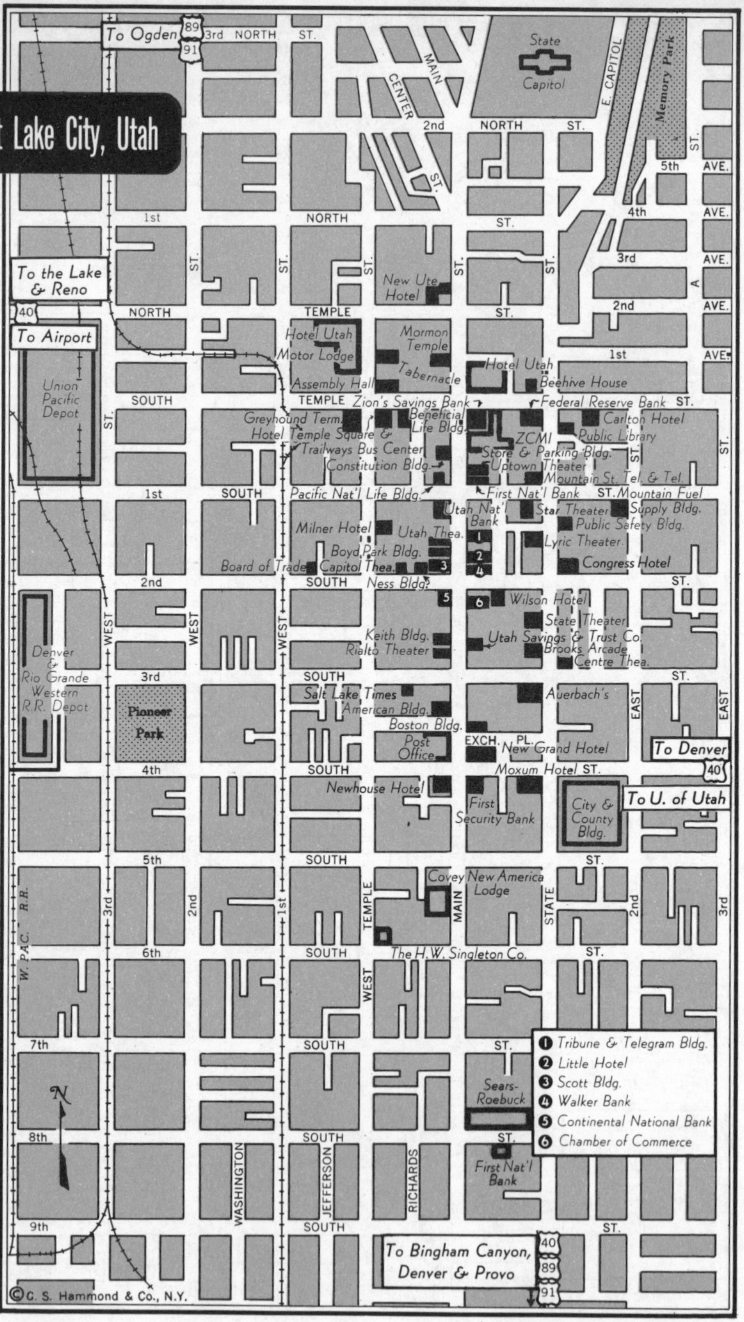

1. Tribune & Telegram Bldg.
2. Little Hotel
3. Scott Bldg.
4. Walker Bank
5. Continental National Bank
6. Chamber of Commerce

SWIMMERS FLOAT like corks on the more than 2,000 square miles of salt water in the Great Salt Lake, the world's great inland sea, where for each 4 gallons of water 1 gallon salt is held in solution

SALT LAKE CITY. When Brigham Young looked across the parched Salt Lake Valley in 1847 and exclaimed in those immortal words, "This is the place," his vision must have carried in its sweep all the valleys and mountains that his people later were to colonize and possess. Since then, Salt Lake City has remained the hub of western colonization and culture in the intermountain region. Salt Lake City is proud of her prestige as a religious center and international headquarters of the Church of Jesus Christ of Latter-Day Saints. In fact, such Mormon monuments as gracious Beehive House, official residence of the church president from the great leader's time until the present century, are among the city's most popular visiting places. She also is universally recognized as a music center, with important contributions by the Tabernacle Choir and organists, as well as by the Utah Symphony Orchestra. With fascinating, mysterious Great Salt Lake to the west, the towering peaks of the Wasatch Range to the east and south and the vast, productive valley stretching for hundreds of miles at her feet, Salt Lake City is not only a city of beauty, she is a city whose future, because of the faith and industry of her residents, will not be denied.

TEMPLE SQUARE, focal point of the entire city, contains the exclusive, six-spired Salt Lake Temple, the famous, turtle-shaped Tabernacle, with its remarkable acoustic properties, and the semi-Gothic Assembly Hall on the left

UTAH STATE CAPITOL, recognized as one of the finest of its kind in the United States, contains notable murals, paintings and sculpture and invaluable decorations in the Gold Room or Governor's Reception Room

Photos: Hal Rumel for Utah Tourist & Publicity Council

EVERY STREET and every building were carefully planned in this unique pioneer city. The basic plan of 10-acre blocks separated by streets 132 feet wide was decided upon within days after the initial company of Mormon emigrants entered the valley

LOOPING, SWIRLING pattern of the cuts at North America's largest open-pit copper mine in nearby Bingham Canyon. Salt Lake City is the mining center of the West

SAN ANTONIO. The flags of Spain, France, Mexico, the Republic of Texas, the Confederate States of America and the United States of America have, at various times, flown over the city of San Antonio. The tall skyscrapers which rise above the modern city spring from ground where some of the most stirring pages of our Southwestern history were written. In the heart of downtown San Antonio, the immortal Alamo, now a national shrine, recalls the gallant bravery and sacrifice of a band of Texas patriots. Hopelessly outnumbered by Mexican forces, they held their tiny makeshift fort for fourteen days, ultimately giving their lives rather than surrender their ideals of freedom. San Antonio, surrounded by numerous historical sites and with its Old World charm, its quaint customs and colorful fiestas, is among our country's most picturesque cities. The time-mellowed adobe walls, the secluded patios of La Villita (a group of San Antonio's earliest homes), have witnessed the transformation of the mission settlement into a modern metropolis. To the south, the ancient missions—Concepción, San Jose, Espada, Capistrano—are preserved today as remnants of Spanish Colonialism. From its early days as capital of the province of Tejas, San Antonio has been an important military establishment.

SPANISH GOVERNORS' PALACE, an old adobe building, was once used as an office and residence by the Spanish Governors of Texas. A wishing well is found inside the inner patio.

SAN JOSE DE AGUAYO is one of the old missions where by patience and trying toil, Franciscans succeeded in teaching the Indians reading, writing, sanitation, art, music and the crafts of those early days

THE ALAMO was originally the old chapel of Mission San Antonio de Valero, founded in 1718. Among the heroes who died here in the war for Texas Independence were James Bowie, James Bonham and Davy Crockett.

SAN ANTONIO RIVER winds its way through the heart of the city. The river's natural beauty is enhanced by winding walks along its grassy banks.

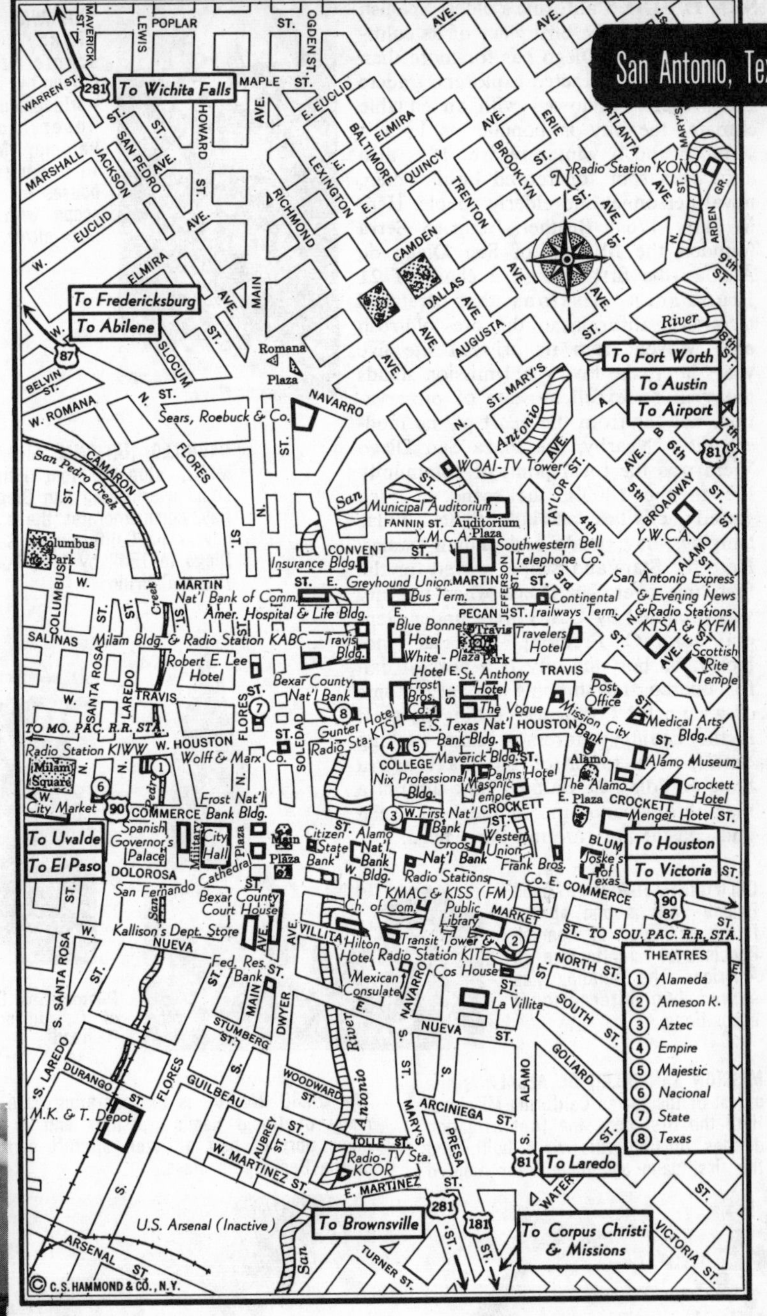

SAN ANTONIO'S SKYLINE is backed by miles of homes set upon the hillsides which stretch to the north, east and west along a lovely river valley

Photos: Texas Highway Depart-mentment, San Antonio Chamber of Commerce

SAN DIEGO. California's oldest Spanish settlement and the birthplace of its colorful history, San Diego has for more than four centuries attracted explorers, traders and settlers. Endowed with an equable climate, the city is popular as both a summer and a winter resort. It is also a favored spot for retired businessmen, naval personnel and elderly people. Here in July, 1769, Brother Junípero Serra founded the Mission of San Diego de Alcalá—the first link in a chain of 21 Franciscan missions that stretched through California in the pre-gold-rush era. Moved from its original site five years later, the lovely old mission stands today in an excellent state of preservation, not far from the heart of the modern city. Nearby, the Plaza San Diego Viejo was the focal point of community life in the 1800's, the scene of such varied activities as bull fights, Judas hangings, law trials and Indian games. Here the Stars and Stripes waved for the first time over San Diego when the city was occupied by U.S. Forces under General John C. Frémont. With its landlocked harbor, the city is a port of call for intercoastal shipping and also home of a colorful Portuguese fishing fleet. It is the country's foremost tuna packing center. The tower of the California State Building in Balboa Park affords a magnificent panorama of the bay, ocean and coastal area around San Diego.

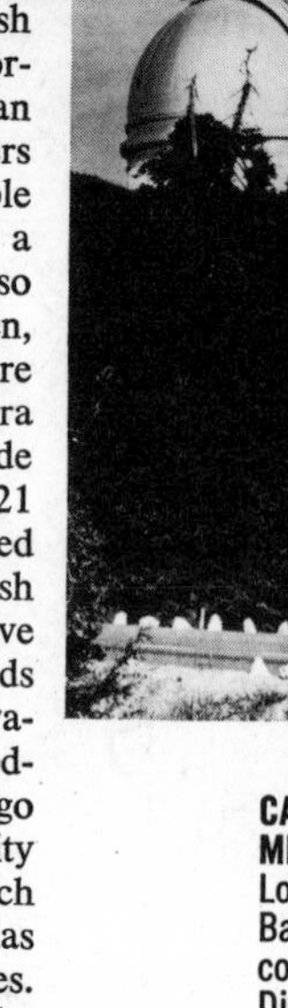

"HIGHWAY OF THE STARS," through scenic San Diego County, leads to world-famous Palomar Observatory atop Palomar Mountain. The huge dome houses the Hale telescope with its 200-inch mirror.

CABRILLO NATIONAL MONUMENT, atop 400-foot Point Loma overlooking San Diego Bay, commemorates the discovery of California at San Diego in 1542 by Juan Rodriguez Cabrillo

CALIFORNIA TOWER in famed Balboa Park is one of the finest examples of Spanish Renaissance architecture in America. The building has served two international expositions.

Photos: San Diego C. of C., Union Pacific Railroad

MISSION SAN DIEGO DE ALCALÁ is the oldest of the famed California Missions. Here the first dam, the first irrigation ditches in California were built, and the first palm and olive trees planted

SAN DIEGO HARBOR is the operating base for many of Uncle Sam's warships and is the home port of half a dozen aircraft carriers of the Bennington class.

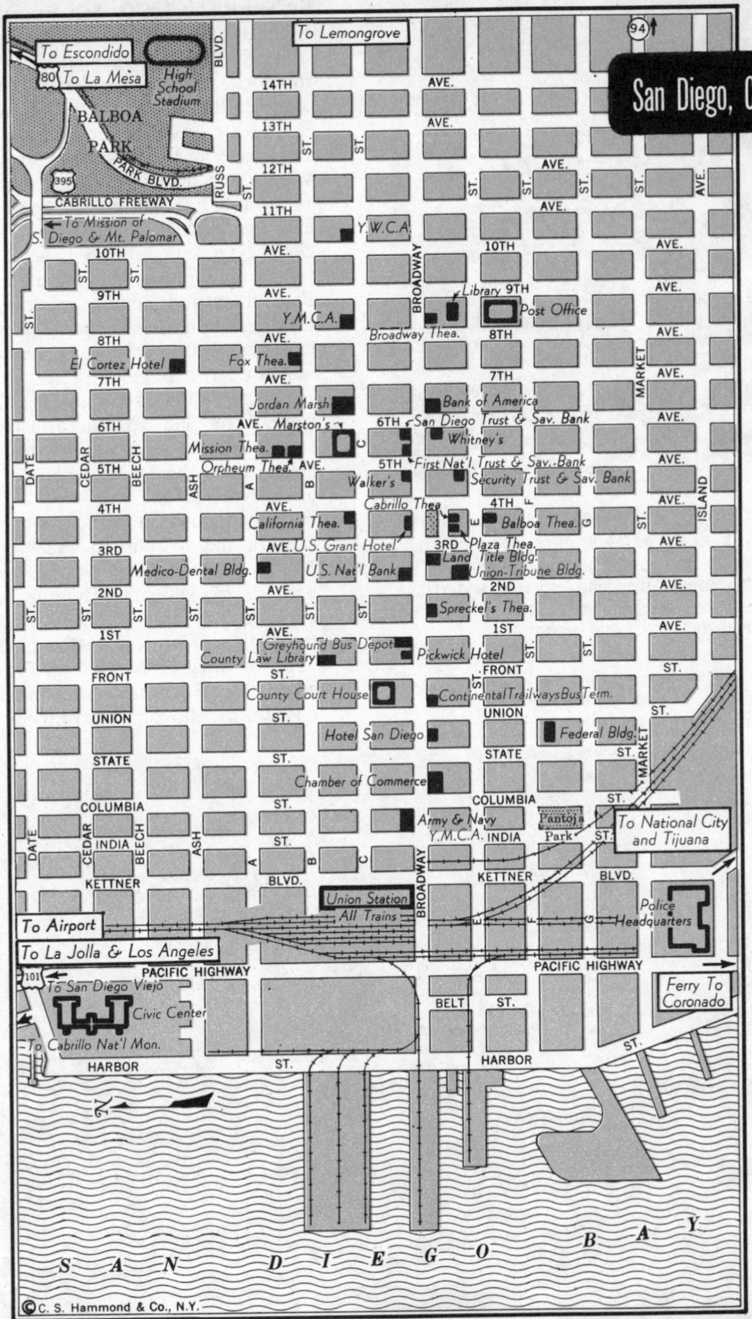

LA JOLLA (pronounced Lah Hoy'-yah), a suburb of San Diego, lies 14 miles north of the city. Its rocky coast and sheltered beaches attract throngs during the summer season.

FISHERMAN'S WHARF, with its wonderful confusion of net menders and swaying blue, white and green boats, is a part of the Embarcadero, the long, curving waterfront, frequented by London, Stevenson, Twain, Kyne, Forester and other writers

SAN FRANCISCO. San Francisco's exhilarating individuality is so well-known as to be almost legendary. Haunted by memories of this wonderful city, people all over the United States harbor intense desires to return permanently to San Francisco and never tire of extolling her virtues to those unfortunates who have never felt her allure. A city of supreme and exotic beauty despite her fogs, her cool, even temperature is a continually refreshing source of pleasure. Her delightful setting amidst sparkling waters and high hills is inspiring. And the cable car, jaunty little relic of bygone days and still a cherished mode of travel over the peaks and dips of the steep hills, is the symbol of San Francisco. Coit Tower stands like a sentinel on storied Telegraph Hill, the lookout station of early days. And no one would dream of leaving San Francisco without sipping cocktails in the twilight at the "top of the Mark" — the Hotel Mark Hopkins — with its magnificent fifty-mile panorama of sparkling cities, mighty bridges and the Golden Gateway to the blue Pacific. Truly a storybook city, San Francisco is colorful and cosmopolitan, with an international flavor contributed by her

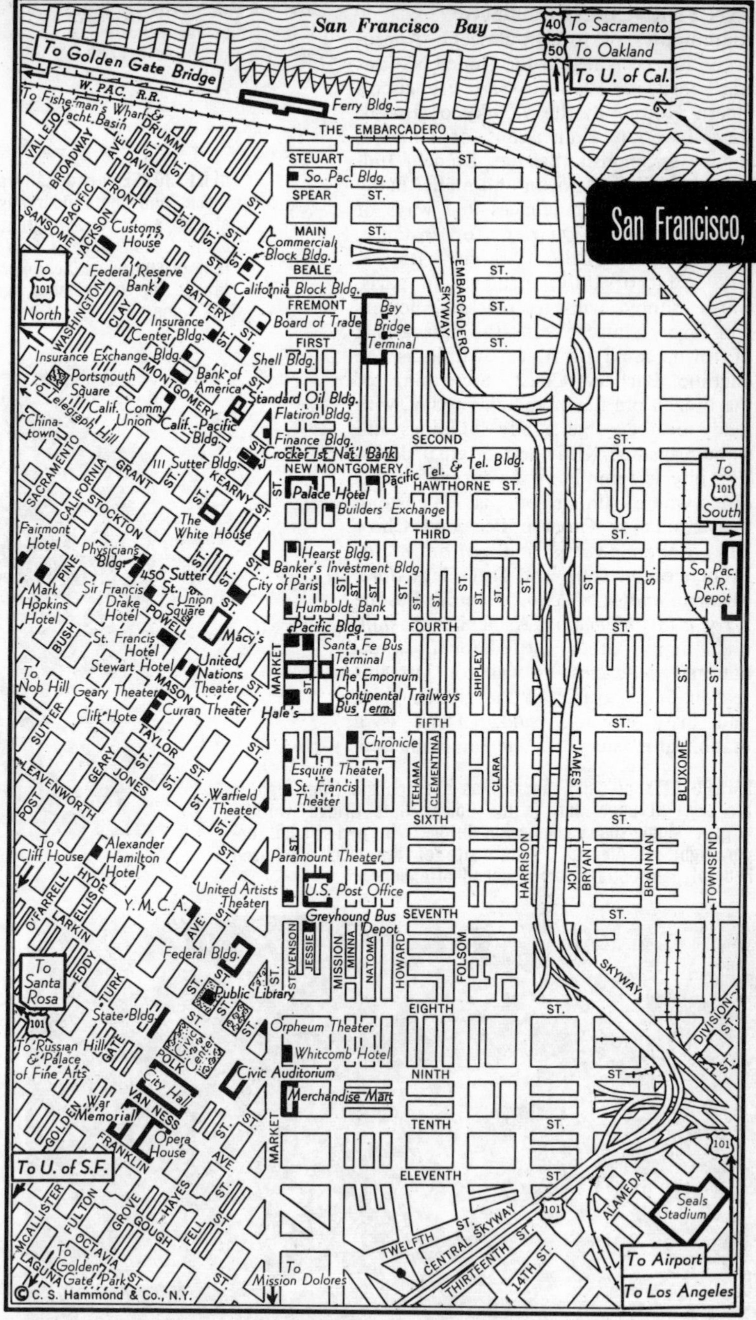

SAN FRANCISCO-OAKLAND BAY BRIDGE is the largest in the world, being 8¼ miles long. This view is toward San Francisco from Yerba Buena. At the east end is Oakland, including Lake Merritt, a wildfowl refuge in the heart of the city, and First & Last Chance Saloon, favorite hangout of Jack London

Photos: San Francisco Chamber of Commerce, Californians Inc.

SAN FRANCISCO Continued

communities of foreign descent. Appropriate indeed is it that the United Nations was born in 1945 in San Francisco's Opera House. In the vicinity of Broadway live San Franciscans of Chinese, Japanese, Spanish, Basque, French, Italian, Hawaiian, Mexican and many, many other ancestries, languages and ways of life. The Latin Quarter for instance, near Telegraph Hill, is a city-within-a-city, a bit of Italy, medieval in parts, warm, sunny, with its markets, flowers and lovely churches. It's the brassy part of town, some of it, for within is the onetime Barbary Coast. Something of the brazen old flavor remains today, with many of the same gaudy buildings still standing, some with their original decor. The city is famous as a gourmet's paradise, where dining out is a custom. Feasters enjoy Chinese Pea Pod Chow Yuk, Italian *pastas* and *cappuccino,* French onion soup and frogs legs *doré,* Mexican *chiles rellenos,* Spanish-Basque *arroz á la Valenciana,* Armenian shashlik and many other little-known, international delicacies. It was for just this reason that Caruso, of the golden voice and lusty appetite, said, "There is a diabolical mystery to your San Francisco.

CLIFF HOUSE, historically a popular resort and the rendezvous of theatrical and literary great, stands along Ocean Beach. Four hundred feet offshore are Seal Rocks, habitat of the polygamous, gregarious sea lions

FABLED CITY of San Francisco as she appears from high in the sky. At upper left is the Golden Gate Bridge, world's largest single-span suspension bridge. In mid-stream, upper right, is Alcatraz Island, site of the much-publicized Federal penitentiary for hardened offenders

ADOBE MISSION DOLORES was founded in 1776 as one of the great California chain of missions. The wooden beams were tied with leather thongs and the Indians painted the interior walls with bright vegetable colors. In the high-walled graveyard are buried many of the famous dead of the early days

BOILING CRAB CAULDRONS are a familiar sight at Fisherman's Wharf. At one of the famous seafood restaurants, diners may watch the fishermen bring their dinners in from the sea, with an aromatic backdrop of coffee, spices and hemp

THE PRESIDENT CLEVELAND is welcomed by a San Francisco fireboat as the ship steams through the Golden Gate to berth in the fabulous port. Picture was taken from the Golden Gate Bridge

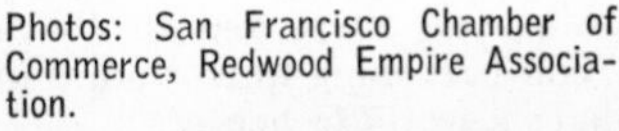
Photos: San Francisco Chamber of Commerce, Redwood Empire Association.

PALACE OF FINE ARTS, a neo-classic structure of brown stucco, stands in majestic but time-worn beauty on the banks of a lazy lagoon, providing inspiration for modern San Franciscan artists

BUFFALO add a strange touch to this peaceful pastoral scene in large Golden Gate Park, which also includes Steinhart Aquarium, De Young Museum, lovely Japanese Tea Garden, Kezar Stadium, giant Dutch windmills and miles of trails and brilliant flower beds

SAN FRANCISCO Continued

Why isn't everyone fat?" And no one has ever been able to answer. Her cosmopolitan character is mirrored, too, in her wealth of cultural activity. Stage-struck San Francisco has recently been undergoing a notable renaissance of the theater, outbidding all other cities, except New York, in dramatic art. In the field of music, she has long been outstanding, with the triumphant San Francisco Opera Company, the Pacific Opera Company, the Cosmopolitan Opera Company, the renowned San Francisco Symphony and her unique summer musical repertoire. Most notable of all, perhaps, is the magnetic attraction she has long held for writers ever since Bret Harte, Jack London and Robert Louis Stevenson reveled in her virile, invigorating atmosphere. Romance? It's everywhere, in this "most exciting city known to man," as mystery writer Leslie Ford has described it. Romance comes in the Golden Gate with ships and trade winds, climbs Nob and Russian Hills and Twin Peaks, lives in the breathtaking views, prowls little Chinatown alleys and strolls the waterfront, beckoning to adventure in the city that's a world in herself.

COLORFUL CALIFORNIA STREET CABLE CAR ascends steep Nob Hill in earlier days the center of elegant living, with sumptuous homes of railroad and mining millionaires, and now the location of fine hotels

GRANT AVENUE in famed Chinatown, the largest Chinese settlement outside the Orient. No one should miss old St. Mary's Church built of bricks brought around the Horn; Waverly Place, "little street of the big tongs," and one of the joss houses, like wondrous Tin How Temple, where Buddha, Tao and Confucius are venerated

YACHT HARBOR, just inside the Golden Gate, gleams with blue water and shining white craft of weekend sailors. This Sunday showplace is a veritable fairyland during Yuletime, when Christmas lights are strung throughout the rigging of the graceful craft

Photos: San Francisco Chamber of Commerce, Redwood Empire Association.

Seattle, Wash.

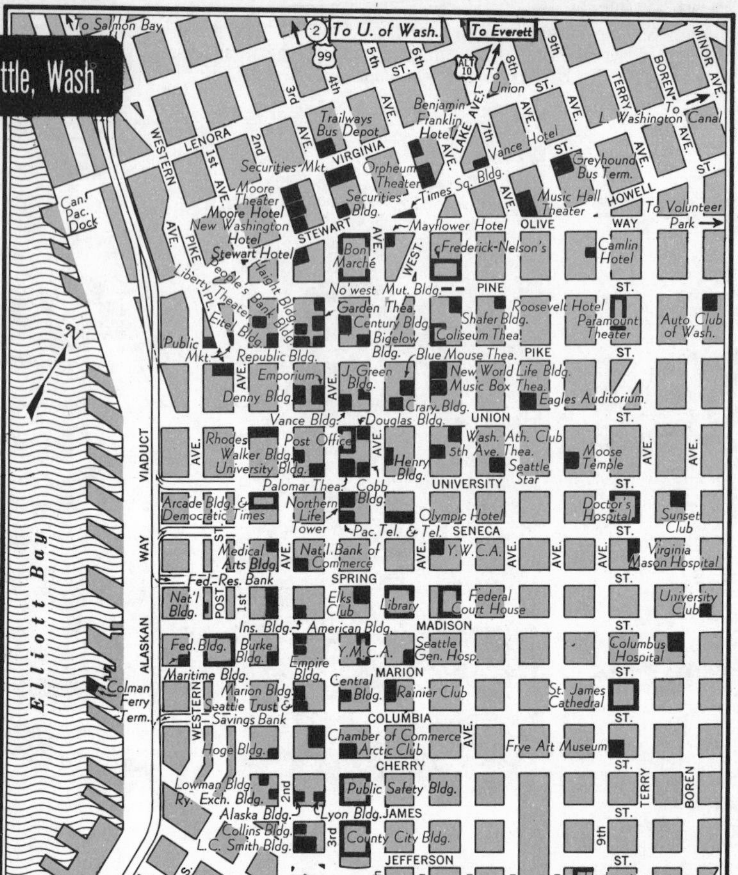

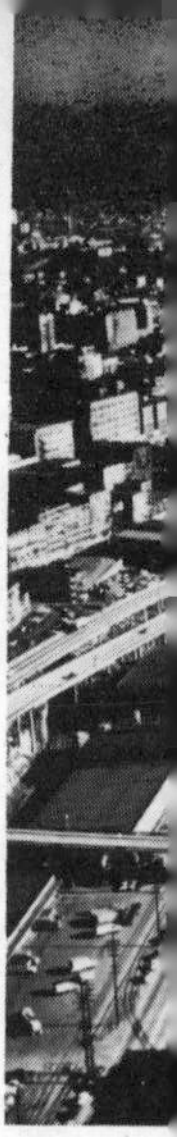

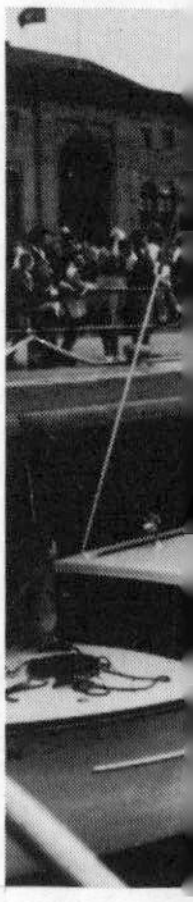

To Salmon Bay
To U. of Wash.
To Everett
To Union L.
To L. Washington Canal
To Volunteer Park
Elliott Bay
Can. Pac. Dock
Trailways Bus Depot
Benjamin Franklin Hotel
Vance Hotel
Greyhound Bus Term.
Securities Mkt.
Orpheum Theater
Times Sq. Bldg.
Moore Theater
Moore Hotel
Securities Bldg.
Music Hall Theater
New Washington Hotel
Mayflower Hotel
Stewart Hotel
Bon Marché
Frederick-Nelson's
Camlin Hotel
People's Bank Bldg.
Haight Bldg.
Liberty Theater
Eitel Bldg.
No'west Mut. Bldg.
Garden Thea.
Century Bldg.
Bigelow Bldg.
Roosevelt Hotel
Shafer Bldg.
Coliseum Thea.
Paramount Theater
Auto Club of Wash.
Public Mkt.
Republic Bldg.
Blue Mouse Thea.
Emporium
J. Green Bldg.
New World Life Bldg.
Music Box Thea.
Denny Bldg.
Crary Bldg.
Eagles Auditorium
Vance Bldg.
Douglas Bldg.
Rhodes
Post Office
Walker Bldg.
University Bldg.
Wash. Ath. Club
5th Ave. Thea.
Henry Bldg.
Seattle Star
Moose Temple
Palomar Thea.
Cobb Bldg.
Arcade Bldg. & Democratic Times
Northern Life Tower
Pac. Tel. & Tel.
Olympic Hotel
Doctor's Hospital
Sunset Club
Medical Arts Bldg.
Nat'l. Bank of Commerce
Y.W.C.A.
Virginia Mason Hospital
Fed. Res. Bank
Nat'l Bldg.
Elks Club
Library
Federal Court House
University Club
Ins. Bldg.
American Bldg.
Fed. Bldg.
Burke Bldg.
Y.M.C.A.
Seattle Gen. Hosp.
Columbus Hospital
Empire Bldg.
Maritime Bldg.
Central Bldg.
Colman Ferry Term.
Marion Bldg.
Seattle Trust & Savings Bank
Rainier Club
St. James Cathedral
Chamber of Commerce
Arctic Club
Hoge Bldg.
Frye Art Museum
Lowman Bldg.
Ry. Exch. Bldg.
Public Safety Bldg.
Alaska Bldg.
Lyon Bldg.
Collins Bldg.
L.C. Smith Bldg.
County City Bldg.
Harborview Hospital
Frye Hotel
Police Station
Greyhound South Depot
Terminal Post Office
New Richmond Hotel
N.P. & G.N. Depot
Un. Pac. and C.M.St.P. & P. Depot
Housing District
Un. Pac. Freight Depot
To Harbor Island
To Boeing Plant
To Airport and Tacoma
To Mt. Baker Park
To Lake Washington Floating Bridge

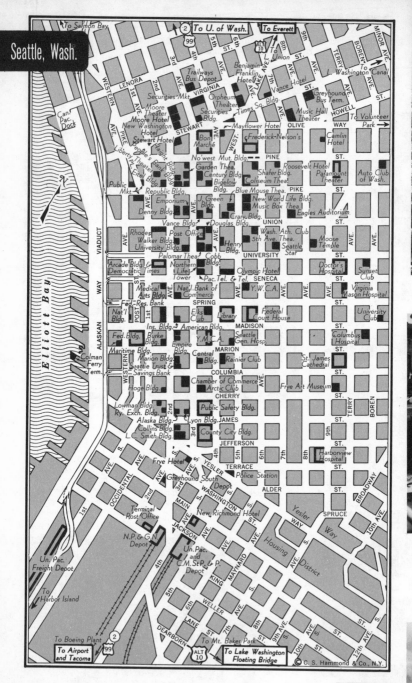

SEATTLE ART MUSEUM, located in Volunteer Park, houses a famed collection of oriental art. The camels which guard its entrance once guarded the approaches to a tomb in China

THE SKYLINE of Seattle's business district towers above the pier-lined rim of Elliott Bay. Seattle's tallest building—the 42-story Smith Tower can be identified by its white cone-shaped roof

Photos: Seattle Chamber of Commerce

GENERAL HIRAM M. CHITTENDEN LOCKS provide entrance to inner harbor of Lake Union and Lake Washington. The locks are capable of accommodating ships with a maximum draft of 30 feet

SEATTLE Seattle, the metropolis of the Pacific Northwest and gateway to Alaska is situated on Puget Sound, along the crescent-shaped, pier-lined rim of Elliott Bay. It is a city of changing vistas; of broken hills, sharp ravines and numerous watercourses. Visible to the west across the blue waters of the Sound, are the distant snow-mantled mountains of the Olympic Range, while to the east and southeast rise the Cascades, their deeply forested slopes dominated by the symmetrical, glacier-ridged cone of Mount Rainier. Nearby are found unrivaled recreational facilities which include fishing, sailing, camping, mountain climbing and year-round winter sports. Within a short distance of Seattle lies the vast untouched wilderness of northern Washington or the magnificent fringes of Pacific seacoast. Seattle's climate, tempered by the warm ocean currents, knows no extremes of heat or cold. Though fog is not uncommon in this region and the rainfall heavy, particularly in winter, the resulting growth of plants, flowers and trees is lush and verdant. Rivaling Seattle's beauty of setting are its outstanding commercial advantages. Its deep and sheltered harbor, the large docks and warehouses lining its waterfront, have long contributed to its importance as a port. During the years 1942 to 1946, great numbers of fighting vessels slid down the ways of its shipyards on Harbor Island at the entrance to Elliot Bay.

LAKE WASHINGTON FLOATING BRIDGE 6,560 feet long, is a 4-lane concrete highway supported by 25 floating pontoons. The bridge is the world's largest floating structure

MOUNT BAKER PARK is situated on the shores of beautiful Lake Washington in the City of Seattle. Mount Rainier's snow-capped peak can be seen in the background

THE UNIVERSITY OF WASHINGTON boasts a handsome, 582-acre campus and an enrollment of more than 14,000 students. The University is the largest in the Pacific Northwest.

FISHERMEN'S TERMINAL, located at Salmon Bay, has a capacity of 1,000 craft and serves as the hub of Seattle's fishing industry. When the fishing fleet is in port, the Terminal looks like a forest of masts

SEATTLE Continued

In World War II, Seattle formed a vital link in our Pacific supply lines; from here thousands of troops embarked for bases in Alaska, the Aleutians and the far-flung islands of the Pacific. Hydroelectric power, generated by dams along the Skagit River of northern Washington, furnish ample electricity for Seattle's rapidly expanding industry, while recent development of western Canadian oil resources have made the city an important refining center. Seattle is the world's largest fur market and the home of the Boeing Airplane Plant—pioneers in the production of larger-type aircraft. Today, four great railroads and eight airlines serve the city. Toward the end of the 19th century, Seattle gained wide renown as a point of departure for the frenzied hordes rushing to the Yukon in search of gold. Though now the gambling joints, cheap saloons and gaudy dance halls have vanished from the scene, Seattle's waterfront still retains some of the flavor of bygone days. Here ship chandlers, picturesque curio shops and the fish and oyster booths are to be found. Lake Washington, 22 miles long and 4 miles wide, lies to the east of Seattle and is connected to Puget Sound by the Lake Washington Ship Canal.

SEATTLE-TACOMA INTERNATIONAL AIRPORT is one of the nation's finest. This 13-million-dollar airport, which is owned and operated by the Port of Seattle, is located about 13 miles outside the city

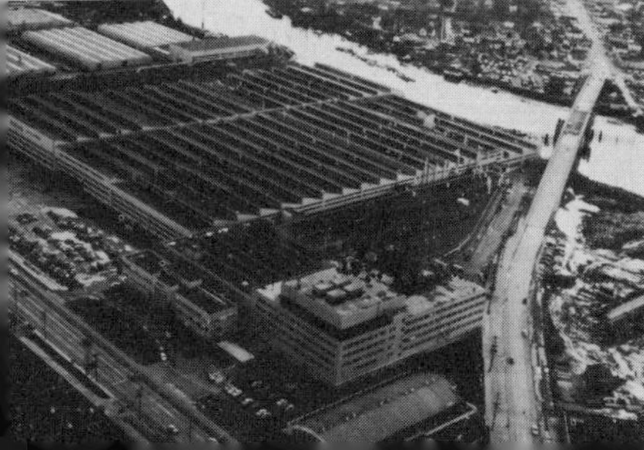

Photos: Seattle Chamber of Commerce

BOEING AIRPLANE PLANT is Seattle's largest industrial building. The plant now produces stratofortresses, the jet bombers and the jet tankers

Shreveport, La.

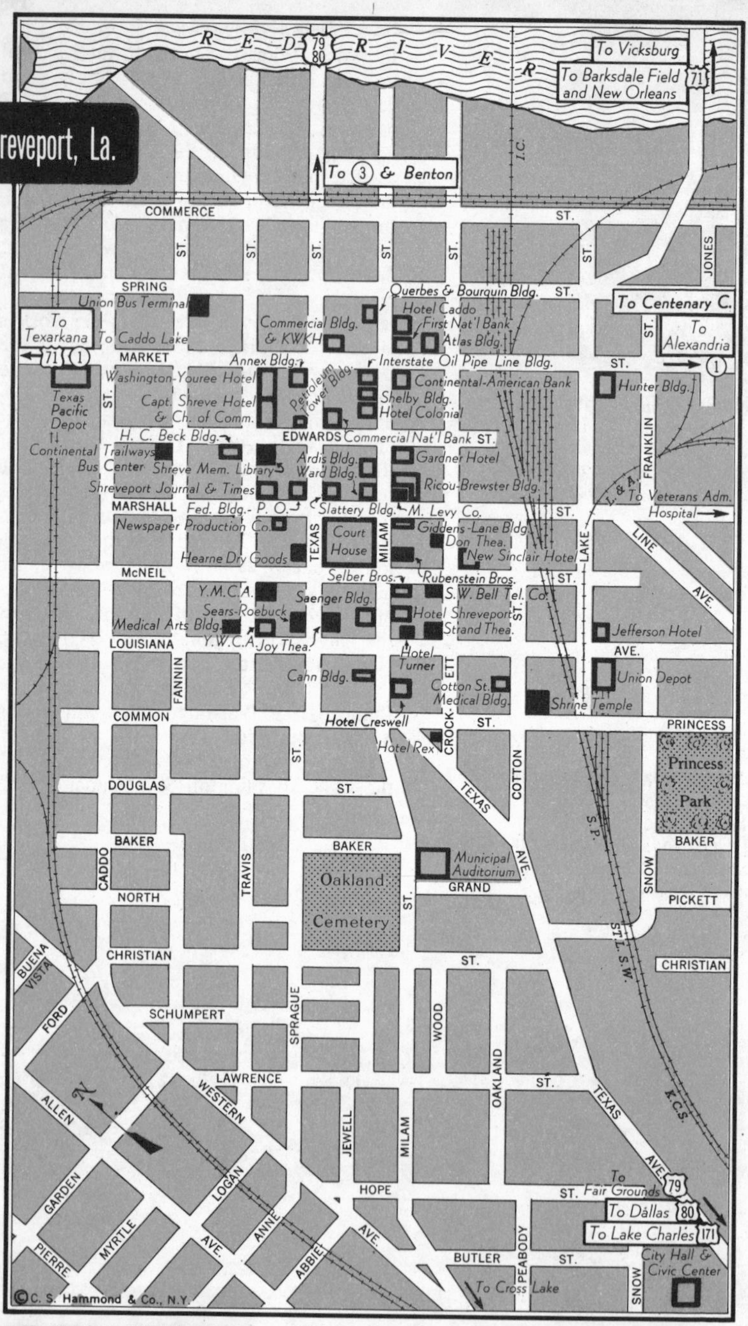

RED RIVER
79 80
To Vicksburg
To Barksdale Field and New Orleans 71
To 3 & Benton
I.C.
COMMERCE ST.
SPRING ST.
JONES
Union Bus Terminal
Querbes & Bourquin Bldg.
Hotel Caddo
First Nat'l Bank
Atlas Bldg.
Commercial Bldg. & KWKH
To Centenary C.
To Alexandria
To Texarkana 71 1
To Caddo Lake
MARKET ST.
Annex Bldg.
Interstate Oil Pipe Line Bldg.
Washington-Youree Hotel
Petroleum Tower Bldg.
Continental-American Bank
Hunter Bldg.
Texas Pacific Depot
Capt. Shreve Hotel & Ch. of Comm.
Shelby Bldg.
Hotel Colonial
H. C. Beck Bldg.
EDWARDS ST.
Commercial Nat'l Bank
FRANKLIN
Continental Trailways Bus Center
Shreve Mem. Library
Ardis Bldg.
Ward Bldg.
Gardner Hotel
Ricou-Brewster Bldg.
Shreveport Journal & Times
L. & A.
To Veterans Adm. Hospital
MARSHALL ST.
Fed. Bldg.- P. O.
Slattery Bldg.
M. Levy Co.
Newspaper Production Co.
Court House
TEXAS
MILAM
Giddens-Lane Bldg.
Don Thea.
New Sinclair Hotel
LAKE
LINE AVE.
Hearne Dry Goods
McNEIL ST.
Selber Bros.
Rubenstein Bros.
Y.M.C.A.
Saenger Bldg.
S. W. Bell Tel. Co.
Sears-Roebuck
Medical Arts Bldg.
Hotel Shreveport
Strand Thea.
Jefferson Hotel
LOUISIANA AVE.
Y.W.C.A.
Joy Thea.
Hotel Turner
FANNIN
Cahn Bldg.
CROCKETT
Cotton St. Medical Bldg.
Union Depot
Shrine Temple
COMMON ST.
Hotel Creswell
PRINCESS
Hotel Rex
Princess Park
DOUGLAS ST.
TEXAS AVE.
COTTON
S.P.
BAKER
CADDO
TRAVIS
Municipal Auditorium
Oakland Cemetery
GRAND
SNOW
NORTH
PICKETT
CHRISTIAN ST.
BUENA VISTA
ST. L. S.W.
SCHUMPERT
SPRAGUE
WOOD
FORD
OAKLAND ST.
LAWRENCE
WESTERN
K.C.S.
ALLEN
N
JEWELL
MILAM
GARDEN
LOGAN
HOPE ST.
To Fair Grounds 79
To Dallas 80
To Lake Charles 171
MYRTLE AVE.
ANNE
ABBIE AVE.
PEABODY
BUTLER ST.
City Hall & Civic Center
PIERRE
To Cross Lake
SNOW

HALL OF SCIENCE is part of Centenary College in Shreveport. Chartered in 1825, Centenary is the oldest college west of the Mississippi River. A Methodist institution, it was named in honor of the centennial celebration of the founding of Methodism

THIS HOME TYPIFIES Shreveport, a city famed for the beauty of its gardens and the quiet charm of its residential areas. It is also a city of churches, boasting over 130 separate congregations

Photos: Shreveport Chamber of Commerce

VETERANS ADMINISTRATION HOSPITAL, a handsome new building, stands on the site of Fort Humbug. The Fort, which once extended for 4 miles along the river, received its "humbug" nickname, when, lacking sufficient artillery, tree trunks were used to simulate cannons

FAIRGOUNDS STADIUM, with a seating capacity of 32,000 persons, is among the many permanent features of the Louisiana State Fairgrounds, which also include exhibit halls, stock barns and a race track. The state fair is held here annually in October

SHREVEPORT. Shreveport, a modern industrial city which has grown up in scarcely more than a century, bears little resemblance to other cities of the South, its skyline of tall buildings suggesting instead the newer cities of Oklahoma and Texas. Until the 1830's, although explored earlier, this region of the Red River Valley remained virtually unsettled by white men, its only inhabitants being the friendly, peace-loving Caddo Indians. Development of the area was hampered by a vast, almost solid jam of driftwood which had accumulated through the centuries and now blocked passage on the Red River for a distance of 160 miles. In 1832, the government appointed Henry Miller Shreve, a steamboat builder and inventor of a twin-hulled snag-boat, to clear the river of the "Great Raft" as the log jam was known. After a year's work Shreve had cleared eighty miles of the river, reaching a point where the city now stands. The townsite, purchased two years later from the Indians, was named in his honor. Shreveport, with an active steamboat trade, flourished in the days of "King Cotton." Later, in 1906, the discovery of oil in Caddo Lake boomed the city to a new and greater prosperity, a prosperity which continues to this day and has made Shreveport second only to New Orleans in the State of Louisiana. In spring the beautiful display of the thousands of redbud trees which bloom around Cross Lake is one of the city's major attractions. Also at this season, Shreveport holds its annual "Holiday in Dixie" celebration which includes yacht races on the river, dances, parades, pageants and a garden tour.

HENRY C. BECK BUILDING, 20 stories high, is the tallest building in Shreveport and the first of its type in the nation. The building is entirely constructed of glass and colored aluminum

SPOKANE. Spokane, second largest city in Washington, is the hub of an extensive wheat farming, lumbering and mining area known as the "Inland Empire." In 1810 in the section east of the Cascade Range chiefly inhabited by the Spokane Indians, Spokane House was built by the North West Fur Company below the falls where the Indians used to pitch their tents on the Spokane River. Two years later, Fort Spokane was built not far away by the Pacific Fur Company. Despite the rivalry of these companies, the posts together were a popular meeting place for trading parties, Indians and company employees until 1821. With the extension of railroad lines and the development of mining in the late 1800's, the place became chief supply point and promotion center for gold miners. Now after the passing of the convivial frontier mining town, this capital of the Inland Empire has grown into a great recreational spot, with its long, sunshiny summers, scores of alluring nearby lakes, open pine forests and mountain wildernesses. A clean, inviting city clinging to the rim of the river's canyon, its northern entrance, the "Lane of Remembrance," is lined on both sides with a series of magnificent trees, making it one of the country's most enchanting roadways.

ENTRANCE to the city from the west prov an awe-inspiring view for visitors of metropolis of eastern Washington and hills beyond of which Mount Spokane is greatest attraction

DOWNTOWN SPOKANE, the metropolitan district, is south of the river. Old National Bank, a few buildings down on the right side of the street, was the city's first skyscraper, built in 1910

LOOKING WEST toward the beautiful Spokane Valley from the Spokane River Bridge gives just a slight idea of the vast ranges of the mighty Inland Empire

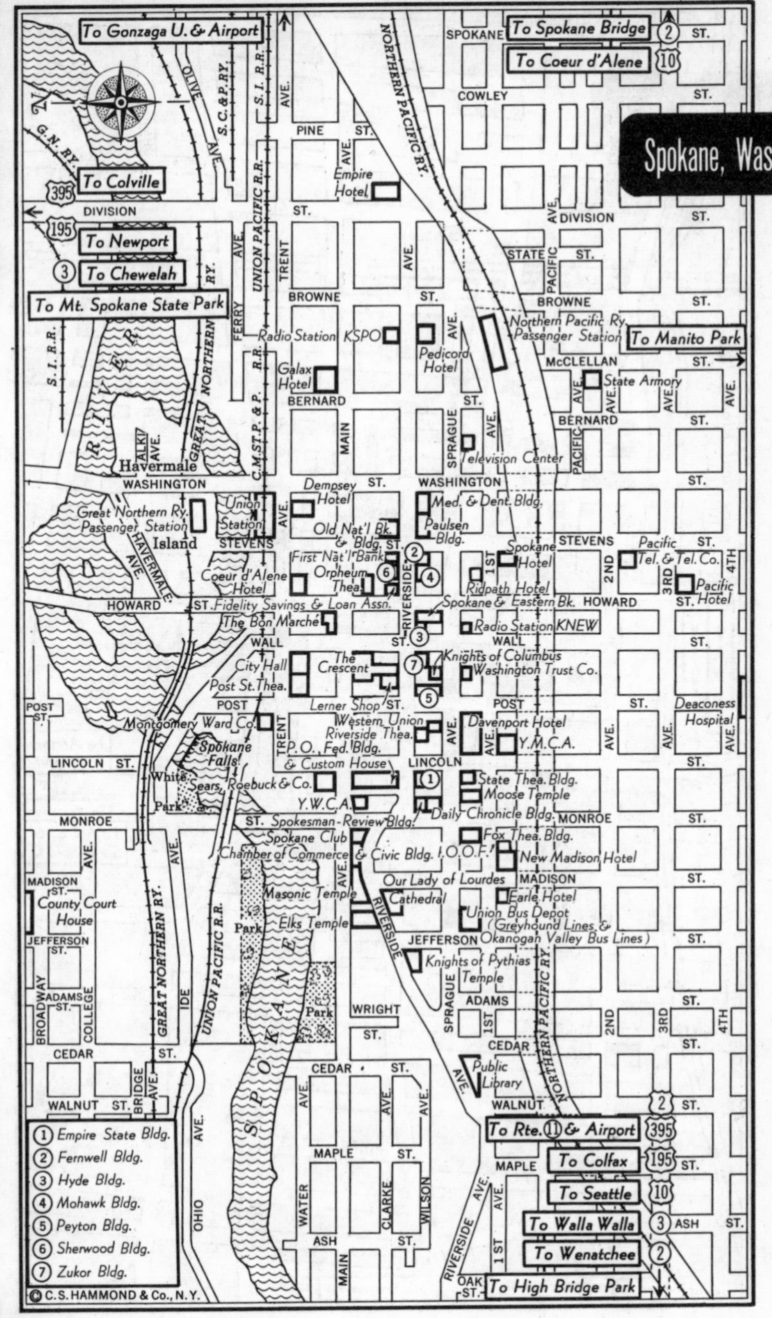

SPOKANE FALLS plunges over the rocks in a glittering rainbow-tinted spray at Monroe Street Bridge, so graceful and large a concrete arch that drawings of it are on display at the Sorbonne in Paris

Photos: Washington State Advertising Commision

Springfield, Mass.

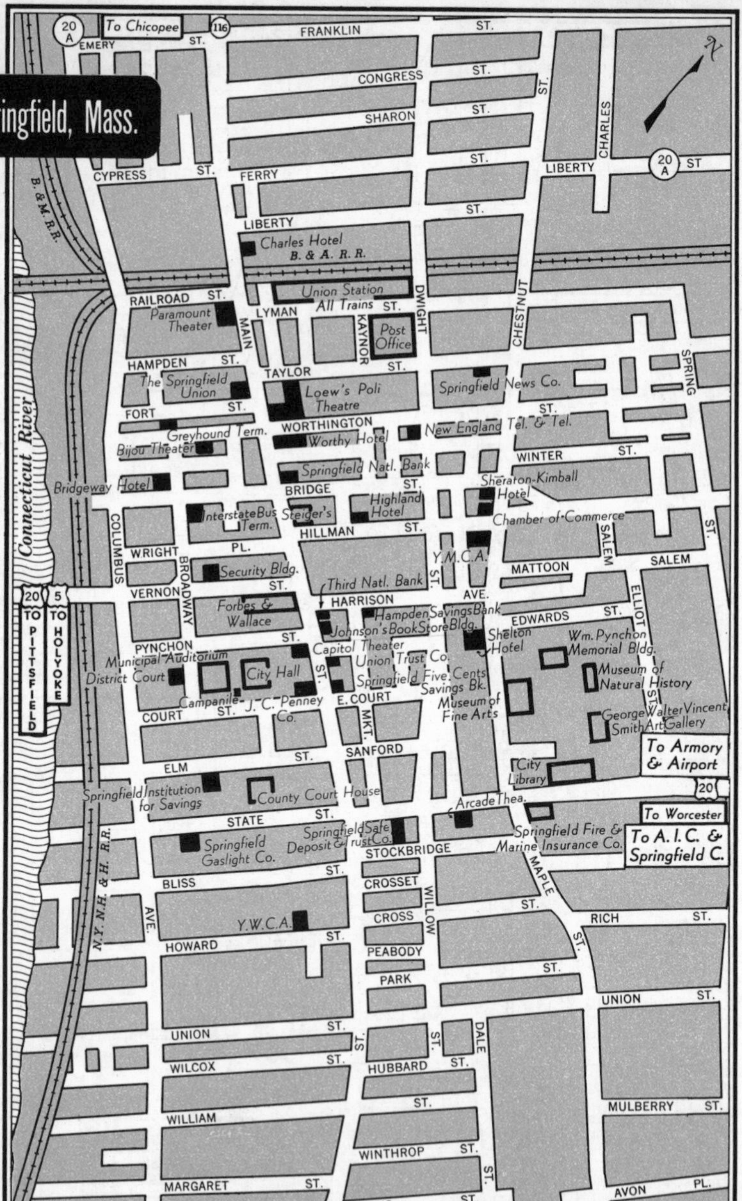

Photos: Greater Springfield Chamber of Commerce, Black Star

THE SPRINGFIELD ARMORY, home of the famous Springfield rifle, stands on a rise commanding a view of the city and river

THE "PURITAN" stands in a little park near the City Library. Created by the sculptor, St. Gaudens, it honors Deacon Samuel Chapin, a founder of Springfield

MOUNTAIN GOATS from Asia are seen at the zoo in Forest Park, one of the country's foremost natural parks covering 756 acres

SPRINGFIELD. From the top of the 300-foot Campanile, a slender bell tower which rises between the classic dignity of Springfield's Administration Building and the Municipal Auditorium, one looks down on a scene comparable in beauty to that of the Rhine Valley of western Germany. Below, the city of Springfield and the elm-shaded streets of its suburbs spread out along the banks of the Connecticut River in a panorama of New England tranquility. Springfield is a city full of vitality, of bustling industry, of handsome buildings and scenic charms. An industrial area for 300 years, Springfield and its surrounding communities are frequently referred to as the "Cradle of Craftsmanship." Home of the popular Springfield Rifle, the city's name has been linked with the manufacture of arms since the establishment of the United States Arsenal here in 1789. Today, Springfield's industries show a healthy diversity of manufacture with small arms, paper and paper products, plastics, textiles, leather goods and various types of machinery among the many products turned out by its factories. Webster's Dictionary, a standard for the English language, has been published here since 1847. The city's museum of natural history houses the first American-made planetarium.

Syracuse, N. Y.

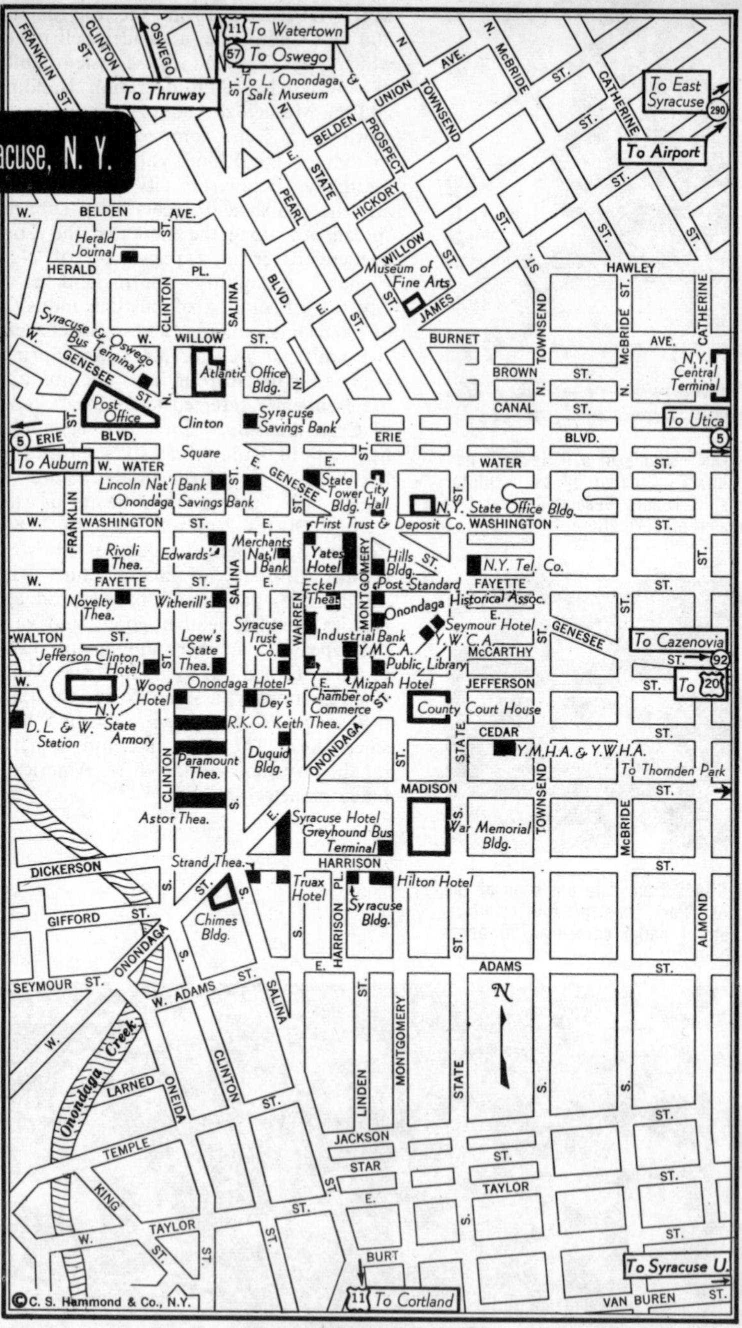

To Watertown
To Oswego
To Thruway
To L. Onondaga & Salt Museum
To East Syracuse
To Airport
Museum of Fine Arts
Herald Journal
Syracuse & Oswego Bus Terminal
Atlantic Office Bldg.
Post Office
Clinton Square
Syracuse Savings Bank
N.Y. Central Terminal
To Utica
To Auburn
Lincoln Nat'l Bank
Onondaga Savings Bank
State Tower Bldg.
City Hall
N.Y. State Office Bldg.
First Trust & Deposit Co.
Rivoli Thea.
Edwards'
Merchants Nat'l Bank
Yates Hotel
Hills Bldg.
N.Y. Tel. Co.
Post-Standard
Novelty Thea.
Witherill's
Eckel Thea.
Onondaga Historical Assoc.
Syracuse Trust Co.
Industrial Bank
Seymour Hotel
Y.W.C.A.
Y.M.C.A.
Loew's State Thea.
Jefferson Clinton Hotel
Public Library
To Cazenovia
Wood Hotel
Onondaga Hotel
Mizpah Hotel
Dey's
Chamber of Commerce
County Court House
N.Y. State Armory
D. L. & W. Station
R.K.O. Keith Thea.
Y.M.H.A. & Y.W.H.A.
Paramount Thea.
Duquid Bldg.
To Thornden Park
Astor Thea.
Syracuse Hotel
Greyhound Bus Terminal
War Memorial Bldg.
Strand Thea.
Truax Hotel
Hilton Hotel
Syracuse Bldg.
Chimes Bldg.
Onondaga Creek
To Syracuse U.
To Cortland
©C. S. Hammond & Co., N.Y.

UNIQUE SALT MUSEUM, built around the last vat house and chimney, contains implements, models, pictures and other reminders of the days when salt was the city's main industry

CLINTON SQUARE, part of the main business section in downtown Syracuse, was once a transfer point for freight on the old Erie Canal

SYRACUSE. Today, as in the days of the red man, Syracuse, the "Salt City," is the hub of the rich orchard, dairy and lake region of central New York. On this site was the village of the Onondaga tribe of the Iroquois and it was this village that was the capital of that remarkable confederacy. Even now, strange as it may seem to some people, there are a number of Indians residing in the Empire State. In fact, near Syracuse is the Onondaga Indian Reservation, still the capital of the Iroquois Confederacy. In 1654 friendly Indians showed Father Le Moyne the salt spring which tradition holds is the spot known as the Jesuit Well. These salt deposits led to the founding a number of years later and early prosperity of the city. They were responsible, too, for her name—the first postmaster suggesting it upon recalling that the ancient city in Sicily had also grown around a marsh and salt springs. Her most recent influence has been in the field of fine arts. Syracuse University's John Crouse College of Fine Arts, organized in 1873, was the first in the United States and the Museum of Fine Arts was the country's first to form a permanent collection devoted exclusively to American painters.

FORT SAINTE MARIE DE GANNENTAHA is a restored stockade and fort built to protect French settlers in 1656. Reconstruction followed plans preserved by the Jesuits and still in existence in France

THORNDEN PARK, near the university, contains famed Mills Rose Garden and a natural amphitheater where pageants and summer concerts are presented

INTERCOLLEGIATE ROWING REGATTAS are exciting annual events on Onondaga Lake. Spread over several hundred acres on the lake's shore are the New York State Fair Grounds

Photos: New York State Department of Commerce

TOLEDO. The territory around Toledo and the Maumee (a corruption of the Indian name "Miami") River in Ohio was long fought over, a prize worth having. Originally explored by one of Champlain's scouts, the river was used as a natural highway by French adventurers and missionaries. General "Mad Anthony" Wayne's victory of 1794 over the federated Indian tribes of the northwest on a battlefield strewn with fallen trees — the Battle of Fallen Timbers — cleared the way for peaceful settlement of this part of the Northwest Territory. The same year, Fort Industry was erected on the present site of Toledo. Later, along the wooded shores of the river, General William Henry Harrison repulsed the British in the War of 1812. It wasn't until the cessation of this warfare that the city got her real start in life. However, in no time at all, Toledo achieved prominence as a leader in reform. While other cities in the throes of the industrial revolution became involved in shameful scandals, Toledo led the way in civic responsibility and advancement, chiefly under her nationally famous mayor, Samuel M. ("Golden Rule") Jones, and she is still recognized for her outstanding achievements in civic affairs.

WHITE MARBLE MUSEUM OF ART ranks among the country's top six. Noteworthy collections include old masters and modern paintings and an exhibit of glass said to be the world's finest. Its colonnaded, acoustically perfect Peristyle is a beautiful concert hall

FEEDING a continuous melting tank with raw material "batch" for the manufacture of plate glass. The glass factories in this city invented many of the processes now used throughout the industry

OUTDOOR AMPHITHEATER in the Zoological Park offers summer orchestral concerts, opera and other entertainment programs. The zoo collection and facilities, including the Museum of Natural Science and History, ranks among the best

ALL-GLASS FOUNTAIN symbolizes Toledo as the "Glass Center of the World" and makes an attractive sight among the beautifully landscaped gardens of the Civic Center

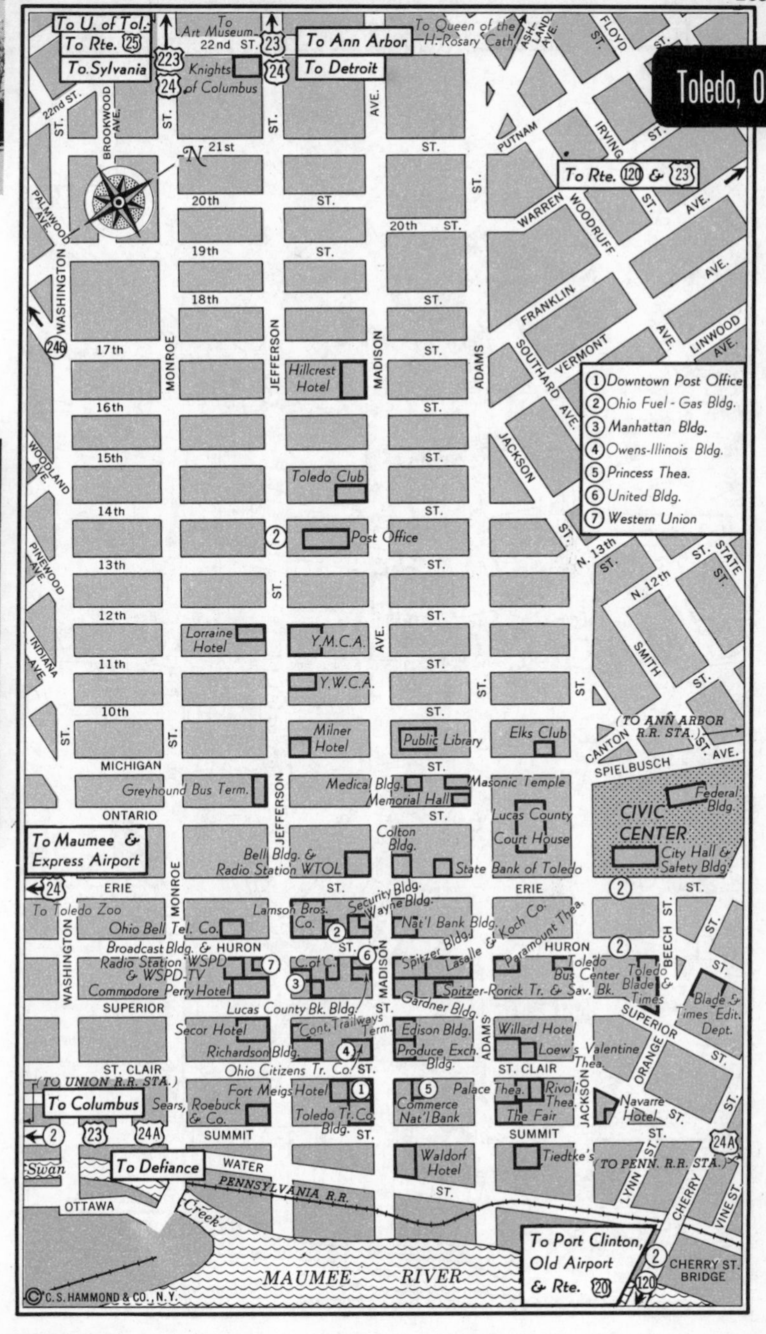

CATHEDRAL of the Queen of the Holy Rosary, built of rainbow-colored granite, limestone and tile in Plateresque, a Spanish architectural style of the 16th-century, is the only Plateresque cathedral in the world

Photos: Toledo Chamber of Commerce, Libby-Owen-Ford, Bob Abodeely Associates

Trenton, N. J.

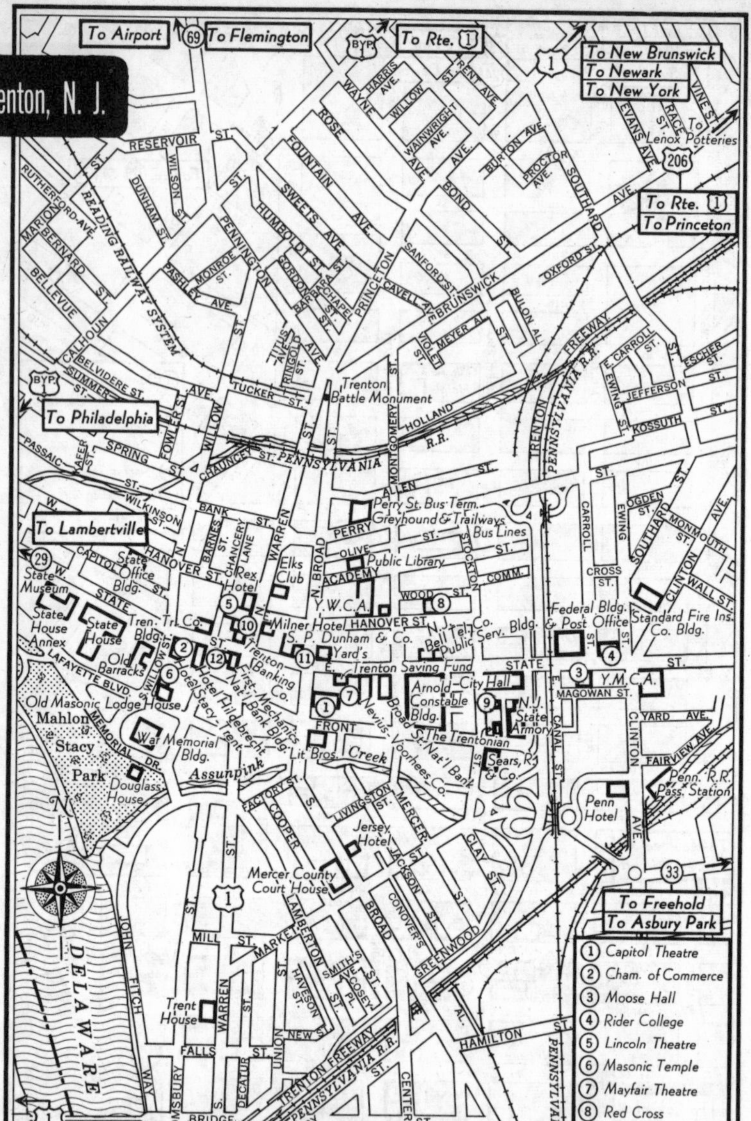

To Airport
To Flemington
To Rte. 1
To New Brunswick
To Newark
To New York
To Lenox Potteries
To Rte. 1
To Princeton
To Philadelphia
To Lambertville
To Freehold
To Asbury Park
To Atlantic City
To Turnpike & Camden
To Roebling Plant
To Philadelphia

1. Capitol Theatre
2. Cham. of Commerce
3. Moose Hall
4. Rider College
5. Lincoln Theatre
6. Masonic Temple
7. Mayfair Theatre
8. Red Cross
9. Trenton Eve. Times
10. Trent Theatre
11. Wallach Bldg.
12. Western Union

SOLDIERS AND SAILORS WAR MEMORIAL, this handsome building with its theater and assembly hall, is a tribute to the faithful service given to their country by Trenton's sons in times of national need

NEW JERSEY STATE CAPITOL has an impressive dome which is covered with gold leaf. An interesting and unique collection of old battle flags is displayed here

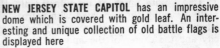

TRENTON. Trenton, New Jersey's capital, has an indelible place in world history. Here, after the memorable "Crossing of the Delaware," Washington's half-starved, half-frozen Continentals ambushed the Hessian forces in a battle that turned the tide of the American Revolution. The Old Barracks, preserved from those war-like times, contributes with its simple architecture in gray stone to the charm of Trenton as a town where history can still be seen and felt. Quiet dignity surrounds the Capitol, with its remarkable dome, near the Delaware river. The beautiful wood carvings in the old building are kept varnished and shiny and the new wing shows, in its delightful copies of colonial styles—for instance in the hall of the Supreme Court—that Trenton proudly preserves its historical atmosphere. This mood meets the visitor also in the rather narrow, winding streets, where, interspersed among busy stores, appear charming colonial residences. The industries which have made Trenton famous beyond the borders of the United States are a kind where tradition of workmanship and quality are essential. In many a fine household, pieces of a creamy, highly glazed pottery testify to the taste of Walter Lenox, the originator of Trenton's famous Lenox Potteries, and to the traditional excellence of the company's craftsmanship. Several famous bridges, some of them the largest ever built, are made of wire ropes and cables from the Roebling plant at Trenton and constructed by its able engineers.

"YE OLDE BARRACKS" built 1758-59 is one of five barracks built to house soldiers in the French and Indian War. Probably the finest example of Colonial barracks in the country, they were also used to quarter Hessian troops in 1776.

Photos: Greater Trenton Chamber of Commerce

TRENTON BATTLE MONUMENT stands on the highest spot in the city. The observatory at the top of the monument is reached by elevator and offers an excellent view of Trenton and its surroundings. The base contains an exhibit of Revolutionary relics

THE TRENT HOUSE was built in 1719 by William Trent from whom the city takes its name. This charming brick house later became the residence of the Royal Governor, Lewis Morris and many other noted families.

TULSA. With much of its industry directly or indirectly associated with petroleum, Tulsa, Oklahoma's second largest city and the center of the mid-continent oil fields, claims the title of "Oil Capital of the World." Over three hundred oil companies make Tulsa their headquarters as do many manufacturers of oil field equipment and supplies. Every four years the International Petroleum Exposition, with displays from all parts of the world, is held here. Situated on the banks of the Arkansas River, Tulsa was founded by Creek Indians before the Civil War. Their council tree, a venerable elm, still stands in the city. Although the extension of the railroad brought white settlers here in 1882, its growth was slow. Tulsey Town, as the place was originally known, remained hardly more than a village until the discovery of oil across the river at Red Fork in 1901. In the boom which followed the oil strike, the city's population rose rapidly; today it ranks among the largest cities in the country. Though its history has been brief, Tulsa's cultural growth has managed to keep pace with its phenomenal industrial development. The University of Tulsa, with its world renowned school of petroleum engineering, is one of the country's outstanding educational institutions. The Gilcrease Museum houses an important collection of American Indian Art as well as collections of American painting and sculpture. Tulsa is the national headquarters of the United States Junior Chamber of Commerce.

PHILBROOK ART CENTER, a gift of Mr. and Mrs. Waite Phillips to the city, is fully endowed and maintains a year-round cultural program for Tulsa and a 4-state area. It is one of the major art galleries in the nation

WEBSTER HIGH SCHOOL is one of Tulsa's five senior high schools. The Tulsa public school system is nationally known and its facilities are valued in excess of $65 million

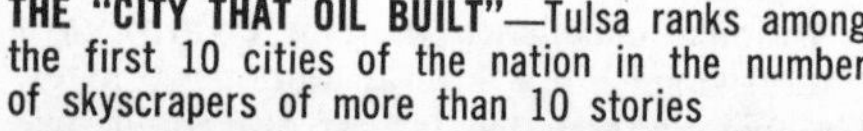

THE "CITY THAT OIL BUILT"—Tulsa ranks among the first 10 cities of the nation in the number of skyscrapers of more than 10 stories

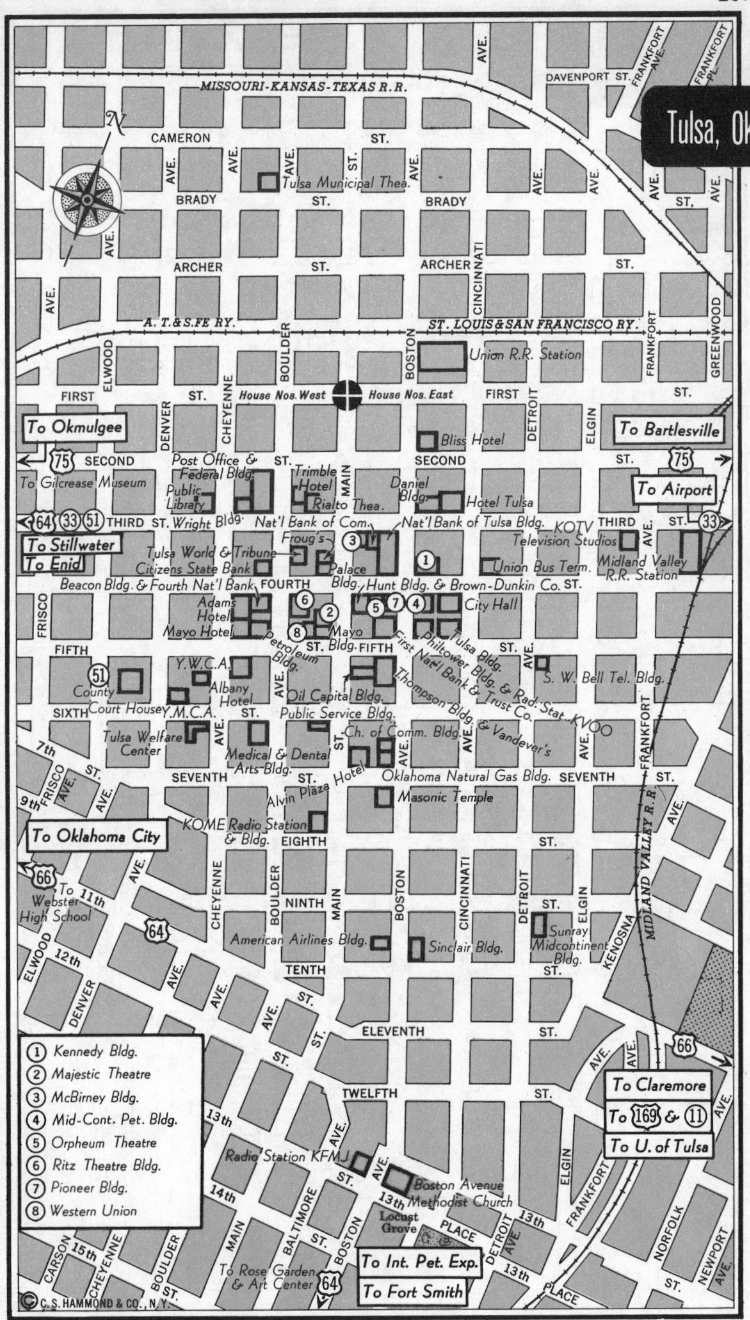

TULSA MUNICIPAL ROSE GARDEN, a six-acre terraced garden containing 11,000 rose plants, centers a 40-acre woodland park in the heart of Tulsa's residential district. It is the official test garden for the South of the All-American Rose Selections Committee

Photos: Tulsa Chamber of Commerce

Washington, D. C.

THE CAPITOL which contains 435 rooms and numerous art works is one of Washington's principal points of interest. The central portion of the building includes the Rotunda, Statuary Hall, and the old Supreme Court Chambers comprise the two wings

WASHINGTON. Washington, our nation's capital, has long been acclaimed one of the most beautiful and cosmopolitan cities in the world. Located in the District of Columbia and co-extensive with it, the city's site was chosen by George Washington and approved by Congress in 1790. Probably possessing more trees than any other capital city, Washington has broad avenues arched by maples, oaks, elms, ginkos and sycamores and its tree-shaded lawns and parks serve to set off the impressive government buildings. Since it is a city where government is the main concern, few industries mar its skyline or fill its air with soot. Washington was among the first great world capitals to be built from a carefully engineered master plan, and while the original plan of its designer, Major Pierre Charles L'Enfant, has not always been followed, the city has come to fulfill the dreams of its creators. Washington's streets which run north and south, also east and west, form a grid pattern which is cut diagonally by wide avenues named for various states. Where streets and avenues intersect are found many small circular or triangular parks. The Capitol Building, home of the legislative branch of the government, stands on the crest of a hill which L'Enfant described as "a pedestal waiting for a monument." Dominating the entire city, the capitol's great dome, illuminated at night by batteries of searchlights, makes an impressive silhouette against the sky. It is surmounted by an heroic statue of "Freedom," and only the slender shaft of the Washington Monument challenges its eminence. To the east, the Library of Congress, with its low cop-

Photos: Washington Board of Trade

WASHINGTON MONUMENT towers 555 feet above the Tidal Basin. An observatory at the top is reached by either an elevator or a flight of 898 steps. This observatory affords an unsurpassed view of the city and its surroundings

per dome, houses one of the world's most outstanding collections of books. Next to the library is the Supreme Court Building, regarded by many as Washington's finest building. Relatively new, it is built of dazzling white marble with a stately columned portico. On the Mall —oldest of the Federal Parks—is the National Gallery of Art. The building, a gift of Andrew Mellon and a showpiece in itself, houses more than 27,000 works of art including the magnificent Mellon, Kress, Widener, Rosenwald and Dale collections. On the other side of the Mall is the Smithsonian Institute, a scattered group of buildings which contain a wide assortment of relics, inventions and curiosities. North of the Mall, between Constitution and Pennsylvania Avenues, is the Federal Triangle, the longest, most expensive and impressive collection of government buildings anywhere. They include the Departments of Commerce, Labor and Justice. The Post Office Department has on exhibition both United States and foreign stamps while its Philatelic Agency in Room 6505 sells commemorative and regular issue stamps at face value. The Archives Building, also in this group, displays in its Exhibition Hall America's greatest historic documents including the Constitution, the

PENTAGON BUILDING, the world's largest office building, is located directly across the river from Washington at Arlington, Virginia. This tremendous structure covers an area of 34 acres and contains 3,333,000 square feet of office space

SMITHSONIAN INSTITUTE is often referred to as the "Nation's Attic." Its several buildings house a tremendous hodge-podge of relics, curiosities and inventions. Famed among its exhibits is Lindbergh's tiny monoplane — The Spirit of St. Louis

LINCOLN MEMORIAL is one of the most impressive structures in Washington. The Doric columns which support the classic pediment symbolize the 36 states of the Union at the time of Lincoln's death

Photos: Washington Board of Trade

JEFFERSON MEMORIAL is patterned after the rotunda of the University of Virginia, one of the several buildings Jefferson himself designed. Within the circular pantheon is a towering statue of the great statesman

"EQUAL JUSTICE UNDER LAW" is the inscription emblazoned across the magnificent façade of the Sureme Court Building. Here our country's highest tribunal holds its sessions

ARLINGTON NATIONAL CEMETERY is the largest and most famous of all national burying grounds, covering over 400 acres. Its best known grave is the Tomb of the Unknown Soldier, guarded day and night by sentries

NATIONAL ART GALLERY contains some of the world's greatest masterpieces. The building's intricate system of air conditioning was designed to maintain the correct temperature for the preservation of the priceless art treasures

THE PRESIDENTIAL MANSION received the name "White House" when, following the fire of 1814, its soot-blackened, light sandstone exterior was restored by a coat of white paint

Photos: Washington Board of Trade

WASHINGTON Continued

Declaration of Independence and the Bill of Rights. The White House on Pennsylvania Avenue has been the home of presidents of the United States since 1799. The dignified Executive Mansion in its setting of rolling lawns has within recent years been completely remodeled and redecorated. A number of its stately rooms on the ground and first floors are open to the public at specified hours. They include the famous East Room where the wife of John Adams is said to have hung her washing, also the Red, Green and Blue Rooms and the State Dining Room. At the western end of the Mall, the Tidal Basin provides a lovely setting for Washington's famed cherry blossoms. Completing the axis of the Mall is the Reflecting Pool and the Lincoln Memorial. This stately building in the form of a Grecian temple with its classic, forty-foot-high columns, contains Daniel Chester French's colossal seated statue of Lincoln and the noble words of the Gettysburg address emblazoned on its walls. The nation's capital and its surroundings offer a wide range of educational, recreational and historical attractions including its excellent park facilities, two outdoor theaters and several of the country's leading universities. Nearby Mount Vernon, the country estate of George Washington, is a national shrine of exceptional charm.

PAN AMERICAN UNION, an organization of the 21 American Republics, occupies a building considered to be among the most beautiful in the world. One of its most charming features is its Aztec Garden

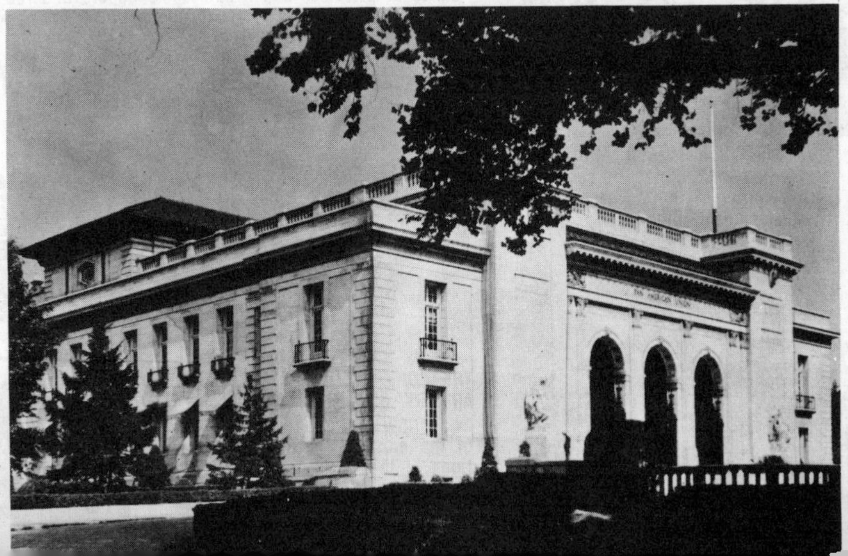

WORCESTER. This city, once called "Heart of the Commonwealth," where New England first heard the Declaration of Independence, certainly shows in its history two very typical New England traits—industriousness and inventiveness at a great variety of subjects, and a spontaneous appreciation for the things of the mind, culture and art. The name of the town is linked with such important inventors as Eli Whitney, inventor of the cotton gin; Elias Howe, inventor of the sewing machine and Erastus Bigelow, inventor of the carpet loom. And it attracted celebrities like Sarah Bernhardt, Edwin Booth, Fanny Kemble and the beautiful Lily Langtry. Emerson spoke here, as did Lincoln, Dickens, John Brown, Thoreau and Thackeray. Today, too, the town is a true New Englander in harboring a variety of industries and several important schools and colleges (Clark University, College of the Holy Cross, State Teachers College, Worcester Polytechnic Institute). Music festivals have been held annually since 1858. The visitor to Worcester can enjoy a remarkable collection of paintings, of stained glass, Japanese prints and early American furniture in the Worcester Art Museum. Or he can enjoy the town's pleasant surroundings on the shore of nearby Lake Quinsigamond.

Photos: Worcester Chamber of Commerce

WORCESTER POLYTECHNIC INSTITUTE is the 3rd oldest engineering school in the country and the Alma Mater of many world-famous industrialists and engineers

HIGH PRECISION QUALITY boring and grinding machines, finishing machines, boring equipment and magnetic chucks are turned out in modern industrial plants such as this

THE AMERICAN ANTIQUARIAN SOCIETY houses thousands of priceless and irreplaceable papers and records of the past. It is a valuable mine of information for writers

WORCESTER'S MEMORIAL AUDITORIUM was erected as a tribute to its service men. It is the center of the Worcester Music Festival and many other civic and cultural affairs

THE JOHN WOODMAN HIGGINS ARMORY of ancient and medieval armor and weapons is one of the most outstanding collections in the world

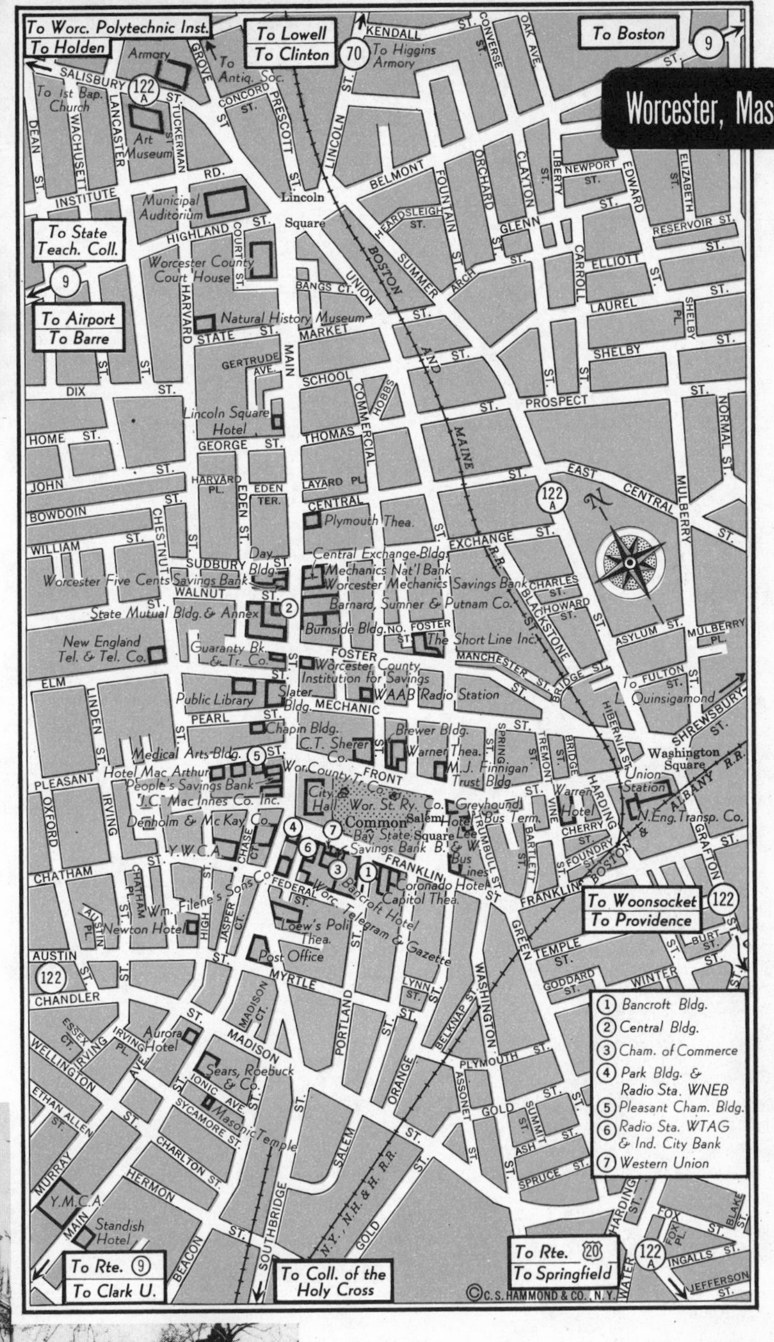

FIRST BAPTIST CHURCH is typical of Worcester's 119 churches. Originally built in 1836, the present-day building is one of the most modern and impressive of church edifices

Other CITIES of the AMERICAS

TALL, MODERN BUILDINGS and broad new thoroughfares endure side by side with the architectural treasures of Bogotá's colonial period. In the course of its transition into a center of commercial and industrial activity, Bogotá has retained its traditional dignity

BOGOTÁ. Bogotá is located on a fertile, four hundred square mile Andean plateau known as the Sabana de Bogotá. Until the inauguration of Colombia's first commercial airline in 1920, Bogotá was probably one of the world's most isolated capitals. To reach the city from Barranquilla on the coast, entailed traveling by boat for more than a week up the Magdalena River and then continuing on by rail across the mountains. Here, the city's inhabitants could at one time boast they spoke the purist Spanish in the Americas. Bogotá was founded in 1538, by Gonzalo Jiménez de Quesada and the ragged, half-starved survivors of an epic trek from the fever-ridden coast, through dense jungles and up the Eastern Cordillera of the Andes. Today, the 8,500-foot high plateau basin in which the city lies, is one of the most densely populated regions of Colombia and Bogotá's Techo Airport links the city with important centers of both Europe and the Americas. Centered around the Plaza Bolívar, the older parts of Bogotá still retain their colonial appearance, their overhanging balconies and narrow streets originally laid out by the Spaniards. In the more modern sections lying to the north and west of the Plaza, 20th century buildings contrast sharply with the red tiled roofs of their surroundings. Cut off from the world for centuries, Bogotá is now the political, social, artistic and commercial center of Colombia.

THE PALACE OF SAN CARLOS was at one time the residence of the liberator, Simón Bolívar. Today, it is occupied by the Ministry of Foreign Affairs

BOGOTÁ'S CHURCHES contain many priceless examples of colonial art and architecture. Pictured is the elaborately carved altar in the Church of La Tercera

BALCONIES with carved balustrades, shadow the narrow streets in the colonial section of Bogotá

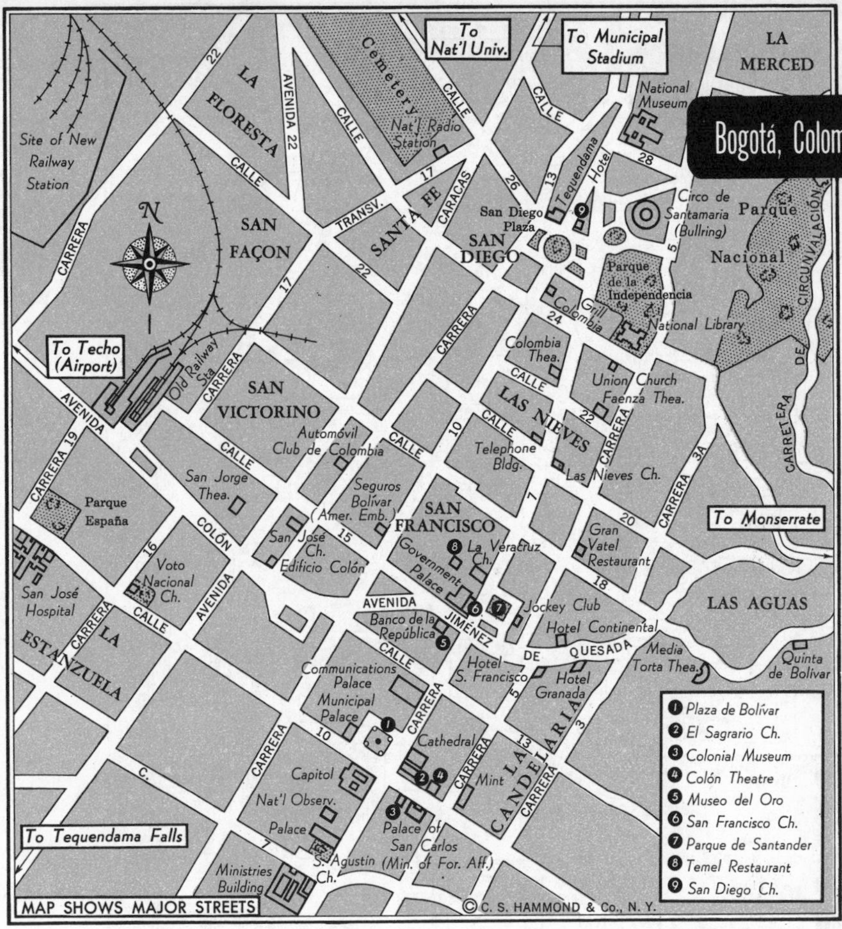

To Nat'l Univ.
To Municipal Stadium
LA MERCED
Cemetery
National Museum
Site of New Railway Station
LA FLORESTA
AVENIDA 22
CALLE
Nat'l Radio Station
SAN FAÇON
TRANSV.
SANTA FE
CARACAS
San Diego Plaza
Tequendama Hotel
Circo de Santamaria (Bullring)
Parque Nacional
SAN DIEGO
Parque de la Independencia
Grill Colombia
National Library
CIRCUNVALACIÓN
To Techo (Airport)
Old Railway Sta.
SAN VICTORINO
Colombia Thea.
Union Church
Faenza Thea.
LAS NIEVES
Automóvil Club de Colombia
Telephone Bldg.
Las Nieves Ch.
CARRETERA DE CIRCUNVALACIÓN
San Jorge Thea.
Seguros Bolívar (Amer. Emb.)
SAN FRANCISCO
To Monserrate
Parque España
COLÓN
San José Ch.
Edificio Colón
La Veracruz Ch.
Government Palace
Gran Vatel Restaurant
Voto Nacional Ch.
San José Hospital
LAS AGUAS
AVENIDA JIMÉNEZ DE QUESADA
Banco de la República
Jockey Club
Hotel Continental
LA ESTANZUELA
Communications Palace
Hotel S. Francisco
Media Torta Thea.
Quinta de Bolívar
Hotel Granada
Municipal Palace
Cathedral
LA CANDELARIA
Capitol
Mint
Nat'l Observ.
Palace
Palace of San Carlos (Min. of For. Aff.)
To Tequendama Falls
S. Agustin Ch.
Ministries Building
MAP SHOWS MAJOR STREETS
© C. S. HAMMOND & Co., N. Y.
1 Plaza de Bolívar
2 El Sagrario Ch.
3 Colonial Museum
4 Colón Theatre
5 Museo del Oro
6 San Francisco Ch.
7 Parque de Santander
8 Temel Restaurant
9 San Diego Ch.

Photos: International Petroleum Ltd., National Register Co.

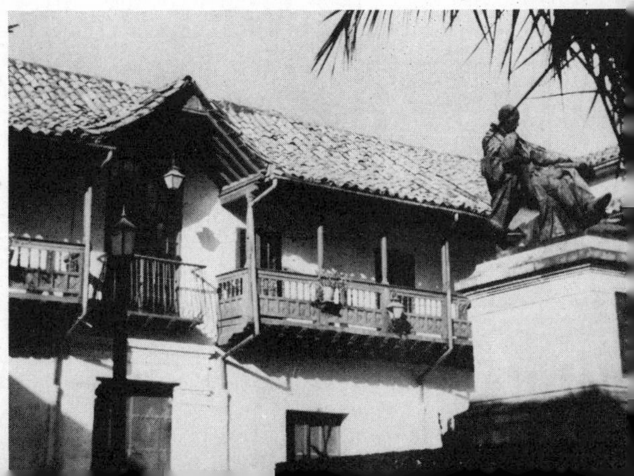

RUFINO JOSÉ CUERVO, who attained international distinction for his unique work in philology, is commemorated by this statue in Bogotá. His **"Critical Notes on the Language of Bogotá,"** constitutes an unsurpassed scientific basis for the study of the Spanish language

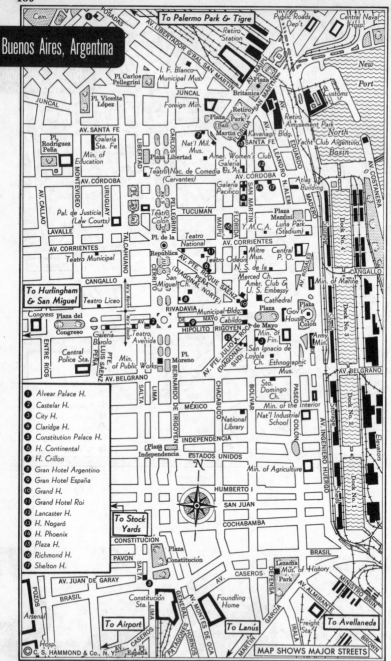

Buenos Aires, Argentina

1. Alvear Palace H.
2. Castelar H.
3. City H.
4. Claridge H.
5. Constitution Palace H.
6. H. Continental
7. H. Crillon
8. Gran Hotel Argentino
9. Gran Hotel España
10. Grand H.
11. Grand Hotel Roi
12. Lancaster H.
13. H. Nogaró
14. H. Phoenix
15. Plaza H.
16. Richmond H.
17. Shelton H.

MAP SHOWS MAJOR STREETS

THE NATIONAL MUSEUM OF FINE ARTS is housed in a building of classic architectural design. It is impossible to visit Buenos Aires without becoming interested in its treasure of marvelous paintings

THE ARGENTINE CONGRESS faces the Plaza del Congreso. A sumptuous building, its magnificent halls and interiors, particularly the Blue Room, are of outstanding elegance

BUENOS AIRES. Many travelers after visiting Buenos Aires with its culture, its elegance and its subtle charm, leave under the conviction that the Argentine capital is the Paris of the Americas. Like Paris, Buenos Aires is a city of many different aspects; it is a modern city of steel and concrete, of skyscrapers and dreams; it is a city full of cozy spots which offer characteristics of the XIX century in the grace of its patios and the artistic beauty of its entrance halls; and it is a merry and daring city with regard to its theaters, cinemas and night clubs. Buenos Aires is a marvelous sight situated on the bank of its great river and surrounded by the vast plains of the Pampas. When Captain Sancho del Campo landed on the bank of the River Plata where the city was founded, he exclaimed, "How good is the fresh and healthy air one breathes in this place." This marked the birth of the new city and established its prophetic name. Almost from that very instant it started to grow, with the certainty of becoming what it is today—the nation's commercial and industrial as well as its political and cultural capital. Today, Buenos Aires astounds the world with its constant expansion, its building activity, its intellectual centers, museums, industries, polyclinics, social works, palaces, universities and churches. Yet here, nature stubbornly refuses to be overcome by progress. It makes itself manifest everywhere amid cement and stones, to form parks and wonderful green gardens thus providing many oases, for dreamers, children and lovers.

Photos: Pan American Union

THE PORT OF BUENOS AIRES, located on the River Plata, is one of the largest seaports in the world. Its export trade is second only to New York in the Western Hemisphere

THE COLÓN THEATER, the National Theater of Argentina, is patterned after the Opera in Paris. The building occupies an entire city block, seats 3,500 persons and its huge stage accommodates more than 600 performers

THE OBELISK a chief point of orientation for sightseeing and a city landmark, commemorates the 400th anniversary of Buenos Aires

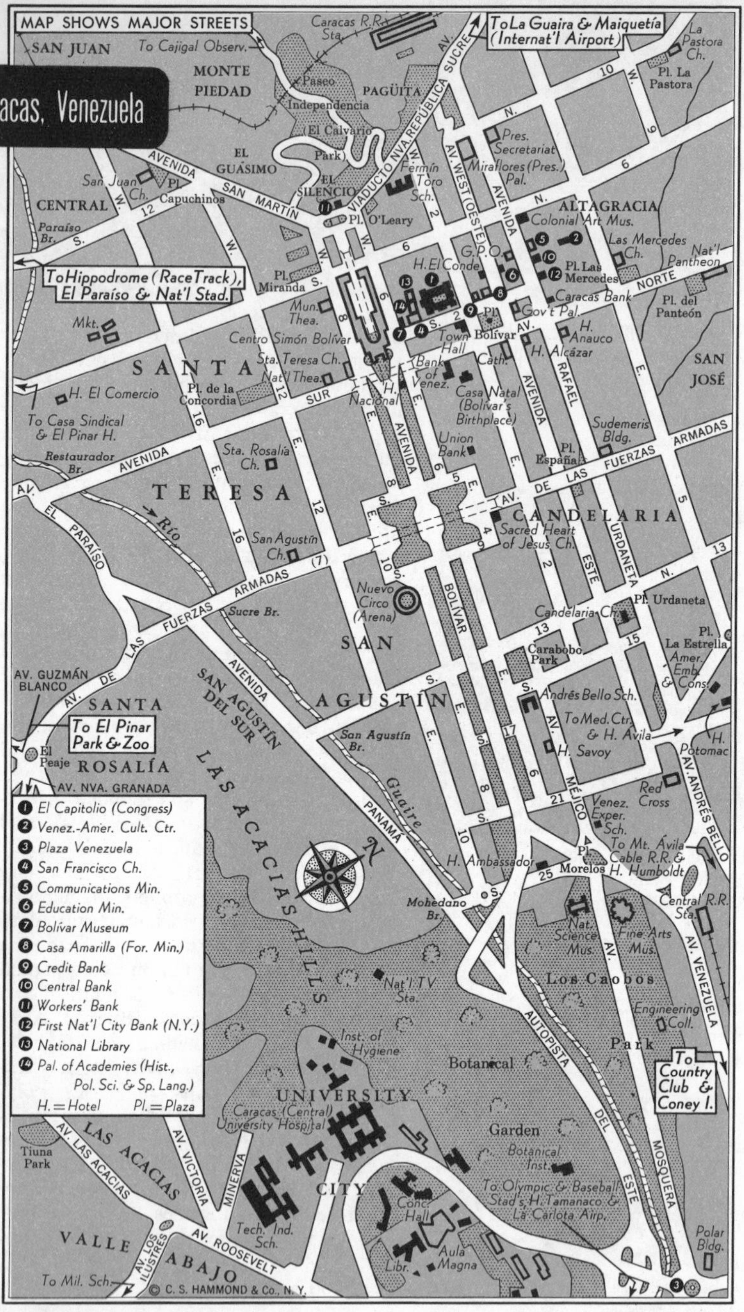

Caracas, Venezuela

MAP SHOWS MAJOR STREETS

1. El Capitolio (Congress)
2. Venez.-Amer. Cult. Ctr.
3. Plaza Venezuela
4. San Francisco Ch.
5. Communications Min.
6. Education Min.
7. Bolívar Museum
8. Casa Amarilla (For. Min.)
9. Credit Bank
10. Central Bank
11. Workers' Bank
12. First Nat'l City Bank (N.Y.)
13. National Library
14. Pal. of Academies (Hist., Pol. Sci. & Sp. Lang.)

H.=Hotel Pl.=Plaza

EL CALVARIO (Calvary), a hill on the outskirts of Caracas, is the site of a famed Observatory. An unexcelled view of the city and surrounding valley is to be had from the crest of the hill

Photos: Pan American Union, Asiatic Petroleum Co. and Creole Petroleum Company

THE PALACE of the ACADEMIES was originally the home of Central University before it was moved to the New University City. The buildings now house the National Library, and the Academies of History, the Spanish Language and Political Science

THE MUSEUM OF FINE ARTS contains excellent collections of sculpture, oil paintings and ceramics created by Venezuelan artists. It is situated at the entrance to the Parque Los Caobos

THE VENEZUELAN CAPITOL occupies an entire city block southwest of Plaza Bolívar. The building contains the famous Elliptical Hall where the presidents of the republic take the oath of office

CARACAS. Half a century ago Caracas was a modest agricultural center but today the old Caracas is vanishing and the city is fast becoming one of the great capitals of the world. When Diego de Losada founded this city in 1567, the entire area was covered with forests but now massive structures of steel and concrete mingle with century old churches and on every hand the venerable landmarks of the past give way to the future. While the city is undergoing an almost complete change its surroundings are the same as when the conquistadores founded the city over 390 years ago. El Avila, with its majestic peak rising in lofty grandeur some 10,000 feet in the air, serves as a spectacular backdrop to the capital of the country. El Avila, it is said, contributed more to the location of the city here than did the mildness of climate, the fertility of the soil or the abundance of water. Caracas is separated into two distinct sectors—the ancient town, with its baroque style of architecture planned by the Spaniards, which now contains the busy commercial and government districts, and the new Caracas, composed of tranquil suburbs spreading into the hillsides and along the valley on properties which were once huge coffee plantations. All the great landmarks of Caracas are retained in the "historic quadrilateral" covering 12 blocks in the center of town.

EDMONTON'S INDUSTRIES are mainly based upon agriculture and other natural resources of the province. Pictured is one of the city's modern industrial plants

EDMONTON. Edmonton, the capital of the Province of Alberta, is built on both sides of the North Saskatchewan River at a point close to the geographical center of the province. It is the seat not only of the Legislature but also of the provincially-owned University of Alberta with its fine schools of agriculture, mining and medicine. It is one of the oldest centers of population in western Canada with a history going back to the 18th century and its beginning as Fort Edmonton, a fur trading post of the Hudson Bay Company. Located twenty miles further down the river, it was moved to the present site of Edmonton when the original fort was destroyed by Indians in 1807. Edmonton lies at the heart of an enormously rich agricultural region and its industries are mainly based on agriculture and other natural resources of the province, with meat packing taking the lead. Edmonton is the gateway to the Mackenzie River country and to the great North generally, with which it enjoys a large and increasing commerce. Discovery of precious metals and other developments in the North, where there are no railroads or highways and where the watercourses are open for only a few months each year, gave a great impetus to commercial flying and Edmonton has become one of the world's important air-freight shipping points.

FORT EDMONTON was established for the Hudson Bay Company in 1795 by William Tomison. The Company as fur traders and merchants has since been active in the life of the community. Pictured is Hudson Bay Company's store on Jasper Avenue.

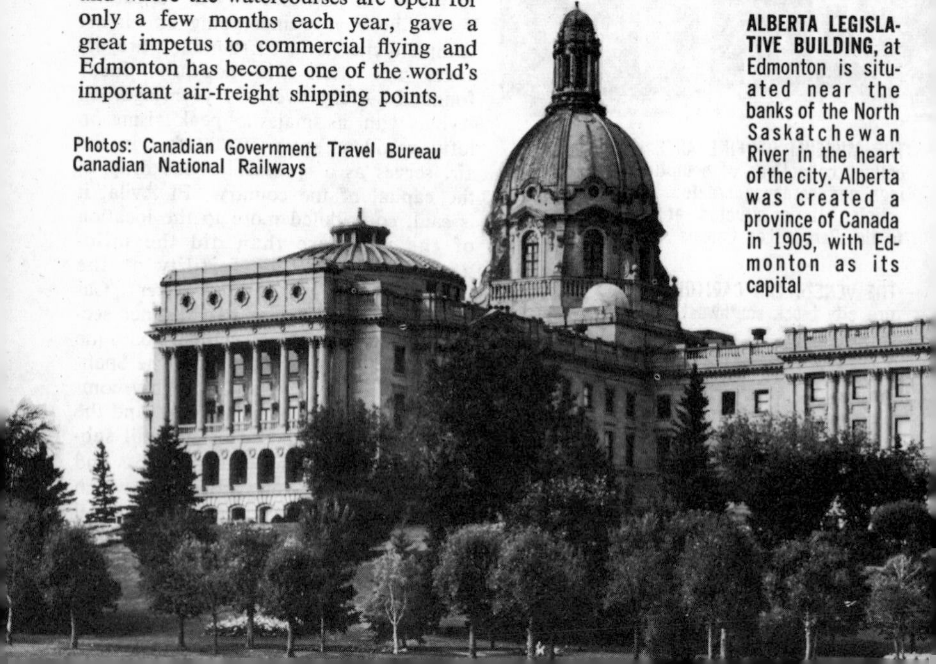

ALBERTA LEGISLATIVE BUILDING, at Edmonton is situated near the banks of the North Saskatchewan River in the heart of the city. Alberta was created a province of Canada in 1905, with Edmonton as its capital

Photos: Canadian Government Travel Bureau
Canadian National Railways

Edmonton, Canada

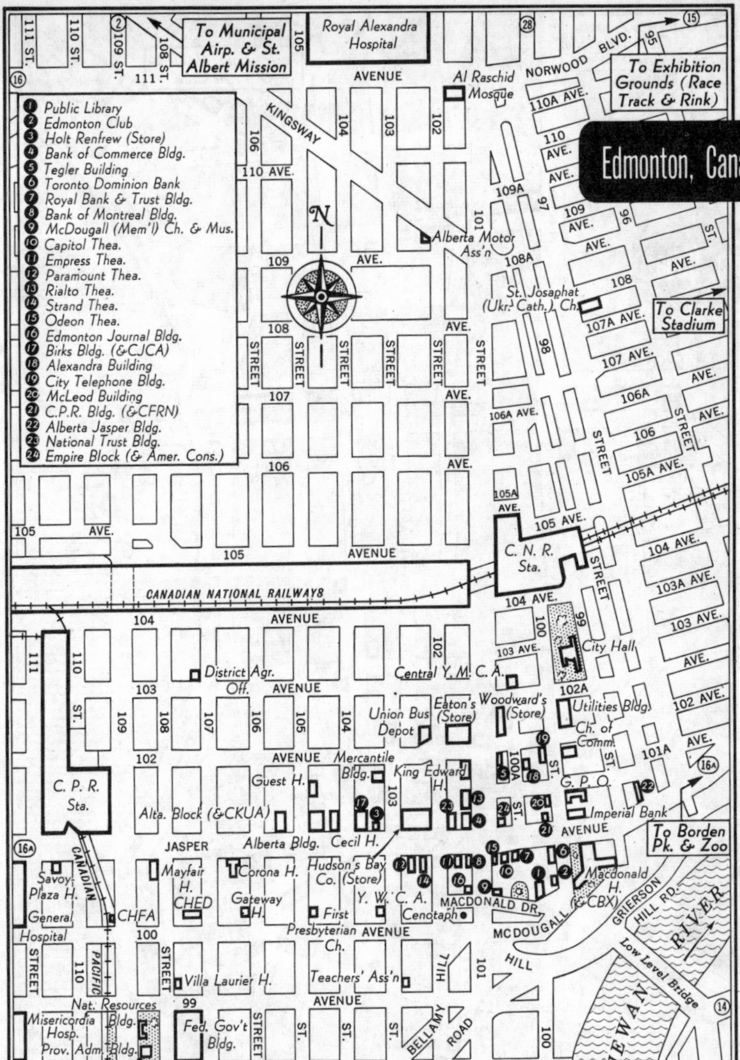

1. Public Library
2. Edmonton Club
3. Holt Renfrew (Store)
4. Bank of Commerce Bldg.
5. Tegler Building
6. Toronto Dominion Bank
7. Royal Bank & Trust Bldg.
8. Bank of Montreal Bldg.
9. McDougall (Mem'l) Ch. & Mus.
10. Capitol Thea.
11. Empress Thea.
12. Paramount Thea.
13. Rialto Thea.
14. Strand Thea.
15. Odeon Thea.
16. Edmonton Journal Bldg.
17. Birks Bldg. (&CJCA)
18. Alexandra Building
19. City Telephone Bldg.
20. McLeod Building
21. C.P.R. Bldg. (&CFRN)
22. Alberta Jasper Bldg.
23. National Trust Bldg.
24. Empire Block (& Amer. Cons.)

MAP SHOWS MAJOR STREETS

THE MILLLING OF CEREALS AND FLOUR from grains grown on the fertile plains of Alberta, is one of the leading industries of Edmonton

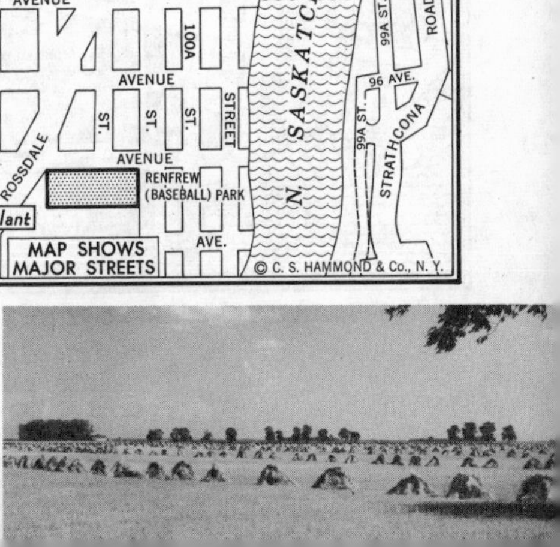

Havana, Cuba

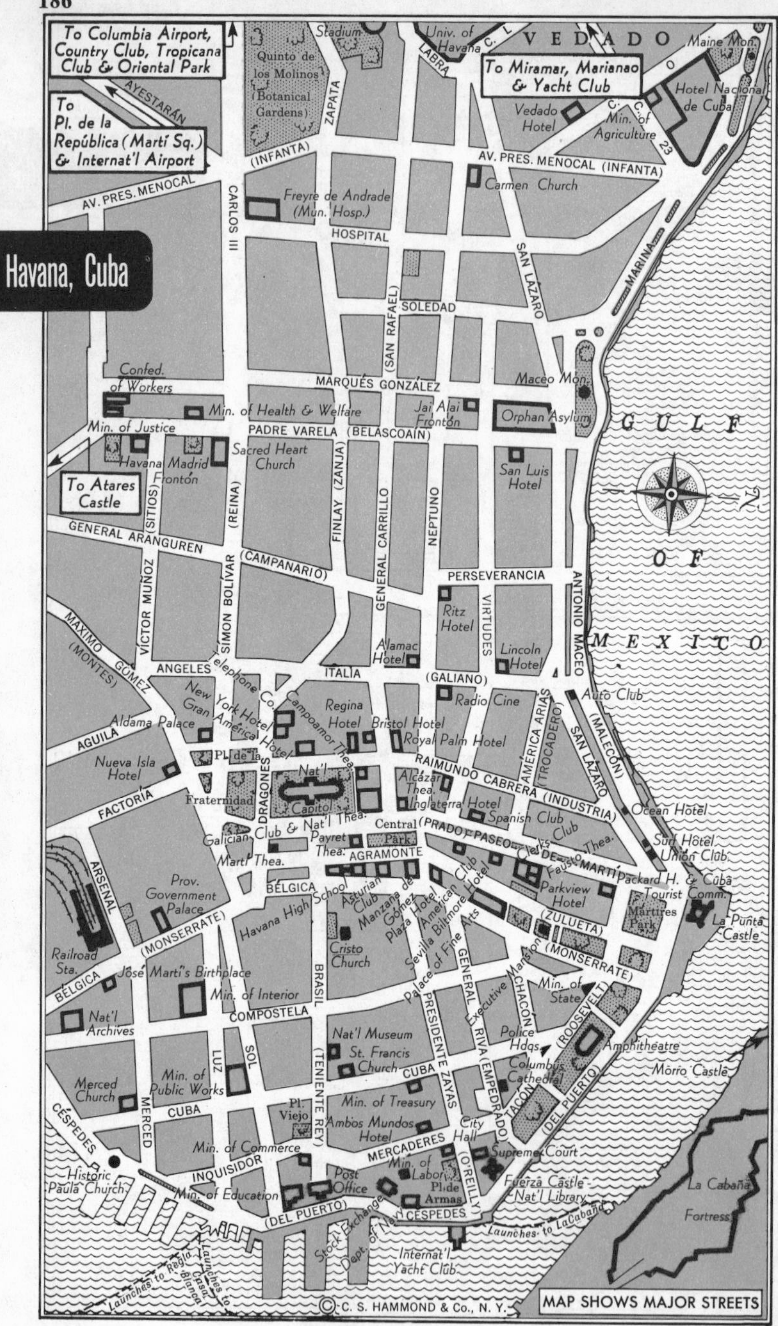

CENTRO ASTURIANO, a popular recreational and educational society located at Central Park, has a beautiful ballroom, magnificent marble stairs and a famous tiled bar

HAVANA. In the course of her four-hundred-odd years of existence, Havana has acquired the customs and activities of a gay, modern cosmopolitan city — reflected in the splendid boulevards, gardens, parks and magnificent buildings of ultramodern architecture. At the same time she has retained all the interesting aspects and charms of colonial times — found in the primitive city of narrow streets, cozy little plazas, forts and ancient churches. Gaiety sounds the keynote for the irrepressible Habañeros, a view of life that is highly infectious even to the dourest visitor in this Cuban capital. Especially is this true during Carnival, when young and old, great and small frolic with happy abandon. Special feature of the fiesta season is the parade of "Compresas," typical Afro-Cuban pageants based on the traditional slave celebration of their one day of freedom granted every year, with passionate songs and dances accompanied by exotic music and the throbbing beat of the tom-toms. Of course, this festive air is most intense throughout the year during the hours of darkness. Favorite promenade, especially

DANCERS carrying fanciful "farolas" (tissue paper lanterns) and gorgeously attired in velvet and satin of vivid colors, set off by sparkling jewels, lead each "Comparsa" in the Carnival parade

Photos: Cuban Tourist Commission

VENERABLE COLUMBUS CATHEDRAL, excellent example of Spanish baroque, whose majestic interior contains a wealth of precious altars, paintings and gorgeous vestments, faces quaint old Cathedral Square

HAVANA Continued

for the romance-bound, is the Prado, the historical boulevard in the heart of Havana. Artistically paved and shaded by splendid laurels, it is rimmed with colonnaded buildings and open-air sidewalk cafes, where native orchestras and wandering minstrels serenade the merry-makers with the rhythm of the rumba, while the Cubans sip *café con leche,* tiny cups of black coffee, beer or long, cool drinks of sweetened fruit juices and visitors enjoy drinks of the exceptionally fine national rum. In the daytime, this lightheartedness extends to a fervent love for sports of all kinds, producing partisan

BREATHLESS MOMENT during a game of "jai alai," the Basque game of handball reputed to be the world's fastest sport, played exclusively by professionals. The greatest stars appear in Havana's two "frontons"

PALACIO MUNICIPAL (City Hall), for centuries the residence of the Spanish governors general of Cuba, has a splendid colonial patio, huge, gently curving stone stairways, richly furnished reception rooms and great oil paintings

aficionados among the Habañeros, whether as spectators or participants. There are several fine professional *beisbol* teams; popular cockfights at smart *villas* or arenas; horse racing at Oriental Park Hippodrome, considered one of the finest tracks in the Western Hemisphere; golfing at the Havana Country Club, a top-flight championship course, and fishing for an enormous variety of game fish. Particularly enjoyable, however, are the many wonderful beaches. With her incomparable climate, constantly refreshed by trade winds and pleasant land breezes, sophisticated Havana combines with the elements to offer exhilarating modern city life of the ultimate in pleasure.

TROPICANA'S floor show and music are as famed as its soaring glass roof and spectacular gardens, making it the most fabulous of Havana's many dazzling night clubs

CITY SKYLINE as seen from Morro Castle, at the entrance to Havana harbor. This exciting fort and La Punta, just visible on the opposite shore, are two of the many huge, stone fortresses built as protection against the dreaded 17th-century buccaneers, in particular the menacing sea rover, Sir Francis Drake

PALACE OF FINE ARTS, with its admirable collections, is one of the newly inauguarated public buildings. Statue in the foreground is of Alfredo Zayas y Alfonso, president of Cuba from 1921 to 1925

EXCLUSIVE HAVANA YACHT CLUB, for which the entrance fee alone is $5,000, typifies the numerous elegant private clubs frequented by well-to-do Habaneros

Photos: Cuban Tourist Commission

La Paz, Bolivia

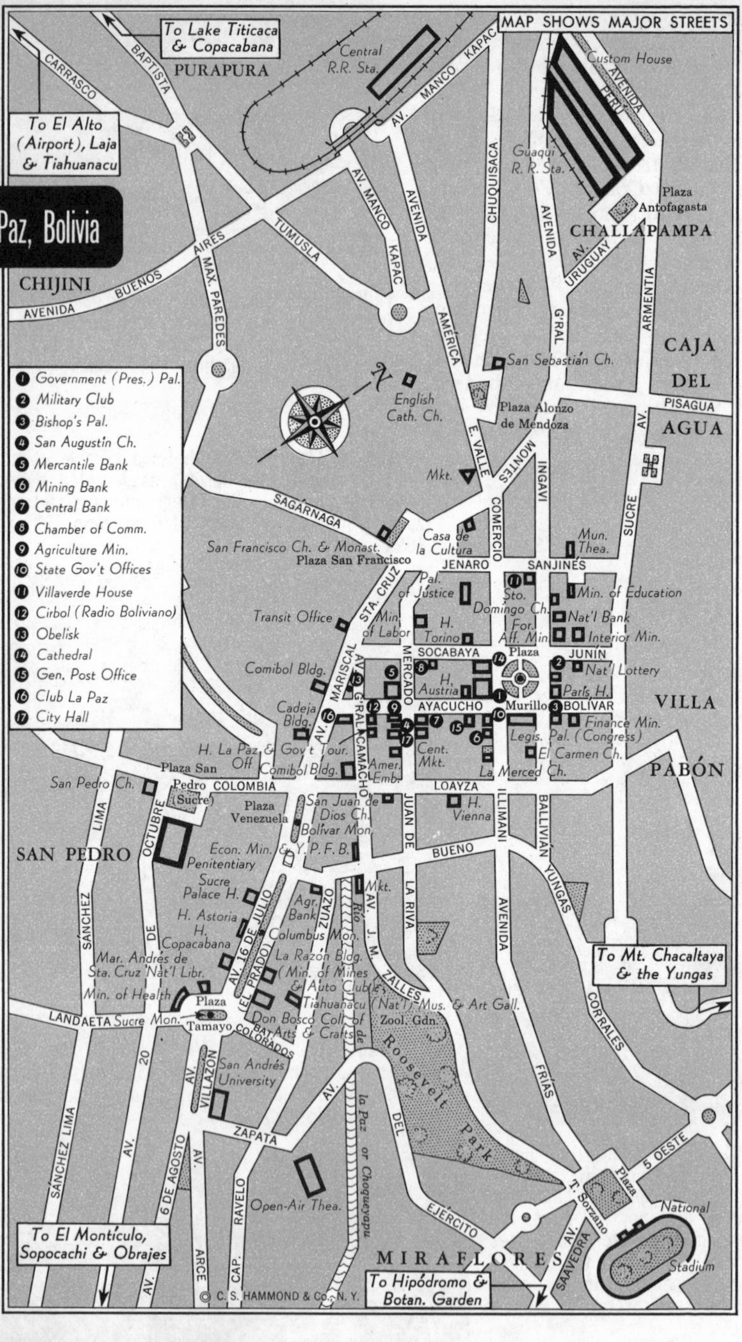

MAP SHOWS MAJOR STREETS

To Lake Titicaca & Copacabana

To El Alto (Airport), Laja & Tiahuanacu

To Mt. Chacaltaya & the Yungas

To El Montículo, Sopocachi & Obrajes

To Hipódromo & Botan. Garden

PURAPURA · CHIJINI · CHALLAPAMPA · CAJA DEL AGUA · VILLA PABÓN · SAN PEDRO · MIRAFLORES

1. Government (Pres.) Pal.
2. Military Club
3. Bishop's Pal.
4. San Augustín Ch.
5. Mercantile Bank
6. Mining Bank
7. Central Bank
8. Chamber of Comm.
9. Agriculture Min.
10. State Gov't Offices
11. Villaverde House
12. Cirbol (Radio Boliviano)
13. Obelisk
14. Cathedral
15. Gen. Post Office
16. Club La Paz
17. City Hall

THE MINISTRY OF HEALTH is one of several modern buildings which face the charming Plaza Tamayo

Photos: Braniff International Airways, Lyn Manouley, I.I.A.A.

HEMMED IN BY THE ANDES, La Paz lies in a narrow mountain valley. The levels of its adjoining streets often vary to conform with the abruptly changing terrain

LA PAZ. Situated in the Altiplano region of western Bolivia, at more than two and a quarter miles above sea level, the air of La Paz is crisp, its natural setting spectacular. To the east, Mount Illimani towers, its rugged slopes clad in the snowy robes of the Royal Andean Cordillera. About the narrow green-carpeted valley in which the city lies are gathered the bare mineral-colored peaks of lesser mountains. From the valley floor, the steep canyon walls rise almost perpendicularly above its cluster of red tiled roofs, its dignified Legislative Palace, and its Greco-Roman cathedral. In 1548, to celebrate the end of a long and bitter struggle between Pizarro and de Almagro, rival conquerors of Peru, the city of La Paz was established. Translated into English the inscription which graces its elaborate coat of arms reads: "With discords and with stubborn rages at length in harmony compounded, the town of peace was thereon founded—a monument for future ages." Belying the name, the history of La Paz, until the end of the 19th century, was far from peaceful. Exploited by the Spaniards, beseiged by Indians, torn by revolutions, unsettled by long periods of political antagonism, yet here a new country emerged from the chaos and in July, 1809, Bolivia declared her independence. Today, although Sucre continues as the official capital of Bolivia, several branches of the government make La Paz their headquarters and the city has become the principal center of her country's industry, commerce and communications.

THE LEGISLATIVE PALACE, Bolivia's capitol, overlooks the Plaza Murillo. The square is dedicated to the memory of Pedro Domingo Murillo, the leader of Bolivia's first independence movement

THE CHURCH OF SAN FRANCISCO, from the point of view of colonial architecture, is among the most interesting of La Paz's ecclesiastical establishments. Consecrated in 1778, it stands on the site of one built in 1549

MAP SHOWS MAJOR STREETS

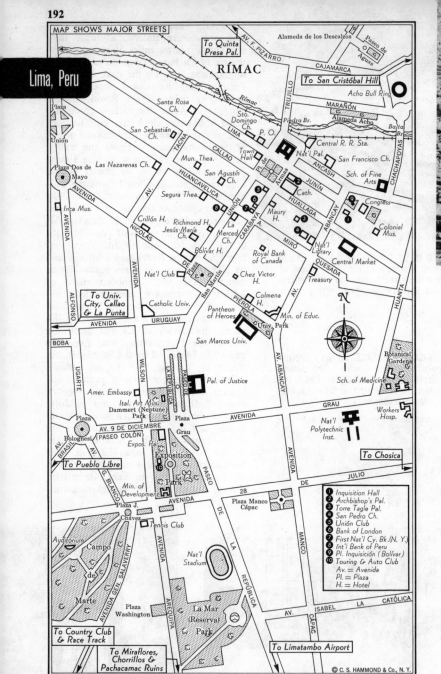

To Quinta Presa Pal.
AV. F. PIZARRO
Alameda de los Descalzos
Paseo de Aguas
RÍMAC
CAJAMARCA
To San Cristóbal Hill
TRUJILLO
Acho Bull Ring
MARAÑÓN
Alameda Acho
Rímac
Piedra Br.
Balta Br.
Santa Rosa Ch.
Sto. Domingo Ch.
P. O.
Plaza Unión
San Sebastián Ch.
LIMA
TACNA
CALLAO
Town Hall
Nat'l Pal.
Central R. R. Sta.
CHACHAPOYAS
San Francisco Ch.
ANCASH
Mun. Thea.
Pl. de Armas
Plaza Dos de Mayo
Las Nazarenas Ch.
San Agustín Ch.
JUNÍN
Sch. of Fine Arts
HUANCAVELICA
Cath.
AVENIDA
Segura Thea.
HUALLAGA
Congress
AV.
UNIÓN
Inca Mus.
Maury H.
ABANCAY
Crillón H.
Richmond H.
CARABAYA
Colonial Mus.
NICOLÁS
Jesús María Ch.
La Merced Ch.
MIRÓ
Nat'l Library
Bolívar H.
Royal Bank of Canada
Central Market
DE
QUESADA
Nat'l Club
Plaza San Martín
Chez Victor H.
Treasury
AVENIDA
PIÉROLA
Colmena H.
AV.
HUANTA
To Univ. City, Callao & La Punta
Catholic Univ.
Pantheon of Heroes
Min. of Educ.
ALFONSO
AVENIDA
URUGUAY
Univ. Park
BOBA
San Marcos Univ.
Botanical Gardens
UGARTE
WILSON
LA REPÚBLICA
PASEO DE
Pal. of Justice
AV. ABANCAY
Sch. of Medicine
Amer. Embassy
Ital. Art Mus.
Dammert (Neptune) Park
GRAU
Plaza Grau
AVENIDA
Workers Hosp.
Nat'l Polytechnic Inst.
Plaza Bolognesi
AV. 9 DE DICIEMBRE (PASEO COLÓN)
Expos. Pal.
AV. BRASIL
AV.
Exposition
AVENIDA
To Chosica
To Pueblo Libre
PASEO
Park
JULIO
DE
Min. of Development
G. BLANCO
28
AVENIDA
Plaza Manco Cápac
Plaza J. Chávez
DE
Tennis Club
Auditorium
Campo de Marte
AVENIDA
LA
MANCO
Nat'l Stadium
AVENIDA GEN. SALAVERRY
REPÚBLICA
AREQUIPA
Plaza Washington
La Mar (Reserva) Park
AV. ISABEL LA CATÓLICA
CAPAC
To Country Club & Race Track
To Miraflores, Chorrillos & Pachacamac Ruins
To Limatambo Airport

1. Inquisition Hall
2. Archbishop's Pal.
3. Torre Tagle Pal.
4. San Pedro Ch.
5. Unión Club
6. Bank of London
7. First Nat'l Cy. Bk. (N. Y.)
8. Int'l Bank of Peru
9. Pl. Inquisición (Bolívar)
10. Touring & Auto Club

Av. = Avenida
Pl. = Plaza
H. = Hotel

Photos: Pan American Union, Grace Line

TORRE TAGLE PALACE which today houses the Foreign Office, preserves much of its storied colonial atmosphere. Pictured is the charming patio of the Palace

THE "CITY OF KINGS" symbolized Spanish power and civilization for almost three centuries. Although modernization has come with expansion, it has followed traditional patterns adding to the beauty of Lima as a whole

THE COLONIAL MUSEUM faces Plaza Bolivar in which stands a statue of the Liberator. In colonial times the beautiful building served as the "House of the Inquisition"

LIMA'S CATHEDRAL faces the Plaza de Armas. The Church was powerful in colonial Peru and the country boasts many examples of religious architecture showing the fusion of Hispanic and Indian art forms

LIMA. Capital of Peru and for centuries the viceroyalty of Spain's vast colonial empire in South America, Lima is a city of proud tradition where on every hand are found the remains of its once fabulous culture. On January 18th, 1535, the great conquistador Francisco Pizarro inscribed its circumference with his famous sword of Gallo, naming his new capital Ciudad de los Reyes—"City of Kings"—in honor of the Epiphany. Later the city became known as Lima, a mispronunciation of Rimac, a river on whose banks the city was founded. Its original checkerboard pattern of 117 squares, designed to provide shade on at least one side of the street at all times, still survives as do many of the colorful names by which the streets were designated. In 1746, a shattering earthquake destroyed most of Lima and its port of Callao, six miles distant on the Pacific coast. Today few of the city's buildings antedate this disaster. Although Lima lies within a few degrees of the equator in a region whose climate should under normal conditions be tropical, the city enjoys little equatorial heat. From May to November, thick clouds caused by the antarctic chill of the Humbolt Current, shroud the bald peak of San Cristobal and obscure the sun. Though little rain falls in the arid coastal region about the city, fog and the heavy mist known as the "Garua" drift inland from the Pacific during the winter months. Today Lima is a harmonious blend of old and new. The churches and houses as well as the clothes worn by her people, reflect the three strains in her culture—Indian, colonial and modern.

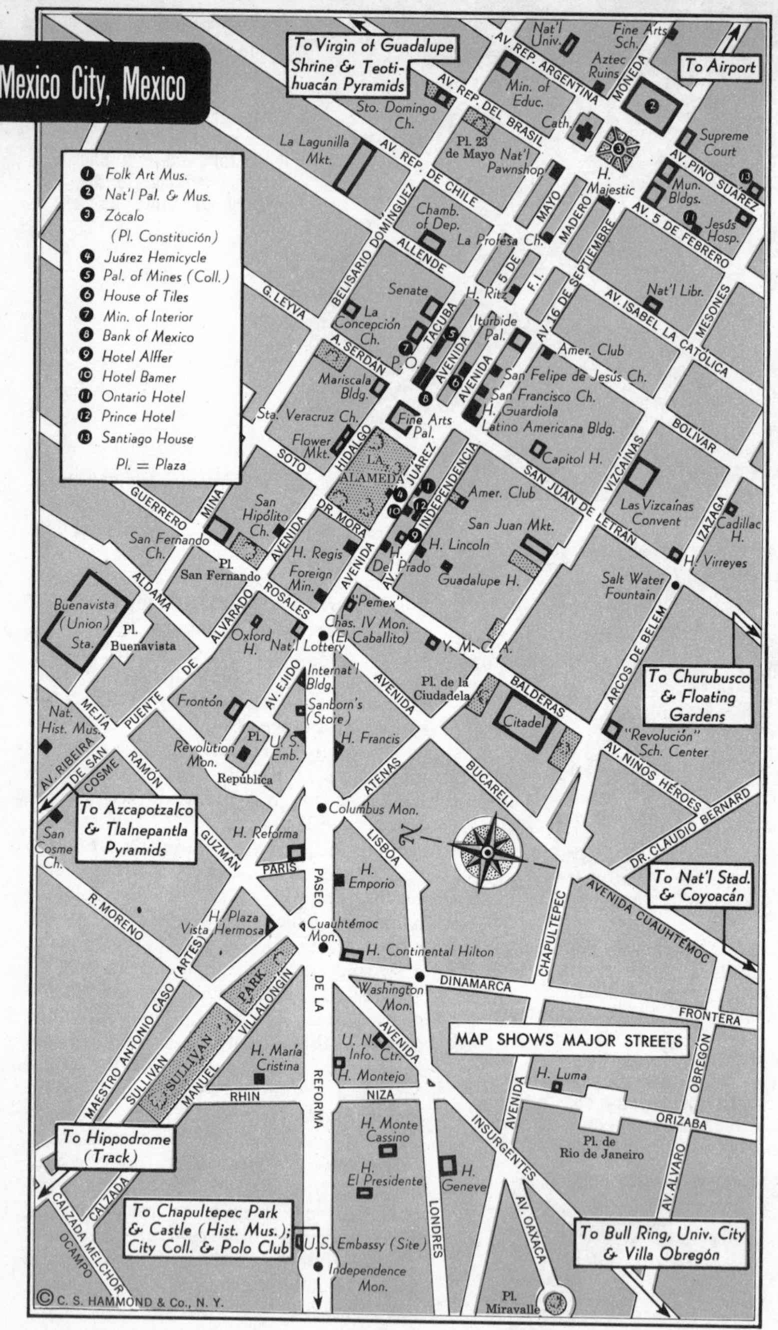

Photos: Pan American Union

THE CATHEDRAL OF MEXICO CITY faces the extensive Plaza de la Constitución, better known as Zócalo. On the north side of the Zócalo, the first church in North America was erected in 1525

XOCHIMILCO and its wonderful floating gardens lies about 15 miles from the center of Mexico City. Visitors may hire flower-decked boats and drift along the canals of this "Venice of Mexico"

THE NATIONAL PALACE occupies the site of Cortez's own house on the east side of the Plaza Constitución. In the picture, the Palace is shown illuminated for the Independence Day celebration

MEXICO CITY. Springing from Tenochtitlán, ancient center of the Aztec Empire, Mexico City, founded about 1325, is the oldest city in North America. When the Spanish conquistadores arrived in 1519, it was a flourishing community with a population of 300,000. With the fall of the Aztec Empire, Hernando Cortez had the main square of the city—now the Plaza de la Constitución—constructed on what had been the very heart of the former Aztec capital. On the north side of the Plaza or Zócalo as it is popularly called, is the Cathedral whose foundations were laid nearly four hundred years ago. It occupies the site of the Teocalli—a great pyramid and temple, where Aztec priests once offered human sacrifices to their gods. The Palacio Nacional, which covers an entire block on the eastern side of the Zócalo, is built where Montezuma's palace once stood. Above the central portal of the Palacio hangs Mexico's Liberty Bell. On September 15th, 1810, in the village of Dolores, the bell was tolled by Father Miguel Hidalgo y Costilla, to summon the Indians from the surrounding hills. Each year at 11 P.M. on the anniversary of the Grito de Dolores, Mexico's president re-enacts the role of the revolutionary priest whose dramatic call to arms marked the end of three hundred years of Spanish rule. The

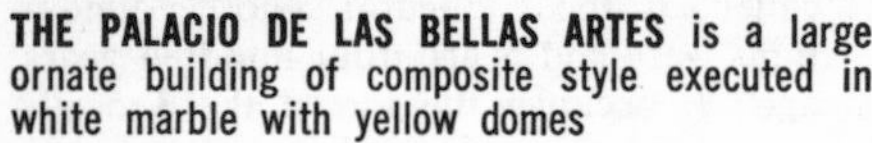

THE PALACIO DE LAS BELLAS ARTES is a large ornate building of composite style executed in white marble with yellow domes

A MONUMENT TO BENITO JUÁREZ, Mexico's national hero, stands in a beautiful park called the Alameda. Juárez forcibly opposed the setting up of a French Empire in Mexico

COLORFUL MURALS adorn many of the exterior walls of buildings in Mexico's new University City. The National University's summer school attracts many students from the United States

CHAPULTEPEC CASTLE, Begun in 1783 and later rebuilt by Maximilian, is the place where the Act of Chapultepec, pledging the American Republics to the collective defense of the Western Hemisphere, was signed

THE INTRICATE STEPS OF A MEXICAN DANCE are demonstrated by a "charro" and his lady. The national association of "charros" (who are best described as gentlemen cowboys) holds public riding exhibitions each Sunday in Mexico City

Photos: Pan American Union, Pan American Airways, Cia. Mexicana, Aero Foto, S. A.

MEXICO CITY Continued

Museo Nacional, on the northeast corner of the Zócalo, has an extensive collection of Indian relics and native handicraft, while the Escuela Nacional de Bellas Artes contains a valuable group of church paintings by such masters as Murillo, Zurbarán and Rubens. Also in the Zócalo quarter is the former School of Medicine; interesting because it was originally the headquarters of the Inquisition, where the cells of its victims still can be seen. The Palacio de las Bellas Artes—of more recent construction—has, because of its tremendous weight, sunk six feet into the spongy lake bed on which Mexico City stands. Executed in white marble with yellow domes, it contains the National Theater whose extraordinary curtain of Tiffany glass cost many thousands of dollars. Mexico City's main boulevard is the Paseo de la Reforma; designed by the Emperor Maximilian to resemble Paris' famed Champs-Elysées. Its three-mile length is interrupted at intervals by "glorietas"—circles containing statues, gardens and fountains. This broad tree-lined avenue leads to Chapultepec Park where the Aztec Emperor Montezuma had his summer palace. Mexico City is situated in a fertile valley, 7,500 feet above the level of the sea. Walled in on three sides by high mountains, the city's altitude tends to offset its tropical location, giving it a climate of eternal spring.

BEAUTIFUL BEACHES, where Uruguayan youngsters are taught to swim at government expense, are only a few minutes ride from the center of the city. Pictured is Pocitos, one of the most popular playgrounds in the Montevideo area

MONTEVIDEO. Montevideo, the capital of Uruguay, lies on the north shore of the Río de la Plata on Montevideo Bay across from El Cerro, a low mountain that is supposed to have given the city its name. When Magellan's ships sailed into the Río de la Plata in 1520, a lookout on seeing El Cerro shouted in Portuguese "Monte vide eu!" (I see a mountain!) Largely because of its salubrious climate but also because of its fine natural facilities for sea and river bathing, Montevideo has become one of the most popular summer resorts in South America. Stretching along the shore of the river for several miles are splendid bathing resorts which attract not only the people of Uruguay but also those of neighboring countries. Within Montevideo are three well defined districts, kept more or less distinct by zoning regulations. The Ciudad Vieja (Old Town) built on the peninsula is the commercial and financial center. Even today, this old section retains its colonial atmosphere. Spreading out from the peninsula is Ciudad Nueva (New City), in which most of the modern architectural development has taken place, including the handsome buildings of the national government, office buildings and churches. The third district in the city is residential, containing beautiful homes with large flowering gardens which front on broad shady streets. Montevideo's excellent transit system connects all sections of the city.

Photos: Pan American Airways, Pan American Union, Moore-McCormack Lines

THE TEATRO SOLIS where world famous artists perform before packed houses during Montevideo's brilliant theatrical and concert season. Books, philosophy and music are an important part of city life

THE PALACIO SALVO HOTEL with its lavish architecture and unique tower, is one of the landmarks of Montevideo

Montevideo, Uruguay

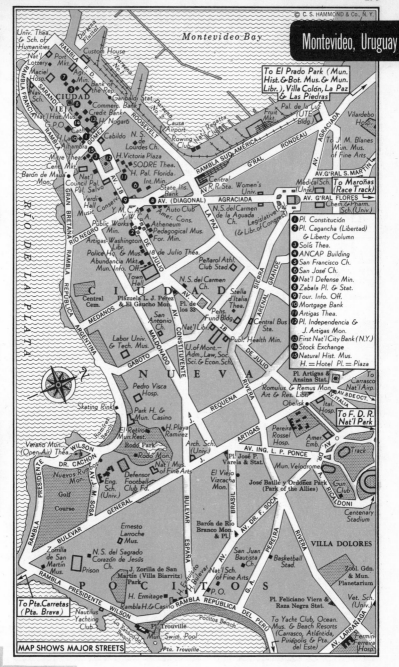

Montevideo Bay

RÍO DE LA PLATA

CIUDAD VIEJA

CIUDAD NUEVA

POCITOS

VILLA DOLORES

To El Prado Park (Mun. Hist. & Bot. Mus. & Mun. Libr.), Villa Colón, La Paz & Las Piedras

To Maroñas (Race Track)

To F. D. R. Nat'l Park

To Carrasco Nat'l Airp.

To Pta. Carretas (Pta. Brava)

To Yacht Club, Ocean. Mus. & Beach Resorts (Carrasco, Atlántida, Piriápolis & Pta. del Este)

Univ. Thea. & Sch. of Humanities · Nat'l Lottery · Maciel Hosp. · Nav. Sch. · Port Mkt. · Custom House · Darsena Fluvial · Darsena No. 1 · Darsena No. 2 · Agr. Min. · Bank of the Rep. · Garibaldi Stat. · Commerc. Bank · Credit Bank · Nat'l Hist. Mus. · H. Nogaró · G.P.O. · Cath. · H. Lafayette · Alhambra · Causa Airport · Nat'l Regatta Club · Rowing Club · Cabildo · N. S. de Lourdes Ch. · Mitre Thea. · Cent. Mkt. · H. Victoria Plaza · SODRE Thea. · H. Pal. Florida · Int. Min. · Barón de Mauá Mon. · Nat'l Council Pal. · Pal. Salvo · State Ins. Bank · Verdi Hall · Music Conserv. · Y.M.C.A. · Y.W.C.A. · Auto Club · Amer. Cons. · Atheneum · Pedagogical Mus. · For. Min. · Public Works Min. · Artigas-Washington Libr. · Police Hq. & Mus. · 18 de Julio Thea. · Abundancia Mkt. · Mun. Info. Off. · Town Hall · Central R.R. Sta. · Women's Univ. · Medical Sch. (Univ.) · Chem. & Pharm. Sch. (Univ.) · Pal. de la Luz (UTE Bldg.) · Fruit Mkt. · Vilardebo Hosp. · To J. M. Blanes Mun. Mus. of Fine Arts · N.S. del Carmen de la Aguada Ch. · Legislative Pal. (& Libr. of Congress) · Peñarol Athl. Club Stad. · N.S. del Carmen Ch. · Stella d'Italia Thea. · Central Cem. · Plazuela L. J. Pérez & El Gaucho Mon. · Pl. de los 33 · San Antonio Ch. · Pens. Fund Bldg. · Central Bus Sta. · Nat'l Libr. · Publ. Health Min. · Labor Univ. & Tech. Mus. · U. of Mont.—Adm., Law, Soc. Sci. & Econ. Sch. · Pl. Artigas & Ansina Stat. · Romulus & Remus Mon. · Art & Res. Libr. · Obelisk · Ital. Hosp. · Pedro Visca Hosp. · Skating Rink · Park H. & Mun. Casino · Ramírez Beach · El Retiro Mun. Rest. · H. Playa Ramírez · Rodó Park · Rodó Mon. · Arch. Sch. (Univ.) · Pereira Rossel Hosp. · Amer. Emb. · Track · Verano Mun. (Open-Air) Thea. · Nuevos Rumbos Mon. · Eng. Sch. (Univ.) · Defensor Football Club Fd. · Nat'l Mus. of Fine Arts · Pl. José P. Varela & Stat. · El Viejo Vizcacha Mon. · Mun. Velodrome · José Batlle y Ordóñez Park (Park of the Allies) · Gun Club · Centenary Stadium · Golf Course · Barón de Río Branco Mon. & Pl. · Ernesto Larroche Mus. · Zorrilla de San Martín Mus. · N. S. del Sagrado Corazón de Jesús Ch. · Prison · J. Zorilla de San Martín (Villa Biarritz) Park · San Juan Bautista Ch. · Basketball Stad. · Nat'l Sch. of Fine Arts · H. Ermitage · H. Exquisito · H. Bulevar · P.O. · Zool. Gdn. & Mun. Planetarium · Vet. Sch. (Univ.) · Pl. Feliciano Viera & Raza Negra Stat. · Rambla H. & Casino · Nautilus Yachting Club · La Estacada Beach · Pl. Trouville · Pocitos Beach · Mun. Swim. Pool · Pta. Trouville · Fermín Ferreira Hosp.

Rambla F. D. Roosevelt · Rambla Francia · Sarandí · Rambla Gran Bretaña · Gomez · Rambla Sud América · G'ral Rondeau · Av. Agraciada · Av. G'ral S. Martín · Av. G'ral Flores · Av. (Diagonal) Agraciada · Av. 18 de Julio · La Paz · Rio Negro · Sierra · Grande · Arenal · Rambla República Argentina · Medanos · Maldonado · Av. Constituyente · Gaboto · Rivera · Requena · Av. 8 de Oct. · Av. Italia · Artigas · Av. Ing. L. P. Ponce · Av. Dr. A. Ricaldoni · Wilson · Dr. Cachon · Av. J. M. Sosa · Rambla Presidente Wilson · Bulevar General Artigas · Bulevar España · Brasil · Av. Dr. F. Soca · Pereira · G. A. Pereira · Av. Brasil · Rambla República del Perú · Av. Larrañaga

1. Pl. Constitución
2. Pl. Cagancha (Libertad) & Liberty Column
3. Solís Thea.
4. ANCAP Building
5. San Francisco Ch.
6. San José Ch.
7. Nat'l Defense Min.
8. Zabala Pl. & Stat.
9. Tour. Info. Off.
10. Mortgage Bank
11. Artigas Thea.
12. Pl. Independencia & J. Artigas Mon.
13. First Nat'l City Bank (N.Y.)
14. Stock Exchange
15. Natural Hist. Mus.

H. = Hotel Pl. = Plaza

MAP SHOWS MAJOR STREETS

LA CARRETA, commemorating Uruguayan pioneers, is an heroic work of José Belloni. The sculpture stands in Batlle y Ordóñez Park where it seems to come to life before the viewer's eyes

Montreal, Canada

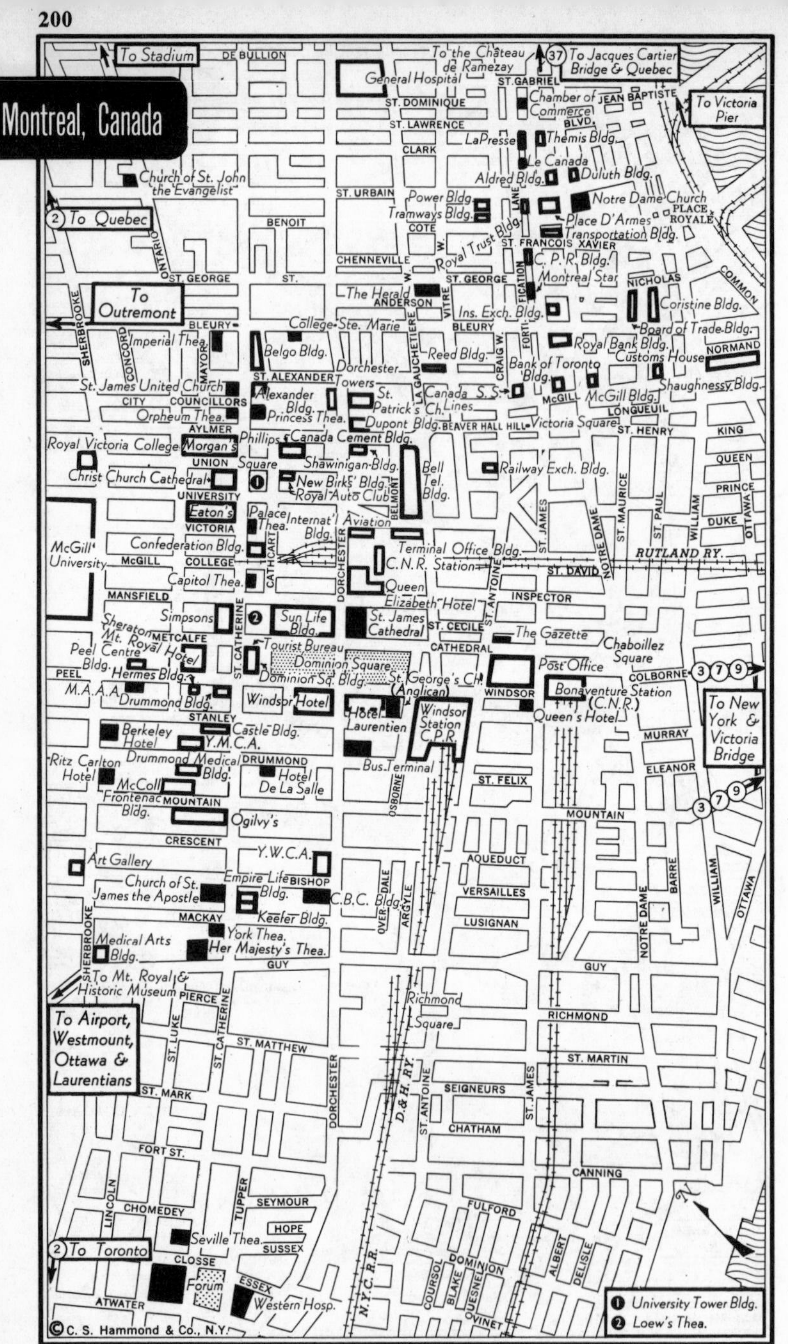

Photos: Canadian National Railways, Canadian Government Travel Bureau

CLOGGED BY ICE and frequently blanketed by snow, the Port of Montreal is closed to navigation from December until April

MONTREAL'S SPACIOUS HARBOR extends for 16 miles along the St. Lawrence River. Ten miles of wharves and unrivaled facilities for handling cargo make Montreal one of the world's busiest ports

MONTREAL. Often called the "Paris of the New World," Montreal, with over two-thirds of her population of French origin, has much the same gaiety and continental charm of her Old World counterpart. Occupying an outstanding position in her nation's economy, Montreal is the metropolis of Canada and its center of transportation, commerce and finance. The city also enjoys the distinction of being the world's largest inland port, and the second largest port on the American Continent. An island, thirty miles long, Montreal lies at the head of ocean navigation in the St. Lawrence River, one thousand miles from the sea. Once the site of the Indian village of Hochelaga, it was discovered in 1535 by the French navigator Jacques Cartier. Originally called Ville-Marie, Montreal is historically associated with the settlement of many American cities. From here ventured forth the makers of the history of New France—Champlain, de La Salle, Marquette, Joliette, Duluth, Maisonneuve, Bienville and other dauntless *voyageurs*. The Château de Ramezay once the seat of government and now a museum, graphically presents the early history of Montreal better than many

THE SUN LIFE BUILDING is among the tallest office buildings in Canada. It faces Dominion Square, a park in the uptown business area of Montreal

MONTREAL Continued

books. Today many buildings in the city's downtown area that were built during the French and early British regimes are marked by tablets which stand as true chronicles dating back to 1642 and the city's founding by Paul Chomedey, Sieur de Maisonneuve. Place Royale was the original site of Ville-Marie chosen by Champlain in 1611. The Canadian Historic Museum contains scenes of early Canadian history realistically depicted in wax. Montreal is in truth a young-old city for though it originated in the 17th century it is more modern than the city of Quebec and its skyline the tallest in the British Empire. Towering over its skyscrapers, Mount Royal rises to 763 feet in the heart of the city. A beautifully wooded park area, its summit is surmounted by a one hundred foot cross. Illuminated at night, the giant cross is visible for many miles. Mount Royal provides within the city wonderful ski trails, toboggan slides and a skating rink located on its slopes at Lac Castor. The park is restricted and no automobiles are allowed within its confines. Calèches and gaily painted horse-drawn sleighs carry visitors to the top of the mountain while trails and paths are provided for hikers. Among the most noted of the city's institutions is McGill University with the stern beauty of its Scottish baronial architecture and its world renowned medical school. On Westmount Mountain, overlooking Montreal, is St. Joseph's Oratory. Another of the city's impressive landmarks, this fabulous shrine venerates the miracle-working Brother André through whose prayers remarkable cures are said to have been wrought. Montreal is renowned for its many beautiful churches, the delight of lovers of religious architecture. The city's bi-lingual atmosphere assures the visitor of merriment and the pleasures of French and Canadian cuisines.

JACQUES CARTIER BRIDGE originally called the Harbour Bridge spans the St. Lawrence at Montreal. Opened in 1930, the bridge carries a heavy load of auto traffic to and from the city

GIANT GRAIN ELEVATORS are located along the river bank at Montreal where grain from the prairies of western Canada is loaded aboard ships for export to England and other nations abroad

STE. CATHERINE STREET, the principal shopping center of Montreal is lined by large department stores and a wide variety of smaller shops which sell furs, woolens, French perfumes, English china and other items popular with the tourist

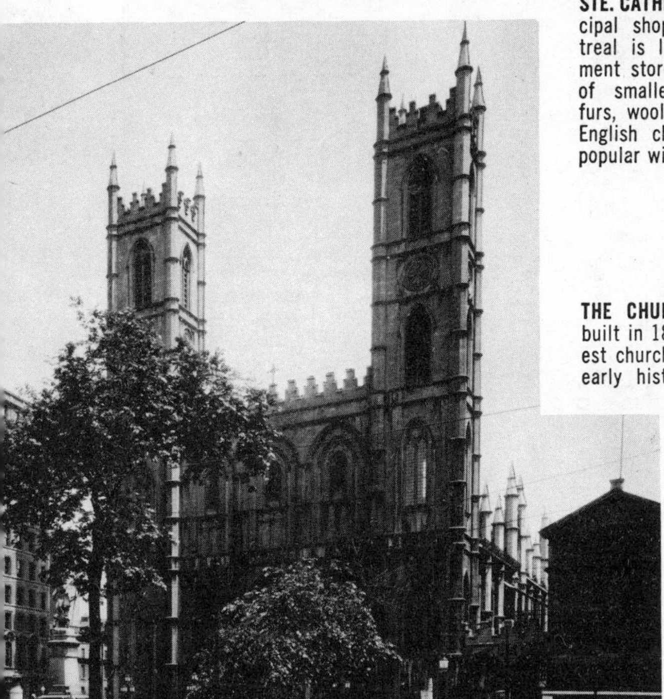

THE CHURCH OF NOTRE DAME built in 1824 is the second largest church in North America. The early history of the parish is depicted in the stained glass of its windows and a museum, adjoining the church, houses an interesting collection of religious and historic relics

Photos: Montreal Tourist and Convention Bureau Inc., Canadian National Railways

McGILL UNIVERSITY with its handsome buildings, imposing gateways and its tree-shaded campus is among the city's most distinguished landmarks. Classes at the university are conducted in English

Ottawa, Canada

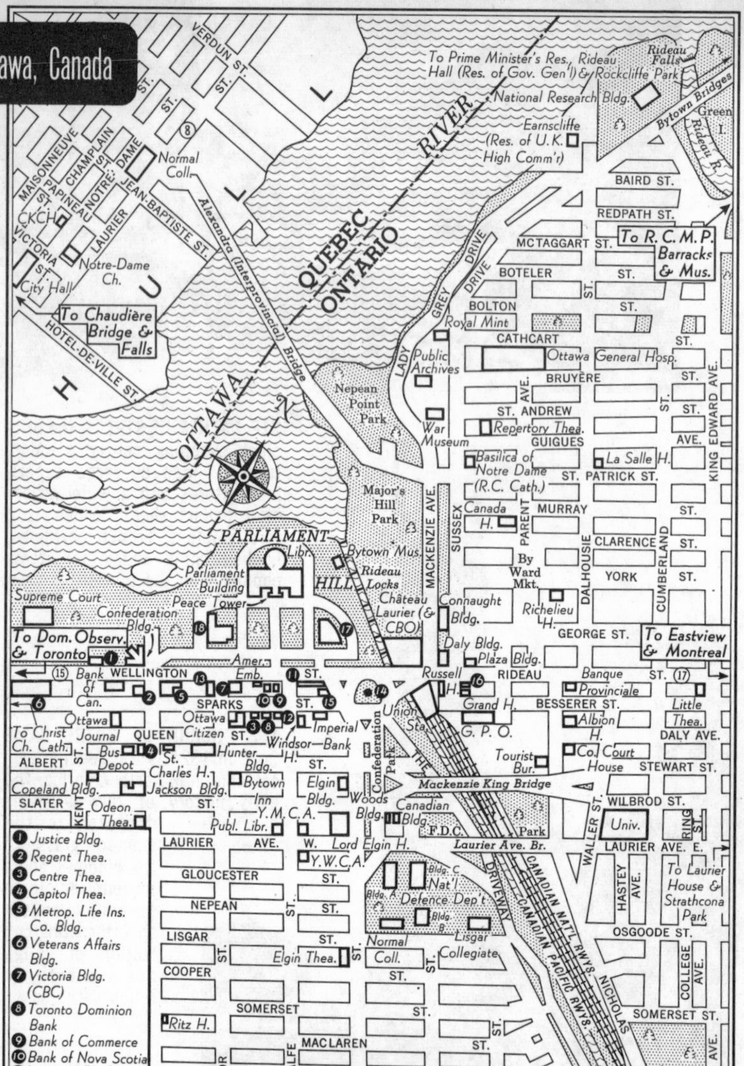

1. Justice Bldg.
2. Regent Thea.
3. Centre Thea.
4. Capitol Thea.
5. Metrop. Life Ins. Co. Bldg.
6. Veterans Affairs Bldg.
7. Victoria Bldg. (CBC)
8. Toronto Dominion Bank
9. Bank of Commerce
10. Bank of Nova Scotia
11. Langevin Block
12. Royal Bank
13. Bank of Montreal
14. Nat'l War Mem'l & Confederation Sq.
15. Uptown P.O. Sta.
16. Transportation Bldg. (City Offices)
17. E. Block (Pr. Min. Off. & Ext. Aff's Dep't)
18. W. Block (Sec. of State Dep't)

H.=Hotel

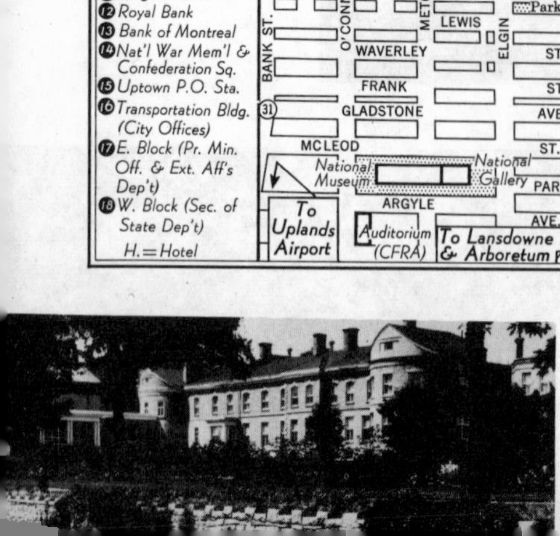

RIDEAU HALL is the official residence of the Governor-General of Canada at Ottawa. The handsome grounds of the mansion are usually open to the public during the summer months when the Governor-General is not in residence

CANADIAN PARLIAMENT BUILDINGS are among the most impressive governmental structures in the world. Central Block was destroyed by fire in 1916. The present building was completed in 1921 at the cost of $12,000,000. It contains 6 floors and 490 rooms

Photos: Canadian Govt. Travel Bureau, Canadian National Railways, Canadian Pacific Railway

RIDEAU CANAL at Ottawa was built originally as a military work. In 1826 the bitterness created by the War of 1812 still poisoned the relations between Canadians and Americans and measures of defense that would be thought absurd today were considered reasonable

THE NATIONAL WAR MEMORIAL in Confederation Square commemorates the heroism and self-sacrifice of the 619,636 Canadians who answered the call of King and Country in the Great War of 1914-1918

OTTAWA. Capital of Canada, Ottawa is a city of stately dignity, a pleasant residential city in a beautiful setting at the meeting of the Ottawa and Rideau Rivers. Ottawa's history like that of many other great cities is almost inseparable from the history of the rivers on which it is situated. Peaceful commerce built Ottawa, and in early days its site served as a place of landing and portage for those intrepid adventurers who first paddled up the Ottawa River's broad stream into the silent forests beyond. The city of Ottawa is dominated by a mass of splendid Gothic buildings. They stand like everlasting sentinels on the summit of Parliament Hill. The architectural perfection of the Peace Tower, reaching 293 feet into the air, catches the eye from a distance before any other part of the city is visible. Canada's greatest carillon (53 bells) peals forth from its tower—a memorial to her heroic sons who gave their lives in service to their country. Among the city's interesting public buildings are the Confederation Building; the Justice Building, headquarters of the Northwest Mounted Police; the Supreme Court Building and the National Art Gallery, containing an excellent collection of paintings by Canadian artists. Throughout the city are scattered the fascinating Royal Mint, the Archives of Canada, the Victoria Museum and other buildings which preserve the records of Ottawa's past or serve the business of the nation today.

QUÉBEC. Imparting a medieval aspect with her picturesque buildings, gables and dormer windows, turreted battlements and French architecture, *Ville de Québec,* "City of Remembrance," is fragrant with the past, fittingly described as the spirit of romance in a materialistic age. White and gray houses front on cobblestone squares, ornamented and weathered, and black, rust-pitted guns peer over the fortified walls. The old city under the French regime consisted of some forty-five streets, the most fashionable sector of which is now known as the Latin Quarter, noted for its quaint little houses, many of them period homes, with small green shutters, red roofs and tiny windows. With more churches to her size than Rome, the ring of church bells sounds a continuous carillon throughout the legendary city on the hill, melodious monuments to the dedicated missionaries who founded Québec, struggling against almost hopeless odds to keep her alive during her infancy. And further enhancing the Old-World atmosphere of these lovely French-Canadian haunts are the *calèches,* the two-wheel bouncing carriages, and old-fashioned buggies skillfully traversing her narrow streets and steep hills.

ST. LOUIS GATE, one of three restored entrances to the old city in the enclosing wall, the city's third, constructed between 1823 and 1832, which made Québec the greatest stronghold of its time

VIEW from the stately, 17th-century, French-renaissance Provincial Parliament Buildings toward the St. Lawrence. On the right is beautiful Isle d'Orleans, whose inhabitants live an age-old French life in old Norman-styled cottages with outdoor ovens

Photos: Canadian National Railways, Canadian Government Travel Bureau.

CITADEL, a diamond-shaped fortress, today houses Quebec's famed Royal 22nd Regiment, which still changes the guard every day in a traditional ceremony

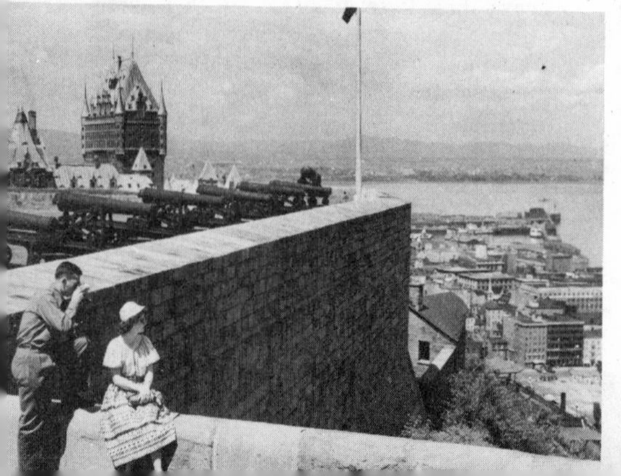

SKIING, ice skating, tobogganing and fashioned sleigh riding may be enjo right within the city's walls. In the ba ground is internationally known Chât Frontenac

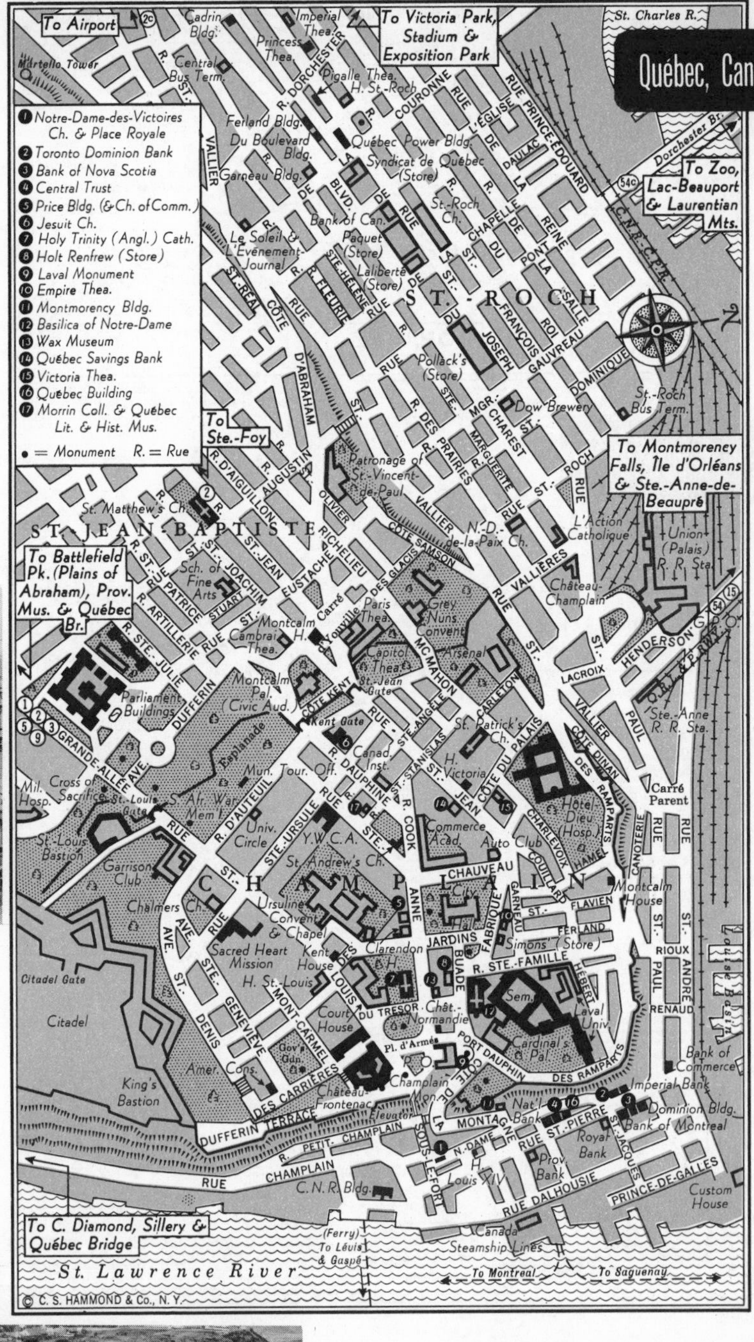

360-FOOT-HIGH CAPE DIAMOND is the huge promontory on whose site perches the "Fortified City," five times beseiged but never taken by storm. On this side of the cape are the Plains of Abraham, where Wolf defeated Montcalm in 1759

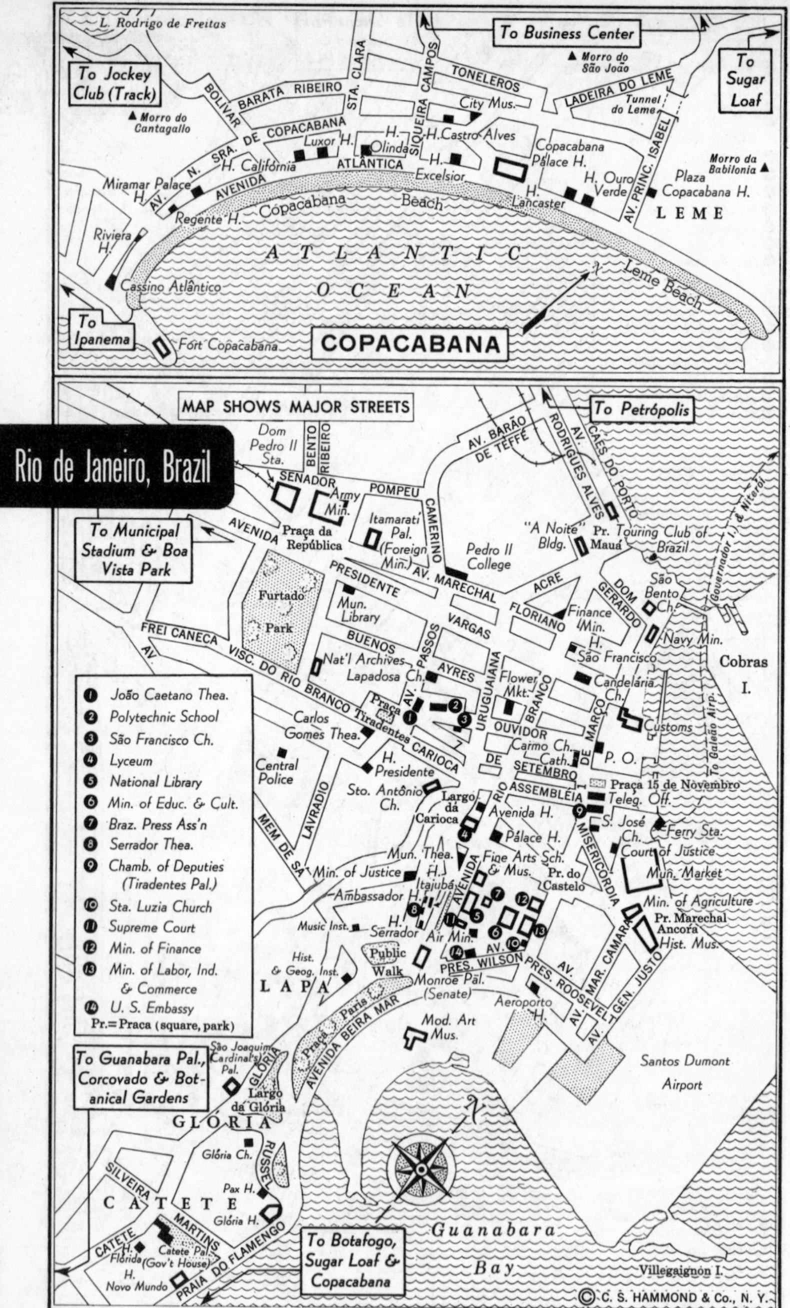
L. Rodrigo de Freitas
To Jockey Club (Track)
Morro do Cantagallo
To Business Center
Morro do São João
To Sugar Loaf
BOLIVAR
BARATA RIBEIRO
STA. CLARA
SIQUEIRA CAMPOS
TONELEROS
City Mus.
LADEIRA DO LEME
Tunnel do Leme
AV. N. SRA. DE COPACABANA
Luxor H.
H. Olinda
H. Castro Alves
Copacabana Palace H.
H. Califórnia
AVENIDA ATLÂNTICA
H. Excelsior
AV. PRINC. ISABEL
Morro da Babilonia
Miramar Palace H.
H. Ouro Verde
Plaza Copacabana H.
Regente H.
Copacabana Beach
H. Lancaster
LEME
Riviera H.
ATLANTIC OCEAN
Leme Beach
Cassino Atlântico
To Ipanema
Fort Copacabana
COPACABANA
MAP SHOWS MAJOR STREETS
To Petrópolis
Dom Pedro II Sta.
BENTO RIBEIRO
AV. BARÃO DE TEFFÉ
RODRIGUES ALVES
AV. CAES DO PORTO
SENADOR POMPEU
Army Min.
CAMERINO
To Municipal Stadium & Boa Vista Park
AVENIDA
Praça da República
Itamarati Pal. (Foreign Min.)
"A Noite" Bldg.
Pr. Mauá
Touring Club of Brazil
(Governador I.) & Niterói
Pedro II College
PRESIDENTE
AV. MARECHAL FLORIANO
ACRE
DOM GERARDO
São Bento Ch.
Furtado Park
Mun. Library
VARGAS
Finance Min.
Navy Min.
FREI CANECA
AV.
BUENOS AYRES
PASSOS
URUGUAIANA
H. São Francisco
Cobras I.
VISC. DO RIO BRANCO
Nat'l Archives
Lapadosa Ch.
Flower Mkt.
BRANCO
Candelária Ch.
AV. Praça Tiradentes
1 João Caetano Thea.
2 Polytechnic School
3 São Francisco Ch.
4 Lyceum
5 National Library
6 Min. of Educ. & Cult.
7 Braz. Press Ass'n
8 Serrador Thea.
9 Chamb. of Deputies (Tiradentes Pal.)
10 Sta. Luzia Church
11 Supreme Court
12 Min. of Finance
13 Min. of Labor, Ind. & Commerce
14 U. S. Embassy
Pr.=Praca (square, park)
Carlos Gomes Thea.
CARIOCA
OUVIDOR
Carmo Ch.
Cath.
DE MARÇO
Customs
Central Police
H. Presidente
DE SETEMBRO
P. O.
To Galeão Airp.
Praça 15 de Novembro
LAVRADIO
Sto. Antônio Ch.
Largo da Carioca
RIO ASSEMBLÉIA
Teleg. Off.
MEM DE SÁ
Avenida H.
S. José Ch.
Ferry Sta.
Pálace H.
MISERICORDIA
Court of Justice
Mun. Thea.
Fine Arts Sch. & Mus.
Mun. Market
Min. of Justice
H.
Pr. do Castelo
Itajubá
AVENIDA
Ambassador H.
Min. of Agriculture
Pr. Marechal Ancora
Music Inst.
H. Serrador
Air Min.
Hist. Mus.
MAR. CAMARA
Public Walk
PRES. WILSON
AV. PRES. ROOSEVELT
GEN. JUSTO
Hist. & Geog. Inst.
LAPA
Monroe Pal. (Senate)
Aeroporto H.
Praça Paris
AVENIDA BEIRA MAR
Mod. Art Mus.
To Guanabara Pal., Corcovado & Botanical Gardens
São Joaquim (Cardinal's) Pal.
GLÓRIA
Largo da Glória
Santos Dumont Airport
GLÓRIA
Glória Ch.
RUSSEL
SILVEIRA MARTINS
CATETE
Pax H.
Glória H.
CATETE
Catete Pal. (Gov't House)
H. Florida
H. Novo Mundo
PRAIA DO FLAMENGO
To Botafogo, Sugar Loaf & Copacabana
Guanabara Bay
Villegaignon I.
© C. S. HAMMOND & Co., N. Y.

Photos: Pan American Union

RIO is a city which must be seen to be believed. Among the impressions which live forever in one's memory, is this view of Copacabana Beach at the left and Praca Vermelha on the right

A STATUE OF DOM PEDRO I commemorates Brazil's first Emperor who with the famous **Grito do Ipiranga** declared his country's independence from Portugal

ITAMARATÍ PALACE, surrounded by royal palms, is the home of the Ministry of Foreign Affairs. The Inter-American Treaty of Reciprocal Assistance, the "Rio Treaty," was signed here in 1947

RIO DE JANEIRO. Surmounting the 2,310 foot summit of the Corcovado, Landowski's great sculpture of Christ the Redeemer, erected to commemorate Brazilian independence, looks serenely out across land-locked Guanabara Bay. In the distance guarding the portals of the South Atlantic, the towering eminence of the Sugar Loaf, Rio de Janeiro's most imposing landmark thrusts its great rock dome above a crescentic sweep of incredibly blue water. The wooded slopes and granite faces of mountains rise from a flat beach-scalloped plain. Here amid one of nature's most spectacular settings, the city of Rio de Janeiro lavishly spreads her panorama of red tiled roofs and pink walled houses, of rococo façades and the starkly denuded shafts of apartment dwellings, of flower filled parks and sprawling factories, of 20th century skyscrapers and mile upon mile of palm-lined boulevards. At dusk the city is transformed by the Midas touch of neon and mazda into long strands of jeweled lights which encircle her bays, adorn her avenues and twine themselves about the shadowed pyramids of her mountains. Rio de Janeiro is a modern city whose dramatic transition from old to new has been accomplished in an amazingly brief period of time. As capital of Brazil which has so recently sprung from an economic obscurity to the stature of a young giant among the industrial nations of the world, her phenomenal growth within the last decade is understandable.

RIO DE JANEIRO is the intellectual as well as the political capital of Brazil. Pictured is the famed National Library, the largest in Latin America, containing over a million volumes

Photos: Pan American Union, Philippa Day

GUANABARA PALACE, set in a lovely park was formerly the official residence of the President of the Republic. Today the Palace serves as the City Hall

THE LOTTERY TICKET VENDOR is a familiar figure in the streets of Rio. **Jogo do bicho** (' animal game") a form of the "numbers game" is the country's most popular lottery

THE GEORGE WASHINGTON STATUE in Rio seems to symbolize the warm friendship which exists between the Brazilians and the people of the United States

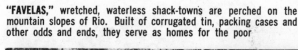

RIO DE JANEIRO Continued

Not only as the seat of government and the center of Brazilian culture but with a spacious harbor providing ample depths for the largest of ocean vessels and Santos Dumont Airport affording speedy access to the widely flung regions of the interior, Rio has now become the hub of her nation's commerce, distribution, and transportation. Long a leader of the modern architecture movement in South America and a pioneer in the use of new and original construction materials, many of Rio's buildings reflect the advanced trends in these fields. The hill known as Morro do Castelo upon which the original walled city was founded has been leveled, making room for the large well-planned commercial and shopping area of the city. A government sponsored project of recent years has given Rio a modern network of broad handsome streets and highways, while another government campaign begun in 1903 and carried out under the direction of Doctor Oswaldo Cruz eliminated through improved sanitation, the ever-present menace of yellow fever and malaria, making Rio one of the most healthful cities in the world. Rio de Janeiro is also one of the most beautiful; its inhabitants proudly refer to it as "cidade maravilhosa" (marvelous city).

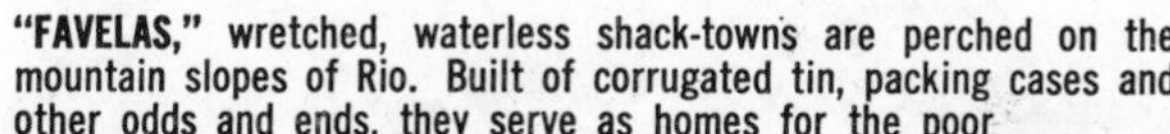

"FAVELAS," wretched, waterless shack-towns are perched on the mountain slopes of Rio. Built of corrugated tin, packing cases and other odds and ends, they serve as homes for the poor

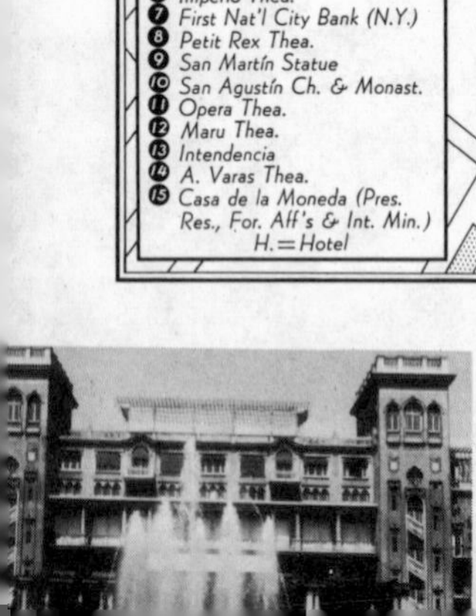

Santiago, Chile

MAP SHOWS MAJOR STREETS

To Observ.

To Los Leones & Farellones

To Nat'l Stad., Tupungato, Lo Valdés & Lagunillas

To Colina & Los Andes

To Hipódromo Chile (Race Track)

To Centenary Park, Valparaíso & Viña del Mar

To Nat'l Mus. of Nat. Hist. & Sci., Sch. of Agr. & Sch. of Arts & Crafts

To Rancagua

To Plaza Argentina, Alameda (Central) Sta., Los Cerrillos Airp. & Cartagena

To Cousiño Park & Club Hípico (Race Track)

1. Supreme Court
2. Auto. Club of Chile
3. Casa Colorada
4. Tomb of the Unknown Soldier
5. Savings Bank
6. Imperio Thea.
7. First Nat'l City Bank (N.Y.)
8. Petit Rex Thea.
9. San Martín Statue
10. San Agustín Ch. & Monast.
11. Opera Thea.
12. Maru Thea.
13. Intendencia
14. A. Varas Thea.
15. Casa de la Moneda (Pres. Res., For. Aff's & Int. Min.)

H.=Hotel

CLUB HÍPICO RACE TRACK is among the finest in South America. Horse racing is one of the most popular pastimes in Chile where thoroughbred horses were introduced from England 300 years ago

SANTIAGO. The North American is often struck with an inexplicable sense of the familiar when he first views the Chilean capital, for in its hustle and bustle, in the shiny newness of its maze of lofty skyscrapers, there is a similarity between Santiago and many of the cities of California or Texas. While in superficial appearance the city is both functional and modern, it possesses many fine examples of Spanish-colonial architecture and a history which goes back more than 400 years. The fourth largest city in South America, Santiago lies at the foot of towering snow-capped mountains in the very heart of Chile's paradise vale, the fertile central plain which furnishes the nation with the bulk of its agricultural produce. The Mapocho River winds through the center of the city and one of its arms which dried up when the river was walled, furnishes the foundation for the Avenida Bernardo O'Higgins or "Alameda" as it is commonly called. Lined with beautiful homes, stately university buildings, clubs, theaters and colorful flower markets, this handsome boulevard is also known as Chile's hall of fame as many statues are found along its shady walks. The Alameda leads to an area known as the Barrio Civico, where an imposing group of buildings house the capital's civic and administrative offices. The Casa de la Moneda, a low graceful colonial building, formerly the Mint, is today the residence of the President of the Republic. Here, one of the most colorful ceremonies in Chile takes place each morning with the changing of the Presidential Guard.

SANTA LUCIA HILL rises from the center of Santiago like a castle in the air. Atop the hill stands Chile's first fort, erected by Valdiva in 1541

Photos: Panagra, Pan American Union, Grace Line

SANTIAGO'S COUNTRY CLUB and golf course is set against a spectacular backdrop of snow-shrouded Andean peaks

THE CASA DE LA MONEDA, a low graceful building, formerly the Mint, is today the residence of the President of the Republic. The changing of the Presidential Guard, one of the most colorful ceremonies in Chile, takes place here each morning

São Paulo, Brazil

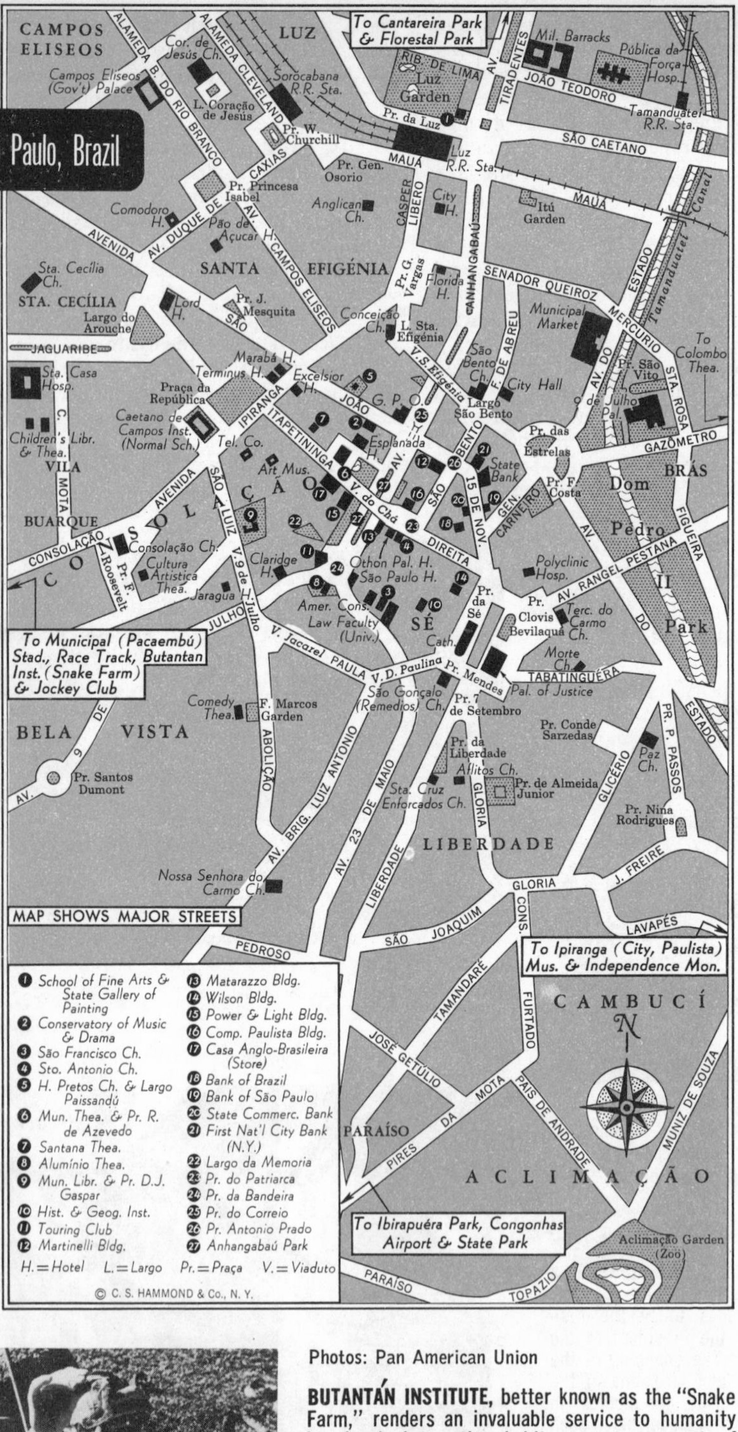

To Cantareira Park & Florestal Park

To Municipal (Pacaembú) Stad., Race Track, Butantan Inst. (Snake Farm) & Jockey Club

To Colombo Thea.

To Ipiranga (City, Paulista) Mus. & Independence Mon.

To Ibirapuéra Park, Congonhas Airport & State Park

MAP SHOWS MAJOR STREETS

1. School of Fine Arts & State Gallery of Painting
2. Conservatory of Music & Drama
3. São Francisco Ch.
4. Sto. Antonio Ch.
5. H. Pretos Ch. & Largo Paissandú
6. Mun. Thea. & Pr. R. de Azevedo
7. Santana Thea.
8. Alumínio Thea.
9. Mun. Libr. & Pr. D.J. Gaspar
10. Hist. & Geog. Inst.
11. Touring Club
12. Martinelli Bldg.
13. Matarazzo Bldg.
14. Wilson Bldg.
15. Power & Light Bldg.
16. Comp. Paulista Bldg.
17. Casa Anglo-Brasileira (Store)
18. Bank of Brazil
19. Bank of São Paulo
20. State Commerc. Bank
21. First Nat'l City Bank (N.Y.)
22. Largo da Memoria
23. Pr. do Patriarca
24. Pr. da Bandeira
25. Pr. do Correio
26. Pr. Antonio Prado
27. Anhangabaú Park

H. = Hotel L. = Largo Pr. = Praça V. = Viaduto

Photos: Pan American Union

BUTANTÁN INSTITUTE, better known as the "Snake Farm," renders an invaluable service to humanity by developing anti-snakebite serums as part of its broad program of scientific research

THE TOWERING SKYLINE OF SÃO PAULO is reflected in the quiet waters of a park lake. The city's phenomenal growth ranks it as one of the fastest-growing cities in the world

SECLUDED GARDENS, beautiful parks and handsome residential areas, make this center of modern progress more than just a city of skyscrapers and factories. Pictured is the lovely garden of the Governor's home

THE PAULISTA MUSEUM, in Ipiranga Park is devoted to history, natural history and ethnography. On a hill nearby, Dom Pedro I, proclaimed Brazil's independence with the immortal cry, "Independence or death," the Grito do Ipiranaga

SÃO PAULO. Often compared with Chicago, São Paulo like her North American counterpart is a vast manufacturing and processing center. Less than fifty years ago, a small provincial town, São Paulo today ranks as the largest industrial city in South America. Located at the very heart of the major coffee, cotton, livestock and mineral producing area of Brazil, the city's enormous development has been due largely to an abundance of hydro-electric power and her close proximity to the export terminus of Santos. Modern highways which link the city with the mineral deposits of Minas Gerais and to the mighty Volta Redonda steel mills also contribute to her growth. Within her ever-lengthening perimeter more than 5,750 mills and factories turn out a diversity of goods ranging from automobiles and heavy machinery to chemicals and plastics. Besides her new wealth of factories and skyscrapers, São Paulo has many handsome public buildings, flower-filled parks and beautiful residences. Among her notable institutions are the University of São Paulo with its medical center, the modern 22-story Municipal Library and the world-renowned Butantán Institute which produces snake-bite and other serums. In addition to playing a leading part in her country's industrial awakening São Paulo has contributed much to its colorful history for here, in 1882, Brazilian independence was declared.

A GENERAL VIEW OF TORONTO'S BUSINESS SECTION, taken from the harbor approach, shows the wharves and sheds of the Canadian Steamship Lines and in the foreground the ferries which connect the islands with the city

TORONTO. On the northern shores of Lake Ontario, where long ago Indian trails converged, stands the city of Toronto—a gateway to a vast lake and forest playground. The Huron Indians gave Toronto its name and their choice was prophetic. In the language of these original inhabitants *Toronto* meant the "meeting place" and since those early days it has grown in size and stature to a city which is now populated by more than a million and a quarter people. Toronto is the capital of the province of Ontario and a great industrial and commercial metropolis which turns out a wide diversity of manufactured goods. Many subsidiaries of American and British firms are located at Toronto. A center of Canadian education, art and culture, the city has many stately churches and public buildings. These, with places of modern and historic interest, form monuments to the courage, resourcefulness and loyalty of her people. In Toronto, mammoth expositions and shows follow each other with the seasons. In early September comes the Canadian National Exposition. The world's largest annual exposition, it is often called the "show window of the nations."

HART HOUSE is the "students union" of the University of Toronto. It includes gymnasia, a swimming-pool, a dining hall, a faculty club, a chapel and numerous other facilities that make it unique among the academic buildings of the world.

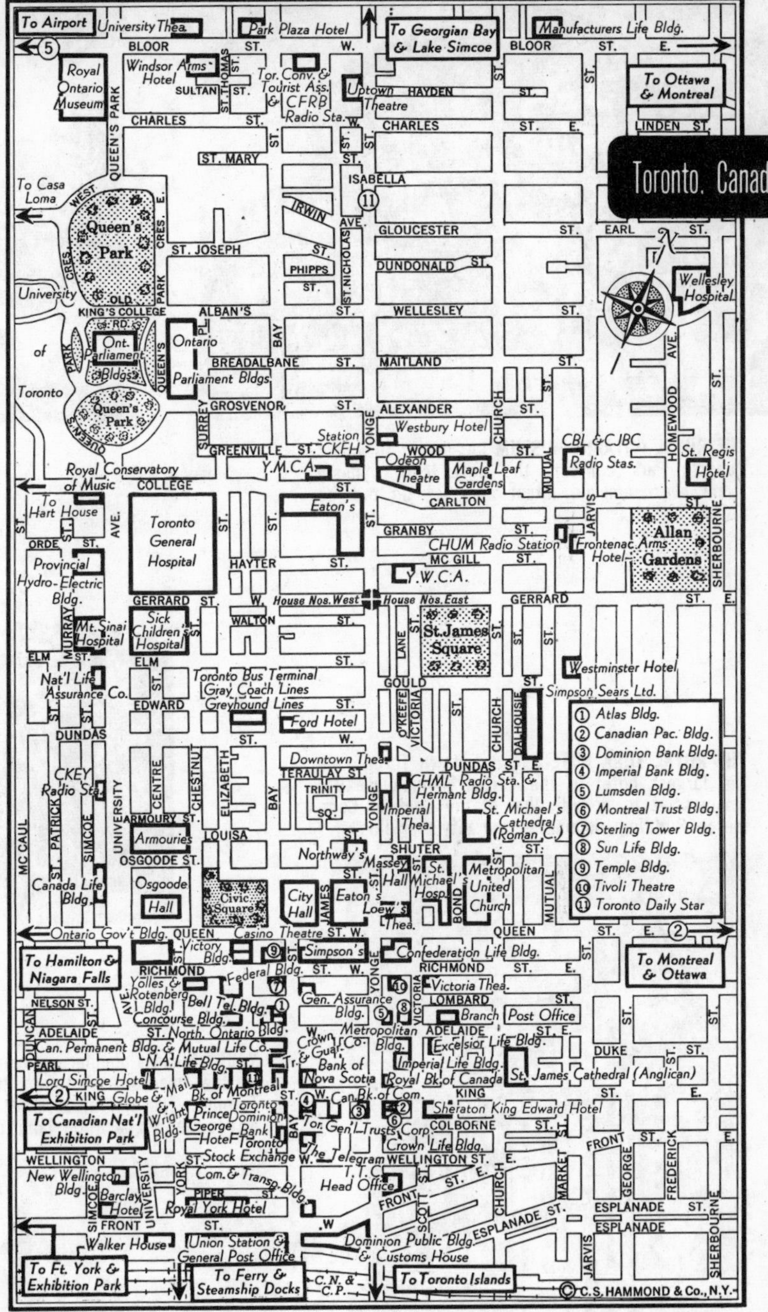

CASA LOMA, the only genuine castle in Canada, is now a tourist attraction of Toronto. It has 98 rooms and 30 baths, as well as a swimming pool and other luxurious appointments. The castle reputedly cost $2,000 a month just to heat. As a night-club, it gave its name to Glen Gray and his Casa Loma orchestra

Photos: Ken Bell, Photographic Survey Corp. Canadian Pacific Railroad

THE ROYAL ONTARIO MUSEUM located in Toronto's Queen's Park contains the only Ming Dynasty Tomb ever removed intact and set up outside China

THE ROYAL YORK HOTEL, in downtown Toronto, is the largest hotel in the British Commonwealth. Its massive tower with that of the Bank of Commerce Building, dominates the city's skyline

YACHTING is a popular summer pastime in the beautiful sheltered harbor of Toronto. The city also serves as gateway to the vast vacation lands of Ontario

THE PROVINCIAL LEGISLATIVE BUILDING of the Province of Ontario, is an impressive red sandstone structure situated in Queen's Park in the heart of Toronto

Photos: National Film Board, Canadian National Airways, Photographic Survey Corp.

THE PRINCE GATE ENTRANCE to the Canadian National Exhibition makes an impressive portal to the world's greatest annual exhibition. A special park on Toronto's lakefront has been set aside for the fair, which attracts as many as two million spectators each fall

TORONTO Continued

In mid-November comes the Royal Agricultural Winter Fair accompanied by a magnificent Horse Show; it is the unrivaled leader of agricultural stock shows. The Canadian National Sportsmen's Show, with emphasis on the great outdoors, is held in mid-March, and early June brings the Canadian International Trade Fair. America's greatest market fair, it displays the industry and commerce of forty nations. Other national and international events of outstanding interest include the Queen's Plate and the National Air Show. Toronto's famous Shakespeare Festival runs all through July in the Trinity College Quadrangle. The city is the home of the Toronto Symphony Orchestra and the Toronto Philharmonic Orchestra. A familiar Toronto landmark is Casa Loma, a formidable stone castle which stands on a hill overlooking the city's downtown area. Built early in the century by a man who hoped to entertain the king, it stands today as a spectacular memento of that grandiose dream. Toronto is filled with fascinating reminders of its history. There is the old lighthouse on Fleet Street, which marked the entrance to Toronto harbor for nearly 100 years; Fort York, whose original blockhouses still bear the bullet scars of colonial warfare and the crumbling walls of the old mill where early settlers started Toronto on its way to becoming the mighty industrial center it is today. Each year thousands of visitors come from near and far to see and enjoy the many attractions of this Canadian "vacation city."

Vancouver, Canada

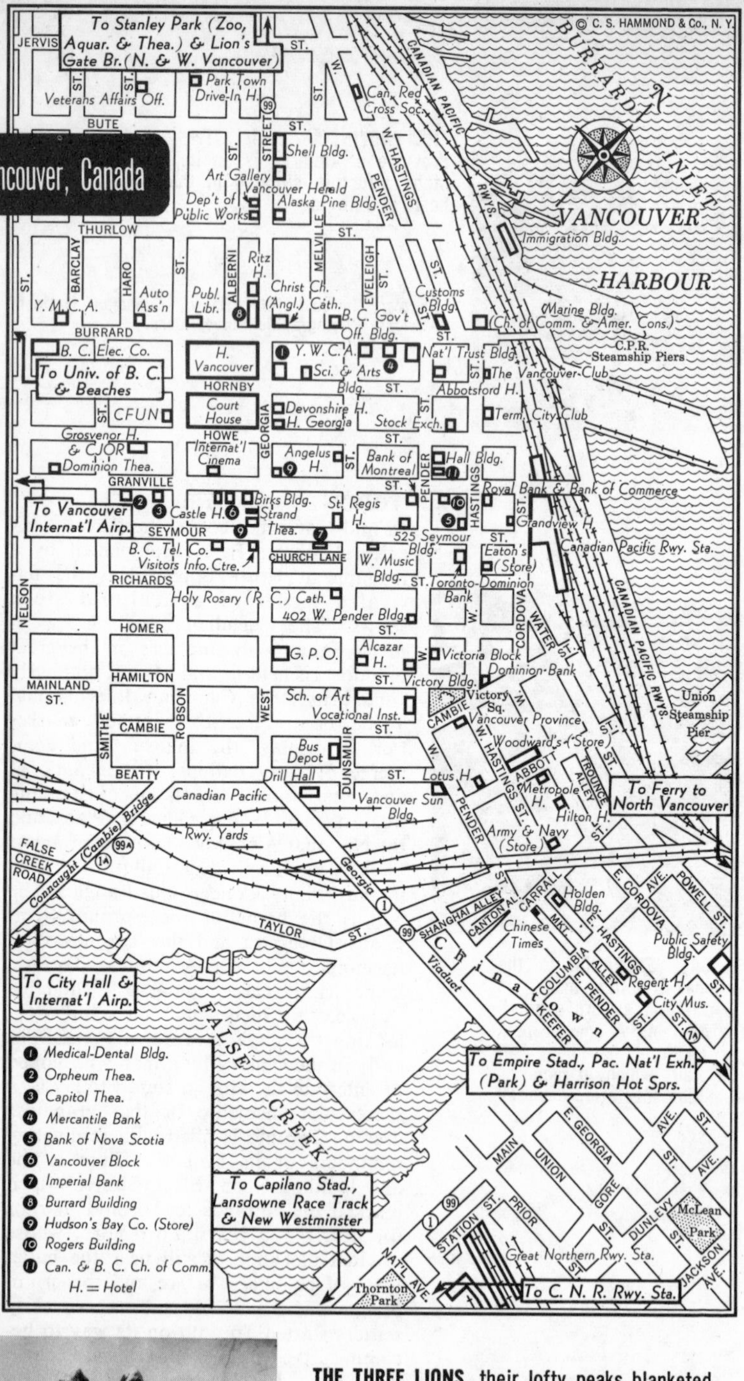

© C. S. HAMMOND & Co., N. Y.
To Stanley Park (Zoo, Aquar. & Thea.) & Lion's Gate Br. (N. & W. Vancouver)
BURRARD INLET
VANCOUVER HARBOUR
CANADIAN PACIFIC RWYS.
JERVIS
BUTE
THURLOW
BURRARD
HORNBY
HOWE
GRANVILLE
SEYMOUR
RICHARDS
HOMER
HAMILTON
MAINLAND ST.
CAMBIE
BEATTY
NELSON
SMITHE
ROBSON
GEORGIA
ALBERNI
MELVILLE
EVELEIGH
BARCLAY
HARO
W. HASTINGS
PENDER
CORDOVA
WATER ST.
DUNSMUIR
WEST
Veterans Affairs Off.
Park Town Drive-In H.
Can. Red Cross Soc.
Shell Bldg.
Art Gallery
Vancouver Herald
Dep't of Public Works
Alaska Pine Bldg.
Immigration Bldg.
Ritz H.
Christ Ch. (Angl.) Cath.
Y. M. C. A.
Auto Ass'n
Publ. Libr.
B. C. Gov't Off. Bldg.
Customs Bldg.
Marine Bldg.
Ch. of Comm. & Amer. Cons.
C.P.R. Steamship Piers
B. C. Elec. Co.
H. Vancouver
Y. W. C. A.
Sci. & Arts Bldg.
Nat'l Trust Bldg.
The Vancouver Club
Abbotsford H.
To Univ. of B. C. & Beaches
Court House
CFUN
Devonshire H.
H. Georgia
Stock Exch.
Term. City Club
Grosvenor H. & CJOR
Internat'l Cinema
Dominion Thea.
Angelus H.
Bank of Montreal
Hall Bldg.
Royal Bank & Bank of Commerce
To Vancouver Internat'l Airp.
Castle H.
Birks Bldg.
Strand Thea.
St. Regis H.
Grandview H.
Canadian Pacific Rwy. Sta.
B. C. Tel. Co.
Visitors Info. Ctre.
CHURCH LANE
W. Music Bldg.
525 Seymour Bldg.
Eaton's (Store)
Toronto-Dominion Bank
Holy Rosary (R. C.) Cath.
402 W. Pender Bldg.
G. P. O.
Alcazar H.
Victoria Block
Dominion Bank
Victory Bldg.
Victory Sq.
Sch. of Art
Vocational Inst.
Vancouver Province
Woodward's (Store)
Union Steamship Pier
Bus Depot
Drill Hall
Lotus H.
Metropole H.
Hilton H.
TROUNCE ALLEY
To Ferry to North Vancouver
Canadian Pacific Rwy. Yards
Vancouver Sun Bldg.
Army & Navy (Store)
FALSE CREEK ROAD
Connaught (Cambie) Bridge
TAYLOR ST.
Georgia Viaduct
SHANGHAI ALLEY
CANTON AL.
CARRALL
Holden Bldg.
Chinese Times
Chinatown
E. CORDOVA
POWELL ST.
Public Safety Bldg.
E. HASTINGS
COLUMBIA
E. PENDER
KEEFER
Regent H.
City Mus.
To City Hall & Internat'l Airp.
FALSE CREEK
To Empire Stad., Pac. Nat'l Exh. (Park) & Harrison Hot Sprs.
MAIN
UNION
E. GEORGIA
PRIOR
GORE
DUNLEVY
JACKSON AVE.
McLean Park
STATION ST.
Great Northern Rwy. Sta.
To Capilano Stad., Lansdowne Race Track & New Westminster
NAT'L AVE.
Thornton Park
To C. N. R. Rwy. Sta.
1 Medical-Dental Bldg.
2 Orpheum Thea.
3 Capitol Thea.
4 Mercantile Bank
5 Bank of Nova Scotia
6 Vancouver Block
7 Imperial Bank
8 Burrard Building
9 Hudson's Bay Co. (Store)
10 Rogers Building
11 Can. & B. C. Ch. of Comm.
H. = Hotel

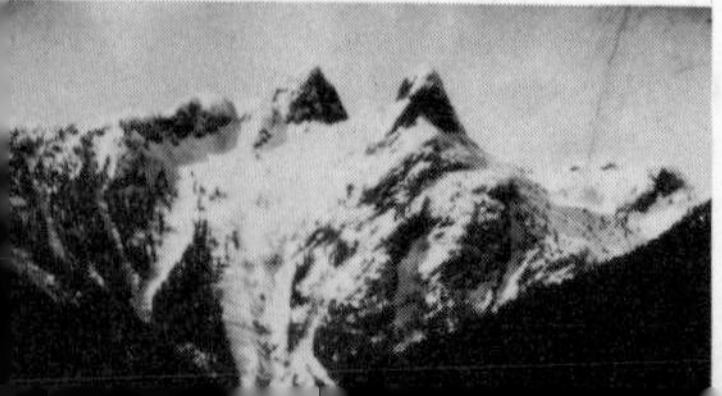

THE THREE LIONS, their lofty peaks blanketed by snow, both in winter and summer, are a part of Vancouver's spectacular mountain backdrop

A BUSTLING PORT, Vancouver possesses one of the world's finest natural harbors. During the winter months, it takes on the additional export trade of ports on the Great Lakes which are forced to close because of ice

VANCOUVER. Built on a peninsula extending into the Strait of Georgia and with one of the finest natural harbors on the west coast, Vancouver serves as Canada's gateway to the Pacific and the bustling commercial center of one of the world's newest industrial empires. To the north and northeast, the protective Coast Range mountains which rise to heights of 5,000 to 6,000 feet, plus the influence of warm ocean currents, provide Vancouver with a moderate climate, making the city and its surroundings the evergreen playground of the Pacific Northwest. In winter, the mercury rarely dips below 30° and has never been below zero while in summer, the pleasant temperatures average in the 60's. Right on the city's doorstep are superb beaches and bays for yachting and bathing while twelve months of the year Vancouver is a fisherman's dream. Just five minutes from the heart of the city, is the entrance to world-famous Stanley Park, a 1,000-acre natural forest playground which includes a children's zoo, cricket field, golf course, bowling green, bathing beach, rose garden, a collection of Totem poles and some 50 miles of roads and bicycle trails. Also in Stanley Park, is the unique Theater Under the Stars where thousands gather on summer evenings to enjoy Broadway-type musical plays. Chairlifts and good highways make it easy for skiers and sightseers to climb Hollyburn, Grouse and Seymour Mountains. Vancouver, with a large British population, has a definite British flavor and such customs as afternoon tea prevail here.

CLOUDS ROLL IN, obscuring the peaks of the Coast Range and bringing frequent rain to the Vancouver area. Although the climate of Vancouver is very wet, the city seldom has snow and on the whole enjoys mild and equable weather

Photos: Canadian Government Travel Bureau, Canadian National Railways

THE SKYLINE OF VANCOUVER, Canada's third largest city, towers above the waters of Coal Harbour. A fast-growing industrial center and the western terminus of Canada's major railway systems, it is also a popular resort

Winnipeg, Canada

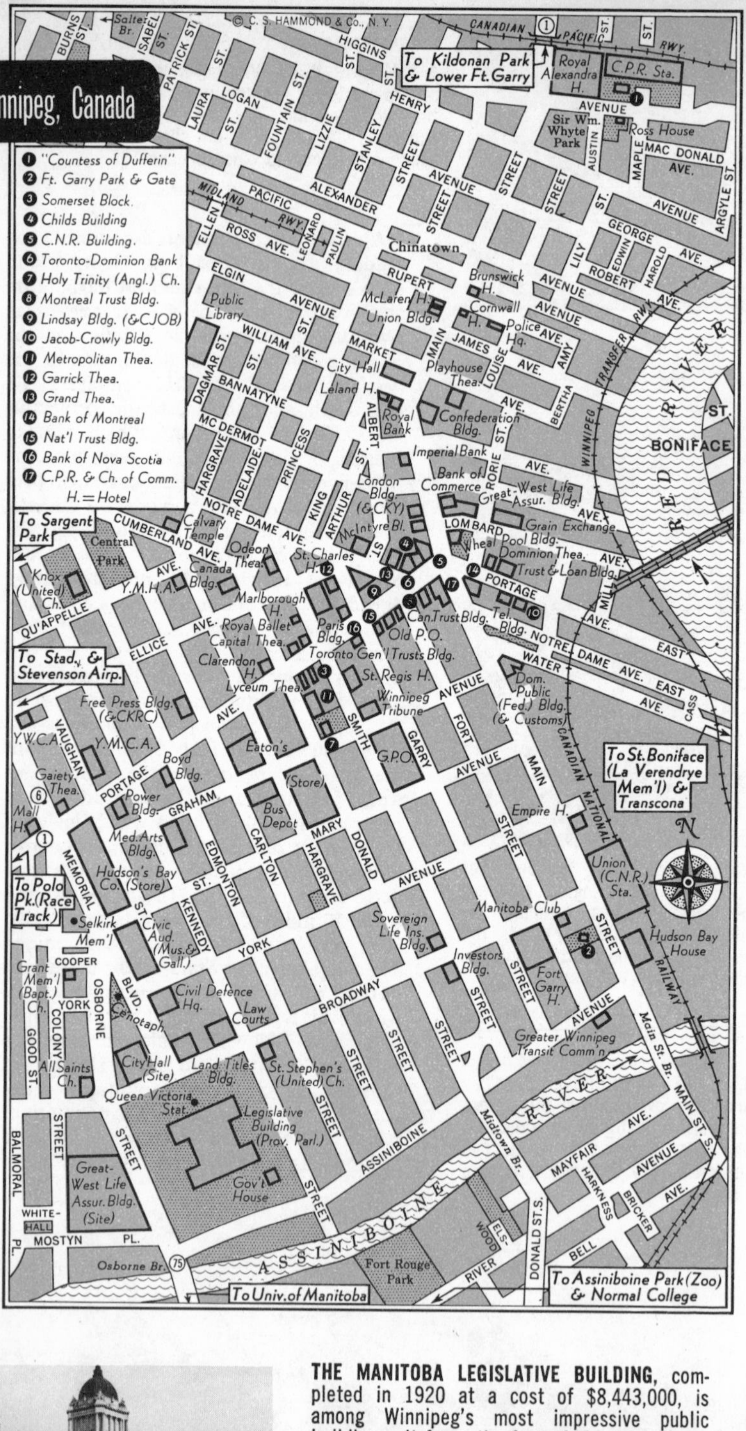

© C. S. HAMMOND & Co., N. Y.

1. "Countess of Dufferin"
2. Ft. Garry Park & Gate
3. Somerset Block
4. Childs Building
5. C.N.R. Building
6. Toronto-Dominion Bank
7. Holy Trinity (Angl.) Ch.
8. Montreal Trust Bldg.
9. Lindsay Bldg. (&CJOB)
10. Jacob-Crowly Bldg.
11. Metropolitan Thea.
12. Garrick Thea.
13. Grand Thea.
14. Bank of Montreal
15. Nat'l Trust Bldg.
16. Bank of Nova Scotia
17. C.P.R. & Ch. of Comm.

H.=Hotel

To Kildonan Park & Lower Ft. Garry

To Sargent Park

To Stad. & Stevenson Airp.

To Polo Pk. (Race Track)

To St. Boniface (La Verendrye Mem'l) & Transcona

To Univ. of Manitoba

To Assiniboine Park (Zoo) & Normal College

THE MANITOBA LEGISLATIVE BUILDING, completed in 1920 at a cost of $8,443,000, is among Winnipeg's most impressive public buildings. It faces the foot of Memorial Boulevard, a handsome thoroughfare which runs through the heart of the city

RAIL LINES, which link the prairies of western Canada with markets in the east have made Winnipeg an important distributing center. Pictured are the extensive yards of the Canadian National Railways

WINNIPEG. Winnipeg, Manitoba's capital, is one of Canada's most cosmopolitan cities. Groups from almost every European country are represented here, each making its contribution to the city's culture. Known as the "Chicago of Canada" Winnipeg is the financial and industrial center of the Prairie Provinces and one of the world's largest grain markets. The city's prosperity is reflected in its towering office buildings, huge factories and handsome public buildings. Fifty-eight parks and playgrounds add beauty to Winnipeg's boulevard streets and attractive residential areas. The Red and Assiniboine rivers meet at Winnipeg and provide the citizens with a waterside vacationland within the city. Canoeing is a popular pastime on the rivers and Winnipeg has produced many experts with the paddle for competition across the country. The winding waterways also provide a scenic background for many points of interest which include historic Lower Fort Garry, Canada's only stone fur trading fort of the early days still intact. The remains of the entrance gate to Upper Fort Garry stand near the Fort Garry Hotel. Upper Fort Garry, a Hudson Bay Company post, was the hub of settlement in early Winnipeg. Around this small nucleus a farming community sprang up which in turn grew into the modern city. Its name, *Winnipeg,* which means "murky water" was derived from Lake Winnepeg located fifty miles to the north.

WINNIPEG which little more than a century and a half ago, was a tiny fur-trading post, is today the chief city of the Prairie Provinces. The picture shows the tall buildings and wide avenues of this modern metropolis

Photos: Canadian Government Travel Bureau, Canadian National Railroads

TOWERING GRAIN ELEVATORS on the city's outskirts are a reminder that Winnipeg is the storage and transportation center of the Prairie Provinces—one of the world's principal granaries

CITIES
of
EUROPE

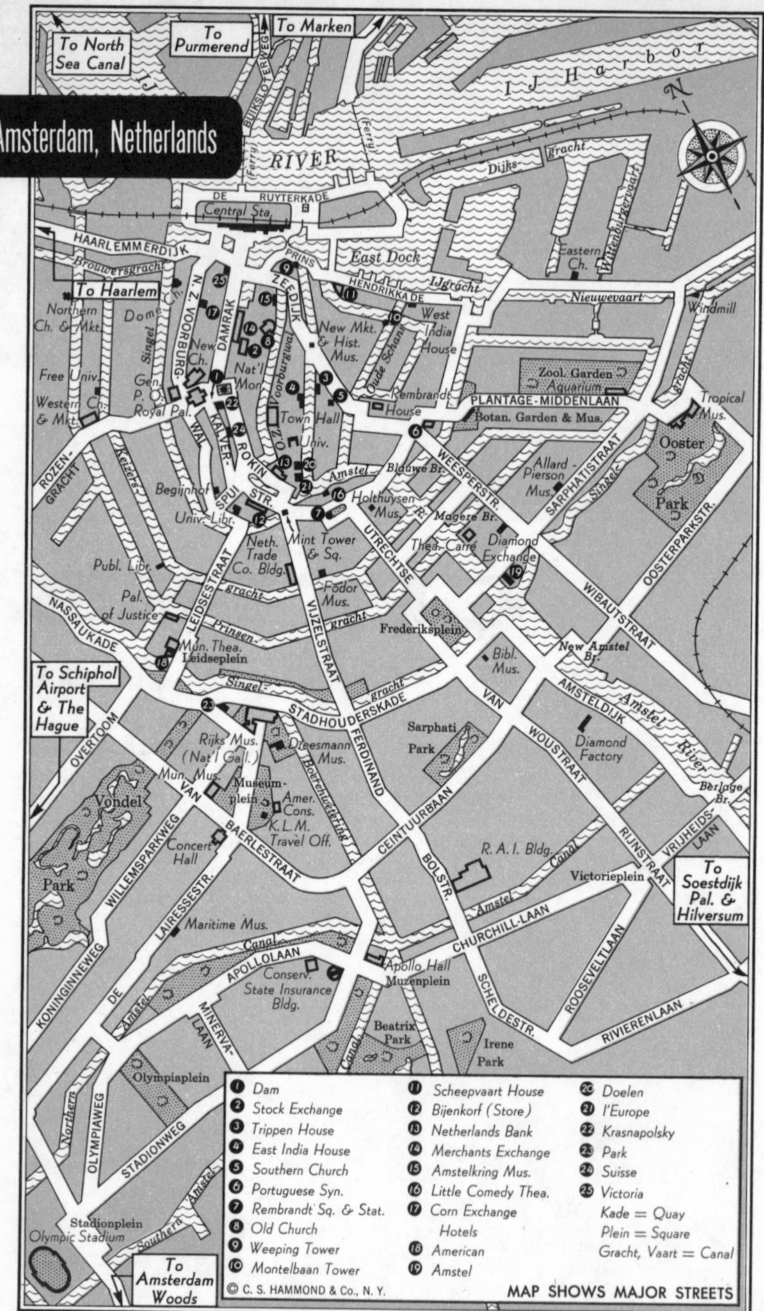

Photos: Philip Gendreau, Netherlands National Tourist Office

THE QUEEN'S PALACE in Amsterdam overlooks Dam Square. Dating from 1648, the Palace was the home of Louis Bonaparte in 1808. Nieuwe Kirk (New Church) can be seen on the right

THE MUNTTOREN (Mint Tower) with its clock and chiming bells, looks down on flower-laden barges plying a canal in the heart of Amsterdam. The tower which dates from 1620 is one of the city's landmarks

A CANAL SYSTEM, laid out in a series of concentric semi-circles, adds to the charm of Amsterdam. The inner canals are bordered by houses dating from the 16th and 17th centuries which today form one of the most attractive architectural features of the city

REMBRANDT'S HOUSE still stands in Amsterdam. Here the great master executed some of his finest works including the "Night Watch" which hangs in the Rijks Museum

AMSTERDAM. The growth of Amsterdam, constitutional capital of the Netherlands, can be traced in the concentric semicircles of its main canals which spread outward like the rings of a tree trunk from the original 13th-century town to its modern 20th-century suburbs. For centuries, Amsterdam has been one of the greatest commercial centers of Europe; here is found one of the world's major stock exchanges and the proud patrician dwellings built by its merchant princes of the 16th and 17th centuries still line its inner canals. Jewish diamond cutters from Spain and Portugal, a part of the large influx of refugees which contributed to the city's growth in the 16th century, made Amsterdam the famed center of the diamond-cutting industry. Amsterdam is the largest city of the Netherlands and an important port connected by a system of canals with both the North Sea and the Rhine delta. The city is also a focal point of its country's art and intellect. The celebrated Rijks Museum, founded by Louis Bonaparte, contains a magnificent collection of masterpieces of the Dutch School. Notable among these paintings is the "Night Watch" by Rembrandt, who made his home in Amsterdam. Painted in 1642, this huge canvas, which today is considered among the artist's most outstanding works, unfortunately marked the decline of Rembrandt's popularity and was received with bitter displeasure by the group that had commissioned its painting.

Athens, Greece

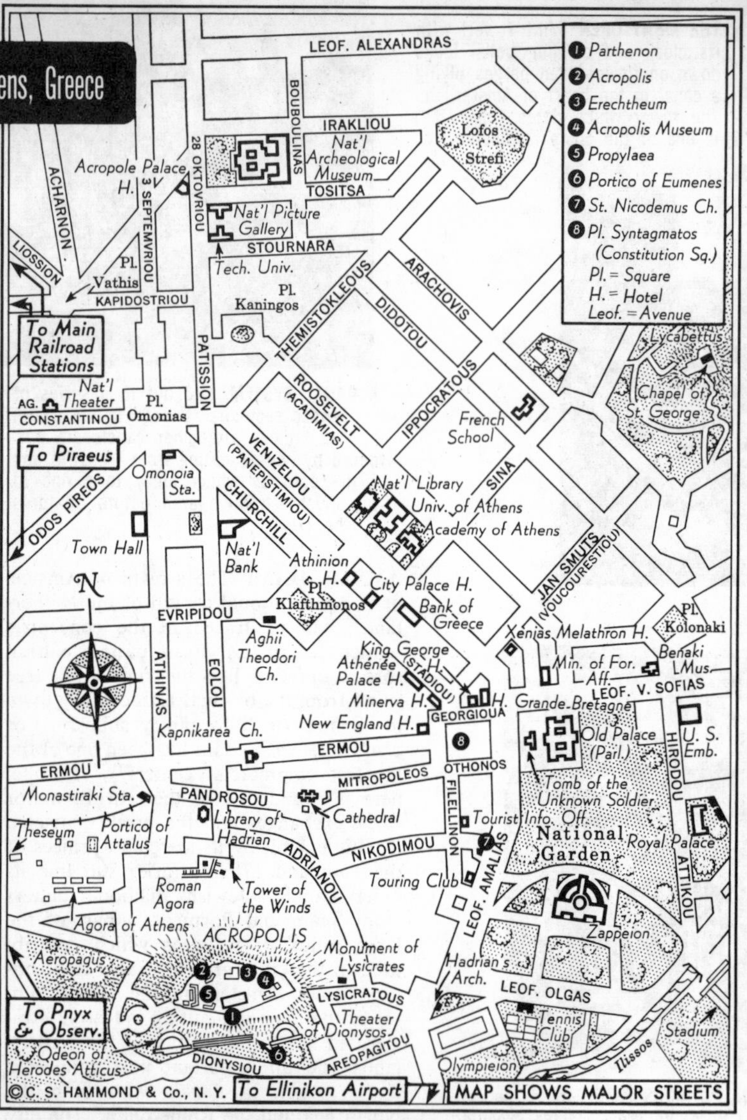

1 Parthenon
2 Acropolis
3 Erechtheum
4 Acropolis Museum
5 Propylaea
6 Portico of Eumenes
7 St. Nicodemus Ch.
8 Pl. Syntagmatos (Constitution Sq.)

Pl. = Square
H. = Hotel
Leof. = Avenue

LEOF. ALEXANDRAS
BOUBOULINAS
IRAKLIOU
Nat'l Archeological Museum
TOSITSA
Lofos Strefi
Acropole Palace H.
28 OKTOVRIOU
3 SEPTEMVRIOU
ACHARNON
Nat'l Picture Gallery
STOURNARA
Tech. Univ.
LIOSSION
Pl. Vathis
KAPIDOSTRIOU
Pl. Kaningos
THEMISTOKLEOUS
ARACHOVIS
DIDOTOU
To Main Railroad Stations
PATISSION
Nat'l Theater
AG. CONSTANTINOU
Pl. Omonias
ROOSEVELT (ACADIMIAS)
IPPOCRATOUS
Lycabettus
Chapel of St. George
French School
To Piraeus
Omonoia Sta.
VENIZELOU (PANEPISTIMIOU)
CHURCHILL
ODOS PIREOS
Nat'l Library
Univ. of Athens
Academy of Athens
SINA
Town Hall
Nat'l Bank
Athinion H.
City Palace H.
Pl. Klafthmonos
JAN SMUTS (VOUCOURESTIOU)
Bank of Greece
N
EVRIPIDOU
Aghii Theodori Ch.
ATHINAS
EOLOU
King George H.
Athénée Palace H.
(STADIOU)
Xenias Melathron H.
Pl. Kolonaki
Min. of For. Aff.
Benaki Mus.
LEOF. V. SOFIAS
Minerva H.
H. Grande-Bretagne
GEORGIOUA
New England H.
Kapnikarea Ch.
ERMOU
Old Palace (Parl.)
U. S. Emb.
HIRODOU
OTHONOS
ERMOU
MITROPOLEOS
Tomb of the Unknown Soldier
Monastiraki Sta.
PANDROSOU
Cathedral
FILELLINON
Tourist Info. Off.
Theseum
Portico of Attalus
Library of Hadrian
National Garden
Royal Palace
ADRIANOU
NIKODIMOU
LEOF. AMALIAS
Roman Agora
Tower of the Winds
Touring Club
ATTIKOU
Agora of Athens
ACROPOLIS
Zappeion
Aeropagus
Monument of Lysicrates
Hadrian's Arch.
LEOF. OLGAS
LYSICRATOUS
To Pnyx & Observ.
Theater of Dionysos
Tennis Club
Stadium
Odeon of Herodes Atticus
DIONYSIOU
AREOPAGITOU
Olympieion
Ilissos
©C. S. HAMMOND & Co., N. Y.
To Ellinikon Airport
MAP SHOWS MAJOR STREETS

Photos: Top and lower left, TWA-Trans World Airlines; others, Royal Greek Embassy

THE FIGHTING EVZONES, light infantrymen famed in legend and song, serve as the royal palace guard of honor, traditionally garbed in the "Foustanella," the kilt of the **Klepht,** or Greek mountaineer

PARTHENON, probably the world's most renowned building and a thrilling creation of perfect symmetry, is often considered man's supreme architectural achievement

ATHENS. Outlined against the sky, overlooking Athens, stands the majestic Acropolis, with its Parthenon, built in the fifth century, B.C., a landmark of extraordinary beauty, grandeur and monumental power, a timeless citadel of the most dynamic period in the history of mankind. During this era of greatness, a remarkable culture flourished in the Greek city states, notably in Athens, which produced the masterpieces that have since inspired art and thought throughout the world. Aeschylus, Sophocles, Euripides and Aristophanes, Ictinus and Phidias, Socrates, Plato and Aristotle — the roll of mighty thinkers and noble artists who walked her dusty, sun-drenched streets is matched by no other city in history. It was here the ideals of democracy were first formulated and Western civilization was born. This heritage of free thought is manifested in the Athenians' pastime: the art of conversation, or more particularly, debating. Everywhere and at all times, they skillfully discuss all questions, disputing this point, upholding that side, expounding their opinions on everything, expressing their love not only of the spoken word but most of all, their fascination with logical argument. The classi-

THEATER OF HERODES ATTICUS, on the south slope of the Acropolis, provides a fitting setting for the peerless masterpieces of the great Athenian dramatists, performed here during the annual festival from August through October

THIS STREET is ample proof of why modern Athenians still passionately love their brilliant white city, the pride and focal point of Greece, on which a welcoming sun shines benignly throughout the year

ATHENS Continued

cal Agora and the Byzantine Hippodrome is the present-day Constitution Square, in front of the Parliament Building, where gesticulating speakers may be seen, during the day and far into the cool of the night, leisurely strolling in pairs or groups or sitting around the tables in outdoor *tavernas,* eating ice cream and sweets, drinking Turkish coffee and the powerful native *ouzo* and discoursing, contending, reasoning. Because of the delightful dry, clear climate, with balmy breezes from the mountains and the sea, and the sociability of these loquacious people, the Athenians live outdoors. In fact, it sometimes seems not a single person has stayed in his own home, for the house is used only for rest; for all other activities — eating, meeting, playing—they go out to the streets, the gardens or the cafés. King of the streets, though, is the donkey, adding still more to the city's unique rural charm. It is this small, proud, plodding donkey who brings in from the bright countryside in his tiny cart the preeminent olives, the glorious Greek grapes and the fragrant royal-hued violets, "the crown of Athens."

BEAUTIFUL GREEK GLASSWARE, supported by generations of superb craftsmanship, is produced both for domestic consumption and for export

Photos: Upper right, V. Papaioannou; lower left, TWA-Trans World Airlines; others, Royal Greek Embassy

ATHENS HARBOR, with its unusually limpid and transparent atmosphere and sapphire-blue Attic sky, provides a colorful haven for fishing boats plying the Aegean Sea

ACROPOLIS, rising grandly over Athens is the most famous monument of all time, in whose shadow democracy was born

ACADEMY OF ATHENS is enhanced by its background of irregularly tiered houses and conical Mt. Lycabettus, topped by a church dedicated to St. George

BYZANTINE CHURCH in the center of the city, a monument to the glory and splendor of the Greek Byzantine Empire, which held the torch of civilization high for more than a thousand years

Barcelona, Spain

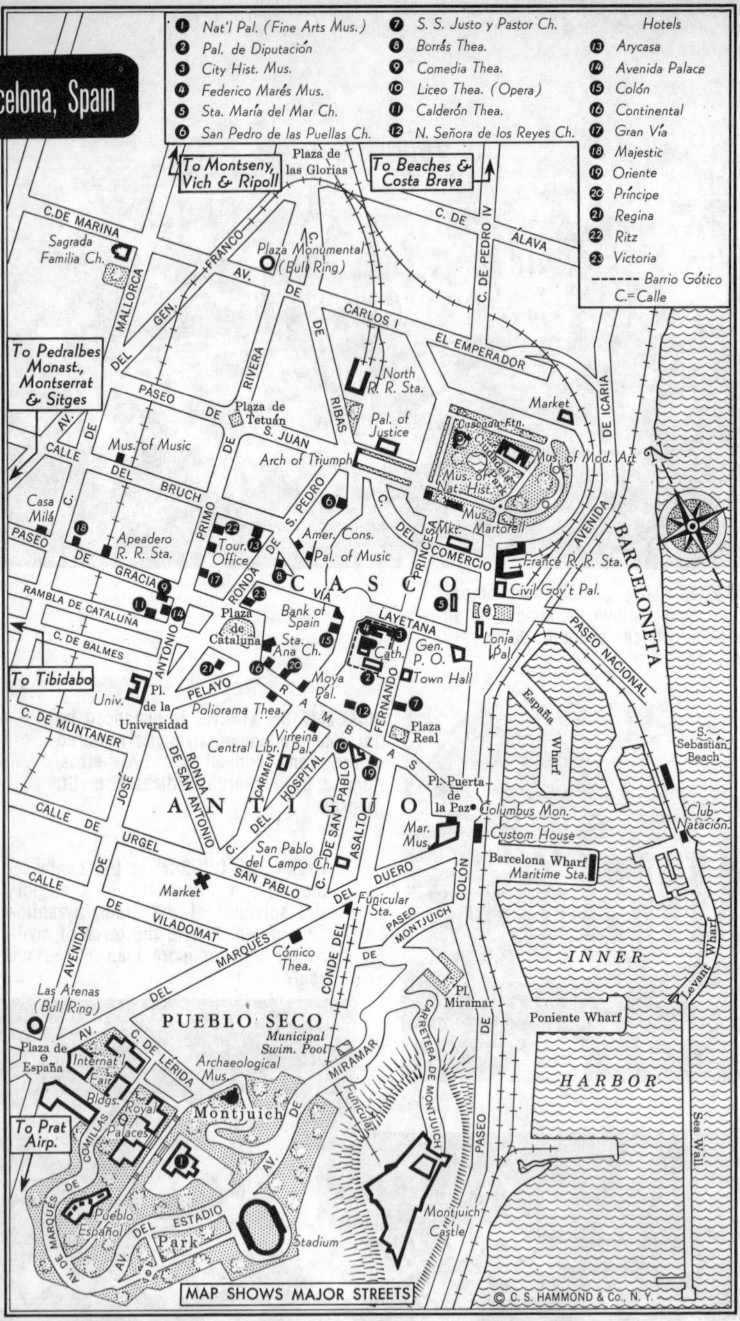

1 Nat'l Pal. (Fine Arts Mus.)
2 Pal. de Diputación
3 City Hist. Mus.
4 Federico Marés Mus.
5 Sta. María del Mar Ch.
6 San Pedro de las Puellas Ch.
7 S. S. Justo y Pastor Ch.
8 Borrás Thea.
9 Comedia Thea.
10 Liceo Thea. (Opera)
11 Calderón Thea.
12 N. Señora de los Reyes Ch.
Hotels
13 Arycasa
14 Avenida Palace
15 Colón
16 Continental
17 Gran Vía
18 Majestic
19 Oriente
20 Príncipe
21 Regina
22 Ritz
23 Victoria
Barrio Gótico
C.=Calle
To Montseny, Vich & Ripoll
Plaza de las Glorias
To Beaches & Costa Brava
To Pedralbes Monast., Montserrat & Sitges
To Tibidabo
To Prat Airp.
C. DE MARINA
Sagrada Familia Ch.
MALLORCA
AV. DEL GEN. FRANCO
Plaza Monumental (Bull Ring)
C. DE ÁLAVA
C. DE PEDRO IV
AV. DE CARLOS I
EL EMPERADOR
RIVERA
RIBAS
North R. R. Sta.
Plaza de Tetuan
PASEO DE S. JUAN
Pal. of Justice
Arch of Triumph
Market
Cascada Ftn.
Ciudadela Park
Mus. of Mod. Art
Mus. of Nat. Hist.
Mus. Martorell
AV. DE ICARIA
AVENIDA
BARCELONETA
Mus. of Music
CALLE DEL BRUCH
Casa Milá
Apeadero R. R. Sta.
PASEO DE GRACIA
Tour. Office
PRIMO DE RIVERA
RONDA DE S. PEDRO
Amer. Cons.
Pal. of Music
C. DEL COMERCIO
PRINCESA
Mkt.
France R. R. Sta.
Civil Gov't Pal.
RAMBLA DE CATALUÑA
C. DE BALMES
CASCO ANTIGUO
VÍA LAYETANA
Plaza de Cataluña
Bank of Spain
Sta. Ana Ch.
Cath.
Gen. P. O.
Town Hall
Lonja Pal.
PASEO NACIONAL
España Wharf
Univ.
Pl. de la Universidad
PELAYO
Moya Pal.
Poliorama Thea.
RAMBLAS
FERNANDO
Plaza Real
C. DE MUNTANER
Virreina Pal.
Central Libr.
CARMEN
HOSPITAL
S. Sebastian Beach
Club Natación
Pl. Puerta de la Paz
Columbus Mon.
Custom House
JOSÉ ANTONIO
RONDA DE SAN ANTONIO
DE SAN PABLO
ASALTO
Mar. Mus.
CALLE DE URGEL
San Pablo del Campo Ch.
Barcelona Wharf Maritime Sta.
CALLE DE VILADOMAT
Market
SAN PABLO
C. DEL DUERO
Funicular Sta.
PASEO DE MONTJUICH
PASEO DE COLÓN
CONDE DEL ASALTO
Cómico Thea.
AV. DEL MARQUÉS
INNER HARBOR
Levant Wharf
AVENIDA
Las Arenas (Bull Ring)
PUEBLO SECO
Municipal Swim. Pool
Pl. Miramar
Poniente Wharf
Plaza de España
Internat'l Fair Bldgs.
C. DE LERIDA
Archaeological Mus.
AV. DE MIRAMAR
CARRETERA DE MONTJUICH
Funicular
Royal Palaces
Montjuich
COMILLAS
Sea Wall
AV. DE MARQUÉS DE COMILLAS
Pueblo Español
AV. DEL ESTADIO
Park
Stadium
Montjuich Castle
MAP SHOWS MAJOR STREETS
© C. S. HAMMOND & Co., N. Y.

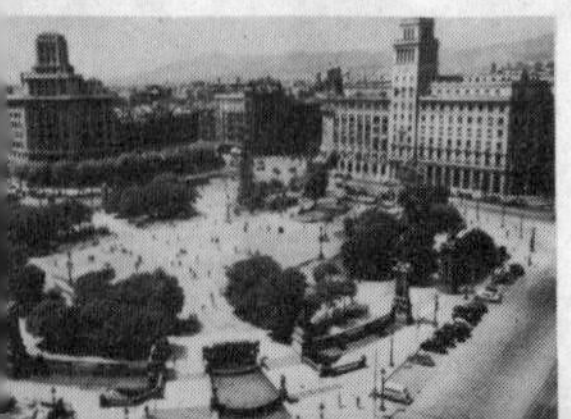

PLAZA DE CATALUÑA with its charming pools, fountains and pigeons serves as the center of Metropolitan Barcelona. From the plaza, the famed Ramblas promenade runs southward to the harbor forming the boundary between the quaint Ciudad and the more modern Arrabal section of the city

Photos: Spanish Tourist Office

CHRISTOPHER COLUMBUS points toward unknown horizons. This lofty monument to the discoverer of America stands at the harbor end of the Ramblas

BARCELONA is Spain's busiest port and largest industrial center, yet the city retains enough old-world charm to make it a popular port-of-call with visitors

THE GOTHIC CATHEDRAL which dates from the 14th century is one of the architectural treasures of Barcelona's Gothic Quarter. The Cathedral contains the tomb of Santa Eulalia, the city's patron saint

CHURCH OF LA SAGRADA FAMILIA is notable for its many unusual architectural features and particularly for its four unique "honeycombed" spires. This modern church is still in the process of construction

BARCELONA. Barcelona, in Catalonia, is Spain's chief manufacturing center and its second largest city. Although founded nearly three centuries before the birth of Christ and possessing a share of Roman ruins, Moorish relics and Medieval churches, Barcelona stands apart from other Spanish cities, somehow lacking their quaint charm, their characteristic atmosphere. Essentially a modern city, well planned and well built, it is for the most part given over to commerce and industry. Only in the "Ciudad" (Old Town) with its narrow streets, its 13th century Gothic Cathedral, has passing time moved at a slower pace. Hugging the shores of the Mediterranean Sea, Barcelona spreads in a narrow crescent between the river Besós on the north and Llobregat on the south, the pink-and-white of its suburbs, the vivid foliage of its gardens contrasting strongly with the huge factories, warehouses and spacious harbor installations that make it Spain's most important seaport. The Catalonian Hills, culminating in the 1,745-foot Tibidabo, form an austere backdrop and afford splendid views of the town's extensive panorama. Barcelona is a city of broad avenues, fine shops, attractive restaurants, numerous cabarets and theaters, several bull rings and a noted university. In contrast to this serene setting Barcelona's history has been marked with violence in frequent and passionate political and social uprising.

Basel, Switzerland

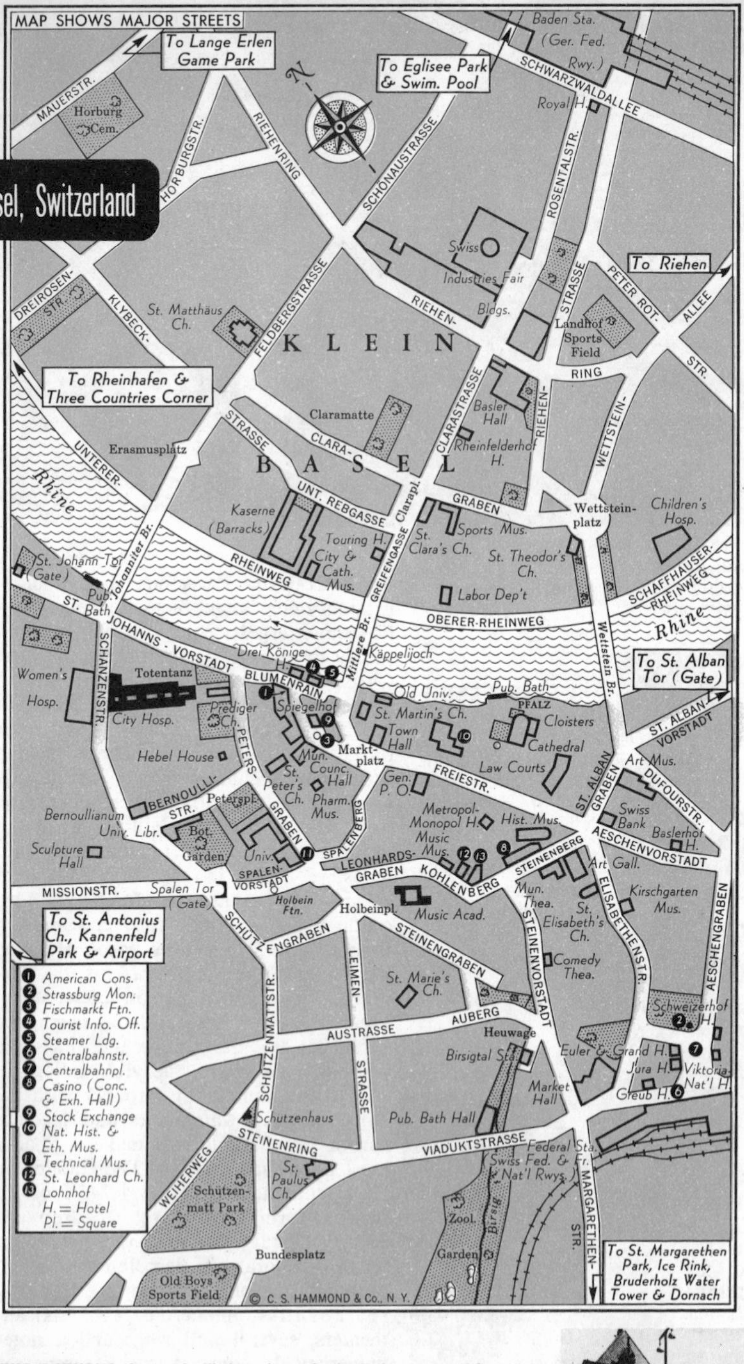

MAP SHOWS MAJOR STREETS

To Lange Erlen Game Park

To Eglisee Park & Swim. Pool

To Riehen

To Rheinhafen & Three Countries Corner

To St. Alban Tor (Gate)

To St. Antonius Ch., Kannenfeld Park & Airport

To St. Margarethen Park, Ice Rink, Bruderholz Water Tower & Dornach

KLEIN BASEL

1. American Cons.
2. Strassburg Mon.
3. Fischmarkt Ftn.
4. Tourist Info. Off.
5. Steamer Ldg.
6. Centralbahnstr.
7. Centralbahnpl.
8. Casino (Conc. & Exh. Hall)
9. Stock Exchange
10. Nat. Hist. & Eth. Mus.
11. Technical Mus.
12. St. Leonhard Ch.
13. Lohnhof

H. = Hotel
Pl. = Square

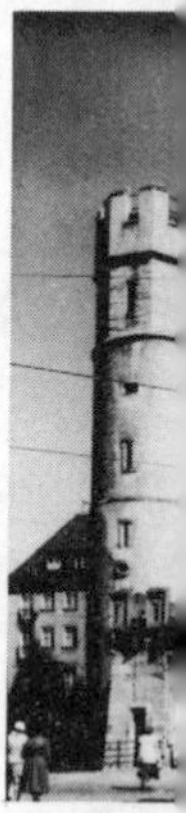

THE RATHAUS (town hall) has long looked down on this square in Basel which on Market Day is filled with colorful stalls and throngs of people. Dating from the 16th century, the old Rathaus with its remarkable court has recently been restored

THE ANCIENT WALLS and medieval ramparts that once guarded Basel are gone and in their place today are handsome tree-shaded promenades laid out along the banks of the Rhine

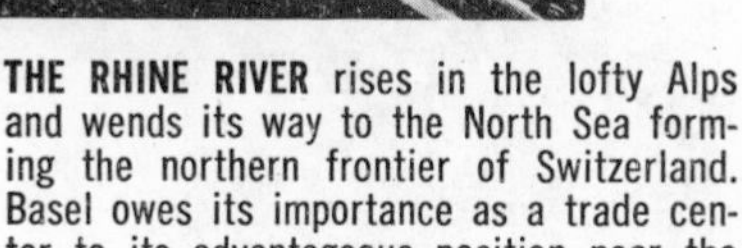

THE RHINE RIVER rises in the lofty Alps and wends its way to the North Sea forming the northern frontier of Switzerland. Basel owes its importance as a trade center to its advantageous position near the point where the river becomes navigable

Photos: Swiss National Tourist Office

BASEL. The city of Basel is located in the northwestern corner of Switzerland at a point almost equidistant from the borders of France and Germany. Its population, second in size only to Zurich in the Swiss Confederation, is, for the most part, German-speaking. The Rhine, which flows through the heart of Basel, divides it into two sections: Gross Basel, the commercial section of the city, lies on the south bank of the river, while Klein Basel, its industrial section, occupies the north bank. The opening of the Gotthard Railway, one of the most impressive railroad constructions in Europe, greatly increased Basel's prosperity, making it an important rail terminus and a distributing point for the goods that funnel into the city from all parts of the continent. Throughout a long history that began in Roman times, Basel has held a prominent place in the intellectual life of Europe and was the residence of such men as Calvin, Holbein and Nietzsche. It was here that the Council of Basel met from 1431 until 1449. Early in the 1500's Basel strongly allied itself with the Reformation and has remained predominantly Protestant ever since. Its most noteworthy structure is the ancient, rosy-red sandstone Cathedral which dominates the entire city from a vantage point high on a bluff overlooking the Rhine. Consecrated in 1019, the main portions of the building were rebuilt following an earthquake in 1356. Erasmus who lived the last 15 years of his life in Basel is buried in the Cathedral. The university, founded by Pope Pius II, is the oldest institution of its kind in Switzerland. Its 250,000-volume library, contains the original documents of the Council of Basel and other valuable writings of the Reformation movement.

THE HANDSOME SPALENTOR has witnessed much of Basel's historic past. Through the massive gateway which was erected in A. D. 1400 passed many of the great figures of the Reformation

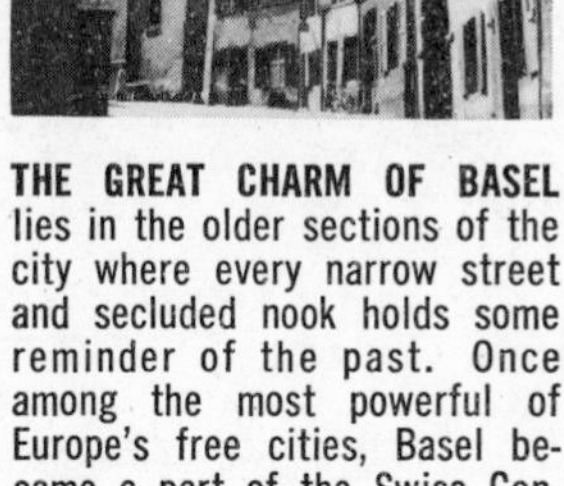

THE GREAT CHARM OF BASEL lies in the older sections of the city where every narrow street and secluded nook holds some reminder of the past. Once among the most powerful of Europe's free cities, Basel became a part of the Swiss Confederation in 1501

Belfast, Northern Ireland

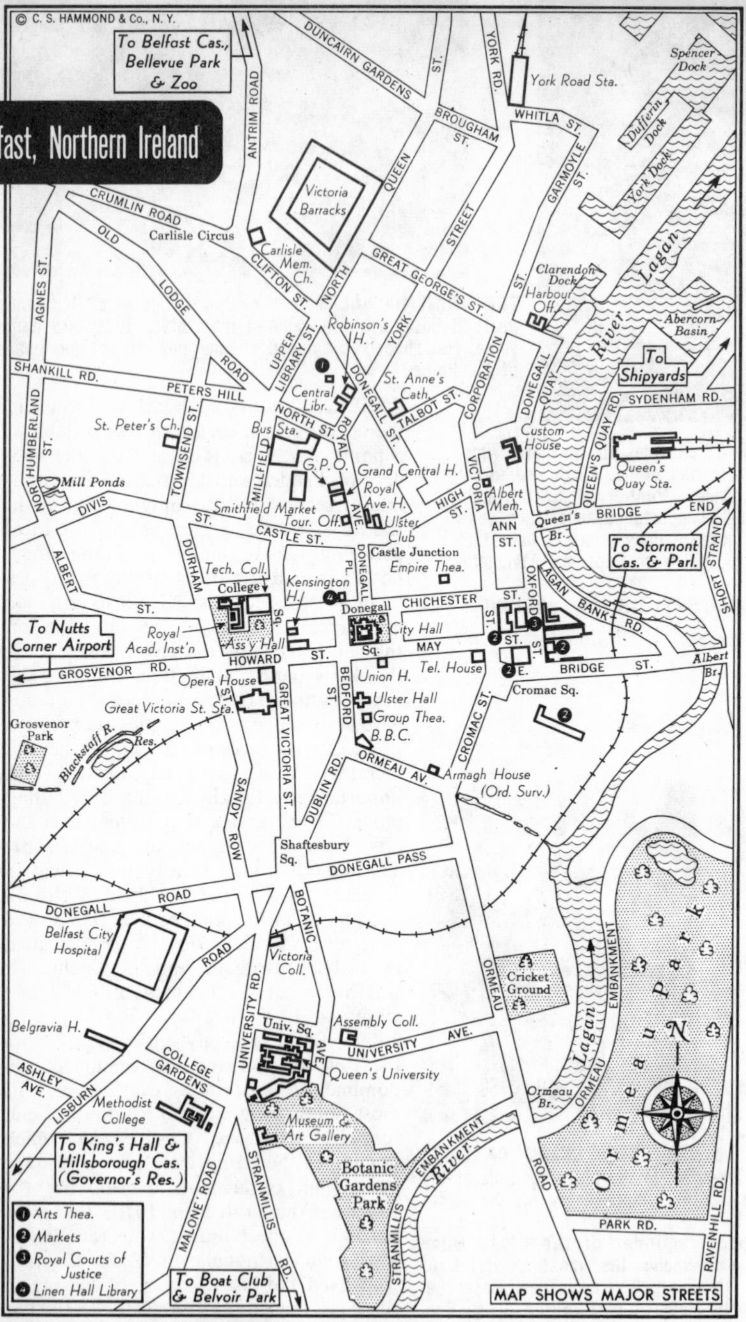

To Belfast Cas., Bellevue Park & Zoo

To Shipyards

To Stormont Cas. & Parl.

To Nutts Corner Airport

To King's Hall & Hillsborough Cas. (Governor's Res.)

To Boat Club & Belvoir Park

1 Arts Thea.
2 Markets
3 Royal Courts of Justice
4 Linen Hall Library

MAP SHOWS MAJOR STREETS

WHITLA HALL, situated on the grounds of Queen's University, represents the most modern trend in architecture. The building was used as the main lecture hall during the British Association Conference of 1952

Photos: British Information Service

ORANGE DAY PROCESSION winds its way through Donegall Place, the main shopping quarters of Belfast. The celebration of Orange Day on July 12th marks a Protestant success of 250 years ago

BELFAST. Belfast, capital and largest city of Northern Ireland, is an industrial center whose large rope and linen factories have made its name almost synonymous with the fine Irish linen cloth and linen cord produced here. Its great shipyards, in operation since the late 18th century, have carried its fame to the corners of the earth. At the head of Belfast Lough, a small arm of the Irish Sea, the city is situated in surroundings of great natural beauty. The rugged glens of Antrim, the pretty farms of County Down and the vast blue expanse of Lough Neagh are close at hand. The focal point of the city is Donegall Square around which are found the Linen Hall Library and the City Hall. In front of City Hall stands a monument commemorating the days which American soldiers, sailors and airmen spent in Northern Ireland prior to the invasion of North Africa and Europe. Royal Avenue and Donegall Place comprise the main shopping thoroughfares where the famous Belfast linens are sold. On the outskirts of Belfast are some of its finest buildings; Queens University, the Art Gallery and Museum in the beautiful botanical gardens and the Parliament buildings in Stormont Park. The people of Belfast are, for the most part, of Scottish and English descent and overwhelmingly Protestant in their religious faith; therefore, the city has long been a hub of opposition to Irish Home Rule.

A TUG STEAMS INTO BELFAST HARBOR. A boat coming up the Lough passes more than a mile of shipyards and docks filled with warships, liners, cargo boats, tankers and tugs in every stage of construction. One shipbuilding firm employs more than 20,000 workers

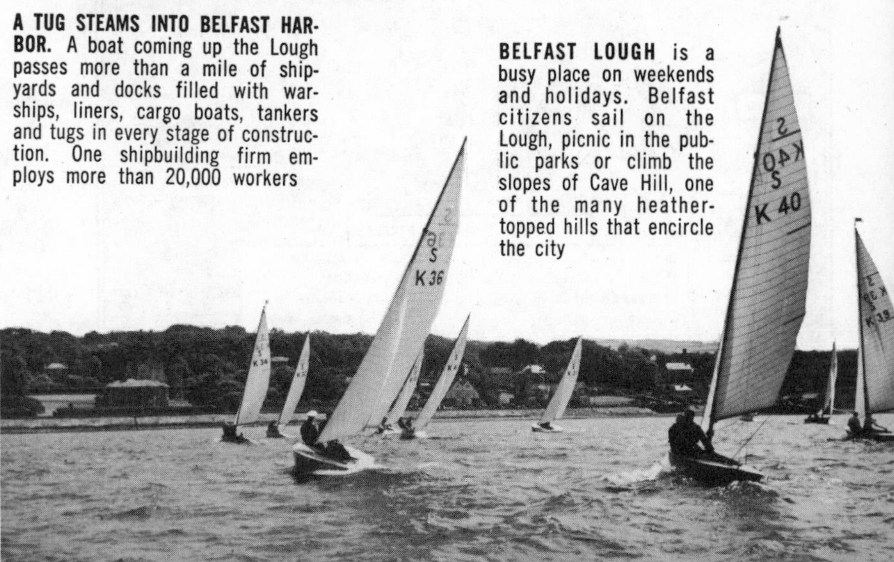

BELFAST LOUGH is a busy place on weekends and holidays. Belfast citizens sail on the Lough, picnic in the public parks or climb the slopes of Cave Hill, one of the many heather-topped hills that encircle the city

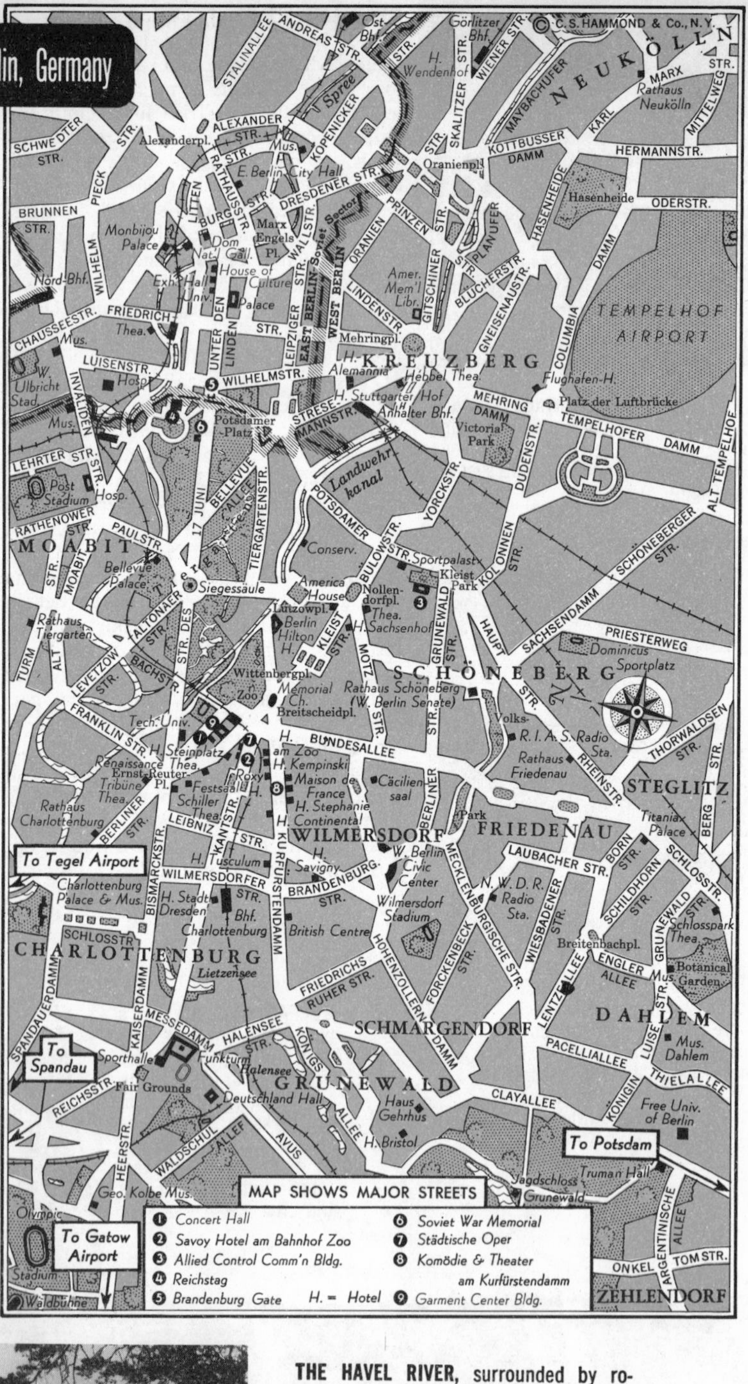

Berlin, Germany

© C. S. HAMMOND & Co., N. Y.

To Tegel Airport

To Spandau

To Gatow Airport

To Potsdam

MAP SHOWS MAJOR STREETS

1. Concert Hall
2. Savoy Hotel am Bahnhof Zoo
3. Allied Control Comm'n Bldg.
4. Reichstag
5. Brandenburg Gate
6. Soviet War Memorial
7. Städtische Oper
8. Komödie & Theater am Kurfürstendamm
9. Garment Center Bldg.

H. = Hotel

THE HAVEL RIVER, surrounded by romantic forests, stretches along western Berlin from north to south. Its idyllic bays form the loveliest of lakes

RUINED TOWER of the Kaiser Wilhelm Memorial Church will stand as a memorial by popular demand of West Berliners who won't allow it to be rebuilt as planned

BERLIN. In its long history, which began in the thirteenth century, Berlin has survived many vicissitudes. At present it is a divided city carved into two sectors, East Berlin and West Berlin. With their widely differing political and administrative policies, each contrasts sharply with the other. There is much in communist-dominated East Berlin that is reminiscent of the Nazi regime; the fear, the drab despair remain, only the uniforms of the ever-present police have changed. On the other hand, West Berlin, isolated as it is in the Soviet Zone of Germany, has become a symbol of freedom and a refuge for those fleeing from communist oppression. More than a decade has passed since bombers and field artillery poured their terrible havoc on the Prussian splendor that was pre-war Berlin, yet even today the former capital of the German Empire still bears the deep scars of battle. With over one-fifth of the city destroyed at the close of World War II, many of its beloved landmarks are gone—the Kaiser Friedrich museum, the Hohenzollern palace, the famed bronze Quadriga statue that once so proudly surmounted Brandenburg Gate. Others, like the charred and gutted ruins of the Kaiser Wilhelm Memorial Church, stand as grim reminders of war's destruction. Yet despite her physical devastation, the industriousness of her people, their intellectual vitality and wit are in many ways responsible for Berlin maintaining her rightful place among the great metropolises of Europe and the world. In the Western sector much has

ILLUMINATED NEWS BOARD at Potsdamer Platz flashes news into East Berlin 24 hours a day. It stands on the spot where the British, French, U.S. and Russian sectors of the city meet

KNAUTSCHKE, the hippo, beloved favorite of the West Berlin Zoo, makes a personal appearance with his daughter Boulette on a warm Sunday afternoon before an admiring crowd. The zoo is located in the famed Tiergarten

Photos: Berlin Tourist Information Office

BERLIN Continued

been done to clear away the rubble, to rebuild and repair the damage. The beautiful Tiergarten which was totally destroyed has been restored to a semblance of its former old-world loveliness by gifts of trees from Great Britain and Japan. The zoological garden is again a major attraction. Modern buildings rise to fill some gaping emptiness; and with the aid of American dollars, Berlin has regained her industrial prowess. Factories are again turning out the electrical, fine mechanical and optical goods that German craftsmen have made world famous. Automobiles and heavy machinery roll from assembly lines and the printing and paper processing industries flourish. Along the Kurfürstendamm and Tauentzienstrasse, West Berlin's main thoroughfares, the many shops are well stocked and bustling with trade in contrast to the shops of East Berlin where only a few commodities are freely sold. Here too, the nightclubs, the restaurants and little sidewalk cafés, the theaters and cinemas are filled once more with the gay crowds and the laughter so long absent from Berlin. And from the New Town Hall in Schöneberg the deep voice of the 20,950-pound Liberty Bell rings out, for all to hear, its daily reminder of a newly-won freedom.

GLITTERING KURFÜRSTENDAMM, Berlin's gay "White Way," lights up at night like a Christmas tree. Kempinski is a newly built hotel, very luxurious but low-priced, with some of the finest food in Europe served at its famous Schloss Marquart café

FUNKTURM, Berlin's 492-foot "Eiffel Tower," is located at the Fairgrounds. Also located here are twelve large exhibition halls and a charming terraced garden restaurant

BERLIN'S FREE UNIVERSITY in Dahlem was constructed with a large grant of funds by the Ford foundation. Pictured is the University's Henry Ford Building

Photos: Berlin Tourist Information Office

BERLIN'S PRIZED FREEDOM BELL, gift of the American people, hangs high in the tower of Schöneberg town hall. The bell rings daily at noon and its tones are broadcast into Communist controlled lands to the east by R.I.A.S., an American broadcasting station in Berlin

THE ENGLISH GARDEN was a gift of the people of England to Berliners after the war. In the background is the Victory Memorial column built in 1873

WESTHAFEN is Germany's second largest inland port and the heart of a barge system that connects Berlin with northern Germany and ports on the North sea

Bern, Switzerland

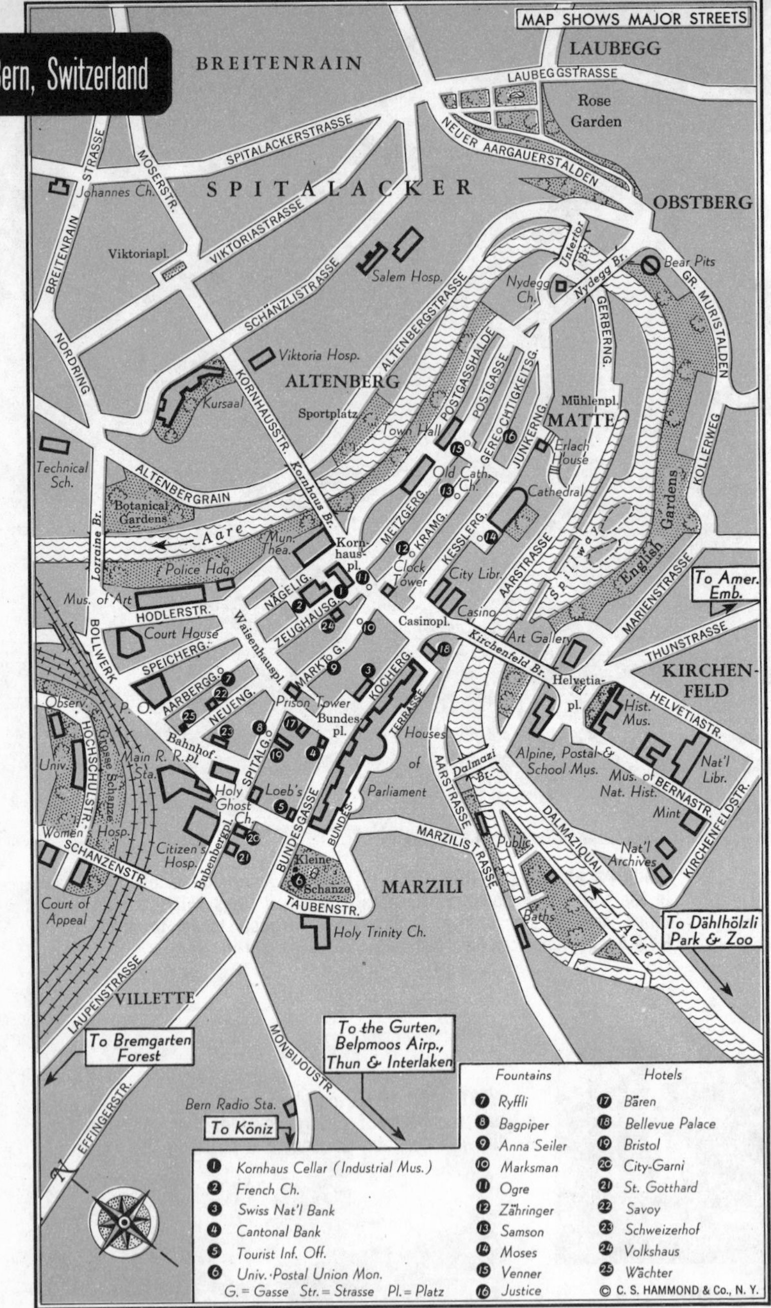

Photos: Swiss National Tourist Office, Official Bern Tourist Association

BEAR PITS' existence can be traced back to the 15th century. Since the city is supposed to have been named from the German word for bear **(Baren),** bears of all shapes and sizes, made of metal, stone, wood and of chocolate and gingerbread, are found all over the city

TOWN HALL, late Gothic in style, stands in the heart of the old town, forming one of the most delightful pictures of medieval architecture in existence. Just below the roof are affixed the coats-of-arms of counties of the Canton of Bern

SOARING, BREATHTAKING interior of the Bernese Cathedral, a fine example of Gothic architecture, showing some of the magnificent stained-glass windows

BERN. Throughout the centuries the Bernese have devoted every care to keeping their beautiful and unique city as it was built in the Middle Ages. It is to this tradition and care that we owe one of the best preserved medieval cities in Europe, a town which can be considered one of the loveliest adornments of the continent. For hundreds of years all households had to manage without water; however, as water is a necessity, fountains were erected in most of the streets. These public fountains naturally became the most popular meeting places and at the wide fountain basins busy clatter mingled with the splashing, sparkling water. It would indeed be fascinating if the figures which adorn them could tell us of the many events they have witnessed since they first stood on their slender perches. But the figures themselves also all have a history and meaning of their own. Most striking feature of Bern's medieval architecture are the arcades, the arched-in pavements on both sides of the streets. Luxurious, tempting shop displays of intricate mechanical devices and other modern items provide for the window-shopper a vivid contrast as he strolls along under the massive, medieval arcades.

OLD ARCADED STREETS with elaborate, carved signs and bay windows show spire of the Cathedral. Although the foundation stone was laid in 1421, final work was completed in 1893

KRAMGASSE with the Zahringer Fountain and the Clock Tower, main tower of the city wall. The figure play and astronomical clock on the tower, built by Caspar Brunner between 1526 and 1530, are known throughout the world as Bern's greatest attraction

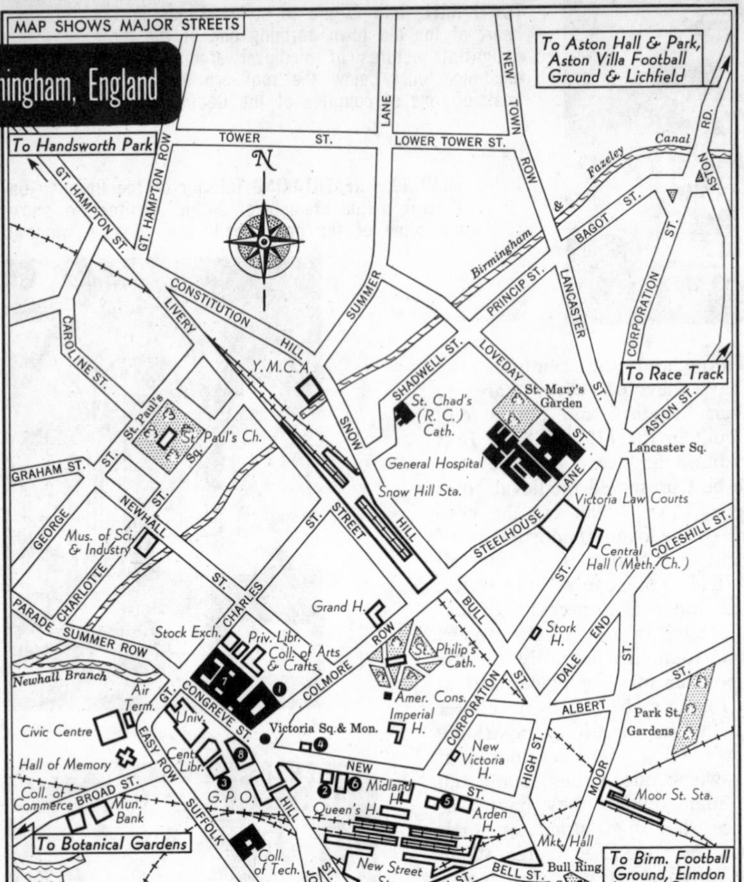

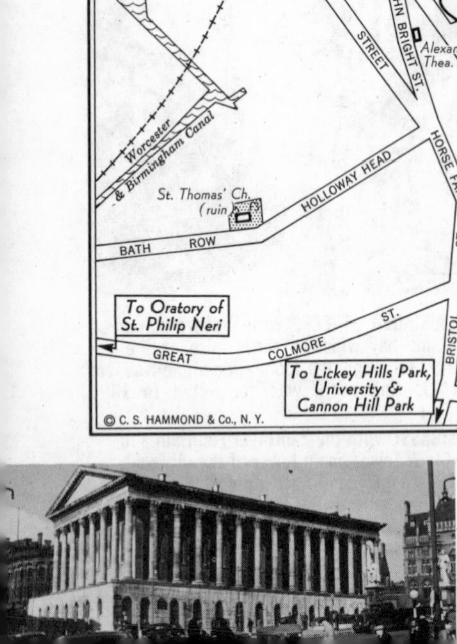

MAP SHOWS MAJOR STREETS

Birmingham, England

To Aston Hall & Park, Aston Villa Football Ground & Lichfield

To Handsworth Park

To Race Track

To Botanical Gardens

To Birm. Football Ground, Elmdon Airp. & Coventry

To Oratory of St. Philip Neri

To Lickey Hills Park, University & Cannon Hill Park

1. Council House
2. Chamber of Commerce
3. Birmingham & Midland Inst.
4. Royal Society of Artists Gall's
5. Birmingham Exchange
6. Theatre Royal
7. Museum & Gallery
8. Town Hall

H. = Hotel

THE TOWN HALL OF BIRMINGHAM was modeled after the Temple of Jupiter Stator in Rome. In 1846, Mendelssohn's oratorio "Elijah" was first performed here under the direction of the composer

THE COUNCIL HOUSE, which faces Birmingham's Victoria Square, is the seat of the city's government

BIRMINGHAM (Eng.) Birmingham, the great industrial giant of Warwick, England, boasts of being able to make anything from "a pin to a powerpress." This metropolis had indeed allied itself with industry as early as the 16th century. Surrounded as it is by districts rich in both coal and iron ore, Birmingham today ranks among such cities as Pittsburgh and its North American "godchild"—Birmingham, Alabama, as one of the greatest steel producing centers of the world. Included also among its major heavy industries are the manufacture of munitions and the large-scale production of automobiles. Many of the copper and brass coins used by Britain and its colonies are minted in Birmingham. This city has often been an ardent crusader in reform movements both political and religious. It was in a suburb of Birmingham that James Watt and his partner Matthew Boulton founded their celebrated Soho metal works; other famous men whose names are associated with Birmingham are Joseph Priestley, John Baskerville and Joseph Chamberlain. Birmingham does not lack for cultural interests; it possesses a modern University, the outgrowth of several smaller institutions, its library probably contains the largest collection of Shakespearean books in the world and its museum houses one of the most important collections of paintings outside London.

BIRMINGHAM, located in Warwickshire is one of the largest cities in England and among the world's greatest industrial centers

Photos: Philip Gendreau, British Info. Services, British Travel Association

ST. MARTIN'S, the parish church of Birmingham, dates from the 13th century and is one of the city's few reminders of its medieval history. In the foreground, is Bull Ring market place

BRUSSELS. Originally called *Broeksele,* or "habitation near the marsh," this Flemish city was renowned during the Middle Ages for its luxury and gaiety of life, as well as for its manufacture of carpets, tapestries and lace. Although centuries have since passed by, the atmosphere of Belgium's capital remains the same. Brussels lace is still among the finest and most delicate in the world, upholding the old Flemish tradition, and is handed down from generation to generation as a cherished family heirloom. Still a happy city, too, she supports excellent musical organizations, usually heard in the handsome Palais des Beaux Arts, one of the finest concert halls in Europe, and not a day goes by when no concert, opera or other performance takes place, indicating the typical Belgian love for music. In fact, all art is treasured in this old city, where many prosperous museums, like the Musées Royaux des Beaux Arts, Cabinet des Estampes and the Belgian Congo Museum, contain opulent collections, especially featuring the magnificent, world-beloved Flemish masters like Jan and Hubert van Eyck, Rubens, Memling, Van Orley, Brueghel the Elder and Brueghel the Younger and Teniers.

PORTE DE HAL (Hal Gate) is the last remaining vestige of the town's second wall, built in the 14th century, was used as a prison during the 18th century and now houses a museum.

PALAIS DE LA NATION is a Louis XVI-style building facing the Parc de Bruxelles, the old gardens of the Duke of Brabant, where parliament meets

HOTEL DE VILLE (Town Hall), a beautiful example of Gothic architecture, is located on the Grand' Place, the cradle of Brussels, originally a halt for merchants or **marche** (market) and one of the most interesting public squares

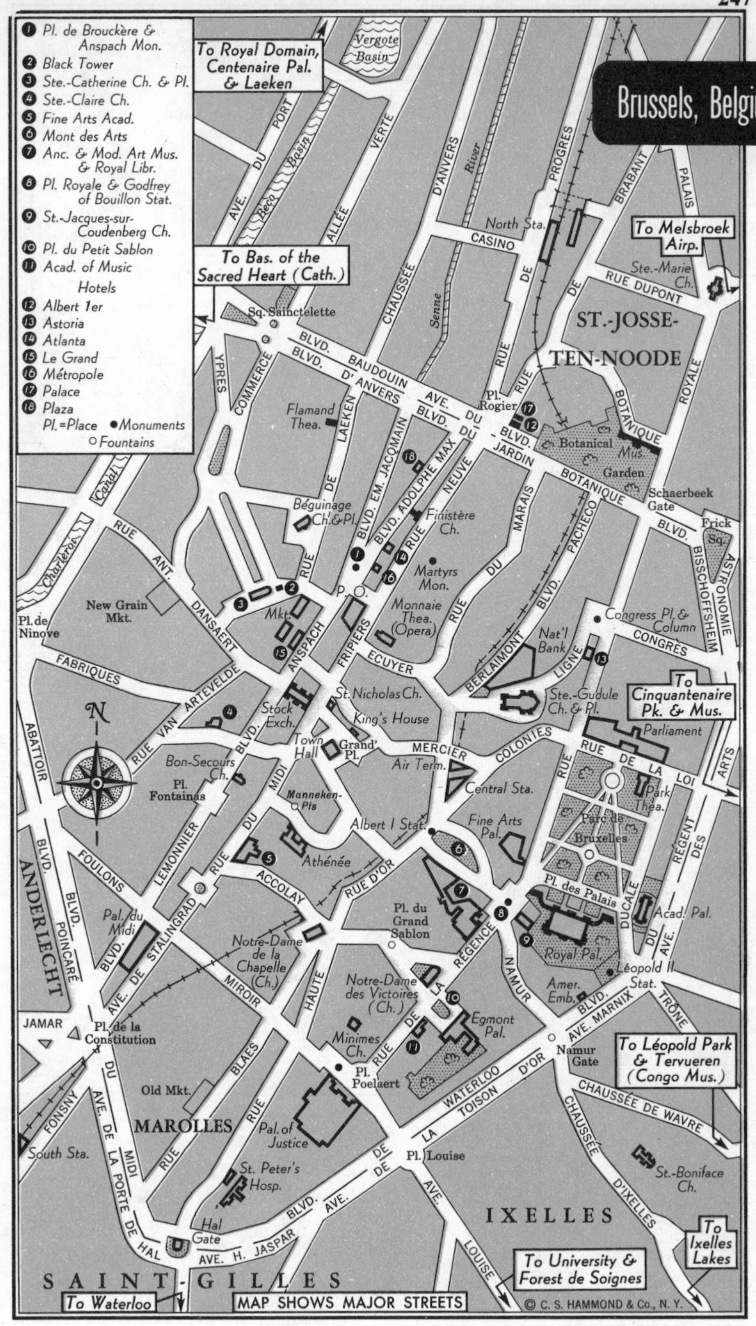

Photos: Belgian National Tourist Office

MASSIVE CINQUANTENAIRE ARCADES, one of the many new structures erected in the last century, on a picturesque avenue lined with fashionable homes

Copenhagen, Denmark

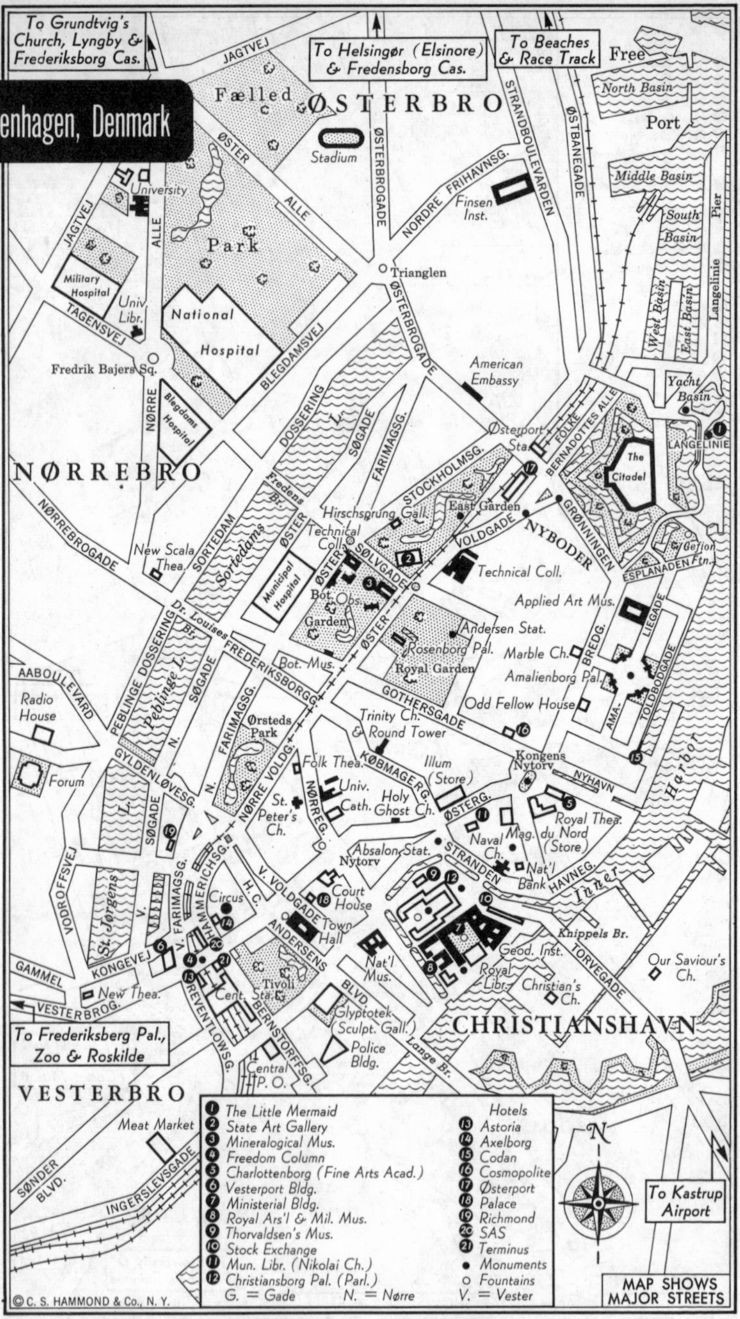

To Grundtvig's Church, Lyngby & Frederiksborg Cas.

To Helsingør (Elsinore) & Fredensborg Cas.

To Beaches & Race Track

To Frederiksberg Pal., Zoo & Roskilde

To Kastrup Airport

1 The Little Mermaid
2 State Art Gallery
3 Mineralogical Mus.
4 Freedom Column
5 Charlottenborg (Fine Arts Acad.)
6 Vesterport Bldg.
7 Ministerial Bldg.
8 Royal Ars'l & Mil. Mus.
9 Thorvaldsen's Mus.
10 Stock Exchange
11 Mun. Libr. (Nikolai Ch.)
12 Christiansborg Pal. (Parl.)

Hotels
13 Astoria
14 Axelborg
15 Codan
16 Cosmopolite
17 Østerport
18 Palace
19 Richmond
20 SAS
21 Terminus

● Monuments
○ Fountains

G. = Gade N. = Nørre V. = Vester

MAP SHOWS MAJOR STREETS

GRUNDTVIG'S CHURCH, whose architecture was inspired by the typical Danish village churches, is built of millions of yellow bricks. American tourists often call it the "organ church" because of its exterior resemblance to a pipe organ

TOWN HALL of Copenhagen is richly ornamented both within and without. The 346-foot tower contains one of the world's most unique clocks which not only tells the hours of the day but shows the astronomic constellations as well

COPENHAGEN. Developing from a 12th century fishing village, friendly and hospitable, Copenhagen has been considered the capital of Denmark since 1416. The city occupies a spot on the eastern shore of Zealand Island and is separated from Sweden by only a 20-mile stretch of water. Because of its fine sheltered harbor and its strategic location at the gateway to the Baltic, Copenhagen has for many years been considered one of the principal ports of Northern Europe. Also, as Copenhagen is a "free port" through which foreign goods can pass duty-free, it is an important transshipping center. A section known as Stroget is the heart of the city's business and commercial life. Here are found concentrated many of the city's office buildings, places of amusement, shops and colorful flower, fruit and vegetable stalls. The Langelinie (Long Line) is probably the most beautiful of Copenhagen's handsome boulevards. A favorite promenade, it sweeps along the edge of the Sound, affording a wonderful panorama of the city's harbor. Along this drive can be seen the famous statue of Hans Christian Andersen's "Little Mermaid." Immortalized in bronze, she gazes thoughtfully across the blue water. Amalienborg Square opens off the Langelinie. Here are found the four rococo mansions which comprise the Amalienborg Palace, residence of the Danish king. Once the

AN OLD DANISH FARM HOUSE is among the quaint buildings which have been transferred from various sections of Denmark to the Open Air Museum near Copenhagen. All are furnished with antiques and household effects typical of the period or region

STOCK EXCHANGE BUILDING, topped by a picturesque spire of four intertwined dragons' tails, is one of the finest of Copenhagen's Renaissance buildings. Built around 1600, it is delightfully situated on a lovely canal

Photos: Danish National Travel Office

homes of four noble families, the mansions were acquired for the king after a fire had destroyed the Christiansborg Palace in 1794. Today Christiansborg Palace, which five times in its long history has been demolished by fire or enêmy attack, houses the Parliament (Rigsdag), the Supreme Court and the Royal Reception Rooms. The present Christiansborg Palace, restored 1907-1915, occupies a site where Bishop Absalon had built a palace in 1167. The crumbling ruins of the Bishop's palace may still be seen beneath the present one. The beautiful renaissance Rosenborg Castle is now a museum containing treasure of the Danish royal family, including the crown jewels and the royal regalia. In the heart of Copenhagen is the famed Tivoli, whose romantic gardens with their idyllic atmosphere, symphony orchestra, ballet, restaurants and scores of amusements and divertisements attract over four million guests during its summer season. Here a charming Pantomime Theater still preserves the commedia dell'arte. The Tivoli, created over a century ago by the genius showman Georg Carstensen, is truly the fairy garden of Denmark. Probably the most noted of Copenhagen's industries is the manufacture of the internationally renowned Copenhagen porcelain. Fired at exceedingly high temperatures, this lovely porcelain is distinguished for its subtle under-glaze colors of blue, brown, green and its exquisite glaze and translucency.

TIVOLI GARDEN is thought by many to be at its best during the day when only a handful of people wander through the quiet, century-old garden admiring the flowers or basking in the sun

AN APARTMENT HOUSE in Copenhagen reflects the modern trend in Danish architecture. Here each apartment is equipped with its own little balcony

NYBORG CASTLE, situated on the fairy-tale island of Funen, was founded around 1170. About 700 to 800 years ago it was the meeting place of the Danehof which was made up of the clergy and the nobility

AMALIENBORG PALACE is the residence of the king of Denmark. To the right, is the equestrian statue of Frederik V. The statue was modeled by Saly at the expense of the Asiatic Company

FREDENSBORG CASTLE, in the town of Fredensborg to the north of Copenhagen, serves as the spring and autumn residence of the Danish Royal Family. Close by is a charming park which was laid out in 1760 and is one of the loveliest of northern Denmark

Photos: Danish National Travel Office

ROSENBORG CASTLE, once the summer residence of the Danish kings was made into the Royal Family Museum in 1833. It contains collections of china, silver and paintings and also the crown jewels

FOUR COURTS, a magnificent pile of superb dignity on the northern quays, was designed by the gifted architect James Gandon in the late 18th century and now houses the Irish Law Courts

DUBLIN. A salt wind blows into the heart of Dublin and the slopes of the Wicklow Hills seem to rise at the end of every street in the southern suburbs, while the Liffey flows down from the hinterland to a truly lovely harbor. The Irish capital, though, is renowned not alone for her exciting location but chiefly as a city of "character." Heart and soul of the fighting Emerald Isle, her turbulent, spirited history and particular flair for backing the losing side have lived up to the name given her by her Norse founders of *Dubh-linn,* "the black pool." In every age a city of vivid personalities, including such stellar literary lights as George Bernard Shaw and William Yeats, her activity has been begotten by a social life that has a strong element of adventure, even of peculiarity. Many of these brilliant men were scholars of the notable Trinity College, Dublin's ancient seat of learning. And greatest Dublin figure of them all was Jonathan Swift; one senses his somber and powerful personality ever imminent behind the life of the city. Gay, quick-witted, eccentric, famous, the Dubliner is embodied in a popular street ballad: "Oh, Dublin City, there is no doubtin',/Is the finest city upon the sea—/'Tis there you may see O'Connell spoutin',/And Lady Morgan making tea."

HISTORIC PARADES, religious ceremonies and the dancers and pipers who gather in St. Stephen's Green for contests and festivals provide exciting fun, satisfying the Irishman's love for colorful pageantry

DUBLINER'S HOME, with the inevitable tiny flower garden, in a municipal housing scheme illustrates what a pleasant, comfortable and wholesome city she is for her inhabitants

Phottos: Irish Tourist Bureau

FRUIT SELLER at the foot of Nelson Pillar, for more than a century the city's best known landmark. Shelley, the poet, resided for some time in a house which stood near here

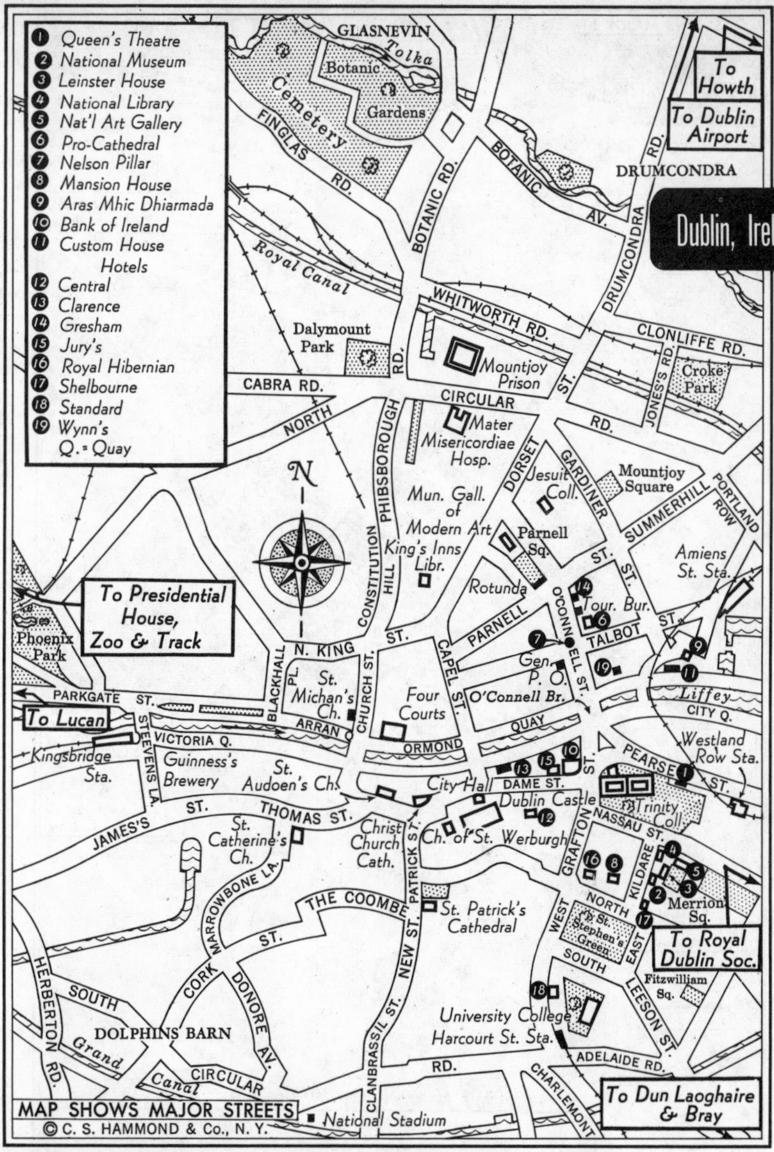

Dublin, Ireland

1 Queen's Theatre
2 National Museum
3 Leinster House
4 National Library
5 Nat'l Art Gallery
6 Pro-Cathedral
7 Nelson Pillar
8 Mansion House
9 Aras Mhic Dhiarmada
10 Bank of Ireland
11 Custom House

Hotels

12 Central
13 Clarence
14 Gresham
15 Jury's
16 Royal Hibernian
17 Shelbourne
18 Standard
19 Wynn's

Q. = Quay

To Howth

To Dublin Airport

To Presidential House, Zoo & Track

To Lucan

To Royal Dublin Soc.

To Dun Laoghaire & Bray

MAP SHOWS MAJOR STREETS

O'CONNELL STREET, finest and most important in Dublin, has witnessed every great national demonstration of triumph or sorrow. In the center is Foley's fine statue of Daniel O'Connell, who secured the Catholic Emancipation Act in 1829. Farther along is the Nelson Pillar

Edinburgh, Scotland

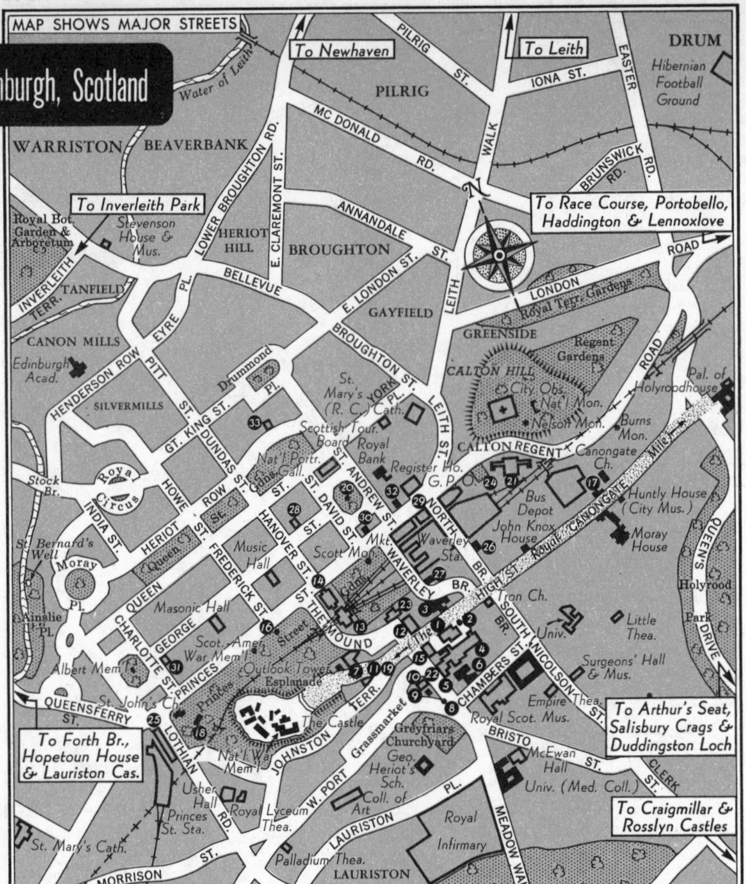

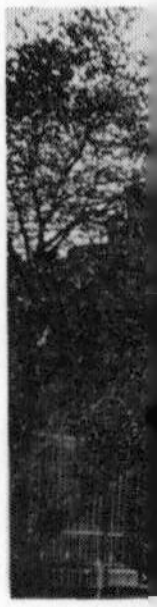

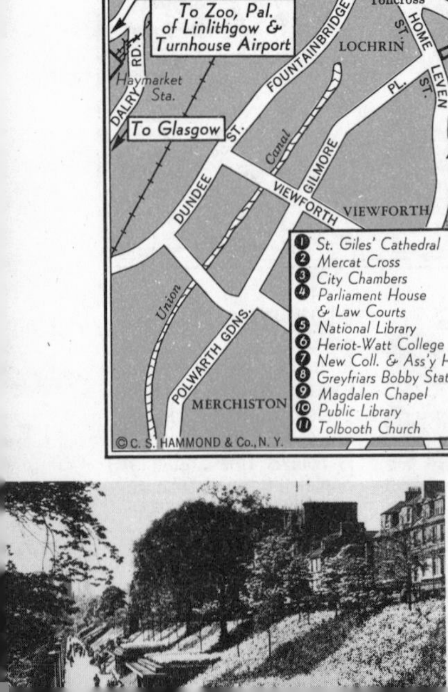

MAP SHOWS MAJOR STREETS
To Newhaven
To Leith
To Inverleith Park
To Race Course, Portobello, Haddington & Lennoxlove
To Arthur's Seat, Salisbury Crags & Duddingston Loch
To Forth Br., Hopetoun House & Lauriston Cas.
To Craigmillar & Rosslyn Castles
To Zoo, Pal. of Linlithgow & Turnhouse Airport
To Glasgow
To Blackford Hill & Royal Observ.
DRUM
Hibernian Football Ground
PILRIG
WARRISTON
BEAVERBANK
BROUGHTON
HERIOT HILL
GAYFIELD
GREENSIDE
CANON MILLS
SILVERMILLS
TANFIELD
LAURISTON
LOCHRIN
Tollcross
VIEWFORTH
BRUNTSFIELD
GRANGE
MERCHISTON
Water of Leith
Royal Bot. Garden & Arboretum
Stevenson House & Mus.
Edinburgh Acad.
CALTON HILL
City Obs.
Nat'l Mon.
Nelson Mon.
Regent Gardens
Royal Terr. Gardens
Burns Mon.
Pal. of Holyroodhouse
Canongate Ch.
Huntly House (City Mus.)
Moray House
Holyrood Park
Little Thea.
Univ.
Surgeons' Hall & Mus.
Empire Thea.
Royal Scot. Mus.
McEwan Hall
Univ. (Med. Coll.)
Royal Infirmary
The Meadows
Bruntsfield Links
King's Thea.
Palladium Thea.
Royal Lyceum Thea.
Usher Hall
Princes St. Sta.
St. Mary's Cath.
Haymarket Sta.
Coll. of Art
Geo. Heriot's Sch.
Greyfriars Churchyard
The Castle
Esplanade
Outlook Tower
Nat'l War Mem'l
Scot.-Amer. War Mem'l
Albert Mem'l
St. John's Ch.
Masonic Hall
Music Hall
Scott Mon.
Mkt.
Waverley Sta.
Register Ho.
G.P.O.
Bus Depot
John Knox House
Tron Ch.
Royal Bank
Scottish Tour. Board
Nat'l Portr. Gall.
St. Mary's (R.C.) Cath.
Royal Circus
Moray Pl.
Ainslie Pl.
St. Bernard's Well
Stock Br.
Canal
Union
Royal Mile
MC DONALD RD.
PILRIG ST.
IONA ST.
EASTER RD.
LEITH WALK
BRUNSWICK RD.
ANNANDALE ST.
LOWER BROUGHTON RD.
E. CLAREMONT ST.
BELLEVUE
E. LONDON ST.
LONDON ROAD
BROUGHTON ST.
LEITH ST.
CALTON REGENT
INVERLEITH TERR.
HENDERSON ROW
EYRE PL.
PITT ST.
GT. KING ST.
DUNDAS ST.
HOWE ST.
INDIA ST.
HERIOT ROW
QUEEN ST.
FREDERICK ST.
HANOVER ST.
ST. DAVID ST.
ST. ANDREW ST.
YORK PL.
NORTH BR.
WAVERLEY BR.
HIGH ST.
CANONGATE
QUEEN'S DRIVE
SOUTH BR.
NICOLSON ST.
CHAMBERS ST.
CLERK ST.
BRISTO ST.
GEORGE ST.
CHARLOTTE ST.
PRINCES ST.
THE MOUND
QUEENSFERRY ST.
LOTHIAN RD.
JOHNSTON TERR.
Grassmarket
W. PORT
LAURISTON PL.
MEADOW WALK
MELVILLE DRIVE
MORRISON ST.
FOUNTAINBRIDGE
HOME ST.
LEVEN ST.
WHITEHOUSE LOAN
MARCHMONT RD.
GRANGE RD.
DALRY RD.
DUNDEE ST.
GILMORE PL.
VIEWFORTH
POLWARTH GDNS.
1 St. Giles' Cathedral
2 Mercat Cross
3 City Chambers
4 Parliament House & Law Courts
5 National Library
6 Heriot-Watt College
7 New Coll. & Ass'y Hall
8 Greyfriars Bobby Statue
9 Magdalen Chapel
10 Public Library
11 Tolbooth Church
12 Sheriff Court House
13 National Gallery
14 Royal Scottish Academy
15 County Buildings
16 Scots-Greys Memorial
17 Canongate Tolbooth
18 St. Cuthbert's Church
19 Lawnmarket
20 St. Andrew Sq. & Melville Mon.
21 St. Andrew's House
22 George IV Bridge
23 Bank of Scotland
24 Calton Old Burying Ground
Hotels
25 Caledonian
26 Carlton
27 Cockburn
28 George
29 North British
30 Old Waverley
31 Roxburghe
32 Royal British
33 Royal Stuart
© C. S. HAMMOND & Co., N. Y.

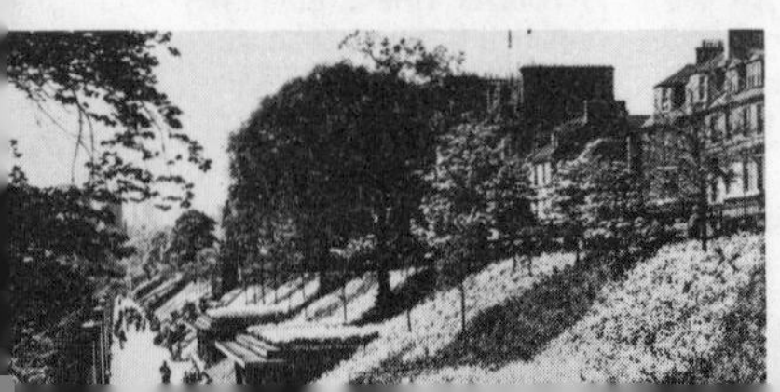

PRINCES STREET GARDENS are laid out in a hollow that was once North Loch, whose waters, before they were drained away, lapped the precipice upon which Edinburgh Castle stands

Photos: British Information Services, British Travel Association.

EDINBURGH — Edinburgh, Scotland's capital and guardian of its ancient history, spreads out upon a series of ridges near the southern banks of the Firth of Forth. South of Princes Street, which divides the old town from the new, Edinburgh's ancient 7th-century Castle looks down from its high, rocky seat on a city considered by many to be the fairest in Europe; a city whose wealth of classic architecture, whose abundance of buildings resembling Grecian temples has won for it the title of "Modern Athens." The Castle around which the city grew has long been famed for its historical associations with such names as Robert the Bruce, Mary Queen of Scots, and Charles Stuart. From it a steep and narrow road leads to the summit of Castle Rock where with the Palace buildings stands Scotland's impressive War Memorial honoring its men and women who gave their lives in two World Wars. Here no detail of service has been forgotten, even mice and carrier pigeons are represented in the various panels and friezes which adorn this shrine. Running eastward, the Royal Mile connects Castle Rock with the Palace of Holyroodhouse which today serves as official residence of the Queen when she visits Edinburgh. Long a center of literature and learning, Edinburgh can count among her famous men: Sir Walter Scott, Lord Lister, Robert Louis Stevenson and Kenneth Grahame.

SCOTT MONUMENT which stands in East Princes Street Gardens is an Edinburgh landmark. Beneath a central tower, supported by four arches is the white marble statue of Scotland's great novelist and poet, Sir Walter Scott

HOLYROODHOUSE is the official residence of the Queen in Edinburgh. Built in 1671, its architecture follows the Renaissance teachings of Inigo Jones and combines Roman Doric, Ionic and Corinthian

PRINCES STREET runs in a straight line through the heart of Edinburgh dividing the Old Town from the New Town. In the foreground, the imposing Royal Scottish Academy bears close resemblance to a classic temple

SCOTTISH REGIMENTS in their colorful regalia rehearsing for the Edinburgh Festival are shown on the Edinburgh Castle Esplanade. Their military displays are a highlight of the Festival

SCHAUSPIELHAUS, or theater, in modern renaissance style, features operatic and dramatic presentations. Frankfurt's stage life now ranks with that of Europe's great cities

FRANKFURT. "Were anyone to ask me if I could think of a place more befitting my birth, more suitable to my conception as a citizen and more agreeable to my poetic feelings, I could name no other town but Frankfurt am Main." Thus wrote Johann Wolfgang Goethe, Frankfurt's greatest son, in 1824. Today, Frankfurt continues to be a city full of life, buzzing with work, an economic center, an international meeting place and a stronghold of culture and science. The *Römer,* venerable City Hall of the late Middle Ages, flanks the famous market square in the Altstadt (old town). This building with its Kaisersaal and the Prince Electors Chamber was the scene of the German emperors' coronation banquets. Nearby is the red-sandstone St. Paul's Church, where the first German National Assembly was held in 1848-1849. The inner city is closely encircled by a garden belt, linking it with the residential sections, and throughout Frankfurt are well-kept gardens and parks with the smell of fresh grass and dainty blossoms in the air, while in the wide woods along the fringe of the city, good forest inns beckon for a leisurely afternoon's rest and conversation, accompanied by good strong coffee and excellent German pastries.

PALM GARDEN offers a wonderful exhibition of plants, with a special subtropical flower show, one of the most important floral displays in Europe

NEW AND OLD in Frankfurt—with modern apartment buildings erected in front of the famous old St. Bartholomew's Cathedral, scene of the elections of German emperors after its completion in 1356 and their coronations from 1562 to 1792

GOETHESAUS, heavily damaged during World War II, has been restored, although the furnishings were preserved intact. In this house, the renowned poet was born and wrote his early works

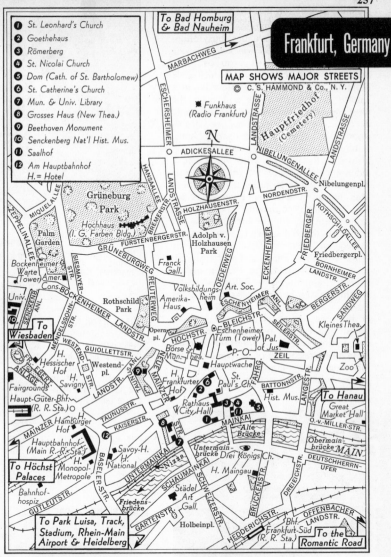

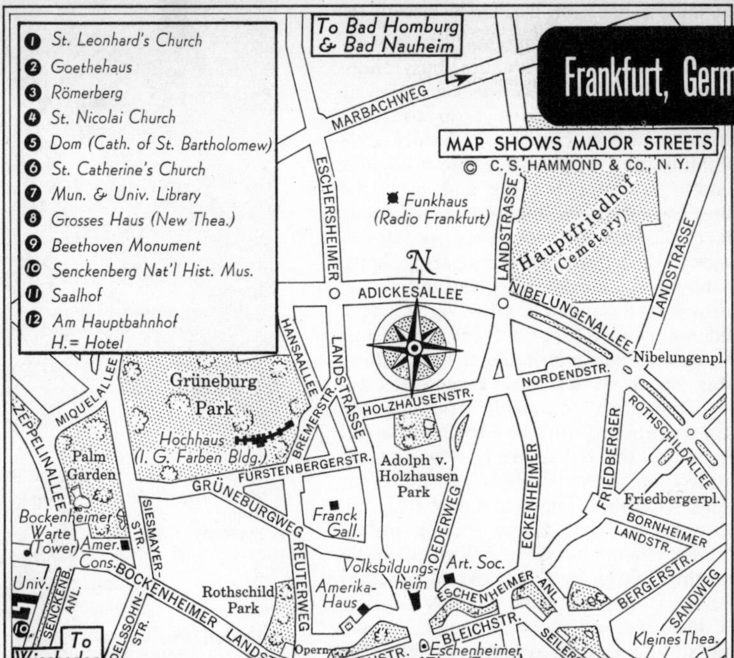

Frankfurt, Germany

MAP SHOWS MAJOR STREETS

1. St. Leonhard's Church
2. Goethehaus
3. Römerberg
4. St. Nicolai Church
5. Dom (Cath. of St. Bartholomew)
6. St. Catherine's Church
7. Mun. & Univ. Library
8. Grosses Haus (New Thea.)
9. Beethoven Monument
10. Senckenberg Nat'l Hist. Mus.
11. Saalhof
12. Am Hauptbahnhof

H. = Hotel

To Bad Homburg & Bad Nauheim
MARBACHWEG
ESCHERSHEIMER LANDSTRASSE
Funkhaus (Radio Frankfurt)
Hauptfriedhof (Cemetery)
LANDSTRASSE
N
ADICKESALLEE
NIBELUNGENALLEE
Nibelungenpl.
HANSAALLEE
NORDENDSTR.
HOLZHAUSENSTR.
Grüneburg Park
MIQUELALLEE
ZEPPELINALLEE
Hochhaus (I. G. Farben Bldg.)
BREMERSTR.
ROTHSCHILDALLEE
FRIEDBERGER LANDSTR.
Palm Garden
FÜRSTENBERGERSTR.
Adolph v. Holzhausen Park
GRÜNEBURGWEG
Franck Gall.
OEDERWEG
ECKENHEIMER
Friedbergerpl.
BORNHEIMER LANDSTR.
Bockenheimer Warte (Tower)
Amer. Cons.
SIESMAYERSTR.
Volksbildungsheim
Art. Soc.
Univ.
BOCKENHEIMER LANDSTR.
REUTERWEG
Rothschild Park
Amerika-Haus
ESCHENHEIMER ANL.
BERGERSTR.
SANDWEG
SENCKENB. ANL.
MENDELSSOHNSTR.
BLEICHSTR.
To Wiesbaden
Opernpl.
HOCHSTR.
Eschenheimer Turm (Tower)
SEILERSTR.
Kleines Thea.
WESTENDSTR.
GUIOLLETTSTR.
Börse & Mun. Thea.
Pal. of Jus.
P. O.
ZEIL
H. Hessischer Hof
Westendpl.
TAUNUSANL.
NEUE MAINZER STR.
Hauptwache
FR. EBERT ANLAGE
H. Savigny
LANDSTR.
H. Frankfurter Hof
St. Paul's Ch.
FAHRG.
BATTONNSTR.
LANGESTR.
Zoo
Fairgrounds
Haupt-Güter-Bhf. (R. R. Sta.)
TAUNUSSTR.
Rathaus (City Hall)
Hist. Mus.
To Hanau
Great Market Hall
H. Hamburger Hof
MAINZER
KAISERSTR.
MAINKAI
Alte Brücke
O.-v.-MILLER-STR.
Hauptbahnhof (Main R. R. Sta.)
Savoy-H.
H. National
Untermainbrücke
Drei Königs Ch.
Obermainbrücke
MAIN
UNTERMAINKAI
Nizza
DEUTSCHHERRNUFER
To Höchst Palaces
H. Monopol-Metropole
SCHAUMAINKAI
H. Maingau
BASELER-STR.
SCHWEIZERSTR.
BRÜCKENSTR.
DREIEICHSTR.
Bahnhof-hospiz
Städel Art Gall.
GUTLEUTSTR.
Friedensbrücke
GARTENSTR.
OFFENBACHER LANDSTR.
To Park Luisa, Track, Stadium, Rhein-Main Airport & Heidelberg
Holbeinpl.
HEDDERICHSTR.
Bhf. Frankfurt-Süd (R. R. Sta.)
To the Romantic Road

AMERICAN SOLDIERS are seen everywhere in Frankfurt, for this is the transportation hub of Western Germany. In the background is the Eschenheimer Turm (tower), a remnant of the medieval fortifications, and the Bayer Building, a modern office structure

Photos: German Tourist Information Office

GENEVA. Since World War I, Geneva has become the international city par excellence. Her broad avenues, busy shopping streets and flower-decked lakeside promenades spread out comfortably around a wide bay. Tall, French-style buildings and innumerable sidewalk cafés lend a cosmopolitan air and even the most casual visitor has a sense of being in the center of things as he sips a smooth drink during the *apéritif* hour, watching the world go by and witnessing history in the making. However, Geneva did not need to wait for the League of Nations to win international recognition. Men began to settle here centuries before the great colonizing priod of the Roman Empire, for the crest of the hill on which the old quarters now rise afforded an ideal strategic position for primitive tribes. She was fairly insignificent, though, until John Calvin, ardent French champion of the Reformed Faith, sought a haven here. As a great religious leader, Calvin attracted famous scholars of his time and received many French, Italian and English refugees, making the city famous as the "Protestant Rome." A favorite residence of foreigners from this time, her reputation was further enhanced with her selection as the seat of

Photos: J. Zimmer-Meylan, F. Villiger, Boissonnas, Swiss National Tourist Office

QUAI WILSON, named in honor of the late President, is one of Geneva's most beautiful lake promenades. The water spout in the harbor is the highest in the world

ANCIENT CATHEDRAL OF ST. PIERRE, the church where Calvin preached from 1536 to 1564, contains a fine modern organ. It and the interesting adjoining chapel of the Macabees are in the old section of town

MONT BLANC BRIDGE crosses a part of Lake Geneva, of which Voltaire said, "This is the most beautiful lake." Beyond the bridge is tiny Rousseau Island

STATUE OF ROUSSEAU, the great Genevese philosopher of the 18th century is set amid his tall poplars on Rousseau Island. His home at No. 40 in the Grand' Rue is open to the public

PALACE OF THE LEAGUE OF NATIONS, now European Headquarters of the United Nations, facing enchanting Mont Blanc from Ariana Park, is the main reason for Geneva's international fame

Geneva, Switzerland

1. Tourist Bureau
2. Mon. Brünswick
3. Salle de la Réformation
4. Pont de la Coulouvrenière
5. Pont de l'Île
6. Pont de la Machine
7. Pont des Bergues
8. Tour de l'Île
9. Reformation Mon.
10. English Ch.

R. = Rue H. = Hotel

MAP SHOWS MAJOR STREETS

the former League of Nations and site of the International Red Cross. Other international associations abound and to the permanent population is added a constantly renewed stratum of political and diplomatic celebrities and their staffs. Consistent with this role is the university's unique School of Interpreters, where linguists are trained for high-ranking jobs in these world organizations. In the late sixteenth century, the craft of watchmaking also began to take root in Geneva, so that by the following centuries Geneva watchmakers had won a remarkable reputation throughout the world, especially for their exquisite enameled and jewel-studded cases, eagerly sought by art connoisseurs as precious collectors' pieces. Today, she is still the world's great watch center and her Watches and Jewels Exhibition, held yearly in August, sets the watch and jewelry style trend for years in advance. Not alone because of her location at the Crossroads of Europe is Geneva an international favorite, but also because of her delightful situation in the midst of verdant hills on the shore of the deep-blue and remarkably transparent Lake Geneva, whose soothing beauty may be luxuriously relished aboard the distinctive, charming lake steamers.

BRUNSWICK MONUMENT, the elaborately decorated mausoleum of Duke Charles II of Brunswick near the lake shore, is a resplendent sight at night

"HUMAN EFFORT" MONUMENT in a splendid setting in front of the International Labor Office pays tribute to working humanity

Photos: Boissonnas, Pilet, Swiss National Tourist Office, F. H. Jullien, J. Zimmer-Meylan

ALABAMA ROOM in the City Hall has been the scene of important historical events, including in 1864 the first International Red Cross convention and in 1871-1872 the Alabama Claims Commission, which settled U. S. claims against Great Britain for the latter's actions during the Civil War

REFORMATION MONUMENT, an impressive, austere wall in the university garden, contains in the center the statues of Calvin, Guillaume Farel, Theodore de Beze and John Knox, flanked by the great Protestant figures of various countries

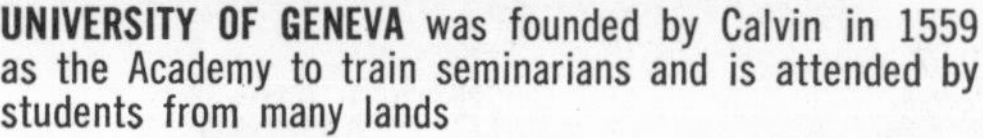

UNIVERSITY OF GENEVA was founded by Calvin in 1559 as the Academy to train seminarians and is attended by students from many lands

CITY HALL is a fine old building with a striking inner courtyard and a quaint, 16th-century, paved spiral pathway, taking the place of a staircase

GLASGOW. Glasgow is a thriving commercial and industrial center in which almost every manufacture in Great Britain is represented. Scotland's most important seaport, the deepening through the years of its long river channel, allows ships from every port in the world to enter and clear its docks. Its colossal shipyards lining both sides of the River Clyde as far down as Greenock are world famous. Here, shipbuilders turn out every conceivable type of vessel from barges to battleships; many a huge Cunard liner has slid down the ways at Glasgow. Textiles too, hold a prominent place among the city's manufactures; it was at Glasgow that Turkey-red dyeing and chlorine bleaching were originated. Much of the famed Scotch whisky is blended and bottled at Glasgow's distilleries. In appearance a modern city, Glasgow has but few buildings of ancient vintage or of particular historic interest. Its oldest and most picturesque building is probably St. Mungo's Cathedral located in the northeastern section of the city. Built over the course of four centuries, it is a fine example of early English architecture and exquisite in its simplicity. Glasgow's famed university occupies a hill overlooking Kelvingrove Park and though founded in 1450, its Gothic buildings are of more recent construction. The university's renowned School of Engineering has established standards that are universally acknowledged. It was while working at Glasgow University that James Watt perfected the steam engine, an invention which helped make possible the modern steamship which has brought fame and prosperity to Glasgow.

GLASGOW is a principal commercial center of Scotland and one of the greatest industrial cities of the United Kingdom

Photos: Philip Gendreau, British Travel Association, British Information Services

GEORGE SQUARE, in Glasgow, contains many monuments including statues of Queen Victoria, Prince Albert, James Watt, Dr. Livingstone and Robert Burns. A statue of Sir Walter Scott stands atop a Doric column in the center of the square

GLASGOW'S ART GALLERY and Museum stand in Kelvingrove Park. They contain many fine examples of the great masters including works by Rubens, Rembrandt, Titian, Botticelli and others

Glasgow, Scotland

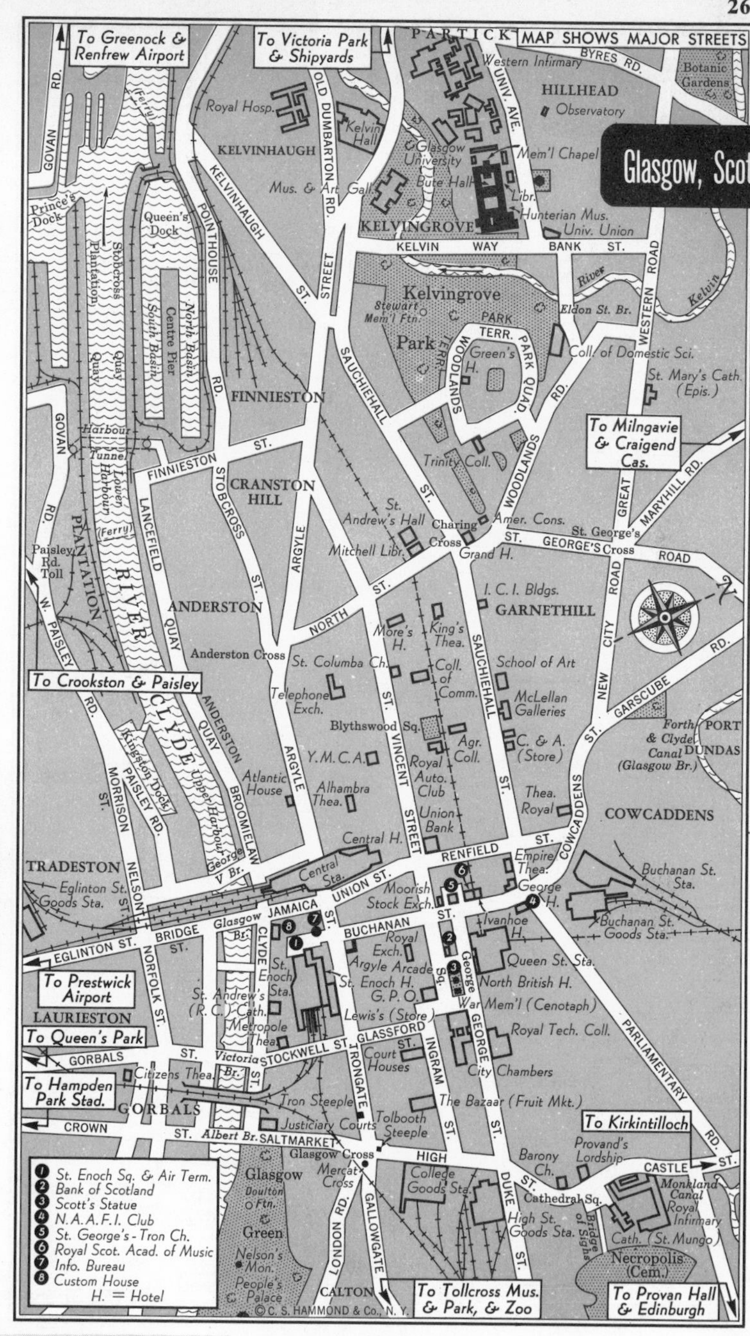
To Greenock & Renfrew Airport
To Victoria Park & Shipyards
PARTICK
MAP SHOWS MAJOR STREETS
Western Infirmary
BYRES RD.
Botanic Gardens
HILLHEAD
Observatory
GOVAN RD.
(Ferry)
Royal Hosp.
OLD DUMBARTON RD.
Kelvin Hall
Glasgow University
Mem'l Chapel
UNIV. AVE.
KELVINHAUGH
KELVINHAUGH ST.
Mus. & Art Gall.
Bute Hall
Libr.
Hunterian Mus.
Univ. Union
KELVINGROVE
Prince's Dock
Queen's Dock
POINTHOUSE RD.
Stobcross Quay
Plantation Quay
North Basin
South Basin
Centre Pier
KELVIN WAY
BANK ST.
WESTERN ROAD
River Kelvin
Kelvingrove Park
Stewart Mem'l Ftn.
PARK TERR.
Eldon St. Br.
WOODLANDS TERR.
PARK QUAD.
Green's H.
Coll. of Domestic Sci.
St. Mary's Cath. (Epis.)
STREET
SAUCHIEHALL ST.
FINNIESTON
WOODLANDS RD.
To Milngavie & Craigend Cas.
Trinity Coll.
GOVAN RD.
Harbour Tunnel
Lower Harbour
(Ferry)
FINNIESTON ST.
CRANSTON HILL
STOBCROSS ST.
St. Andrew's Hall
Charing Cross
Amer. Cons.
GREAT
MARYHILL RD.
St. George's Cross
ST. GEORGE'S ROAD
Mitchell Libr.
Grand H.
Paisley Rd. Toll
PLANTATION
RIVER
LANCEFIELD QUAY
ARGYLE
NORTH ST.
I. C. I. Bldgs.
GARNETHILL
NEW CITY ROAD
ANDERSTON
More's H.
King's Thea.
Anderston Cross
St. Columba Ch.
Coll. of Comm.
School of Art
W. PAISLEY RD.
To Crookston & Paisley
Telephone Exch.
McLellan Galleries
ANDERSTON QUAY
GARSCUBE RD.
CLYDE
Blythswood Sq.
C. & A. (Store)
Forth & Clyde Canal (Glasgow Br.)
PORT DUNDAS
Y.M.C.A.
Agr. Coll.
Kingston Dock
Upper Harbour
Royal Auto. Club
MORRISON ST.
PAISLEY RD.
BROOMIELAW
Atlantic House
Alhambra Thea.
ST. VINCENT STREET
Thea. Royal
COWCADDENS
Union Bank
TRADESTON
Central H.
RENFIELD ST.
Empire Thea.
Buchanan St. Sta.
NELSON ST.
George V Br.
Central Sta.
UNION ST.
Moorish Stock Exch.
George H.
Eglinton St. Goods Sta.
JAMAICA ST.
Ivanhoe H.
Glasgow Br.
BUCHANAN ST.
Buchanan St. Goods Sta.
BRIDGE ST.
EGLINTON ST.
Royal Exch.
Queen St. Sta.
Argyle Arcade
St. Enoch Sta.
St. Enoch H.
George Sq.
North British H.
To Prestwick Airport
NORFOLK ST.
St. Andrew's (R.C.) Cath.
G.P.O.
War Mem'l (Cenotaph)
LAURIESTON
Lewis's (Store)
GEORGE ST.
Metropole Thea.
GLASSFORD ST.
Royal Tech. Coll.
To Queen's Park
GORBALS ST.
Victoria Br.
STOCKWELL ST.
Court Houses
INGRAM ST.
City Chambers
PARLIAMENTARY RD.
To Hampden Park Stad.
Citizens Thea.
TRONGATE
GORBALS
Tron Steeple
The Bazaar (Fruit Mkt.)
CROWN ST.
Albert Br.
SALTMARKET
Justiciary Courts
Tolbooth Steeple
To Kirkintilloch
Provand's Lordship
Glasgow Cross
HIGH ST.
Barony Ch.
CASTLE ST.
Mercat Cross
College Goods Sta.
Cathedral Sq.
Monkland Canal
Royal Infirmary
Glasgow Green
Doulton Ftn.
DUKE ST.
High St. Goods Sta.
Bridge of Sighs
Cath. (St. Mungo)
LONDON RD.
GALLOWGATE
Necropolis (Cem.)
Nelson's Mon.
People's Palace
CALTON
To Tollcross Mus. & Park, & Zoo
To Provan Hall & Edinburgh
© C. S. HAMMOND & Co., N. Y.
1 St. Enoch Sq. & Air Term.
2 Bank of Scotland
3 Scott's Statue
4 N.A.A.F.I. Club
5 St. George's - Tron Ch.
6 Royal Scot. Acad. of Music
7 Info. Bureau
8 Custom House
H. = Hotel

THE UNIVERSITY OF GLASGOW is situated atop a hill on the north side of Kelvingrove Park. Of collegiate Gothic architecture, its impressive buildings are among the city's most famous landmarks

The Hague, Netherlands

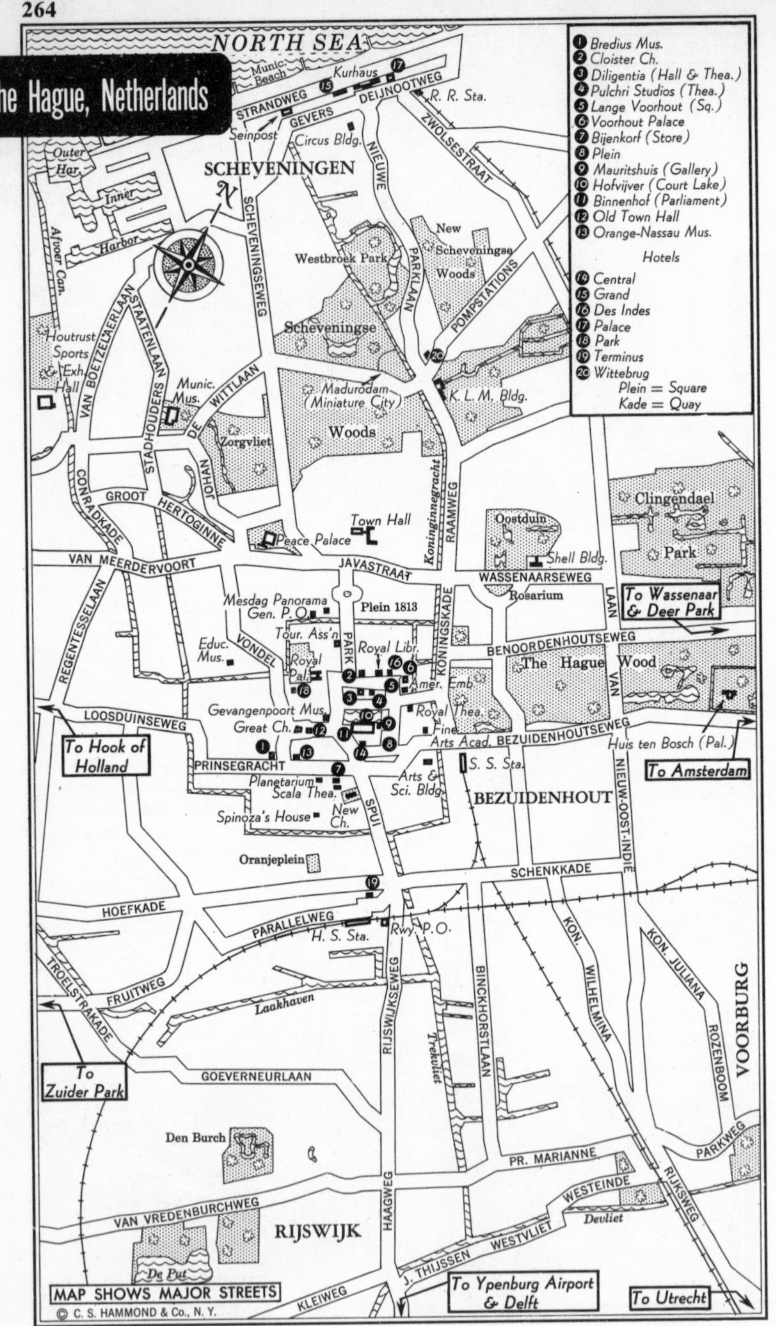

Photos: Netherlands National Tourist Office

THE RIDDERZAAL or Hall of Knights is a picturesque 13th-century building where the states of the Netherlands renounced their alliance with Philip II of Spain. Today the Ridderzaal houses the archives of the Netherlands home office.

THE HAGUE. Seat of the Netherlands' government and of its sovereigns, The Hague, or 's Gravenhage, is a city renowned for the dignified charm of its Gothic and Renaissance architecture, its fine avenues and its lovely parks and gardens. Built as a stronghold by William, Count of Holland, in 1250, it was once the site of a hunting lodge and its name, 's Gravenhage, means literally "the Count's woods." The Binnenhof (Inner Court), with its majestic gabled Ridderzaal (Hall of Knights), grew from the original palace and today houses both chambers of the Netherlands' legislature. Each year on the third Tuesday of September, the colorful opening of Parliament takes place amid the only pomp and pageantry associated with the Dutch Royal House. On this occasion the Queen rides through the streets of The Hague in a Golden Coach pulled by eight ebony horses. Adjoining the Binnenhof is the Mauritshuis Museum which contains several of Rembrandt's finest paintings and also works of Vermeer and Potter. The city centers about a square known as the Plein, around which are grouped many government buildings; but on the whole The Hague is a residential city. The Vredespalais (Peace Palace), completed in 1913, houses The International Court of Justice. Among other notable buildings of The Hague are its royal palace and the Groote Kerk (Great Church), dating back to the 15th century.

THE PEACE PALACE is among the many notable buildings of The Hague. Designed by Cordonnier, its construction was begun in 1907 with the aid of a one and a half million dollar fund donated by the American Industrialist, Andrew Carnegie

THE BINNENHOF or Inner Court is the oldest part and the center of The Hague. Here are found many remarkable buildings dating from all periods of the town's development. Pictured is the Parliament Building; the octagonal tower to the left contains the office of the Prime Minister.

THIS ATTRACTIVE BOOKSTAND also serves as an information center. Here visitors to The Hague may obtain information about tours of the city and the many interesting places that lie in its immediate vicinity.

Photos: German Tourist Information Office

LARGE OFFICE BUILDINGS are representative of the initiative, enterprise and world-wide experience handed down from generation to generation in the export-import trade

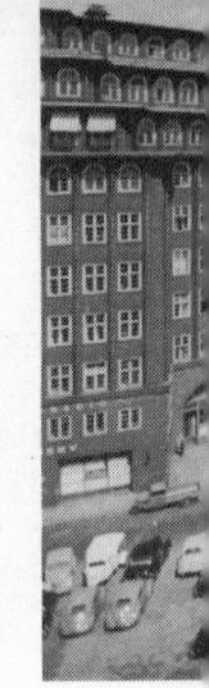

Hamburg, Germany

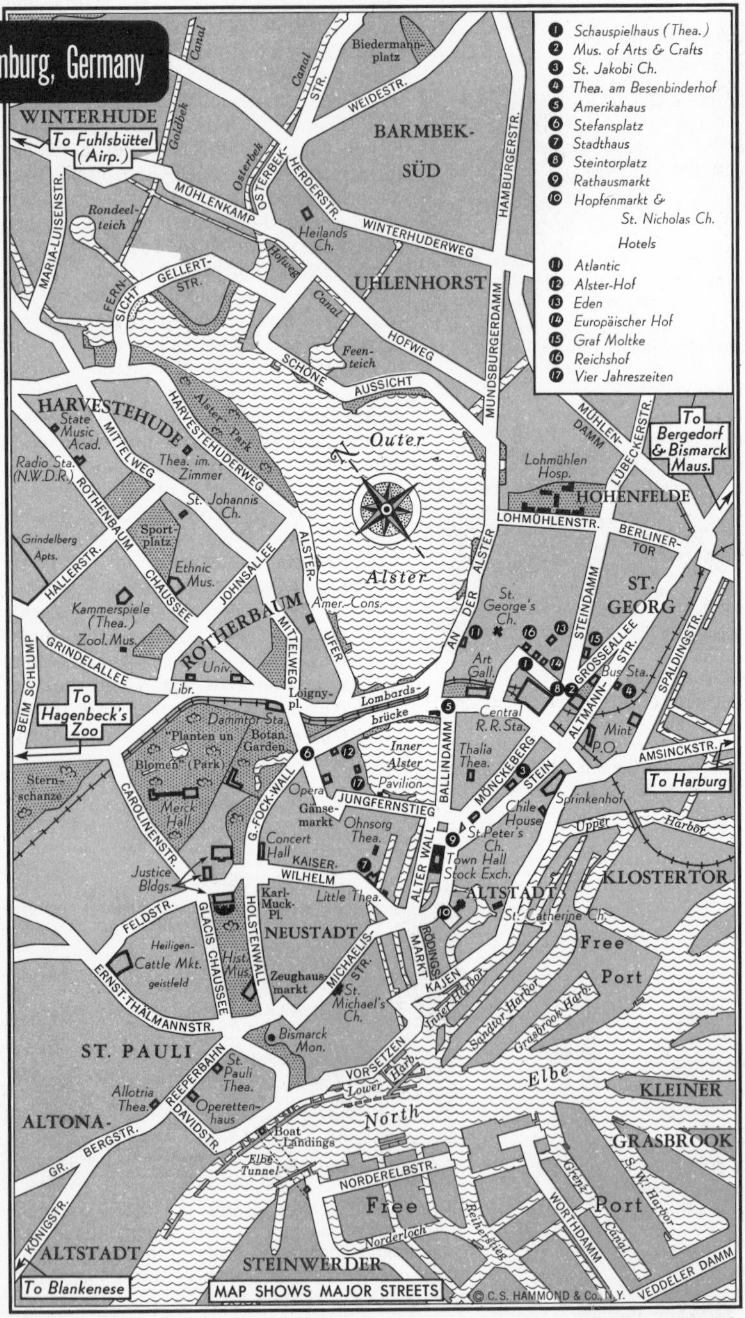

1 Schauspielhaus (Thea.)
2 Mus. of Arts & Crafts
3 St. Jakobi Ch.
4 Thea. am Besenbinderhof
5 Amerikahaus
6 Stefansplatz
7 Stadthaus
8 Steintorplatz
9 Rathausmarkt
10 Hopfenmarkt & St. Nicholas Ch.
Hotels
11 Atlantic
12 Alster-Hof
13 Eden
14 Europäischer Hof
15 Graf Moltke
16 Reichshof
17 Vier Jahreszeiten
WINTERHUDE
To Fuhlsbüttel (Airp.)
BARMBEK-SÜD
UHLENHORST
HARVESTEHUDE
ROTHERBAUM
HOHENFELDE
ST. GEORG
Outer Alster
Inner Alster
To Bergedorf & Bismarck Maus.
To Hagenbeck's Zoo
To Harburg
NEUSTADT
ALTSTADT
KLOSTERTOR
Free Port
ST. PAULI
ALTONA-ALTSTADT
Elbe
North
KLEINER GRASBROOK
STEINWERDER
To Blankenese
MAP SHOWS MAJOR STREETS
© C.S. HAMMOND & Co., N.Y.

THE JUNGFERNSTIEG (Maiden's Walk), the real heart of the town, forms a broad and stately promenade facing the cheerful water, separating the teeming business area from the fascinating residential area with its classical villas

APARTMENT BLOCKS at Grindelberg provide pleasant, clean, sun-filled housing for modern Hamburg families

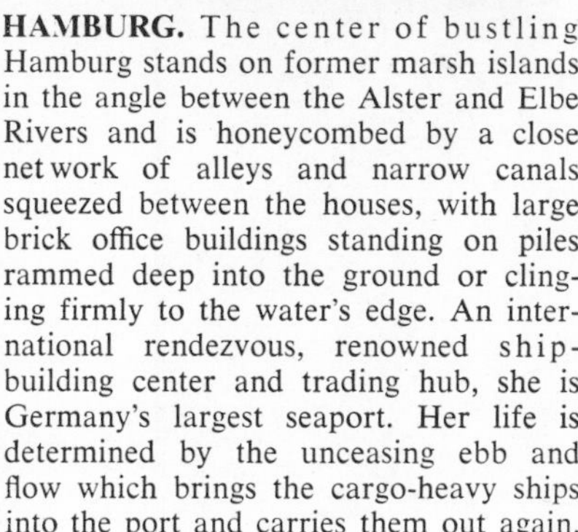

HAMBURG. The center of bustling Hamburg stands on former marsh islands in the angle between the Alster and Elbe Rivers and is honeycombed by a close network of alleys and narrow canals squeezed between the houses, with large brick office buildings standing on piles rammed deep into the ground or clinging firmly to the water's edge. An international rendezvous, renowned shipbuilding center and trading hub, she is Germany's largest seaport. Her life is determined by the unceasing ebb and flow which brings the cargo-heavy ships into the port and carries them out again, a characteristic shared by those other towns in the North German Lowlands whose amazing vitality and spirit were fused into the powerful Hanseatic League. Today Hamburg is still a Free and Hanse Town, one of the two in the German Confederation. Upon this independent tradition, a self-confident and orderly town has been developed by her hard-working, enterprising, self-reliant citizens. Especially revealing of this vital Hamburg spirit is the section known as "Twieten," where even the old streets are named for foreign countries, well-known trading firms or shipping companies.

HARBOR SCENE, taken from the Free Port area, showing in the background the neo-Gothic tower of burnt-out Nicolai Church; the square Town Hall tower, Hamburg's landmark, and the graceful copper tower of St. Petri

Helsinki, Finland

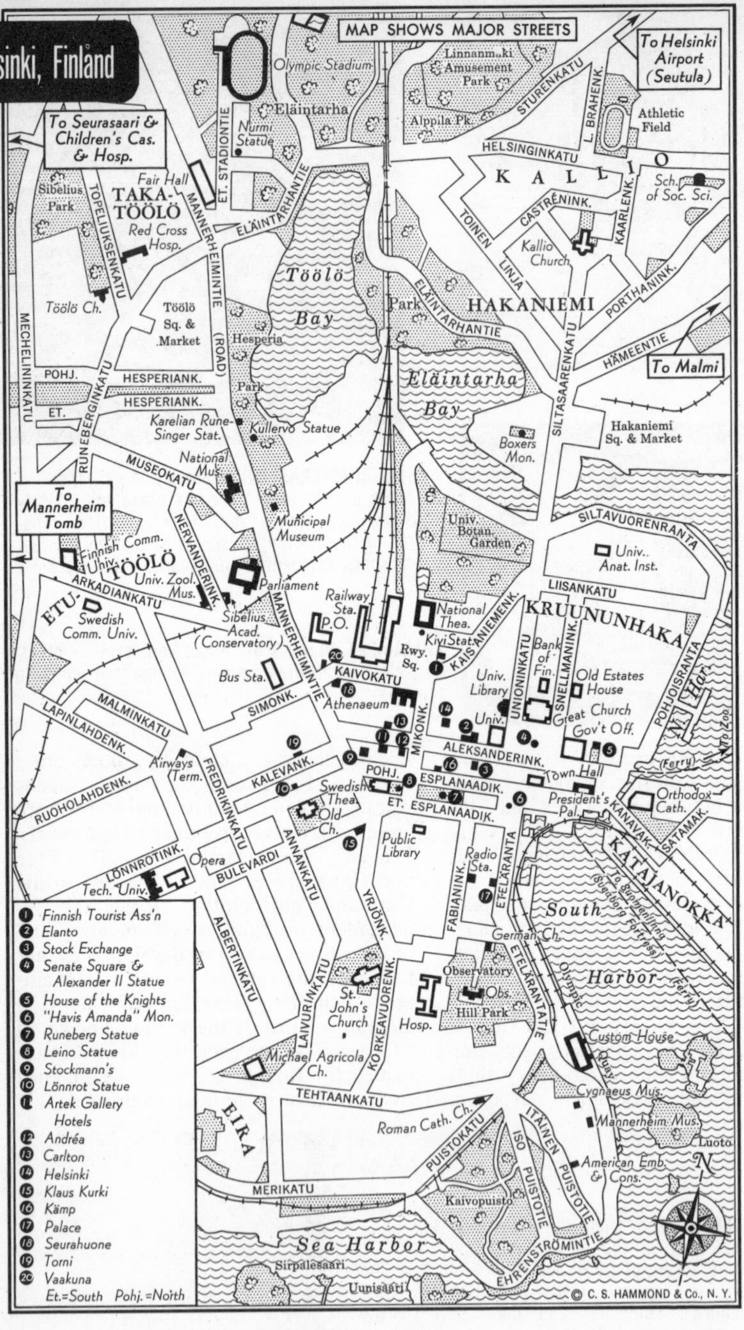

MAP SHOWS MAJOR STREETS

To Helsinki Airport (Seutula)

To Seurasaari & Children's Cas. & Hosp.

To Mannerheim Tomb

To Malmi

Olympic Stadium

Linnanmäki Amusement Park

Eläintarha

Nurmi Statue

Alppila Pk.

Athletic Field

KALLIO

Sch. of Soc. Sci.

Kallio Church

HAKANIEMI

Hakaniemi Sq. & Market

TAKA-TÖÖLÖ

Sibelius Park

Fair Hall

Red Cross Hosp.

Töölö Ch.

Töölö Sq. & Market

Töölö Bay

Hesperia Park

Eläintarha Bay

Boxers Mon.

Karelian Rune-Singer Stat.

Kullervo Statue

National Mus.

Municipal Museum

Univ. Botan. Garden

Univ. Anat. Inst.

KRUUNUNHAKA

TÖÖLÖ

Finnish Comm. Univ.

Univ. Zool. Mus.

Parliament

Sibelius Acad. (Conservatory)

Swedish Comm. Univ.

Railway Sta.

P.O.

National Thea.

Kivi Stat.

Rwy. Sq.

Bus Sta.

Athenaeum

Univ. Library

Bank of Fin.

Old Estates House

Great Church

Univ.

Gov't Off.

Town Hall

President's Pal.

Orthodox Cath.

N. Har.

(Ferry)

To Zoo

Airways Term.

Swedish Thea.

Old Ch.

Public Library

Radio Sta.

Opera

Tech. Univ.

KATAJANOKKA

South Harbor

To Suomenlinna (Sveaborg Fortress) (Ferry)

German Ch.

Observatory

Obs. Hill Park

Hosp.

St. John's Church

Michael Agricola Ch.

Custom House

Quay

Olympic

Cygnaeus Mus.

Mannerheim Mus.

Luoto

American Emb. & Cons.

Roman Cath. Ch.

EIRA

Kaivopuisto

Sea Harbor

Sirpalesaari

Uunisaari

MANNERHEIMINTIE · ET. STADIONTIE · ELÄINTARHANTIE · STURENKATU · L. BRAHENK. · HELSINGINKATU · CASTRÉNINK. · KAARLENK. · TOINEN LINJA · PORTHANINK. · HÄMEENTIE · SILTASAARENKATU · MECHELININKATU · TOPELIUKSENKATU · RUNEBERGINKATU · POHJ. HESPERIANK. · ET. HESPERIANK. · MUSEOKATU · NERVANDERINK. · ARKADIANKATU · ETU · SILTAVUORENRANTA · LIISANKATU · KAISANIEMENK. · UNIONINKATU · SNELLMANINK. · POHJOISRANTA · KAIVOKATU · SIMONK. · MALMINKATU · LAPINLAHDENK. · RUOHOLAHDENK. · KALEVANK. · FREDRIKINKATU · MIKONK. · ALEKSANDERINK. · POHJ. ESPLANAADIK. · ET. ESPLANAADIK. · KANAVAK. · SATAMAK. · LÖNNROTINK. · BULEVARDI · ANNANKATU · ALBERTINKATU · YRJÖNK. · FABIANINK. · ETELÄRANTA · ETELÄRANTATIE · LAIVURINKATU · KORKEAVUORENK. · TEHTAANKATU · PUISTOKATU · ISO PUISTOTIE · ITÄINEN PUISTOTIE · MERIKATU · EHRENSTRÖMINTIE

1. Finnish Tourist Ass'n
2. Elanto
3. Stock Exchange
4. Senate Square & Alexander II Statue
5. House of the Knights
6. "Havis Amanda" Mon.
7. Runeberg Statue
8. Leino Statue
9. Stockmann's
10. Lönnrot Statue
11. Artek Gallery

Hotels

12. Andréa
13. Carlton
14. Helsinki
15. Klaus Kurki
16. Kämp
17. Palace
18. Seurahuone
19. Torni
20. Vaakuna

Et.=South Pohj.=North

Photos: Finish National Travel Office

MORNING MARKET PLACE, one of the liveliest squares in Scandinavia, is at picturesque South Harbor. In the center is the Swedish Embassy and to its far left the President's Palace, while at the picture's far right is Uspenskij (Orthodox) Cathedral.

SUOMENLINNA, the island fortress once called the "Gibraltar of the North," has had a long, stirring history and still retains the special atmosphere of former centuries.

HELSINKI. An airy, ultramodern, progressive city, Helsinki's impressive modern buildings — like the delightfully unusual Children's Castle Hospital and the famous Railroad Station, greatest masterpiece of the period — demonstrate the dynamic new designs of the imaginative young Finns who have so advanced twentieth-century architecture. Most outstanding is Alvar Aalto, whose clean, graceful furniture of Finnish birch, as influential as his buildings, may be seen at the Artek Gallery. In modern sculpture, too, Helsinki has been the leader, especially with the pioneer works of renowned Wäinö Aaltonen, including the monument to writer Aleksis Kevi at the National Theater, the four figures in the council chamber of the austere, red-granite Parliament Building and others collected in the Ateneum Art Gallery and the National Museum. The city is also the scene of the greatest annual music event in Scandinavia: the Sibelius Festival, usually held in early June during the nightless northern summer, in tribute to her most famous resident, Jean Sibelius, world's greatest living composer. And no one should ever leave Helsinki without the marvelous stimulation of a Finnish sauna, or steam bath.

SCENE on Mannerheim Road, the main thoroughfare, is illustrative of the well-planned city's clean, broad, open boulevards, lined with up-to-date, glass-encircled buildings.

GREAT CHURCH, focal point of Senate Square, heart of the city, is the mighty architectural achievement of C. L. Engel, who designed the entire square in the neoclassical Empire style.

OLYMPIC STADIUM, one of Helsinki's new pure, unaffected buildings, features a tower commanding a sweeping view of the city and its environs.

İstanbul, Turkey

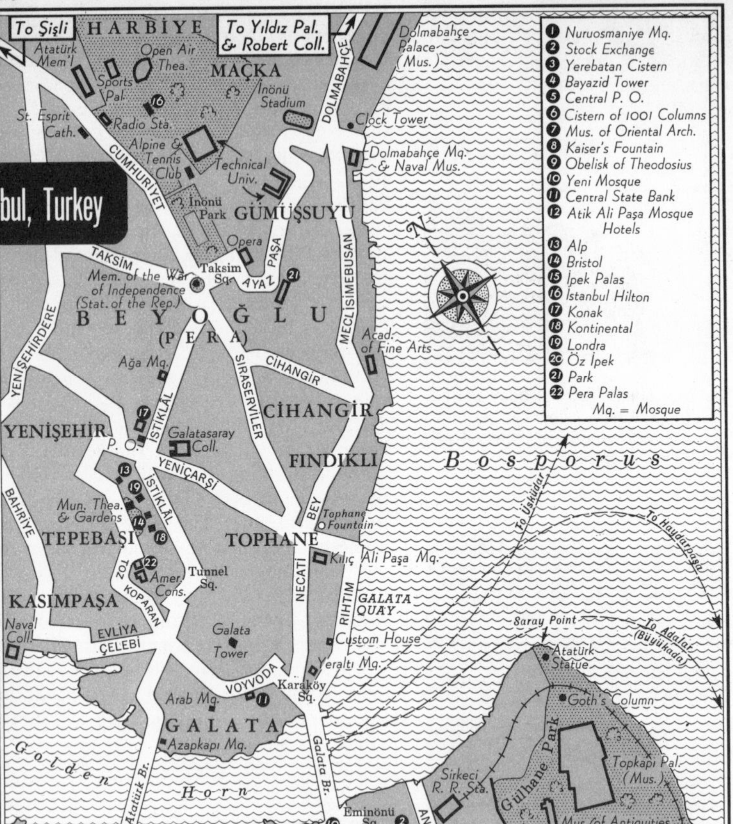

1. Nuruosmaniye Mq.
2. Stock Exchange
3. Yerebatan Cistern
4. Bayazid Tower
5. Central P. O.
6. Cistern of 1001 Columns
7. Mus. of Oriental Arch.
8. Kaiser's Fountain
9. Obelisk of Theodosius
10. Yeni Mosque
11. Central State Bank
12. Atik Ali Paşa Mosque

Hotels

13. Alp
14. Bristol
15. İpek Palas
16. İstanbul Hilton
17. Konak
18. Kontinental
19. Londra
20. Öz İpek
21. Park
22. Pera Palas

Mq. = Mosque

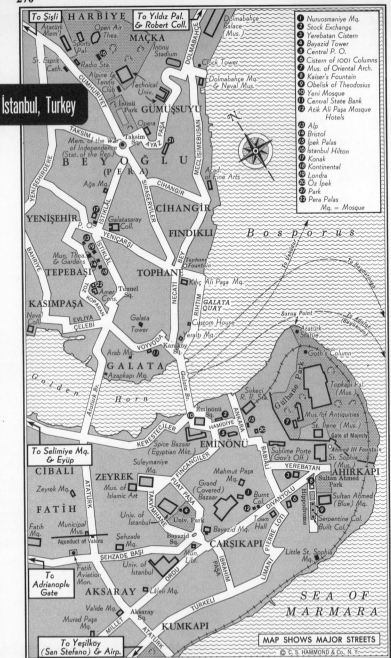

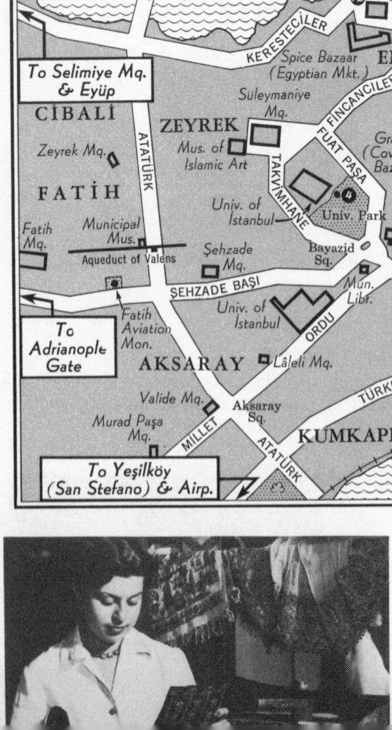

To Şişli
HARBİYE
To Yıldız Pal. & Robert Coll.
MAÇKA
Dolmabahçe Palace (Mus.)
Atatürk Mem'l
Open Air Thea.
Sports Pal.
İnönü Stadium
St. Esprit Cath.
Radio Sta.
Clock Tower
Alpine & Tennis Club
Technical Univ.
Dolmabahçe Mq. & Naval Mus.
CUMHURİYET
İnönü Park
GÜMÜŞSUYU
Opera
TAKSİM
Taksim Sq.
AYAZ PAŞA
Mem. of the War of Independence (Stat. of the Rep.)
MECLİSİMEBUSAN
BEYOĞLU (PERA)
Acad. of Fine Arts
YENİŞEHİRDERE
Ağa Mq.
SIRASERVİLER
CİHANGİR
İSTİKLÂL
YENİŞEHİR
P. O.
Galatasaray Coll.
FINDIKLI
Bosporus
YENİÇARŞI
To Üsküdar
To Haydarpaşa
BAHRİYE
Mun. Thea. & Gardens
BEY
Tophane Fountain
TEPEBAŞI
TOPHANE
Kılıç Ali Paşa Mq.
TOZ KOPARAN
Amer. Cons.
Tunnel Sq.
NECATİ
RIHTIM
GALATA QUAY
KASIMPAŞA
Naval Coll.
EVLİYA ÇELEBİ
Galata Tower
Saray Point
To Adalar (Büyükada)
Custom House
Atatürk Statue
Yeraltı Mq.
VOYVODA
Karaköy Sq.
Arab Mq.
Goth's Column
GALATA
Azapkapı Mq.
Golden Horn
Galata Br.
Atatürk Br.
Sirkeci R. R. Sta.
Gülhane Park
Topkapı Pal. (Mus.)
Eminönü Sq.
ANKARA
Mus. of Antiquities
KERESTECİLER
HAMİDİYE
St. Irene (Mus.)
Gate of Majesty
Spice Bazaar (Egyptian Mkt.)
EMİNÖNÜ
BABIÂLİ
Sublime Porte (Gov't Off.)
Ahmed III Fountain
St. Sophia (Mus.)
To Selimiye Mq. & Eyüp
Süleymaniye Mq.
FİNCANCILER
YEREBATAN
AHIRKAPI
CİBALİ
ZEYREK
Mahmut Paşa Mq.
Sultan Ahmed Park
Zeyrek Mq.
Mus. of Islamic Art
FUAT PAŞA
Grand (Covered) Bazaar
Burnt Col.
Hippodrome
Sultan Ahmed (Blue) Mq.
ATATÜRK
TAKVİMHANE
DİVANYOLU
FATİH
Univ. of İstanbul
Univ. Park
Town Hall
Serpentine Col.
Built Col.
Fatih Mq.
Municipal Mus.
Bayazid Mq.
PİERRE LOTİ
Aqueduct of Valens
Şehzade Mq.
Bayazid Sq.
ÇARŞIKAPI
ŞEHZADE BAŞI
Mun. Libr.
Little St. Sophia Mq.
To Adrianople Gate
Fatih Aviation Mon.
Univ. of İstanbul
ORDU
İBRAHİM PAŞA
LİMANI
AKSARAY
Lâleli Mq.
SEA OF MARMARA
Valide Mq.
Aksaray Sq.
TÜRKELİ
Murad Paşa Mq.
MİLLET
KUMKAPI
ATATÜRK
To Yeşilköy (San Stefano) & Airp.
MAP SHOWS MAJOR STREETS

SHOPPING in the Grand Bazaar for renowned Turkish embroidery, carpets, copperware, black and amber cuff links, filigree work in silver or meerschaum pipes intrigues both resident and visitor

ISTANBUL. Istanbul — Constantinople — Byzantium — no matter what her name (and she has been called by all three), each conjures up visions of Eastern splendor and might. Only city bridging two continents — Europe and Asia — her shores are washed by the Marmara Sea, the Bosporus and the Golden Horn, whose sparkling waters add still more enchantment to her fabulous fame. Proud jewel of emperors, she was the glittering prize city of the Byzantines, of the Eastern Roman Empire and upon her capture in 1453 — signalizing the end of the European Middle Ages — of the mighty Ottoman Empire. Her great walls withstood many an heroic assault, but when the city succumbed — only three times in her history — she brought such wealth and authority that commanders and kings thought any blood sacrifice worth such dazzling rewards. Today, her breath-taking skyline symbolizes both her impressive past and future influence—a skyline whose magic is the thousands of minarets that, with pious, slender fingers, aspire to heaven and the majestic domes of the 444 mosques that sit like crowns on the summits of her seven hills. Truly it may be said now as in ages gone, "If one had but a single glance to give the world, one should gaze at Istanbul."

GALATA BRIDGE over the Golden Horn connects Old Istanbul with Beyoglu and more people cross it daily than any other bridge in the world. Dominating the right-hand side are the Yeni (New) Mosque's tiers and tiers of domes

GARDENS of the Topkapi Palace, historic seat of the Ottoman sultans from 1472 to 1853, afford memorable views of the Bosporus and the Asian part of the city

Photos: Turkish Information Office

ST. SOPHIA, world-famous basilica built by Justinian the Great in the 6th century, has a unique massive dome and houses glorious priceless mosaics

SULTAN AHMED MOSQUE, 17th-century masterpiece of Turkish religious architecture, is also known as the Blue Mosque because of the brilliant tilework adorning its interior. To its right is the ancient Hippodrome, while in the background is St. Sophia

Lisbon, Portugal

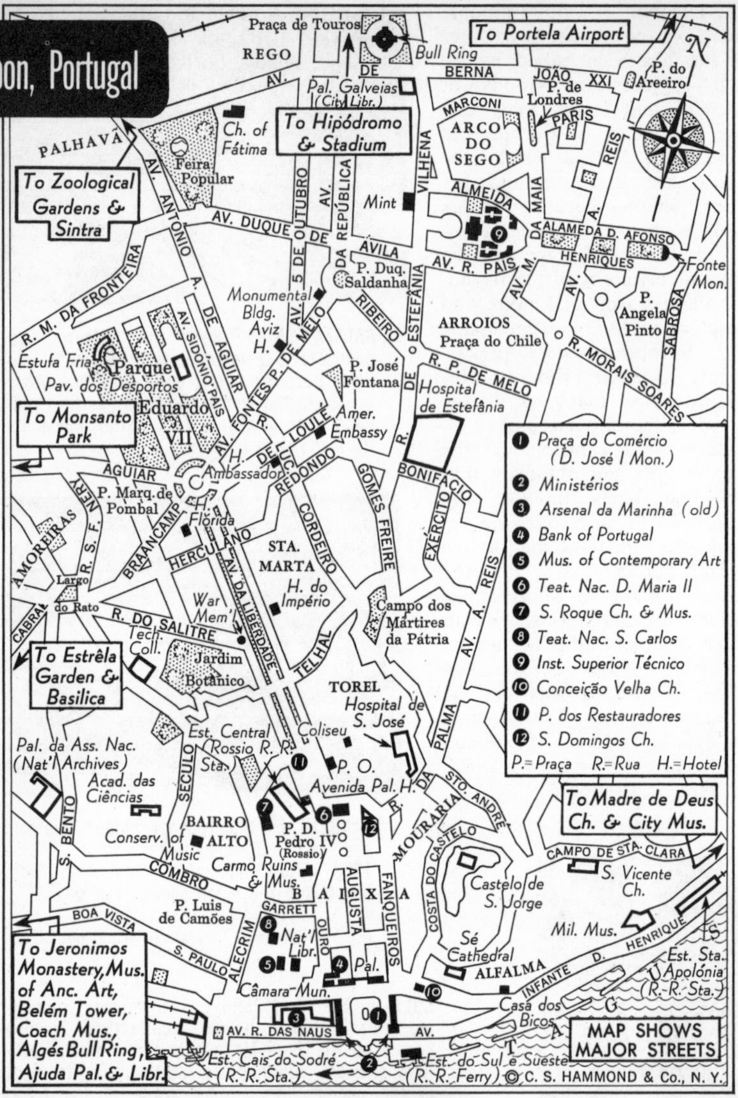

To Portela Airport

To Hipódromo & Stadium

To Zoological Gardens & Sintra

To Monsanto Park

To Estrêla Garden & Basilica

To Madre de Deus Ch. & City Mus.

To Jeronimos Monastery, Mus. of Anc. Art, Belém Tower, Coach Mus., Algés Bull Ring, Ajuda Pal. & Libr.

1. Praça do Comércio (D. José I Mon.)
2. Ministérios
3. Arsenal da Marinha (old)
4. Bank of Portugal
5. Mus. of Contemporary Art
6. Teat. Nac. D. Maria II
7. S. Roque Ch. & Mus.
8. Teat. Nac. S. Carlos
9. Inst. Superior Técnico
10. Conceição Velha Ch.
11. P. dos Restauradores
12. S. Domingos Ch.

P.= Praça R.= Rua H.= Hotel

MAP SHOWS MAJOR STREETS

PRAÇA de DOM PEDRO QUARTO, one of Lisbon's spacious plazas, is bordered by the Ionic columned Teatro de Dona Maria Segunda. The royal national theater stands on a site formerly occupied by the Inquisition Buildings. In the center of the great plaza is a pillar surmounted by a statue of Dom Pedro IV

A CITY OF SEVEN HILLS, Lisbon rises in the manner of a terraced amphitheater. above a broad sweep of the Tagus. Castelo de São Jorge, a Moorish fortress, crowns the background. Elevators aid in reaching the city's various levels

LISBON. A noble and gracious city, Lisbon rises tier upon tier above the ship-studded waters of its fine harbor. Located where the river Tagus widens to meet the Atlantic, Lisbon, like Rome, is a city built upon seven hills. It is a place of white or pastel-colored houses, of broad tree-lined avenues and little winding streets overhung by Moorish balconies. Although many of its medieval buildings have been destroyed by earthquakes, Alfama, the older section of the city in the vicinity of the cathedral, still contains many magnificent relics of Lisbon's past history. A number of the city's buildings display excellent examples of Manueline-style architecture, which, influenced by the Age of Discovery, consists of intricate decorations and nautical symbols such as globes, twisted cables and the Templar cross which was displayed on the sails of early ships. The Monastery at Belém facing the sea from the north shore of the Tagus was built by Manuel I to commemorate Vasco da Gama's discovery of a sea route to India. The Tower of Belém, originally a fortress, marks the spot where the great explorer landed after his adventurous voyage. The city of Lisbon is dominated by the Castelo de São Jorge, a fort which majestically crowns the highest of the seven hills and may occupy the site of ancient Roman fortifications. From its high perch, the Castelo looks out upon a breath-taking panorama of sea, harbor and city.

JERONIMOS MONASTERY ranks among the finest of ecclesiastical structures. The massive white marble buildings, designed by João de Castilho, the foremost Manueline architect, contain the tombs of many of Portugal's kings, queens and heroes

Photos: Joaquim De Vasconcellos, Casa de Portugal

TWO BEAUTIFUL BRONZE FOUNTAINS stand in the Praça de Dom Pedro Quarto, also known as the Rossio. The square itself is paved with mosaics, laid in intricate geometric designs and wavelike patterns

LIVERPOOL. Liverpool is the chief port of Lancashire; indeed it is the second seaport of England and the fourth largest city of the United Kingdom. Although Liverpool is a manufacturing center with many different types of industries, its wealth and its commercial importance have always come from the sea. Its basins, docks and graving docks along the Mersey estuary cover an area of over six hundred acres and there are nearly forty miles of quays. Also included in its harbor facilities is a vast system of warehouses. These, as well as the docks and quays, are administered by the Liverpool Dock Board and all are public property. One of the outstanding features of the city is its magnificent cathedral which, when completed, will be the largest in England. It was designed by Sir Giles Gilbert Scott, whose winning design was accepted in 1904 when the architect was no more than twenty-one years old. The Walker Art Gallery contains one of the finest collections of paintings in the provinces. The University of Liverpool is renowned for its School of Tropical Medicine, which has made valuable contributions to the study of such diseases as yellow fever, malaria and sleeping sickness. Five miles from Liverpool is Aintree, the famous racecourse where, in March of each year, is run the Grand National Steeplechase over a track which presents bigger and stiffer hurdles than appear on any other racecourse in the world.

ROYAL LIVER BUILDING stands overlooking the Mersey river at the Pier Head. Liverpool is remarkable for its number of imposing office buildings built chiefly of stone

THE HEAD OFFICE of the Mersey Docks and Harbour Board, a public trust which administers the Port of Liverpool, is housed in this impressive building

BRUNSWICK GARDENS is one of Liverpool's modern municipal housing schemes. Since the beginning of the century the city has carried out an extensive program of slum clearance and housing improvement

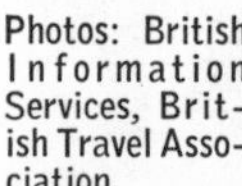

Photos: British Information Services, British Travel Association

LIVERPOOL in Lancashire is one of Britain's greatest seaports. The city carries on an extensive maritime trade with the United States

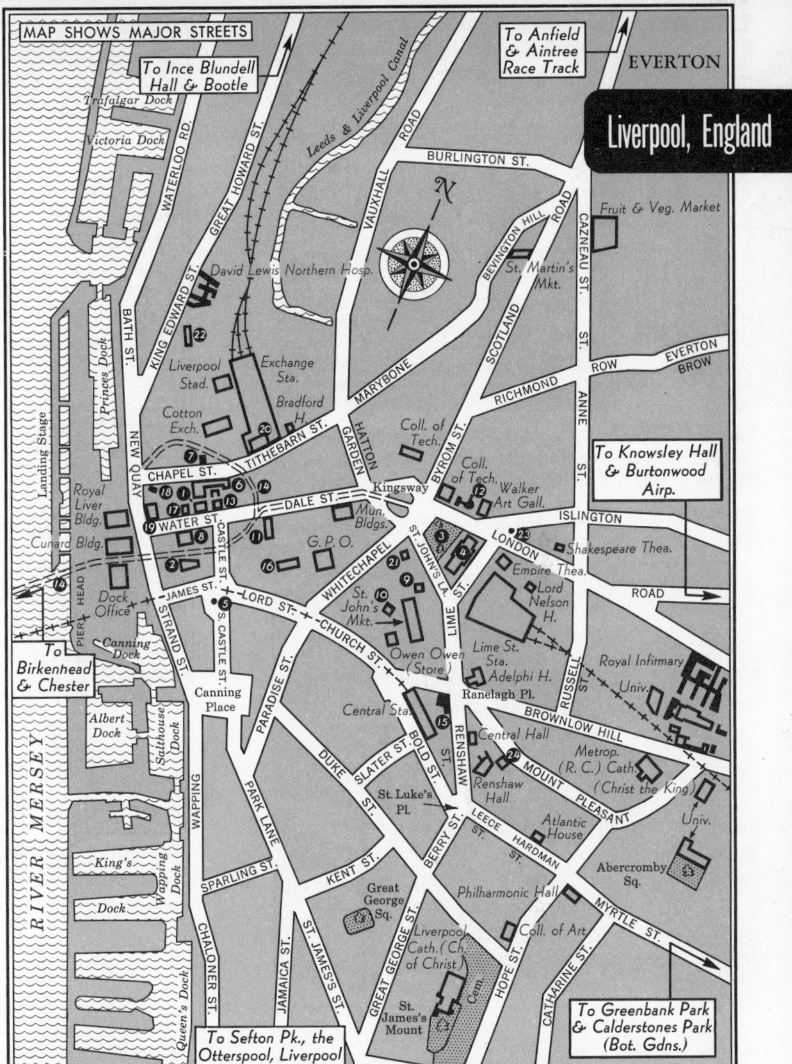

Liverpool, England

MAP SHOWS MAJOR STREETS

To Ince Blundell Hall & Bootle

To Anfield & Aintree Race Track

To Knowsley Hall & Burtonwood Airp.

To Birkenhead & Chester

To Greenbank Park & Calderstones Park (Bot. Gdns.)

To Sefton Pk., the Otterspool, Liverpool Airp., Speke Hall, Kirkby & Sudley

1. Martins Bank
2. Corn Exchange
3. St. John's Garden
4. St. George's Hall (Law Courts & Concert Hall)
5. Derby Sq. & Victoria Mem'l
6. Exchange Buildings
7. Chamber of Commerce
8. India Buildings
9. Royal Court Thea.
10. Playhouse Thea.
11. Royal Insurance Bldg.
12. Cent. Libr. & Picton Hall
13. Town Hall
14. Queensway (Mersey Tunnel)
15. Lewis's (Store)
16. Fruit & Produce Exch.
17. Barclays Bank
18. St. Nicholas's Ch.
19. Tower Bldg.
20. Exchange Hotel
21. Stork Hotel
22. Lancaster House
23. Wellington Column
24. Y.M.C.A.

H. = Hotel

ST. GEORGE'S HALL, a modern example of Graeco-Roman architecture, stands in the heart of Liverpool. It is one of an imposing group of buildings which include the law courts, Walker Art Gallery, the Picton Library and a museum

GODFREY STREET, with its variety of architecture and design, its gaily colored decorations and well tended window boxes, is characteristic of Chelsea's little streets

REGENT STREET, one of the arteries leading into Piccadilly, is known as the best shopping district in London

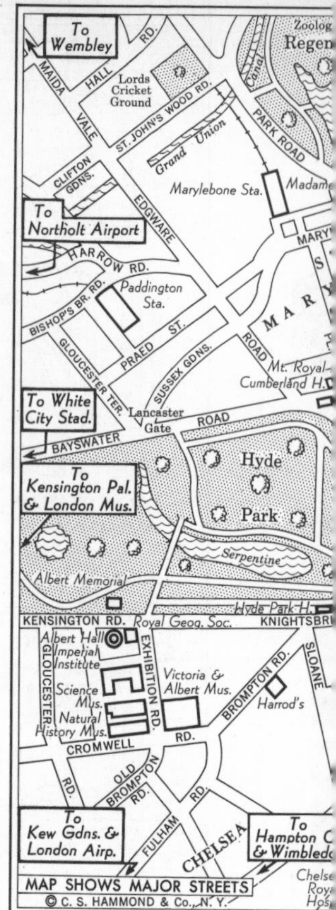

Photos: British Information Services

FROM ADMIRALTY ARCH, the broad Mall stretches up through St. James Park toward Buckingham Palace, providing an imposing route for the Royal carriages which travel this way on State occasions to Parliament and Westminster Abbey

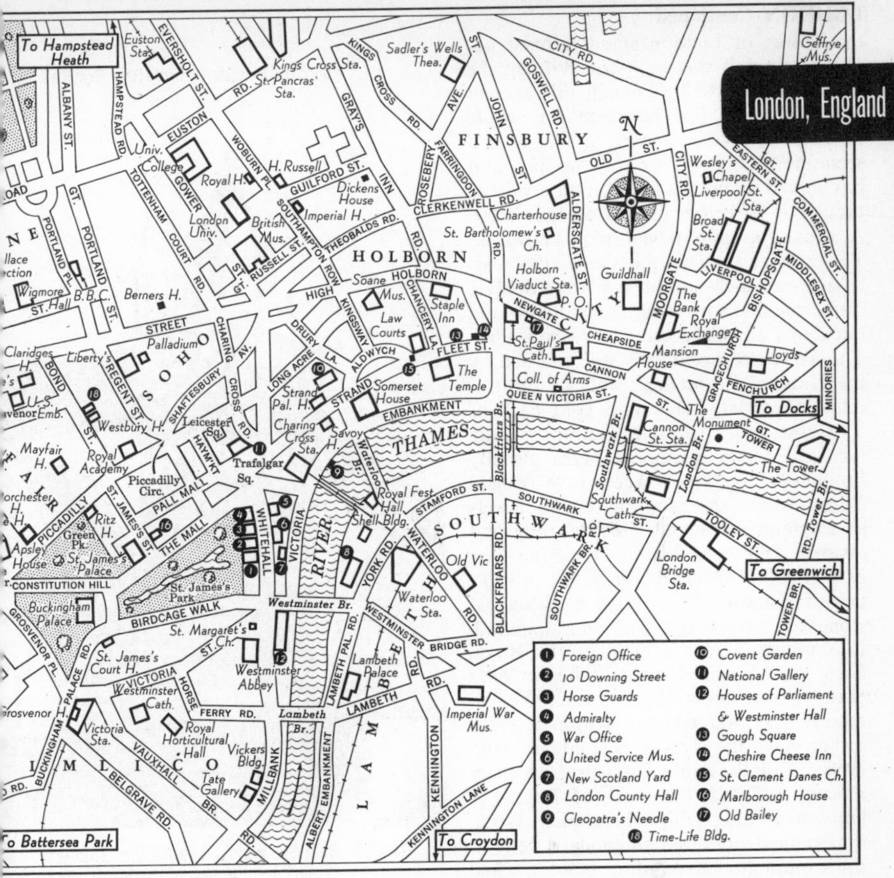

LONDON. Dr. Samuel Johnson, the 18th-century lexicographer, once wrote "when a man is tired of London, he is tired of life; for there is in London all that life can afford." Though the city, let it be admitted, does not contain all that Dr. Johnson's broad statement claims for it, London can provide such a wealth of interest, so many beautiful, ancient, historic, impressive and curious sights, so many diversions, occupations, entertainments and pursuits, that to live in London might almost be considered a profession. The character of London, like that of any other great city, does not reveal itself at first glance but requires at least a short acquaintanceship before it can be appreciated. With increased knowledge there will grow a deep affection for its jumble of past and present, practical and obsolete, beautiful and commonplace, majestic and homely, that together make up the London of today. This pulsing heart of the British Empire, so vast it comprises a country within itself, probably possesses the largest metropolitan area of any city in the world. With a history going back to Roman times, its people and its institutions have shaped the world's destinies for a thousand years. The oldest part of London, the tiny mile-square nucleus around which the sprawling metropolis grew, is known as the "City of London" or just simply "The City." Today the "City's" government which is endowed with greater powers than the surrounding twenty-eight boroughs, retains many features of the past. Its Lord Mayor, elected by the various trade guilds, takes office each year on November ninth, in a ritual whose pomp and pageantry dates back to medieval times. Just outside the original walled city, known in the days of the Romans as Londinium, are found a number of London's most notable landmarks. Here

LONDON Continued

the Tower of London stands almost unaltered since it was built for William the Conqueror in 1078. Though this ancient Norman castle has not seen the whole of London's long history, it has indeed seen most of it. Through the years, it has served as both a palace and a prison, though it is better known as the latter. A square granite paved plot known as Tower Green marks the site of the scaffold where such notables as Anne Boleyn, Catherine Howard and the pathetic and talented Lady Jane Grey were beheaded. The Tower of London is still guarded by the famous "Beefeaters" wearing the traditional scarlet, black and gold garb of a by-gone era. Adjoining Traitor's Gate, through which prisoners were usually brought to the Tower keep, is Wakefield Tower where the fabulous crown jewels of England are kept. This dazzling and historic collection includes the First Star of Africa, a 530 carat gem, the world's largest diamond. The biggest of several stones cut from the Cullinan diamond, it is mounted in the head of the Royal Scepter. Also on display is the Imperial State Crown containing some 3,000 diamonds and 300 pearls. Within a short distance of the Tower is Ludgate Hill, crowned by St. Paul's Cathedral. A magnificent building, the work of England's greatest architect, Sir Christopher Wren, it remained obscured to modern generations until the surrounding buildings had been reduced to a pile of rubble in the London Blitz. Also in the vicinity of the Tower are Tower Bridge and London Bridge, both spanning the Thames

Photos: British Information Services

TOWER BRIDGE which spans the Thames, can be raised by means of hydraulic machinery to allow for the passage of large vessels

THE TOWER OF LONDON, on the left bank of the Thames, has weathered nearly a thousand years of crowded history. To the left is Traitor's Gate, while at the rear, to the left, is the tower of the Port of London Authority Building

WAKEFIELD TOWER was the scene of the stabbing of Henry IV, founder of Eton College. To this day, boys from the college mark the anniversary of his death by placing a wreath of lilies on the spot where he died

ST. PAUL'S CATHEDRAL, the greatest work of England's greatest architect, Sir Christopher Wren, stands on the summit of Ludgate Hill. Work on the Cathedral was completed in 1710. It occupies the site of Old St. Paul's destroyed in the Great Fire of London

LONDON Continued

River. From the vantage point of London Bridge, the loiterer may view the busy scene of ships unloading in the Pool, a part of the Port of London which extends along the Thames for nearly seventy miles. Near the northern end of the bridge is the seething maelstrom of the City's business district where the Bank of England and the Royal Exchange with its golden grasshopper perched on top, look at each other across a vortex of purposeful traffic. But even at the conjunction of the city's busiest streets—Throgmorton Street, Threadneedle Street, Lombard Street and Cornhill with their temples of finance—romance and the old world are not far distant. The most historic building in the West End section is Westminster Abbey, which contains more historical treasures than any other building in Britain. Built in the year 800, it was originally used as a royal mausoleum and until the reign of George II only the kings of England were buried here. Outside the Abbey, a short distance from its north door, is a stone slab on which is engraved *T II*. This Roman boundary mark is over a thousand years older than the oldest stone in the Abbey. Across the roadway from the Abbey is the Palace of Westminster, the official name for the Houses of Parliament. When Parliament is sitting, a flag flies from Victoria Tower by day; by night a light burns in the clock tower from which the deep-throated bell—"Big Ben"—tolls each passing hour.

BIG BEN, the great bell whose deep voice tolls the passing hour, is hung in the Clock Tower at the north end of the Parliament Buildings. This 13½ ton bell is flanked by smaller bells which mark the quarter hours

THE VICTORIA EMBANKMENT which borders the left bank of the Thames, offers a wonderful view of ships passing along London's busy waterway. In the background is the tall obelisk known as Cleopatra's Needle

Photos: British Information Services

WESTMINSTER ABBEY, originally used as a mausoleum, contains the tombs of no less than 28 royal personages. The Abbey also contains the tomb of the Unknown Warrior of the First World War

THE PALACE OF WESTMINSTER is the official name of the British Houses of Parliament. These huge buildings contain eleven hundred rooms and two miles of passages

LONDON Continued

Running due north from the Houses of Parliament, in a straight line to Trafalgar Square, is the broad thoroughfare known as Whitehall; and here flourishes the machinery of government—the Home Office, the Treasury, the War Office, the Admiralty and other governmental offices each housed in its own majestic and rather pompous palace. From Trafalgar Square the avenued Mall leads to Buckingham Palace. First used as a royal residence by Queen Victoria, it is the London home of Queen Elizabeth. Today on occasions of national rejoicing, Londoners gather in thousands in front of the palace gates to give vociferous vent to their happiness, their affection, their loyalty, and their hope that their Queen will appear on the balcony of the palace. Nearby, St. James' Palace is a mellow red brick Tudor building which is the official residence of the court. Englishmen have an aptitude for forming clubs, but nowhere do they cluster in such profusion as in St. James

No. 10 DOWNING STREET is perhaps the most widely known address in London. Though unpretentious in appearance, it serves as the official residence of the British Prime Minister

BUCKINGHAM PALACE and its gardens stand on the site of the mulberry gardens of James I who hoped to encourage the silk industry in England. One of the original mulberry trees is still growing in the palace gardens today.

CLARENCE HOUSE is the London home of Queen Elizabeth, the Queen Mother and Princess Margaret Rose

Photos: British Information Services

PARK LANE, which forms the western boundary of Mayfair, is noted for its many luxurious hotels, with spacious ballrooms, suites and restaurants

THE STATUE OF EROS looks down on a flower girl as she sells her colorful wares in Piccadilly Circus. It is said that if you stand long enough in Piccadilly Circus, you will meet the person you are looking for

PETTICOAT LANE, in the East End, is now officially called Middlesex Street. Though its name has changed, it still retains its noisy Sunday street market where items, both new and second-hand, are sold to a milling throng of bargain hunters

OXFORD STREET, with its large department stores and furniture shops, is a leading London shopping center

TRAFALGAR SQUARE is named for Lord Nelson's great naval victory. At the south end of the square is the 185-foot Nelson Monument

Photos: British Information Services

LONDON Continued

Street. They form, as it were, a link between the cold formalities of official Whitehall and the garish distractions of irrepressible Piccadilly. All London is summed up in Piccadilly and to walk along it is almost to become a Londoner. Piccadilly contains everything — shops, hotels, restaurants, art galleries, clubs, private houses—and into it lead the main arteries of shopping—Regent Street, Haymarket, Bond Street, Albemarle Street, Dover Street and Knightsbridge. At one end is Piccadilly Circus where Eros presides and flower girls sell their scented wares, where traffic rushes around the fountain only because it is not allowed to rush over it. At the other end of Piccadilly is Hyde Park where ducks swim about on the Serpentine and where Londoners can lie on their backs in the grass and gaze up at the trees and the clouds beyond. And through the length of Piccadilly are Londoners going about their daily business, their daily pleasures and their daily lives.

ALZETTE RIVER winds its way through a section of Luxembourg city called Grund. Here the river's banks are lined by distilleries and tanneries which turn out some of the spirits and high quality leathers for which Luxembourg is famous

LUXEMBOURG. "This is a spot, where so much grandeur and grace, somber solemnity and exquisite loveliness are found side by side that one can only wish Poussin [17th century French artist] had seen and painted it." In these words, the German poet Goethe wrote of the charm of Luxembourg. Later the English artist, Turner, immortalized the beauty of this quaint cathedral city in a group of his famous, deftly-executed watercolor sketches. Through the years, many have been enchanted by this "picture-book" town whose massive ramparts thrust out high above the Rham Plateau where once the Romans are said to have camped. With its double walls, its impenetrable fortifications, and its labyrinth of "casemates" — subterranean tunnels and corridors—carved into the solid rock beneath the city—Luxembourg was once known as the "Gibraltar of the North." The city, whose history goes back nearly one thousand years, grew up in the protecting shadow of a 10th century castle. Her strong defenses were long coveted by France, Spain and Austria, who, in turn, ruled Luxembourg for over 400 years. Today it is a unique combination of ancient town, 18th-century fortress and prosperous 20th-century city. Many of Luxembourg's buildings date back to medieval times while others reflect the influence and tastes of the nations which, at various times, have ruled over this capital of the diminutive Grand Duchy of Luxembourg.

GRAND DUCAL PALACE, a relic of Spanish occupation, was built by Peter Ernst, Count of Mansfeld, the most distinguished of the governors of Luxembourg. The magnificent residence is a striking example of Spanish Renaissance architecture

Photos: Luxembourg National Tourist Office

ADOLPHE BRIDGE, the longest single stone span bridge in Europe, links the newer section of the city of Luxembourg with the older section

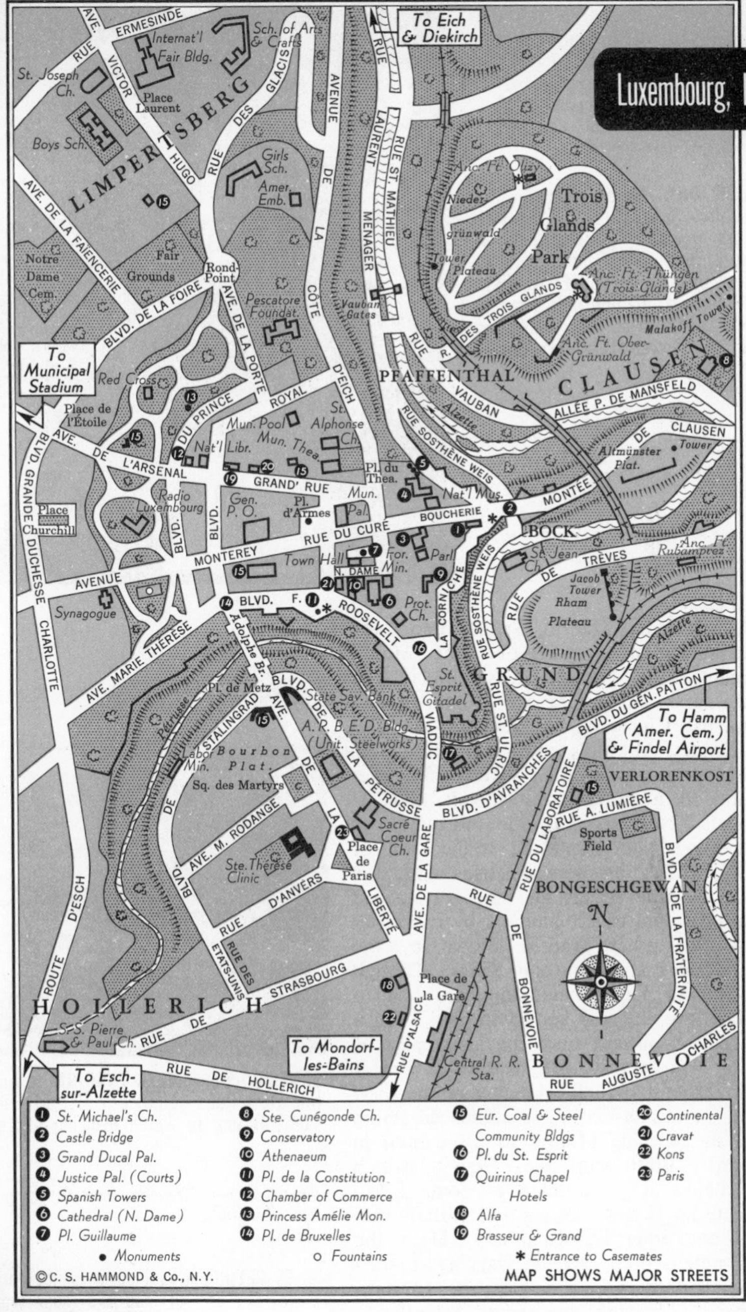

SPANISH TURRET is a part of a system of defenses that once made Luxembourg an impregnable stronghold around whose walls wars raged for more than 100 years

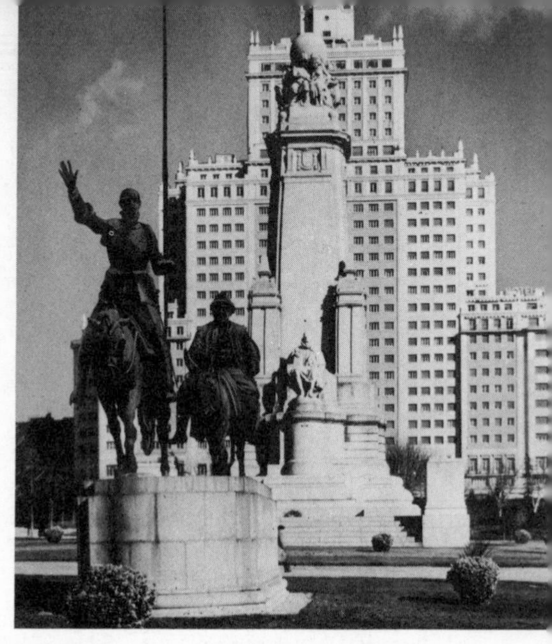

DON QUIXOTE and his faithful squire, Sancho Panza, bid visitors welcome to their land of adventure. This monument to Cervantes is located at Plaza de España. Behind it is a monument to Christopher Columbus and the tower of Europe's tallest building

MADRID. Madrid, Spain's handsome capital, is often spoken of as the "Monumental City" because of its abundance of statuary and impressive public monuments. City gates, bridges and fountains complete Madrid's traditional landmarks. Few towns offer such variety of scenes and so many different moods and aspects. Next to the wide thoroughfares teeming with onrushing traffic, full of noise, dazzling with electric signs, are sleepy little streets and squares steeped in profound peace, haunted by memories of that other Madrid known by the Hapsburg and Bourbon Kings. Though Madrid's actual beginnings are lost in time, the city was known to have been a Moorish outpost until the latter part of the 11th century. Its location at almost the exact geographical center of the Iberian peninsula may have influenced Philip II in choosing Madrid as his capital in 1561. Built atop the New Castilian Plateau, at an altitude of some 2,150 feet, its skyline towers taller than that of any other European city. Here, the climate is often extreme, varying as much as 50 degrees in a single day. In summer, a blazing sun beats relentlessly down from cloudless skies on the barren red plain, while in winter the city is swept by icy winds from the Sierra de Guadarrama. Although Madrid is Spain's capital and its administrative center, it

SANTIAGO BERNABEAU STADIUM is but one of the attractions of modern Madrid. Here thousands throng to watch exciting soccer games

Photos: Screen Traveler, from Gendreau, Spanish Tourist Office

EL RETIRO, a vast park, is not only beautiful but one of Madrid's most typical features since the days when Philip IV's court used to repair there for merrymaking and to stage theatrical shows. The monument to Alfonso XII is but one of the handsome statues that grace this sylvan spot

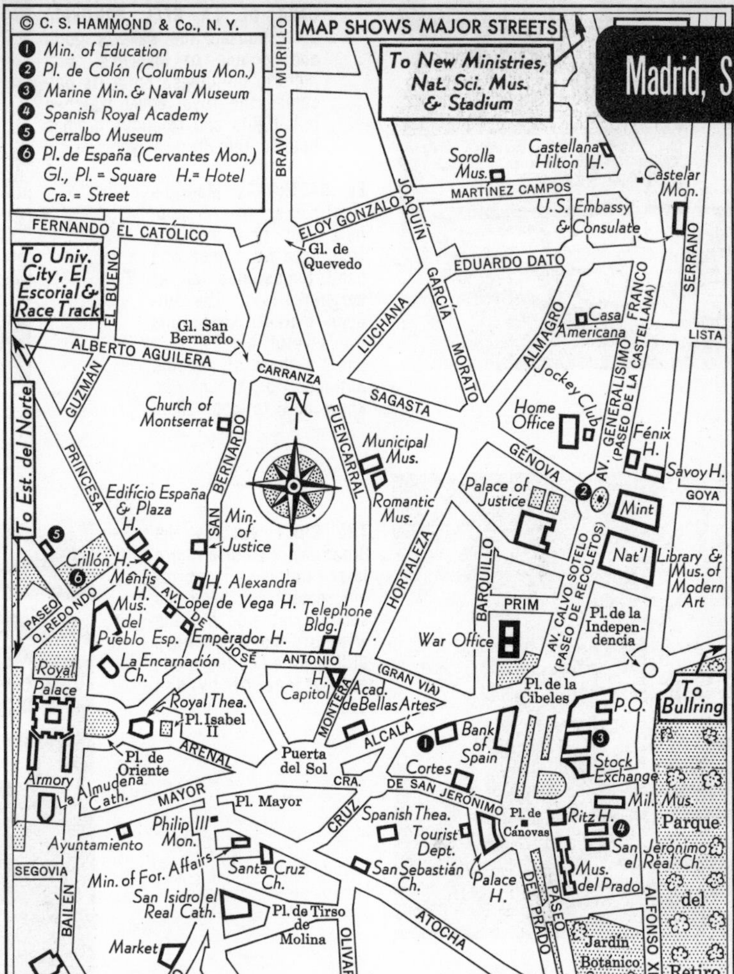

Madrid, Spain

© C. S. HAMMOND & Co., N. Y.

MAP SHOWS MAJOR STREETS

1. Min. of Education
2. Pl. de Colón (Columbus Mon.)
3. Marine Min. & Naval Museum
4. Spanish Royal Academy
5. Cerralbo Museum
6. Pl. de España (Cervantes Mon.)

Gl., Pl. = Square H.= Hotel
Cra. = Street

To New Ministries, Nat. Sci. Mus. & Stadium

To Univ. City, El Escorial & Race Track

To Est. del Norte

To Bullring

MURILLO
BRAVO
FERNANDO EL CATÓLICO
EL BUENO
ELOY GONZALO
Gl. de Quevedo
JOAQUÍN
MARTÍNEZ CAMPOS
Sorolla Mus.
Castellana Hilton H.
Castelar Mon.
U.S. Embassy & Consulate
SERRANO
EDUARDO DATO
GARCÍA
MORATO
LUCHANA
ALMAGRO
Casa Americana
AV. GENERALISIMO FRANCO (PASEO DE LA CASTELLANA)
LISTA
Gl. San Bernardo
ALBERTO AGUILERA
GUZMÁN
CARRANZA
SAGASTA
Jockey Club
Home Office
Church of Montserrat
SAN BERNARDO
FUENCARRAL
Municipal Mus.
Romantic Mus.
GÉNOVA
Fénix H.
Savoy H.
GOYA
PRINCESA
Edificio España & Plaza H.
Min. of Justice
Palace of Justice
Mint
Nat'l Library & Mus. of Modern Art
AV. CALVO SOTELO (PASEO DE RECOLETOS)
HORTALEZA
BARQUILLO
Crillón H.
Ménfis H.
H. Alexandra
Lope de Vega H.
PRIM
PASEO O. REDONDO
Mus. del Pueblo Esp.
AV. DE JOSÉ ANTONIO
Emperador H.
Telephone Bldg.
War Office
Pl. de la Independencia
Royal Palace
La Encarnación Ch.
(GRAN VIA)
Capitol H.
Acad. de Bellas Artes
MONTERA
Pl. de la Cibeles
P.O.
Royal Thea.
Pl. Isabel II
ALCALA
Bank of Spain
ARENAL
Puerta del Sol
Pl. de Oriente
Armory
La Almudena Cath.
MAYOR
Cortes
CRA. DE SAN JERÓNIMO
Stock Exchange
Mil. Mus.
Pl. Mayor
CRUZ
Spanish Thea.
Pl. de Cánovas
Ritz H.
Parque del Retiro
Philip III Mon.
Tourist Dept.
San Jerónimo el Real Ch.
Ayuntamiento
SEGOVIA
Min. of For. Affairs
Santa Cruz Ch.
San Sebastián Ch.
Palace H.
Mus. del Prado
BAILEN
San Isidro el Real Cath.
Pl. de Tirso de Molina
ATOCHA
PASEO DEL PRADO
ALFONSO XII
Jardín Botánico
Market
OLIVAR
San Francisco el Grande Ch.
TOLEDO
EMBAJADORES
Gl. Emp. Carlos V Hospital
Min. of Public Works
RONDA DE SEGOVIA
Rastro
Pl. de Lavapiés
ARGUMOSA
Estación de Atocha (R.R. Sta.)

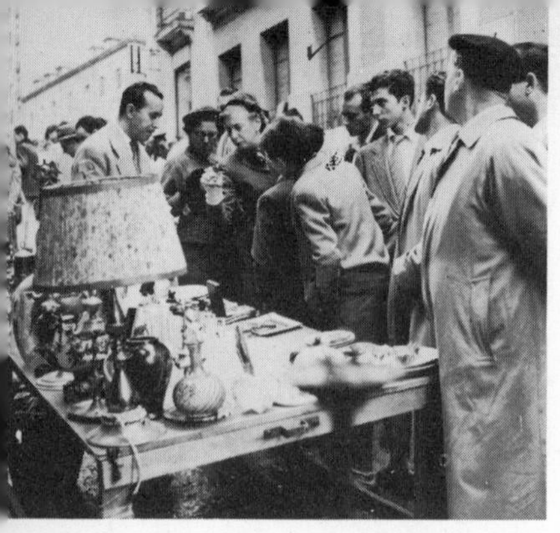

CASA DE LA REAL PANDERÍA once housed the baker's guild and is one of Madrid's most historic buildings. From its balconies the royal court watched bull fights and religious dramas held in the Plaza Mayor

EL RASTRO is Madrid's flea market, where shoppers can find anything from used nails to second hand tombstones, all at bargain prices. The outdoor market, that runs for several blocks, also has its share of genuine antiques for those who know how to spot them

THE GRAN VIA, is the Broadway of Madrid where large hotels, places of amusement and luxurious shops exist side by side with old-world corners still haunted by the steps and voices of bygone ages

PLAZA DE ORIENTE, near the Royal Palace is lavishly laid out in formal, boxwood-bordered gardens. Also in this splendid square is the famed equestrian statue of Philip IV by Velazquez

Photos: Spanish Tourist Office

PLAZA DE LA VILLA, a typical corner of old Madrid, is formed by the Casa and Torre of the Lujanes, where Francis I of France was kept prisoner; the Casa de Cisneros where the famous cardinal and regent of Spain lived; and the beautiful 17th-century Ayuntamiento

MADRID Continued

is still considered only a "villa" (town) never having received the official designation "ciudad" (city). Madrid became a Loyalist stronghold during the Civil War (1936-1939) and was heavily bombed by Nationalist forces before its surrender. During the twenty-nine day siege, with four columns of Nationalist troops converging on Madrid, Nationalist sympathizers who awaited their arrival within the city made up the original "Fifth Column." Modern Madrid has its skyscrapers, its towering buildings and its newest source of pride, the Ciudad Universitaria (University City), erected against a background characteristic of Velasquez's canvases. Madrid is an excellent starting point for many very pleasant excursions. For the lover of nature, the imposing Sierra de Guadarrama is close at hand offering good mountain climbing and winter sports facilities in an atmosphere of restful quietness. The art and history lover has at short distances from the capital, such points of interest as Escorial, Alcalá de Henares, Ávila, Segovia, Toledo—which add to Madrid's interest by making it the center of a large area studded with priceless landmarks.

PRADO MUSEUM is known throughout the world for merit and number of pictures within its walls. Here the Spanish School is well represented by Velazquez, El Greco, Goya, Murillo and others

CALLE DE SACRAMENTO is one of the oldest streets in Madrid. Close to it are the Royal Theater and the Royal Palace, built in the 18th century, which was the envy of Napoleon. Also close by is the Plaza Mayor

Manchester, England

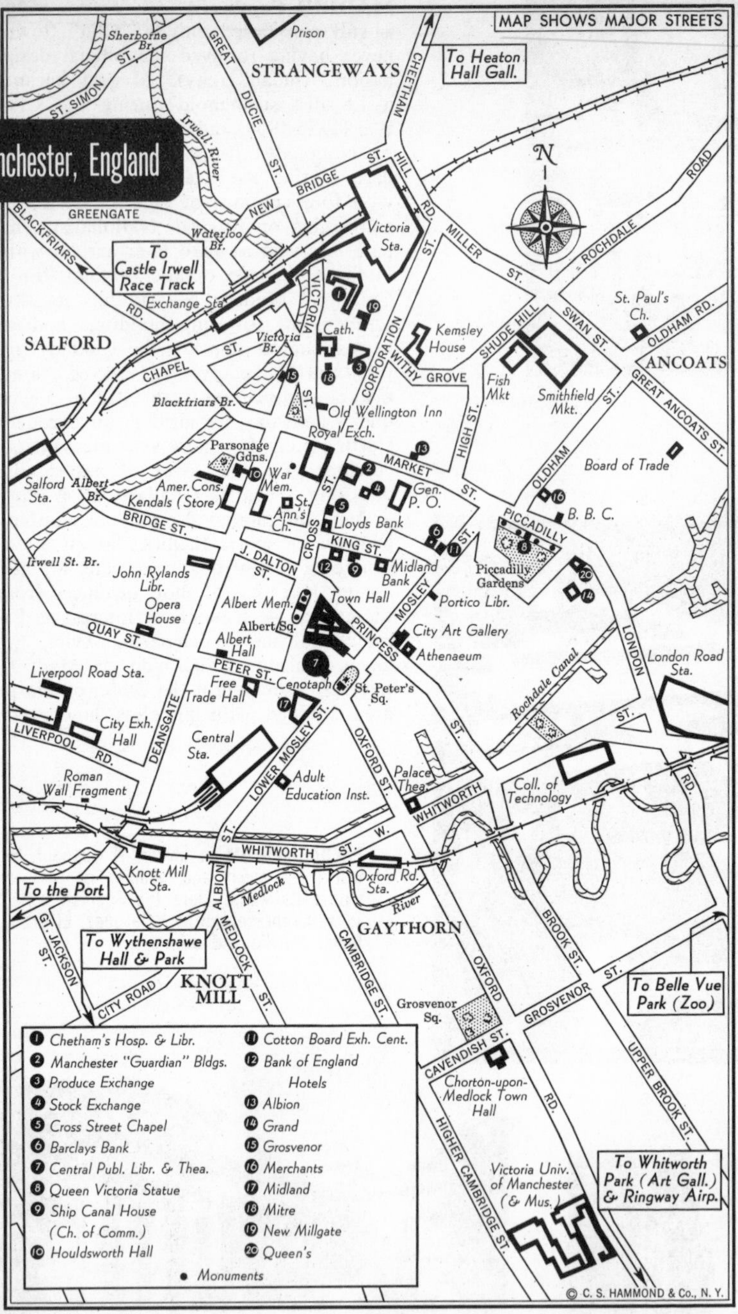

MAP SHOWS MAJOR STREETS

1. Chetham's Hosp. & Libr.
2. Manchester "Guardian" Bldgs.
3. Produce Exchange
4. Stock Exchange
5. Cross Street Chapel
6. Barclays Bank
7. Central Publ. Libr. & Thea.
8. Queen Victoria Statue
9. Ship Canal House (Ch. of Comm.)
10. Houldsworth Hall
11. Cotton Board Exh. Cent.
12. Bank of England

Hotels

13. Albion
14. Grand
15. Grosvenor
16. Merchants
17. Midland
18. Mitre
19. New Millgate
20. Queen's

• Monuments

Photos: British Travel Association, British Information Services

SUNKEN GARDENS at Piccadilly, in the heart of the city, rivals the larger parks in its fine flower displays, providing a welcome oasis and pleasant contrast to the somber buildings

MARKET STREET, converging on Piccadilly, is the street of tightly packed humanity, with its good-humored pushing and thrusting, for this is the principal shopping center

MANCHESTER. Manchester is possibly better known as the center of Britain's great cotton industry, but she always has been the center of many of the great political and cultural reform movements. The city has become a musical center of international standing, and home of her world-renowned Halle Orchestra is the Free Trade Hall, which "for decades symbolised the traditional independence of Manchester people, their love of liberty, their tolerance and their fearless loyalty to the great ideals." In the field of journalism, too, the city has achieved a world-wide reputation through *The Manchester Guardian*. Even so, the story is probably apocryphal which relates how a certain Nonconformist minister began a prayer one Sunday with the words: "Oh Lord, as thou wilt yesterday have seen in the Manchester Guardian . . . " It isn't an area famous for beauty, but an area in which the stress is laid on people and there is a rugged clarity about the Mancunian which is never quite shed. He prides himself on plain speaking and on driving a hard bargain. It would be a surprise to him if he ever discovered what most people found out long ago, that behind a somewhat laconic humor there is a curiously warm heart.

CENTRAL LIBRARY houses five specialized libraries and a theater. Also in Manchester is the famous John Rylands Library a gathering of many matchless treasures

SMOKE-BLACKENED CATHEDRAL is not imposing, but the interior has exquisitely carved, 13th-century choir stalls, beautiful roofs of the choir and nave and 18th-century iron screens

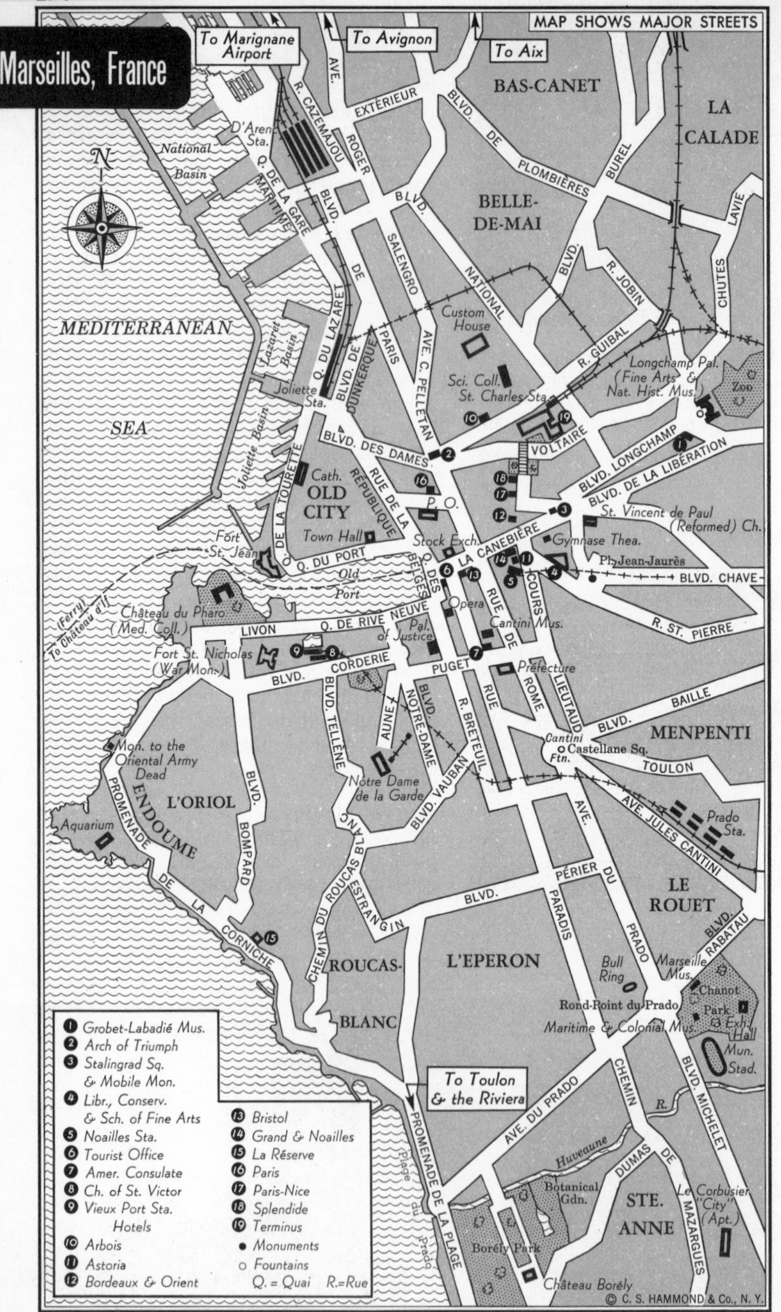

Photos: French Government Tourist Office

VIEUX PORT, the old port where fishermen tie up to repair nets, was protected on the far-side cliff by the 17th-century Fort St. Jean. On the hill is the 12th-century old cathedral of la Major (Sainte-Marie-Majeure), built on ruins of a temple to Diana

WATERFRONT district of France's chief seaport, lusty meeting place of all races, accounts for much of the city's rugged individualism

NOTRE DAME DE LA GARDE, celebrated basilica dominating a Marseilles hill, is surmounted by a 30-foot-high, bronze statue of the Virgin Mary, first landmark seen by ships approaching the harbor

GIGANTIC, ULTRAMODERN apartment house on stilts was designed by the pioneer Swiss architect, painter and writer, Le Corbusier. This unconventional, functional structure is a complete little city within itself

MARSEILLES. 2500-year-old Marseilles, France's oldest city, is a colorful, bustling port on the ageless Mediterranean. As an international sea station and long-time favorite with sailors, her whole atmosphere is permeated with the lusty flavor of the sea, giving her a definite charm and personality all her own, just as the seafarer's salty tang distinctly marks him from the landlubber. Even the accent and manner of speech of her inhabitants is unique. And since most of her trade is with the north coast of Africa, the eastern Mediterranean and the Far East, this teeming setting has an almost Oriental cast. Marseilles is noted for her world-famous bouillabaisse, that incomparable fish soup with an unusual flavor achieved here alone, because it is made with fish peculiar to this region. One of her most interesting buildings is the curious stone church of St. Victor, with catacombs ranking among the earliest Christian evidences in Gaul. Most exciting of all, however, is the tiny island in the harbor containing the forbidding Chateau d'If, built as a castle in 1524 and later used as a state prison, made famous by the swashbuckling *Le Comte de Monte-Cristo,* by Alexandre Dumas, as the miserable dungeon from which the Count escaped.

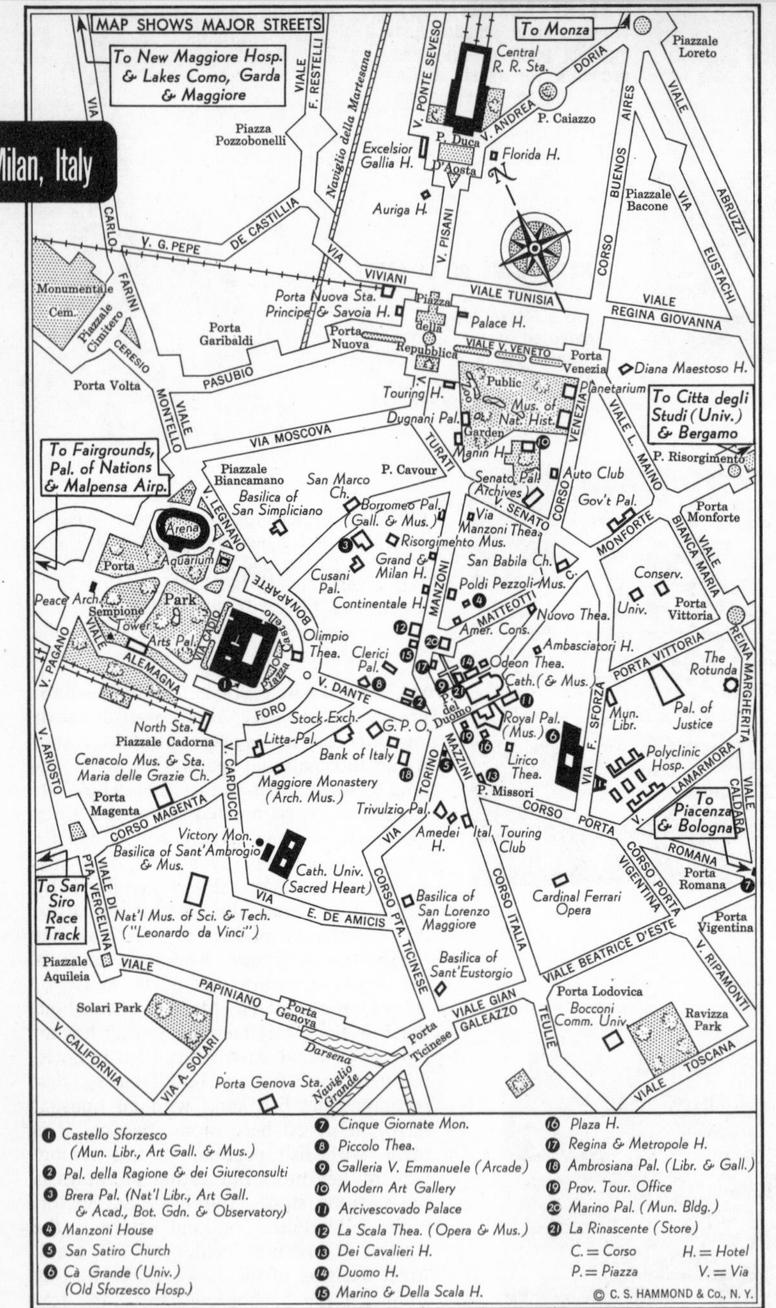

Photos: Italian State Tourist Office, TWA-Trans World Airlines

THE ARCO DELLA PACE (Arch of Peace), directly opposite the Castel Sforzesco in the Parco Nuovo was begun by Napoleon in 1806 and later finished by the Austrians

THE CATHEDRAL OF MILAN is considered one of the great wonders of the world. Its construction was begun in 1386 and its elaborate façade was designed by Tibaldi

MILAN. The second largest city in Italy and its greatest industrial, commercial and financial center, Milan rises imposingly above the rich garden of the Lombard plain. Since 222 B.C. when the original Gallic town fell to the invading Roman legions, Milan has known many aggressors and her history has been one of repeated devastations. Today, few buildings remain from Roman and early medieval times, although it is still possible to distinguish the tiny rectangular nucleus of the ancient town within the boundaries of the modern city. Because of Milan's strategic position at the confluence of numerous rail lines and its importance in the industrial field, it was the target, in World War II, for both German and Allied bombs. Many of its famous landmarks were destroyed or damaged during the war. Perhaps the city's most impressive structure is its Gothic cathedral located at one end of the spacious Piazza del Duomo. Among the largest in Europe, the cathedral is elaborately ornamented with over 100 pinnacles and 4,400 statues of various periods. The main tower, which rises 354 feet above the street, is surmounted by a golden figure of the Virgin. The cathedral's roof, reached by stairs carried up the buttresses, commands an excellent view of the city as well as the surrounding plain with its tidy checkerboard of fields and roads bordered by symmetrical rows of Lombardy poplars.

MILAN Continued

To the south, can be seen the long line of the Apennines stretching along the horizon, while to the north and west rise the snowy peaks of the Alps. Two splendid palaces also face the Piazza del Duomo. These are the palace of the archbishops of Milan and the Palazzo Reale which is built on the site of the Viscontis' mansion. Milan's notable buildings include the church of San Ambrogio, founded by St. Ambrose in the 4th century and restored during the 11th century in the style of a Romanesque basilica; the 15th century Casa dei Borromei with its exquisite Gothic courtyard; the beautiful Loggia degli Osii and the famed 17th-century Biblioteca Ambrosiana. Besides a great treasure of architectural masterpieces, Milan possesses a wealth of painting and sculpture. The renowned Brera picture gallery contains works by such masters as Veronese, Bellini, Raphael, Luini and Bramantino, while Leonardo da Vinci's immortal fresco "The Last Supper" adorns the refectory wall of the convent of Santa Maria delle Grazie. Milan is a noted center of music and the theater, as well as the home of various educational institutions including a university and a school of engineering.

ROOFED WITH GLASS, the 320-yard-long Galleria Vittorio Emanuele is built in the form of a cross, its center crowned by a great glass cupola. The Gallery contains some of Milan's finest shops

PIAZZA DEL DUOMO is one of the focal points of Milan. Here great flocks of pigeons gather for a daily handout from kind-hearted passersby

THE CASTEL SFORZESCO, "the Castle of Milan" stands in the Parco Nuovo. The building now houses the archaeological museum with its Roman, medieval and Renaissance relics

A SIDEWALK CAFE in the Galleria Vittorio Emanuele is a wonderful spot from which to view the passing scene. Here the Milanesi gather to talk business or exchange gossip over a cup of black Italian coffee

Photos: Italian State Tourist Office, Philip Gendreau

LA SCALA, Milan's renowned Opera House, is the second largest theater in Europe with a seating capacity of 3,600. Besides keeping alive the great traditions of Italian opera, it contains an interesting theatrical museum

Munich, Germany

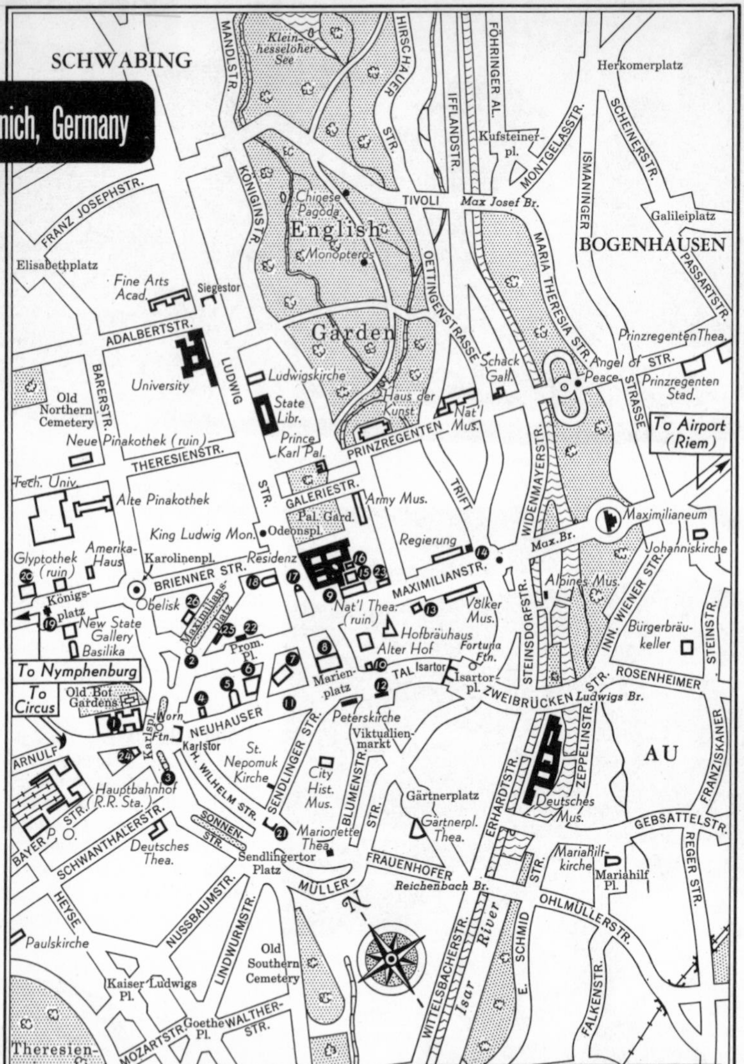

SCHWABING
Klein-hesselöher See
MANDLSTR.
HIRSCHAUER STR.
FÖHRINGER AL.
IFFLANDSTR.
Kufsteiner-pl.
MONTGELASSTR.
Herkomerplatz
SCHEINERSTR.
ISMANINGER STR.
Galileiplatz
BOGENHAUSEN
PASSARTSTR.
FRANZ JOSEPHSTR.
KÖNIGINSTR.
Chinese Pagoda
English Garden
Monopteros
TIVOLI
Max Josef Br.
OETTINGENSTRASSE
MARIA THERESIA STR.
Elisabethplatz
Fine Arts Acad.
Siegestor
ADALBERTSTR.
University
LUDWIG STR.
Ludwigskirche
State Libr.
Haus der Kunst
Nat'l Mus.
Schack Gall.
Angel of Peace
PrinzregentenThea.
PRINZREGENTEN STRASSE
Prinzregenten Stad.
To Airport (Riem)
Old Northern Cemetery
BARERSTR.
Neue Pinakothek (ruin)
Prince Karl Pal.
THERESIENSTR.
Tech. Univ.
Alte Pinakothek
GALERIESTR.
Army Mus.
Pal. Gard.
TRIFT
WIDENMAYERSTR.
Maximilianeum
Johanniskirche
King Ludwig Mon.
Odeonspl.
Regierung
Max.Br.
Glyptothek (ruin)
Amerika-Haus
Karolinenpl.
Residenz
BRIENNER STR.
MAXIMILIANSTR.
Königsplatz
Obelisk
Maximilians-platz
Nat'l Thea. (ruin)
Völker Mus.
Albines Mus.
WIENER STR.
INN.
STEINSTR.
New State Gallery
Basilika
Prom. Pl.
Hofbräuhaus
Alter Hof
STEINSDORFSTR.
Bürgerbräu-keller
To Nymphenburg
Marien-platz
TAL
Isartor
Fortuna Ftn.
Isartor-pl.
ROSENHEIMER STR.
To Circus
Old Bot. Gardens
Worn Ftn.
Karlspl.
Karlstor
NEUHAUSER
ZWEIBRÜCKEN STR.
Ludwigs Br.
Peterskirche
Viktualien-markt
ARNULF
H. WILHELM STR.
St. Nepomuk Kirche
SENDLINGER STR.
City Hist. Mus.
BLUMENSTR.
ERHARDTSTR.
ZEPPELINSTR.
Deutsches Mus.
AU
FRANZISKANER
Hauptbahnhof (R.R. Sta.)
SCHWANTHALERSTR.
BAYER STR.
SONNEN-STR.
Gärtnerplatz
Gärtnerpl. Thea.
Marionette Thea.
GEBSATTELSTR.
Deutsches Thea.
Sendlingertor Platz
FRAUENHOFER
Mariahilf-kirche
Mariahilf Pl.
REGER STR.
MÜLLER-
Reichenbach Br.
HEYSE
NUSSBAUMSTR.
LINDWURMSTR.
OHLMÜLLERSTR.
Paulskirche
Old Southern Cemetery
WITTELSBACHERSTR.
Isar River
E. SCHMID STR.
FALKENSTR.
Kaiser Ludwigs Pl.
Goethe Pl.
WALTHER-STR.
MOZARTSTR.
Theresien-wiese
MATT.-PSCHORR
Bavaria Statue
AVARIARING
THERESIENHÖHE
To Zoo

1. Pal. of Justice
2. Wittelsbacher Fountain
3. Brunnenbuberl (Ftn.)
4. Bürgersaal
5. Michaelskirche
6. Old Acad. of Sciences
7. Frauenkirche (Cathedral)
8. New Town Hall (Neues Rathaus) & Glockenspiel
9. Max-Joseph Platz
10. Old Town Hall (Altes Rathaus)
11. Kaufingerstrasse
12. Heiliggeistkirche
13. Schauspielhaus
14. Max.II Mon. & Little Comedy Thea.
15. Residenz Thea.
16. Allerheiligen-Hofkirche
17. Feldherrnhalle
18. Theatinerkirche
19. Propyläen
20. City Art Gallery
21. Sendlinger Tor Hotels
22. Bayerischer Hof
23. Vier Jahreszeiten
24. Der Koenigshof
25. Park
26. Regina-Palast

MAP SHOWS MAJOR STREETS

NYMPHENBURG, a suburb of Munich, is noted for its fine porcelain, has a lovely 17th-century castle. Its formal gardens are laid out in a semblance of the famed English parks. A statue, "Vanity," is one of the decorative features of the gardens

THE GERMAN MUSEUM of Science and Technology stands on the banks of the River Isar. Founded by Oscar von Miller, a renowned electrical engineer, the museum contains a library of 300,000 volumes and the German Patent Office. Its observation tower affords an excellent view of the city

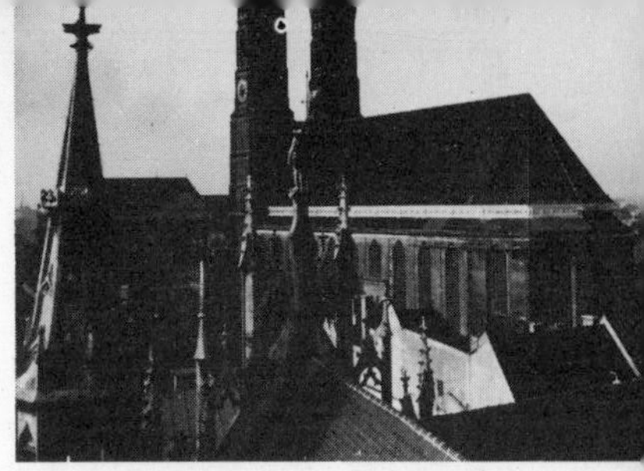

LIEBFRAUENKIRCHE (Church of Our Lady), which dates from the 15th century, is a fine specimen of late Gothic red brick architecture. It was severely damaged in the past war; only the two belfries of this Munich landmark escaped unscathed

THE UNIVERSITY, originally founded at Ingolstadt in 1472, faces this "old world" square at Munich. In the background are the towers of the Ludwigskirche which contains Cornelius' "Last Judgment," the largest altar painting in Germany

Photos: German Tourist Information Office

THE CITY OF MUNICH as it appears from the tower of the Rathaus on the Marienplatz. In the foreground is the Talstrasse with the ruined 11th-century Peterskirche on the right

MUNICH. Munich, the gateway to the Bavarian Alps, is a city with a great many historical associations—past and present—a city with an atmosphere completely unspoiled by bustling modernity. Lying midway between Strassbourg and Vienna, it is the most important town in southern Germany, also one of the largest European towns to be situated at so high an altitude. Founded in 1158, Munich was for centuries the capital of the independent kingdom of Bavaria, and in more recent times the birthplace of Nazidom. A heavy ring of munitions factories built by the Hitler regime made it an important target for allied bombings in World War II; however its protected location prevented much of the devastation suffered by other large German cities. After the Americans liberated Munich in 1945, the Temple of Honor, a memorial to the 16 Nazis killed in the "beerhall putsch," as well as other remnants of Nazi rule, were destroyed. Today, Munich has regained much of its former prominence as a cultural center of world fame. This is a city rich in museums, art collections and exhibitions, theaters and concert halls. Especially famous are the Munich Opera, the art treasures of the Old Pinakothek and the Deutsche Museum. Every year the inherent "joie de vivre" of Munich is expressed in three typical festivals—the Munich Carnival, the bock beer festival held each spring and the gay and colorful Oktoberfest.

Naples, Italy

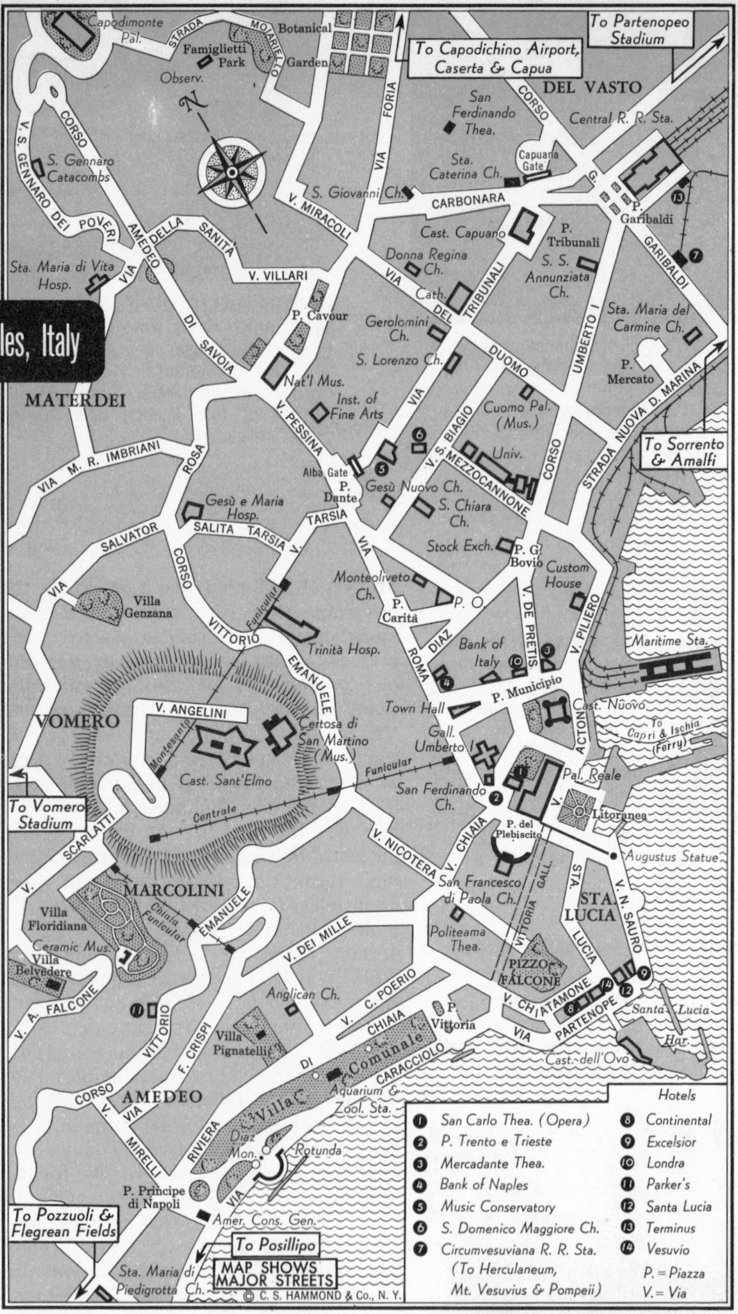

Capodimonte Pal.
STRADA
MOIARIELLO
Botanical Garden
Famiglietti Park
Observ.
To Capodichino Airport, Caserta & Capua
To Partenopeo Stadium
DEL VASTO
CORSO
S. Gennaro Catacombs
V. S. GENNARO DEI POVERI
San Ferdinando Thea.
Central R. R. Sta.
VIA FORIA
Sta. Caterina Ch.
Capuana Gate
S. Giovanni Ch.
CARBONARA
P. Garibaldi
G. GARIBALDI
V. MIRACOLI
Cast. Capuano
P. Tribunali
VIA DELLA SANITÀ
AMEDEO
Donna Regina Ch.
S. S. Annunziata Ch.
Sta. Maria di Vita Hosp.
V. VILLARI
VIA DEL TRIBUNALI
Cath.
Sta. Maria del Carmine Ch.
P. Cavour
Gerolomini Ch.
UMBERTO I
DI SAVOIA
S. Lorenzo Ch.
DUOMO
P. Mercato
Nat'l Mus.
STRADA NUOVA D. MARINA
MATERDEI
Inst. of Fine Arts
VIA
Cuomo Pal. (Mus.)
V. PESSINA
V. S. BIAGIO
Univ.
To Sorrento & Amalfi
VIA M. R. IMBRIANI
ROSA
MEZZOCANNONE
CORSO
Alba Gate
P. Dante
Gesù Nuovo Ch.
Gesù e Maria Hosp.
S. Chiara Ch.
TARSIA
SALVATOR
SALITA TARSIA
Stock Exch.
P. G. Bovio
Custom House
VIA
Monteoliveto Ch.
CORSO
P. O.
V. DE PRETIS
V. PILIERO
Villa Genzana
P. Carità
Funicular
DIAZ
Bank of Italy
Maritime Sta.
VITTORIO EMANUELE
Trinità Hosp.
ROMA
P. Municipio
V. ANGELINI
Town Hall
Cast. Nuovo
VOMERO
Certosa di San Martino (Mus.)
Gall. Umberto I
To Capri & Ischia (Ferry)
ACTON
Montesanto
Cast. Sant'Elmo
Funicular
Pal. Reale
San Ferdinando Ch.
To Vomero Stadium
Centrale
V. Litoranea
SCARLATTI
P. del Plebiscito
CHIAIA
V. NICOTERA
Augustus Statue
MARCOLINI
San Francesco di Paola Ch.
GALL. VITTORIA
STA. LUCIA
V. N. SAURO
STA. LUCIA
Villa Floridiana
Chiaia Funicular
EMANUELE
V. DEI MILLE
Politeama Thea.
Ceramic Mus.
Villa Belvedere
PIZZO FALCONE
V. A. FALCONE
V. C. POERIO
Anglican Ch.
V. CHIATAMONE
PARTENOPE
Santa Lucia Har.
VITTORIO
Villa Pignatelli
CHIAIA
P. Vittoria
VIA
F. CRISPI
DI
Villa Comunale
CARACCIOLO
Cast. dell'Ovo
CORSO
AMEDEO
VIA
Aquarium & Zool. Sta.
V. MIRELLI
RIVIERA
Diaz Mon.
Rotunda
P. Principe di Napoli
VIA
Amer. Cons. Gen.
To Pozzuoli & Flegrean Fields
To Posillipo
Sta. Maria di Piedigrotta Ch.
MAP SHOWS MAJOR STREETS

		Hotels
1 San Carlo Thea. (Opera)		8 Continental
2 P. Trento e Trieste		9 Excelsior
3 Mercadante Thea.		10 Londra
4 Bank of Naples		11 Parker's
5 Music Conservatory		12 Santa Lucia
6 S. Domenico Maggiore Ch.		13 Terminus
7 Circumvesuviana R. R. Sta. (To Herculaneum, Mt. Vesuvius & Pompeii)		14 Vesuvio
		P. = Piazza
		V. = Via

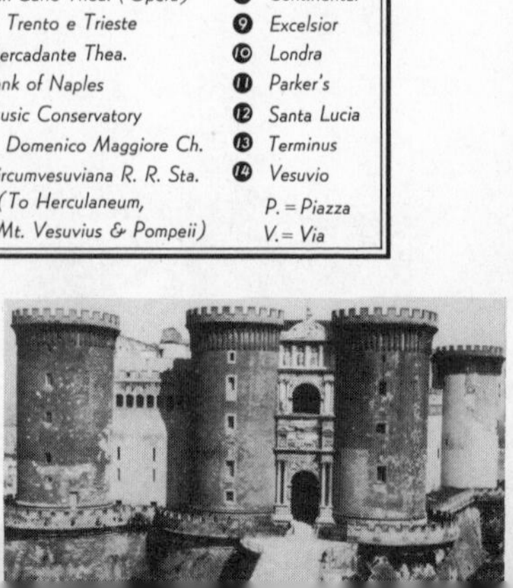

CASTEL NUOVO contains between its grim, round towers one of the glories of Italian Renaissance architecture, the triumphal arch of Alfonso I of Aragon. In the interior is the beautiful church of Santa Barbara

SANTA LUCIA, an old quarter of the city with an exciting view of the rippling sea, is the area of seafood restaurants. Much of the section was damaged during the Second World War

ELABORATE SAN CARLO Opera House, one of the largest in Europe, is a renowned musical institution in the city of song and country of avid opera lovers.

NAPLES. "The farther I am from you, the nearer you are to my heart" — this is the passionate, homesick song of the Neopolitan away from his illustrious city, with her mild, caressing climate and striking scenery. Dating back to the Greeks in origin and a source of deep fascination for the rich people of Rome, the city has always been a favored summer resort. Many masterpieces of the Greek and Roman eras are preserved in her National Museum, Europe's most important archeological museum, whose art collection is also famous. A gay, festive city of song, feasting and revelry, with a deep love and extraordinary flair for life, her most beloved festival is the Piedegrotta Feast, a devout homage to a miraculous Madonna and at the same time, a song contest marking the birth of the most catching popular Neopolitan songs of the year. Favorite pastime of her merry-makers is dining on mouth-watering *pizze alla napolitana,* topped later by a tangy sweet *pastiera napolitana* and refreshed with sweet Capri or some other wine, in a charming restaurant overlooking the enchanting bay. The men and women—dark-haired, vivacious and passionate — keep singing and dreaming through the years, eternally in love with their smiling "Napoli."

PIAZZA DEL PLEBISCITO, flanked by the enormous, 17th-century Palazzo Reale, belonging to the most pompous Naples period, a colonnade and the round-shaped, neoclassic church of San Francesco di Paola

BAY OF NAPLES lays claim to being one of the world's loveliest. Dominating the sweeping bay is the gently sloping Mt. Vesuvius

Photos: Italian State Tourist Office, TWA-Trans World Airlines

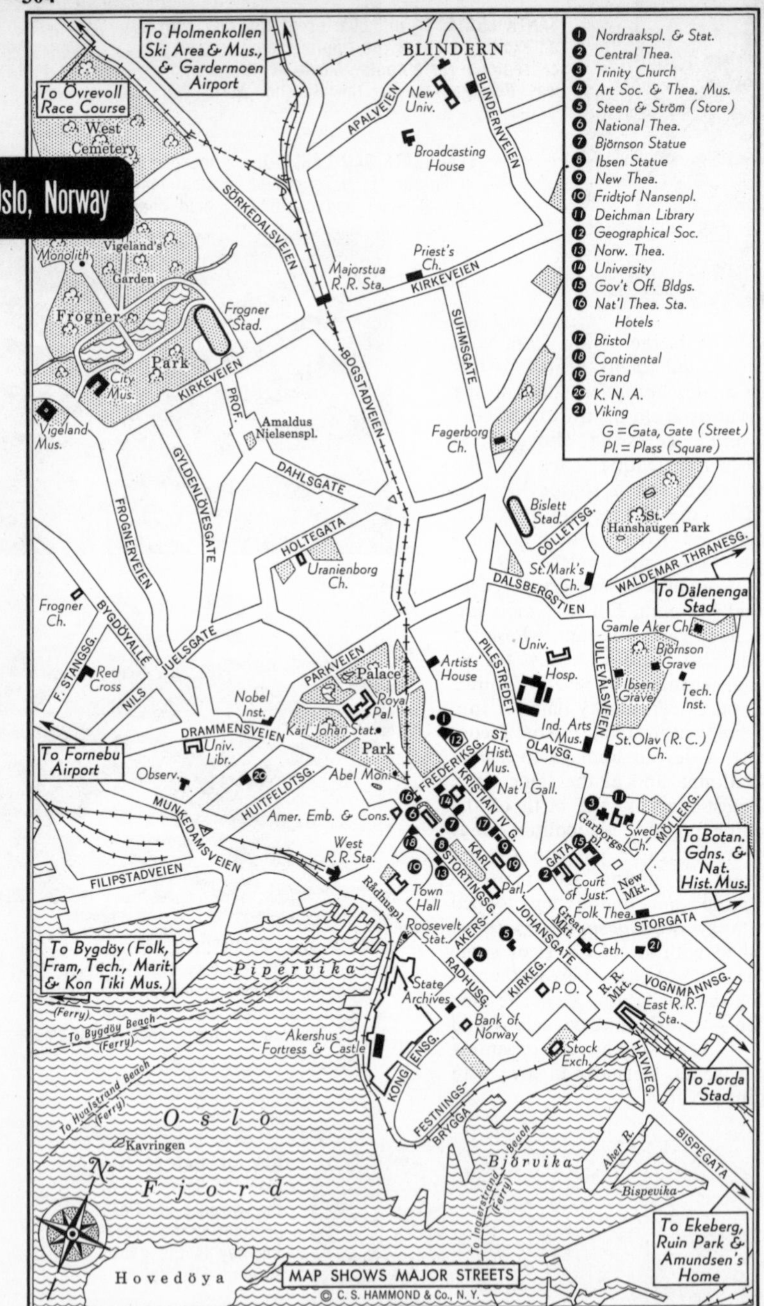

1 Nordraakspl. & Stat.
2 Central Thea.
3 Trinity Church
4 Art Soc. & Thea. Mus.
5 Steen & Ström (Store)
6 National Thea.
7 Björnson Statue
8 Ibsen Statue
9 New Thea.
10 Fridtjof Nansenpl.
11 Deichman Library
12 Geographical Soc.
13 Norw. Thea.
14 University
15 Gov't Off. Bldgs.
16 Nat'l Thea. Sta.
Hotels
17 Bristol
18 Continental
19 Grand
20 K. N. A.
21 Viking
G = Gata, Gate (Street)
Pl. = Plass (Square)
To Holmenkollen Ski Area & Mus., & Gardermoen Airport
To Övrevoll Race Course
BLINDERN
New Univ.
Broadcasting House
West Cemetery
APALVEIEN
BLINDERNVEIEN
SÖRKEDALSVEIEN
Vigeland's Garden
Monolith
Frogner Park
Frogner Stad.
City Mus.
Vigeland Mus.
Majorstua R.R. Sta.
Priest's Ch.
KIRKEVEIEN
SUHMSGATE
BOGSTADVEIEN
PROF.
Amaldus Nielsenspl.
Fagerborg Ch.
DAHLSGATE
GYLDENLÖVESGATE
FROGNERVEIEN
HOLTEGATA
Uranienborg Ch.
Bislett Stad.
COLLETTSG.
St. Hanshaugen Park
WALDEMAR THRANESG.
St. Mark's Ch.
DALSBERGSTIEN
To Dälenenga Stad.
Gamle Aker Ch.
Björnson Grave
Ibsen Grave
Tech. Inst.
ULLEVÅLSVEIEN
PILESTREDET
Univ. Hosp.
Artists' House
Frogner Ch.
BYGDÖYALLÉ
F. STANGSG.
Red Cross
NILS
JUELSGATE
PARKVEIEN
Palace
Royal Pal.
Park
Nobel Inst.
Karl Johan Stat.
DRAMMENSVEIEN
Univ. Libr.
To Fornebu Airport
Observ.
HUITFELDTSG.
Abel Mon.
Amer. Emb. & Cons.
MUNKEDAMSVEIEN
FILIPSTADVEIEN
West R.R. Sta.
Rådhuspl.
Town Hall
Roosevelt Stat.
FREDERIKSG.
KRISTIAN IV G.
ST. OLAVSG.
Hist. Mus.
Nat'l Gall.
Ind. Arts Mus.
St. Olav (R.C.) Ch.
MÖLLERG.
Swed. Ch.
Garborgs pl.
To Botan. Gdns. & Nat. Hist. Mus.
KARL JOHANSGATE
STORTINGSG.
Parl.
Court of Just.
New Mkt.
Folk Thea.
Great Mkt.
STORGATA
Cath.
AKERSG.
KIRKEG.
RÅDHUSG.
P.O.
R. R. Mkt.
VOGNMANNSG.
East R.R. Sta.
State Archives
Bank of Norway
Stock Exch.
Akershus Fortress & Castle
KONG ENSG.
HAVNEG.
To Jorda Stad.
To Bygdöy (Folk, Fram, Tech., Marit. & Kon Tiki Mus.)
Pipervika
(Ferry)
To Bygdöy Beach (Ferry)
To Hvalstrand Beach (Ferry)
Oslo Fjord
Kavringen
FESTNINGS-BRYGGA
Björvika
Aker R.
BISPEGATA
Bispevika
To Ingierstrand Beach (Ferry)
To Ekeberg, Ruin Park & Amundsen's Home
N
Hovedöya
MAP SHOWS MAJOR STREETS
© C. S. HAMMOND & Co., N. Y.

Photos: Norwegian National Travel Office

VIEW OF KARL JOHANSGATE, in front of the venerable Grand Hotel, whose elegant Mirror Room and spacious Grand Cafe are both noted for superb cuisine

OSLO. Since the time of the intrepid Vikings, life in fjord-bordered Norway has been influenced by the sea and Norsemen have been skillful and fearless seafarers. From the unbelievable voyages of Leif Eriksson to modern luxury cruises, these heroic sailors have recorded proud deeds of courage and daring on the earth's indomitable oceans. And Oslo, capital and coveted home port at the head of beautiful Oslo Fjord, is a city dominated by the water, containing many relics of their sailing tradition. Here, for instance, are three remarkable Viking ships, invoking exciting thoughts of that amazing early age. Here, too, is the *Fram*, which has been further south and north than any other ship in the world, since she was built for Nansen's polar expedition, was also used on Otto Sverdrup's expedition and, finally, by Roald Amundsen on his expedition to the South Pole in 1910. And more up-to-date, here is the renowned Kon Tiki balsa-log raft of Thor Heyerdahl. This love for the sea extends even into Oslo's sports life, for she has many excellent harbors for sailing and fishing craft and glorious beaches on her numerous lakes, rivers and the fjord.

ROYAL PALACE, commanding the hill in Palace Park at the center of the city, overlooks Karl Johansgate, the main thoroughfare

THE STAVE CHURCH is Norway's unique contribution to medieval architecture

NATIONAL THEATER, which presents a varied repertoire of classical and modern plays, is above all the theater of the great dramatist and poet,. Henrik Ibsen, whose bronze statue flanks the entrance

FORTRESS OF AKERSHUS, built by King Haakon V in 1300 as a royal residence, looks down from its ancient battlements onto the inner harbor

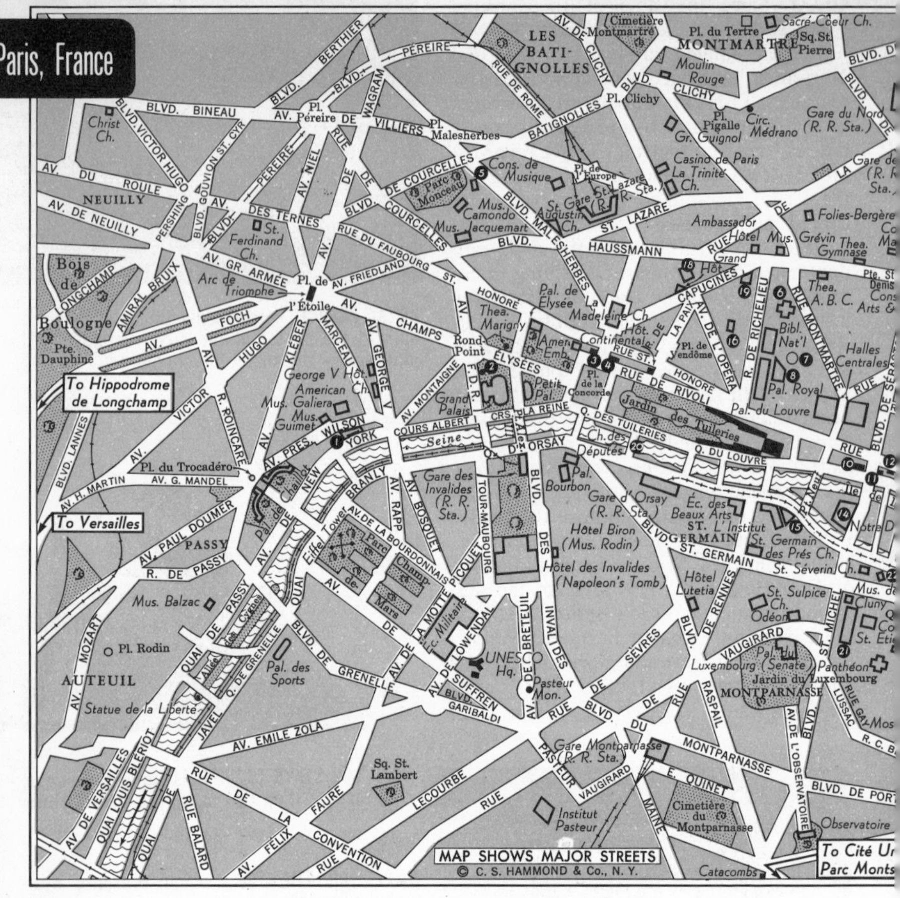

PARIS. Synonymous with gaiety, good food for gastronomes, gorgeous gowns, delectable wine, all the good things of life, is unrivaled, appealing Paris. The early morning mists on the Seine, the lazy-plying barges, the ever-patient fishermen, the spellbinding orators in the Chamber of Deputies, the gaunt, leafless trees along the quays in the fall, the flowering horse-chestnut trees in the spring, the breath-taking vistas from the bridges, the ageless, awe-inspiring beauty of the churches, the avid poets and painters, all this and much, much more is Paris. For centuries generation after generation of people from all over the world have gravitated to her narrow alleys and wide boulevards, for Paris "is not just a city, she is a world." To women, she is the undisputed center of high fashion, the acknowledged authority on what well-dressed beauties everywhere should wear. As style leader, the showings of top Paris dress designers draw all the editors, manufacturers and buyers of the fashion world, while their collections continually attract wealthy shoppers and less-wealthy window-shoppers. The noted Rue de la Paix is identical with Parisian elegance, an air every woman openly or secretly strives to exude. Not only the epitome of glamour, this fabulous capital has been a focal point of culture, too. In Paris, history, poetry and art sit on every doorstep, set the backdrop for everyday living, and great painters, musicians and writers have all been caught in the seductive web she weaves. The left bank of the Seine, lined by the famous open-air book stalls, is the intellectual and governmental section. Here is the Sorbonne, center of the University of Paris, perhaps the most influential and greatest school of liberal arts

CELEBRATED LOUVRE, "Queen of all the Museums," is on the Place du Carrousel. Here are the "Mona Lisa," Vermeer's "Lace Maker," Whistler's "Mother," the renowned Winged Victory of Samothrace, the Venus de Milo and other priceless masterpieces

ÎLE DE LA CITÉ, heart and earliest cradle of Paris, contains the enormous Palais de Justice, the revolutionary prison of the Conciergerie, Sainte Chapelle, the lovely bird market and Notre Dame

QUAY along the riverbank near Pont des Arts, one of the city's three foot bridges over the Seine, provides, like the quays all along the river, a lovely, peaceful setting for relaxation, promenades or lovers' rendezvous

Pan American World Airways Photo

in Europe; the classical Church of Saint-Sulpice, with famous paintings by Delacroix, and noteworthy Saint-Germain-de-Prés, oldest church in Paris, dating from the eleventh century. The gallery of nearby Ecole des Beaux Arts, scene of the annual wild Art Students' Ball, displays works of Fragonard, David and Ingres. Radiating from the university is the Latin Quarter, second oldest and one of the most picturesque sections in the city. For centuries these streets around Boulevard Saint-Michel have been the haunt of university students and teachers. Also in this area are the Cluny Museum, one of the fine medieval buildings still standing in Paris, housing a rare collection of medieval arts and crafts, and the Luxembourg Palace and Museum, surrounded by its beautiful gardens, housing contemporary painting and sculpture. The Quai d'Orsay is the center of government agencies, notably the foreign office, and the Chamber of Deputies sits in the Palais Bourbon. Although Frenchmen enjoy the luxury of disparaging their elected representatives and other parliaments sometimes are astonished at the instability of French governments, attendance at a session of the Deputies is a most exciting experience, for the powerful, fiery oratory heard everyday in this hall is the most brilliant of any such gathering on earth. The right bank also contains a number of cultural attractions, including the Palais Royal, the Cardinal Richelieu palace where Louis XIV lived as a boy. In one wing is the Théâtre Français, or Comédie Français, France's great national theater, which was founded by Louis. Avenue de l'Opéra, leading

PANTHÉON, built in the form of a Greek cross, is a grandiose sepulchre for great citizens, containing, among others, the tombs of Rousseau, Voltaire, Victor Hugo and Zola

THESE COMMEMORATIVE CANNONS stand at Les Invalides, which shelters the red granite tomb of Napoleon I. The church is a fine building with a noble dome

MOULIN ROUGE, in the heart of the amusement quarter, is one of the French music halls where the can-can was born, but is chiefly remembered as the favorite hangout of the unhappy painter, Toulouse-Lautrec

PLACE DU TERTRE, Montmartre's little main square covered with sun-shaded café tables and surrounded by picturesque houses, is a favorite haunt of Parisian artists

Photos: French Government Tourist Office, Pan American World Airways

L'OPÉRA, world's largest, personifies the ornate sumptuousness of the Second Empire, with its decorated exterior, gilt and scrollwork interior, magnificent grand staircase and majestic foyer

from the palace to the Opera House, was the crowning achievement in the city planning of Baron Haussmann, Napoleon's prefect who inaugurated huge municipal improvements, concentrating particularly on the handsome wide boulevards and public garden parks, trademarks of modern Paris. Across from the Palais Royal is the enormous Bibliothèque Nationale, probably the best in the world, with especially fine collections in the Medals and Antiquities Room. Of course, no one ever forgets the glittering, clamorous Paris, the night life of Gay Paree. Here the streets are dark and menacing, figures hover in dimly lighted passageways and your imagination can easily recapture the atmosphere of stealth, brutality, robbery and murder in this, the heart of the former Paris underworld. Cabarets once frequented by notorious night birds are still found in the quarter, where apache and adagio dancers whirl in wild abandon — a dramatic contrast to the equally famous, smart night clubs with their atmosphere of discreet elegance. Most bewitching of all, however, is the Parisian himself. Shop girl, professor, sophisticated mannequin, artist or subway conductor, no matter what his profession, he is a special brand of exuberance, ironic gaiety and careless indifference — a unique combination of endless fascination. The ancient winding streets of Paris, the sidewalk cafés, the fine shops, the lovely public gardens and parks, the scintillating crowds unite to form a colorful mosaic of human warmth and culture.

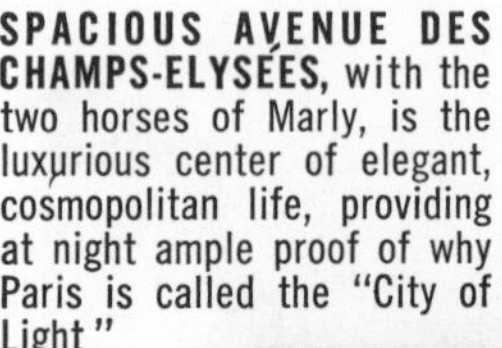

PALAIS DE CHAILLOT, sweeping, white-limestone building erected in 1937 and seat of United Nations Paris conferences, commands a fine view of Paris' unusual, world-renowned landmark, the Eiffel Tower, a masterpiece of metal architecture

SPACIOUS AVENUE DES CHAMPS-ELYSÉES, with the two horses of Marly, is the luxurious center of elegant, cosmopolitan life, providing at night ample proof of why Paris is called the "City of Light"

ROOFS OF HOUSES in the cluttered workers' residential district, on the right bank of the Seine, paint a haphazard, striped foreground for Montmartre (The Mount of Martyrs)

Photos: French Government Tourist Office

MONTPARNASSE QUARTER, on the left bank, which has replaced Montmartre as the center of artistic life, is known for its gay, cosmopolitan night life and large cafés

STATUE OF LIBERTY by Bartholdi, who created the identical but more colossal figure presented by the French people to the U. S. and now standing in New York Harbor

PLACE VENDÔME, begun in the 17th century, features the Vendôme Column, with spiraling bas-reliefs made from German and Austrian cannons captured at Austerlitz, topped by a statue of Napoleon as Caesar

OYSTER PEDDLER prepares for his day's sale. All sea food is popular with Frenchmen and many tasty sea-food dishes are served in the outstanding Parisian restaurants and cafés

SACRÉ COEUR, a Romanesque-style basilica on the top of the hill of Montmartre, highest point in Paris, has a lofty, white, Byzantine dome with an unmatched view of the city

CATHEDRAL OF NOTRE DAME, one of the greatest masterpieces of Gothic art, was begun in 1163 and finished 200 years later. From it there is a wonderful view of the serpentine Seine.

TUILERIES GARDEN, prettiest in the city, was laid out with chestnut, linden and plane trees and adorned with playing fountains, basins and statues. This view is looking toward the imperial-style Arc de Triomphe du Carrousel and the Louvre

Photos: TWA — Trans World Airlines, French Government Tourist Office

ARC DE TRIOMPHE is a symbol of national honor, for it was ordered by Napoleon to commemorate the victories of the French army, and under the arch rest the ashes of the French Unkown Soldier marked by an eternal flame

OBELISK OF LUXOR, an Egyptian monolith over 3,000 years old, is in the middle of the Place de la Concorde, largest and most beautiful square in Paris, where Louis XVI, Marie Antoinette, Danton and Robespierre were guillotined

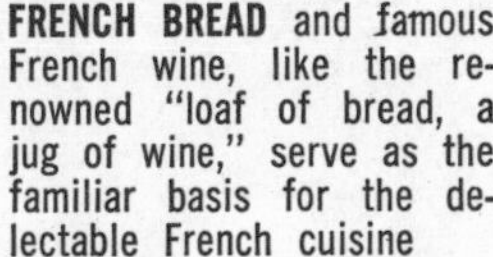

FRENCH BREAD and famous French wine, like the renowned "loaf of bread, a jug of wine," serve as the familiar basis for the delectable French cuisine

ROME. Much of the fascination of modern Rome lies in its historic past; in its long association with Christianity; in fragments of its ancient grandeur unearthed from the dust of time. Perhaps no city on earth has enjoyed a longer, more continuous importance, both politically and religiously, than Rome, seat of the Italian government and former capital of the Roman Republic and Empire For this the "eternal city" belongs not to Italy alone but to the world at large. A museum of grandiose proportions, few places have so many objects of religious and historical interest to attract the student, the pilgrim, the artist or the sightseer. This is the "city of the seven hills" founded by

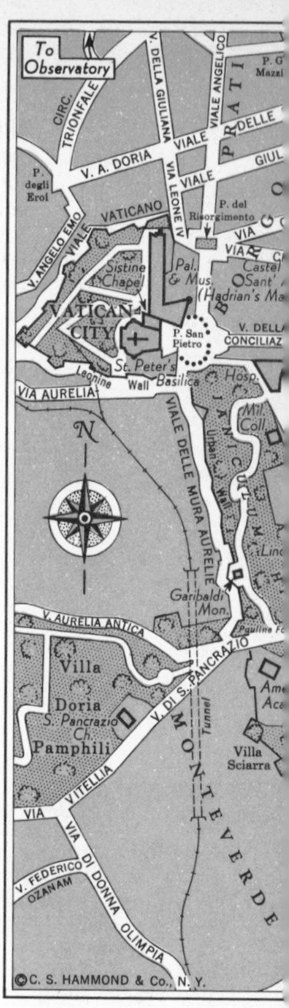

ROME IS A CITY OF FOUNTAINS. In the heart of the city a statue of Neptune watches over the famous Fontana di Trevi where legend states a coin dropped into the crystal waters will assure return to the "Eternal City"

Photos: Colosseum, Arch of Constantine, Vendors, TWA; all others to Italian Tourist Office

THE RIVER TIBER lazily winds its way through Rome, its clay-colored waters held in check by broad, tree-shaded embankments

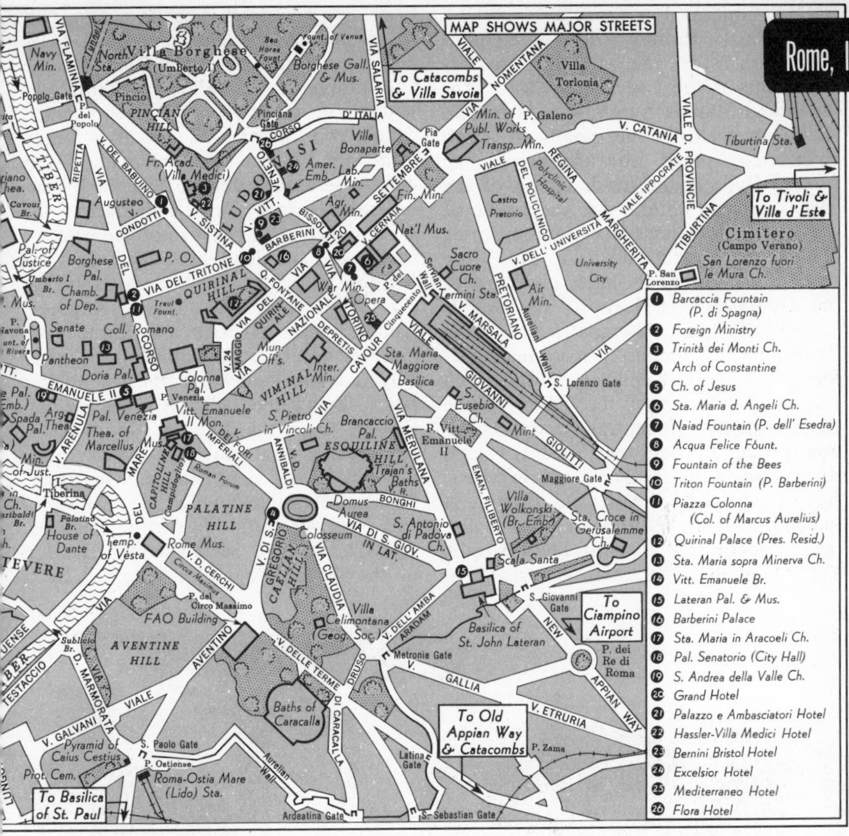
MAP SHOWS MAJOR STREETS
To Catacombs & Villa Savoia
To Tivoli & Villa d'Este
To Ciampino Airport
To Old Appian Way & Catacombs
To Basilica of St. Paul
Villa Borghese
Borghese Gall. & Mus.
Villa Torlonia
PINCIAN HILL
QUIRINAL HILL
VIMINAL HILL
ESQUILINE HILL
PALATINE HILL
CAELIAN HILL
AVENTINE HILL
TEVERE
TIBER
Colosseum
Baths of Caracalla
Cimitero (Campo Verano)
San Lorenzo fuori le Mura Ch.
Termini Sta.
Tiburtina Sta.
Nat'l Mus.
Sta. Maria Maggiore Basilica
Basilica of St. John Lateran
Scala Santa
Pyramid of Caius Cestius
Rome Mus.
FAO Building
Pantheon
Villa Celimontana (Geog. Soc.)
1 Barcaccia Fountain (P. di Spagna)
2 Foreign Ministry
3 Trinità dei Monti Ch.
4 Arch of Constantine
5 Ch. of Jesus
6 Sta. Maria d. Angeli Ch.
7 Naiad Fountain (P. dell' Esedra)
8 Acqua Felice Fount.
9 Fountain of the Bees
10 Triton Fountain (P. Barberini)
11 Piazza Colonna (Col. of Marcus Aurelius)
12 Quirinal Palace (Pres. Resid.)
13 Sta. Maria sopra Minerva Ch.
14 Vitt. Emanuele Br.
15 Lateran Pal. & Mus.
16 Barberini Palace
17 Sta. Maria in Aracoeli Ch.
18 Pal. Senatorio (City Hall)
19 S. Andrea della Valle Ch.
20 Grand Hotel
21 Palazzo e Ambasciatori Hotel
22 Hassler-Villa Medici Hotel
23 Bernini Bristol Hotel
24 Excelsior Hotel
25 Mediterraneo Hotel
26 Flora Hotel

THE COLOSSEUM, probably the most symbolic of Rome's ancient structures, is particularly effective when viewed at night by moonlight. Started by Vespasian and finished by his son, Titus, in A.D. 80, it was used for gladiatorial combats

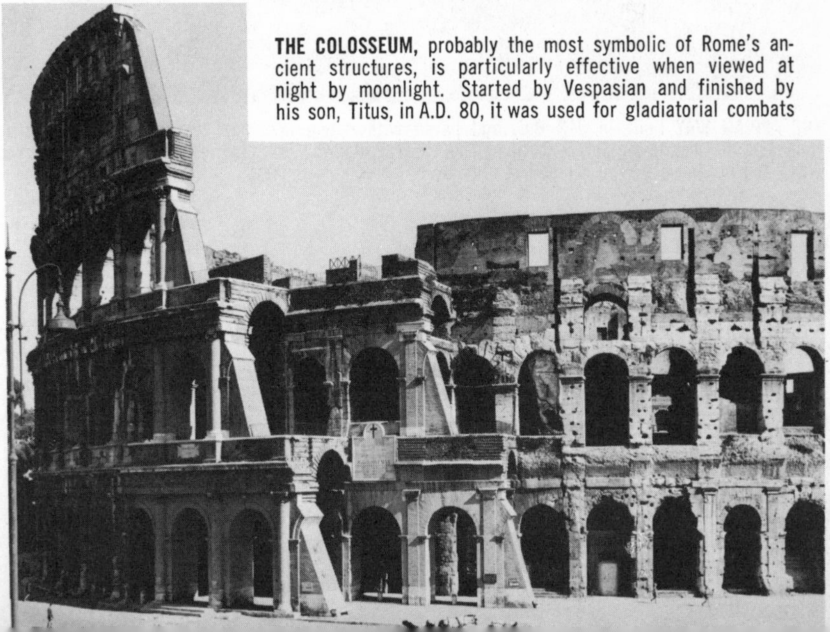

ROME Continued

the legendary Romulus over seven hundred years before the birth of Christ. It is the city of the Caesars; of Mark Anthony and Marcus Aurelius; of Nero and Diocletion. This is the spot from which civilization spread outward across the face of Europe; the headquarters of the early Christian church and the cradle of the Italian Renaissance. Modern Rome lies within a wide bend of the Tiber River about seventeen miles northeast of the Mediterranean Sea. Its situation is strategically unimportant, the city owing its prominence to purely man-made factors. Originally Rome stood on seven ridges to the east of the Tiber, in the Latium region of central Italy. Gradually through the centuries, the city spread downward to the level of the plain where, by the period of the Roman Empire, it encompassed the entire Campus Martius. The modern city is built literally atop the ancient one, which careful excavations reveal lying as four street levels beneath an accumulation of volcanic ash. Archaeology is a vital part of the Roman scene and much of Rome's expansion and building in recent years has been planned with a consideration to the city's famed ruins. On the Palatine (one of the seven hills) where according to legend, Romulus traced the city's first boundaries, still stand the colossal remains of the palaces, stadia and gardens built first for the wealthy patricians and later for the Emperors. Here it is said that Augustus "found a city of brick and left one of marble." Nearby, the Colosseum is probably the best known, of ancient Roman relics. Below the Palatine is the Roman Forum, once the hub of Roman life. Here it was that the large public meetings and games were held and the triumphant processions of Rome's Emperors and generals returning from conquest passed along the Sacred Way. The top of the Capitoline Hill is reached by a

THE APPIAN WAY built in 312 B.C. and paved with native lava has survived the passage of time and the weathering of centuries. The ancient highway is shadowed by spreading cypress trees and bordered by the crumbling remains of early Roman tombs

THE ARCH OF CONSTANTINE in Rome was erected in 312 A.D. to celebrate Constantine's liberation of the country from the tyrant Maxentius. The stone as well as many of the friezes were taken from former arches

THE ROMAN FORUM, when studied from the vantage point of Capitol Hill seems to fall into a pattern revealing much of its former grandeur. Once the center of ancient Rome, the Forum contains such monuments as the Arch of Septimus, Trajan's Column, and the house of the vestals

Photos: Colosseum, Arch of Constantine, Vendors, TWA; all others to Italian Tourist Office

THE ARCH OF TITUS which dates from A.D. 82, stands along Rome's Sacred Way. The passing centuries have left much of the amazing detail of its stonework intact.

THE SPANISH STEPS sweep gracefully upward to the Trinita dei Monti from an open square known as the Piazza di Spagna. The Church of the Trinity which stands above the magnificent staircase was built in the 15th century by Charles the VIII of France

Photos: Colosseum, Arch of Constantine, Vendors, TWA; all others to Italian Tourist Office

THE MONUMENT OF VICTOR EMANUEL II, dominates the square known as the Piazza Venezia. Designed by Giuseppe Sacconi, the monument was begun in 1885 and dedicated in 1911. It also contains Italy's tomb of the unknown soldier

ROME Continued

broad flight of stone stairs. On the summit is Capitol Square, in the center of which rises the bronze equestrian statue of Marcus Aurelius while in the background the City Hall is flanked by the Piazza Conservatori and the famed Museo Capitolino. Designed by Michelangelo the Museo contains a spectacular collection of Roman sculpture. In the center of the city is the Pantheon best preserved of the ancient monuments; it has been used as a church continuously for more than 2,000 years. Built by Marcus Agrippa to celebrate the victory over Anthony and Cleopatra, and completely rebuilt by Hadrian, both Roman and Pagan gods were worshipped here until its final consecration as a Christian church in A.D. 609. Today it contains the tombs of the Kings of Italy. The Vatican, seat of the papacy, lies to the west of the Tiber. This "City Within a City" contains the Basilica of St. Peter, the world's largest Christian church and the culmination of designs by some of the most celebrated architects of the Renaissance including San Gallo, Peruzzi and Raphael. Michelangelo designed its magnificent dome and Maderna its façade. Before the Basilica is an immense square surrounded by an elliptical colonnade consisting of four rows of 284 columns. Among the various buildings which comprise the Vatican Palace is the Sistine Chapel on the ceiling and the altar wall of which Michelangelo painted his greatest masterpieces; "The Last Judgment" and "The Creation." Next to St. Peters the most famous of Rome's medieval churches are St. John Lateran, Santa Maria Maggiore and St. Pauls Without the Walls.

THE BASILICA OF ST. MARY MAJOR is one of Rome's seven Catholic pilgrimage churches. With 400 churches and many other relics of religious significance, Rome is the greatest religious center of the world

STREET VENDORS are a familiar sight in Rome. Many of the city's small streets and alleys have their outdoor markets where in the early hours of the morning peddlers display fresh fruit, vegetables, fish and meat at colorful stalls

HADRIAN'S TOMB, now known as Castel Sant' Angelo, stands on the west bank of the Tiber. Here, Pope Gregory the Great, saw a vision of the archangel Michael which was interpreted as a sign that a plague which ravaged Rome would end. A statue of the Saint atop the Castel commemorates the miraculous event

Rotterdam, Netherlands

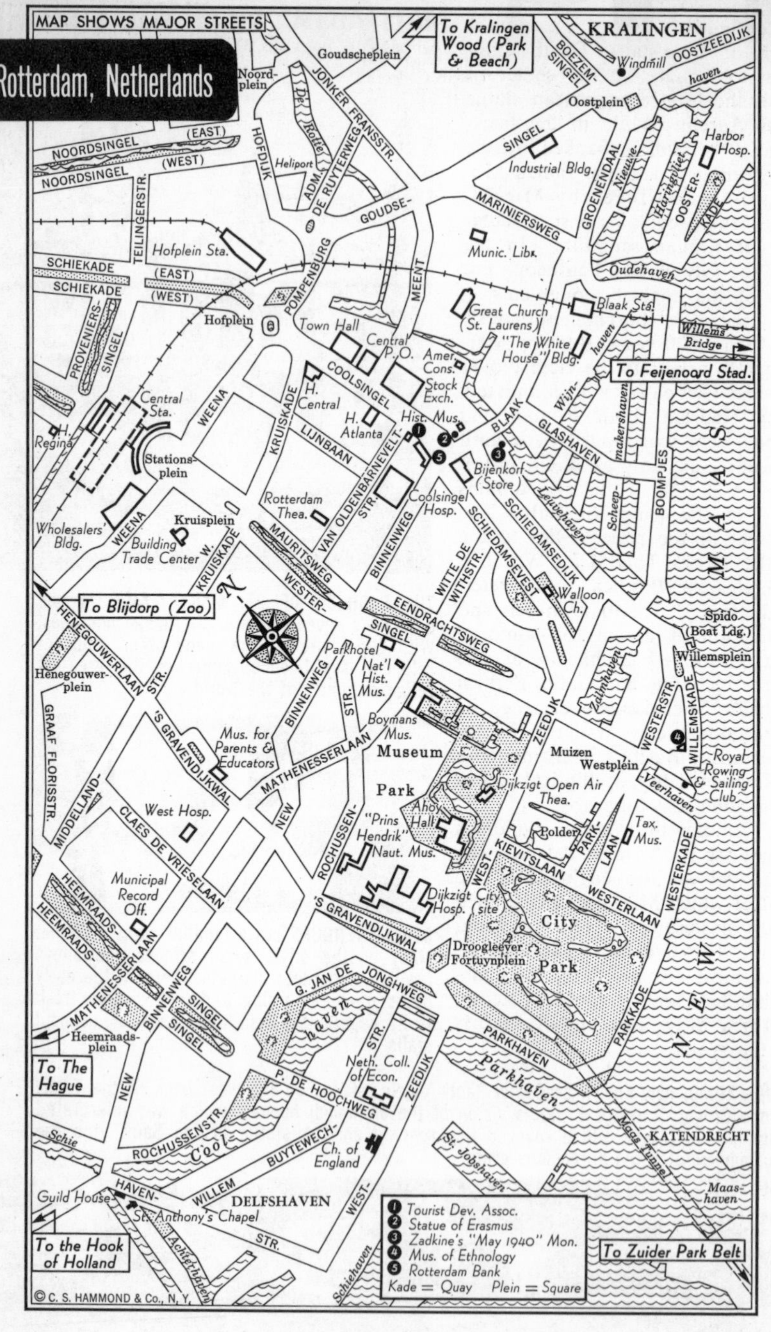

Photos: Philip Gendreau, Netherlands National Tourist Office

THE TOWN HALL, in the heart of Rotterdam, was one of the few buildings which survived the terrible bombing on May 14, 1940

THE MANY MODERN BUILDINGS, new parks, broad boulevards and extensive harbor improvements in Rotterdam are a tribute to the courage and resourcefulness of its people

ROTTERDAM. With its original charter dating back to the early part of the 14th century, Rotterdam, principal port of the Netherlands, is in reality an old city. Yet today, with but a few remnants of its antiquity among its scores of modern buildings, Rotterdam is, at least in appearance, a new city conceived in the latest and most functional of 20th century architecture. On May 14th, 1940, shortly after the people of Rotterdam had ceased their active resistance and surrendered their city to the Nazi invaders, wave after wave of German bombers showered Rotterdam with brutal and unjustifiable destruction. In less than three hours, the entire commercial heart of the city had been reduced to a vast wasteland with over 25,000 people lying dead beneath the rubble. As the tides of war changed, allied bombing of enemy installations brought further destruction, particularly to Rotterdam's extensive harbor facilities. Faced with an almost overwhelming task of reconstruction, Rotterdam's remarkable re-birth is a tribute to the indomitable courage and resourcefulness of her people. Today, the city whose primary concern is commerce, maintains her place among the foremost ports and trans-shipping centers of Europe. Past its door flows the New Maas River, a mighty water-highway leading inland from the North Sea to the industrial cities of the Netherlands, Belgium and the Ruhr basin of northwestern Germany.

"RUINED CITY," a memorial statue by Ossip Zadkine, stands in a spacious plaza overlooking Rotterdam's harbor. The statue expresses the sentiments felt on seeing the terrible destruction

THE RECONSTRUCTION OF ROTTERDAM has taken place at an unprecedented rate and visitors are amazed to find that few signs of the city's destruction remain

Stockholm, Sweden

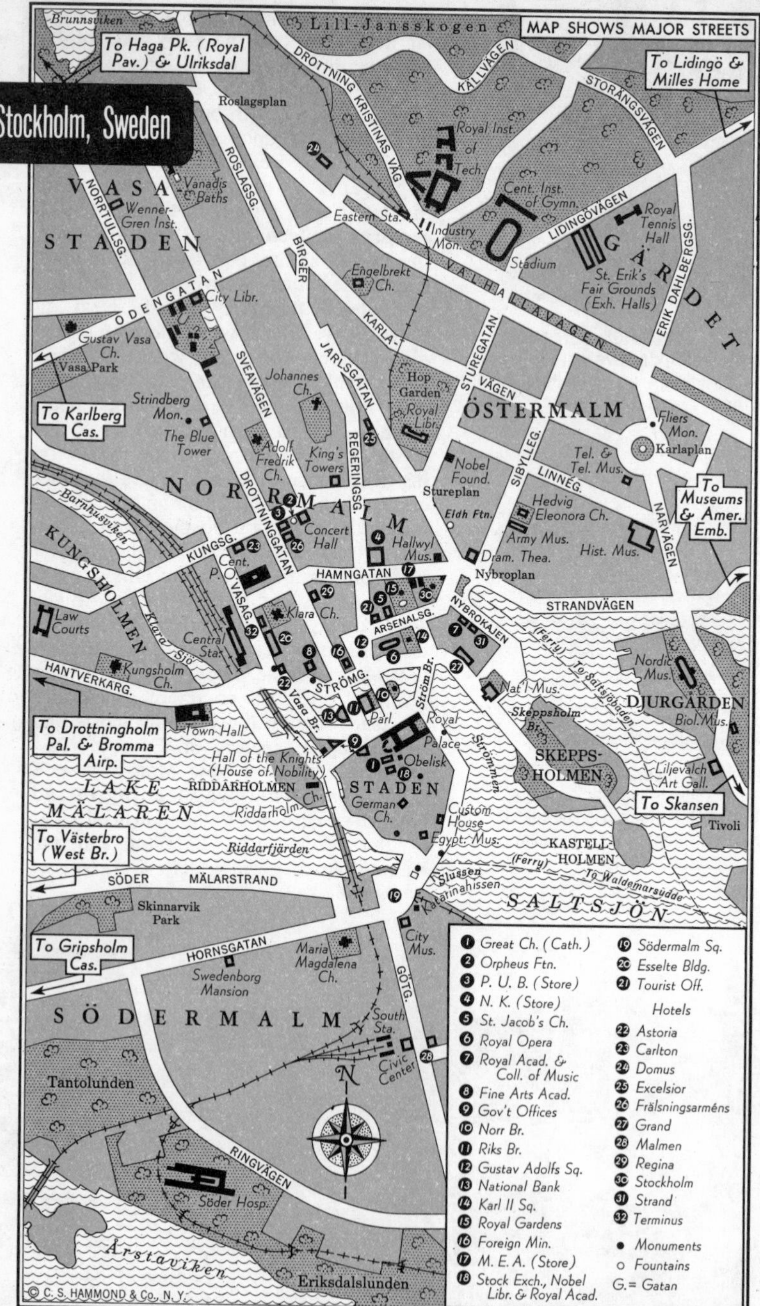

Photos: Swedish National Travel Office

OLD TOWN, on an island in the turbulent outlet of Lake Malaren into the Baltic with the modern sections on the mainland beyond, presents from the Town Hall tower a pinkish, miniature, model-like appearance

TOWN HALL, completed in 1923 on the banks of Lake Malaren, is a brick masterpiece by Ragnar Ostberg and is considered Europe's most artistic contemporary building

SKANSEN, famous out-of-door, living museum and zoo, contains old buildings from all over the country. Open-air concerts, folk dances and theatrical performances take place during the summer

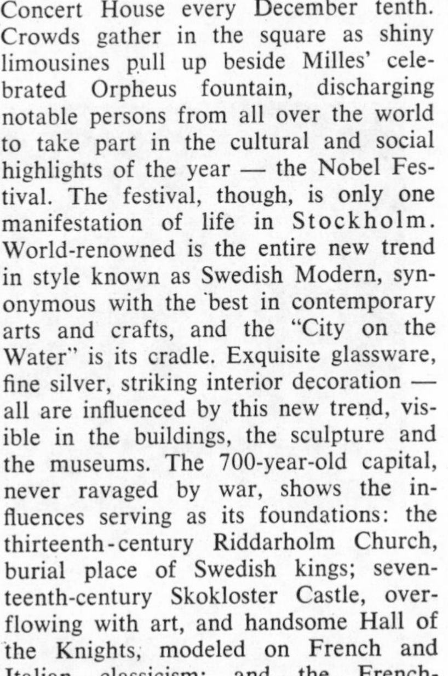

STOCKHOLM. A row of blazing torches lights up the classic columns of the Concert House every December tenth. Crowds gather in the square as shiny limousines pull up beside Milles' celebrated Orpheus fountain, discharging notable persons from all over the world to take part in the cultural and social highlights of the year — the Nobel Festival. The festival, though, is only one manifestation of life in Stockholm. World-renowned is the entire new trend in style known as Swedish Modern, synonymous with the best in contemporary arts and crafts, and the "City on the Water" is its cradle. Exquisite glassware, fine silver, striking interior decoration — all are influenced by this new trend, visible in the buildings, the sculpture and the museums. The 700-year-old capital, never ravaged by war, shows the influences serving as its foundations: the thirteenth-century Riddarholm Church, burial place of Swedish kings; seventeenth-century Skokloster Castle, overflowing with art, and handsome Hall of the Knights, modeled on French and Italian classicism; and the French-influenced, eighteenth-century, unique Court Theater of Drottningham Palace, and extraordinarily imposing and symmetrically satisfying Royal Palace.

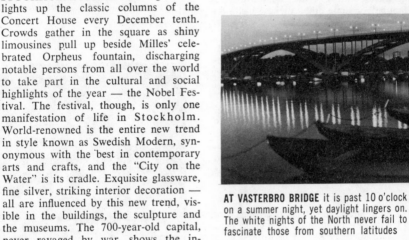

AT VASTERBRO BRIDGE it is past 10 o'clock on a summer night, yet daylight lingers on. The white nights of the North never fail to fascinate those from southern latitudes

STUREPLAN, with its circular rain shelter, is a traffic center in this large, industrialized city, which has its commuter problem

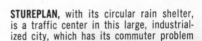

VIENNA. Vienna, dating back to the Roman era and beyond, has become over the centuries a symbol of European culture. Strategically located on the lovely, legend-haunted Danube, Austria's river of fate, this gay, glamorous city of the Hapsburgs is the world's capital of glorious music and bewitching dance. Her beautiful concert halls have resounded to the most majectic music on earth, for she has embraced the brightest galaxy of composers any city has ever known — Mozart, Beethoven, Haydn, Schubert, Schumann, to name only the greatest of them all. And what woman has never dreamed of romantically swirling to the entrancing strains of the "Beautiful Blue Danube" or some other Vienese waltz on a moon-drenched terrace or crystal-chandeliered ballroom in the very city where Johann Strauss composed his lilting melodies. Center of intellectual accomplishment, with her famed university, and other artistic achievement, as well as the home of magical music, Vienna's splendid art galleries and imposing buildings characterize all periods of artistic styles, from the Romanesque through the Gothic, renaissance and early baroque, culmininating in the famous Vienna Baroque, to which the city gave its individual style.

UNRIVALLED OPERA HOUSE, world's most impressive, with its famous staircase, is on the Ringstrasse, Europe's finest boulevard. Vienna is the only city boasting two first-rank symphony orchestras of international reputation

THE ROSE ROOM, one of the richly ornate rooms in the Hofburg, or Imperial Palace of the House of Hapsburg, which formed the background for some of history's most dramatic scenes

RATHAUS (CITY HALL) is one of the finest buildings of its period, the last half of the 19th century, where the elements of Gothic and Renaissance have been combined

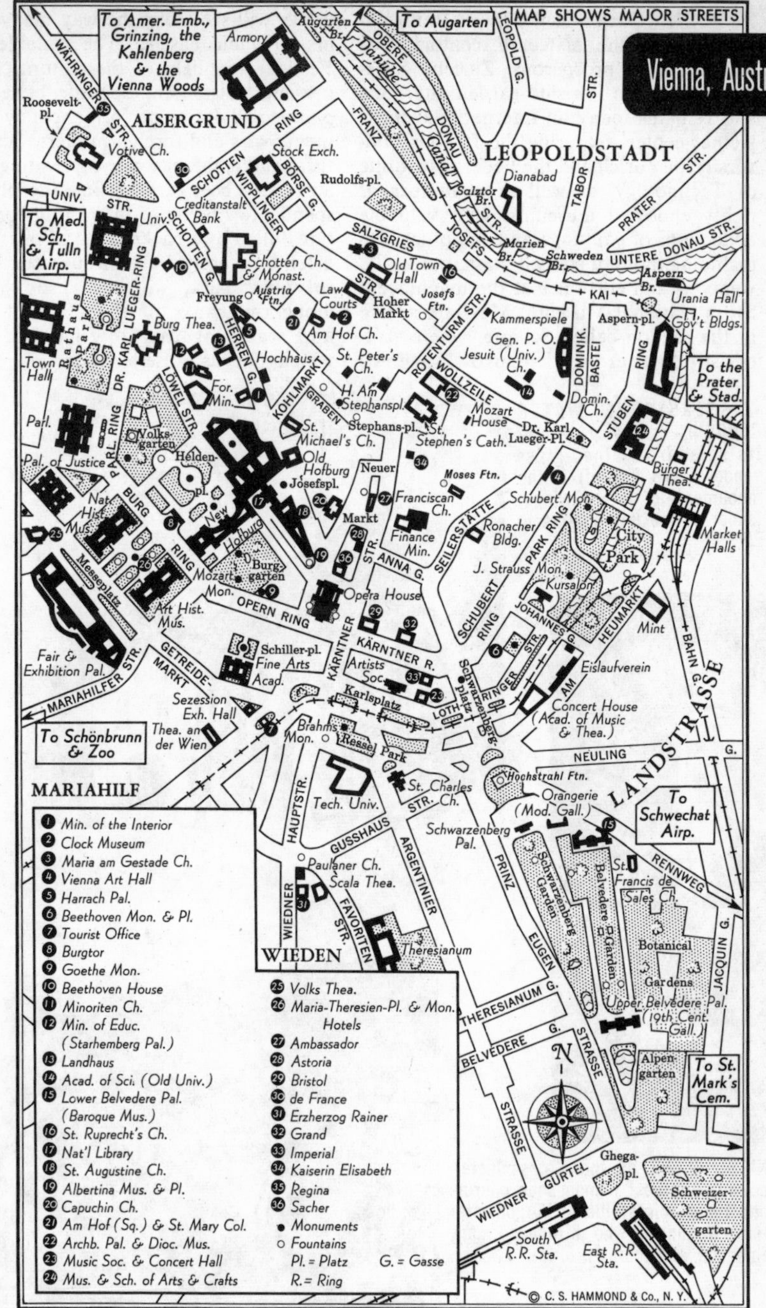

ST. STEPHEN'S CATHEDRAL, the city's landmark and one of the most important Gothic buildings in Europe, has played a central part in many historical legends. The dome is that of Karlskirche, the Coronation Church of St. Charles

Photos: Austrian State Tourist Department

ZÜRICH. Center of the Swiss Reformation during the sixteenth century was wealthy and prosperous Zürich, Swiss metropolis and lakeside garden city. She still remains today an international intellectual center, featuring the famous University of Zürich and the Federal Institute of Technology, as well as a number of richly endowed museums, with valuable collections of paintings and sculpture also including those of stained glass, porcelain, weapons and costumes at the magnificent Swiss National Museum. Most artists live in the section called Schipfe, where visitors strolling through its narrow, shadowy alleys will see along the way many painters at their easels. The notable June Festival, highlight of the cultural season, presents outstanding operatic, ballet, symphonic and drama performances by prominent Swiss and foreign masters. Scattered throughout the city are captivating openair terrace beer gardens; inviting places to spend a few hours of interesting conversation lulled by a background of soft music, after a leisurely walk through the beautiful quiet park, with its rustic bridges, along the banks of the peaceful canal, and watching the slow-moving punts which dot its waters.

WASSERKIRCHE (WATER CHURCH), indicating two of its splendid stained-glass windows. To the left is the monument to Ulrich Zwingli, leader of the Reformation in Zürich

NIGHT SCENE of the Grossmünster, country's largest Romanesque church, and the heroic statue of burgomaster Hans Waldmann, who introduced many financial and moral reforms

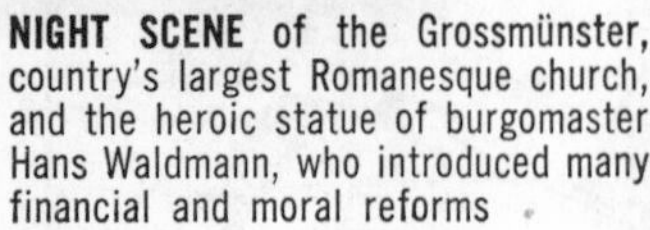

LEFT BANK OF THE LIMMAT, dominated by the spire of the Fraumünster church containing frescoes by Paul Bodmer representing legends of the city's history

Photos: Window, Gemmerli; all others, Swiss Nat'l Tourist office

ORIEL WINDOWS are an attractive feature of "Zimmerleuten," one of the historic guild houses along both sides of the river

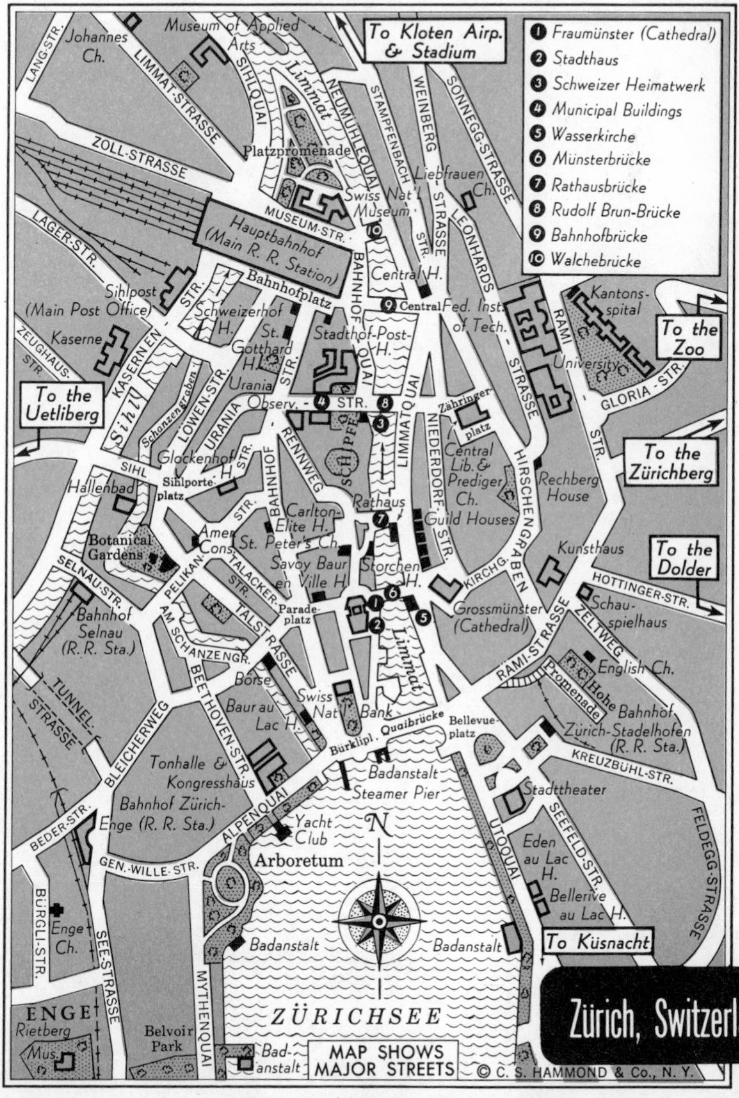

VIEW OF BELLEVUE PLATZ shows street scene typical of this clean, attractive city, largest and finest in Switzerland

1. Fraumünster (Cathedral)
2. Stadthaus
3. Schweizer Heimatwerk
4. Municipal Buildings
5. Wasserkirche
6. Münsterbrücke
7. Rathausbrücke
8. Rudolf Brun-Brücke
9. Bahnhofbrücke
10. Walchebrücke

To Kloten Airp. & Stadium

To the Zoo

To the Zürichberg

To the Dolder

To the Uetliberg

To Küsnacht

ZÜRICHSEE

MAP SHOWS MAJOR STREETS

Zürich, Switzerland

CITIES
of
AFRICA

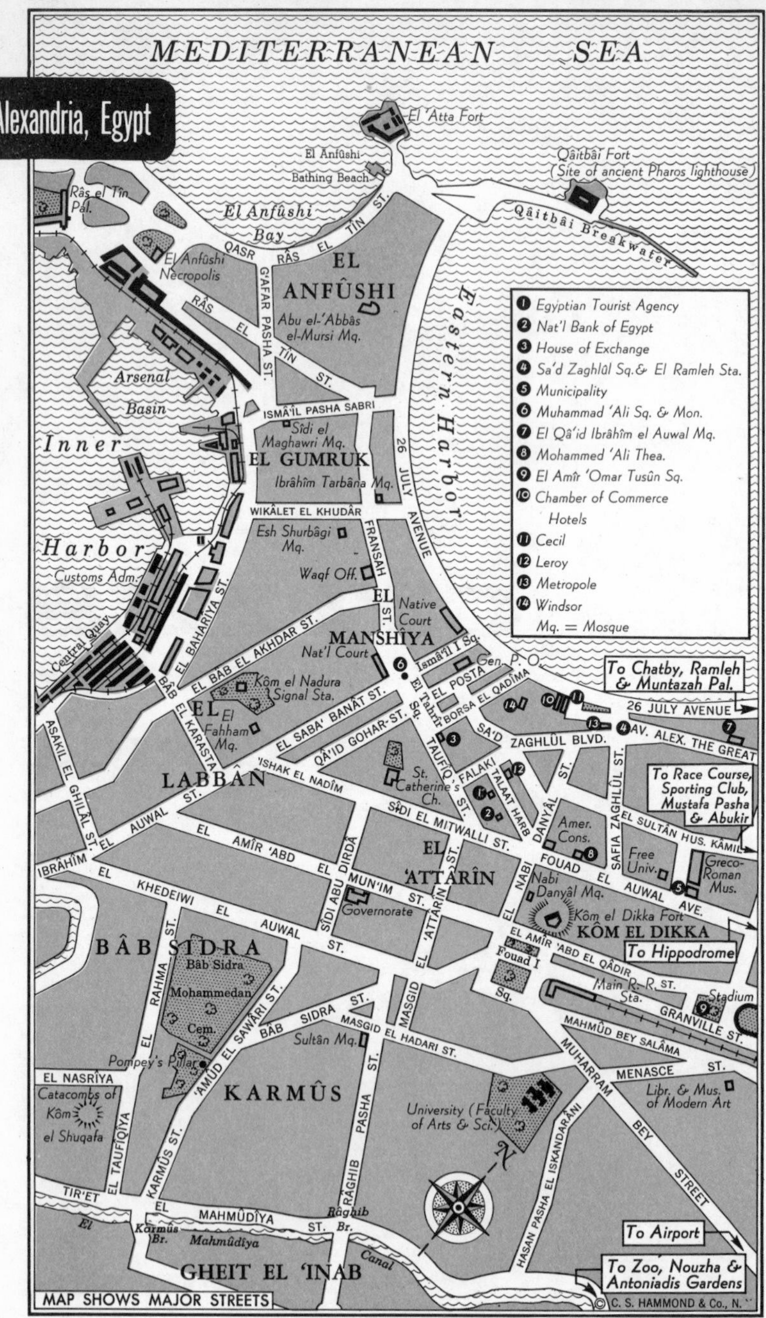

Photos: Egyptian State Tourist Administration

YACHTING is a popular pastime in Alexandria with its fine sheltered harbors and its swank yacht club overlooking the waterfront from Ras et-Tin (the Cape of Figs)

CORNICHE DRIVE, which follows the curve of Alexandria's eastern harbor, is a handsome boulevard lined by villas and bathing beaches

ALEXANDRIA'S ARCHITECTURE is a strange yet pleasing combination of Oriental, Italian and 20th-century modern styles

ALEXANDRIA. When Alexander the Great traced his proposed plan for a new city on the ground of Pharos Island in 332 B.C. the Great Conqueror could hardly foresee that this city, in less than a century, would become the largest and most magnificent in the known world. Alexander never saw the great city he had founded and which still bears his name. Leaving Egypt, he entrusted its construction to his viceroy. Strategically located just west of the Nile Delta on a narrow strip of land between Lake Mareotis and the Mediterranean Sea, Alexandria soon became the "Gateway to Egypt" and the hub of trade between Europe and the Middle East. The rocky island, where stood the wonderful Pharos lighthouse, was joined to the mainland by a narrow causeway and incorporated into the city. Here Euclid wrote his famous geometry; here Hellenistic and Jewish culture flourished. Its two libraries were said to have contained nearly 700,000 scrolls. Through the centuries Alexandria's importance declined with the loss of shipping, due in part to silt closing a channel which linked the city with the Nile. Not until the 19th century did it regain some of its former importance. Today with its modern harbor installations, it is Egypt's foremost port through which most of this country's foreign trade passes. Much of the ancient city now lies beneath the water and the eastern part of its divided harbor is suitable only for small fishing boats. Except for a tall red granite shaft known as "Pompey's Pillar" almost nothing remains of Alexandria's antiquity.

Algiers, Algeria

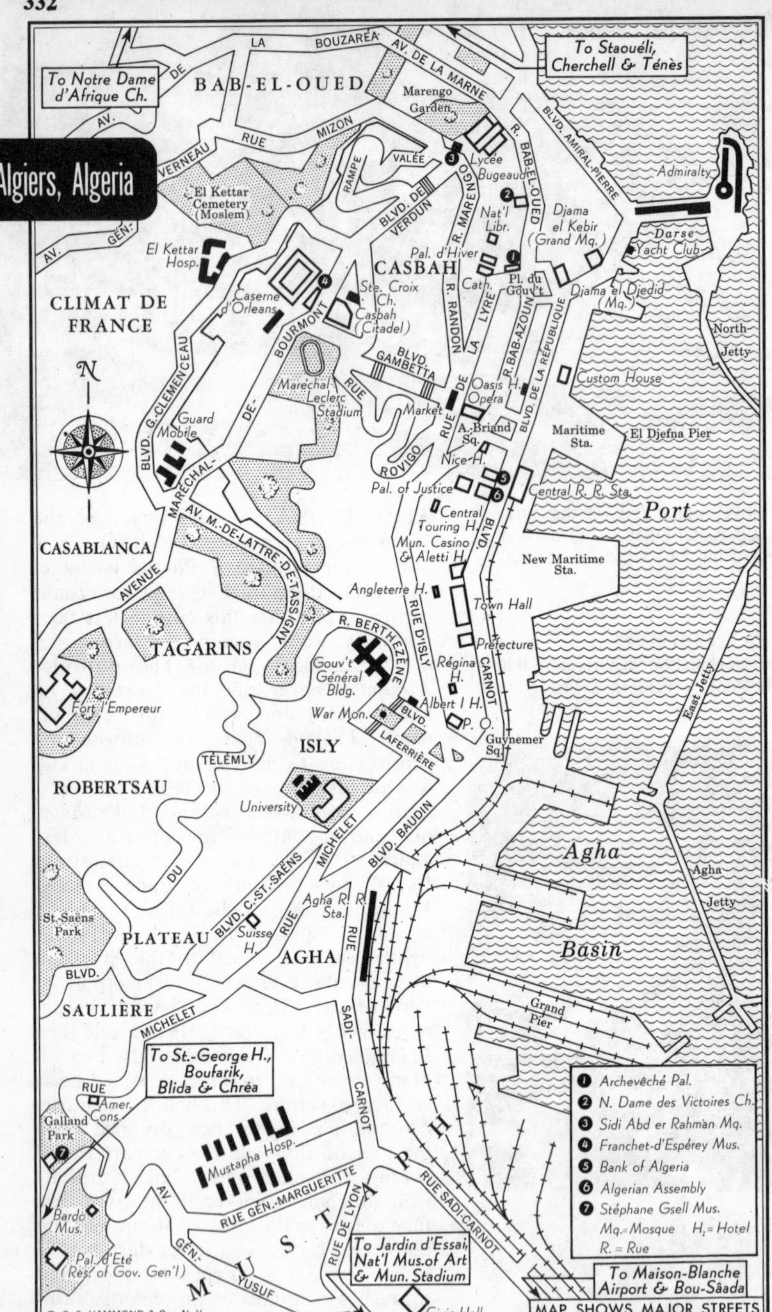

Photos: TWA-Trans World Airline, French Government Tourist Office

MODERN FRENCH QUARTER has up-to-date, luxurious shops, lovely gardens and parks and elegant residential quarters, including the palatial Governor General's Residence

ALGIERS. Stretching along a bay for ten miles in the shape of an amphitheater, at the foot and on the slopes of coastal hills, exotic Algiers appears from the sea as gorgeous tier upon tier of brilliant white, so dazzlingly beautiful in the surrounding luxuriant verdure that the Arabs liken her to a diamond set in an emerald frame. Her story, too, is almost as violently exciting as her appearance is ravishing. Founded by Berbers, she became important after Turkish rule was established by the fiery Barbarossa in 1518. From this time she became the chief seat of the Barbary pirates, scourge of the Mediterranean, who menaced shipping or exacted tribute from all those plying the sea until the French captured the city in the last century. A land of mystery, of the white burnoosed Arab and his veiled lady, a land of high adventure, Algiers still retains her spinetingling but exaggerated reputation as the haunt of spies and fugitives and the scene of whispered intrigue. Today, as capital of Algeria and the core of bitter Arab opposition to French rule, her halls and avenues often do resound with the sharp, staccato sounds of noisy street fighting or violent political battles.

SUBURBAN ORANGE GROVES provide abundant supply of excellent fruit, fine accompaniment to tasty meals of mutton or chicken **couscous** or **Mechoui du Sud** (barbecued sheep), mint tea or Moorish coffee

CASBAH, or old town, with its labyrinthine pattern of narrow, arcaded streets and steep, cobblestoned, dead-end alleys, twists up to the citadel, palace of the last two deys of Algiers

ADMIRALTY BUILDINGS and remains of the old fort, constructed on the long dyke built by Barbarossa to link the small offshore islets, formed the old harbor, now used by yachtsmen

Cairo, Egypt

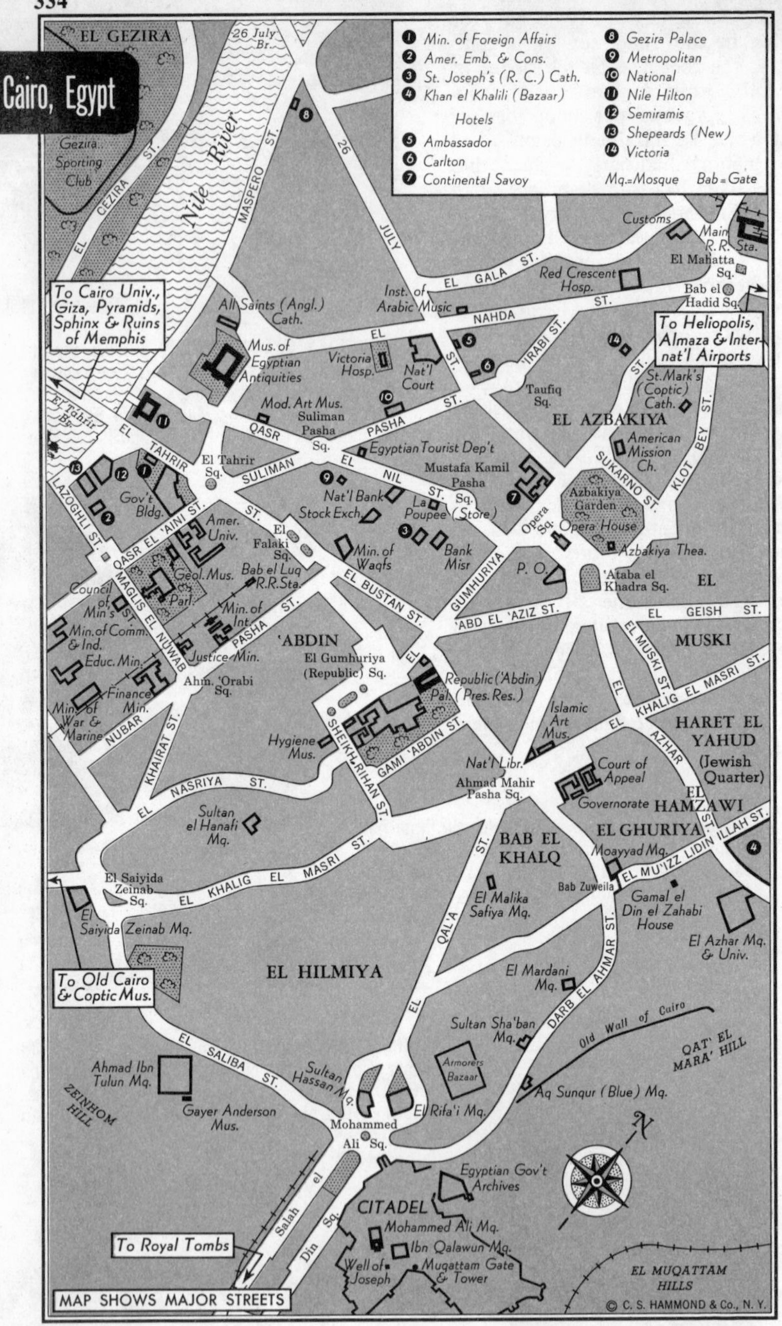

Photos: Trans World Airline, Egyptian State Tourist Administration

PYRAMIDS at Giza, each one built in the 27th century B. C. by 100,000 men working for 20 years, are gigantic royal tombs whose construction remains a puzzle even today

SPHINX, nicknamed this by the Greeks, is a monumental Pharaohic riddle, classified with the Pyramids as one of the seven wonders of the world

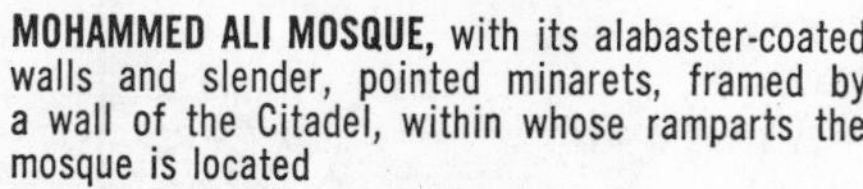

MOHAMMED ALI MOSQUE, with its alabaster-coated walls and slender, pointed minarets, framed by a wall of the Citadel, within whose ramparts the mosque is located

A MODERN EGYPTIAN GIRL views the Pyramids via the age-old mode of transportation—camelback—thus symbolizing all of Cairo, where ancient and modern exist side by side

HELIOPOLIS PALACE, one of Cairo's beautiful, luxurious hotels, is on a palm-bordered street in the airy, comfortable suburb of Heliopolis, an early capital of Egypt

CAIRO. Sophisticated Cairo, on the banks of the ageless Nile, contains vestiges of the more than 8,000 years that civilizations have flourished in this land of sunshine, culture and beauty. She illustrates, too, the flowering vitality and power of the modern Arab world, of which she is the largest city. At the base of the twelfth century Citadel is the old part, with winding, narrow, arcaded streets, steep, dead-end alleys, clamorous, crowded bazaars and venerable mosques, including El Azhar Mosque, "the splendid mosque," intellectual fountainhead of the Arab world. In the center of the city is the newer, cosmopolitan part with theaters, dancing halls with exotic, elusive perfumes permeating the air, oriental music and clever gally-gally men, and the simple, shining modern buildings. Here, too, are the priceless treasure troves of golden furniture, ebony statues, alabaster goblets, gem-studded jewelry and other royal trappings in the Museum of Egyptian Antiquities and others. At Giza, on the other side of the slow-moving Nile, are the huge, amazing Pyramids and the fabulous, mysterious Sphinx, Cairo's greatest lure for many, many centuries.

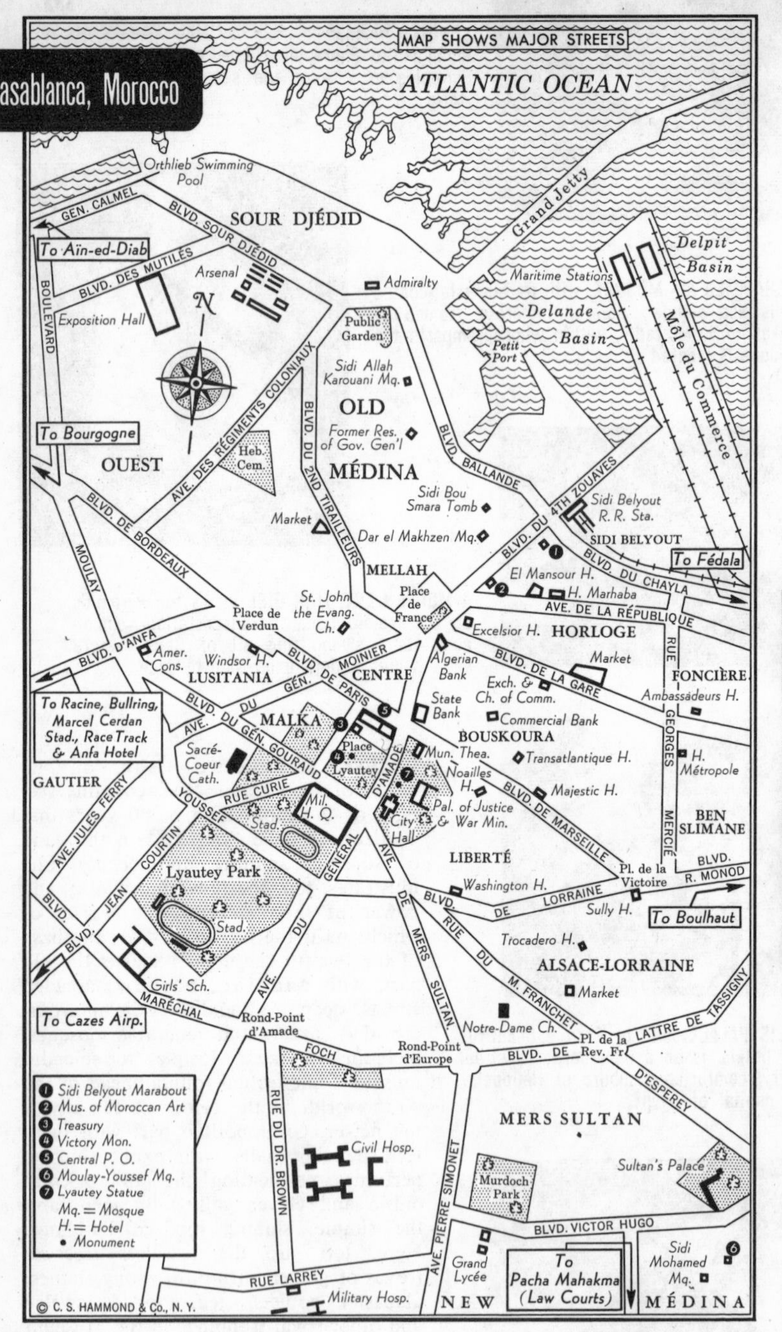

Photos: French Government Tourist Office, Screen Traveler, From Gendreau

PLACE DE FRANCE serves as hub of Casablanca. From this square, located in the commercial and entertainment area, radiate the city's main thoroughfares

PALACE OF JUSTICE is one of the beautiful buildings of Casablanca. Because of its mild Mediterranean-type climate, many of the city's public buildings as well as its attractive private residences are built around an open courtyard

CASABLANCA. With its contemporary architecture, its broad neon-lighted streets, its extensive harbor installations and its cosmopolitan atmosphere, Casablanca is a modern city; yet its Moroccan setting changed but little in the past six centuries. Outside the city, Berbers and Arabs live in much the same manner as their ancestors lived in the 14th century. Founded by the Portuguese in 1515, Casablanca occupies the site of the ancient city of Anfa, which was destroyed by them in 1465. French forces gained control of Casablanca in 1907. On the ruins of the town which their naval guns had reduced to rubble, the French erected a gleaming new city. Under the direction of Marshal Lyautey, first resident general of Morocco, the city's economic future was secured by the building of jetties to protect its exposed position. Its harbor thus sheltered from the northeast winds and the Atlantic, Casablanca has become one of the great ports of the African continent and probably the most spacious artificial seaport in the world. The Cazes airport, also of major importance to the city's commerce, handled much of the Allied military traffic for the North African campaign in World War II.

CASABLANCA'S ARCHITECTURE is a happy blend of ancient and modern. Pictured is the impressive City Hall which combines the design forms of old Morocco with modernistic French

CASABLANCA'S ARAB INHABITANTS live mainly in two sections known as New Médina and Old Médina while the city's large European population dwells in the Racine, Bourgogne, Maarif and Mers Sultan districts. Pictured is a courtyard in modern New Médina

THE EQUESTRIAN STATUE of Marshal Lyautey, first resident-general of Morocco, stands in Casablanca's Administrative Square. The Marshal was famed not only for his successful defense of Morocco against Rifi attack but also his successful methods of colonial administration

Johannesburg, South Africa

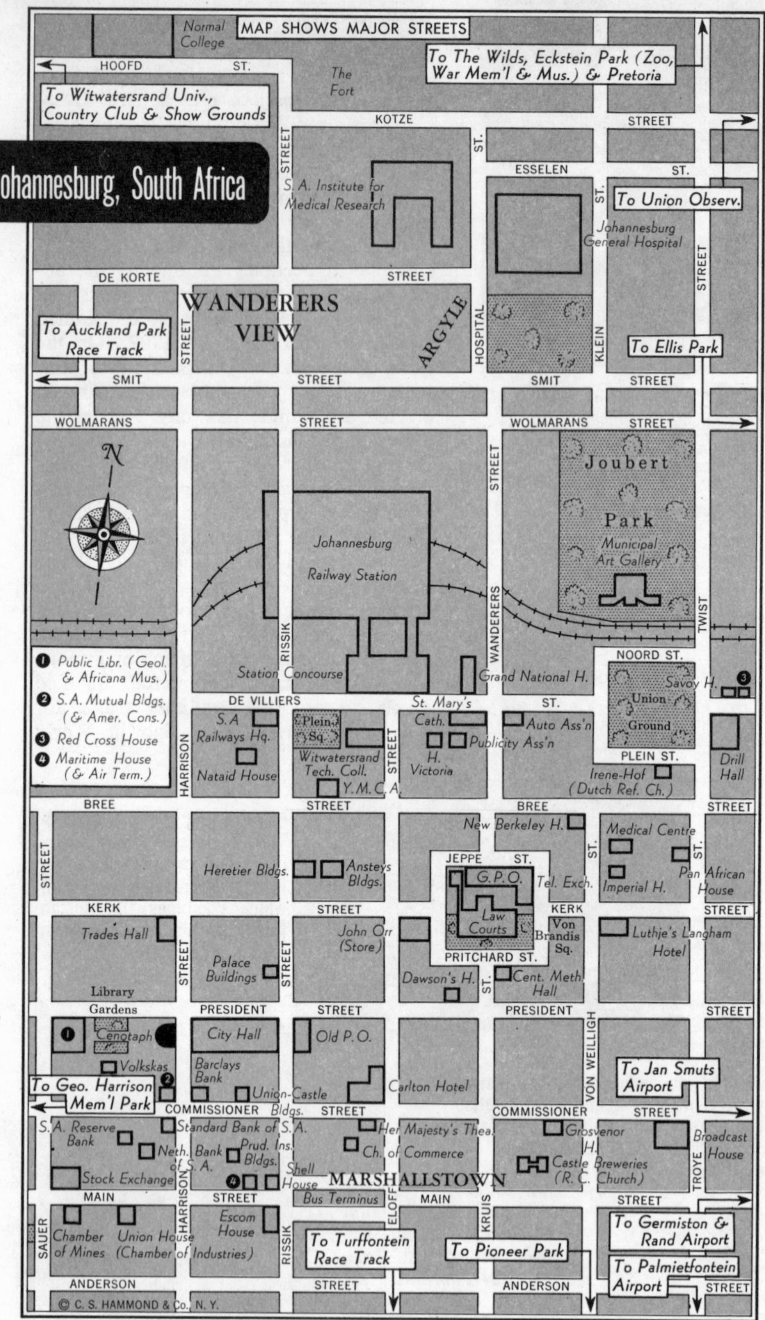

Photos: Union of South Africa, Gov't Information Office

MAIN FEEDER CONVEYOR BELT is delivering ore to a mill from a shaft bin on a Witwatersrand gold mine. In sixty years the Rand mines have yielded fabulous wealth from the golden veins, 8,000 feet below the earth's surface

JOHANNESBURG is a metropolis of massive architecture, great gold mines, many races and customs. Rich and triumphant, the city today is virtually the "powerhouse" of the African continent

JOHANNESBURG. With its foundations literally springing from the world's richest reef of gold-bearing ore, Johannesburg is truly the realization of the ancient dream of Eldorado. The "City of Gold," with the raw newness of its massive buildings etched against the sky, is the largest and wealthiest city in South Africa, yet scarcely sixty years have passed since its beginnings. Many a hardy pioneer still living today can recall the early gold rush era when, as a tiny mining camp with a huddled group of prospectors' huts and its streets mere wagon ruts, Johannesburg attracted fortune-seekers from all parts of the world. The city stands on the high, barren Witwatersrand (Ridge of White Waters) of the South African Transvaal, beneath which lies the fabulous Rand "diggings," which at present yield one third of the world's gold supply. South, east and west of the city rise the steel headgear of mines whose shafts probe to depths of more than 8,000 feet to tap the vast wealth of the golden veins. On every hand the dumps, huge and golden, make Johannesburg unique. Now, recent discoveries of uranium are adding to the city's amazing prosperity. Among the many attractions of this "city of strange contrasts" are the spectacular tribal dances of the native mine workers at the various mine compounds. Also a must for visitors is the Africana Museum containing many relics of the Voortrekkers and the colony's early history.

TOWERING HEADGEAR of gold mines is a familiar sight around the city of Johannesburg. It has been calculated that half of the people of South Africa derive all their income—directly or indirectly—from the gold mining industry

COMMISSIONER STREET, today, with its huge white business blocks, theaters and cinemas, is the throbbing artery of urban life. One of the most cosmopolitan cities in the world, Johannesburg has built up a great entertainment industry

CITIES of ASIA and OCEANIA

Auckland, New Zealand

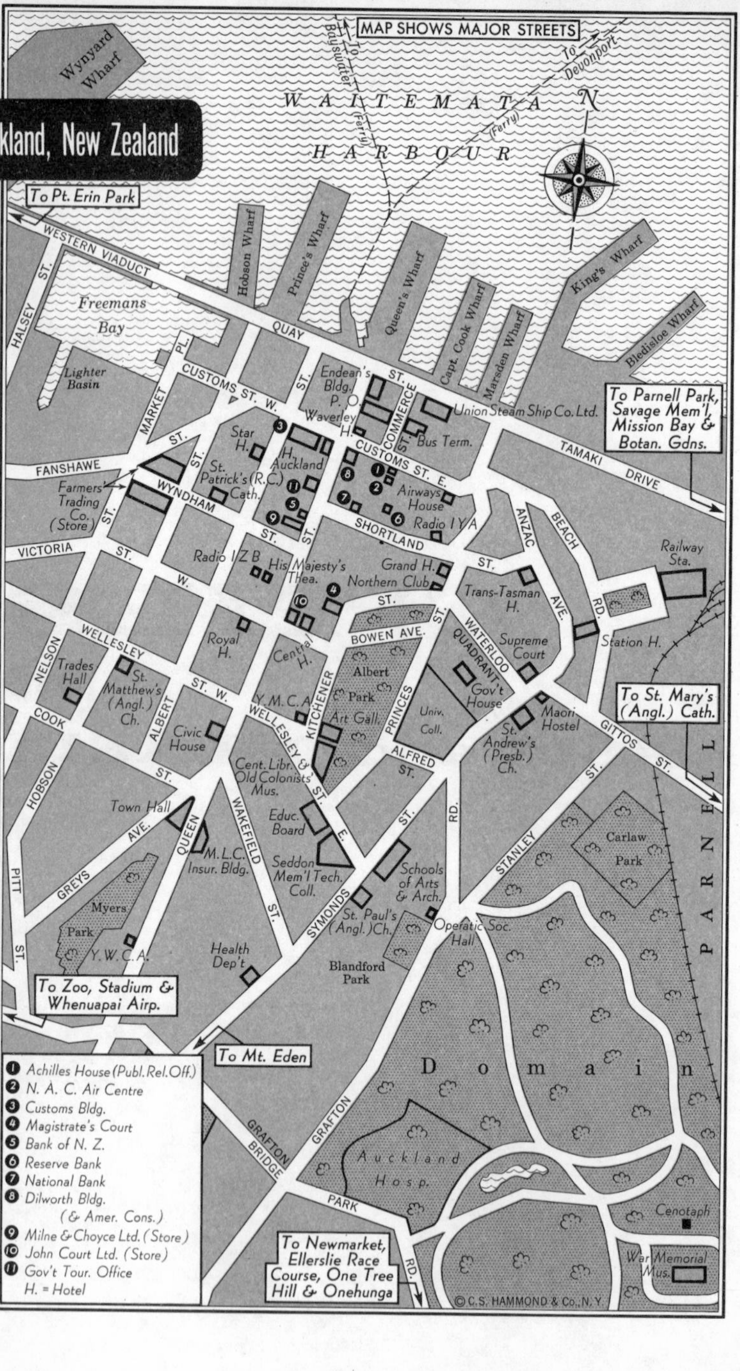

MAP SHOWS MAJOR STREETS

WAITEMATA HARBOUR

To Pt. Erin Park

To Parnell Park, Savage Mem'l, Mission Bay & Botan. Gdns.

To St. Mary's (Angl.) Cath.

To Zoo, Stadium & Whenuapai Airp.

To Mt. Eden

To Newmarket, Ellerslie Race Course, One Tree Hill & Onehunga

1. Achilles House (Publ. Rel. Off.)
2. N. A. C. Air Centre
3. Customs Bldg.
4. Magistrate's Court
5. Bank of N. Z.
6. Reserve Bank
7. National Bank
8. Dilworth Bldg. (& Amer. Cons.)
9. Milne & Choyce Ltd. (Store)
10. John Court Ltd. (Store)
11. Gov't Tour. Office

H. = Hotel

© C.S. HAMMOND & Co., N.Y.

Photos: New Zealand Embassy

QUEEN STREET, main commercial thoroughfare, was formed in the bed of a stream which 100 years ago meandered between scrub-covered slopes to empty in Waitemata Harbour

OVERSEAS VESSELS dock at warves abutting on the main commercial area in Auckland's fine natural harbor, to which the city owes its rapid growth and high position

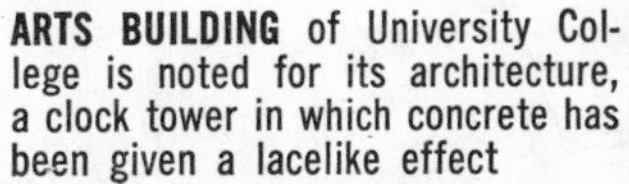

ARTS BUILDING of University College is noted for its architecture, a clock tower in which concrete has been given a lacelike effect

VIEW from a southeastern suburb shows homes of well-to-do suburban dwellers. In the background, dominating the harbor, is the island sentinel Rangitoto, composed entirely of lava, whose summit is a cone inside a broken-down crater

AUCKLAND. Auckland, largest metropolis of New Zealand, is a two-ocean city in the north of the North Island, her eastern flank touching the Pacific, while her western boundary is embraced by the Tasman Sea. A subtropical city, she closely resembles a British provincial town, nevertheless, and Aucklanders still proudly, warmly call themselves British. The city is in an extremely beautiful location, for she is built on hills, many of which are extinct volcanoes, among the world's finest examples of spatter cones. A number of these sixty volcanic hills, once used by the Maoris as forts, are now parks of great beauty, with sheep, or four-legged lawn mowers, grazing serenely on the undulating slopes and summits. In one of these, the Domain, is the fine War Memorial Museum, commemorating those Anzacs who served in both World Wars and containing one of the best existing Maori collections. A sprawling city that has grown like Topsy, Auckland has virtually no apartment buildings and almost everybody lives in one-story bungalows with yellow walls and red roofs. Thus, as you gaze out over the outstretched city from the surrounding hills, before your eyes spreads one vast, bright, scarlet sea.

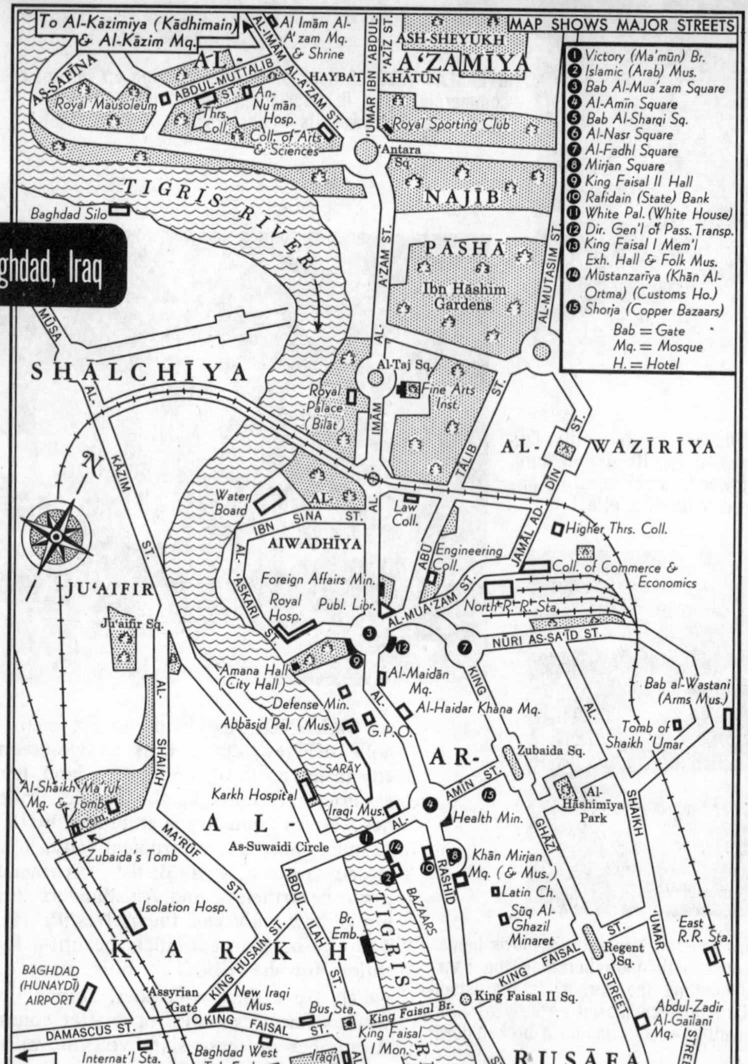

Baghdad, Iraq

MAP SHOWS MAJOR STREETS

1. Victory (Ma'mūn) Br.
2. Islamic (Arab) Mus.
3. Bab Al-Mua'zam Square
4. Al-Amīn Square
5. Bab Al-Sharqi Sq.
6. Al-Nasr Square
7. Al-Fadhl Square
8. Mirjan Square
9. King Faisal II Hall
10. Rafidain (State) Bank
11. White Pal. (White House)
12. Dir. Gen'l of Pass. Transp.
13. King Faisal I Mem'l Exh. Hall & Folk Mus.
14. Mūstanzarīya (Khān Al-Ortma) (Customs Ho.)
15. Shorja (Copper Bazaars)

Bab = Gate
Mq. = Mosque
H. = Hotel

To Al-Kāzimīya (Kādhimain) & Al-Kāzim Mq.
Al Imām Al-A'zam Mq. & Shrine
ASH-SHEYŪKH
AL-A'ZAMĪYA
HAYBAT KHĀTŪN
AS-SAFINA
Royal Mausoleum
ABDUL-MUTTALIB ST.
An-Nu'mān Hosp.
Thrs. Coll.
Coll. of Arts & Sciences
AL-IMĀM AL-A'ZAM ST.
'UMAR IBN 'ABDUL-'AZIZ ST.
Royal Sporting Club
Antara Sq.
TIGRIS RIVER
Baghdad Silo
NAJĪB PĀSHĀ
Ibn Hāshim Gardens
AL-MUTASIM ST.
AL-IMĀM AL-A'ZAM ST.
MŪSA AL-KĀZIM ST.
SHĀLCHĪYA
Al-Taj Sq.
Royal Palace (Bilāt)
Fine Arts Inst.
TALIB ST.
AL-WAZĪRĪYA
JAMĀL AD-DIN ST.
Water Board
AL-IBN SINA ST.
Law Coll.
AIWADHĪYA
Higher Thrs. Coll.
Engineering Coll.
ABU
Coll. of Commerce & Economics
Foreign Affairs Min.
JU'AIFIR
AL-'ASKARI ST.
Royal Hosp.
Publ. Libr.
AL-MUA'ZAM ST.
North R. R. Sta.
Ju'aifir Sq.
NŪRI AS-SA'ĪD ST.
Amana Hall (City Hall)
Al-Maidān Mq.
KING GHĀZI ST.
Defense Min.
Al-Haidar Khāna Mq.
Bab al-Wastani (Arms Mus.)
Abbāsid Pal. (Mus.)
G.P.O.
Tomb of Shaikh 'Umar
AL-SHAIKH MA'RŪF ST.
SARĀY
AR-RUSĀFA
Zubaida Sq.
Al-Shaikh Ma'rūf Mq. & Tomb
Cem.
Karkh Hospital
AMIN ST.
Al-Hāshimīya Park
Iraqi Mus.
Health Min.
AL-RASHID
SHAIKH 'UMAR STREET
AL-KARKH
Zubaida's Tomb
As-Suwaidi Circle
Khān Mirjan Mq. (& Mus.)
Latin Ch.
Isolation Hosp.
ABDUL-ILAH ST.
BAZAARS
Sūq Al-Ghazil Minaret
Br. Emb.
TIGRIS RIVER
East R.R. Sta.
Regent Sq.
KING FAISAL ST.
BAGHDAD (HUNAYDĪ) AIRPORT
Assyrian Gate
KING HUSAIN ST.
New Iraqi Mus.
King Faisal II Sq.
Bus Sta.
Abdul-Zadir Al-Gailānī Mq.
DAMASCUS ST.
KING FAISAL ST.
King Faisal Br.
King Faisal I Mon.
Internat'l Sta.
Baghdad West Tel. Exch.
Iraqi Radio Sta.
RUSĀFA
Mosul R.R. Sta.
West (Basra) R.R. Sta.
St. George Ch.
AL-MANSŪR ST.
Sinbad H.
South Baghdad P.O.
To Ar-Rihāb & Zohūr Palaces & Al-Mansūr
Semiramis H.
Tigris H.
Zia H.
Aviation Sq.
Ghāzī Park
Dir. Gen'l of Survey
KARRĀDAH MARYAM
Bab Al-Sharqi Br.
AL-GHAFIQI ST.
BATTĀWIYIN
Dir. of Nationality & Travel
To New Baghdad & Race Track
To New Parliament Bldg.
To King Faisal I Mq., Amer. Emb. & Ctesiphon
TUNIS ST.
Y.M.C.A.

Photos: Arab Information Center, Royal Consulate General of Iraq

RASHID STREET, one of the old narrow, twisting alleys, is now a heavily traveled main thoroughfare of the growing city

ROYAL MAUSOLEUM, impressive tomb of King Faisal I, first king of Iraq, King Ghazi I and his wife, Allyah, is an outstanding example of the fine tradition of Arab ornament adapted to modern architecture

BAGHDAD. Storied scene of the *Arabian Nights,* Baghdad lies in an extensive desert plain between the ageless waters of the Tigris and Euphrates, within whose coils, tradition says, the Garden of Eden was found and lost. Founded in 762 A.D., she has been from Sumerian times a focal point of desert travel and trade. It was under the Abbasid caliphate and before the thirteenth-century Mongol invasion that the "Abode of Peace" was the center for poets, musicians, philosophers, scientists and literary men and the preserver, during the European Dark Ages, of the treasures of ancient Greece. Little is now visible of this old city, except for the walls on her three sides, some of the citadel, including the partially restored Abbasid Palace, and excellent collections in the Iraqi Museum. At the beginning of this century, Baghdad had shrunk to the dimensions of a small Arab market town of twisting lanes and rickety houses of mud and reeds. With the birth of Iraq, the capital has become one of the world's most rapidly expanding cities — broad, imaginative, with flower-lined boulevards and notable new buildings, like the Opera House, Karkh Hospital and wonderful spacious, well-lighted, modern homes and schools.

BARGAINING is a traditional, beloved Arab art in the bustling bazaars of Baghdad, like this copper bazaar

KHADIMAIN MOSQUE, built by the Shah of Persia in the 16th century and one of the most sacred shrines of the Shiite sect, boasts lovely Persian-style mosaics and glittering golden domes and minarets, the first objects seen by the traveler approaching Baghdad

Bangkok, Thailand

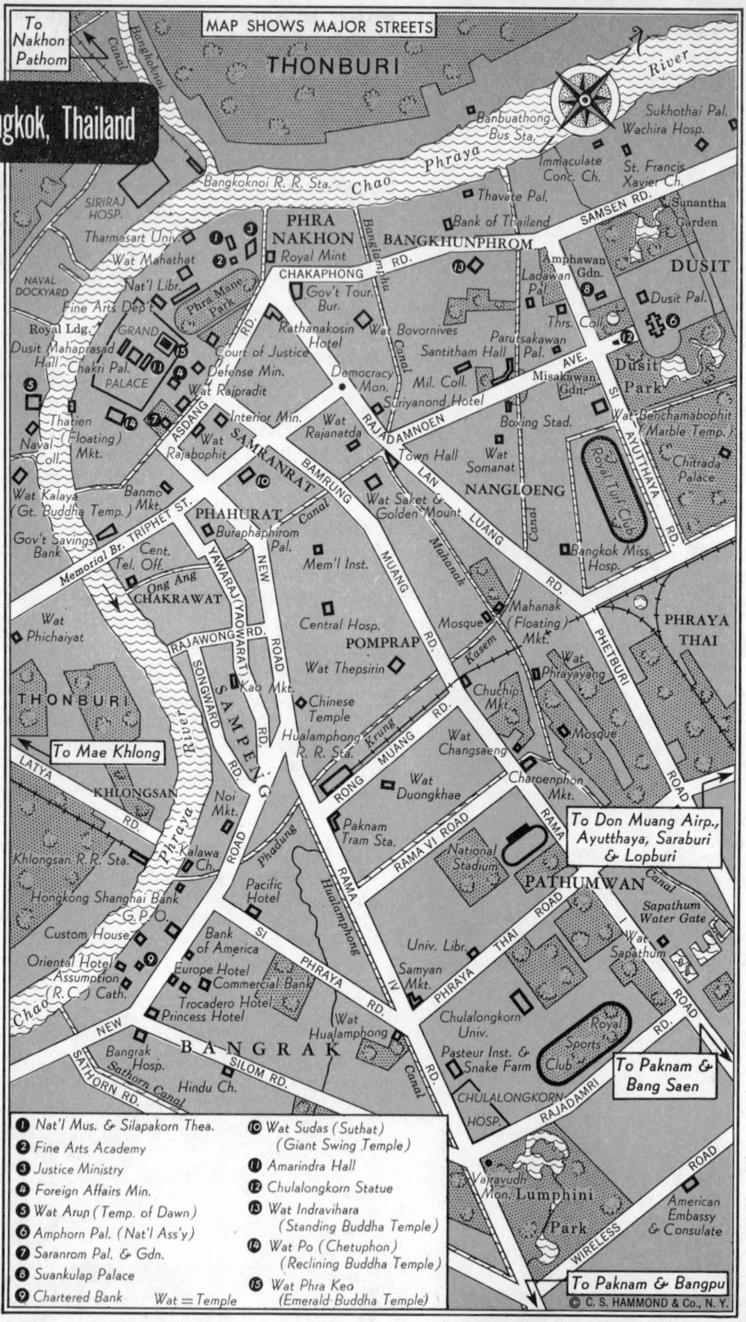

MAP SHOWS MAJOR STREETS

1. Nat'l Mus. & Silapakorn Thea.
2. Fine Arts Academy
3. Justice Ministry
4. Foreign Affairs Min.
5. Wat Arun (Temp. of Dawn)
6. Amphorn Pal. (Nat'l Ass'y)
7. Saranrom Pal. & Gdn.
8. Suankulap Palace
9. Chartered Bank
10. Wat Sudas (Suthat) (Giant Swing Temple)
11. Amarindra Hall
12. Chulalongkorn Statue
13. Wat Indravihara (Standing Buddha Temple)
14. Wat Po (Chetuphon) (Reclining Buddha Temple)
15. Wat Phra Keo (Emerald Buddha Temple)

Wat = Temple

"A CITY OF TEMPLES" is a fitting title for Bangkok. Wherever located, the Thai temple is an eloquent testimony to the great religious devotion of the Thai Buddhist. Pictured is the Sri Mahatat Temple

THE TEMPLE OF DAWN is a famous sanctuary on the right bank of the Chao Phraya River, opposite the Grand Palace. This temple is a famous landmark, its central pagoda towering to a height of 74 meters

BANGKOK (Krung Thep). Bangkok with its network of canals jutting from the Chao Phraya River is sometimes likened to Venice. Until the innovation of motor vehicles these canals or "klongs" served as the city's principal thoroughfares. Even today, despite Bangkok's modern paved streets the klongs carry a heavy volume of water traffic. They are also the site of fabulous "floating markets" where in the early hours of the morning, sampans laden with fish and farm produce gather, offering their varied wares to Bangkok's housewives who move through the colorful maze in their own little boats. Capital of Thailand (Siam), Bangkok lies in the center of the world's greatest rice producing area. This commodity with tin, teak and rubber are the city's exports. Although too shallow to accommodate the larger ocean-going vessels, the harbor of Bangkok nevertheless attracts ships from every corner of the globe. Probably the city's most noted feature is its Buddhist monasteries with their lance-like spires and roofs of gleaming tile or ornately fashioned teakwood. These monasteries, over 400 in number, serve as homes for the yellow-clad Buddhist monks and also as schools, hospitals, clubs, playgrounds and centers of artistic and educational development. Most famous of Bangkok's shrines is the Temple of the Emerald Buddha containing a beautiful collection of art works associated with Thailand's ruling house, and the Emerald Buddha carved from a large piece of the precious green gem.

WORSHIPPERS are dwarfed by these giant figures guarding the Temple of the Emerald Buddha. Apart from its unique distinction as a work of art, the Emerald Buddha is regarded as the palladium of Thailand

Photos: Philip Gendreau, TWA Trans World Airlines

THAILAND'S NATIONAL ASSEMBLY, formerly the Ananta Samakom Throne Hall is an impressive structure of white marble. It is situated at the northern end of Rajadamnern Avenue in the Amporn Garden

BEIRUT. "The devastating discord among nations will only cease to compromise peace when Beryte [Beirut], protecting the right to tranquillity in life, rules in spirit over land and sea, fortifies towns with a bulwark of unalterable and eternally valid laws." The world conflicts referred to in this quotation make it seem quite up-to-date, when actually it is by Nonnus, a Greek writer living about the end of the fourth century A.D. The Phoenicians, who inhabited Lebanon as early as 4000 B.C., were noted as traders, not warriors, and gave to the world the first alphabet, the first principles of architecture and the industry of dyes (in particular, that of purple), transparent glass, timber and metallurgy. The port of modern Beirut is still the Middle East trading axis, and her cultural heritage is as alive today as it was in Roman days, when the Beirut School of Law was the acknowledged authority throughout the empire. Led by the American University of Beirut, the University of St. Joseph, the Lebanese Academy of Fine Arts, with its choir and symphonic orchestra, the National Museum and the National Library, Beirut — probably the area's only capital where illiteracy is almost nonexistent — is the intellectual center of the Middle East.

MODERN BUILDINGS are not unusual in Beirut, since her very old buildings were destroyed over the years by earthquakes or enemy assaults. In fact, because her leadership in trade and culture has increased her contacts with other nations, she is the most westernized of all Middle East towns

SPLENDID BEACHES along the blue-green Mediterranean, like this one at the St. George Club, contribute to Beirut's fame as a fine summer resort

CAMPUS playing fields and tennis courts of the 89-year-old American University of Beirut, largest American institution of learning outside the United States and perhaps the world's most cosmopolitan group of students and faculty

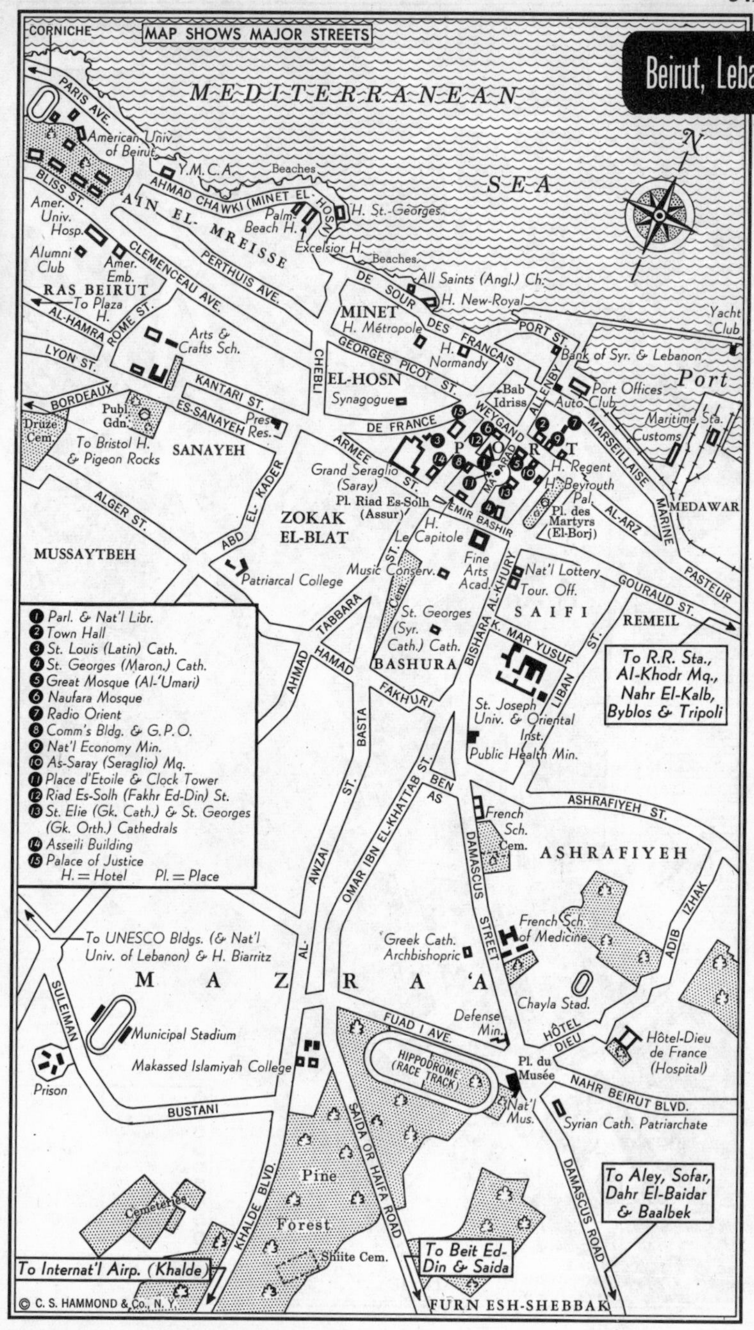

PANORAMA of the clean, attractive buildings of the capital, looking toward the pine-studded slopes of Mt. Lebanon. It is only a few minutes' drive to the cool fastnesses of the ski slopes and mountain resorts

Photos: Philip Gendreau, N. Y., Arab Information Center

Bombay, India

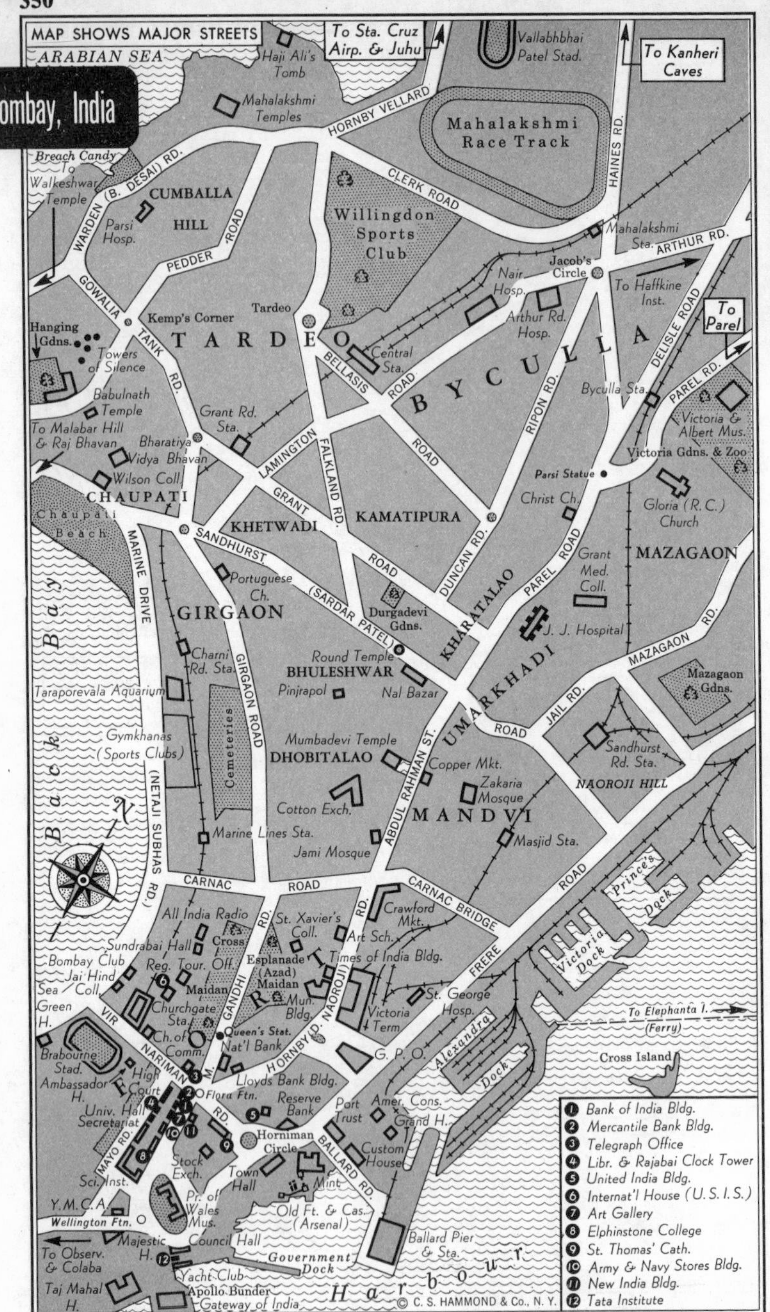
MAP SHOWS MAJOR STREETS
ARABIAN SEA
Haji Ali's Tomb
To Sta. Cruz Airp. & Juhu
Vallabhbhai Patel Stad.
To Kanheri Caves
Mahalakshmi Temples
HORNBY VELLARD
Mahalakshmi Race Track
HAINES RD.
Breach Candy
To Walkeshwar Temple
WARDEN (B. DESAI) RD.
CUMBALLA HILL
Parsi Hosp.
PEDDER ROAD
CLERK ROAD
Willingdon Sports Club
Mahalakshmi Sta.
ARTHUR RD.
Jacob's Circle
Nair Hosp.
To Haffkine Inst.
GOWALIA TANK RD.
Kemp's Corner
Tardeo
TARDEO
Arthur Rd. Hosp.
DELISLE ROAD
To Parel
Hanging Gdns.
Towers of Silence
Central Sta.
BELLASIS ROAD
BYCULLA
Babulnath Temple
Byculla Sta.
PAREL RD.
To Malabar Hill & Raj Bhavan
Grant Rd. Sta.
RIPON RD.
Victoria & Albert Mus.
Bharatiya Vidya Bhavan
LAMINGTON
FALKLAND RD.
ROAD
Victoria Gdns. & Zoo
Wilson Coll.
Parsi Statue
CHAUPATI
Chaupati Beach
GRANT ROAD
Christ Ch.
Gloria (R.C.) Church
KHETWADI
KAMATIPURA
MARINE DRIVE
SANDHURST (SARDAR PATEL) ROAD
DUNCAN RD.
PAREL ROAD
Grant Med. Coll.
MAZAGAON
Portuguese Ch.
KHARATALAO
GIRGAON
Durgadevi Gdns.
J. J. Hospital
Back Bay
Charni Rd. Sta.
Round Temple
UMARKHADI
MAZAGAON RD.
BHULESHWAR
Mazagaon Gdns.
Taraporevala Aquarium
Pinjrapol
Nal Bazar
JAIL RD.
Cemeteries
GIRGAON ROAD
ROAD
Gymkhanas (Sports Clubs)
Mumbadevi Temple
DHOBITALAO
ABDUL RAHMAN ST.
Sandhurst Rd. Sta.
Copper Mkt.
(NETAJI SUBHAS RD.)
Zakaria Mosque
NAOROJI HILL
Cotton Exch.
MANDVI
Marine Lines Sta.
Masjid Sta.
Jami Mosque
ROAD
Prince's Dock
CARNAC ROAD
CARNAC BRIDGE
All India Radio
St. Xavier's Coll.
Crawford Mkt.
Art Sch.
Sundrabai Hall
Cross
Victoria Dock
Bombay Club
Reg. Tour. Off.
Esplanade (Azad) Maidan
Times of India Bldg.
FRERE
Jai Hind Coll.
Sea Green H.
Maidan
GANDHI RD.
Mun. Bldg.
St. George Hosp.
Churchgate Sta.
Victoria Term.
Alexandra Dock
To Elephanta I. (Ferry)
VIR NARIMAN RD.
Queen's Stat.
Ch. of Comm.
Nat'l Bank
HORNBY (D. NAOROJI) RD.
G. P. O.
Brabourne Stad.
Cross Island
High Court
Lloyds Bank Bldg.
Ambassador H.
Flora Ftn.
Reserve Bank
Port Trust
Amer. Cons.
Univ. Hall
Secretariat
Grand H.
Horniman Circle
MAYO RD.
Stock Exch.
Custom House
BALLARD RD.
Sci. Inst.
Town Hall
Mint
Y.M.C.A.
Pr. of Wales Mus.
Wellington Ftn.
Old Ft. & Cas. (Arsenal)
Majestic H.
Council Hall
Ballard Pier & Sta.
To Observ. & Colaba
Government Dock
Yacht Club
Taj Mahal H.
Apollo Bunder
Gateway of India
Harbour
© C. S. HAMMOND & Co., N. Y.
1 Bank of India Bldg.
2 Mercantile Bank Bldg.
3 Telegraph Office
4 Libr. & Rajabai Clock Tower
5 United India Bldg.
6 Internat'l House (U. S. I. S.)
7 Art Gallery
8 Elphinstone College
9 St. Thomas' Cath.
10 Army & Navy Stores Bldg.
11 New India Bldg.
12 Tata Institute

Photos: Philip Gendreau

MALABAR HILL affords a splendid view of Bombay Harbour, the beauty of which is said to rival the harbors of Venice and Rio de Janeiro

CRAWFORD MARKET and the whole network of lanes that surround it is one of the most colorful sections of Bombay. Here shoppers can buy all manner of varied and attractive wares

INDIAN PRINCES' PALACE boasts an ornate façade embellished with iron lace and elaborately carved stonework. Within recent years, dwellings of a more modern and functional architecture have taken their place among buildings whose architecture reflects the florid styles of by-gone days

BOMBAY. Bombay, the "Gateway to India" and the principal city of the western region, provides the traveler coming by sea with the first glimpse of the country. Its beautiful harbor is studded with hilly islands and its palm-fringed shore rises gradually to meet the misty-blue peaks beyond. Besides being India's chief port of entry, Bombay is a modern commercial city, so cosmopolitan in appearance and habits that the visitor feels at home immediately. The city is also an industrial center where throughout the day a constant stream of people flows in and out of its busy textile mills, smart business premises, palatial hotels and streamlined transport. In the evening, the center of interest is the city's splendid promenade by the sea, the Marine Drive, to which sophisticated ladies, elegantly dressed in "saris," lend color and gaiety. Of interest to the visitor are the Hanging Gardens on Malabar Hill which offer a panoramic view of the bay and the imposing buildings of the city below. Also noteworthy is the Parsi Tower of Silence, the Prince of Wales Museum and Art Gallery, the Brabourne Stadium and the seaside resort of Juhu. At Mahalakshmi, Bombay has the best race course in Asia. A good deal of Bombay's local color derives from the mixed nature of its population. Apart from the local inhabitants, there are thousands from other parts of India who come here to make a living. The different customs, languages and even the food eaten can make a fascinating study.

GATEWAY TO INDIA was erected to commemorate the landing of King George V and Queen Mary in 1911. It consists of a central hall with great archways and side halls which can accommodate up to 600 people

Calcutta, India

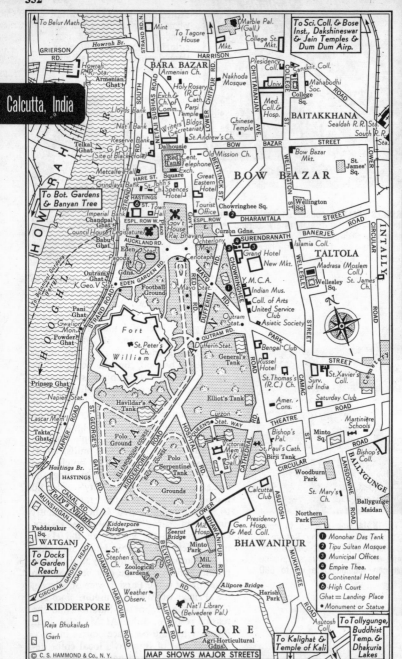

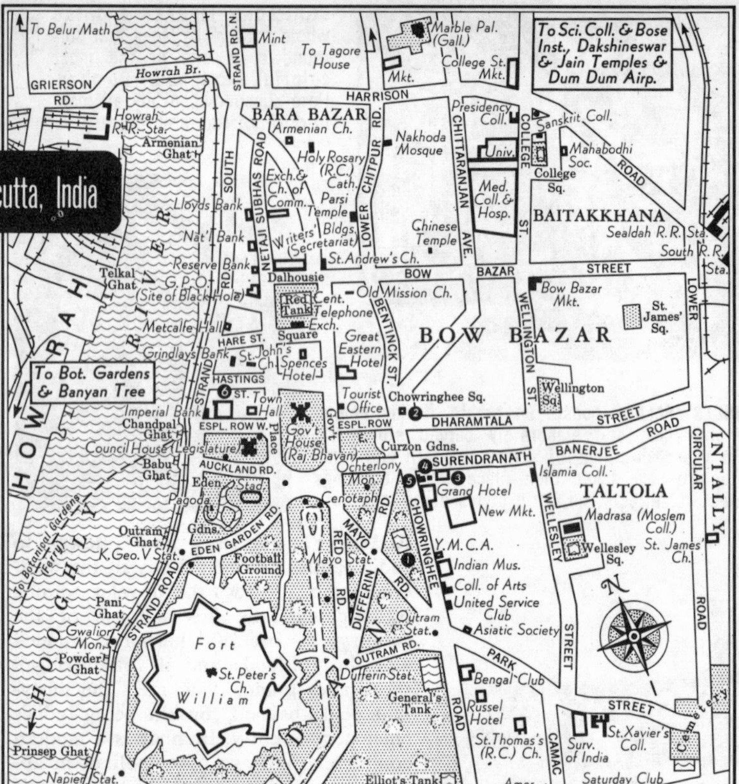

To Belur Math
GRIERSON RD.
Howrah Br.
Howrah R.R. Sta.
STRAND RD. N.
Mint
To Tagore House
Marble Pal. (Gall.)
Mkt.
College St. Mkt.
To Sci. Coll. & Bose Inst., Dakshineswar & Jain Temples & Dum Dum Airp.
HARRISON
BARA BAZAR
Armenian Ch.
Armenian Ghat
Presidency Coll.
Sanskrit Coll.
Nakhoda Mosque
Holy Rosary (R.C.) Cath.
Exch. & Ch. of Comm.
Parsi Temple
Univ.
Mahabodhi Soc.
College Sq.
Med. Coll. & Hosp.
Lloyds Bank
Nat'l Bank
Writers' Bldgs. (Secretariat)
Chinese Temple
BAITAKKHANA
Sealdah R.R. Sta.
South R.R. Sta.
SOUTH
NETAJI SUBHAS ROAD
LOWER CHITPUR RD.
CHITTARANJAN AVE.
COLLEGE ST.
ROAD
St. Andrew's Ch.
Reserve Bank
Telkal Ghat
G.P.O. (Site of Black Hole)
Dalhousie
Red Tank
Cent. Telephone Exch.
Old Mission Ch.
BOW BAZAR STREET
Bow Bazar Mkt.
BOW BAZAR
St. James' Sq.
Metcalfe Hall
HARE ST.
Square
St. John's Ch.
Great Eastern Hotel
Grindlays Bank
Spences Hotel
BENTINCK ST.
WELLINGTON ST.
LOWER CIRCULAR ROAD
To Bot. Gardens & Banyan Tree
HASTINGS ST.
Town Hall
Tourist Office
Chowringhee Sq.
Wellington Sq.
Imperial Bank
Chandpal Ghat
ESPL. ROW W.
ESPL. ROW E.
Govt. Place
DHARAMTALA STREET
Gov't. House (Raj Bhavan)
Curzon Gdns.
BANERJEE ROAD
SURENDRANATH
Council House (Legislature)
Babu Ghat
AUCKLAND RD.
Ochterlony Mon.
Islamia Coll.
TALTOLA
Eden Gdns.
Stad.
Pagoda
Cenotaph
Grand Hotel
New Mkt.
Madrasa (Moslem Coll.)
Outram Ghat
K. Geo. V Stat.
EDEN GARDEN RD.
Football Ground
Mayo Stat.
RED RD.
MAYO RD.
CHOWRINGHEE RD.
Y.M.C.A.
Indian Mus.
WELLESLEY
Wellesley Sq.
St. James' Ch.
INTALLY
HOOGHLY RIVER
HOWRAH
To Botanical Gardens (Ferry)
Pani Ghat
STRAND ROAD
DUFFERIN RD.
Coll. of Arts
United Service Club
Gwalior Mon.
Fort William
St. Peter's Ch.
Outram Stat.
Asiatic Society
WELLESLEY STREET
Powder Ghat
OUTRAM RD.
Dufferin Stat.
PARK STREET
Bengal Club
General's Tank
Russel Hotel
MAIDAN
St. Thomas's (R.C.) Ch.
Surv. of India
St. Xavier's Coll.
Cemetery
Prinsep Ghat
Napier Stat.
Elliot's Tank
Amer. Cons.
CAMAC ST.
Saturday Club
Havildar's Tank
THEATRE ROAD
Lascar Mem'l
NAPIER ROAD
ST. GEORGE'S GATE RD.
Curzon Stat.
QUEEN'S WAY
Martinière Schools
Takta Ghat
Polo Ground
Bishop's Pal.
Minto Sq.
Victoria Mem'l (& Gall.)
St. Paul's Cath.
CATHEDRAL RD.
Birji Tank
Bishop's Coll.
ELLENBOROUGH COURSE
KIDDERPORE ROAD
HOSPITAL RD.
RACE COURSE
Polo
Serpentine Tank
Grounds
CIRCULAR ROAD
Woodburn Park
LANSDOWNE ROAD
BALLYGUNGE
Hastings Br.
HASTINGS
CANAL RD.
Tolly's Nullah
MUNSHIGANJ RD.
Calcutta Club
St. Mary's Ch.
Ballygunge Maidan
Kidderpore Bridge
LOWER BHAWANIPUR RD.
Presidency Gen. Hosp. & Med. Coll.
ASUTOSH MUKHERJEE ROAD
Northern Park
Paddapukur Sq.
WATGANJ
Zeerut Bridge
Mil. Hosp.
Minto Park
BHAWANIPUR
To Docks & Garden Reach
St. Stephen's Ch.
Zoological Gardens
Mil. Cem.
BELVEDERE RD.
CIRCULAR GARDEN REACH ROAD
DIAMOND HARBOUR ROAD
Alipore Bridge
Weather Observ.
Harish Park
Nat'l Library (Belvedere Pal.)
KIDDERPORE
ALIPORE RD.
Raja Bhukailash Garh
ALIPORE
Asutosh Coll.
To Tollygunge, Buddhist Temp. & Dhakuria Lakes
Agri-Horticultural Gdns.
To Kalighat & Temple of Kali

1. Monohar Das Tank
2. Tipu Sultan Mosque
3. Municipal Offices
4. Empire Thea.
5. Continental Hotel
6. High Court

Ghat = Landing Place
• Monument or Statue

MAP SHOWS MAJOR STREETS

VICTORIA MEMORIAL is an enormous yet symmetrical pile of white marble which stands at the southern end of the Maidan. Reputed to be the finest building in Bengal, it is a rich storehouse of Indian history, especially of the Victorian era

GLEAMING MARBLE WALLS of Calcutta's handsome post office are reflected in the tranquil waters of a lake in Dalhousie Square. Because of its many imposing buildings, Calcutta is often referred to as a "city of palaces"

Photos: Screen Traveler from Gendreau, Gov't of India

CALCUTTA PORT is situated on the left bank of the Hooghly River about 80 miles from the river's mouth. The port handles about half of the total seaborne trade of India

AT BELUR MATH, a small village on the opposite banks of the Hooghly River a short distance from Calcutta, is enshrined the memory of Swami Vivekanand. Belur is the headquarters of the Ramakrishna Mission

CALCUTTA. Calcutta is young as Indian cities go. It owes its origin to an agent of the East India Company who, in 1690, chose this site for a British trade settlement. The settlement prospered both because of its excellent trade position and its importance as the headquarters of British administration until 1912. Today, Calcutta is the second largest city in India. As it has grown up in comparatively recent times, Calcutta has none of the ancient historical monuments that characterize Indian towns. There are, however, more relics here of British rule than anywhere else in India, some dating back to the earliest days of the East India Company's settlement. A modern city, Calcutta offers all the amenities a visitor can desire. In Chowringhee, the densely populated city area, are excellent hotels, cinemas, restaurants, and a shopping center capable of meeting every conceivable requirement. The Maidan, a vast park, two miles long by a mile wide, might be called the lungs of this heavily populated area. Here Calcutta citizens spend much of their leisure time. Within the park are beautiful drives, gardens and a section known as the Brigade ground where ceremonial parades are held. The two Dhakuria Lakes, which have a combined frontage of about a mile and are lined with tall palm trees and surrounded by parkland, is another spot popular with the people of Calcutta. Regattas and rowing championships are regularly held on the lakes.

FAMOUS JAIN TEMPLES, four in number, stand on Buddree Das Temple Street. The most important one is dedicated to Shree Shree Sheetalnathji, the 10th of the 24 Jain deities. This temple stands amid one of the prettiest gardens in Calcutta

TWIN MINARETS of Sultan Suleyman Mosque. As the sun sinks behind the mountains and stars begin to sparkle in the clear skies of the Levant, the chant of the muezzin rises from some 250 minarets scattered throughout this holy city, calling the faithful to prayer

DAMASCUS. To the Arab world, Damascus is the cradle of Islamic culture and the symbol of Islamic glory. As the world's oldest continuously inhabited community, she has always been the highway of nations, and in ancient times the great camel caravans found shelter and comfort in her hospitable khans, or caravan inns. The "street called Straight" (Acts IX:11) is where Paul stayed while in the great and flourishing capital of Biblical times. Little changed today, the broad, gloomy, cobblestoned street is lined with *souks,* or bazaars, where shrewd craftsmen sell the exquisite jewelry and gold or silver thread brocades for which the city has been justly distinguished throughout the ages. At the foot of the peaks of Anti-Lebanon, the copious gardens and orchards, watered by the Barada River, the "Golden River" of the Greeks, make Syria's capital a luxuriant oasis in the surrounding forsaken desert and the succulent "Fruits of Damascus" harvested in this fecund valley have a flavor fit for the gods. The glorious fertility and richness in the midst of desolation is said to have caused the Prophet Mohammed to decline to enter this garden city, explaining that no man is entitled to enter paradise twice.

THE BEAUTIFUL GARDEN SPOT on the extensive green plain over which the numerous streams of the Barada spread, bestowing life, greenness, abundance and prosperity, is the great oasis of Damascus

BAB CHARKI, the Eastern Gate to the Old City, was built by the Romans and leads to the street called Straight. Near this gate are made many of the famous Damascene silk brocades, inlaid arabesque furniture and articles of copper and brass

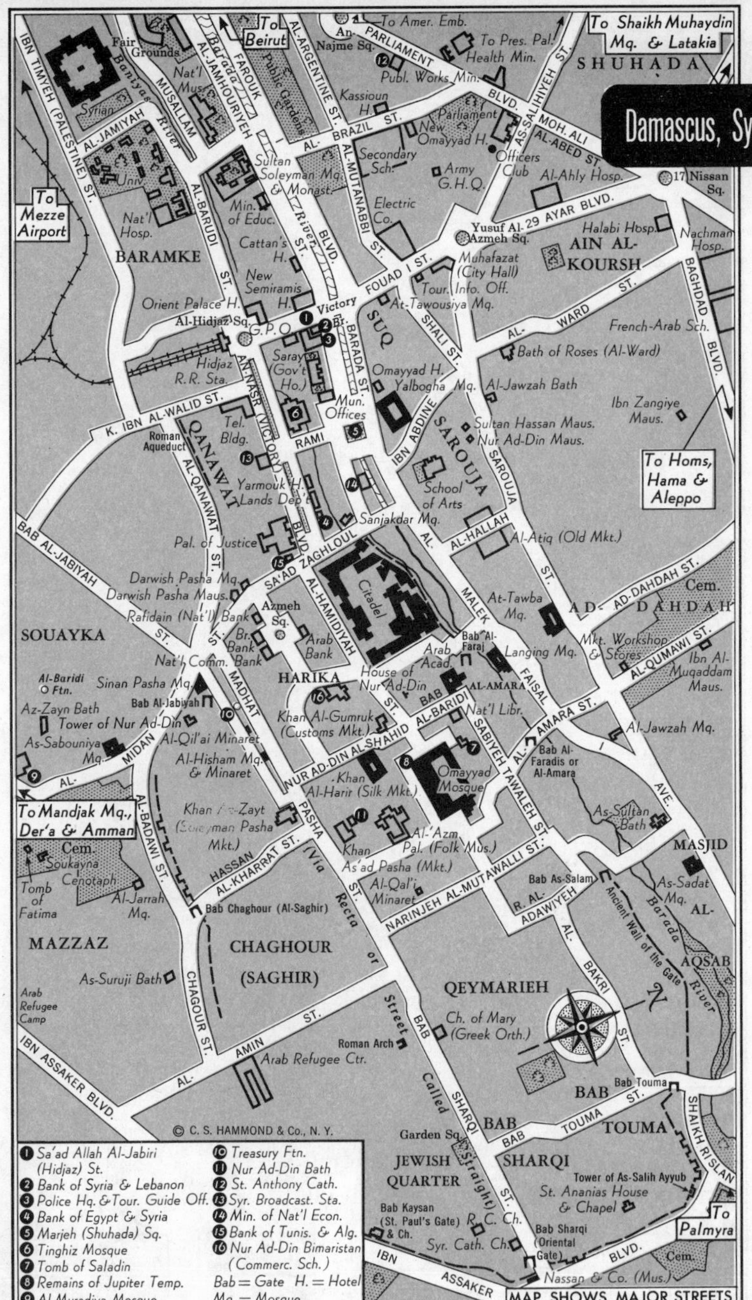

EL NASR, or Victory, Boulevard gives a small glimpse of the community's ambitious plan to give its profile a new look while preserving the graciousness of the old

Photos: Philip Gendreau, N. Y., Arab Information Center

Djakarta, Indonesia

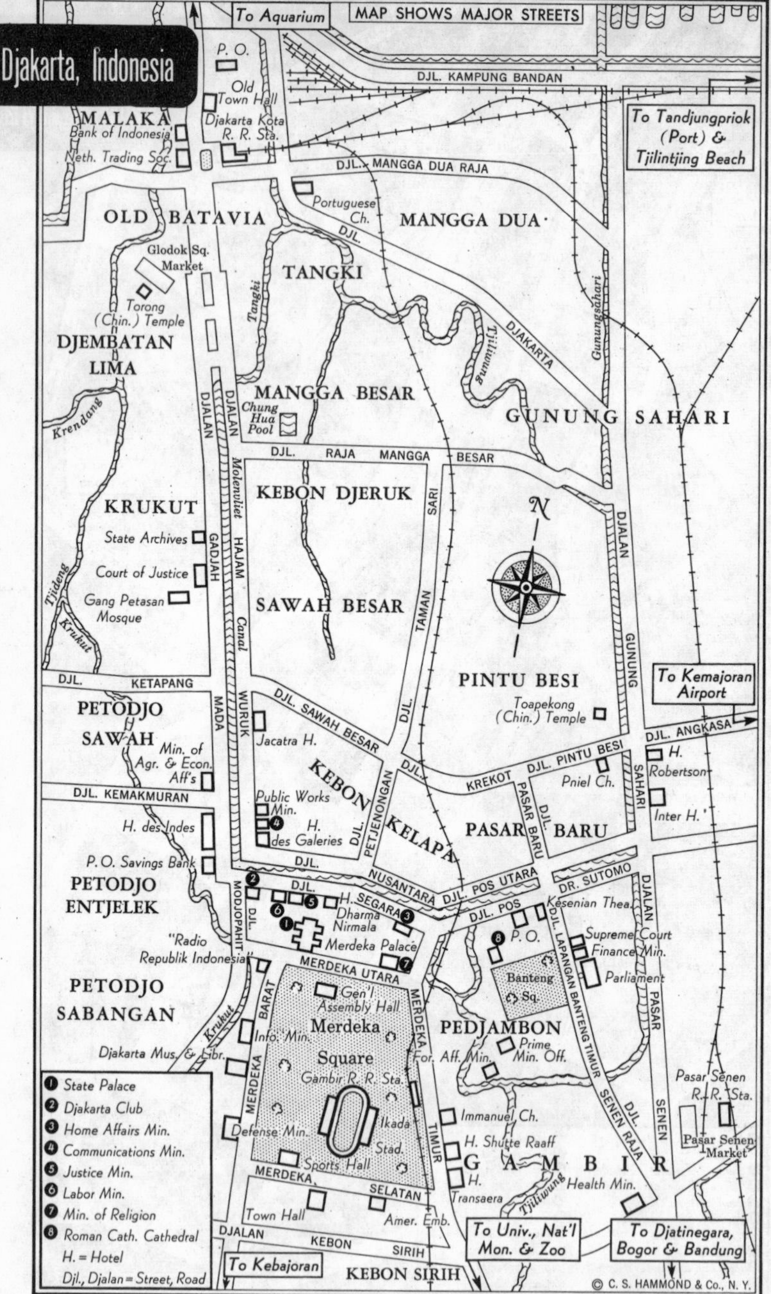

To Aquarium
MAP SHOWS MAJOR STREETS
P. O.
Old Town Hall
MALAKA
Bank of Indonesia
Neth. Trading Soc.
Djakarta Kota R. R. Sta.
DJL. KAMPUNG BANDAN
To Tandjungpriok (Port) & Tjilintjing Beach
DJL. MANGGA DUA RAJA
Portuguese Ch.
OLD BATAVIA
MANGGA DUA
DJL.
Glodok Sq. Market
TANGKI
Torong (Chin.) Temple
Tangki
DJEMBATAN LIMA
DJAKARTA
Gunungsahari
Tjiliwung
Krendang
MANGGA BESAR
Chung Hua Pool
GUNUNG SAHARI
DJALAN
DJALAN
Molenvliet
DJL. RAJA MANGGA BESAR
KEBON DJERUK
SARI
KRUKUT
State Archives
GADJAH
HAJAM
Court of Justice
Gang Petasan Mosque
Canal
SAWAH BESAR
TAMAN
DJALAN
GUNUNG
Tjideng
Krukut
PINTU BESI
To Kemajoran Airport
DJL. KETAPANG
PETODJO SAWAH
MADA
WURUK
DJL. SAWAH BESAR
DJL.
Toapekong (Chin.) Temple
DJL. ANGKASA
Jacatra H.
Min. of Agr. & Econ. Aff's
KEBON KELAPA
DJL. PINTU BESI
H. Robertson
DJL. KEMAKMURAN
KREKOT
PASAR BARU
DJL.
Pniel Ch.
SAHARI
Public Works Min.
H. des Galeries
DJL.
PETJENONGAN
Inter H.
H. des Indes
PASAR BARU
P.O. Savings Bank
DJL.
NUSANTARA
DJL. POS UTARA
DR. SUTOMO
PETODJO ENTJELEK
MODJOPAHIT
DJL.
DJL.
H.
SEGARA
Dharma Nirmala
DJL. POS
Kesenian Thea.
DJALAN
Merdeka Palace
P. O.
DJL. LAPANGAN BANTENG TIMUR
Supreme Court
Finance Min.
"Radio Republik Indonesia"
MERDEKA UTARA
Parliament
Banteng Sq.
PETODJO SABANGAN
BARAT
Gen'l Assembly Hall
MERDEKA
Krukut
Merdeka Square
PEDJAMBON
PASAR
Info. Min.
Djakarta Mus. & Libr.
For. Aff. Min.
Prime Min. Off.
Gambir R. R. Sta.
SENEN RAJA
DJL.
Pasar Senen R. R. Sta.
MERDEKA
Defense Min.
Ikada Stad.
Immanuel Ch.
SENEN
TIMUR
H. Shutte Raaff
Pasar Senen Market
Sports Hall
G A M B I R
H. Transaera
Health Min.
MERDEKA SELATAN
Tjiliwung
Town Hall
Amer. Emb.
DJALAN KEBON SIRIH
To Univ., Nat'l Mon. & Zoo
To Djatinegara, Bogor & Bandung
To Kebajoran
KEBON SIRIH
1 State Palace
2 Djakarta Club
3 Home Affairs Min.
4 Communications Min.
5 Justice Min.
6 Labor Min.
7 Min. of Religion
8 Roman Cath. Cathedral
H. = Hotel
Djl., Djalan = Street, Road
© C. S. HAMMOND & Co., N. Y.

Photos: Indonesian Information Office.

NEW HOUSES are constantly being erected in the suburbs to provide accommodations for the ever-increasing population of the capital.

RAILROAD STATION provides terminal facilities for twelve tracks coming into Djakarta. To the right on the same square is the Netherlands Trading Society and to the left the oblong Bank of Indonesia.

AT A RAILWAY CROSSING, both horse-drawn, two-wheeled carts and burly trucks wait for the passage of the spanking-new electric trains.

DJAKARTA. In Djakarta coconut palms are common, lovely dark-skinned women are found and the spellbinding moon shines warmly in a tropical sky. But much more is found, too, in this city of Indonesia on the bewitching island of Java. As capital of one of the youngest nations, chief city of the former Dutch colony and pre-colonial port, she appears as an unusual Low-Country village set on a lava island, a raucous, newly awakened, Asiatic town of expectant vitality trying to overcome the humiliations of the past. Here then is a kaleidoscope of contrasts. Streamlined cars line up in traffic jams. Someone gives a *slametan* party in celebration of his baby's first footfall upon soil, complete with old traditions and symbolism whose meaning stretches far back into antiquity. Hungry office workers lick ice-cream cones. Peddlers roam from door to door, bargaining loudly over every sale. Girls wearing cosmetics and "new look" dresses walk down the streets. People carry market purchases in baskets slung to the back or on shoulder poles. Diamond-paned, shuttered, gabled houses overlook peaceful Dutch canals. And betjaks, the tricycle-taxis, are decorated with spotlessly clean feather dusters and padded, brightly covered, leather seats.

BANTENG SQUARE has fronting on it—the white, columned building in the background with a fountain before its entrance—the building of Parliament, once a club for officers of the Dutch army. Next to it is the Ministry of Finance.

A NARROW STREET in Hong Kong's native quarter is lined by tiny tenement-topped shops between which flows a stream of jinrikishas, street vendors and Chinese dressed in their colorful native·garb

QUEEN'S ROAD is the main thoroughfare of Hong Kong. The broad street is lined with modern commercial establishments, fine hotels, restaurants and shops

Photos: Screen Traveler, from Gendreau

HONG KONG. Although bearing the official name Victoria, this renowned port is better known by the misnomer Hong Kong, the name of the British Crown Colony of which it is the administrative headquarters. Crowded into a narrow strip on the north shore of Hong Kong Island, it is only a mile from the Chinese mainland and is strategically situated for trade with that country. Hong Kong's island setting is one of the loveliest in the southern seas while its latitude gives it a climate much like that of Hawaii. Silhouetted against a cloud-capped mountain wall, its skyline is a unique mixture of ancient Eastern and modern Western architecture. Buildings, seemingly piled one atop the other, climb to precarious heights on Victoria Peak while others overflow onto land reclaimed from the fringes of its harbor. The narrow streets, the little shops, the docks and crowded quays are a teeming hodge-podge of humanity drawn from the corners of the earth. Bustling with activity, the harbor is a world within itself, pulsing with a never-ending flow of commerce that is the life blood of Hong Kong. Originally founded as a safe base from which opium could be smuggled into China, the city has now risen through legitimate trade to become one of the world's greatest seaports where the twain of Orient and Occident meet and merge in a kaleidoscopic scene of color and contrast.

20th CENTURY SKYSCRAPERS thrust their steel and concrete shafts above Hong Kong, a city whose skyline is a unique blend of ancient eastern and modern western architecture. Pictured is the tower of the Bank of East Asia, one of Hong Kong's tallest buildings.

JUNKS AND SAMPANS serve to carry goods between Kowloon on the Chinese mainland and Hong Kong Island. These craft also serve as homes for a large portion of Hong Kong's Chinese population. This strange community has its own floating shops and its own set of customs

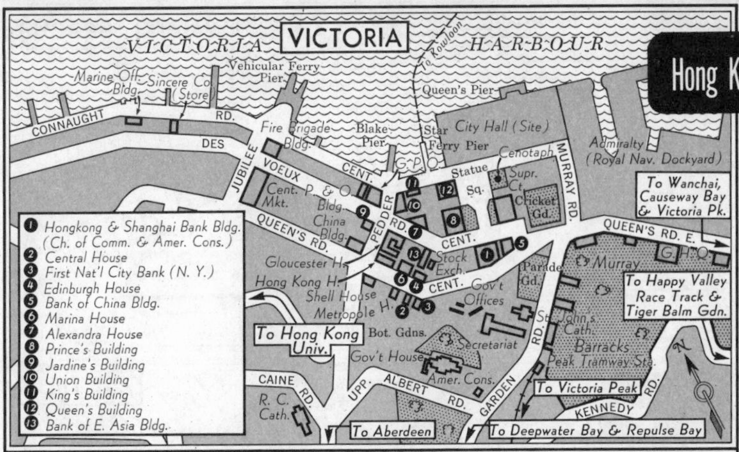

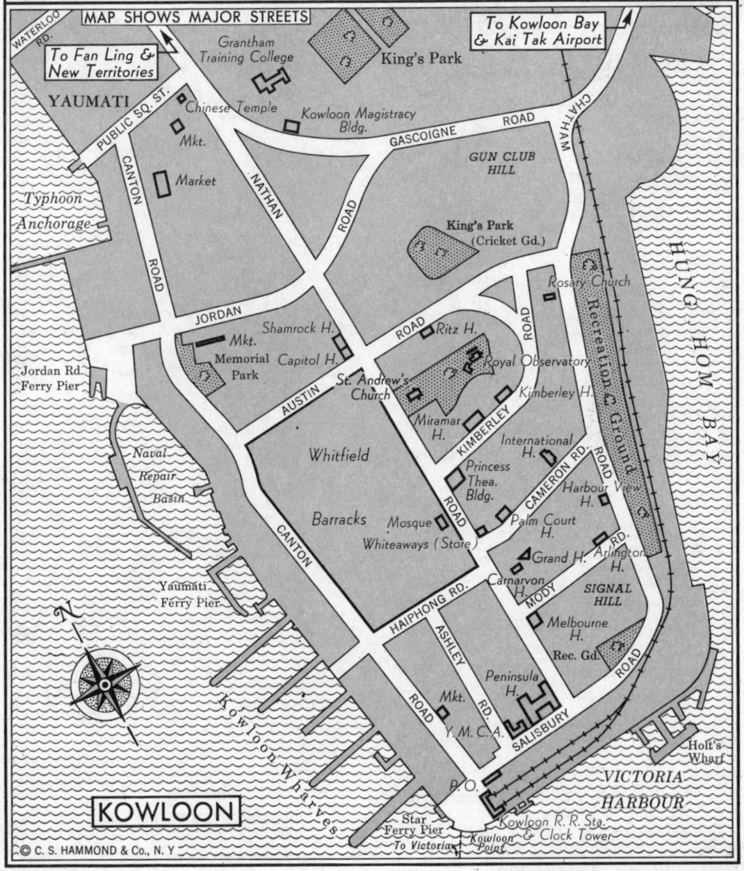

VICTORIA

VICTORIA HARBOUR

1. Hongkong & Shanghai Bank Bldg. (Ch. of Comm. & Amer. Cons.)
2. Central House
3. First Nat'l City Bank (N. Y.)
4. Edinburgh House
5. Bank of China Bldg.
6. Marina House
7. Alexandra House
8. Prince's Building
9. Jardine's Building
10. Union Building
11. King's Building
12. Queen's Building
13. Bank of E. Asia Bldg.

To Kowloon · Vehicular Ferry Pier · Marine Off. Bldg. · Sincere Co. (Store) · Queen's Pier · Connaught Rd. · Des Voeux Rd. Cent. · Jubilee · Fire Brigade Bldg. · Blake Pier · Star Ferry Pier · City Hall (Site) · G. P. O. · Cenotaph · Statue Sq. · Supr. Ct. · Cricket Gd. · Murray Rd. · Admiralty (Royal Nav. Dockyard) · To Wanchai, Causeway Bay & Victoria Pk. · Cent. Mkt. · P. & O. Bldg. · China Bldg. · Pedder Rd. · Queen's Rd. Cent. · Queen's Rd. E. · G. H. Q. · Gloucester H. · Hong Kong H. · Shell House · Metropole H. · Stock Exch. · Gov't Offices · Parade Gd. · Murray Barracks · To Happy Valley Race Track & Tiger Balm Gdn. · St. John's Cath. · Peak Tramway Sta. · To Hong Kong Univ. · Bot. Gdns. · Secretariat · Gov't House · Amer. Cons. · Caine Rd. · R. C. Cath. · Upr. Albert Rd. · Garden Rd. · To Victoria Peak · Kennedy Rd. · To Aberdeen · To Deepwater Bay & Repulse Bay

KOWLOON

MAP SHOWS MAJOR STREETS

Waterloo Rd. · To Fan Ling & New Territories · Grantham Training College · King's Park · To Kowloon Bay & Kai Tak Airport · Yaumati · Public Sq. St. · Chinese Temple · Kowloon Magistracy Bldg. · Gascoigne Road · Chatham · Mkt. · Market · Canton Road · Nathan Road · Gun Club Hill · Typhoon Anchorage · King's Park (Cricket Gd.) · Hung Hom Bay · Rosary Church · Recreation Ground · Jordan Road · Shamrock H. · Ritz H. · Mkt. · Memorial Park · Capitol H. · Royal Observatory · Jordan Rd. Ferry Pier · Austin Road · St. Andrew's Church · Kimberley H. · Miramar H. · Kimberley Road · International H. · Naval Repair Basin · Whitfield Barracks · Princess Thea. Bldg. · Cameron Rd. · Harbour View H. · Mosque · Whiteaways (Store) · Palm Court H. · Grand H. · Arlington H. · Carnarvon H. · Signal Hill · Yaumati Ferry Pier · Haiphong Rd. · Mody Rd. · Ashley Rd. · Melbourne H. · Rec. Gd. · Kowloon Wharves · Peninsula H. · Mkt. · Y. M. C. A. · Salisbury Road · Holt's Wharf · P. O. · Victoria Harbour · Star Ferry Pier · To Victoria · Kowloon Point · Kowloon R. R. Sta. & Clock Tower

VICTORIA PEAK rises to a height of 1,823 feet, forming a splendid backdrop for the city of Hong Kong. Many fine homes stand on the mountain's heights or nestle on its wooded slopes. Victoria Peak is a popular resort during the warm summer months

Honolulu, Hawaii

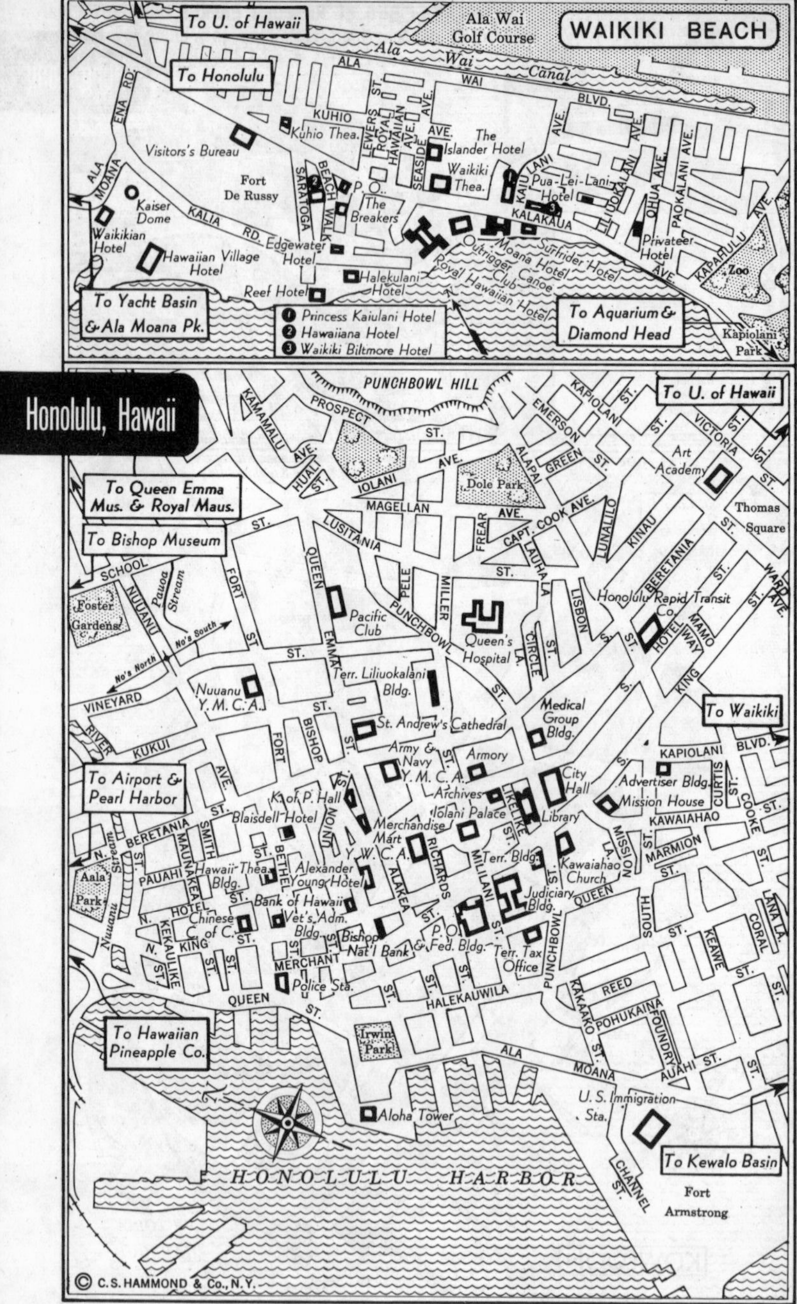

Photos: Hawaii Visitors Bureau, Hawaiian Pineapple Co.

KAWAIAHAO CHURCH, built more than a century ago, with coral from Hawaiian waters and lumber brought from New England around Cape Horn in clipper ships, is known as the Westminster Abbey of Hawaii

IOLANI ("Bird of Heaven") PALACE, only royal palace on American soil, was the home of Hawaii's old-time rulers and is now the government seat of the territory.

STATUE of King Kamehameha I, the Great, in front of the Judiciary Building, honors the "Napoleon of the Pacific," who founded the united Hawaiian kingdom

HONOLULU. Beaches secret in the palm shadows of tropic night, warm sunshine tempered by cooling trade winds—this is Honolulu, city of inspiring loveliness, incomparable scenery and majestic spectacles. Here is world-famous Waikiki Beach, where ancient outrigger canoes landed and royalty enjoyed surfing under the watchful eyes of the crouching lion of Diamond Head, the island's celebrated landmark. In this land of festivity, holidays are climaxed by the *luau,* or typical Hawaiian feast. Pigs roasted in the *imu* (underground oven), with sweet potatoes and fish wrapped in ti-leaf parchment, are served with coconut pudding, fresh pineapple, shellfish and other exotic dishes. Meanwhile, the diners are entertained by dark-haired, smiling girls dancing the hula, one of the most graceful and expressive dances in the world, every movement of the body speaking of joy or sadness, of a great love or the death of a mighty chief. An enchanting city of joy and romance, Honolulu is bright with rich purple orchids, brilliant red Chinese or rosy coral hibiscus, blooming in gay, colorful medley or worn by island women tucked in their hair and strung in fragrant leis around their necks.

BISHOP STREET—big business with a tropical look—is headquarters of plantation, shipping, import-export, banking and merchandising interests

PACKERS in the world's largest fruit cannery carefully sort pineapple slices into cans. The pineapple industry is second only to sugar in the territory

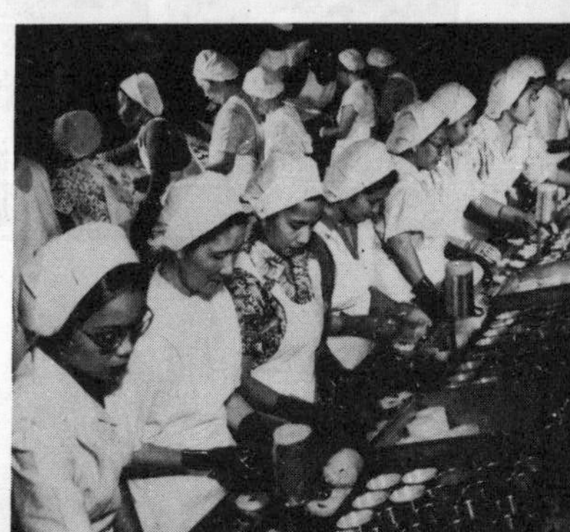

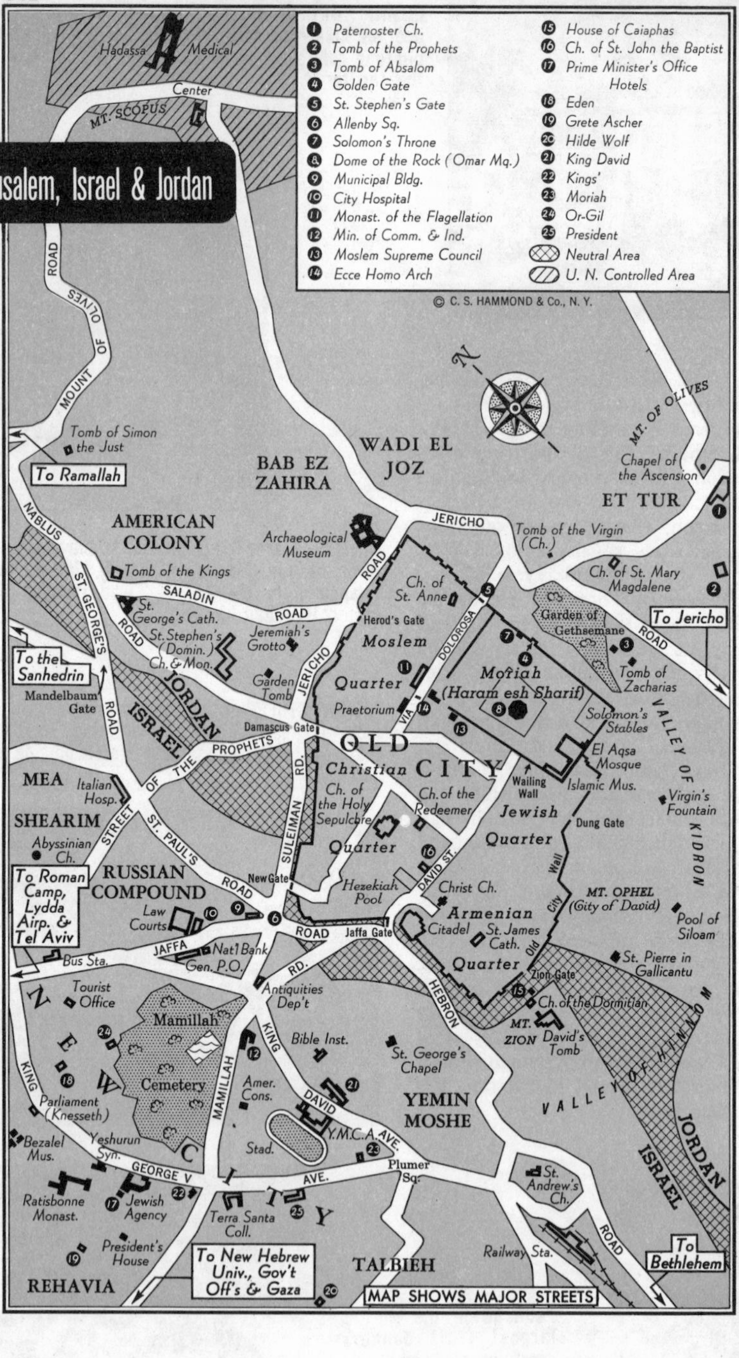

Jerusalem, Israel & Jordan

1. Paternoster Ch.
2. Tomb of the Prophets
3. Tomb of Absalom
4. Golden Gate
5. St. Stephen's Gate
6. Allenby Sq.
7. Solomon's Throne
8. Dome of the Rock (Omar Mq.)
9. Municipal Bldg.
10. City Hospital
11. Monast. of the Flagellation
12. Min. of Comm. & Ind.
13. Moslem Supreme Council
14. Ecce Homo Arch
15. House of Caiaphas
16. Ch. of St. John the Baptist
17. Prime Minister's Office

Hotels

18. Eden
19. Grete Ascher
20. Hilde Wolf
21. King David
22. Kings'
23. Moriah
24. Or-Gil
25. President

Neutral Area
U. N. Controlled Area

MAP SHOWS MAJOR STREETS

Photos: Oriental Institute, University of Chicago, TWA—Trans World Airlines, Israel Gov't Tourist Office

DOME OF THE ROCK, the 7th-century "Noble Sanctuary" of the Moslems, is located where Solomon erected his magnificent, rich Temple

PANORAMIC VIEW shows Mount Zion—hallowed ground to Christians, Jews and Moslems alike—rising above the homes and gardens of modern Jerusalem

JERUSALEM. Throughout three millenia of history, Jerusalem the Eternal, city of David, in the Judean Hills has been revered in the hearts and minds of men. Within her precincts were nurtured the world's greatest monotheistic religions and her ancient stones have formed a backdrop to some of the greatest dramas on the stage of history. The Holy City of the Jews — site of Solomon's Temple and the Wailing Wall — and Christians alike — scene of much of Jesus' ministry, his death, burial and resurrection — she is also venerated by the Moslems as next in holiness to Mecca and Medina. She envelopes such noble shrines as Mount Zion with the Cenacle, probably the scene of the Last Supper, and the traditional Tomb of David; Sanhedria, rock-hewn catacombs where the Sanhedrin, high priests of ancient Israel, were buried; the Mount of Olives; Romena, camp of the Roman Tenth Legion, and the Dome of the Rock, or Mosque of Omar. Three thousand years old and still a beautiful city, Jerusalem's charm lies not only in her regality, her Biblical surroundings, her rose-pink stone buildings and her human kaleidoscope, but in her atmosphere of holy serenity.

TOWER of the Church of the Dormition, marking the traditional site of the death of Mary, adjoins the Cenacle on Mount Zion

TOWER OF DAVID, near the Jaffa Gate, in the modern Citadel, is really the tower Phaselus, built by Herod the Great as part of his palace, residence of Pontious Pilate at the time of the crucifixion of Jesus

Karachi, Pakistan

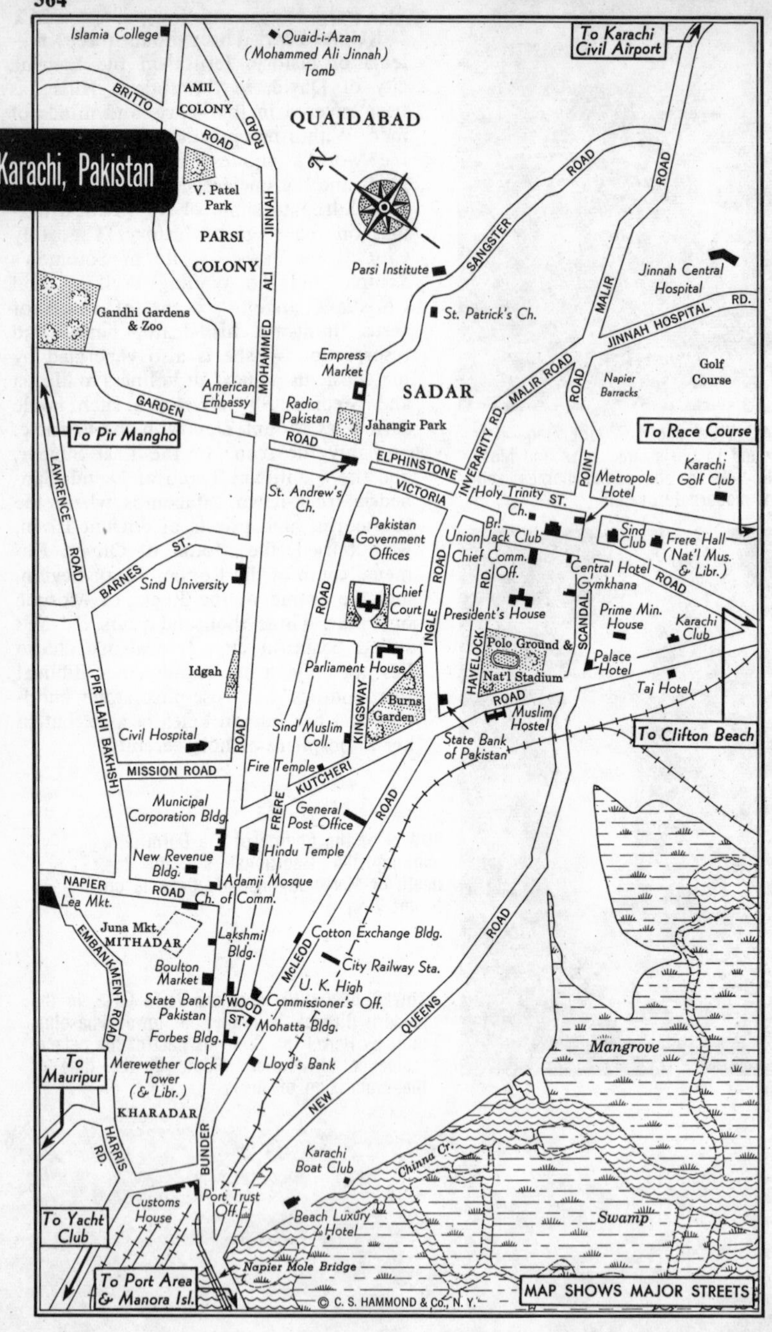

CLOTH MARKET BAZAAR, one of the tantalizing bazaars prevalent throughout the city, where brass and silver-engraved articles, embroideries, textiles, tapestries and carpets may be purchased, is a colorful reminder of ancient Karachi

Photos: Consulate General of Pakistan, New York.

GLEAMING FRERE HALL, across the street from the residence of the United States ambassador, houses a library and the National Museum

KARACHI. "From a fishing village to a metropolis" — that is the story of Karachi. Since selected in 1947 as capital of the new state of Pakistan, she has doubled her size and more. And only three centuries ago, when known as Kalachi, "the land of the sand dunes," she was just a small fishing port with a long history, including identification as Alexander the Great's Haven, the Korokula of the Greek travelers and the site where the first Moslem invaders landed on this subcontinent. Now a clean, thriving trading center, cooled by a brisk sea breeze, her picturesque past and bright future are both reflected in the donkey and camel carts proceeding side by side with high-powered cars and modern buildings like the Cotton Exhange bordering the same streets as the narrow, crowded, stall bazaars. Too, the dedicated crowds paying homage at the tomb of Mohammed Ali Jinnah, founder and first governor-general of Pakistan, are as large as those attending the classic Quaid-e-Azam's Gold Cup race. And the Mithadar (Sweet Water) and Kharadar (Salt Water) Gates still remain from the old wood and mud fort, while the young Pakistani parliament conducts its weighty discussions in English.

FAMOUS BUNDER ROAD, the city's longest road and biggest and busiest shopping district, showing the fine Municipal Corporation Building, representative of new local architecture.

MEREWETHER TOWER, a busy center of town, proudly stands in a contrasting setting of donkey, bullock and handcarts, automobiles and buses

Manila, Philippine Is.

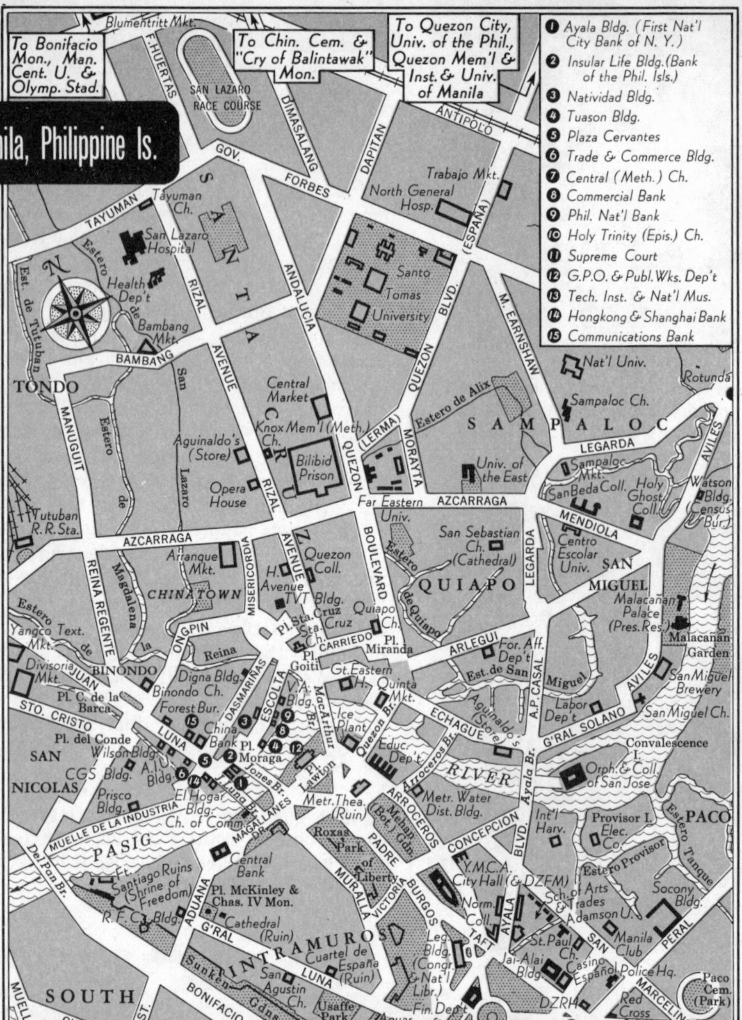

To Bonifacio Mon., Man. Cent. U. & Olymp. Stad.

To Chin. Cem. & "Cry of Balintawak" Mon.

To Quezon City, Univ. of the Phil., Quezon Mem'l & Inst. & Univ. of Manila

1. Ayala Bldg. (First Nat'l City Bank of N. Y.)
2. Insular Life Bldg. (Bank of the Phil. Isls.)
3. Natividad Bldg.
4. Tuason Bldg.
5. Plaza Cervantes
6. Trade & Commerce Bldg.
7. Central (Meth.) Ch.
8. Commercial Bank
9. Phil. Nat'l Bank
10. Holy Trinity (Epis.) Ch.
11. Supreme Court
12. G.P.O. & Publ. Wks. Dep't
13. Tech. Inst. & Nat'l Mus.
14. Hongkong & Shanghai Bank
15. Communications Bank

To Yacht Club, Ft. San Antonio Abad & Internat'l Airport (Parañaque)

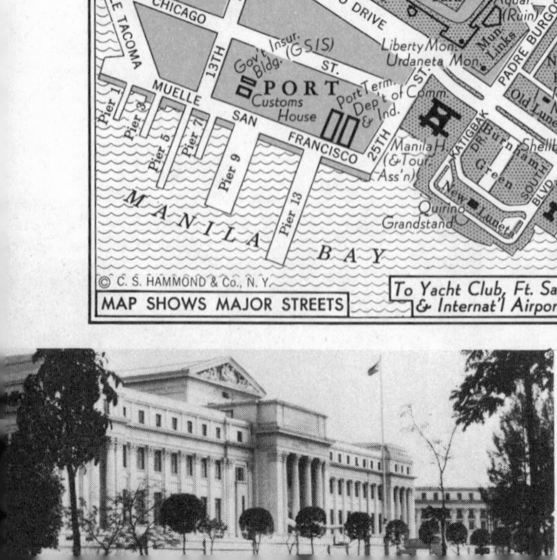

MAP SHOWS MAJOR STREETS

THE PHILIPPINES' LEGISLATURE meets in this handsome building. Although Quezon City is now the official capital of the Republic, most of the government buildings are located in Manila.

HORSE DRAWN VEHICLES are a familiar sight in the Tondo district of Manila. This semi-slum area is inhabited mainly by native workers

MANILA'S NATIVE BAZAARS are noisy, colorful and crowded with bargain hunters

MANILA. With its background deeply rooted in Western civilization, Manila is an Occidental city in an Oriental setting. Manila's streets are lined by modern concrete and steel structures and with its many uniquely Western features it more closely resembles an American city than do the other cities of the Philippines. On the western coast of Luzon, largest of the Islands, the city spreads outward from both banks of the Pasig River at a point where the river empties into Manila Bay. A tiny fishing village until the arrival of the Spaniards in 1571, Manila, with one of the world's finest land-locked harbors, soon became a leading Oriental port. The University of Santo Tomas, twenty-five years older than Harvard, played a large part in the city's growth as cultural and educational center of the Islands. The original inner town, known as the Intramuros, was a relic of its 400 years of Spanish rule. Once a veritable museum of Spanish architecture, little of the Intramuros remains intact today. Demolished and burned by the retreating Japanese when American forces liberated Manila in 1945, only the massive walls that once encircled it still stand. After Admiral Dewey's destruction of the Spanish fleet in 1898, Manila as well as the Philippines came under United States protection. During this period the fortifications on Corregidor, which guard the entrance to Manila Bay were strengthened and the system of tunnels that honeycomb the island were carved in its volcanic rock.

Photos: Philip Gendreau

THE POST OFFICE, of classic design, is among Manila's finest public buildings. Other notable structures within the city include the General Hospital, the new Scottish Rite Temple and the Jai-alai Building

Melbourne, Australia

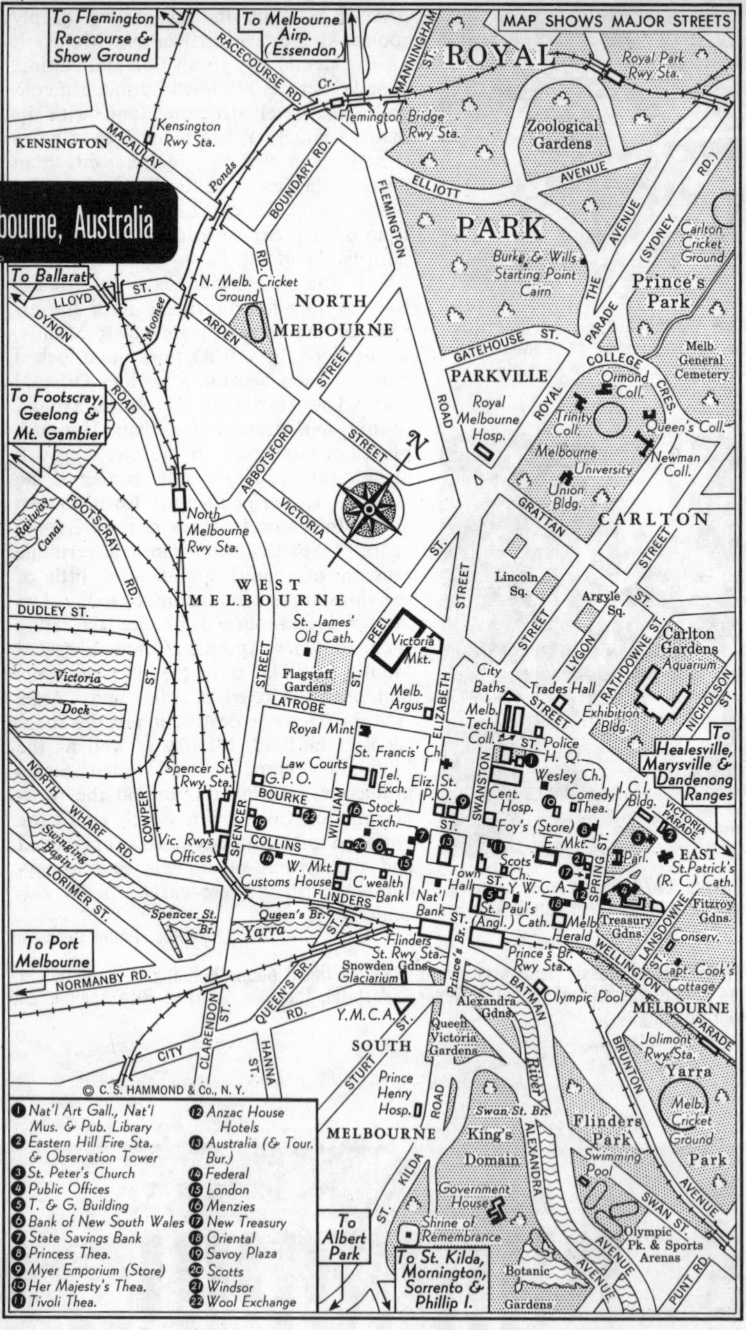

MAP SHOWS MAJOR STREETS

To Flemington Racecourse & Show Ground
To Melbourne Airp. (Essendon)
ROYAL PARK
Royal Park Rwy. Sta.
Zoological Gardens
Kensington Rwy. Sta.
KENSINGTON
Flemington Bridge Rwy. Sta.
Racecourse Rd.
Macaulay Rd.
Manningham St.
Cr.
Ponds
Boundary Rd.
Flemington Rd.
Elliott Avenue
The Avenue
(Sydney Rd.)
Carlton Cricket Ground
Burke & Wills Starting Point Cairn
Prince's Park
To Ballarat
Lloyd St.
Dynon Road
Moonee
Arden St.
N. Melb. Cricket Ground
NORTH MELBOURNE
Gatehouse St.
Parade
College Cres.
Melb. General Cemetery
PARKVILLE
Ormond Coll.
Royal Parade
Royal Melbourne Hosp.
Trinity Coll.
Queen's Coll.
Melbourne University
Newman Coll.
Union Bldg.
To Footscray, Geelong & Mt. Gambier
Abbotsford Street
Street
Victoria St.
N
Railway Canal
Footscray Rd.
North Melbourne Rwy. Sta.
Grattan St.
CARLTON
Street
WEST MELBOURNE
Lincoln Sq.
Argyle Sq.
Dudley St.
St. James' Old Cath.
Peel St.
Victoria Mkt.
Street
Lygon Street
Rathdowne St.
Carlton Gardens
Aquarium
Victoria Dock
Flagstaff Gardens
City Baths
Trades Hall
Nicholson St.
Latrobe
Melb. Argus
Elizabeth
Melb. Tech. Coll.
Exhibition Bldg.
Royal Mint
St. Francis' Ch.
Police H. Q.
To Healesville, Marysville & Dandenong Ranges
North Wharf Rd.
Law Courts
Tel. Exch.
Eliz. St. P. O.
Swanston St.
Wesley Ch.
I. C. I. Bldg.
Spencer St. Rwy. Sta.
G. P. O.
Bourke
William
Stock Exch.
Cent. Hosp.
Comedy Thea.
Victoria Parade
Cowper
Spencer
Foy's (Store)
EAST
Swinging Basin
Vic. Rwys Offices
Collins
E. Mkt.
Parl.
St. Patrick's (R. C.) Cath.
W. Mkt.
Scots Ch.
Customs House
C'wealth Bank
Town Hall
Y. W. C. A.
Spring St.
Lorimer St.
Flinders
Nat'l Bank
St. Paul's (Angl.) Cath.
Melb. Herald
Treasury Gdns.
Fitzroy Gdns.
Spencer St. Br.
Queen's Br.
Yarra
Flinders St. Rwy. Sta.
Prince's Br.
Prince's Br. Rwy. Sta.
Wellington
Lansdowne St.
Conserv.
To Port Melbourne
Snowden Gdns.
Glaciarium
Capt. Cook's Cottage
Normanby Rd.
Batman
Olympic Pool
Clarendon St.
Queen's Br.
Rd.
Y. M. C. A.
Alexandra Gdns.
MELBOURNE
Parade
Sturt St.
Queen Victoria Gardens
River
Brunton
Jolimont Rwy. Sta.
City
Hanna St.
SOUTH MELBOURNE
Yarra Park
© C. S. HAMMOND & Co., N. Y.
Prince Henry Hosp.
Road
Swan St. Br.
Alexandra
Flinders Park
Melb. Cricket Ground
King's Domain
Swimming Pool
Avenue
Kilda St.
Government House
Swan St.
Shrine of Remembrance
Olympic Pk. & Sports Arenas
To Albert Park
To St. Kilda, Mornington, Sorrento & Phillip I.
Botanic Gardens
Avenue
Punt Rd.

1. Nat'l Art Gall., Nat'l Mus. & Pub. Library
2. Eastern Hill Fire Sta. & Observation Tower
3. St. Peter's Church
4. Public Offices
5. T. & G. Building
6. Bank of New South Wales
7. State Savings Bank
8. Princess Thea.
9. Myer Emporium (Store)
10. Her Majesty's Thea.
11. Tivoli Thea.
12. Anzac House Hotels
13. Australia (& Tour. Bur.)
14. Federal
15. London
16. Menzies
17. New Treasury
18. Oriental
19. Savoy Plaza
20. Scotts
21. Windsor
22. Wool Exchange

Photos: Australian News & Information Bureau

COLLINS STREET, the main thoroughfare and typical of Melbourne's wide, tree-shaded avenues, provides an attractive setting not usually available to city dwellers

MELBOURNE'S SKYLINE, as seen from across the River Yarra, looks much like any city's in the United States, except possibly for the rural-like park fronting the calm water

MELBOURNE. A great industrial and financial center of Australia, Melbourne also is one of her chief ports. Despite the heavy industrialization, though, the city has an air of quiet and dignity reminiscent of Boston, coupled with an attractive symmetry of wide streets, pleasant parks and beautiful gardens. In fact, in Fitzroy Gardens is Captain Cook's Cottage, where Australia's discoverer lived, re-erected after shipment intact from Yorkshire, England. All these elements combine to produce an excellent background for leisure as well as work. And Melbourne is not staid and dull; on the contrary, recreation is most important to her. It is here that the Melbourne Cup race is run in November — one of the country's greatest sporting events and a day of national festivity — and the finals of the Australian Rules season are played in September — one of the world's fastest football games. Thus, it is fitting that Melbourne was chosen as the site of the 1956 Olympic Games, and for the first time in history the symbolic Olympic flame was carried by plane from Greece into the Southern Hemisphere, to the Melbourne Cricket Ground, beginning the sixteenth modern Olympiad.

BOURKE STREET leads to the noble State Parliament House, backed by the ornate rising spires of St. Patrick's Church

SHRINE OF REMEMBRANCE, one of the city's main attractions, is the state of Victoria's striking memorial to her sons who served in World War II

Rangoon, Burma

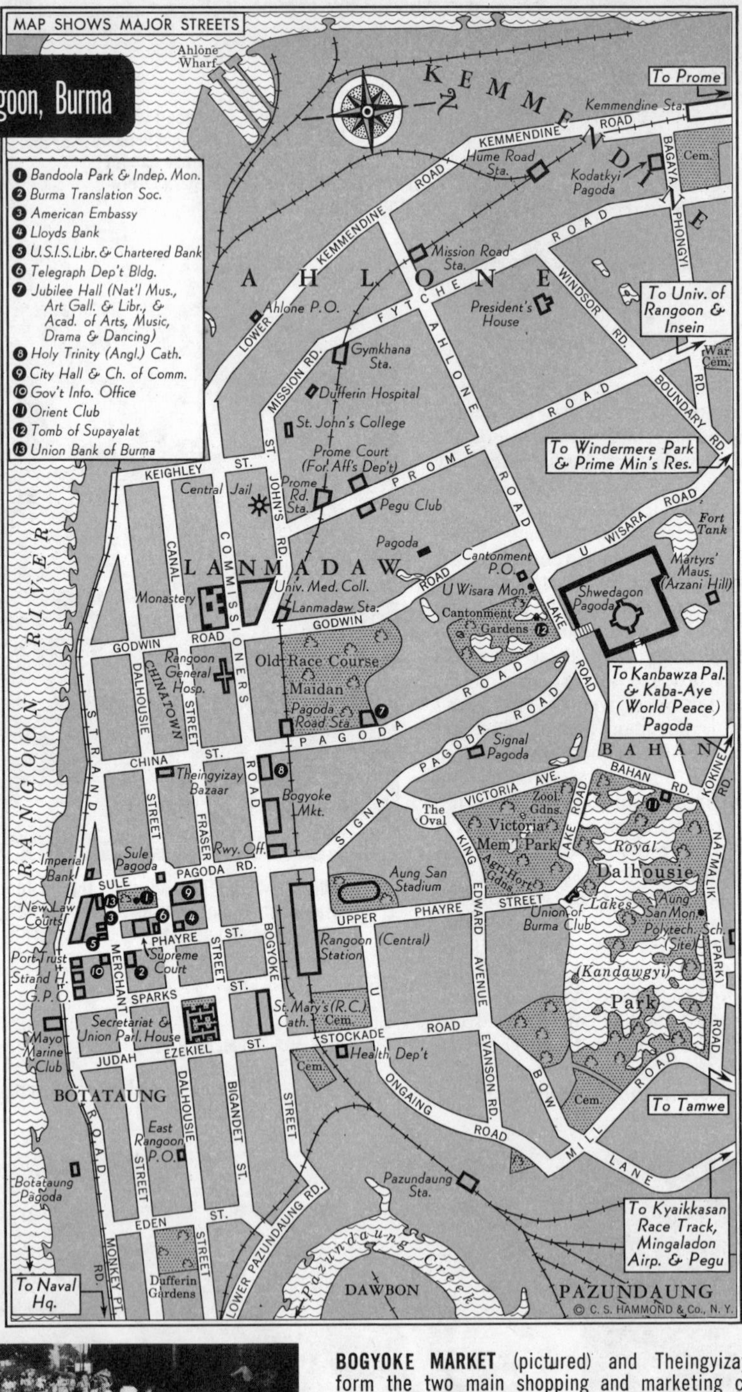

MAP SHOWS MAJOR STREETS

1. Bandoola Park & Indep. Mon.
2. Burma Translation Soc.
3. American Embassy
4. Lloyds Bank
5. U.S.I.S. Libr. & Chartered Bank
6. Telegraph Dep't Bldg.
7. Jubilee Hall (Nat'l Mus., Art Gall. & Libr., & Acad. of Arts, Music, Drama & Dancing)
8. Holy Trinity (Angl.) Cath.
9. City Hall & Ch. of Comm.
10. Gov't Info. Office
11. Orient Club
12. Tomb of Supayalat
13. Union Bank of Burma

To Prome

To Univ. of Rangoon & Insein

To Windermere Park & Prime Min's Res.

To Kanbawza Pal. & Kaba-Aye (World Peace) Pagoda

To Tamwe

To Kyaikkasan Race Track, Mingaladon Airp. & Pegu

To Naval Hq.

BOGYOKE MARKET (pictured) and Theingyizay Market form the two main shopping and marketing centers of Rangoon while business, commercial, banking and government offices are centered in the Sule Pagoda area. Sule Pagoda Road serves as the entertainment center of the city

SHIVEDAGON PAGODA, Kipling's "walking, winking, wonder," is a picturesque landmark greeting every traveler arriving by land, sea or air in Rangoon

RANGOON. Capital of the Independent Republic of the Union of Burma, Rangoon has a history which goes back over 2,500 years when it was known as Okkala. When King Alungpaya conquered Lower Burma in 1775, the small settlement was renamed Yangon, meaning "the end of strife." Subsequent British influence transformed Yangon to Rangoon. Planning for the city provided for both unity and mathematical uniformity, resulting in perfectly straight streets and roads that intersect at right angles. With these well formulated streets, imposing buildings, soothing lakes and gold-encrusted pagodas, Rangoon is considered among the most attractive cities in the Orient, combining the mystic and religious charm of the East with the modern living facilities of the West. Towering over the city is the golden cone of the Shivedagon Pagoda with its spire rising to a height of 326 feet. It is the world's largest and most venerated Buddhist shrine. Another picturesque pagoda is the Sule Pagoda in the very heart of the city. Theingyizay and the Bogyoke Market form the two main shopping centers of Rangoon while business, commercial, banking and governmental offices are concentrated in the Sule Pagoda area. Spacious Sule Pagoda Road serves as the entertainment center of the city. The sprawling campus of the University of Rangoon on the banks of the Inya Lakes, the well organized race course at Kyaikkasan, the Aung San Stadium and the well laid out golf links are other points of more than scenic interest.

GILDED BUDDHAS stand in Rangoon's ancient Shivedagon Pagoda. The Pagoda also contains the 8½ foot high Maha Tissada Ganda bell and a jeweled canopy valued at 62,000 pound sterling

STRAND ROAD, 250 feet wide, parallels the waterfront along the Rangoon River and provides access for truck traffic to all points in the city

Photos: Philip Gendreau

CLAY AND STRAW are popular building materials in Korea. Pictured are typical native huts on the outskirts of Seoul

Photos: Philip Gendreau, I.P.L. Korea

THE NAMDAEMUN GATE, one of three ancient gateways, stands as a reminder that Seoul was at one time enclosed by a high wall. Through the years the wall has been gradually torn down to make way for the city's expansion

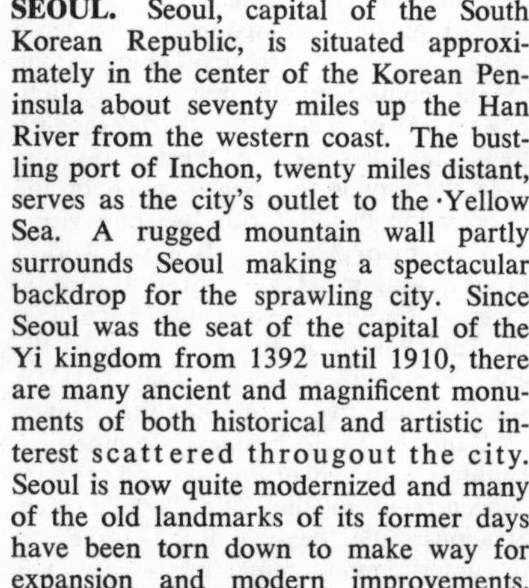

SEOUL. Seoul, capital of the South Korean Republic, is situated approximately in the center of the Korean Peninsula about seventy miles up the Han River from the western coast. The bustling port of Inchon, twenty miles distant, serves as the city's outlet to the ·Yellow Sea. A rugged mountain wall partly surrounds Seoul making a spectacular backdrop for the sprawling city. Since Seoul was the seat of the capital of the Yi kingdom from 1392 until 1910, there are many ancient and magnificent monuments of both historical and artistic interest scattered througout the city. Seoul is now quite modernized and many of the old landmarks of its former days have been torn down to make way for expansion and modern improvements. One of the outstanding landmarks, a lofty wall which once enclosed Seoul in the ages of the old kingdom has gradually been removed through the years. However, three of the main gates belonging to the wall remain intact. Notable among the city's buildings are its three imperial palaces, Changgyong, Toksu and Kyongbok. Also outstanding are the capitol building, Myongdong Catholic Church and Kyongjong Throne Hall, an old administration building of the Yi dynasty. During the recent Korean War, Seoul was invaded twice—first by Communist North Koreans· then by the Red Chinese forces, laying the whole city in ruins. While it is now under reconstruction, it will take many years to restore Seoul to a pre-war condition.

SEOUL, Capital of Korea, is now quite modern in appearance with paved and lighted streets, and western-type buildings of steel and concrete construction

Seoul, Korea

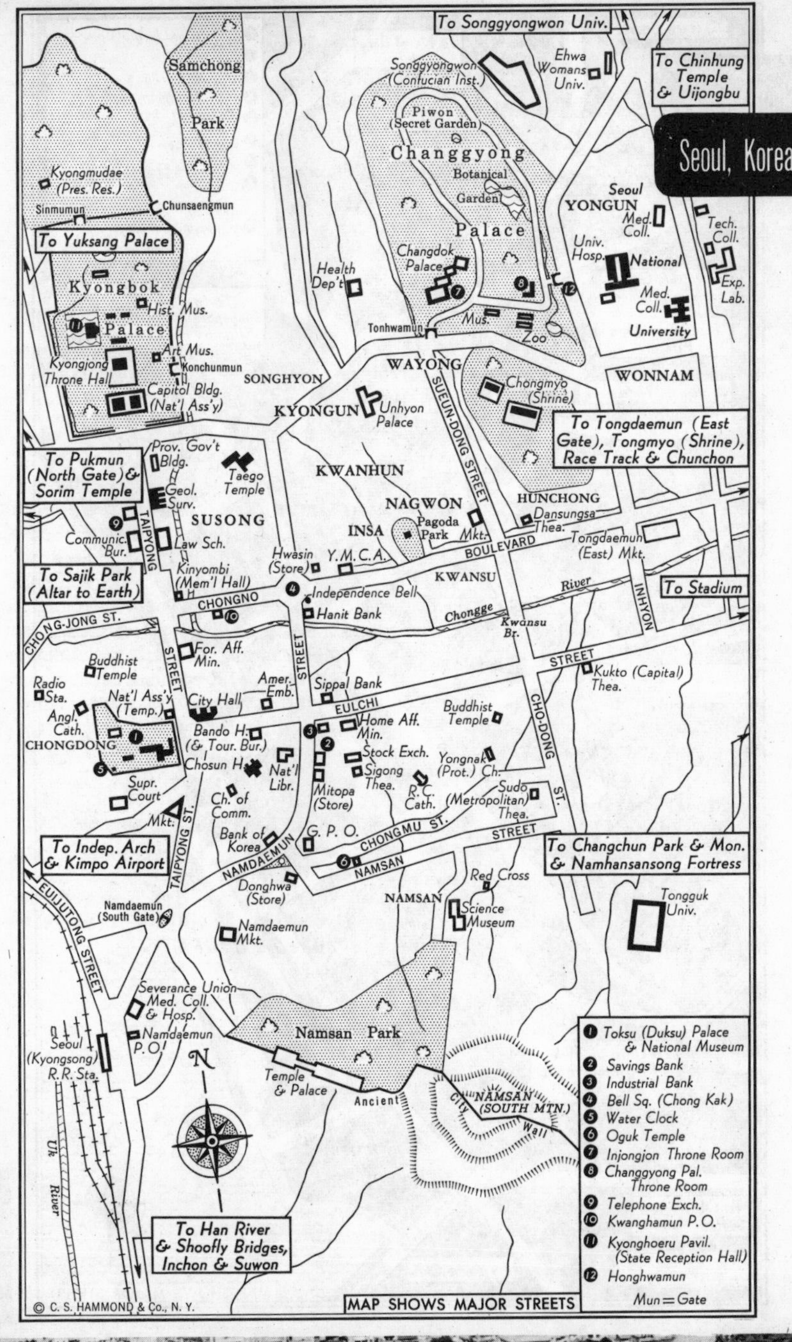
To Songgyongwon Univ.
To Chinhung Temple & Uijongbu
To Yuksang Palace
To Pukmun (North Gate) & Sorim Temple
To Sajik Park (Altar to Earth)
To Tongdaemun (East Gate), Tongmyo (Shrine), Race Track & Chunchon
To Stadium
To Indep. Arch & Kimpo Airport
To Changchun Park & Mon. & Namhansansong Fortress
To Han River & Shoofly Bridges, Inchon & Suwon
Samchong Park
Kyongbok Palace
Changgyong Palace
Namsan Park
NAMSAN (SOUTH MTN.)
MAP SHOWS MAJOR STREETS
1 Toksu (Duksu) Palace & National Museum
2 Savings Bank
3 Industrial Bank
4 Bell Sq. (Chong Kak)
5 Water Clock
6 Oguk Temple
7 Injongjon Throne Room
8 Changgyong Pal. Throne Room
9 Telephone Exch.
10 Kwanghamun P.O.
11 Kyonghoeru Pavil. (State Reception Hall)
12 Honghwamun
Mun = Gate
© C. S. HAMMOND & Co., N. Y.

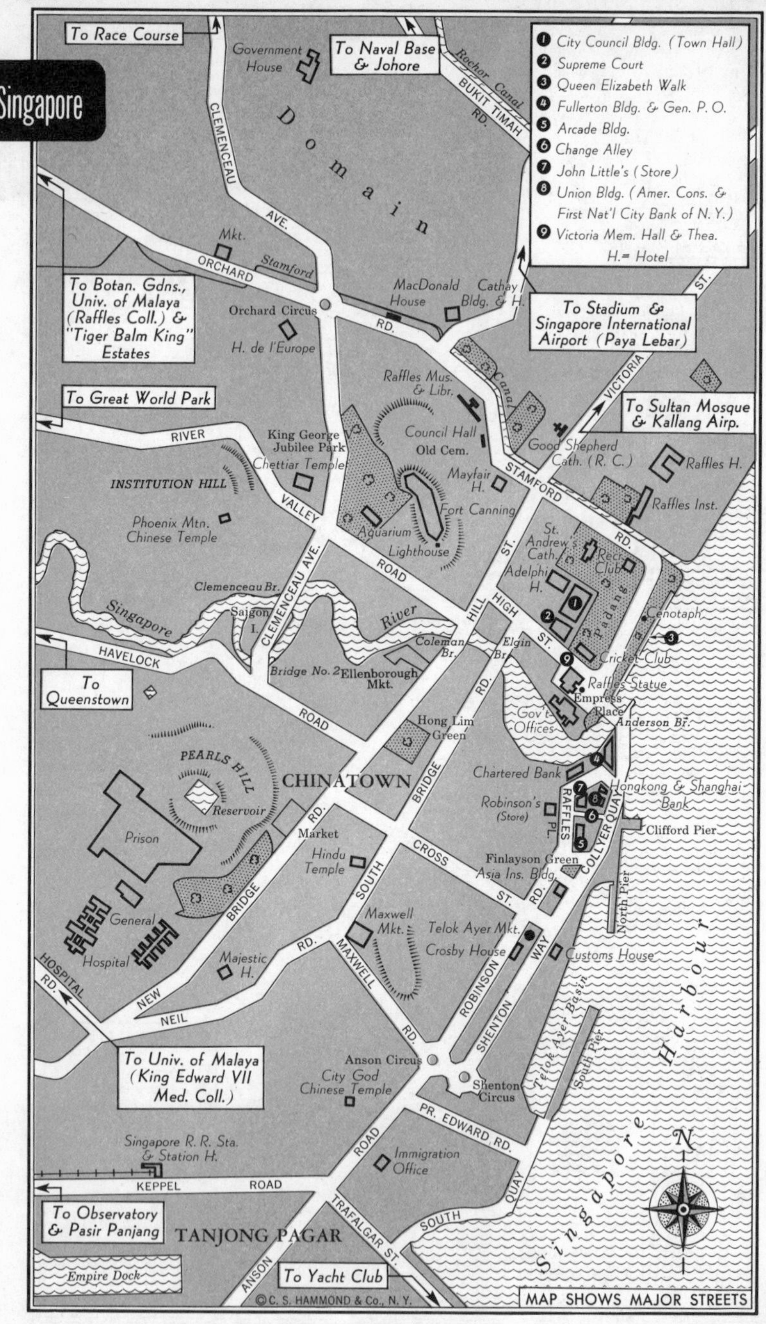

SINGAPORE RIVER, important factor in the colony's entrepot trade and a favored subject for artists, is lined on both sides by hundreds of Chinese godowns and warehouses. Native junks hug its banks, transporting Malaya's rich produce to oceangoing ships in the inner roads

MARKET SCENE in one of the Singapore Improvement Trust housing estates, modern apartments for middle-class families. Vegetable vendors, who have come from nearby farms, are seen squatting, waiting for customers

SINGAPORE. One of the most colorful ports in the world, the diamond-shaped island of Singapore lies on the southernmost tip of the Asiatic continent. It is the Occident's gateway to the East and the Orient's gateway to the West. Malays, Chinese, Indians, Pakistanis and Europeans, Moslems, Buddhists and Christians live side by side in peace and goodwill. Singapore is called with justice the melting pot of East and West. The name comes from two Sanskrit words, "Singa Pura," meaning the "Lion City," recalling the time before the arrival of Islam when Indian influence was predominent. Although the history of the colony trails back into the mists of time, it had fallen into obscurity when Sir Thomas Stamford Raffles landed here in 1819 and began to develop it from a mangrove swamp. As the "emporium and pride of the East," Singapore is a fascinating city where beautiful Eastern works of art, lavish carpets, carvings, jewelry, exotic Malay sarongs and Oriental slippers are sought. Famous Change Alley emits an atmosphere and glamour all its own, with a reputation as a bargain hunter's paradise. Comprising a motley collection of roadside stalls, the narrow alleyway is the place to find anything, from a needle to a bale of cloth or a Persian carpet.

TRISHAS, or pedicabs, have replaced the traditional rickshas, a more novel cheaper mode of travel than the taxi. Thousands of these strange contraptions weave through the city's traffic

Photos: Public Relations Office, Singapore.

CREPE RUBBER GRADERS at work in a rubber factory. Skilled Chinese women snip out defects in crepe rubber sheets before they are exported overseas. Rubber is Singapore's chief export

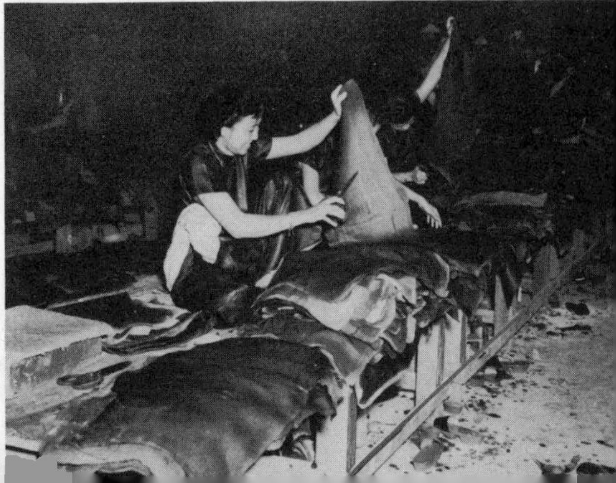

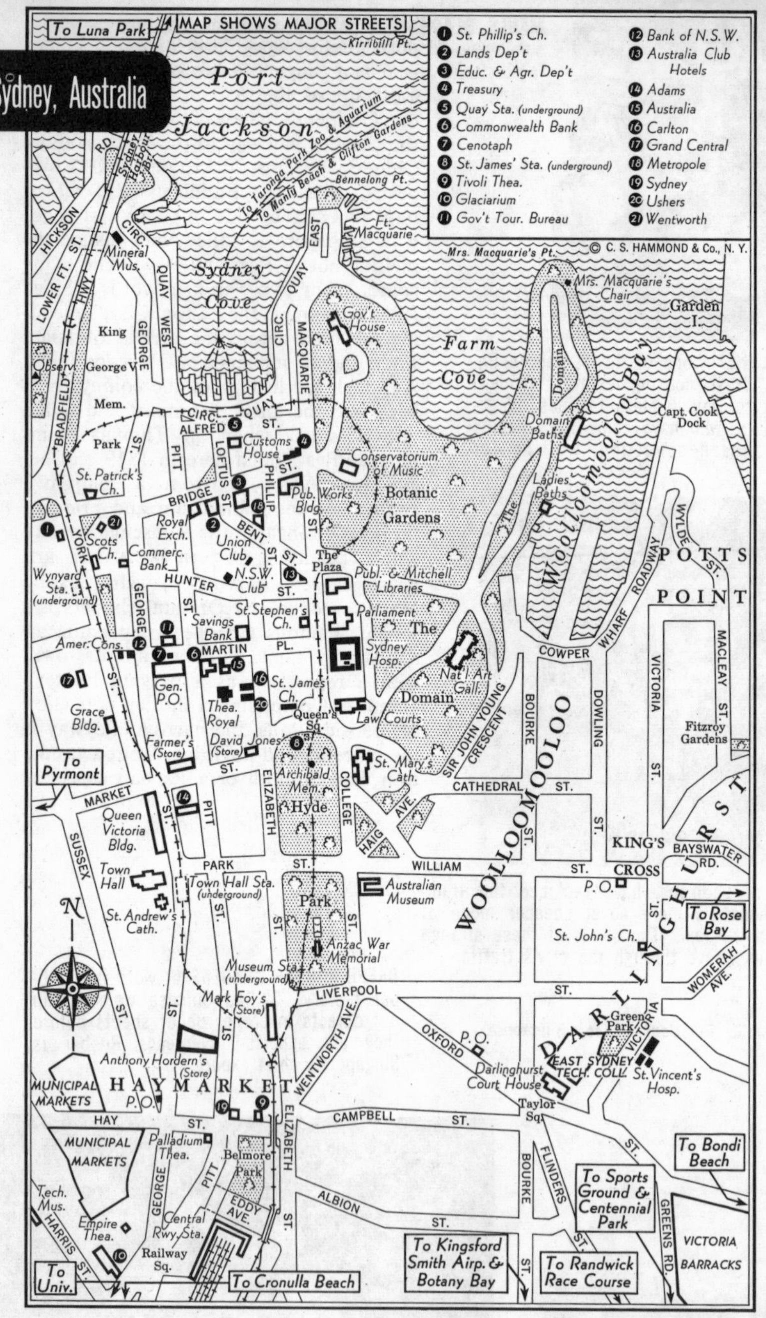

Photos: Australian News & Information Bureau

BEAUTIFUL HARBOR, which Captain Phillip, who brought the first settlers, described as "the finest harbour in the world," features famous Sydney Harbour Bridge

MANLY BEACH is a popular rendezvous for the sun-loving inhabitants, for wherever there is water in Australia, there is a playground. Shark-proof netting keeps the swimmers safe

TARONGA PARK, with its specially designed animal pits, is outstanding because of its fine location, natural setting and good accommodations

SAILING CRAFT of all description find perfect water in lovely Sydney harbor. With her thousands of miles of shoreline, Australia provides full opportunity for the people to indulge their love of summer sports

SYDNEY. Of all cities outside the United States, visiting Americans probably feel most at home in Sydney. With the same language and heritage, plus similar characteristics of youthful vigor and rugged vitality, Australia is much like our own country, anyway, and with her skyline and tempo of living, fashionable stores, good night clubs and up-to-date theaters, Sydney resembles an American city more than any other "down under." Cradle of Australia and her largest city, as well as the third city of the British Commonwealth, this trade and transportation center is situated on one of the world's finest and most beautiful harbors, dominated by her famous landmark, the Sydney Harbour Bridge. Because of her relatively venerable age in relation to other Australian settlements, she embraces old historical buildings situated along the picturesque winding streets that follow the former cattle-wagon paths near the harbor in addition to new modern buildings along the outskirts of this area. Sydney is also a well-known resort, with no less than twenty-one ocean surf beaches and at least half a dozen other beaches on the harbor or Botany Bay — all free to the public.

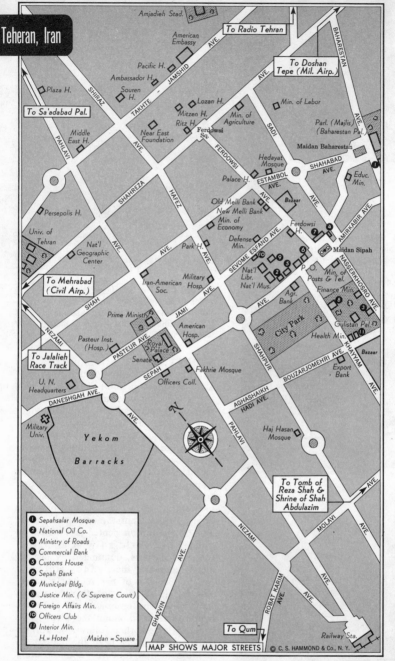

Teheran, Iran

To Radio Tehran

To Doshan Tepe (Mil. Airp.)

To Sa'adabad Pal.

To Mehrabad (Civil Airp.)

To Jalalieh Race Track

To Tomb of Reza Shah & Shrine of Shah Abdulazim

To Qum

1. Sepahsalar Mosque
2. National Oil Co.
3. Ministry of Roads
4. Commercial Bank
5. Customs House
6. Sepah Bank
7. Municipal Bldg.
8. Justice Min. (& Supreme Court)
9. Foreign Affairs Min.
10. Officers Club
11. Interior Min.

H. = Hotel Maidan = Square

MAP SHOWS MAJOR STREETS

NEW MELLIS BANK Building shows the influence of the clean, uncluttered lines of modern architecture. On the opposite side of the street are the tentlike stalls of a bazaar

Photos: Philip Gendreau, N. Y.

TEHERAN AIRPORT, an international gathering place, faces toward the snow-capped mountains, with ideal slopes for winter sports. Suburban summer resorts cluster at the foot of the mountains

TEHERAN. Teheran was an insignificant village until chosen as the capital of Persia, now Iran, at the end of the eighteenth century. But history from the beginning mentions Persia. Evidences of her glories fill museums the world over, but especially her own National Museum. Her sculpture, pottery, carpets and miniatures, her gardens and her poetry have inspired ensuing generations and civilizations, and so her glorious heritage remains. Teheran reflects both her own history as a small village and her later fame as the capital of an important Near East country with a rich, exciting past. One section retains a typical Oriental aspect of crooked, narrow streets and clamorous bazaars, while another consists of broad, tree-lined avenues and European-style buildings. In this latter district is the marble royal palace and splendid foreign legations. Popular meeting place of the gregarious Teheranis is the Maidan Baharistan, for this square is adjoined by the parliament buildings. Most famous of all the Persian treasures is the resplendent Peacock Throne, brought from Delhi, India, in 1739 by Nadir Shah. This is now in the museum in the collection of gardens, courts and buildings known as the Gulistan (Rose Garden).

OLD MELLIS BANK Building is reminiscent of the imposing, decorated buildings of former days. Up its broad steps walk Teheranis in modern, Western-style dress and those in long, flowing Eastern robes

MAIDAN SIPAH is the civic and government center and several ministries face on this principal large square at the city's heart

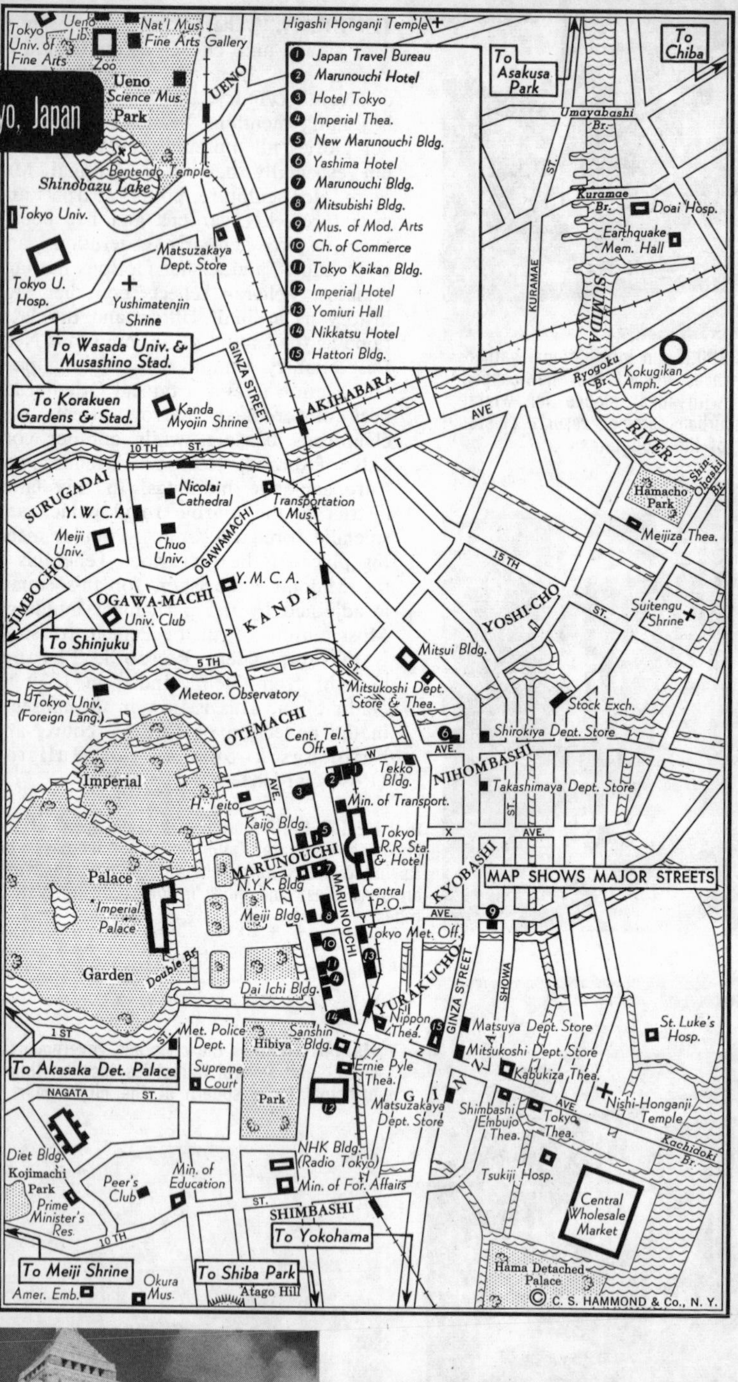

Tokyo, Japan

1. Japan Travel Bureau
2. Marunouchi Hotel
3. Hotel Tokyo
4. Imperial Thea.
5. New Marunouchi Bldg.
6. Yashima Hotel
7. Marunouchi Bldg.
8. Mitsubishi Bldg.
9. Mus. of Mod. Arts
10. Ch. of Commerce
11. Tokyo Kaikan Bldg.
12. Imperial Hotel
13. Yomiuri Hall
14. Nikkatsu Hotel
15. Hattori Bldg.

Tokyo Univ. of Fine Arts
Ueno Lib.
Nat'l Mus.
Fine Arts Gallery
Zoo
Ueno Science Mus.
Ueno Park
Bentendo Temple
Shinobazu Lake
Tokyo Univ.
Tokyo U. Hosp.
Matsuzakaya Dept. Store
Yushimatenjin Shrine
To Wasada Univ. & Musashino Stad.
To Korakuen Gardens & Stad.
Kanda Myojin Shrine
Higashi Honganji Temple
UENO
To Asakusa Park
To Chiba
Umayabashi Br.
Kuramae Br.
Doai Hosp.
Earthquake Mem. Hall
KURAMAE ST.
SUMIDA RIVER
Kokugikan Amph.
Ryogoku Br.
AKIHABARA
GINZA STREET
AVE. T
10 TH ST.
SURUGADAI
Nicolai Cathedral
Transportation Mus.
Y. W. C. A.
Meiji Univ.
Chuo Univ.
OGAWAMACHI
Hamacho Park
Shin-Ohashi Br.
Meijiza Thea.
15 TH ST.
JIMBOCHO
OGAWA-MACHI
Univ. Club
Y. M. C. A.
KANDA
YOSHI-CHO
Suitengu Shrine
To Shinjuku
5 TH
Mitsui Bldg.
A ST.
Tokyo Univ. (Foreign Lang.)
Meteor. Observatory
Mitsukoshi Dept. Store & Thea.
Stock Exch.
OTEMACHI
Cent. Tel. Off.
W AVE.
Shirokiya Dept. Store
Tekko Bldg.
NIHOMBASHI
Imperial
H. Teito
AVE.
Min. of Transport.
Takashimaya Dept. Store
Kaijo Bldg.
Tokyo R.R. Sta. & Hotel
X AVE.
ST.
MARUNOUCHI
N.Y.K. Bldg
KYOBASHI
MAP SHOWS MAJOR STREETS
Palace
Imperial Palace
Meiji Bldg.
Central P.O.
Y
AVE.
Tokyo Met. Off.
Garden
Double Br.
Dai Ichi Bldg.
YURAKUCHO
GINZA STREET
SHOWA
1 ST
Met. Police Dept.
Hibiya
Sanshin Bldg.
Nippon Thea.
Matsuya Dept. Store
St. Luke's Hosp.
To Akasaka Det. Palace
Supreme Court
Ernie Pyle Thea.
Z
Mitsukoshi Dept. Store
GINZA
Kabukiza Thea.
NAGATA ST.
Park
Matsuzakaya Dept. Store
Shimbashi Embujo Thea.
Tokyo Thea.
AVE.
Nishi-Honganji Temple
Kachidoki Br.
Diet Bldg.
NHK Bldg. (Radio Tokyo)
Tsukiji Hosp.
Kojimachi Park
Peer's Club
Min. of Education
Min. of For. Affairs
Central Wholesale Market
Prime Minister's Res.
ST.
SHIMBASHI
To Yokohama
10 TH
To Meiji Shrine
To Shiba Park
Hama Detached Palace
Amer. Emb.
Okura Mus.
Atago Hill

THE DIET BUILDING stands on an eminence in the heart of Tokyo. Completed in 1936, it is a three-storied concrete structure with a massive central tower.

TOKYO. An Oriental city that has been westernized, Tokyo, capital city of Japan since 1869, still retains much of her old eastern flavor and charm. Thus, she offers the most impressive exhibitions of unique Japanese attractions like the classical Kabuki dramas and Noh plays and *sumo,* or Japanese wrestling, along with fine modern accommodations, outstanding baseball games in Ueno Park, fashionable stores on Ginza and Nihombashi Streets and the bustling business center of Marunouchi. Since the dress, too, reflects both influences, women wearing *yofuku* (western clothing) may be seen walking along the streets with others in the traditional *kimono.* Geisha dancers and ritualistic tea ceremonies, Oriental art and architecture, Buddhist and Shinto temples, ancient popular festivals, gorgeous landscape gardens and Tokyo's famous cherry trees, lovely pearl jewelry, exquisite silks, costumed dolls, glistening lacquerware, delicate china and carved ivory are just a few fascinating features. In Japan, flower arrangement is a loving art and the people are true artists in the medium, so, throughout the city, unusual floral displays provide an additional pleasing touch to the colorful scene.

MASSIVE WALLS and a moat surround the Imperial Palace in Tokyo. The palace is not open to the public except on New Year's Day and the Emperor's birthday

"DEZOME-SHIKI," a parade of fire brigades, is held in front of the Imperial Palace in Tokyo. The firemen give various demonstrations of acrobatic feats, including ladder-climbing

Photos: Philip Gendreau, Japan Tourist Association

TOKYO'S THEATER DISTRICT is attractively lit at night by colored lights and neon signs.

INDEX AND LIST OF PRINCIPAL CITIES OF THE WORLD

This list of cities, with latest population figures, includes all cities for which there is an article in the book, as well as other important world cities. Page numbers in parentheses refer to the pages on which the articles appear.

† Population includes suburbs. * Capital of country.

City	Population
Halifax,* N. S.	93,301
Halle, Ger.	222,505
Hälsingborg, Sweden	71,718
Hamburg, Ger. (266-267)	1,605,606
Hamilton, Ont.	239,625
Hangchow, China	700,000
Hankow, China	749,952
Hannover, Ger.	444,296
Hanoi,* No. Vietnam	237,150
Harbin, China	1,200,000
Harrisburg,* Pa.	89,544
Hartford,* Conn. (58-59)	177,397
Havana,* Cuba (186-189)	787,448
Havre, Le, France	137,175
Heidelberg, Ger.	116,488
Helena,* Mont.	17,581
Helsinki, Finland (268-269)	363,834
Hindenburg (Zabrze), Pol.	132,888
Hiroshima, Japan	285,712
Hobart, Tas.	195,206
Hollandia,* Neth. N. Guinea	13,911
Hong Kong, (358-359)	2,250,000
Honiara,* Sol. Is. Prot.	2,000
Honolulu,* Hawaii (360-361)	248,034
Houston, Texas (60-61)	596,163
Howrah, India	433,630
Hué, Vietnam	407,000
Hull, Eng.	299,105
Hyderabad, India	1,085,722
Hyderabad, Pak.	241,801
Ibadan, Nigeria	459,196
Inch'on, Korea	265,767
Indianapolis,* Ind. (62-63)	427,173
Indore, India	310,859
Irkutsk, U.S.S.R.	314,000
Istanbul, Turkey (270-271)	1,000,022
Ivanovo, U.S.S.R.	319,000
Izmir, Turkey	230,508
Jackson,* Miss.	98,271
Jacksonville, Fla. (64-65)	204,517
Jaffa-Tel Aviv, Israel	335,000
Jefferson City,* Mo.	25,099
Jerusalem, Jord. and *Israel (362-363)	120,000
Jesselton,* No. Borneo	11,704
Johannesburg, Transv. (338-339)	†880,573
Juneau,* Alaska	5,956
Kabul,* Afgh.	206,208
Kaifeng, China	303,422
Kalinin, U.S.S.R.	240,000
Kanazawa, Japan	252,017
Kanpur, India	705,383
Kansas City, Kans.	129,553
Kansas City, Mo. (66-67)	456,622
Karachi,* Pak. (364-365)	1,009,438
Karlsruhe, Ger.	198,840
Kassel, Ger.	162,132
Katmandu,* Nepal	108,805
Kazan, U.S.S.R.	565,000
Khabarovsk, U.S.S.R.	280,000
Khar'kov, U.S.S.R.	877,000
Khartoum,* Sudan	75,000
Kiel, Ger.	254,449
Kiev, U.S.S.R.	991,000
Kingston,* Jamaica	109,056
Kingston-upon-Hull (Hull), Eng.	299,105
Kirov, U.S.S.R.	211,000
Knoxville, Tenn.	124,769
Kobe, Japan	765,435
Köln, Ger.	594,941
Kolozsvár (Cluj), Rum.	117,915
Kraków, Poland	347,517
Krasnoyarsk, U.S.S.R.	328,000
Kuala Lumpur,* Mal. Fed.	175,961
Kuching,* Sarawak	37,949
Kumamoto, Japan	267,506
Kunming, China	500,000
Kuybyshev, U.S.S.R.	600,000
Kyoto, Japan	1,101,854
Lagos,* Nigeria	267,407
Lahore, Pak.	849,476
Lansing,* Mich.	92,129
La Paz,* Bolivia (190-191)	321,073
Las Palmas,* Canary Is., Spain	†153,856
Lausanne, Switz.	106,807
Leeds, Eng.	505,219
Leghorn (Livorno), Italy	134,513
Le Havre, France	137,175
Leicester, Eng.	285,181
Leipzig, Ger.	607,655
Leningrad, U.S.S.R.	2,814,000
Léopoldville,* Belg. Congo	257,197
Lille (Lisle), France	190,078
Lima,* Peru (192-193)	628,821
Lincoln,* Nebr.	98,884
Linz, Austria	184,685
Lisbon,* Port (272-273)	783,226
Little Rock,* Ark. (68-69)	102,213
Liverpool, Eng. (274-275)	788,659
Livorno, Italy	134,513
Ljubljana, Yugo.	138,211
Łódź, Poland	622,495
London,* Eng. (276-285)	3,347,982
London* (Greater), Eng.	8,348,023
London, Ont.	101,693
Long Beach, Calif.	250,767
Los Angeles, Calif. (70-73)	1,970,358
Louisville, Ky. (74-75)	369,129
Lourenço Marques,* Moz.	93,303
Luanda,* Angola	141,722
Lübeck, Ger.	238,276
Lucknow, India	496,861
Luxembourg,* Lux. (286-287)	61,996
Luzern (Lucerne), Switz.	60,526
L'vov (Łwów), U.S.S.R.	387,000
Lyon, France	462,657
Macao (Port.), China	187,772
Maceió, Brazil	99,088
Madison,* Wis.	96,056
Madras, India	1,416,056
Madrid,* Spain (288-291)	†1,618,435
Madurai, India	361,781
Magdeburg, Ger.	236,326
Magnitogorsk, U.S.S.R.	284,000
Málaga, Spain	†274,847
Malmö, Sweden	192,498
Managua,* Nicar.	109,352
Manaus, Brazil	89,612
Manchester, Eng. (292-293)	703,082
Mandalay, Burma	182,367
Manila, P. I. (366-367)	983,906
Mannheim, Ger.	245,634
Maracaibo, Venez.	235,750
Marrakech, Mor.	215,695
Marsala, Sicily, Italy	42,488
Marseilles, France (294-295)	605,577
Mecca,* Saudi Arabia	150,000
Medellín, Col.	328,294
Melbourne,* Victoria (368-369)	†1,524,111
Memphis, Tenn. (76-77)	396,000
Mexico City, Mex. (194-197)	2,234,795
Miami, Fla. (78-81)	249,276
Milan, Italy (296-299)	1,267,040
Milwaukee, Wis. (82-83)	637,392
Minhow (Foochow), China	328,434
Minneapolis, Minn. (84-85)	521,718
Minsk, U.S.S.R.	412,000
Miskolc, Hungary	103,724
Mogadiscio,* Som.	58,000
Molotov, U.S.S.R.	538,000
Monrovia,* Liberia	14,000
Monterrey, Mex.	333,422
Montevideo,* Uruguay (198-199)	850,000
Montgomery,* Ala.	106,525
Montpelier,* Vt.	8,599
Montreal, Que. (200-203)	1,109,439
Moscow (Moskva),* U.S.S.R.	4,839,000
Mukden, China	2,300,000
Munich, Ger. (300-301)	831,937
Murcia, Spain	†217,934
Nagoya, Japan	1,030,635
Nagpur, India	449,099
Nairobi,* Kenya	18,976
Nanchang, China	258,692
Nancy, France	120,484
Nanking, China	1,200,000
Nantes, France	197,915
Naples, Italy (302-303)	984,684
Nashville,* Tenn. (86-87)	174,307
Nassau,* Bahama Is.	13,231
Newark, N. J. (88-89)	438,776
New Bedford, Mass. (90-91)	109,189
Newcastle, N. S. W.	178,144
Newcastle-on-Tyne, Eng.	291,724
New Delhi,* India	276,314
New Haven, Conn. (92-93)	164,443
New Orleans, La. (94-97)	570,445
New York, N. Y. (98-103)	7,891,957
New York, N. Y. (met. area)	12,911,994
Nice, France	208,453
Ninghsien (Ningpo), China	249,633
Nizhni Novgorod (Gor'kiy), U.S.S.R.	876,000
Norfolk, Va. (104-105)	213,513
Norrköping, Sweden	84,939
Nottingham, Eng.	306,055
Nouméa,* New Cal.	10,500
Novosibirsk, U.S.S.R.	731,000
Nürnberg, Ger.	362,459
Oakland, Calif. (106-107)	384,575
Odessa, U.S.S.R.	607,000
Oklahoma City,* Okla. (108-109)	243,504
Olympia,* Wash.	15,819
Omaha, Nebr. (110-111)	251,117
Omdurman, Sudan	126,650
Omsk, U.S.S.R.	505,000
Oporto (Porto), Port.	281,406
Oradea, Rum.	82,282
Oran, Algeria	274,772
Osaka, Japan	1,956,136
Oslo,* Norway (304-305)	434,047
Ostrava, Czech.	171,064
Ottawa,* Canada (204-205)	222,129
Pago Pago, Amer. Samoa	1,586
Palermo, Sicily, Italy	477,421
Palmas, Las,* Canary Is., Spain	†153,856
Panamá,* Panama	127,874
Papeete,* Tahiti, Soc. Is.	12,417
Para (Belém), Brazil	225,218
Paramaribo,* Surinam	67,381
Paris,* France (306-313)	2,820,534
Peiping (Peking),* China	2,768,149
Penang, Mal. Fed.	189,068
Penza, U.S.S.R.	231,000
Perm (Molotov), U.S.S.R.	538,000
Pernambuco (Recife), Brazil	512,370
Perth,* W. Australia	348,647
Philadelphia, Pa. (112-115)	2,071,605
Phnom Penh,* Cambodia	110,600
Phoenix,* Ariz. (116-117)	106,818
Pierre, S. Dak.	5,715
Pilsen (Plzeň), Czech.	120,753
Pinkiang (Harbin), China	1,200,000
Piraeus, Greece	210,722
Pittsburgh, Pa. (118-119)	676,806
Ploeşti, Rum.	95,632
Plovdiv, Bulgaria	125,440
Plymouth, Eng.	208,985
Plzeň, Czech.	120,753
Poona, India	480,982
Port-au-Prince,* Haiti	142,840
Port Elizabeth, C. of G. H.	†188,892
Portland, Me. (120-121)	77,634
Portland, Oreg. (122-123)	373,628
Port Louis, Mauritius	57,466
Port Moresby,* Pap. Terr.	17,546
Porto, Port.	281,406
Pôrto Alegre, Brazil	375,049
Port of Spain,* Trinidad	92,793
Port Said, Egypt	178,432
Portsmouth, Eng.	233,464
Poznań (Posen), Poland	327,192
Prague (Praha), Czech.	934,933
Pretoria,* U. of S. Afr.	283,535

City	Population
Providence,* R. I. (124-125)	248,674
Puebla, Mex.	211,331
Pusan, Korea	473,619
Québec,* Quebec (206-207)	170,703
Quezon City,* P. I.	107,977
Quito,* Ecuador	209,932
Rabat,* Mor.	155,993
Rabaul, New Brit., Terr. N. G.	7,600
Raleigh,* N. C.	65,679
Rangoon,* Burma (370-371)	711,520
Recife, Brazil	512,370
Reggio di Calabria, Italy	120,021
Reims, France	114,682
Rennes, France	112,553
Reno, Nev. (126-127)	32,497
Reykjavik,* Iceland	56,096
Richmond,* Va. (128-129)	230,310
Riga, U.S.S.R.	565,000
Rio de Janeiro,* Brazil (208-211)	2,303,063
Riyadh,* Saudi Arabia	80,000
Rochester, N. Y. (130-131)	332,488
Rome,* Italy (314-319)	1,610,467
Rosario, Arg.	467,937
Rostov, U.S.S.R.	552,000
Rotterdam, Neth. (320-321)	646,248
Sacramento,* Calif. (132-133)	137,572
Saigon,* So. Vietnam	1,179,000
Saint Étienne, France	154,283
Saint John, N. B.	52,491
Saint John's, Nfld.	57,078
Saint Louis, Mo. (134-135)	856,796
Saint Paul,* Minn. (136-137)	311,349
Salem,* Oregon	43,140
Salisbury,* So. Rhod.	†118,772
Salonika, Greece	224,748
Salt Lake City,* Utah (138-139)	182,121
Salvador, Brazil	389,422
San Antonio, Texas (140-141)	52,093
San Diego, Calif. (142-143)	334,387
San Francisco, Calif. (144-149)	775,357
San Jose,* C. R.	86,718
San Juan,* P. R.	224,767
San Salvador,* El Sal.	161,951
Santa Cruz de Tenerife,* Canary Is., Spain	†103,110
Sante Fé, Arg.	168,791
Sante Fe,* N. Mex.	27,998
Santiago,* Chile (212-213)	1,348,283
Santos, Brazil	198,405
São Paulo, Brazil (214-215)	2,017,025
Sapporo, Japan	313,850
Saragossa (Zaragoza), Spain	244,015
Sarajevo, Yugo.	135,657
Saratov, U.S.S.R.	518,000
Seattle, Wash. (150-153)	467,591
Sendai, Japan	341,685
Seoul,* So. Korea (372-373)	1,446,019
Seville (Sevilla), Spain	†376,627
Seyhan (Adana), Turkey	117,799
Shanghai, China	6,204,417
Sheffield, Eng.	512,834
Shenyang (Mukden), China	2,300,000
Sherbrooke, Que	58,668
Shreveport, La. (154-155)	127,206
Singapore,* Sing. (374-375)	679,659
Skopje, Yugo.	91,557
Smyrna (Izmir), Turkey	230,508
Sofia (Sofiya),* Bulg.	366,925
Southampton, Eng.	178,343
Spokane, Wash. (156-157)	161,721
Springfield,* Ill.	81,628
Springfield, Mass. (158-159)	162,399
Srinagar, Kash.	207,847
Stalingrad, U.S.S.R.	525,000
Stalino, U.S.S.R.	625,000
Stettin (Szczecin), Poland	200,217
Stockholm,* Sweden (322-323)	745,936
Stoke-on-Trent, Eng.	275,115
Strasbourg, France	192,353
Stuttgart, Ger.	497,677
Subotica, Yugo.	115,402
Sucre,* Bolivia	40,128
Sunderland, Eng.	181,524
Surabaja, Java, Indon.	925,617
Suva,* Fiji Is.	36,967
Sverdlovsk, U.S.S.R.	707,000
Swansea, Wales	160,988
Sydney,* N. S. W. (376-377)	†1,863,161
Syracuse, N. Y. (160-161)	220,583
Szczecin, Poland	200,217
Taegu, Korea	313,765
Tainan, Formosa, China	243,098
Taipei, Formosa, China	599,189
Taiyuan, China	700,000
Talien, China	1,000,000
Tallahassee,* Fla.	27,237
Tampere, Finland	103,043
Tananarive,* Madag.	187,330
Tashkent, U.S.S.R.	778,000
Tbilisi, U.S.S.R.	635,000
Tegucigalpa,* Hond.	72,385
Teheran (Tehran),* Iran (378-379)	554,372
Tel Aviv-Jaffa, Israel	335,000
The Hague*, Neth. (264-265)	532,998
Thessalonikē (Salonika), Greece	224,748
Tientsin, China	2,693,831
Tiflis (Tbilisi), U.S.S.R.	635,000
Timişoara, Rum.	111,987
Tirana (Tiranë),* Albania	59,887
Tokyo,* Japan (380-381)	6,969,104
Tokyo* (Greater), Japan	8,037,084
Toledo, Ohio (162-163)	303,616
Topeka,* Kans.	78,791
Torino, Italy	711,2
Toronto,* Ont. (216-219)	667,7
Toulon, France	125,5
Toulouse, France	217,6
Trenton,* N. J. (164-165)	128,9
Tripoli,* Libya	130,2
Trois Rivières, Que.	50,4
Troy, N. Y.	72,3
Tsinan, China	700,0
Tsingtao, China	1,000,0
Tucumán, Arg.	194,1
Tula, U.S.S.R.	320,0
Tulsa, Okla. (166-167)	182,7
Tunis, Tunisia	364,5
Turin (Torino), Italy	711,2
Ufa, U.S.S.R.	265,0
Ulan Bator,* Mong. Rep.	50,0
Urga (Ulan Bator),* Mong. Rep.	50,0
Üsküb (Skopje,) Yugo.	91,5
Valencia, Spain	†509,0
Valletta,* Malta	18,6
Valparaiso, Chile	218,8
Vancouver, B. C. (220-221)	365,8
Venice (Venezia), Italy	291,6
Victoria,* Br. Col.	54,5
Victoria,* Hong Kong	887,4
Vienna,* Austria (324-325)	1,766,1
Vientiane,* Laos	10,0
Vladivostok, U.S.S.R.	265,0
Voronezh, U.S.S.R.	400,0
Voroshilovgrad, U.S.S.R.	251,0
Warsaw (Warszawa),* Pol.	641,8
Washington, D. C.,* U.S.A. (168-173)	802,1
Waterbury, Conn.	104,4
Wellington, N. Z.	†133,4
Wenchow, China	153,3
Wichita, Kans.	168,2
Wiesbaden, Ger.	220,7
Wilkes-Barre, Pa.	76,8
Willemstad,* Neth. Ant.	40,5
Windsor, Ont.	121,9
Winnipeg,* Man. (222-223)	255,0
Wolverhampton, Eng.	162,6
Worcester, Mass. (174-175)	203,4
Wrocław, Poland	341,4
Wuppertal, Ger.	363,2
Yangku (Taiyuan), China	700,0
Yaroslavl', U.S.S.R.	374,0
Yerevan, U.S.S.R.	385,0
Yokohama, Japan	951,1
York, Eng.	105,3
Youngstown, Ohio	168,3
Yunnan (Kunming), China	500,0
Zabrze, Poland	132,8
Zagreb, Yugo.	350,4
Zaragoza, Spain	†244,0
Zhdanov, U.S.S.R.	273,0
Zürich, Switz. (326-327)	390,0

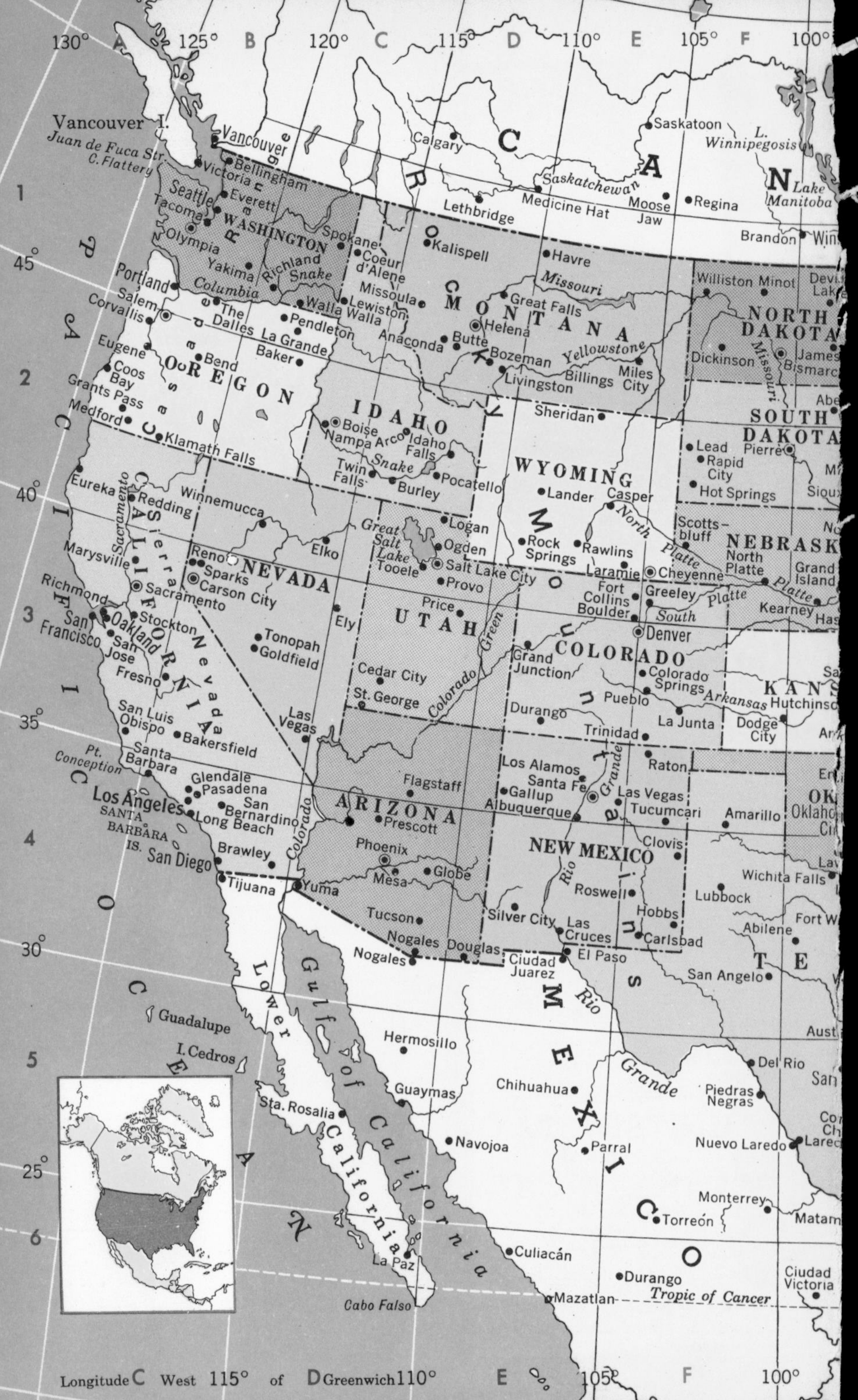

130° A 125° B 120° C 115° D 110° E 105° F 100°
Vancouver I.
Juan de Fuca Str.
C. Flattery
Vancouver
Victoria
Bellingham
Seattle
Everett
Tacoma
Olympia
WASHINGTON
Spokane
Yakima
Richland
Snake
Columbia
Coeur d'Alene
Walla Walla
Lewiston
Missoula
Kalispell
Calgary
Lethbridge
Medicine Hat
Saskatchewan
Saskatoon
Moose Jaw
Regina
L. Winnipegosis
Lake Manitoba
Brandon
C A N
Havre
Missouri
Great Falls
MONTANA
Helena
Butte
Anaconda
Bozeman
Livingston
Billings
Yellowstone
Miles City
Williston
Minot
NORTH DAKOTA
Dickinson
Bismarck
SOUTH DAKOTA
Pierre
Lead
Rapid City
Hot Springs
Portland
Salem
Corvallis
Eugene
Coos Bay
Grants Pass
Medford
The Dalles
Pendleton
La Grande
Baker
Bend
OREGON
Klamath Falls
IDAHO
Boise
Nampa
Arco
Idaho Falls
Snake
Twin Falls
Burley
Pocatello
Sheridan
WYOMING
Lander
Casper
North Platte
Rock Springs
Rawlins
Laramie
Cheyenne
Scottsbluff
NEBRASKA
North Platte
Grand Island
Platte
Kearney
Eureka
Redding
Sacramento
Winnemucca
Elko
Marysville
Reno
Sparks
Carson City
NEVADA
Great Salt Lake
Logan
Ogden
Salt Lake City
Tooele
Provo
Richmond
San Francisco
Oakland
San Jose
Stockton
Fresno
CALIFORNIA
Sierra Nevada
Tonopah
Goldfield
Ely
Price
UTAH
Green
Fort Collins
Greeley
Boulder
South
Denver
Grand Junction
COLORADO
Colorado Springs
Pueblo
Arkansas
La Junta
Hutchinson
Dodge City
Cedar City
St. George
Colorado
Durango
Trinidad
San Luis Obispo
Bakersfield
Las Vegas
Pt. Conception
Santa Barbara
Los Alamos
Santa Fe
Raton
Gallup
Albuquerque
Las Vegas
Tucumcari
Amarillo
Glendale
Pasadena
Los Angeles
San Bernardino
Long Beach
SANTA BARBARA IS.
San Diego
Brawley
Flagstaff
ARIZONA
Prescott
Phoenix
Mesa
Globe
NEW MEXICO
Clovis
Rio Grande
Roswell
Lubbock
Wichita Falls
Tijuana
Yuma
Tucson
Silver City
Las Cruces
Hobbs
Carlsbad
Nogales
Douglas
Ciudad Juarez
El Paso
Abilene
San Angelo
ROCKY MOUNTAINS
PACIFIC OCEAN
Guadalupe
I. Cedros
Lower California
Gulf of California
Hermosillo
Guaymas
Sta. Rosalia
Navojoa
Chihuahua
Parral
MEXICO
Rio Grande
Del Rio
Piedras Negras
Nuevo Laredo
Monterrey
Torreon
Culiacán
La Paz
Durango
Ciudad Victoria
Cabo Falso
Mazatlan
Tropic of Cancer
1 2 3 4 5 6
45° 40° 35° 30° 25°
Longitude C West 115° of D Greenwich 110° E 105° F 100°